Cemeteries of Cranberry Isles and the Towns of Mount Desert Island

a record of names and dates
on gravestones in cemeteries
of Bar Harbor, Cranberry Isles,
Mount Desert, Southwest Harbor,
and Tremont

Thomas F. Vining

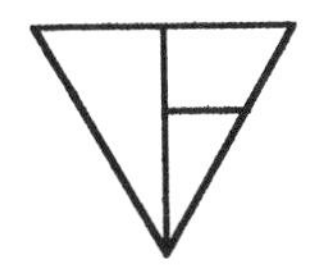

V. F. Thomas Co.
P. O. Box 281
Bar Harbor, Maine 04609-0281

cover illustration by Judy Hazen-Connery

Library of Congress Catalog Card Number: 00-190962

ISBN 0-9664874-1-9

DEDICATION

to my parents, Thomas Frank Vining and Phyllis May (Boothby) Vining,

and

to those persons, past, present, and future, who preserve our cemeteries.

TABLE of CONTENTS

ACKNOWLEDGMENTS

Many individuals and groups helped in this project, often by pointing the way to an obscure cemetery or a helpful book. Some who knew the history of a particular site took time to share it. Alphabetically they are:

Acadia National Park
Joyce Barr
Jim Bartlett
John Clark
Kathy Combs
Bar Harbor Assessors' Office
Bar Harbor Public Works Department
Bar Harbor Town Office
Barbara Craighead
Owen Craighead
Martha Farley
Michael Farley
Jonathan Gormley
Peter and Jenny Gott
Pat Gray
Ruth Gortner Grierson
Hilda Hale
Kathy Hamor
Ruth Higgins Horsman
Sharon Ingram
Milford Jackson
Jesup Memorial Library
Barbara Kramp
Diana Lawson
Edwin "Ned" Lawson
Jean Marshall
Sally Merchant
George McKay
David Milliken
David Mills
Jennifer Monat
Wanda Moran
Tina Morris
Mount Desert Island Historical Society
Mount Desert Town Office
May Nebius
Northeast Harbor Library
Robert Pyle
John and Evie Pyne
Emma Richards
Peggy Richardson
Raymond Robbins Jr.
David Rockefeller Sr.
Clarence and Esther Rodick
Jaylene Roths
Peter and Isabelle Schweitzer
Heidi Smallidge
Elaine R. Smith
Southwest Harbor Town Office
Smuggler's Den Campground
Spruce Valley Campground
Ted Spurling
Lyford and Norma Stanley
Ralph Stanley
Carl and Louise Strandberg
Tremont Historical Society
Tremont Town Office
Bob and Ruth Williams

Special thanks go to Joyce Barr, Jim Bartlett, John Clark, and Raymond Robbins Jr. who took an active interest and spent much time helping with this project.

INTRODUCTION

This book records names and dates on all gravestones and other markers in all cemeteries in the towns of Bar Harbor, Cranberry Isles, Mount Desert, Southwest Harbor, and Tremont. There were three steps involved in writing this book—locating cemeteries, recording all the names and dates on the stones, and researching the history of selected cemeteries.

Location of cemeteries was determined primarily by the use of older 15' topographic maps and the more recent 7.5' ones. There are, however, several cemeteries that are not identified on either type (Bar Harbor - 21, for example). Fortunately, people who knew of such places were willing to share that information. It is not impossible, perhaps not even unlikely, that other cemeteries will come to light as a result of this book. Only cemeteries with engraved stones or other clear identification (Tremont - 18, for example) are included in this book. Names and birth and death dates of the many individuals in unmarked graves in these cemeteries are not included. Also beyond the scope of this book are burial grounds of Native Americans, historic cemeteries whose "inhabitants" have been moved to other cemeteries, and homestead burial grounds that do not contain any stones bearing names and dates.

Recording names and dates involved two principal steps. First, names and dates were written on paper during a visit to a cemetery and later entered into a computer. Second, one or more follow-up visits were made to proof the work. During this step, errors in copying and typing were revealed as well as discovery of new stones and/or new inscriptions since the previous visit(s). In spite of this proofing, there are probably still some errors. These should be pointed out to the author in order they may be corrected in future editions as well as in any ancillary material. Errors, data from new stones or new engraving, plus additional information about cemeteries and individuals buried in them will be posted on http://www.vfthomas.com.

Research into the history of the cemeteries was limited by time and by the intent to keep the focus of this book, or at least this first edition, on the identification of cemeteries and on recording the names and dates. Information on history is, therefore, somewhat brief or absent.

This book will likely serve a variety of functions. First and foremost, it is a reference for genealogists and historians. Although care was taken to insure accuracy, anyone interested in the **Names and dates on gravestones and other markers** should visit the cemetery or cemeteries of interest to verify the information of interest. Second, it is a record of what can be lost if such an accounting is not made. At one cemetery a child's gravestone was found discarded into the woods. Within a year following a visit to another cemetery, two footstones disappeared. At a third cemetery, a stone (or other marker) denoting an individual's grave can no longer be found, and a new grave and stone for another person are now in its place. Further, stones themselves can become buried in time. Third, this book may stimulate towns, organizations, and/or individuals to preserve these historic places and perhaps to identify other burial grounds.

PART ONE

The thousands of gravestones in the more than 100 cemeteries covered in this book contain more than just the names and dates recorded in Part Two—even more than the symbols or words of epitaphs and other verses. The following short units of Part One result from observation of cemeteries themselves as well as the gravestones they contain.

GONE AND SOMETIMES FORGOTTEN

There is a considerable range in quantity and quality of maintenance—from manicured lawns with sprinkler systems to total abandonment. Even in some "maintained" cemeteries, footstones and, in two cases, even headstones, have been found in a pile by themselves or discarded into nearby woods.

There is little or no provision for proper disposal of material such as styrofoam, plastic, foil, *etc.* Consequently, nearby woods are often littered with plastic flowers and flower pots, deteriorating wreaths, ribbons, and a host of other unwanted material. Found on a hill adjacent to one cemetery was a vehicle battery and in the woods next to another one were two mattresses and an old window frame.

There is a great need for proper repair of stones, including use of correct materials. In one cemetery, a substance used to mend broken stones was applied so carelessly that it obscured some of the stone's inscription. Fortunately, that information had been recorded in this book before the "repair" took place.

There is also a need for research into proper location of a stone when the stone is clearly, or perhaps not so clearly, out of place. In one cemetery, there were three graves in a row. The first was marked by the broken base of a stone, the next by a stone of a wife/mother, and the third by a stone of a son. It seemed apparent that the missing stone probably belonged to the husband/father. A broken stone bearing his name was laying elsewhere in that cemetery in a place that was clearly incorrect—both at an angle oblique to nearby graves and too near to a properly placed stone. When the person employed to repair/reset broken and/or toppled stones in that cemetery was questioned about the seemingly incorrect location of this man's stone, he indicated that he *was* puzzled by the number of stones standing or laying so close together. Upon hearing the suggestion for the correct location mentioned above, he carried the stone to the broken base and found a perfect fit. The father's stone is now in its correct place next to his wife and one of his sons.

WRITTEN IN STONE

Correcting errors during the writing of this book was a simple matter thanks to computers and word processing software. Correcting an error that has been cut into a gravestone is another matter. On the gravestones of the cemeteries covered in this book, some errors were allowed to stand, and others were corrected.

The most common uncorrected error is the backwards or upside down letter or numeral. An upper case *N* can be seen backwards on the stone of Sylvanus Higgins in Hillside Cemetery (Bar Harbor - 6). In Mount Height Cemetery (Southwest Harbor - 4) an upside down *7* appears on the stone of Agnes B. Reynolds. Included in this category of uncorrected errors is the occurrence of conflicting death or birth dates on two stones. Variant spellings of a surname are not at all unusual as different families may spell the name differently. However, occasionally two spellings were given for the same individual. In Salisbury Cove Cemetery (Bar Harbor - 5), Upton Salisbury's wife is called Thankful on some stones and Thankfull on others. Also, although they spelled their last name with an *i*, their son, George M., (or perhaps the person engraving the stone) preferred Salsbury instead. In at least one instance, an incorrect letter is used in a word. On the stone marking Lucretia E. Birlen's grave in Mount Height Cemetery (Southwest Harbor - 4) the first *d* of *died* is an upper case *B* producing the word *Bied*.

Two methods of correcting a mistake have been found in the cemeteries covered in this book—"erase" the error and engrave the correct character(s), or leave the error and superimpose the correction on the mistake.

Evidence of erasure is found on several stones. The surface is scooped out to remove the offending character. This method appears on relatively recent stones. A variation of the erasure method is to fill in the error with a substance that hardens to imitate the rest of the stone and then to engrave the correct information. The outline of the earlier error is still visible, but it does not affect in any appreciable way the ability to read the correct information.

A second method of correcting an error, and one that usually leaves genealogists and historians puzzled, is to engrave a correction on top of an error. In at least one case, however, engraving a correction on top of an error did not cause confusion. In Mount Height Cemetery (Southwest Harbor - 4), the second letter of the month of Emma J. Dolliver's death was originally (and incorrectly) engraved as *u*, presumably with the intent to engrave the month of June. After noticing the error, the worker engraved an *a* on top of the *u*. The *y* that was added to the end of the abbreviation of the corrected month, *Jany*, makes the result unambiguous, although interesting.

BEFORE THEIR TIME

Infant and child mortality were notably higher a hundred years ago, and safety and navigational aids were minimal. It should not be unexpected, therefore, to find many graves of children and young adults, especially from the 1800s. In spite of this, there were some deaths, from natural causes or accidents, that stood out during the research for this book.

In the Mount Desert Street Cemetery in Bar Harbor is a stone marking the grave of a Lucreatia [sic] K. Douglass (dau. of Rev. William S. and Priscilla [no stones]) who died in 1853 at the age of 12 years. Her gravestone reports that she "was killed by falling from cliffs on Newport Mt. Eden Me." Newport is an earlier name for Champlain Mountain. The term "cliffs" likely referred to the east side. Until recently, her stone laid on the ground obliquely to nearby graves.

Accidents occasionally claimed multiple individuals in a single family. For people in the Mount Desert Island region, these accidents often involved the sea. James Bartlett and two of his sons (Bartlett Island Cemetery 1 [Mount Desert - 15]) were all lost at sea on 24 April 1846. Three young Hadlock men (Cranberry Isles - 5) were also lost at sea—one in 1829 and two in January 1831. A fourth died in the West Indies in 1828.

Disease often took the lives of several children in a family over a relatively brief span of time. Three Rosebrook children (Cranberry Isles - 4) died within a seven day period in late September of 1898. An extreme case is recorded in the Otter Creek Cemetery (Mount Desert - 10). From 28 February to 28 March 1862, a 29-day period, six children of William and Elizabeth S. Stanley died. They were two girls and four boys and ranged in age from about 4 years and 2 months through nearly 18 years and 8 months.

Although nothing can compensate for the death of a child, some parents dealt with this loss by naming a subsequent child for the deceased one. A headstone in Ledgelawn Cemetery (Bar Harbor - 20) gives the name of a mother and father and two children, both named Elmar [sic] J. The first Elmar J. was born in 1909 and died the next year. The second Elmar J. was born in 1913 and died in 1918. Similarly, a gravestone in Mount Height Cemetery (Southwest Harbor - 4) reports that Frederick Lawler (son of William and Elizabeth C.) died in February of 1864 at the age of 9 years and 10 months. In the early summer of 1865 Elizabeth gave birth to another son, whom they named Freddie (probably Frederick, but the gravestone says Freddie). Similar to the Ledgelawn Cemetery example, this second Frederick died just over three years later.

DEATH BY ANY OTHER NAME

The word *died* seems a harsh word to many people, so numerous alternatives are used in its place, often coupled with references to a belief in something beyond death. These other words and phrases, not unexpectedly, have found their way onto gravestones. Among them are:

asleep
at rest
called home
cease[d] to be
cross[ed] the cold dark river
crossed alone the narrow sea
departed this life
entered the higher life
fell asleep
gone before [temporally]
gone (but not forgotten)
gone home
gone to mansions above yonder sky
gone to the mansions of rest
gone to rest
gone to sleep
lost
passed from life to his home in the grave
passed to rest
passed to the higher life
passed to the mansions of rest
plucked
safely reached the other shore
sleeping in her lonely grave
transition

HOW THEY DIED

A cause of death other than illness or old age is occasionally reported on a gravestone. Three that can be observed in cemeteries covered in this book are “lost at sea”, “killed in action” (mostly, but not exclusively, diring the Civil War), and “drowned”.

NOTABLE PERSONS

Charles W. Eliot, long-time president of Harvard University, subtitled his book about the life of John Gilley “one of the forgotten millions.” Truly the lives of many people are apparently forgotten after a generation or two. Indeed, one hundred years after anyone’s death, there is no living recollection of that person’s life. Only photographs or occasionally audio tapes or films may remain, and without careful preservation, these, too, are lost. Nevertheless, there are in each generation a few notable individuals who, by some act of their own or circumstance of history or a combination of the two, rise above the anonymity that is the fate of most.

Some of these people are, alphabetically:

Harriet (Blaine) Beale and Margaret (Blaine) Damrosch (Ledgelawn Cemetery, Bar Harbor - 20) - daughters of James G. Blaine, U. S. Statesman and former owner of the home that is now the Governor's residence.

Walter Damrosch (Ledgelawn Cemetery, Bar Harbor - 20) - musician, whose radio concerts were familiar fare in the first half of the 20th century.

Wendell Gilley (Mount Height Cemetery, Southwest Harbor - 4) - birdcarver, whose work is celebrated in the Gilley Museum in Southwest Harbor.

Nellie Thornton (Mrs. Seth) (Mount Height Cemetery, Southwest Harbor - 4) - author of a history of Somesville and Southwest Harbor.

Marguerite Yourcenar (Brookside Cemetery, Mount Desert - 6) - French author and first woman elected to the Académie Français.

There are also persons who share a name with a famous individual of history or fiction. Some of these are: Charles Dickens, John Hancock, Ruth Moore, William Faulkner, Henry Higgins, James Joyce, Horace Mann, and Thomas Paine.

LAUGHING IN THE FACE OF DEATH?

It is, perhaps, difficult to be optimistic in the face of death, but one stone seems to exhibit that outlook. In the Seal Harbor Cemetery (Mount Desert - 18) is a stone into which has been carved the familiar "smiley face". Of all the dates marking death, only one was found that has not yet arrived. In the Ledgelawn Cemetery (Bar Harbor - 20) is an individual's stone giving a birth date of 1924 and a death date of 2024. The dates of the life of one person, now buried in the Hodgdon Cemetery (Tremont - 1), is simply "20th century".

Footstones are not an expected place for anything whimsical, if for no reason other than their diminutive size. However, someone's apparent sense of humor can be seen in the "First Public Cemetery" on the High Road in Southwest Harbor. A footstone is so-named because it is located at the end of a grave nearest the feet of the deceased. It may be blank or simply bear the person's initials, usually of the first and last names, but sometimes including the middle name(s). The footstone of David E. F. G. Hopkins bears not only 5 initials, but they are alphabetically consecutive: D. E. F. G. H.

In Mount Height cemetery is an occurrence common in cemeteries. A husband and wife's names are on a large stone on a lot. In addition, each individual has a separate stone marking his or her grave and indicating his or her relationship to the couple's children. The rhyming couplet "Man's work is from sun to sun, but woman's work is never done" is unintentionally, but nonetheless humorously, displayed by two such stones, one reading "Father/at rest" and the other, simply "Mother".

PART TWO

Part two is a record of names and dates on all stones found in all cemeteries in the towns of Bar Harbor, Cranberry Isles, Mount Desert (including Bartlett Island and Sheep Island) Southwest Harbor, and Tremont (including Great Gott Island and Tinker Island).

EXPLANATION OF CONTENTS

Name/number. Cemetery names are primarily from topographic maps, signs, and popular usage. In some cases, names were given to cemeteries only for convenience of reference in this book. These names are based on geographical location (*e.g.*, Schooner Head Cemetery [Bar Harbor - 19]) or surname of predominant family (*e.g.*, Thomas Cemetery [Bar Harbor - 16]). Numbers assigned to the cemeteries will provide continuity through subsequent editions of this book when research reveals a need to change a name applied to a cemetery in this first edition.

Location/directions. The location of each cemetery is noted. Directions are given to the cemetery and mileage from easily identifiable points, usually intersections of roads. These directions do not always follow the shortest route, but are intended to be the easiest to follow for a person unfamiliar with the area. Many cemeteries are on privately owned land. The directions given in this book should in no way be construed as permission to visit these cemeteries if a landowner does not want such activity.

History. This section contains only a small fraction of the history of any cemetery. A comprehensive history of each cemetery is not an objective of this book, but is part of ongoing research that some day may find its way into print. All referenced books and pages in deeds and wills are found in the Hancock County Registry of Deeds, Ellsworth, Maine.

Notes. Here are observations of the general condition of each cemetery. Occasionally notes are included regarding particular stones.

Names and dates on gravestones and other markers. Material in parentheses, such as (husb. of Lelia), is from information found on the gravestones or that can be deduced confidently (*e.g.*, a man and a woman's name on a headstone with individual stones on the same lot that read "mother" and "father" are assumed to be husband and wife). Bracketed material, such as [dau. of Henry and Anna], indicates information strongly suggested by the gravestones (*e.g.*, adjacent stones of the same design are probably a husband and wife) and sometimes supported by supplemental material such as census records, vital records, and obituaries. Material followed by a question mark and enclosed in brackets, such as [son of Thomas and Releaf?], are educated guesses by the author. All dates and ages are recorded here as they are found on the stones. As mentioned in the introduction, this book, in spite of care taken to insure its accuracy, constitutes a secondary source and should be treated as such. Finally, the bracketed phrase [no stone] means that there is no stone for the person whose name immediately precedes the brackets, and the bracketed phrase [no stones] indicates the absence of stones for both persons whose names precede the brackets.

The date of the most recent visit for the purpose of checking names and dates on *all* stones is placed in brackets at the end of the heading to this section. Occasionally a later visit for other purposes allowed recording information from a new stone, but this date is not reported.

LITERATURE CITED

Colby and Stuart. 1881. Colby's Atlas of the State of Maine. Houlton, Maine.

Robbins, Raymond E. Jr. 1994. A History of the Houses of West Tremont, Maine. Volume One.

Thornton, Mrs. Seth. [Nellie C.]. 1938. Traditions and records of Southwest Harbor and Somesville, Mount Desert Island, Maine. Acadia Publishing Company, Bar Harbor, Maine.

BAR HARBOR

On a Monday, the sixth of April, in 1795, the inhabitants of the town of Mount Desert voted to divide their town into two towns. Their vote further called for the selectmen to determine a dividing line and report back to a town meeting to be held the next month. On May 6, the selectmen's report was accepted, and on 23 February 1796, the new town was incorporated as Eden. Bar Harbor, one of the villages of Eden, replaced the name Eden as the official name on 4 March 1918. There are twenty-two cemeteries in Bar Harbor, ranging in size from a single stone (Bar Harbor - 22) to the largest, Ledgelawn (Bar Harbor - 20). Some are owned and maintained by the town; others are owned and maintained by a non-profit organization, usually a cemetery association; the rest are private. A few are owned by the town but maintained by a non-profit organization. Some private cemeteries are cared for either by individuals who own the land that contains or surrounds the cemetery or by descendants of individuals buried in the cemetery; other private cemeteries are generally abandoned. The following cemeteries are grouped according to the entity that maintains them.

Town:
- Hamilton Station Cemetery (Bar Harbor - 3)
- Salisbury Cove Cemetery (Bar Harbor - 5)
- Higgins Cemetery (Bar Harbor - 9)
- Mount Desert Street Cemetery (Bar Harbor - 11)

Non-profit organization:
- Hadley Point Cemetery (Bar Harbor - 2)
- Leland Cemetery (Bar Harbor - 4)
- Hillside Cemetery (Bar Harbor - 6)
- Mountain View Cemetery (Bar Harbor - 8)
- Holy Redeemer Cemetery (Bar Harbor - 12)
- Ledgelawn Cemetery (Bar Harbor - 20)

Private or unknown oversight:
- Old County Road Cemetery (Bar Harbor - 1)
- Emery Cemetery (Bar Harbor - 7) - maintained by owner of surrounding land
- Higgins-Marcyes Burial Ground (Bar Harbor - 10) - maintained by landowner
- Peach Cemetery (Bar Harbor - 13) - maintained by relatives of some persons buried in the cemetery
- Deacon Oliver's Cemetery (Bar Harbor - 14) - maintained by descendants of Deacon Oliver Higgins
- Hadley Cemetery (Bar Harbor - 15) - no apparent care
- Thomas Cemetery (Bar Harbor - 16) - recently restored; future oversight unknown
- Burn[e]s-Richardson Burial Ground (Bar Harbor - 17) - no apparent care
- Paine Cemetery (Bar Harbor - 18) - maintained by landowner
- Schooner Head Cemetery (Bar Harbor - 19) - unknown oversight
- Emery Family Burial Ground (Bar Harbor - 21) - unknown oversight
- Newman grave (Bar Harbor - 22) - no apparent care

Previously buried stone (at right) of Ruth Higgins, wife of William Higgins whose stone is at left (Old County Road Cemetery, Bar Harbor - 1).

Old County Road Cemetery

(Bar Harbor - 1)

Location/directions. Along west side of Old County Road. From the traffic light at the north end of Mount Desert Island, turn right onto Old County Road. The cemetery is on the right in approximately 0.2–0.3 miles. Across the road from this cemetery is (2000) an old house in poor condition.

History. —

Notes. There appears to be no regular maintenance of this cemetery. During the past few years, however, a few small trees have been cut down, and some lichens have been removed from the stones. There is no enclosure, nor are there any apparent boundary markers. It is likely that there are more stones than reported below, but they have become buried over time. Indeed, when I returned to unearth a partially buried stone that I had observed during an earlier visit, I was initially unable to locate it. I remembered, however, that it was near the road and, by removing leaves here and there, found it. Only part of the inscription was visible. The remaining portion, including the person's name, was covered with packed soil and a tree root. Using an old wood-handled paintbrush, I removed the dirt to reveal the name Ruth Higgins [see below]. The root continues to prevent returning the stone to an upright position. Less than a year later, leaves cover all but one corner of the stone.

Names and dates on gravestones and other markers. [2 May 1999]

C.
  A.M.[3] [footstone only]
  J. O. [footstone only]
COLLINS
  [Cynthia M. - see COUSINS]
COUSINS
  Asenath (dau. of Elisha and Thankful) - d. 15 March 1830 Æ 20 y.
  Cynthia M. (COLLINS; adopted dau. of Capt. Samuel H. [no stone] and Martha A.) - d. 31 January 1880 Æ 22 y., 3 m.
  Elisha (husb. of Thankful) - d. 25 September 1850 Æ 79 y.
  Martha A. (wife of Capt. Samuel H. [no stone]) - d. 14 February 1896 Æ 73 y., 2 m.
  Thankful (wife of Elisha) - d. 23 January 1852 Æ 80 y.
GILLEY
  Mary A. ("infant" dau. of L. W. and Mary [no stones]) - [b. and?] d. 10 August 1837
HALEY
  Jennie M. (MAYO; wife of Patrick [no stone]) - d. 16 September 1901 Æ 63 y.
HIGGINS
  Jesse (husb. of Priscilla) - d. 12 December 1814 Æ 74 y.
  Priscilla - d. 12 August 1878 Æ 80 y., 2 m.
  Priscilla (wife of Jesse) - d. 20 February 1843 Æ 86 y., 9 m.
  Ruth (wife of William) - d. 20 September 1877 Æ 80 y., 3 m., 4 d.
  William (husb. of Ruth) - d. 27 October 1869 Æ 74 y.
MAYO
  Cynthia M. (dau. of Joseph and Maria [S. or L.][1]) - d. 14 October 1884 Æ 29 y., 17 d.
  Flora M. (dau. of Joseph and Maria [S. or L.][1]) - d. 24 March 1879 Æ 20 y., 10 m., 18 d.
  [Jennie M. - see HALEY]
  Joseph (husb. of Maria [S. or L.][1]) - d. 20 August 1878 Æ 56 y., 1 m., 17 d.

Maria [S. or L.][1,2] (wife of Joseph) - d. 4 January 1886 Æ 60 y., 4 m., 18 d.
Mary F. (wife of Israel [no stone]) - d. 18 April 1854 Æ 79 y., 5 m., 28 d.
Sherman L. (son of Joseph and Maria [S. or L.][1]) - d. 27 October 1887 Æ 15 y., 7 m., 24 d.

PHIPIN

Eben - d. 3 April 1863 Æ 58 y., 4 m., 20 d.

R.

C. [footstone only]

RICHARDSON

Joseph (husb. of Mercy S.) - d. 9 August 1899 Æ 84 y.
Julia T. (dau. of Joseph and Mercy S.) - d. 30 October 1875 Æ 18 y., 10 m., 20 d.
Mercy S. (wife of Joseph) - d. 1 January 1894 Æ 70 y.
Thomas (Capt.) - d. 10 September 1849, "at sea", Æ 27 y.

S.

D. H. [footstone only]

SNOW

Cordelia (wife of Giles) - d. 15 August 1887 Æ 68 y., 10 m.
Giles (husb. of Cordelia) - d. 27 June 1870 Æ 59 y., 11 m., 27 d.

Notes:

[1]Different middle initial on different stones.
[2]The *q* in the word *quiet* on this stone is backwards.
[3]The initial of the last name is probably C. This footstone is broken into two main pieces with a small fragment missing. Two sets of initials appear on this footstone—J. O. C. and A. M. [...], this last initial being on the missing piece.

Hadley Point Cemetery

(Bar Harbor - 2)

Location/directions. Along west side of Hadley Point Road. From the traffic light at the north end of Mount Desert Island, bear left on Route 3. In approximately 3.0–3.1 miles, turn left onto Hadley Point Road. The cemetery is on the left in about 0.2–0.3 miles.

History. —

Notes. Part of this cemetery's boundary is marked by a chain-link fence, and part is marked by iron stakes driven into rocks. A portion of the cemetery is somewhat overgrown, and many gravestones are laying on the ground. A map drawn from a survey by Herrick & Salsbury, Inc., of Ellsworth is on file in the Hancock County Registry of Deeds (17:180, 15 January 1982). See 1501:343–345 for a description of the property.

Names and dates on gravestones and other markers. [30 April 1999]

BUTLER
Sheila M. - b. 1948; d. 1980

CLEAVES
C. Lester - b. 14 May 1867; d. [...][1]
Harriet Alice - [b. and d.?] 2 August 1907; ("our baby")

COUSINS
Edward E. [husb. of Iva E.] - b. 1879; d. 1951
Iva E. [wife of Edward E.] - b. 1879; d. 1957

EMERY
Jane (RICHARDSON) - b. 1815; d. 1910

FARINELLA
Salvatore III - b. 8 August 1940; d. 24 July 1988

FARRIN
Ella P. [wife of Eugene E.] - b. 1923; d. 1994
Eugene E. [husb. of Ella P.] - b. 1919

HADLEY
Orville ("infant son" of Capt. Z. [K.?][2] and C. E. [no stones]) - [b. and?] d. 16 October 1870

INGALLS
Charlotte S. [wife of Sheldon A.] - b. 1914
Sheldon A. [husb. of Charlotte S.] - b. 1912; d. 1979

LELAND
Clifford V. (husb. of Lizzie A.) - b. 1860; d. 1937
David H. (husb. of Sophia) - d. 12 February 1876 Æ 58 y., 5 m., 12 d.
Everett E. (husb. of Mary Deane) - b. 1864; d. 1911
Harlan D. (son of Everett E. and Mary Deane) - b. 3 March 1906; d. 30 September 1920
Hollis C. [husb. of Mary E.] - b. 1 April 1897; d. 3 April 1971
Lizzie A. (wife of Clifford V.) - d. 21 August 1901 Æ 33 y., 4 m., 11 d.
Margaret M. - b. 1888; d. 1940
Mary Deane (wife of Everett E.) - b. 1870; d. 1960
Mary E. [wife of Hollis C.] - b. 1886; d. 1957
Otis B. [husb. of Sarah R.?] - b. 1849; d. 1929
Sarah R. [wife of Otis B.?] - b. 1855; d. 1932
Sophia (wife of David H.) - b. 13 November 1826; d. 24 March 1915

LINSCOTT
Charlotte I. [wife of Russell E.] - b. 1929
Russell E. [husb. of Charlotte I.] - b. 1929; d. 1986
MANCK
Edward A. [husb. of Elizabeth R[ODICK?].] - b. 1865; d. 1949
Elizabeth R[ODICK?]. [wife of Edward A.] - b. 1871; d. 1949
RICHARDS
Elizabeth R. (wife of Samuel H.) - d. 29 April 1888 Æ 74 y., 10 m., 8 d.
Frank P. [husb. of Julia A.] - d. 19 October 1885 Æ 33 y., 28 d.
Fred (son of Simeon H. and Etta [no stone]) - d. 26 May 1869 Æ 2 d.
George B. (Capt.; husb. of Hannah Caroline) - d. 26 May 1898 Æ 74 y., 6 m.
George H. (son of James H. and H. C. [no stone]) - b. 1875; d. 1914
[H. Ann - see RODICK]
Hannah Caroline (wife of Capt. George B.) - b. 13 November 1829; d. 10 March 1915
James H. (husb. of H. C. [no stone]) - b. 1833; d. 1914
Julia A. [wife of Frank P.] - b. 1853; d. 1930
Mary - d. 28 July 1848 Æ 87 y., 10 m.
Phila [RICHARDS?] - [no dates]
Samuel 2nd - d. 24 February 1894 Æ 50 y., 11 m., 9 d.
Samuel H. (husb. of Elizabeth R.) - d. 13 July 1899 Æ 88 y., 4 m., 23 d.
Simeon H. (husb. of Etta [no stone]) - d. 26 January 1889 Æ 69 y., 7 d.
William (Capt.; husb. of [...][3]) - d. 2[1?][4] March 1862 Æ 84 y., 9 m., 14 d.
William B. - b. 1862; d. 1943
[...][3] (wife of Capt. William) - d. 16 September 1867 Æ 80 y., 7 m., 11 d.
RICHARDSON
[Jane - see EMERY]
Roscoe G. S. (son of William S. and Susan L.) - d. 30 May 1877, "Chelsea Hospital", Æ 22 y., 5 m., 13 d.
Ruth Eliza [wife of William S.?] - d. 17 April 1851 Æ 36 y., 11 m.
Susan L. (wife of William S.) - d. 21 January 1875 Æ 48 y., 7 d.
William S. (husb. of [Ruth Eliza and?] Susan L.) - d. 4 May 1876 Æ 76 y., 5 m., 9 d.
RODICK
Daniel - d. 6 August 1897 Æ 39 y., 7 m.
[Elizabeth R[ODICK?]. - see MANCK]
Fountain - b. 1865; d. 1947
H. Ann (RICHARDS; wife of Thomas [no stone]) - b. 1826; d. 1901
SERONDE
Dorothea (wife of Joseph) - b. 1890; m. 1916; d. 1945
Joseph (husb. of Dorothea) - b. 1883; m. 1916; d. 1979
SMITH
Gerard K. - b. 25 December 1923; d. 15 September 1943
Gordon E. [son of Howe C. and Linnie A.?] - b. 1921; d. 1943
Howe C. (husb. of Linnie A.) - b. 1885; d. 1965
infant (son [of Howe C. and Linnie A.?]) - [b. and d.?] 28 October 1916
Linnie A. (wife of Howe C.) - b. 1887; d. 1948
Mary Lois ("infant" dau. of Howe C. and Linnie A.) - [b. and d.?] 3 March 1929
Sherrold Leland - b. 20 April 1918; d. 23 February 1999
STEARNS
Geraldine [STEARNS?] - b. 1922; d. 1979

THOMAS
Benjamin (Capt.; husb. of Polly) - d. 2 April 1867 Æ 86 y., 10 m., 27 d.
Betsey (dau. of Capt. Benjamin and Polly) - d. [...][4,5] August 1823 Æ 16 y.
Betsey M. (dau. of Capt. Benjamin and Polly) - d. 15 October 1825 Æ 5 d.
Cornelius T. (Capt.; husb. of Mary Ann [no stone]) - d. 22 April 1887 Æ 75 y., 3 m.
Emer[li?]ne[4] (dau. of Capt. Benjamin and Polly) - d. 1[...][4] January 1829 Æ 13 y.
Juliaan [sic] (son of Capt. Benjamin and Polly) - d. 22 May 1818 Æ 2 m.
Lewis (son of Capt. Benjamin and Polly) - d. 9 August 1834 Æ 25 y.
Lewis M. (son of Capt. Cornelius T. and Mary Ann [no stone]) - d. 14 September 1862 Æ 8 y., 9 m., 11 d.
Polly (wife of Capt. Benjamin) - d. 29 August 1873 Æ 87 y., 7 m., 11 d.
S. Bernice (dau. of Capt. Cornelius T. and Mary Ann [no stone]) - d. 9 April 1850 Æ 1 y., 7 m., 24 d.

WASGATT
John (husb. of Julia A.) - d. February 1892 Æ 78 y., 8 m., 27 d.
Julia A. (wife of John) - d. 6 March 1889 Æ 69 y., 8 m., 2 d.

YOUNG
Arvilla [O. or T.][6] (wife of William H.) - b. 1859; d. 1917
Charlie E. (son of William H. and Arvilla [O. or T.][6]) - d. 27 February 1890 Æ 8 y., 6 m., 7 d.
William H. (husb. of Arvilla [O. or T.][6]) - b. 1857; d. 1959

[...]
[...][3,7]

Notes:
[1] Both numbers and letters for the date of death are missing from the metal marker that is set in a concrete base on this grave. On an adjacent grave, a similar metal marker set in a concrete base is broken, with only the bottom remaining.
[2] Difficult to read.
[3] Stone crumbling.
[4] Stone broken.
[5] Digit for the day is round-topped.
[6] Different middle initial on different stones.
[7] Base for stone in good condition.

Hamilton Station Cemetery

(Bar Harbor - 3)

Location/directions. Hamilton Station. From the traffic light at the north end of Mount Desert Island, bear left on Route 3. In approximately 3.2–3.3 miles, two long, red buildings set back from the left side of the road. The cemetery is to the right of these buildings when they are viewed from Route 3.

History. Owned by town of Bar Harbor.

Notes. This cemetery is composed of two parts—a mowed portion enclosed by chain suspended between granite posts and an unmaintained portion.

Names and dates on gravestones and other markers. [2 August 1999]

EMERY
- Agnes Mabel (wife of Raymond [no stone]) - d. 5 February 1899 Æ 19 y., 5 m., 12 d.
- infant (dau. of Raymond [no stone] and Agnes Mabel) - d. 9 January 1899 Æ [not given]

H.
- L. H.[1] - d. 17 September 1862 Æ 26 y., 8 m., 16 d.
- U. [footstone only]

HIGGINS
- Ansel B. (son of Capt. Eben L. and Hannah D.) - d. 12 July 1839 Æ 8 m.
- [B. Frank or Frank B.][2] (husb. of Hattie M. [no stone]) - d. 9 January 1899 Æ 46 y., 9 m., 27 d.
- Benjamin L. - d. 25 January 1891 Æ 77 y.
- Charles H. (son of Eben L. 2nd and Lucy M.) - d. 13 October 1888 Æ 20 y.
- Clarion F. (wife of Z. H.) - d. 4 April 1895 Æ 58 y., 8 m.
- Eben L. (Capt.; husb. of Hannah D.) - d. 28 December 1900 Æ 92 y., 9 m.
- Eben L. 2nd (husb. of Lucy M.) - b. 1845; d. 1916; ("G. A. R." [Civil War])
- Eve[r]line[2] C. (dau. of Capt. Eben L. and Hannah D.) - d. 4 November 1857 Æ 21 y., 5 m.
- Hannah D. (wife of Capt. Eben L.) - d. 10 September 1893 Æ 88 y., 9 m.
- Johnny H. (son of [B. Frank or Frank B.][2] and Hattie M. [no stone]) - d. 25 December 1893 Æ 6 y., 7 m.
- Lucy M. (wife of Eben L. 2nd) - d. 14 November 1887 Æ 40 y., 4 m., 4 d.
- [Nancy L. - see JONES]
- Nehemiah - d. 28 October 1818 Æ 51 y.
- Z. H. (husb. of Clarion F.) - [no dates]

JONES
- Nancy L. (HIGGINS; wife of Charles A. [no stone]) - d. 27 February 1890 Æ 49 y.

LELAND
- Almira H. (dau. of William and Lydia [no stones]) - d. 15 February 1866 Æ 25 y., 6 m.
- Amariah M. ("twin son" of Capt. Amariah and Martha [no stones]) - d. 28 April 1852 Æ 6 m.
- Josephine A. (wife of Capt. H. D. [no stone]) - d. 28 December 1863, Eden, Æ 21 y., 10 m.
- Milford A. (son of Capt. H. D. [no stone] and Josephine A.) - d. 18 January 1864, Eden, Æ [not given]

[for Notes, please see next page]

Notes:

[1]A portion of the headstone is missing. The footstone reads "L. H. H.".

[2]Different on different stones.

Leland Cemetery
(Bar Harbor - 4)

Location/directions. Leland Point. From the traffic light at the north end of Mount Desert Island, bear left on Route 3. In approximately 3.7–3.8 miles, and just before the Coach Stop Inn, turn left onto fire road 411. Follow this road to the cemetery.

History. Land was added to an already extant cemetery by deed to the Leland Cemetery Association in 1911 (483:401–402; "one-third acre more or less") and twice in 1915 (521:82–83 and 521:84–85), the second 1915 addition being a "triangular strip of land containing twelve hundred and ninety-five square feet more or less".

Notes. This cemetery is not enclosed, but one old wood post with a decorative top was found indicating the likelihood of an earlier fence. Several iron pipes are apparent boundary markers. The grass is mowed and trimmed.

Names and dates on gravestones and other markers. [5 July 1999]
A.
P.[1]
ALLEY
Amelia Frances (dau. of Jason and Nancy) - d. 30 June 1883 Æ 27 y., 11 m., 21 d.
Ephraim [husb. of Lulu B.] - b. 9 November 1858; d. 17 February 1911
Jason (husb. of Nancy) - d. 19 November 1882 Æ 67 y., 24 d.
Laura F. (dau. of H. O. and T. P. [no stones]) - b. 14 October 1930; d. 12 November 1930
Lulu B. [wife of Ephraim] - b. 12 January 1868; d. 9 October 1932
Milton E. [son of Ephraim and Lulu B.?] - b. 23 January 1895; d. 13 April 1900
Nancy (wife of Jason) - d. 26 October 1886 Æ 70 y., 3 m.
BAILEY
Elizabeth C. (wife of Samuel D.) - b. 1875; d. 1959
Samuel D. (husb. of Elizabeth C.) - b. 1871; d. 1935
BOWDEN
Ann Katherine - b. 8 November 1922; d. 20 September 1995
Caroline S. [wife of Frank O.] - b. 1853; d. 1927
Frank O. [husb. of Caroline S.] - b. 1851; d. 1918
Gail J. - b. 23 October 1927
Jennie L. [wife of Lewis F.] - b. 1889; d. 1956
Lewis F. [husb. of Jennie L.] - b. 24 September 1888; d. 28 October 1947
BREWER
Lillian A. (dau. of Perry H. [no stone] and Orilla A.) - d. 17 May 1861 Æ 2 y., 8 m.
Marcelles E. (son of Perry H. [no stone] and Orilla A.) - d. 16 July 1864 Æ 5 m.
Orilla A.[2] (wife of Perry H. [no stone]) - d. 20 March 1866 Æ 29 y., 11 m.
CARPENTER
Edward S. (husb. of Mattie A.) - b. 1867; d. 1947
Mattie A. (wife of Edward S.) - b. 1857; d. 1935
CONNERS
Sarah E. (SALISBURY; dau. of John S. SALISBURY and Endora [no stone]) - d. 11 February 1900 Æ 41 y., 4 m., 2 d.
COOK
Georgia (McFARLAND; [wife of Lawrence H.]) - b. 1902; d. 1985
Lawrence H. [husb. of Georgia (McFARLAND)] - b. 10 October 1899; d. 20 September 1960

DILLON
Isabel (SALISBURY; [wife of William E. Sr.]) - b. 1920; d. 1996
William E. Sr. [husb. of Isabel (SALISBURY)] - b. 1921; d. 1997
DOYLE
Joseph W. - b. 1907; d. 1979
Leland - b. 1936; d. 1983
DYER
infant [son of Marguerite (LELAND)] - [no dates]
Marguerite (LELAND) - b. 1892; d. 1981
EMERY
Albion J. (husb. of Ellen E.) - b. 1909; d. 1992
Alta V. - b. 1854; d. 1940
Anita Faye - b. 1 April 1938; d. 3 September 1938
Ashpeline (wife of Thomas P.) - b. 1834; d. 1912
Ellen E. (wife of Albion J.) - b. 1910; d. 1982
Elnora (wife of Rufus R.) - b. 13 November 1835; d. 13 June 1906
Eunice (JELLISON) - b. 19 August 1877; d. 5 February 1941
Frank O. - b. 1856; d. 1893
Fred O. - b. 15 March 1879; d. 2 September 1909
[Julia Ann - see FOGG]
Lona (RICH) - b. 1868; d. 1947
Lydia H. (wife of Thomas P.) - b. 1818; d. 1883
Nancy (PEACH) - b. 15 November 1853; d. 18 June 1933
Rufus R. (husb. of Elnora) - b. 30 April 1832; d. 23 December 1916
Sally E. (wife of William) - d. 15 July 1849 Æ 61 y.
Thomas P. (husb. of Lydia H. and Ashpeline) - b. 1827; d. 1913
William (husb. of Sally E.) - d. 21 June 1857 Æ 78 y.
William H. - b. 29 October 1880; d. 18 November 1940
FOGG
Julia Ann (EMERY; dau. of William EMERY and Sally E.; wife of Isaac [no stone]) - d. 23 November 1836 Æ 23 y.
GRAY
Carmelita L. [GRAY?] - b. 1898; d. 1952
Linwood C. - b. 20 May 1888; d. 17 August 1971
H.
M[...][3] - d. 20 March 1866 Æ 29 y., 11 m.
HAMOR
Alice M. (wife of Robert B.) - b. 20 September 1858; d. 19 May 1899
Ansel L. [son of Robert B. and Alice M.?] - b. 1888; d. 1978
Charles A. [husb. of Henrietta T.?] - d. 26 May 1921 Æ 74 y., 5 m., 20 d.
Denvill B. - b. 1845; d. 1865
Georgia E. - b. 29 April 1885; d. 31 October 1971
Henrietta T. [wife of Charles A.?] - d. 2 April 1909 Æ 58 y., 5 m., 7 d.
Robert B. (husb. of Alice M.) - b. 1836; d. 1917
HOMER
[Alice - see McFARLAND]
HOPKINS
Archie C. (son of George W. and Linda Myra (YOUNG)) - b. 1868; d. 1962
George W. (husb. of Linda Myra (YOUNG)) - b. 14 September 1834; d. 27 February 1922
Linda Myra (YOUNG; wife of George W.) - b. 23 October 1834; d. 5 March 1912
Mary (wife of Smith [no stone]) - d. 3 March 1871 Æ 75 y., 5 m., 15 d.

Seth H. (son of George W. and Linda Myra (YOUNG)) - b. 1863; d. 1957
[Zena - see RICH]

JELLISON
[Eunice - see EMERY]

JORDAN
infant (son of William R. and Anna S. [no stones]) - d. 15 June 1891 Æ 1 m.

KARST
Cora [wife of George] - [no dates]
George [husb. of Cora] - [no dates]

LELAND
A. Maxwell (husb. of Ruby S.) - b. 1895; d. [no date]
Adelbert H. - d. 5 August 1888 Æ 31 y.
Alston H. - b. 1853; d. 1917
Clara R. (dau. of Frederick A. and Sarah M.) - d. 18 March 1848 Æ 3 y., 4 m., 22 d.
D[avid?].[4] (husb. of Susan) - [...][4]
E. A. - [no dates]; (member of Co. E, 30th Massachusetts Infantry [Civil War])
Eben L. (husb. of Thankful) - d. 14 October 1849 Æ 71 y., 6 m.
Eben L. (son of Eben L. and Thankful) - d. 18 May 1833 Æ 14 y.
Eben L. [son of Capt. Thomas H. and Mary A. [no stone]] - d. 19 October 1849 Æ 16 y., 3 m.
[Elisabeth - see WATERMAN]
Eliza A. (wife of Capt. William T.) - d. 15 September 1884 Æ 66 y., 11 m.
Elizabeth S. (wife of Frank I.) - b. 30 March 1865; d. 25 May 1940
Elmiretta R. (wife of Capt. Orien H.) - b. 1839; d. 1922
Elvin Y. [husb. of Mary J.] - b. 1867; d. 1946
Ezra (husb. of Hannah) - d. 26 November 1833 Æ 57 y., 10 m., 24 d.
Ezra L. (son of Eben L. and Thankful) - d. 17 June 1857, "at sea", Æ 23 y.
Frank I. (husb. of Elizabeth S.) - b. 20 March 1855; d. 11 January 1913
Frederick A. (husb. of Sarah M.) - b. 30 April 1812; d. 25 January 1893
Geneva R. (wife of Capt. P. R.) - d. 16 October 1879 Æ 29 y., 5 m., 16 d.
Hannah (wife of Ezra) - d. 19 December 1840 Æ 57 y., 10 m., 2 d.
Haynes P. (son of Roswell and Jane) - d. 28 October 1849 Æ 1 y., 22 d.
Herman S. (husb. of Laura A.) - b. 16 April 1897; d. 14 July 1959
infant [LELAND?] - [no dates]
Ira B. (son of Eben L. and Thankful) - d. 10 September 1830, New York, Æ 22 y.
J. Watson - b. 4 September 1843; d. 8 May 1902
Jane (wife of Roswell) - d. 12 September 1872 Æ 68 y., 9 m.
John R. (son of Frederick A. and Sarah M.) - d. 29 August 1871 Æ 22 y., 10 m., 14 d.
John S. K. - b. 26 November 1906; d. 15 December 1982
Josephine H. (dau. of Frederick A. and Sarah M.) - d. 30 November 1885 Æ 32 y., 10 m.
Laura A. (wife of Herman S.) - b. 1902; d. 1973
Lester (son of Capt. William T. and Eliza A.; twin brother of William) - d. 12 November 1849 Æ 1 y., 7 m.
Louise - b. 31 August 1888; d. 21 August 1971
[Marguerite - see DYER]
Martha A. (wife of Washington M.) - d. 20 January 1918 Æ 68 y., 11 m.
Mary J. [wife of Elvin Y.] - b. 1871; d. 1944
Mizie T. (son of Capt. Orien H. and Elmiretta R.) - d. 23 April 1863 Æ 3 y., 5 m., 13 d.
Orien H. (Capt.; husb. of Elmiretta R.) - b. 1828; d. 1906

P. R. (Capt.; husb. of Geneva R.) - b. 1842; d. 1916
Roswell (husb. of Jane) - d. 5 February 1877 Æ 68 y., 11 m.
Ruby S. (wife of A. Maxwell) - b. 1889; d. 1968
Sarah M. (wife of Frederick A.) - d. 30 July 1883 Æ 68 y., 1 m.
Susan (wife of David [see D.]) - d. 11 February 1880 Æ 84 y., 16 d.
Thankful - d. 30 October 1850 Æ 26 y.
Thankful (wife of Eben L.) - d. 31 May 1854 Æ 69 y., 2 m.
Thomas H. (Capt.; husb. of Mary A. [no stone]) - d. 14 June 1888 Æ 83 y., 5 m.
Washington M. (husb. of Martha A.) - d. 4 February 1907 Æ 70 y.
William (son of Capt. William T. and Eliza A.; twin brother of Lester) - d. 6 April 1848 Æ 7 d.
William T. (Capt.; husb. of Eliza A.) - d. 1 September 1892 Æ 74 y.

LISCOMB

George Olin - b. 11 August 1879; d. 27 September 1918
Helen W. [wife of Wayman C.] - b. 1887; d. 1955
Lawrence [LISCOMB?] - b. 1898; d. 1938
Susan L. (wife of Willard H.) - b. 1858; d. 1932
Wayman C. [husb. of Helen W.] - b. 1884; d. 1943
Willard H. (husb. of Susan L.) - b. 1855; d. 1939

MCFARLAND

Abbie D. (wife of Vernon H.) - b. 28 June 1874; d. 19 June 1950
Agnes Mabel (dau. and "only ... child" of Capt. Ira L. and Columbia L.) - d. 20 January 1879 Æ 11 y., 3 m., 5 d.
Alice (HOMER; wife of Sherman P.) - b. 1877; d. 1935
Alvaro R. - b. 1865; d. 1941
Columbia L. (wife of Capt. Ira L.) - b. 1836; d. 1906
Conrad (son of Lester M. and Mabel [L. or D.][5]) - d. 10 April 1889 Æ 6 m.
E. H.[7] (son of Capt. John M. and Sarah) - [no dates]
[Georgia - see COOK]
Hannah A. (dau. of Capt. John M. and Sarah) - d. 25 October 1849 Æ 1 y., 7 d.
infant (dau. of Lester M. and Mabel [L. or D.][5]) - d. 4 February 1895 Æ 1 m.
Ira L. (Capt.; husb. of Columbia L.) - b. 1830; d. 1899
John M. (Capt.; husb. of Sarah) - d. 12 December 1888 Æ 87 y., 7 m.
Lester M. (husb. of Mabel [L. or D.][5]) - b. 12 February 1857; d. 27 March 1926
Mabel [L. or D.][5] (wife of Lester M.) - b. 4 November 1871; d. 6 March 1942
Marian H. (wife of Sanford M. H.) - b. 1837; d. 1920
Mary J. S. (dau. of Capt. John M. and Sarah) - d. 8 November 1849 Æ 4 y., 7 m., 13 d.
Sanford M. H. (son of Capt. John M. and Sarah; husb. of Marian H.) - b. 1833; d. 5 August 1867 Æ 34 y., 10 m., "in Cuba of yellow fever"
Sarah (wife of Capt. John M.) - d. 20 April 1893 Æ 89 y., 7 m.
Sherman P. (husb. of Alice (HOMER)) - b. 1861; d. 1923
Vernon H. (husb. of Abbie D.) - b. 18 July 1859; d. 14 September 1923
[...][6] (son of Capt. John M. and Sarah) - d. 15 November [...][6] Æ 30 y., 10 m., 10 d.

MILLS

Abbie S. (wife of Andrew J.) - b. 1826; d. 1912
Andrew J. (husb. of Abbie S.) - b. 1829; d. 1907

PALMER

Addie S. (wife of A. F. [no stone]) - b. 28 March 1859; d. 5 October 1892

PEACH

[Nancy - see EMERY]

PETTINGILL
- Charles E. (husb. of Elba H.) - b. 1843; d. 1917
- Elba H. (wife of Charles E.) - b. 1849; d. 1907
- Percy Morton (son of Charles E. and Elba H.) - d. [no date] Æ 23 y.

RICH
- Anna H. [wife of Chester M.] - b. 22 February 1884; d. 14 May 1964
- Chester M. [husb. of Anna H.] - b. 5 June 1878; d. 11 October 1960
- Emma A. [wife of Samuel N.] - b. 18 August 1843; d. 8 March 1908
- John (husb. of Zena (HOPKINS)) - b. 16 February 1813; d. 23 September 1893
- [Lona - see EMERY]
- Margaret - b. 1870; d. 1939
- Samuel N. [husb. of Emma A.] - b. 23 February 1844; d. 1 December 1929
- Zena (HOPKINS; wife of John) - b. 25 December 1816; d. 13 March 1897

RICHARDSON
- M. W. - d. 19 January 1903 Æ 22 y., 4 m., 19 d.

RUSSELL
- Alice B. (wife of Walter G.) - b. 1898; d. 1982
- Mary Virginia (dau. of Walter G. and Alice B.) - b. 30 May 1924; d. 26 August 1925
- Oliver R. - b. 23 April 1927; d. 22 April 1991
- Walter G. (husb. of Alice B.) - b. 1886; d. 1952

SALISBURY
- George L. (son of Marston B. and Sarah E.) - b. 1884; d. 1902
- [Isabel - see DILLON]
- John S. (husb. of Endora [no stone]) - b. 13 April 1829; d. 2 February 1894
- Marston B. (husb. of Sarah E.) - b. 1852; d. 1945
- Mary G. (wife of Persis M.) - b. 1895; d. 1981
- Persis M. (husb. of Mary G.) - b. 1885; d. 1952
- [Sarah E. - see CONNERS]
- Sarah E. (wife of Marston B.) - b. 1861; d. 1918
- Warren S. - b. 14 December 1864; d. 21 August 1866

SMITH
- Charles C. - b. 1848; d. 1927
- Harry L. - b. 1867; d. 1925
- Olive E. - b. 1849; d. 1937

SUGATT [includes SUGETT]
- E. Harris (son of Capt. Samuel H. and Joanna H.) - d. 6 August 1860 Æ 1 y., 2 m., 8 d.
- Eugene H. (son of Capt. Samuel H. and Joanna H.) - "lost at sea" 25 April 1874 Æ 28 y.
- Joanna H. (wife of Capt. Samuel H.) - d. 24 October 1877 Æ 52 y.
- John - d. 19 May 1837 Æ 27 y.
- Lemuel G. M. (son of Capt. Samuel H. and Joanna H.) - d. 27 October 1849 Æ 1 y., 8 m.
- Samuel H. (Capt.; husb. of Joanna H.) - d. 21 May 1889 Æ 72 y., 2 m.
- Walter P. - b. 10 June 1856; d. 1 October 1887

THOMAS
- Agnes M. [wife of Linwood W.] - b. 1908; d. 1986
- Amanda J. (wife of John S.) - b. 1868; d. 1962
- Edgar E. - b. 1902; d. 1974
- George P. [THOMAS?] - b. 1891; d. 1959
- John S. (husb. of Amanda J.) - b. 1867; d. 1971

Linwood W. [husb. of Agnes M.] - b. 1910
Lloyd M. (son of John S. and Amanda J.) - d. 31 January 1919 Æ 18 y., 6 m.
Myrtle C. (dau. of John S. and Amanda J.) - d. 19 February 1894 Æ 1 m.

THURSTON
J. Granville - b. 1879; d. 1936

TROTT
Harriet M. (wife of Henry E.) - b. 1862; d. 1914
Henry E. (husb. of Harriet M.) - b. 1853; d. 1913
Ralph Henry - b. 1896; d. 1942

WATERMAN
Elisabeth (LELAND) - b. 23 January 1902; d. 3 April 1986

YOUNG
[Linda Myra - see HOPKINS]

Notes:

[1]Headstone is laying on the ground and crumbling. Footstone reads "P. A.".

[2]This stone is laying on the ground, and the portion that contained Orilla's name is badly deteriorated. That it is her stone can be inferred from its position relative to the stones of her son and daughter and from the two remaining letters *f* and *o* in "wi*f*e *o*f". Also, in the four lines of verse on the stone is a reference to the husband and family of the deceased.

[3]This stone is laying on the ground, and the upper portion containing the name of the deceased is completely worn off.

[4]The headstone on a grave adjacent to Susan LELAND likely marks her husband David's grave. The footstone on that grave reads "D. L." and her stone notes that she is the "wife of David".

[5]Different middle initial on different stones. Mabel's maiden name was DALTON, which is the likely source of the middle initial D.

[6]Stone broken.

[7]Top of stone is missing. Initials are from footstone.

Salisbury Cove Cemetery
(Bar Harbor - 5)

Location/directions. Set back from the north side of Old Bar Harbor Road. From the traffic light at the north end of Mount Desert Island, bear left on Route 3. In approximately 4.6–4.7 miles, turn left onto Norway Drive. Follow this road to the end (about 0.1 miles). Turn right onto Old Bar Harbor Road, and the cemetery is on the left in approximately 0.2–0.3 miles (and immediately after fire road #342, also on the left).

History. Owned by town of Bar Harbor.

Notes. A large stone along the approach to the cemetery bears a plaque with the inscription "In memory of our pioneers/This tablet marks the/site of/the first town house/erected in Eden/built in 1842/razed in 1931/This memorial erected by/the town of Bar Harbor/1932". No fence encloses the cemetery, although there are remnants of a former wood fence. Many stones are laying on the ground. The grass is mowed and trimmed.

Names and dates on gravestones and other markers. [18 January 1999]

BURK

Annie ("of Philadelphia") - d. July 1890 Æ [not given]

BURNS

George W. - d. 19 May 1864 Æ 23 y., 2 m.; (member of Co. C, 1st Maine Heavy Artillery [Civil War])

Lewis M. - d. 20 January 1872 Æ 15 y., 6 m.

CAMPBELL

Alberta R. (wife of James) - b. 8 September 1832; d. 28 August 1889

Betsey (dau. of John and Margaret [no stones]) - d. 22 January 1841 Æ 9 y.

Fayette - b. 20 January 1872; d. 15 April 1898

Hannah [...][1] - d. 20 March 1862 Æ 1 y., 3 m.

James (husb. of Alberta R.) - b. 3 May 1837; d. 29 January 1901

Julia M. (dau. of James and Alberta R.) - d. 20 August 1881 Æ 22 y.

Sarah E. (wife of Capt. Timothy) - d. 3 April 1893 Æ 87 y., 7 m.

Timothy (son of John and Margaret [no stones]) - d. 25 February 1847 Æ 8 m., 5 d.

Timothy (Capt.; husb. of Sarah E.) - d. 31 December 1844, Savannah, Georgia, Æ 39 y., 10 m.

DOANE

Sarah (wife of Jonathan [no stone]) - d. 9 April 1856 Æ 68 y., 8 m., [12?][2] d.

FISH

Caroline (dau. of Capt. Gilbert B. and Penelope H. "Nellie" (YOUNG)) - d. 13 June 1849 Æ 17 y., 11 m.

Gilbert B. (Capt.; husb. of Penelope H. "Nellie" (YOUNG)) - b. 1798; d. 1863

Penelope H. "Nellie" (YOUNG; wife of Capt. Gilbert B.) - b. 1805; d. 1888

Rebecca (dau. of Samuel and Jane [no stones]) - d. 22 November 1849 Æ 15 y., 9 m.

Susan Y. (dau. of Capt. Gilbert B. and Penelope H. "Nellie" (YOUNG)) - d. 20 September 1848 Æ 19 y., 2 m., 10 d.

FREEMAN

John W. - d. 14 July 1889 Æ 34 y.

T. O. - [no dates]; (member of Co. G, 16th Maine Regiment [Civil War])

GOODRIDGE

Hannah (THOMAS; wife of Uriah) - d. 4 January 1896 Æ 68 y., 3 m., 8 d.

Uriah (husb. of Hannah (THOMAS)) - d. 15 April 1880 Æ 58 y., 3 m., 25 d.

HARDEN
Abbie M. (wife of David N. [no stone]) - d. 21 March 1875 Æ 25 y., 11 m., 12 d.
HIGGINS
Fred E. - d. 19 July 1889 Æ 22 y., 5 m.
Orinton A. - d. 24 July 1864, Alexandra, Æ 23 y., 8 m.; (member of Co. D, 31st Maine Regiment [Civil War])
Otis A. - d. [...][2] 1864 Æ 20 y., 5 m.; (member of Co. D, 31st Maine Regiment [Civil War])
HODGKINS
Jennie R. (wife of Daniel W. [no stone]) - d. 21 October 1872 Æ 20 y., 11 m., 25 d.
HOPKINS
Adelaide V. (dau. of Capt. Isaac [no stone] and Delia F.) - d. 20 November 1864 Æ 6 y., 10 m., 2 d.
Clarissa C. (dau. of Capt. Seth and Jane) - d. 12 October 1837 Æ 6 m.
Delia F. (wife of Capt. Isaac [no stone]) - d. 25 August 1863 Æ 3[0 or 9?][2] y., 10 m.
Giles (husb. of Martha) - d. 3 April 1847 Æ 66 y.
Jane (wife of Capt. Seth) - d. 3 May 1870 Æ 78 y., 2 m.
Jane (dau. of Capt. Seth and Jane) - d. 2 November 1833 Æ 12 y.
Jonathan N. (son of Capt. Isaac [no stone] and Delia F.) - d. 6 January 1865 Æ 14 y., 4 m., 21 d.
Martha (wife of Giles) - d. 18 July 1864 Æ 87 y.
Seth (Capt.; husb. of Jane) - d. 29 April 1879 Æ 88 y.
Winfield S. (son of Capt. Isaac [no stone] and Delia F.) - d. 1 December 1873 Æ 25 y., 6 m., 19 d.
JAMESON
[Eleanor - see STAFFORD]
LELAND
Albert J. (son of Pembroke and Irene [no stones]) - d. 16 September 1850 Æ 9 y., 9 m.
Gilman P. (son of Pembroke and Irene [no stones]) - d. 13 September 1850 Æ 3 y., 7 m.
LISCOMB
Abby M. (dau. of Gideon Jr. and Sarah A.) - d. 18 April 1847 Æ 3 y.
Annie (wife of Horace T. [no stone]) - d. 2 March 1886 Æ 17 y.
Aphia (wife of Gideon) - d. 20 November 1871 Æ 93 y., 7 m., 20 d.
Francis H. (son of Gideon Jr. and Sarah A.) - d. 3 April 1892 Æ 38 y., 5 m., 15 d.
Gideon (husb. of Aphia) - d. 30 June 1843 Æ 76 y.
Gideon Jr. (husb. of Sarah A.) - d. 2 June 1895 Æ 78 y., 2 m., 28 d.
infant (dau. of Thomas S. and Mary Ella) - [no dates]
infant[s?][3] (son[s?][3] of Gideon Jr. and Sarah A.) - [no dates]
John M. - d. 12 August 1863 Æ 20 y.; (member of Co. C, 1st Maine Heavy Artillery [Civil War])
Mary Ella (wife of Thomas S.) - d. 19 July 1879 Æ 23 y.
Rosa S. (dau. of Gideon Jr. and Sarah A.) - d. 9 February 1903 Æ 50 y.
Sarah A. (wife of Gideon Jr.) - d. 2 May 1905 Æ 81 y., 3 m.
Thomas S. (husb. of Mary Ella) - b. 8 March 1845; d. 21 August 1915
MANCHESTER
Fred W. "Freddie" (son of Wilber I. and Nellie T. [no stones]) - d. 12 September 1887 Æ 9 m., 18 d.
NEWMAN
H. H. - [no dates]; (member of Co. L, 1st Maine Heavy Artillery [Civil War])

PEACH
Clara H. (wife of Eben) - d. 25 July 1886 Æ 63 y., 6 m., 21 d.
Eben (husb. of Clara H.) - b. 9 September 1825; d. 17 February 1900
Ebenezer W. (husb. of Sarah) - d. 20 November 1862 Æ 82 y., 1 m., 14 d.
[Hannah [R. or K][6] - see YOUNG]
Marina (wife of Capt. William) - d. 23 April 1884 Æ 72 y., 8 m., 22 d.
Sarah (wife of Ebenezer W.) - d. 21 April 1861 Æ 82 y., 1 m., 20 d.
William (Capt.; husb. of Marina) - "lost at sea" 20 March 1850 Æ 46 y., 2 m., 16 d.
PENDLETON
Adeline T. (wife of J. H. [no stone]) - d. 11 April 1885 Æ 56 y.
RATNER
Jeffrey H. - b. 1945; d. 1978
RICHARDSON
Emma A. (dau. of Capt. Nicholas T. and Hannah) - d. 15 February 1854 Æ 4 y.
George (Capt.; "formerly of Mount Desert") - d. 16 November 1822 Æ 27 y.
Hannah (wife of Capt. Nicholas T.) - d. 10 January 1887 Æ 73 y.
Nicholas T. (Capt.; husb. of Hannah) - d. 16 June 1854 Æ 45 y.
Orlando - [no dates]; (member of Co. E, 26th Maine Regiment [Civil War])
SALISBURY [includes SALSBURY]
Abbie F. (wife of Capt. S. A. [no stone]) - d. 21 May 1867 Æ 19 y., 1 m., 8 d.
Abigail (wife of Ebenezer) - d. 9 February 1821 Æ 44 y.
Albert F. (son of Upton G. and Thankful[l][4]) - d. 9 February 1859 Æ 5 y., 10 m., 16 d.
Alburn (husb. of Sarah C. [no stone]) - d. 10 January 1873 Æ 30 y., 7 m.
Allie E. (son of Alburn and Sarah C. [no stone]) - d. 10 February 1874 Æ 1 y., 3 m., 12 d.
Auther [sic] L. (son of Upton G. and Thankful[l][4]) - d. 20 July 1867 Æ 21 y., 11 m.
Bethuel (son of Upton G. and Thankful[l][4]) - d. 24 August 1873 Æ 23 y.
Ebenezer (husb. of Abigail) - d. 6 April 1848 Æ 74 y.
Ebenezer [husb. of Mehitable] - b. 1739; d. 1825
Erastus B. (Capt.) - b. 1835; d. 1924
George M. (son of Upton G. and Thankful[l][4]) - d. 30 August 1869 Æ 22 y.
infant (dau. of Upton G. and Thankful[l][4]) - d. 5 [...][5] 18[4?][5]0
infant (dau. of Upton G. and Thankful[l][4]) - d. 9 September 1852 Æ 4 w., 1 d.
infant (son of Elbridge and Mehitabel [no stones]) - d. 5 July 1847 Æ 3 w.
infant (son of Upton G. and Thankful[l][4]) - d. 12 September 1852 Æ 4 w., 4 d.
[infant?][2] (son of [Upton G. and?][2] Thankful[l][4]) - d. 17 May 18[...][2] Æ 3 [...][2]
John (husb. of Julia [no stone]) - d. 26 December 1853 Æ 50 y., 1 m., 4 d.
Mehitable [wife of Ebenezer] - b. 1740; d. 1825
Nathan M. (son of John and Julia [no stone]) - d. [...][2] Æ 18 y., 6 m.; ("was drowned")
Ruany W. (dau. of Elbridge and Mehitabel [no stones]) - d. 30 March 1846 Æ 1 y., 17 d.
Samuel (Capt.; son of Upton G. and Thankful[l][4]) - d. 24 August 1873 Æ 34 y.
Thankful[l][4] (wife of Upton G.) - d. 15 March 1880 Æ 70 y.
Upton G. (husb. of Thankful[l][4]) - d. 28 May 1901 Æ 86 y.
STAFFORD
Eleanor (JAMESON; "from Northumberland Eng."; wife of Andrew [no stone]) - d. 10 April 1889 Æ 49 y.; (died "on her 49 birthday")
Ruth A. [wife of Samuel L.?] - b. 2 June 1894; d. 7 August 1973
Samuel L. [husb. of Ruth A.?] - b. 27 September 1902; d. 1 October 1966

THOMAS
[Hannah - see GOODRIDGE]
THOMPSON
Thankful (wife of William [no stone]) - d. 3 February 1821 Æ 20 y., 11 m.
THURBER
Emma J. (wife of Alexander [no stone]) - d. 22 June 1877 Æ 25 y.
WILCOMB
John [husb. of Mary A.] - b. 1806; d. 1865
Mary A. [wife of John] - b. 1808; d. 1880
WOOD
Albert W. (son of Joseph A. and Emma J. [no stones]) - d. 7 October 1882 Æ 6 m., 19 d.
infant (son of Joseph A. and Emma J. [no stones]) - d. 10 July 1888 Æ 13 d.
YOUNG
Abner (husb. of Susannah and Lucy) - d. 2 January 1864 Æ 84 y.
Addie P. (son [sic] of Edward H. and Hannah [R. or K.][6] (PEACH)) - d. 12 September 1881 Æ 6 y., 11 m., 27 d.
Alice J. ("only dau." of Owen S. [no stone] and Zena [H. or R.][6] "Zeny") - d. 29 October 1866 Æ 4 y., 27 d.
Eben S. (Capt.; husb. of Prudence T.) - b. 8 May 1803; d. 3 December 1894
Edward H. (husb. of Hannah [R. or K.][6] (PEACH)) - b. 12 May 1843; d. 1 November 1902
Emeline (Mrs.) - d. 31 May 1890 Æ 61 y.
Hannah [R. or K.][6] (PEACH; wife of Edward H.) - b. 1851; d. 1942
infant (son of Owen S. [no stone] and Zena [H. or R.][6] "Zeny") - d. 1858 Æ [not given]
Lucy (wife of Abner) - d. 29 September 1837 Æ 43 y.
Minnie W. (dau. of Capt. Peleg H. and Etta [no stones]) - d. 2 March 1896 Æ 22 y., 4 m., 22 d.
Orient C. - b. 4 September 1855; d. 9 April 1914
[Penelope H. "Nellie" - see FISH]
Prudence T. (wife of Capt. Eben S.) - b. 15 July 1808; d. 9 September 1903
Susannah (wife of Abner) - d. 18 September 1834 Æ 54 y.
William Thomas (son of Capt. Eben S. and Prudence T.) - d. 26 November 1838 Æ 10 m.
Zena [H. or R.][6] "Zeny" (wife of Owen S. [no stone]) - d. 19 February 1870 Æ 38 y., 4 m.
[...]
Anna D. (dau. of Elisha and [...][2]) - d. [28?][2] January 18[...][2] Æ 17 y., [...][2] m.
[...][2]inso[...][2] [...][2]xani[...][2] [...][2]ayne[...][2] - [no dates]
[...][2] [3 stones]
[...][7] - [...][7]

Notes:
[1]Middle initial broken; name very worn.
[2]Stone worn, cracked, and/or broken.
[3]Stone reads, "an infant sons of".
[4]Variable spelling found on stones.
[5]Inscription partly below ground.
[6]Different on different stones.
[7]Stone crumbling.

Hillside Cemetery

(Bar Harbor - 6)

Location/directions. West of Route 3, Hulls Cove. From the traffic light at the north end of Mount Desert Island, bear left on Route 3. In approximately 6.6–6.7 miles on the right, two short driveways (separated by about 0.1 miles) lead to this cemetery. Alternatively, from the intersection of Route 3 and Crooked Road in Hulls Cove, travel north (ocean on your right) approximately 0.5–0.6 miles to the driveways on the left.

History. This cemetery is found in the 1881 Colby Atlas. In 1920, "a portion of the James M. Richardson estate and homestead" was conveyed (556:309–310) to the Hillside Cemetery Association. A 1942 deed (687:350–351) added 111,197.5 square feet to the cemetery and referred to a "portion of Hillside Cemetery now or heretofore known as the Stanley Burying Ground" (687:350).

Notes. This cemetery is not enclosed. The grass is mowed and trimmed. Many older stones are leaning or laying on the ground.

Names and dates on gravestones and other markers. [8 September 1999]

ABBOTT
- Alvah L. [husb. of Mabel] - b. 1873; d. 1944
- Arthur L. [husb. of Grace P.] - b. 1907; d. 1962
- Charles M. [husb. of Gertrude W.] - b. 1911; d. 1974
- Esther S. - b. 10 February 1908; d. 12 November 1983
- George C. [husb. of Rosa B.] - b. 1904; d. 1983
- Gertrude W. [wife of Charles M.] - b. 1910; d. 1988
- Grace P. [wife of Arthur L.] - [no dates]
- Jean Burr - b. 22 December 1938; d. 3 April 1978
- Lawrence F. - b. 8 August 1908; d. 13 February 1986
- Leonard Lee - b. 4 September 1894; d. 14 March 1952
- Mabel [wife of Alvah L.] - b. 1886; d. 1947
- Rosa B. [wife of George C.] - b. 1906; d. 1997
- [Ruth A[BBOTT?]. - see MURPHY]

ALLEN
- Alvah R. - b. 1884; d. 1951
- [Violet - see HARDING]

ALLEY
- Charles E. [husb. of Flora L.] - b. 1877; d. 1954
- Clara A. - b. 1861; d. 1931
- Flora L. [wife of Charles E.] - b. 1884; d. 1951
- Herman F. Sr. - b. 1900; d. 1968
- Michael - [b. and d.?] 1950
- Nina R[OBBINS?]. [[dau. of Byron F. ROBBINS and Effie N.?]; wife of Nowell D.] - b. 1904; d. 1973
- Nowell D. [husb. of Nina R[OBBINS?].] - b. 1906; d. 1972
- S. Elizabeth [wife of William H.] - b. 1909; d. 1984
- Stella L. - b. 1955
- Thelma T. - b. 1897; d. 1995
- William H. [husb. of S. Elizabeth] - b. 1898; d. 1972

ANTONISEN
- Andrew K. - b. 1883; d. 1937

APPLEBY
infant (dau.) - [b. and d.?] November 1961
AREY
[Maude L. or L. Maude][1] (wife of Milton Stanley) - b. 1871; d. 1965
Milton Stanley (husb. of [Maude L. or L. Maude][1]) - b. 1871; d. 1928
ASHWORTH
Elizabeth C. [wife of Harold] - b. 1890; d. 1957
Harold [husb. of Elizabeth C.] - b. 1885; d. 1964
[Jane - see DENTART]
Myrle - b. 1894; d. 1985
BABSON
Angenoria (wife of John Somes) - d. 31 [sic] September 1865 Æ 23 y., 6 m., 9 d.
Frank Irving (son of John Somes and Angenoria) - d. 26 July 1870 Æ [...][2]
John Somes (husb. of Angenoria) - d. 17 September 1868 Æ 35 y., 3 m., 5 d.
BAKER
Dorothy V. [wife of Earle F.] - b. 1898; d. 1982
Earle F. [husb. of Dorothy V.] - b. 1896; d. 1966
BARSTOW
Genevieve C. - b. 1922; d. 1941
Oscar - b. 1887; d. 1950
BENEDICT
Harry Earl (husb. of Florence Mae (EMERY)) - b. 1 January 1892; d. 16 November 1956
Florence Mae (EMERY; wife of Harry Earl) - b. 24 September 1900; d. 19 December 1995
BENNETT
Esther C. - b. 1911; d. 1964
BRADLEY
Hallie C. [wife of Harry L.] - b. 1880; d. 1936
Harry L. [husb. of Hallie C.] - b. 1875; d. 1940
BREWER
Abbie E. [wife of Frank L.] - b. 1862; d. 1946
Agnes P. - b. 1881; d. 1968
Alburn S. [husb. of Mae H.] - b. 1872; d. 1942
Alma R. - b. 1876; d. 1962
Annie W. (wife of C. Leslie) - b. 1896; d. 1948
Archie L. [husb. of Harriet P.] - b. 1879; d. 1944
[Betsey - see RODICK]
Bryant S. (son of Everett K. and Nellie (LELAND)) - d. 11 September 18[...][3] Æ [at least 2][3] m., 10 d.
C. Leslie (husb. of Annie W.) - b. 1891; d. 1972
[Charlotte M. - see ELLS]
Chester S. (husb. of Lillian B.) - b. 1856; d. 1918
Daniel W. (husb. of Melinda S.) - b. 4 September 1829; d. 4 June 1895
Dora E. - b. 1889; d. 1965
Edith E. - b. 1875; d. 1963
Edward (husb. of Sarah and Mary) - d. 14 March 1868 Æ 70 y.
[Effie E. - see HAMOR]
Eliza C. - b. 1896; d. [no date]
Elmore G. (husb. of Frances A.) - d. 18 September 1897 Æ 53 y.
[Emeline - see CARPENTER]
Ernest M. - b. 5 December 1886; d. 22 June 1950

Everett K. (husb. of Nellie (LELAND)) - b. 1857; d. 1932
Fountain (son of Edward and Mary) - d. 31 July 18[44?][9] Æ 2 y., 3 m.
Frances A. (wife of Elmore G.) - d. 21 April 1935 Æ 86 y.
Frances H. - b. 1905; d. 1966
Frank L. [husb. of Abbie E.] - b. 1859; d. 1934
Fred J. [husb. of Georgia S.?] - b. 1861; d. 1947
Genevieve H. "Gerry" [wife of Merrill F. "Dinger"?] - b. 1910; d. 1990
Georgia S. [wife of Fred J.?] - b. 1861; d. 1937
[Hannah - see HAMOR]
Harriet P. [wife of Archie L.] - b. 1881; d. 1952
Herbert - b. 1900; d. 1900
Herman - b. 1900; d. 1900
Hiram S. (son of Porter [no stone] and Sophia B.) - d. 5 April 1864 Æ 5 y., 4 m.
infant (son of Loren F. and Lizzie L. [no stones]) - d. 18 March 1885 Æ 3 m., 18 d.
Johnie [sic] (son of Daniel W. and Melinda S.) - d. 17 October 187[...][3] y., 8 m.
Josie H. (dau. of Everett K. and Nellie (LELAND)) - d. 17 January 18[...]5[3] Æ 3 y., 4 m.
Lawrence A. - b. 1897; d. 1971
[Lillian - see FITZGERALD]
Lillian B. (wife of Chester S.) - b. 1863; d. 1920
Mae H. [wife of Alburn S.] - b. 1878; d. 1971
Margaret (dau. of Clarence A. and Myrtle L. [no stones]) - b. 1921; d. 1922
Mary (wife of Edward) - d. 7 January 1876 Æ 76 y., 1 m., 7 d.
Mary F. - d. 6 July 1955 Æ 82 y.
Melinda S. (wife of Daniel W.) - b. 20 February 1835; d. 15 March 1922
Merrill F. "Dinger" [husb. of Genevieve H. "Gerry"?] - b. 1904; d. 1968
Nellie (LELAND; wife of Everett K.) - b. 1861; d. 1927
Orient E. - b. 1877; d. 1963
Otis (husb. of Rebecca A.) - d. 20 April 1884 Æ 60 y., 4 m., 14 d.
Rebecca A. (wife of Otis) - d. 25 July 1885 Æ 60 y.
Sarah (wife of Edward) - d. 9 July 185[8?][3] Æ [...][3]
Shirley M. [male] - [d.?] 10 May 1934
Sophia B. (wife of Porter [no stone]) - d. 1 August 1882 Æ 45 y., 7 m.

BROWN
Arthur W. [husb. of Ruby M.] - b. 1875; d. 1956
[Emeline B[ROWN?]. - see BRYANT]
Henry W.[10] [son of Arthur W. and Ruby M.?] - b. 1905; d. 1919
Ruby M. [wife of Arthur W.] - b. 1880; d. 1969

BRYANT
Ellen (SIMPSON; [wife of Samuel H.?]) - b. 18 August 1923
Emeline B[ROWN?]. - b. 1908; d. 1999
Samuel H. [husb. of Ellen (SIMPSON)?] - b. 9 April 1906; d. 25 May 1966

BULEY
Lura L. - b. 1886; d. 1927

BURCH
Lawrence E. - b. 1935; d. 1971

BURKE
Florence G. - b. 1913; d. 1940

BURNS
Edna E. (wife of Sylvester L.) - b. 1873; d. 1941
Howard E. (son of Sylvester L. and Edna E.) - b. 1907; d. 1920
Sylvester L. (husb. of Edna E.) - b. 1876; d. 1958

BUZZELL
Fulton G. [husb. of Mertice V.] - b. 1915; d. 1987
Mertice V. [wife of Fulton G.] - b. 1920
CAMPBELL
Alexander S. (husb. of Lucy M.) - b. 24 October 1834; d. 21 February 1915
Camilla S. (EVELETH; wife of LeRoy A.) - b. 1890; d. 1945
LeRoy A. (husb. of Camilla S. (EVELETH)) - b. 1894; d. 1971
Lucy M. (wife of Alexander S.) - d. 4 April 1893 Æ 50 y.
CANDAGE
Chester E. [husb. of Gladys H.] - b. 1893; d. 1975
Chester E. Jr. [son of Chester E. and Gladys H.] - b. 8 October 1923; d. 3 September 1984
Gladys H. [wife of Chester E.] - b. 1895; d. 1968
CARPENTER
Emeline (BREWER; wife of Orient H.) - d. 18 December 1885 Æ 57 y., 3 m., 20 d.
Fernie Althea [CARPENTER?] - b. 14 February 1946; d. 14 March 1946
Katherine L. - [b. and d.?] 1930
Orient H. (husb. of Emeline (BREWER)) - d. 9 April 1898 Æ 78 y.
CARTER
Ella F. [wife of Lester P.] - b. 1865; d. 1902
Florence E. - b. 1849; d. 1932
Henryette [sic] J. - b. 1896; d. 1968
Lester P. [husb. of Ella F.] - b. 1870; d. 1933
Lester P. Jr. [son of Lester P. and Ella F.] - b. 1910; d. 1969
Lue [sic] - b. 1877; d. 1958
CHADBOURNE
Medville [sic] L. - d. 28 January 1900 Æ 26 y.
CHAKALIS
Marion (CHANEY; [dau. of Nelson W. CHANEY and Bertha F.?]) - b. 1890; d. 1948
CHANDLER
Delia W. [wife of William T.?] - b. 1882; d. 1937
William T. [husb. of Delia W.?] - b. 1867; d. 1958
CHANEY
Bertha F. (wife of Nelson W.) - b. 1874; d. 1937
[Marion - see CHAKALIS]
Nelson W. (husb. of Bertha F.) - b. 1858; d. 1937
CIRARD
Alice M. (wife of John) - b. 1924
John (husb. of Alice M.) - b. 1920; d. 1977
CLARK
Ervena - d. 24 September 1942 Æ 89 y.
CLOUDMAN
[...] [headstone only "CLOUDMAN/STIMPSON"]
CONNERS
Alonzo W. - b. 1909; d. 1942
Carl E. - b. 1907; d. 1956
CROCKER
Lewis F. [husb. of Sylvia D.] - b. 1912; d. 1994
Sylvia D. [wife of Lewis F.] - b. 1910; d. 1995
CROWELL
[Anne S. - see SULLIVAN]

Isabelle (HAMOR; wife of F. M. [no stone]) - b. 22 April 1865; d. 10 May 1886
CUMMINGS
Irene Emma (STEWART; dau. of Lionel S. STEWART and Violet M.; mother of Peter W. DOUGLAS [no stone] and Paul A. DOUGLAS [no stone]) - b. 6 February 1909; d. 30 March 1988; bur. "at sea"
CUNNINGHAM
Anson P. (husb. of Drusilla H.) - d. 28 February 1900 Æ 80 y.
Arthur [husb. of Josie] - b. 1877; d. 1938
Drusilla H. (wife of Anson P.) - d. 23 February 1910 Æ 86 y., 5 m., 15 d.
Ella (DRISKO; [wife of Roger S.]) - b. 1911; d. 1997
Eunice M. [wife of William H.] - b. 1888; d. 1954
Frances M. [wife of George E.?] - b. 1877; d. 1967
George E. [husb. of Frances M.?] - b. 1870; d. 1946
George E. - b. 1909; d. 1998
Hannah L. [wife of Irving L.] - b. 1902; d. 1980
Irving L. [husb. of Hannah L.] - b. 1906; d. 1975
Josie [wife of Arthur] - b. 1876; d. 1959
Lillian M. [dau. of George E. and Frances M.?] - b. 1907; d. 1987
Philip R. [son of Roger S. and Ella (DRISKO)?] - b. 1948
Roger S. [husb. of Ella (DRISKO)] - b. 1913
Walter R. [son of Arthur and Josie?] - b. 1904; d. 1935
William H. [husb. of Eunice M.] - b. 1888; d. 1964
CUSHING
George J. (husb. of Ida F. [no stone]) - d. 10 August 1899 Æ 57 y., 10 m.; (member of Co. C, 2nd Maine Regiment [Civil War])
Mazzie A. E. (dau. of George J. and Ida F. [no stone]) - d. 21 December 1898 Æ 3 y., 10 m.
DAMROSCH
Elizabeth H. [wife of Leopold Priest] - b. 1915
Leopold Priest [husb. of Elizabeth H.] - b. 1912; d. 1990
DAVIES
[Bessie - see WILLIAMS]
DAVIS
Ansel R. [husb. of Jennie B.] - b. 1884; d. 1967
Bernard C. [husb. of Gertrude S.] - b. 1917; d. 1996
Doris A. - b. 1912; d. 1943
Earle N. (husb. of Thelma J.) - b. 24 September 1897; d. 4 May 1983
Gertrude S. [wife of Bernard C.] - b. 1914; d. 1982
Hiram (husb. of Minnie) - b. 1875; d. 1940
Jennie B. [wife of Ansel R.] - b. 1889; d. 1980
Minnie (wife of Hiram) - b. 1871; d. 1956
Thelma J. (wife of Earle N.) - b. 13 October 1900; d. 2 March 1983
DE GREGOIRE
[no name(s)] - [d.] 1811 Æ [not given]
DENTART
Jane (ASHWORTH; [dau. of Harold ASHWORTH and Elizabeth C.?]) - b. 1925; d. 1961
DICKEY
Cyrus W. (husb. of Mary J.) - b. 1850; d. 1915
Ivan E. - b. 24 April 1897; d. 23 December 1961
Mary J. (wife of Cyrus W.) - b. 1863; d. 1933

DITTMAN
Ashley Ann - [b. and d.?] 7 February 1988
DIXON
A. Elizabeth (dau. of Rufus S. and Mary [L.?][3] [no stones]) - d. 8 March 1853 Æ 8 m., 17 d.
infant (son of Rufus S. and Mary [L.?][3] [no stones]) - [b. and?] d. 2 November 1850
DORITY
Millard Lee - b. 17 April 1920; d. 3 November 1952
DORR
Agnes K. (wife of Russell S.) - b. 1870; d. 1945
[Agnes K. - see TARTAGLIA]
Arlene [wife of Phillip [sic] H.] - b. 1914; d. 1988
Asta O. [wife of Elliott B.] - b. 1886; d. 1959
[Bessie C. [DORR?] - see LOWRIE]
Elliott B. [husb. of Asta O.] - b. 1890; d. 1965
James B. (son of Russell S. and Agnes K.) - d. 29 May 1894 Æ 7 w.
Phillip [sic] H. [husb. of Arlene] - b. 1907; d. 1972
Russell S. (husb. of Agnes K.) - b. 1858; d. 1939
Timothy Phillip [sic] [son of Phillip [sic] H. and Arlene] - b. 1 October 1951
DOUGLAS
[Irene Emma - see CUMMINGS]
Marty L. - b. 5 December 1977; d. 4 August 1988
[Paul A. - see CUMMINGS]
[Peter W. - see CUMMINGS]
DRISKO
[Ella - see CUNNINGHAM]
DUFFY
Deliah [sic] (wife of William) - [no dates]
William (husb. of Deliah [sic]) - [no dates]
DUNTON
Adelma C. (wife of Walter H.) - b. 1859; d. 1930
Austin Leslie [son of Walter H. and Adelma C.?] - b. 1881; d. 1888
Dorothy A. (wife of Leslie I.) - b. 1905; d. 1967
infant (dau. [of Walter H. and Adelma C.?]) - b. 1882; d. 1882
infant ("twin son" [of Walter H. and Adelma C.?]) - b. 1892; d. 1892
Jeffrey P. - b. 3 July 1961; d. 9 July 1985
Leslie I. (husb. of Dorothy A.) - b. 1898; d. 1974
Lottie A. [dau. of Walter H. and Adelma C.?] - b. 1894; d. 1894
Walter H. (husb. of Adelma C.) - b. 1852; d. 1938
ELLIOTT
Charlotte M. - [no dates]
ELLS
Charlotte M. (BREWER; [dau. of Frank L. BREWER and Abbie E.?]; wife of John B. [no stone]) - b. 1891; d. 1949
Julia H. - b. 1853; d. 1928
Roy - b. 1882; d. 1953
EMERY
[Florence Mae - see BENEDICT]
George L. - b. 1863; d. 1934
Minnie A. - b. 1873; d. 1944
ENGMAN
Beatrice - [no dates]

Gustaf F. (husb. of Margaret C.) - b. 1874; d. 1937
Margaret C. (wife of Gustaf F.) - b. 1884; d. 1985
ERICKSON
Clara C. - b. 16 August 1877; d. 15 October 1965
EVELETH
[Camilla S. - see CAMPBELL]
FARNSWORTH
Betsey M. (wife of Bion D.) - b. 1892; d. 1979
Bion Calvin - b. 1930; d. 1989
Bion D. (husb. of Lydia E. and Betsey M.) - b. 1893; d. 1980
Ira Burton - b. 26 October 1916; d. 31 March 1976
Lydia E. (wife of Bion D.) - b. 1898; d. 1943
FARRAR
Dorris [sic] G. (WOOD; wife of Raymond M.) - b. 1906
Raymond M. (husb. of Dorris [sic] G. (WOOD)) - b. 9 August 1908; d. 22 April 1981
FARRELL
Atwood R. [husb. of Viola P.] - b. 1899; d. [no date]
Cassie L. (wife of James R.) - b. 5 November 1912
Corrine Elizabeth (dau. of James R. and Cassie L.) - b. 1940; d. 1959
James R. (husb. of Cassie L.) - b. 15 April 1910; d. 12 July 1992
Viola P. [wife of Atwood R.] - b. 1902; d. 1973
FEARON
[Kathleen - see GERRISH]
FENWICK
Iver [sic] J. (wife of Charles H. [no stone]) - b. 1882; d. 1930
FERRY
Isa M. [wife of Mentor B.] - b. 1888; d. 1968
Mentor B. [husb. of Isa M.] - b. 1881; d. 1952
FITZGERALD
Lillian (BREWER; wife of Patsy J.) - b. 22 July 1865; d. 5 January 1909
Patsy J. (husb. of Lillian (BREWER)) - b. 17 April 1867; d. 27 July 1904
FORDAN
Eleanor S. (wife of Capt. John T.) - b. 1910; d. 1976
John T. (Capt.; husb. of Eleanor S.) - b. 1906; d. 1978
FOWLER
Charles H. [husb. of Edith W.] - b. 1877; d. 1964
Edith W. [wife of Charles H.] - b. 1875; d. 1966
FRANCIS
Dorothy P. [wife of Percy M.] - b. 1913; d. 1991
Percy M. [husb. of Dorothy P.] - b. 1914; d. 1973
FRENCH
Wilma (dau. of Jessie [no stone]) - b. 1932; d. 1938
FROST
[Ina C. - see GRAVES]
FRYE
Robert Samuel [husb. of Signey M.] - b. 8 November 1925; d. 26 June 1993
Signey M. [wife of Robert Samuel] - b. 14 August 1927
GARDINER
Lulu M. - b. 17 November 1890; d. 6 April 1891
Mary E. - b. 16 March 1871; d. 20 July 1911

GEREMIA
Samuel J. - b. 1953; d. 1971
GERRISH
Ace - b. 3 January 1979; d. 24 September 1989
Kathleen (FEARON; [wife of Lewis Everett]) - b. 19 March 1917; d. 5 December 1979
Lewis Everett [husb. of Kathleen (FEARON)] - b. 24 July 1917; d. 15 July 1998
GETCHELL
Abner S. - b. 1851; d. 1925
Bertram I. - b. 1881; d. 1899
Effie B. - b. 1854; d. 1930
GOOCH
Evelyn L. - b. 1926
Horace E. [husb. of Lena M.] - b. 1893; d. 1970
Lena M. [wife of Horace E.] - b. 1893; d. 1981
GRACE
Inez B. - b. 1894; d. 1951
GRAHAM
Barbara A. (wife of Robert F. [no stone]) - b. 25 March 1933; d. 25 January 1986
Constance M. (wife of Ernest R.) - b. 10 September 1913
Ernest R. (husb. of Constance M.) - b. 27 December 1907; d. 30 December 1980
Frank M. (husb. of Margaret) - b. 1875; d. 1950
Margaret (wife of Frank M.) - b. 1874; d. 1964
GRANT
Florence S[UMINSBY?]. [dau. of Colimore SUMINSBY and Hannah?] - b. 1875; d. 1958
GRATEN
Geneva H. [wife of Oney S.] - b. 1914
Oney S. [husb. of Geneva H.] - b. 1912; d. 1963
GRAVES
Chandler E. [husb. of Ina C. (FROST) and Gladys M.] - b. 1897; d. 1971
Gladys M. [wife of Chandler E.] - b. 1912
Ina C. (FROST; [wife of Chandler E.]) - b. 1886; d. 1964
GRAY
Adelbert [husb. of Lelia E.] - b. 1850; d. 1940
Arthur C. - b. 1884; d. 1972
Bertha A. - b. 1887; d. 1974
Bertha C. - b. 1898; d. 1963
Clarence A. - b. 1904; d. 1963
Edward J. (husb. of Ella L.) - b. 1851; d. 1937
Ella L. (wife of Edward J.) - b. 1861; d. 1920
[Fannie - see MORRISON]
Fred D. [husb. of Zelphia E.] - b. 1886; d. 1937
Irving S. - b. 10 November 1891; d. 29 December 1986
Lelia E. [wife of Adelbert] - b. 1855; d. 1937
Myron H. - b. 1894; d. 1931
Thelma I. [GRAY?] - b. 1920; d. 1937
Waldon E. - b. 1915; d. 1935
Walter R. - b. 1840; d. 1902
William E. - b. 21 September 1928; d. 30 September 1928
Zelphia E. [wife of Fred D.] - b. 1894; d. 1987

GRINDLE
Alice C. [wife of Alonzo H.] - b. 1873; d. 1945
Alice M. [wife of Chester H.[8]] - b. 1885; d. 1956
Allen V. [son of Chester H.[8] and Alice M.] - b. 27 July 1918; d. 23 July 1945
Alonzo H. [husb. of Alice C.] - b. 1859; d. 1944
Amy D. [wife of Morris W.] - b. 1889; d. 1979
Betty [GRINDLE?] - [b. and d.?] 1924
Chester H.[8] [husb. of Alice M.] - b. 1884; d. 1970
Cora B. - b. 1868; d. 1954
Edward A. - b. 1863; d. 1952
Ermine M. - b. 7 September 1928; d. 16 December 1987
Gertrude M. [wife of Theodore W.] - b. 1903; d. 1973
Kenneth [son of Ermine M.?] - b. 1966; d. 1966
Leland [GRINDLE?] - b. 1893; d. 1945
Mabel D. [wife of Winn] - b. 1884; d. 1952
Maud - b. 1888; d. 1950
Morris W. [husb. of Amy D.] - b. 1888; d. 1957
Richard M. [GRINDLE?] [son of Theodore W. and Gertrude M.?] - b. 1933; d. 1973
Thelma A. - b. 1905; d. 1955
Theodore W. [husb. of Gertrude M.] - b. 1900; d. 1958
Theodore W. Jr. - b. 30 September 1925; d. 1 July 1999
Theodore W. III - b. 10 July 1948; d. 26 May 1992
Winn [husb. of Mabel D.] - b. 1879; d. 1959
GROSS
Alton H. [husb. of Louise H.] - b. 1890; d. 1955
Louise H. [wife of Alton H.] - b. 1900; d. 1979
H.
E. [footstone only]
HADLEY
[Harriett [sic] M. - see WOOD]
HAFFCKE
William H. - b. 1897; d. 1965
HALL
Ada O. (wife of Lewis H.) - b. 1874; d. 1937
Charles E. (son of George H. and Lillie G.) - b. 1921; d. 1937
Ethel Y. - b. 1910; d. 1953
George H. (husb. of Lillie G.) - b. 1872; d. 1956
Herbert G. (son of George H. and Lillie G.) - b. 1903; d. 1991
Hylie K. Sr. [husb. of Thelma L.] - b. 1910; d. 1995
Lester J. - b. 1912; d. 1990
Lewis H. (husb. of Ada O.) - b. 1875; d. 1948
Lillie G. (wife of George H.) - b. 1882; d. 1970
Margaret T. - b. 1969; d. 1969
Thelma L. [wife of Hylie K. Sr.] - b. 1907; d. 1994
Walter E. [son of Lewis H. and Ada O.?] - b. 23 December 1909; d. 10 April 1972
HAMOR
Abbie A. (wife of Jeremiah C.) - b. 1 April 1846; d. 14 October 1914
[Agnes - see SALISBURY]
Alden S. [husb. of Tryphena N.] - b. 1815; d. 1913
Alfonzo G. (son of Capt. Ezra L. and Eliza R.) - d. 11 February 1854 Æ 14 y., 9 m., 26 d.
Alice M. (dau. of Jeremiah C. and Abbie A.) - b. 1868; d. 1934

Alice M. (wife of Clarence N.) - b. 1904; d. 1963
Alice M. [wife of George H.] - b. 7 February 1889; d. 30 December 1973
Alpheus A. - d. 22 October 1883, Lawrence, Æ 49 y., 5 m., 6 d.
Angelia T. (wife of John S.) - b. 1835; d. 1913
Annie B. [wife of Edward R.] - b. 4 July 1873; d. 17 October 1935
Annie P. - b. 6 April 1881; d. 5 November 1973
Arthur H. (son of Dean H. and Sophia J. [no stone]) - d. 29 August 1884 Æ 12 y., 9 m.
Bertha M. - b. 1869; d. 1949
C. Augusta [dau. of Alden S. and Tryphena N.] - b. 1844; d. 1926
Calvert G. - b. 1857; d. 1934
Carroll W. (son of Eugene W. and Ethel M.) - b. 1901; d. 1901
Charles A. (son of Augustus and Eliza H. [no stones]) - d. 26 February 1880 Æ 24 y., 24 d.
Chastena (wife of John W.) - d. 7 April 1916 Æ 71 y., 7 m.
[Chastena M. - see LELAND]
Clarence N. (husb. of Alice M.) - b. 1908; d. 1990
Cornelius T. (husb. of Sally D. (HOPKINS)) - d. 14 May 1885 Æ 78 y., 9 m.
Daniel (husb. of Polly [who d. 1851]) - d. 22 November 1847 Æ 81 y.
Daniel (husb. of Polly [who d. 1894]) - d. 5 November 1894 Æ 72 y., 6 m.
David (husb. of Experience) - b. 11 March 1757, Arundel, Maine; d. 25 October 1836, Hulls Cove, Maine; ("A. S. R. 1775" [Revolutionary War])
Dean H. (husb. of Sophia J. [no stone]) - d. 25 August 1880 Æ 39 y., 4 m.
Edward (Capt.; husb. of Elmenia (THOMAS)) - d. 7 February 1842 Æ 39 y., 1 m., 1 d.
Edward H. (son of Cornelius T. and Sally D. (HOPKINS)) - d. 18 June 1864 Æ 20 y.; ("killed in battle before Petersburg"[11]; member of Co. L, 1st Maine Heavy Artillery [Civil War])
Edward R. - b. 1904; d. 1963
Edward R. [husb. of Annie B.] - b. 14 August 1873; d. 13 September 1946
Edward W. [son of Daniel [who d. 1894] and Polly [who d. 1894]] - b. 1854; d. 1928
Effie E. (BREWER; wife of Frank A.) - b. 1 June 1875; d. 1 November 1960
Elihu T. (husb. of Isiphine) - b. 10 July 1844; d. 14 June 1908
[Eliza - see WILCOMB]
Eliza R. (wife of Capt. Ezra L.) - d. 13 August 1884 Æ 82 y., 7 m., 17 d.
Ella F. [dau. of Daniel [who d. 1894] and Polly [who d. 1894]] - b. 1851; d. 1928
Elmenia (THOMAS; wife of Capt. Edward) - d. 29 March 1839 Æ 30 y., 1 m., 28 d.
Ethel M. (wife of Eugene W.) - b. 1879; d. 1940
Eugene W. (husb. of Ethel M.) - b. 1875; d. 1959
Eugenia H. (wife of Granville H.) - b. 1866; d. 1894
[Everline [sic] C. - see RICHARDSON]
Experience (wife of David) - d. 26 October 1856 Æ 85 y.
Experience (LELAND; wife of David [no stone]) - b. 1799; d. 1886
Ezra L. (Capt.; husb. of Eliza R.) - d. 28 April 1870 Æ 71 y., 4 m., 4 d.
F. E. - [no dates]
Frank A. (husb. of Effie E. (BREWER)) - b. 25 December 1878; d. 2 February 1919
George Byron [husb. of Lucy Ann] - b. 1837; d. 1898; ("He was a soldier in the war for the Union 1861–65. Serving as a Volunteer from the State of Massachusetts, in 'Nims Battery Light Artillery'." [Civil War])
George Byron - b. 26 June 1899; d. 7 February 1948

George E. (son of Cornelius T. and Sally D. (HOPKINS)) - d. 11 July 1876 Æ 21 y., 3 m., 20 d.
George H. [husb. of Alice M.] - b. 13 August 1887; d. 9 May 1962
Gerald [HAMOR?] - [no dates]
Granville H. (husb. of Eugenia H. and Louise S.) - [no dates]
H. D. [HAMOR?] - [no dates]
Hannah (BREWER; wife of Capt. Jonathan) - d. 17 September 1875 Æ 64 y.
Hattie E. - b. 1859; d. 1916
Hester Elmenia - b. October 1892; d. December 1893
Hester L. [dau. of Eugene W. and Ethel M.?] - b. 1906; d. 1967
Hosea K. [husb. of Louise C.] - b. 1 June 1829; d. 30 August 1917
Hoyt P. [son of Millard L. and Ida J.?] - b. 1892; d. 1918
Ida J. (wife of Millard L.) - b. 1851; d. 1922
infant [male] - b. December 1889; d. December 1889
infant [child of Cornelius T. and Sally D. (HOPKINS)] - [no dates]
infant [son of Elihu T. and Isiphine?] - d. 27 August 1883 Æ 6 m., 1 d.
Irving G. - b. 1880; d. 1962
Irving N. (son of John W. and Chastena) - d. 3 April 1882 Æ 1 y., 10 m.
[Isabelle - see CROWELL]
Isiphine (wife of Elihu T.) - b. 28 January 1847; d. 7 March 1883
J. A. [HAMOR?] [footstone only]
J. S. [HAMOR?] [footstone only]
Jeremiah C. (husb. of Abbie A.) - b. 4 September 1838; d. 15 July 1919
John (husb. of Mercy) - d. 1 November 1880 Æ 82 y., 1 m., 16 d.
John - b. 1857; d. 1931
John C. - d. 11 October 1850 Æ 22 y., 4 m.
John S. (husb. of Angelia T.) - b. 1832; d. 1863; (member of 26th Maine Regiment [Civil War])
John W. (husb. of Chastena) - d. 20 April 1884 Æ 37 y., 17 d.
Jonathan (Capt.; husb. of Hannah (BREWER)) - d. 8 July 1860 Æ 64 y.
[Julia A. - see SALISBURY]
Julia Ann (dau. of David and Experience) - d. Ma[...][3]
Katherine R. [wife of Leslie I.] - b. 1896; d. 1972
Lena - [no dates]
Leota Adelia - b. December 1889; d. October 1904
Leslie I. [husb. of Katherine R.] - b. 1888; d. 1967
Louise C. [wife of Hosea K.] - b. 21 April 1839; d. 1 January 1927
Louise S. (wife of Granville H.) - b. 1859; d. 1911
Lucy Ann [wife of George Byron] - b. 1840; d. 1915
Maria M. [dau. of Daniel [who d. 1894] and Polly [who d. 1894]] - b. 1857; d. 1936
Marjorie Maker - b. 6 January 1914; d. 18 August 1984
Mary A. [wife of Orington [sic]] - b. 1839; d. 1915
Mary Ann (wife of Capt. Richard) - b. 1 June 1817; d. 27 December 1889
Mercy (wife of John) - d. 6 July 1852 Æ 46 y.
Millard L. (husb. of Ida J.) - b. 1852; d. 1936
Orington [sic] [husb. of Mary A.] - b. 1835; d. 1911
Peleg (son of David and Experience) - d. 18 November 1839 Æ 29 y.
Percie A. - b. 28 March 1879; d. 6 February 1911
Phyllis - b. 7 May 1910; d. 12 July 1966
Polly (wife of Daniel [who d. 1847]) - d. 6 June 1851 Æ 80 y.
Polly (wife of Daniel [who d. 1894]) - d. 9 September 1894 Æ 64 y., 1 m., 9 d.
Ralph (husb. of Sarah D.) - b. 1867; d. 1948

Richard (Capt.; husb. of Mary Ann) - b. 24 March 1812; d. 21 June 1891
Roy - b. 1875; d. 1946
Ruth E. - b. 10 August 1912; d. 12 August 1971
Sally D. (HOPKINS; wife of Cornelius T.) - b. 1812; d. 1897
Sarah D. (wife of Ralph) - b. 1873; d. 1947
[Sarah J. - see SPURLING]
Tryphena N. [wife of Alden S.] - b. 1822; d. 1902

HANSCOM [includes HANSCOME]
Alice C. [wife of E. Colon] - b. 1912; d. 1975
E. Colon [husb. of Alice C.] - b. 1915; d. 1964
Ella A. ([1st] wife of N. Lee) - b. 1893; d. 1944
Elwood V. [husb. of Emily V.] - b. 1906; d. 1974
Gladys (2nd wife of N. Lee) - b. 1901; d. 1955
Emily V. [wife of Elwood V.] - b. 1910; d. 1977
Marguerite [dau. of N. Lee and Ella A.] - b. 1912; d. 1913
N. Lee (husb. of Ella A. and Gladys) - b. 1892; d. 1962
Robert E. - b. 18 September 1952; d. 16 January 1981
Virginia [dau. of N. Lee and Ella A.] - b. 1927; d. 1927
Wallace C. - b. 1904; d. 1975

HARADEN
[Helen - see ROBERTS]
Katherine V. (wife of Linwood C.) - b. 1896; d. 1972
L. Chandler [son of Linwood C. and Katherine V.?] - b. 4 August 1924; d. 10 April 1996
Linwood C. (husb. of Katherine V.) - b. 1891; d. 1946
Louis W. (husb. of Rena H.) - b. 1904; d. 1985
Rena H. (wife of Louis W.) - b. 1909; d. 1953
Richard Scott - b. 26 January 1951; d. 11 March 1951
Shirley E. [husb. of Sylvia B.] - b. 23 December 1892; d. 31 May 1980
Sylvia B. [wife of Shirley E.] - b. 1899; d. [no date]

HARDEN
Alice May (dau. of A. and D. E. [no stones]) - b. 13 December 1883; d. 27 August 1900
Alton [son of A. and D. E. [no stones]] - b. 13 December 1883; d. 9 September 1884

HARDING
Alice A. [wife of William H.] - b. 7 April 1862; d. 18 April 1935
Edna L. [wife of Vaughn [sic] L.] - b. 1915; d. 1943
Pauline A. - b. 1900; d. 1950
Percy A. (husb. of Violet (ALLEN)) - b. 19 February 1897; d. 20 September 1968
Vaughn [sic] L. [husb. of Edna L.] - b. 1910; d. 1961
Violet (ALLEN; wife of Percy A.) - [no dates]
William H. [husb. of Alice A.] - b. 27 April 1879; d. 29 May 1939

HARDY
G. Daryl - b. 1888; d. 1935
George - d. 18 December 1915 Æ [not given]

HARRIS
Dorothea (WHITE; wife of Elijah P.) - b. 1888; d. 1976
Elijah P. (husb. of Dorothea (WHITE)) - b. 1886; d. 1953

HAVENER
Mary A. - b. 1879; d. 1960

HERSEY
Floy A. (wife of George W.) - b. 1880; d. 1948

George W. (husb. of Floy A.) - b. 1880; d. 1957
George W. Jr. [son of George W. and Floy A.] - b. 24 December 1908; d. 1 March 1964
Mary L. (mother of George, Laura, and Iver [no stones]) - b. 1908; d. 1984

HIGGINS
Ada A. (wife of Serenus H.) - b. 1868; d. 1950
Albion [Capt.; husb. of Sophia H.] - d. 7 June 1871 Æ 60 y.
Albion L. (son of Serenus H. and Ada A.) - b. 19 August 1887; d. 6 October 1887
Bertha H. - b. 1900; d. 1985
Dalma A. [dau. of Serenus H. and Ada A.] - b. 6 March 1902; d. 16 September 1902
Earl W. - b. 22 December 1892; d. 16 October 1922
Edgar S. - b. 1903; d. 1970
Emily L. - d. 23 March 1952 Æ 89 y.
Ezra H. - b. 1855; d. 1941
Guy A. [son of Serenus H. and Ada A.] - b. 4 July 1903; d. 16 October 1903
Harry J. [husb. of Ruth C.] - b. 1900; d. 1973
infant ("son") - d. 19 May 1861 Æ 1 m., 15 d.
infant (son of Serenus H. and Ada A.) - b. 27 January 1891; d. 14 February 1891
Jessie L. (wife of Warren F.) - b. 1865; d. 1933
Josephine E. - b. 1867; d. 1948
Krystal V. - b. 1 September 1963; d. 24 April 1969
Levi (Lieut.) - b. 1743; d. 1825; (member of 6th Massachusetts Regiment [Revolutionary War])
[Maisie - see TRUITT]
Mary R. - d. 15 November 1878 Æ 30 y.
Nathan [son of Capt. Albion and Sophia H.?] - d. 7 June 1878 Æ 33 y.
R. [HIGGINS?] [footstone only]
Rebecca ([wife] of [...][3]) - [...][3]
Richard (son of S. and [H.?][3] [C.][3] [no stone(s)?]) - d. 28 April 1833 Æ 1[1 or 4?][3] m., 28 d.
Ruth C. [wife of Harry J.] - b. 1907; d. 1983
Sarah D. - d. 18 September 1830 Æ 3 y.
Serenus (Capt.) - d. 8 February 1846, Mobile, Æ 38 y.
Serenus H. (husb. of Ada A.) - b. 1853; d. 1933
Sophia H. [wife of Capt. Albion] - d. 16 April 1888 Æ 68 y.
Warren F. (husb. of Jessie L.) - b. 8 November 1855; d. 27 November 1892

HINCKLEY
C. Herbert [husb. of Isabelle B.] - b. 1906; d. 1986
Charles W. [husb. of Effie B.] - d. 8 July 1915 Æ 37 y., 1 m., 11 d.
Effie B. [wife of Charles W.] - b. 1884; d. 1978
Isabelle B. [wife of C. Herbert] - b. 1906
John B. (husb. of Mary B.) - d. 26 June 1888 Æ 50 y., 20 d.
Marion V. (SMITH; dau. of Arthur A. SMITH and Mable S. [no stones]; wife of John C. [no stone]) - b. 21 January 1920; d. 2 February 1967
Mary B. (wife of John B.) - d. 16 June 1904 Æ 65 y., 8 m.

HODDLE
Edwin Walter - b. 1917; d. 1975

HODGKINS
Earl Littlefield (son of Ludolph [sic] Frank and Ruby (SALISBURY); husb. of Martha (PAGE)) - b. 10 February 1919
Emma F. (dau. of Greenleaf L. and Rachel A.) - d. 17 May 1903 Æ 36 y., 6 m., 4 d.
Greenleaf L. (husb. of Rachel A.) - d. 11 December 1900 Æ 66 y., 11 m., 24 d.

[Julia A. - see LELAND]
Ludolph [sic] Frank (husb. of Ruby (SALISBURY)) - b. 21 November 1887; d. 12 May 1982
Martha (PAGE; wife of Earl Littlefield) - b. 15 January 1921
Rachel A. (wife of Greenleaf L.) - d. 17 May 1896 Æ 71 y., 10 m., 3 d.
Ruby (SALISBURY; wife of Ludolph [sic] Frank) - b. 24 July 1901; d. 18 November 1988

HOLLIS
Lewis D. - b. 19 September 1891; d. 7 February 1937

HOOPER
Effie M. - b. 1884; d. 1958

HOPKINS
Clyde L. Jr. - b. 11 December 1926; d. 17 August 1947
Euphemia M. (wife of Gerard D.) - b. 1896; d. 1968
Gerard D. (husb. of Euphemia M.) - b. 1899; d. 1992
Reliance - b. 25 July 1811; d. 10 January 1887
[Sally D. - see HAMOR]

HORTON
Malcolm R. Sr. [husb. of Mildred P.] - b. 1901; d. 1975
Mildred P. [wife of Malcolm R. Sr.] - b. 1903; d. 1996

HUMPHREY
Edwin R. (husb. of Julia A.) - d. 24 March 1901 Æ 63 y., 6 m., 16 d.
Julia A. (wife of Edwin R.) - b. 11 April 1835; d. 21 February 1921

HUNTLEY
Charlie B. - b. 1897; d. 1973

HUTCHINS
Gerald Dewey [husb. of Joy Louise] - b. 14 February 1897; d. 14 August 1989
Joy Louise [wife of Gerald Dewey] - b. 26 July 1901; d. 10 June 1990

JACKSON
Charlotte (PAINE; dau. of Marguerite (OBER) PAINE) - b. 26 October 1931; d. 2 October 1956

JELLISON
Fontaine R. - b. 7 September 1876; d. 27 January 1961
Jeremiah W. - b. 16 November 1931; d. 30 October 1990

JOHNSON
Albert C. - b. 1891; d. 1953
Edward A. - b. 15 September 1916; d. 24 May 1973
Elizabeth B. (wife of Lloyd C. [no stone]) - b. 1911; d. 1951
Helen W. [wife of Kenneth C.] - b. 7 September 1913; d. 8 December 1995
Kenneth C. [husb. of Helen W.] - b. 17 March 1904; d. 13 April 1973

JOHNSTON
E. Carlton - b. 1897; d. 1899
John - b. 1830; d. 1896

JONES
Maurice Lewis - b. 22 April 1949; d. 11 May 1971

JORDAN
Arno W. (husb. of Eloise (PORTNER)) - b. 1856; d. 1917
Benjamin S. (husb. of Carolyn A.) - d. 1 April 1894 Æ 73 y.
Carolyn A. (wife of Benjamin S.) - b. 1828; d. 1907
Eloise (PORTNER; wife of Arno W.) - b. 1860; d. 1916
Jennie L. - d. 18 June 1919 Æ 15 y., 5 m., 18 d.
Jennie L. (wife of Frank M. [no stone]) - d. 1 January 1904 Æ 28 y., 7 m., 6 d.

Jos[e]phine[4] S. (wife of Waldo A.) - b. 1891; d. 1992
Nathan W. [son of Frank M. [no stone] and Jennie L.] - b. 21 June 1895; d. 6 August 1909
Waldo A. (husb. of Jos[e]phine[4] S.) - b. 1897; d. 1972
William N. (son of Waldo A. and Jos[e]phine[4] S.) - b. 1919; d. 1937

KEARNEY
Agnes - b. 1876; d. 1938

KELLEY
Albertena P[IERCE?]. (wife of Hudson O.) - b. 1867; d. 1950
Beatrice (dau. of Hudson O. and Albertena P[IERCE?].) - b. 1888; d. 1960
Hudson O. (husb. of Albertena P[IERCE?].) - b. 1867; d. 1950

KINTER
William Boardman - b. 1926; d. 1978

LACROSSE
Thomas V. Sr. - b. 1932; d. 1989

LARKIN
[Adelaide - see TAYLOR]
Arthur E. - b. 1911; d. 1943

LARRABEE
Clark B. - b. 1945; d. 1973
Clifton W. - b. 11 November 1912; d. 7 December 1980
Elizabeth L. - b. 1916; d. 1959

LAWRY
Charles W. [husb. of Elizabeth?] - b. 1897; d. 1957
Elizabeth [wife of Charles W.?] - b. 6 November 1903; d. 25 April 1993

LEACH
Elmer F. [husb. of Helena S.] - b. 1885; d. 1960
Helena S. [wife of Elmer F.] - b. 1888; d. 1949

LEATHERS
Doris M. [wife of Leon H.] - b. 1921
Leon H. [husb. of Doris M.] - b. 1918; d. 1989

LEE
[Mattie H. - see WHITE]

LELAND
Ansel H. (husb. of Chastena M. (HAMOR) and Julia A. (HODGKINS)) - d. 26 October 1916 Æ 76 y., 10 m.
Chastena M. (HAMOR; wife of Ansel H.) - d. 2 September 1877 Æ 37 y., 4 m., 14 d.
Clara E. - b. 1874; d. 1962
[Experience - see HAMOR]
infant [LELAND?] [child of Shepard L. and Myra E.?] - [no dates]
infant (son of Ansel H. and Chastena M. (HAMOR)) - [b. and?] d. 5 October 1865
Jennie - b. 1869; d. 1935
Jennie K. [wife of Shirley E.] - b. 1904; d. 1994
Julia A. (HODGKINS; wife of Ansel H.) - d. 6 May 1912 Æ 53 y., 8 m.
[Linda - see ROBBINS]
Mattie P. (wife of Oscar F.) - b. 1896; d. 1956
Myra E. (wife of Shepard L.) - b. 1861; d. 1923
[Nellie - see BREWER]
Oscar F. (husb. of Mattie P.) - b. 1884; d. 1958
Shepard L. (husb. of Myra E.) - b. 1858; d. 1932
Shirley E. [husb. of Jennie K.] - b. 5 September 1891; d. 1 January 1960

LINSCOTT
Alice S. [wife of Milton O.?] - b. 21 October 1917; d. 26 July 1997
Annie C. [wife of Hollis M. Jr.] - b. 1901
Hollis M. Jr. [husb. of Annie C.] - b. 1898; d. 1993
Milton O. [husb. of Alice S.?] - b. 24 April 1912; d. 16 June 1990
LISCOMB
Arthur [husb. of Ina S.] - b. 1876; d. 1949
Bruce D. [son of Donald C. and Edna B.] - b. 20 October 1941; d. 2 October 1958
Donald C. [husb. of Edna B.] - b. 14 October 1912; d. 14 November 1996
Edna B. [wife of Donald C.] - b. 13 February 1920; d. 26 August 1978
Ina S. [wife of Arthur] - b. 1876; d. 1949
LOCKEY
Elizabeth - b. 1909; d. 1955
LOWRIE
Bessie C. [[DORR?]; wife of Walter M.] - b. 1887; d. 1974
Walter M. [husb. of Bessie C. [DORR?]] - b. 1889; d. 1950
LUNDMARK
Frederick H. - b. 29 January 1923; d. 25 May 1987
MACDONALD
Alexander [husb. of Elizabeth H.] - b. 11 January 1878; d. 3 January 1965
Elizabeth H. [wife of Alexander] - b. 30 January 1880; d. 4 July 1971
Finlay A. [husb. of Florence M.] - b. 18 October 1904; d. 3 August 1972
Florence M. [wife of Finlay A.] - b. 29 May 1918; d. 15 June 1985
William - b. 1905; d. 1935
MACPIKE
Bertha I. (wife of Richard E.) - b. 1883; d. 1948
Inez D. [wife of Richard E.] - b. 1905; d. 1988
Lilla M. [dau. of Richard E. and Bertha I.?] - b. 1903; d. 1983
Richard E. (husb. of Bertha I.) - b. 1870; d. 1950
Richard E. [husb. of Inez D.] - b. 1902; d. 1978
MACQUINN [see also MCQUINN]
Carlton M. [husb. of Thelma B.] - b. 1903; d. 1960
Cora B. [wife of Edward A.?] - b. 1868; d. 1954
Edward A. [husb. of Cora B.?] - b. 1863; d. 1952
Harold J. [husb. of Henrietta R.] - b. 1910; d. 1984
Henrietta R. [wife of Harold J.] - b. 1912; d. 1997
[Hildreth M[ACQUINN?]. - see PERRY]
Maud [dau. of Edward A. and Cora B.?] - b. 1888; d. 1950
Ruth I. [dau. of Harold J. and Henrietta R.?] - b. 1946; d. 1977
Thelma B. [wife of Carlton M.] - b. 1912; d. 1990
MAGNUSSON
Anna E. [wife of Carl J.] - b. 1891; d. [no date]
Carl J. [husb. of Anna E.] - b. 1876; d. 1959
John - b. 1880; d. 1950
MARCYES
C. E. (husb. of Mary I.) - [no dates]
Danforth P. (husb. of Helen A.) - d. 30 October 1899, Bar Harbor, Maine, Æ 75 y., 7 m., 14 d.
Helen A. (wife of Danforth P.) - d. 29 February 1904, Bar Harbor, Maine, Æ 67 y., 2 m., 17 d.
infant - [no dates]
Mary I. (wife of C. E.) - b. 1875; d. 1939

MAYO
Harriet W. - b. 1888; d. 1947
McFARLAND
Beulah M. [wife of Sherman F.] - b. 1912
Edward F. - d. 22 November 1864, "at Andersonvill [sic] Prison Ga.", Æ 25 y., 7 m.; (member of Co. G, 8th Maine Regiment [Civil War])
[Emeline M[cFARLAND?]. - see MURPHY]
Howard H. [husb. of Josephine A.] - b. 1898; d. 1966
infant (dau. of Leonard and Sarah "Sally") - d. February 1853 Æ 1 d.
John F. (son of Leonard and Sarah "Sally") - d. 6 November 1851 Æ 10 m., 15 d.
John H. [son of Howard H. and Josephine A.?] - b. 1937; d. 1997
Josephine A. [wife of Howard H.] - b. 1900; d. 1969
Leonard (husb. of Sarah "Sally") - b. 1813; d. 1890; (member of Co. E, 26th Maine Regiment [Civil War])
Sarah "Sally" (wife of Leonard) - b. 1823; d. 1901
Sherman F. [husb. of Beulah M.] - b. 1908; d. 1995
Washburn - b. 4 July 1861; d. 28 February 1926
[...][2]
McINTOSH
Dorothy H. - b. 1900; d. 1963
McKAY
Colin A. - b. 12 September 1906; d. 4 March 1970
Ronald G. - b. 8 March 1907; d. 22 May 1980
McPHETERS
Ruth S. - b. 1900; d. 1968
McQUINN [see also MacQUINN]
Arthur L. [husb. of Tillie J.] - b. 1878; d. 1961
Arthur L. Jr. [son of Arthur L. and Tillie J.] - b. 1906; d. 1971
Douglas A. - b. 1933; d. 1974
Maybelle F. (wife of Vernon A.) - b. 1904; d. 1993
Tillie J. [wife of Arthur L.] - b. 1878; d. 1936
Vernon A. (husb. of Maybelle F.) - b. 30 August 1897; d. 3 May 1957
MINNICH
Charles H. [husb. of Elizabeth E.] - b. 1916
Elizabeth E. [wife of Charles H.] - b. 1916; d. 1972
MITCHELL
Amy Frances - [b. and d.?] 1895
Clarence H. [husb. of Corice A.] - b. 1882; d. 1949
Corice A. [wife of Clarence H.] - b. 1879; d. 1935
Donald B. [husb. of Fernie A.] - b. 1906; d. 1947
Eleta I. - b. 1904; d. 1952
Elsa J. [wife of Ralph H.] - b. 13 January 1909; d. 15 November 1992
Fernie A. [wife of Donald B.] - b. 1913; d. 1945
Mary S. (SARGENT; wife of Nelson S.) - b. 1831; d. 1901
Maxwell M. - b. 1899; d. 1984
Nelson S. (husb. of Polly, Polly, and Mary S. (SARGENT)) - d. 18 January 1899 Æ 81 y., 2 m., 15 d.
Polly (wife of Nelson S.) - d. 7 May 1848 Æ 29 y., 3 m.
Polly (wife of Nelson S.) - d. 7 January 1858 Æ 28 y.
Ralph H. [husb. of Elsa J.] - b. 18 October 1898; d. 1 May 1985
Robert Henry - b. 1904; d. 1936
Sabra Corthell - b. 1867; d. 1952

MORRISON
Fannie (GRAY) - b. 1850; d. 1926
Helen T. [wife of James] - b. 1887; d. 1955
James [husb. of Helen T.] - b. 1885; d. 1959
MUNRO
Isabelle H. - b. 1886; d. 1973
MURPHY
Emeline M[cFARLAND?]. - b. 22 February 1887; d. 12 August 1921
Ruth A[BBOTT?]. [wife of Winfield P. Jr. [no stone]] - b. 1930; d. 1956
MUSHERO
Henry J. [husb. of Mildred U.] - b. 1904; d. 1980
Mildred U. [wife of Henry J.] - b. 1897; d. 1980
MYRICK
[Jestina E. - see ROBBINS]
Joseph (son of Anthony and Aurilla [no stones]) - b. 1855; d. 1895
NELSON
Dorothy L. [wife of George S.?] - b. 20 September 1927; d. 24 February 1994
George S. [husb. of Dorothy L.?] - b. 1921; d. 1988
NICHOLS
David E. - b. 10 July 1965; d. 3 November 1965
NICKERSON
George A. (husb. of Lizzie (STANLEY)) - b. 1876; d. 1938
Kathleen Ann - b. 1946; d. 1948
Lizzie (STANLEY; wife of George A.) - b. 1883; d. 1961
OBER
Allen E. (husb. of Georgia S.) - b. 1871; d. 1936
Georgia S. (wife of Allen E.) - b. 1868; d. 1935
[Marguerite - see PAINE]
O'HEARN
Merle Chaney - b. 1884; d. 1950
OTT
Joseph W. [husb. of Margaret D.] - b. 1861; d. 1946
Margaret D. [wife of Joseph W.] - b. 1871; d. 1942
PAGE
[Martha - see HODGKINS]
PAINE
[Charlotte - see JACKSON]
Marguerite (OBER) - b. 25 November 1902; d. 6 October 1991
PALMER
Madeline (PARSONS; dau. of John E. PARSONS and Annie H. [no stones]) - b. 21 January 1923; d. 24 April 1972
PARRITT
Gordon A. [husb. of Eleanor G.?] - b. 1917; d. 1969
Gordon A. Jr. [son of Gordon A. and Eleanor G.] - b. 1943
Eleanor G. [wife of Gordon A.?] - b. 1921
Nancy J. - b. 1943
Martha B. [wife of Warren A.] - b. 1881; d. 1967
Warren A. [husb. of Martha B.] - b. 1881; d. 1947
PARSONS
Bruce H. - b. 1956; d. 1977
Clara E. (wife of Herbert W.) - b. 1908; d. 1980
Clara H. (wife of Linwood E.) - b. 1860; d. 1921

Clarence E. (son of Eben E. and Nellie E.) - d. 16 October 1894 Æ 16 y., 1 m., 16 d.
Eben E. (husb. of Nellie E.) - b. 1855; d. 1934
Gerald H. - b. 1933; d. 1976
Herbert W. (husb. of Clara E.) - b. 1904; d. 1982
Linwood E. (husb. of Clara H.) - b. 1857; d. 1940
[Madeline - see PALMER]
Nellie E. (wife of Eben E.) - b. 1856; d. 1937

PERRY
Benjamin M. [husb. of Ida E.] - b. 1868; d. 1946
Hildreth M[ACQUINN]. [wife of Willis L.] - b. 1905; d. 1995
Ida E. [wife of Benjamin M.] - b. 1876; d. 1945
Willis L. [husb. of Hildreth M[ACQUINN?].] - b. 1907; d. 1988

PETER
Ellen (WILLIAMS; [wife of Louis]) - b. 1903; d. 1976
Louis [husb. of Ellen (WILLIAMS)] - b. 1904; d. 1959

PETTINGILL
Mabel G. - b. 1883; d. 1984

PHILLIPS
Angie L. - b. 17 October 1866; d. 21 June 1882
Levi F. (husb. of Melinda) - b. 20 May 1829; d. 11 July 1915
Melinda (wife of Levi F.) - b. 13 February 1836; d. 11 February 1913
William H. - b. 1860; d. 1943

PHINNEY
Bertha L. - b. 7 January 1911; d. 6 October 1988
Donald R. - b. 1912; d. 1972
Russell[6] - [no dates]

PIERCE
[Albertena P[IERCE?]. - see KELLEY]
Alvah H. - b. 1862; d. 1938
Cynthia M. (wife of Joseph H. [no stone]) - d. 23 January 1876 Æ 33 y., 7 m., 3 d.
Hannah E. (wife of John M.) - b. 12 October 1842; d. 20 September 1908
John M. (husb. of Hannah E.) - b. 2 August 1836; d. 29 December 1912
Lenora J. - b. 1868; d. 1948
Marie B. - b. 1893; d. 1946

POIRIER
[...] [headstone only "SARGENT/POIRIER"]

PORTER
Theodore R. - b. 1928; d. 1928

PORTNER
[Eloise - see JORDAN]

PRESTON
Charles W. [husb. of Goldie A.] - b. 1875; d. 1948
Goldie A. [wife of Charles W.] - b. 1884; d. 1959

REMICK
Hannah (wife of Seth D.) - d. 27 November 1850 Æ 47 y., 5 m.
Seth D. (husb. of Hannah) - d. 15 October 1846, Newport, Rhode Island, Æ 47 y., 5 m.

REYNOLDS
Daniel L. [husb. of Madora B.] - b. 14 September 1896; d. 31 October 1968
David (husb. of Mary E.) - b. 1836; d. 1923; (member of Co. C, 11th Maine Regiment [Civil War])

J. Henry - d. 18 April 1896 Æ 66 y., 9 m., 12 d.
Madora B. [wife of Daniel L.] - b. 1899; d. 1983
Mary E. (wife of David) - d. 11 August 1894 Æ 54 y.
Minnie E. (TENNEY; adopted dau. of David and Mary E.) - d. 11 April 1896 Æ 19 y., 9 m., 27 d.

RICHARDSON
Abiathair L. [husb. of Margaret M.] - b. 17 March 1874; d. 31 January 1940
Benjamin (husb. of Everline [sic] C. (HAMOR)) - d. 20 September 1895 Æ 57 y., 3 m.; (member of Co. A, 1st Maine Heavy Artillery [Civil War])
Everline [sic] C. (HAMOR; wife of Benjamin) - d. 24 May 1910 Æ 62 y., 3 m.
Margaret M. [wife of Abiathair L.] - b. 4 April 1874; d. 1 April 1955
William T. - d. 3 February 1895 Æ 38 y., 16 d.

RIDDELL
George T. - b. 1936; d. 1978
John [husb. of Margaret C.] - b. 1903; d. 1982
John C. ([son of John and Margaret C.]; husb. of Annie M. [no stone]) - b. 30 May 1931; d. 10 November 1973
Margaret C. [wife of John] - b. 1907
Thomas K. - b. 1909; d. 1983
Vicki Lee (dau. of John C. and Annie M. [no stone]) - b. 18 May 1954; d. 18 January 1957

RIDER
Amy - [no dates]
George - [no dates]
Grace - [no dates]
infant - [no dates]

RINALDO
C. Leslie [husb. of Norma M.] - b. 1909; d. 1986
Charles - b. 20 February 1837; d. 28 December 1913
Norma M. [wife of C. Leslie] - b. 1907; d. 1986

ROBBINS
Byron F. [husb. of Effie N.] - b. 1872; d. 1946
Cecil L. (husb. of Hazel M.) - b. 1897; d. 1960
Cecil L. Jr. (son of Cecil L. and Hazel M.; [husb. of Florence M.]) - b. 1926; d. 1992
Effie N. [wife of Byron F.] - b. 1879; d. 1951
Florence M. [wife of Cecil L. Jr.] - b. 1924
Hazel M. (wife of Cecil L.) - b. 1906; d. 1976
Jestina E. (MYRICK; former wife of Joseph H. MYRICK [no stone]; wife of Nelson [no stone]) - b. 1867; d. 1918
Linda (LELAND; [dau. of Shepard L. LELAND and Mrya E.?]; wife of Ralph E.) - b. 1899; d. 1963
Mary A. - d. 25 March 1905 Æ 62 y., 1 m.
Nettie E. [wife of Ralph] - b. 1876; d. 1960
[Nina R[OBBINS?]. - see ALLEY]
Ralph [husb. of Nettie E.] - b. 1871; d. 1941
Ralph E. (husb. of Linda (LELAND)) - b. 1901; d. 1979

ROBERTS
Austin D. [husb. of Marion E.] - b. 1922
Helen (HARADEN; wife of Fred L. [no stone]) - b. 1914; d. 1996
Marion E. [wife of Austin D.] - b. 1925

RODICK
Alice M. (wife of David 2nd) - d. 30 May 1929 Æ 75 y.
Betsey (BREWER; wife of David [no stone]) - d. 8 April 1885 Æ 59 y., 7 m.
David 2nd (husb. of Alice M.) - d. 19 September 1895 Æ 51 y., 8 m., 15 d.
Heman C. [son of David 2nd and Alice M.?] - b. 1872; d. 1936
RONALD
Byron H. [husb. of Josie P.] - b. 1885; d. 1942
Josie P. [wife of Byron H.] - b. 1886; d. 1984
RUSSELL
Paul L. (husb. of Rose B.) - b. 1892; d. 1953
Rhoda H. - b. 1853; d. 1920
Robert A. (son of Paul L. and Rose B.) - b. 1920; d. 1936
Rose B. (wife of Paul L.) - b. 1900; d. 1988
SALISBURY
Agnes (HAMOR; [wife of Everett J.]) - b. 1910; d. 1989
Camilla H. - d. 17 November 1888 Æ 17 y., 7 m.
Cornelia E. (wife of Warren [no stone]) - b. 1832; d. 1914
Everett J. [husb. of Agnes (HAMOR)] - b. 1906; d. 1950
Fannie M. (wife of George E.) - b. 1877; d. 1936
George E. (husb. of Fannie M. and Grace E.) - b. 1878; d. 1960
George L. Jr. - b. 1915; d. 1975
Grace E. (wife of George E.) - b. 1883; d. 1964
infant (son of Wilbur R. and Julia A. (HAMOR)) - [b. and d.?] 19 June 1890
Julia A. (HAMOR; wife of Wilbur R.) - b. 30 April 1855; d. 7 October 1930
[Ruby - see HODGKINS]
Sarah E. (wife of Stephen S.) - d. 22 September 1928 Æ 81 y., 8 m., 4 d.
Stephen S. (husb. of Sarah E.) - d. 14 June 1887 Æ 47 y., 4 m., 5 d.
Wilbur R. (husb. of Julia A. (HAMOR)) - b. 10 July 1855; d. 24 December 1947
SARGENT
[Mary S. - see MITCHELL]
Grace L. (wife of Walter W. Sr.) - b. 1867; d. 1936
Ruth A. [wife of Walter W. Jr.] - b. 1907
Walter W. Jr. (son of Walter W. Sr. and Grace L.; [husb. of Ruth A.]) - b. 1903; d. 1988
Walter W. Sr. (husb. of Grace L.) - b. 1874; d. 1958
[...] [headstone only "SARGENT/POIRIER"]
SAVIN
Frances G. [wife of William A.] - b. 24 December 1909; d. 13 June 1995
William A. [husb. of Frances G.] - b. 25 July 1910; d. 2 September 1978
SAWYER
Ada M. (wife of Fred H.) - b. 1893; d. 1929
Burnell F. - b. 3 April 1928; d. 29 March 1977
Erland L. [son of Fred H. and Ada M.?] - d. 12 September 1919 Æ 7 m., 27 d.
Fred H. (husb. of Ada M.) - b. 1888; d. 1972
Frederick H. [son of Fred H. and Ada M.?] - d. 2 April 1921 Æ 6 y., 8 m., 14 d.
Harrison P. - b. 8 June 1921; d. 31 March 1972
Lowell J. [son of Fred H. and Ada M.?] - d. 28 October 1919 Æ 2 y., 4 m., 28 d.
Madeline L. [dau. of Fred H. and Ada M.?] - d. 27 May 1927 Æ 2 m., 5 d.
SCANKS
Charlie E. - b. 23 January 1889; d. 26 February 1908
William H. - b. 25 July 1879; d. 21 March 1898

SHAW

Asenath - d. 4 June 1913 Æ 60 y., 4 m.

SHEA

Anna K. - b. 16 April 1895; d. 24 February 1900
Charles W. (husb. of Elizabeth P. "Lizzie") - b. 1877; d. 1961
Elizabeth P. "Lizzie" (wife of Charles W.) - b. 1875; d. 1962
infant (son of Charles W. and Elizabeth P. "Lizzie") - [b. and?] d. 19 August 1902
James M. - b. 22 April 1867; d. 26 May 1963
James W. - b. 30 April 1904; d. 17 May 1955
Mildred H. - b. 1900; d. 1944
Ruth E. - b. 18 May 1882; d. 23 March 1941

SIMPSON

Edgar L. [husb. of Emma H.] - b. 1859; d. 1942
[Ellen - see BRYANT]
Emma H. [wife of Edgar L.] - b. 1863; d. 1937
Harry L. (husb. of Sarah A.) - b. 1873; d. 1929
Sarah A. (wife of Harry L.) - b. 1890; d. 1962

SLEEPER

David A. - b. 1905; d. 1958
Percival W. - b. 1912; d. 1995

SMITH

Addie (wife of William E.) - b. 1852; d. 1931
Blanche B. (dau. of H. and F. D. [no stones]) - b. 19 May 1897; d. 8 February 1898
Clarence K. (husb. of Mona A.) - b. 1885; d. 1968
Frank H. [husb. of Mamie E.] - b. 27 February 1914; d. 17 January 1972
Mamie E. [wife of Frank H.] - b. 1 August 1916; d. 13 July 1966
[Marion V. - see HINCKLEY]
Mona A. (wife of Clarence K.) - b. 1888; d. 1970
William E. (husb. of Addie) - b. 1862; d. 1935

SPRAGUE

Hattie M. [wife of Kenneth C.] - b. 1897; d. 1994
Kenneth C. [husb. of Hattie M.] - b. 1903; d. 1971

SPURLING

John (husb. of Sarah J. (HAMOR)) - b. 23 September 1836; d. 20 May 1890
Sarah J. (HAMOR; wife of John) - b. 15 March 1843 d. 4 March 1903
[...]rd[5] Anderson (son of A. E. and [...]ry[5] [no stones?][5]) - b. 29 [...]c.[5] 1901; d. 15 September 1902

STANLEY

Alice D. [wife of N. Leroy] - b. 1892; d. 1957
C. Estella [wife of John N.] - b. 1863; d. 1954
Carrie V. (wife of Tyler W.) - b. 17 September 1868; d. 4 August 1907
Dorothea M. - b. 14 June 1892; d. 5 December 1987
Eliza (wife of Joseph) - b. 1837; d. 1926
Elizabeth - b. 26 September 1881; d. 7 January 1972
Eva (wife of James C.) - b. 21 October 1857; d. 29 July 1945
Hannah M. (wife of Wilbert W.) - d. 19 January 1890 Æ 41 y., 6 m.
infant (son of Nathan S. and Alice R. [no stone]) - d. [no date] Æ 9 d.
James C. (husb. of Eva) - b. 18 July 1856; d. 13 September 1936
John N. [husb. of C. Estella] - b. 1863; d. 1947
Joseph (husb. of Eliza) - b. 1830; d. 1910
Katie L. (dau. of James C. and Eva) - d. 3 October 1893 Æ 19 y.
[Lizzie - see NICKERSON]

Louise Ray [STANLEY?] - b. 1868; d. 1954
Marion T. - b. 13 June 1882; d. 27 July 1971
Melicent [sic] F. - b. 27 May 1884; d. 24 January 1961
N. Leroy [husb. of Alice D.] - b. 1901; d. 1974
Nathan S. (husb. of Alice R. [no stone]) - d. 21 June 1864 Æ 31 y.; ("died of wounds received in battle before Petersburg"[11]; member of Co. L, 1st Maine Heavy Artillery [Civil War])
Tyler W. (husb. of Carrie V.) - b. 2 November 1860; d. [no date]
Veston [sic] F. (son of Nathan S. and Alice R. [no stone]) - d. 1 March 1862 Æ 2 y., 3 m.
Wilbert W. (husb. of Hannah M.) - d. 18 April 1933 Æ 82 y., 8 m., 18 d.

STEARNS
Harry E. (husb. of Lena M.) - b. 3 January 1877; d. 17 October 1948
Lena M. (wife of Harry E.) - b. 29 June 1875; d. 10 September 1941
[Margaret B. - see WHITE]

STEVENS
Eunice (wife of Jeremiah [no stone]) - d. 17 February 1820 Æ 27 y.

STEWART
Avis Pearl (wife of Lionel L.) - b. 1905; d. 1976
[Irene Emma - see CUMMINGS]
John L. (son of Lionel L. and Avis Pearl) - b. 1936
Lionel L. (husb. of Avis Pearl) - b. 1907; d. 1996
Lionel S. (husb. of Violet M.) - b. 1868; d. 1961
Violet M. (wife of Lionel S.) - b. 1888; d. 1962

STIMPSON
[...] [headstone only "CLOUDMAN/STIMPSON"]

STROUT
Adfer A. (husb. of Ida M. and Helen L.) - b. 1883; d. 1970
Adfer A. Jr. (son of Adfer A. and Helen L.) - b. 1922; d. 1922
Dennis R. - b. 1953; d. 1971
Edith G. [wife of Seldon] - b. 17 October 1889; d. 28 December 1956
Edward L. [husb. of Herthel T.] - b. 1919
Edwin A. [husb. of Pauline M.] - b. 30 November 1919
Helen L. (wife of Adfer A.) - b. 1896; d. 1987
Herthel T. [wife of Edward L.] - b. 1926; d. 1970
Ida M. (wife of Adfer A.) - b. 1882; d. 1916
Ira Leroy - b. 1921; d. 1979
Pauline M. [wife of Edwin A.] - b. 19 May 1919
Peggie S. [dau. of Edward L. and Herthel T.?] - b. 1958; d. 1970
Ruth L. [dau. of Seldon and Edith G.?] - b. 22 April 1922; d. 3 June 1926
Seldon [husb. of Edith G.] - b. 26 October 1887; d. 12 September 1956
Tena J. - b. 10 June 1870; d. 2 February 1911

SULLIVAN
Anne S. (CROWELL; [wife of Edward J.?]) - b. 1879; d. 1961
Edward J. [husb. of Anne S. (CROWELL)?] - b. 23 December 1887; d. 21 November 1966
Elizabeth D. [wife of Frederick A.?] - b. 1903; d. 1979
Frederick A. [husb. of Elizabeth D.?] - b. 27 June 1898; d. 6 April 1959

SUMINSBY
Charles E. [son of Colimore and Hannah?] - b. 1869; d. 1954
Colimore [husb. of Hannah] - b. 1846; d. 1897
[Florence S[UMINSBY?]. - see GRANT]

Hannah [wife of Colimore] - b. 1849; d. 1927
Harriett (Miss) - d. 27 September 1882 Æ 62 y., 1 m., 20 d.
SWANSON
Alice - b. 1906; d. 1977
Lilliy [sic] O. [wife of Oke] - b. 1871; d. 1961
Oke [husb. of Lilliy [sic] O.] - b. 1863; d. 1943
SWEET
Charlotte J. [wife of Sherley [sic] M.?] - b. 1896; d. 1985
Henry C. [husb. of Lena H.?] - b. 1884; d. 1970
Lena H. [wife of Henry C.?] - b. 1890; d. 1984
Richard C. [son of Sherley [sic] M. and Charlotte J.?] - b. 1921; d. 1936
Sherley [sic] M. [husb. of Charlotte J.?] - b. 1891; d. 1969
TARTAGLIA
Agnes K. (DORR; [dau. of Elliott B. DORR and Asta O.?]) - b. 1912; d. 1962
TAYLOR
Adelaide (LARKIN; wife of Russell W.) - b. 11 July 1912
Russell W. (husb. of Adelaide (LARKIN)) - b. 26 January 1911; d. 8 September 1986
TENNEY
[Minnie E. - see REYNOLDS]
TEWELL
John R. - b. 1949; d. 1988
THOMAS
[Elmenia - see HAMOR]
Harry W. J. - b. 25 September 1892; d. 29 March 1956
infant [THOMAS?] - [no dates]
Oliver C. (Capt.; husb. of Sarah S.) - d. 26 September 1868 Æ 83 y.
Ruth M. - b. 6 October 1891; d. 10 February 1920
Sarah S. (wife of Capt. Oliver C.) - d. 10 March 1871 Æ 82 y.
THOMPSON
Carrie B. [wife of Frank W.] - b. 1861; d. 1950
Frank W. [husb. of Carrie B.] - b. 1858; d. 1930
TRACY
Alice M. (dau. of Elwyn Boyd and Alice Marguerite) - d. 11 October 1920 Æ 4 d.
Alice Marguerite (wife of Elwyn Boyd) - b. 4 July 1899; d. 24 February 1998
Dora A. [wife of George W.] - b. 1872; d. 1948
Elwyn Boyd (husb. of Alice Marguerite) - b. 1 November 1892; d. 1 March 1954
George W. [husb. of Dora A.] - b. 1875; d. 1941
TRUITT
Maisie (HIGGINS; [wife of William Harrison]) - b. 1895; d. [no date]
William Harrison [husb. of Maisie (HIGGINS)] - b. 1886; d. 1968
TURNBULL
Emma [wife of Howard] - b. 1907; d. 1993
Howard [husb. of Emma] - b. 1897; d. 1982
UNDERWOOD
Freddie E. (son of T. W. and Alice M. [no stones]) - d. 5 September 1895 Æ 6 m.
infant (child of T. W. and Alice M. [no stones]) - d. 3 January 1894 Æ 3 d.
WAGNER
Marjorie - b. 19 June 1926; d. 21 June 1953
WEBBER
Allen G. - b. 26 April 1941; d. 28 July 1995
Earl L. [husb. of Virginia B.] - b. 1909; d. 1961

Earl L. - b. 1908; d. 1960
Virginia B. [wife of Earl L.] - b. 1915; d. 1999
WHITE
Alfred L. (son of Ralph L. and Mattie H. (LEE)) - [b. and d.?] 1920
[Dorothea - see HARRIS]
Howard C. - b. 1916; d. 1962
Laura O. - b. 1890; d. 1960
Leon W. - b. 1911; d. 1969
Leslie W. - b. 1908; d. 1940
Lloyd H. - b. 1885; d. 1964
Margaret B. (STEARNS) - b. 1894; d. 1983
Mattie H. (LEE; wife of Ralph L.) - b. 1881; d. 1929
Ralph L. (husb. of Mattie H. (LEE)) - b. 1876; d. 1958
[...] [headstone only]
WHITING
Julia Beverley [sic] - b. 5 August 1892; d. 11 January 1967
WHITNEY
Arden L. - b. 8 August 1915; d. 14 August 1985
Georgia (WORCESTER; wife of Capt. Harold C.) - b. 27 October 1891; d. 13 February 1986
Harold C. (Capt.; husb. of Georgia (WORCESTER)) - b. 25 August 1885; d. 2[5 or 1][4,7] April 1959
WIGHT
[...] [headstone only]
WILCOMB
Alliene T. [wife of Ernest D.?] - b. 13 November 1892; d. 14 August 1979
Carroll A. [son of Ernest D. and Alliene T.?] - b. 1922; d. 1977
Charles A. (husb. of Eliza (HAMOR)) - b. 6 April 1846; d. 19 May 1925
Eliza (HAMOR; wife of Charles A.) - b. 22 February 1848; d. 1 March 1930
Ernest D. [husb. of Alliene T.?] - b. 27 January 1888; d. 29 November 1963
infant (son of Charles A. and Eliza (HAMOR)) - [b. and d.?] 5 September 1877
WILKINSON
Dolores T. - b. 1955; d. 1961
Ellen M. [wife of Manly E.] - b. 1902; d. 1993
Manly E. [husb. of Ellen M.] - b. 1899; d. 1967
WILLIAMS
Bennett J. (husb. of Bessie (DAVIES)) - b. 1875; d. 1946
Bessie (DAVIES; wife of Bennett J.) - b. 1874; d. 1941
Ella May - b. 1917; d. 1948
[Ellen - see PETER]
Madeline A. [wife of Theodore K.] - b. 1913; d. 1966
Theodore K. [husb. of Madeline A.] - b. 1906; d. 1970
WOOD
A. H. - d. 18 April 1898 Æ 30 y.
[Dorris [sic] - see FARRAR]
Foster J. [husb. of Nettie M.] - b. 1884; d. 1963
George F. (husb. of Harriett [sic] M. (HADLEY)) - b. 1878; d. 1945
Harriett [sic] M. (HADLEY; wife of George F.) - b. 1881; d. 1956
Nettie M. [wife of Foster J.] - b. 1894; d. 1963
Olin D. - b. 1880; d. 1945

WOODWARD
  Ethelyn Ward [wife of Maxwell G.] - b. 1907
  Maxwell G. [husb. of Ethelyn Ward] - b. 1910; d. 1988
WOODWORTH
  Frances S. - b. 1907
  Geneva L. [wife of Henry W.?] - b. 1882; d. 1982
  Henry W. [husb. of Geneva L.?] - b. 1879; d. 1918
  Linwood P. - b. 1936; d. 1987
  Preston L. - b. 1904; d. 1970
WORCESTER
  [Georgia - see WHITNEY]
WRIGHT
  Gertie M. (wife of E. W. [no stone]) - b. 9 April 1876; d. 14 November 1899
YORK
  Josephine M. - b. 31 July 1853; d. 22 May 1908
YOUNG
  Daniel J. [husb. of Ella S.] - b. 26 November 1907; d. 14 May 1970
  David Augustus - b. 28 March 1894; d. 11 November 1954
  Ella S. [wife of Daniel J.] - b. 3 January 1916; d. 19 October 1984
  Edith May - b. 31 December 1871; d. 20 January 1911
  Joseph E. (husb. of Laura E.) - b. 1839; d. 1919; ("G. A. R." [Civil War])
  Julia M. [wife of Theodore M.?] - b. 23 November 1906; d. 21 December 1979
  Laura E. (wife of Joseph E.) - b. 1836; d. 1888
  Maria - d. 19 November 1904 Æ 38 y., 10 m., 6 d.
  Theodore M. [husb. of Julia M.?] - b. 4 July 1907; d. 23 March 1968
  William - d. 23 May 1902 Æ 68 y.

Notes:
[1]Different order on different stones.
[2]Remainder of stone below ground.
[3]Stone worn, cracked, and/or broken.
[4]Different on different stones.
[5]A tall monument that is laying on the ground with one side completely unobservable and one side partially buried.
[6]The name "Russell Phinney" is carved into an unpainted, deteriorating, wooden cross. This cross is now broken off at the base, but it once stood at a grave on the same lot—but not the same grave—as Donald R. PHINNEY.
[7]25 on Harold and Georgia's stone; 21 on Harold's Coast Guard stone.
[8]Originally engraved "Chester J.", but then the "J." was filled in and H. engraved in its place.
[9]Spacing of the numbers suggests that both the ten's digit and unit's digit are 4.
[10]Henry W. BROWN's marker was on the same lot as Arthur W. and Ruby M. in 1998. In February 2000, it was no longer on the lot, and there was a recent grave with a new stone of Emeline B[ROWN?]. BRYANT (*q.v.*).
[11]Much of the time spent by Union troops in the vicinity of Petersburg was outside the city, generally referred to as "in front of Petersburg" or "before Petersburg".

Emery Cemetery
(Bar Harbor - 7)

Location/directions. In pasture southwest of intersection of Norway Drive and Crooked Road. From the traffic light at the north end of Mount Desert Island, bear left on Route 3. In approximately 4.6–4.7 miles, turn right onto Norway Drive. Travel 1.2–1.3 miles to a stop sign at the intersection of Norway Drive and Crooked Road. Turn right onto Crooked Road, and the cemetery is in the pasture on the left in approximately 0.1 miles.

History. Although this cemetery is called the Emery Cemetery on the 1981 7.5' Salsbury [sic] Cove topographic map, the earliest graves belong to the Thompson family.

Notes. During the summer of 1999, major improvements were made to this cemetery—brush was cleared; fallen gravestones were propped up when possible; and a fence was repaired to protect both the cemetery and the remains of an old iron fence.

Names and dates on gravestones and other markers. [4 March 2000]

EMERY

Arthur L. (son of Jared and Sophia) - d. 24 August 1873 Æ 19 y., 3 m., 7 d.
Charley M. (son of Hiram J. and Rose B. [no stones]) - d. 29 July 1876 Æ 11 m., 3 d.
Clarence D. (son of Isaac H. and Clarissa H.) - b. 1870; d. 1893
Clarissa H. (wife of Isaac H.) - [no dates]
Edward E. (son of Jared and Sophia) - d. 17 May 1864 Æ 19 y.; ("killed in the battle of the Wilderness"; member of Co. C, 1st Maine Heavy Artillery [Civil War])
E. W. [EMERY?] - [footstone only[2]]
[H.?][1] E[MERY?]. (Mrs.; wife of [...][1]) - [...][1]
infant (son of H. F. and N. M. [no stones]) - [no dates]
Isaac H. (husb. of Clarissa H.) - [no dates]; (member of Co. E, 26th Maine Regiment [Civil War])
Jane H. (dau. of Jared and Sophia) - d. 9 September 1840 Æ 6 y.
Jared (husb. of Sophia) - d. 4 June 1883 Æ 72 y.
Joel (husb. of Martha) - d. 19 February 1867 Æ 86 y.
Joel Jr. (husb. of Abby [no stone]) - d. 13 December 1866 Æ 37 y., 7 m., 12 d.
John L. (son of Jared and Sophia) - d. 23 July 1866 Æ 23 y., 2 m., 13 d.; (member of Co. C, 1st Maine Heavy Artillery [Civil War])
Josiah M. - d. 6 July 1859 Æ 25 y., 3 m., 21 d.
Lorenzo J. (son of Joel Jr. and Abby [no stone]) - d. 14 March 1852 Æ 2 y., 7 d.
Margaret A. (dau. of Jared and Sophia) - d. 20 September 1840 Æ 2 y.
Martha (wife of Joel) - d. [...][1] 1872 Æ 79 y., 2 m., 9 d.
Onslow Y. (son of Jared and Sophia) - d. 17 April 1876 Æ 24 y., 2 m., 5 d.
Sophia (wife of Jared) - b. 1814; d. 1903

HALL

Daniel G. [husb. of Elva M.] - b. 1863; d. 1939
Elva M. [wife of Daniel G.] - b. 1864; d. 1946

PAINE

Addie M. (wife of Edgar M.) - b. 14 February 1867; d. 24 December 1903
Charles Sargent - d. 28 June 1894 Æ 18 y.
Edgar M. (husb. of Addie M.) - b. 18 September 1859; d. 23 January 1941
James R. (son of M. W. and Hattie L. [no stones]) - d. 10 February 1890 Æ 3 d.
Phebe A. (wife of Richard H.) - d. 28 February 1892 Æ 47 y., 6 m.

Richard H. (husb. of Sophia A. and Phebe A.) - b. 1828; d. 1913; (member of Co. E, 26th Maine Regiment [Civil War])
Sophia A. (wife of Richard H.) - d. 22 October 1864 Æ 28 y., 7 m.

THOMPSON

Cornelius (husb. of Sally) - d. 1 November 1862 Æ 74 y., 8 m.
Cornelius Jr. [son of Cornelius and Sally] - d. 21 February 1850, “at sea”, Æ 19 y., 9 m.
Eben T. (son of Cornelius and Sally) - d. 13 April 1845 Æ 20 y., 29 d.
Joel E. (son of Cornelius and Sally) - d. 21 August 1838 Æ 18 y., 6 m., 13 d.
Meltiah T. (son of Cornelius and Sally) - d. 24 August 1839 Æ 7 y., 8 m., 8 d.
Sally (wife of Cornelius) - d. 22 April 1846 Æ 49 y., 8 d.

Notes:

[1]Stone worn, cracked, and/or broken.

[2]A headstone that is broken and crumbling, with only remnants of verse at bottom remaining, is probably associated with the footstone: “E. W. E.”.

Mountain View Cemetery

(Bar Harbor - 8)

Location/directions. Along east side of Routes 102/198, Town Hill. From the traffic light at the north end of Mount Desert Island, go straight ahead (south) onto Routes 102/198. In approximately 2.4 miles, the cemetery is on the left. Alternatively, from the traffic light at the intersection of Routes 3/198 and 102/198 (just north of the village of Somesville), go north approximately 1.8–1.9 miles, and the cemetery is on the right.

History. This cemetery is found in the 1881 Colby Atlas. Thornton (1938) called this the Town Hill or West Eden Cemetery and noted that "many flags flutter in this yard on Memorial Day showing the graves of those who served their country in the Civil War" (p. 234). Today, the West Eden Village Improvement Society oversees its maintenance that includes mowing, trimming, and raking. The Society owns the new section of the cemetery and the right to sell the 91 lots that have been developed.

Notes. This cemetery is enclosed by a gated chain-link fence, and has a U-shaped gravel road. Many older stones are tipping or laying on the ground. One stone that had been completely covered with dirt and vegetation was discovered during research for this book.

Names and dates on gravestones and other markers. [18 January 1999]

ABBOTT
- George W. [husb. of Phena B.] - b. 1876; d. 1963
- Phena B. [wife of George W.] - b. 1887; d. 1949

ADAMS
- John R. - b. 19 July 1932; d. 15 December 1992

AHLBLAD
- Charles P. (husb. of Elida W.) - b. 1866; d. 1936
- Elida W. (wife of Charles P.) - b. 1869; d. 1947
- George E. [AHLBLAD?] - b. 1864; d. 1924
- Harold (son of Charles P. and Elida W.) - b. 1899; d. 1907

ALLEN
- Charles D. (husb. of Julia E.) - b. 1867; d. 25 October 1940
- Climenia (wife of Capt. Frederick) - [no dates]
- Delmon [son of Capt. Frederick and Climenia?] - d. 15 October 1875, Havana, Cuba, Æ 22 y.
- Flora B. (wife of Harvey F.) - b. 1867 d. 1951
- Frederick (Capt.; husb. of Climenia) - d. 30 October 1885 Æ 72 y.
- Harvey F. (husb. of Flora B.) - b. 1863; d. 1901
- Julia E. (wife of Charles D.) - b. 1859; d. 1 February 1944

ALLEY
- Howard O. [husb. of Thelma P.] - b. 1896; d. 1979
- Ronald E. - b. 1922; d. 1978
- Thelma P. (sister of Dorothy P. DOW; [wife of Howard O.]) - b. 1901; d. 1978

ANDREWS
- Charlotte M. - b. 1875; d. 1944
- Frances A. - b. 1839; d. 1918
- Frank L. - b. 1868; d. 1933
- Frank P. - b. 1896; d. 1982
- Henrietta B. - b. 1902; d. 1957

ARNOLD
Chucky [son of Ruth A.] - b. 1950; d. 1958
Ruth A. - b. 1918; d. 1995
ASH
Annie N. (MAYO; dau. of Isaac MAYO and Mary H. (CALLANAN)) - b. 25 April 1878; d. 15 September 1903
ASHLEY
[Louise - see LURVEY]
BARTLETT
Georgia L. [wife of Henry D.] - b. 1899; d. 1987
Henry D. [husb. of Georgia L.] - b. 1893; d. 1962
BRANSCOM [includes BRANSCOMB]
Alice W. (wife of David U.) - b. 5 July 1874; d. 4 February 1949
Charles (Capt.; husb. of Elizabeth G.) - d. 29 October 1856, Port au Prince, San Domingo, W. I., Æ 36 y., 2 m., 28 d.
David (Capt.; husb. of Emily (KNOWLES)) - d. 24 July 1873 Æ 55 y.
David U. (husb. of Alice W.) - b. 23 April 1875; d. 23 September 1932
Elizabeth G. (wife of Capt. Charles) - d. 10 April 1884 Æ 58 y., 4 m., 18 d.
Emily (KNOWLES; wife of Capt. David) - d. 12 November 1922 Æ 87 y., 6 m., 14 d.
James N. (Capt.; husb. of Maranda M.) - b. 18 August 1832; d. 4 June 1900
Maranda M. (wife of Capt. James N.) - b. 1837; d. 1926
BRALEY
Edward E. (husb. of Nettie C.) - b. 1879; d. 1953
Nettie C. (wife of Edward E.) - b. 1891; d. 1927
BROWN
Ida A. (HARDING; wife of William S. [no stone]) - d. 4 July 1876 Æ 21 y., 4 m., 1 d.
Lorenette (dau. of Lorenzo and Sylvia F. [no stones]) - b. 20 July 1850; d. 22 November 1855
BUNKER
Aaron S. (husb. of Arletta A. (MAYO)) - b. 1845; d. 1931
Arletta A. (MAYO; wife of Aaron S.) - b. 1847; d. 1913
Hattie D. (wife of William H. [no stone]) - d. 23 November 1872 Æ 21 y., 1 m., 25 d.
Phebe L. (wife of William H. [no stone]) - d. 12 August 1870 Æ 51 y., 10 m.
BURNS
Agnes Louise (dau. of John W. and Ella F. (KNOX)) - d. 6 January 1891 Æ 5 y., 6 m., 9 d.
Carrie A. (wife of Eben F.) - b. 4 August 1848; d. 20 May 1917
[Cora - see LISCOMB]
Eben F. (husb. of Carrie A.) - b. 22 March 1843; d. 15 September 1911; (member of Co. C, 1st Maine Heavy Artillery [Civil War])
Ella F. (KNOX; wife of John W.) - b. 1856; d. 1934
John W. (husb. of Ella F. (KNOX)) - b. 1849; d. 1930
Richard C. - b. 1933; d. 1979
Sylvester [R. or W.][5] (son of Eben F. and Carrie A.) - b. 25 May 1867; d. [3 or 4][5] April 1874 Æ 6 y., 10 m.
Victor E. (son of John W. and Ella F. (KNOX)) - d. 25 November 1880 Æ 2 y., 2 m., 6 d.
Willie R. (son of John W. and Ella F. (KNOX)) - d. 5 February 1901 Æ 18 y., 7 m., 24 d.

BUTLER
Elizabeth M. [wife of Woodrow W.] - b. 1916
Woodrow W. [husb. of Elizabeth M.] - b. 1914; d. 1985
BUTTERFIELD
Effie H[ODGKINS?]. (wife of John H. [no stone]) - b. 1883; d. 1952
CALLANAN
[Mary H. - see MAYO]
CANDAGE
Doris E. [wife of Percy L.] - b. 1909; d. 1995
Percy L. [husb. of Doris E.] - b. 1909; d. 1996
CARTER
Annie (wife of Charles I.) - b. 1868; d. 1924
Charles I. (husb. of Annie) - b. 1862; d. 1943
John H. [husb. of Nettie M.] - b. 1902; d. 1989
Nettie M. [wife of John H.] - b. 1906; d. 1984
CHURCHILL
Edythe R[ICHARDS?]. [wife of Llewellyn E.] - b. 8 May 1926
Llewellyn E. [husb. of Edythe R[ICHARDS?].] - b. 11 November 1921; d. 3 July 1995
CIRARD
Mary G. - b. 14 April 1913; d. 28 October 1982
CLARK
Franklin W. (husb. of Martha C.) - b. 1859; d. 1926
Gertrude L. (wife of Walter F.) - b. 1883; d. 1953
Martha C. (wife of Franklin W.) - b. 1865; d. 1954
Walter F. (husb. of Gertrude L.) - b. 1884; d. 1929
CLINKARD
Ella F. [wife of William H. Jr.] - d. 22 December 1901 Æ 48 y., 4 m., 7 d.
William H. Jr. [husb. of Ella F.] - d. 6 May 1912 Æ 65 y., 9 m., 3 d.
COLLIER
Alice Jean (wife of Louis Walter) - b. 24 July 1905; d. 10 March 1999
Louis Walter (husb. of Alice Jean) - b. 25 August 1907; d. 1 July 1978
CORSIAR [sic]
Elmyra - d. 11 January 1916 Æ 87 y., 2 m., 11 d.
COUSINS
Cornelia (wife of Nathaniel) - [no dates]
George L. [husb. of Theresa E.] - b. 1902; d. 1966
Hoyt - d. 1 October 1941 Æ [not given]
Nathaniel (husb. of Cornelia) - [no dates]
Theresa E. [wife of George L.] - b. 1921
COX
Mary C. - b. 24 September 1952; d. 20 October 1993
CROWLEY
[Christine Elaine - see STAPLES]
CUMMINGS
Frank W. Jr. [husb. of Susie J.] - b. 12 December 1892; d. 20 August 1968
Harold Bertram - b. 18 April 1920; d. 26 October 1999
Susie J. [wife of Frank W. Jr.] - b. 7 November 1900; d. 29 April 1994
DAVIS
Stephen - [b. and d.?] 31 August 1970
Susan - [b. and d.?] 31 August 1970

DICKENS
Charles E. [husb. of Geneva R.] - b. 1883; d. 1963
Geneva R. [wife of Charles E.] - b. 1885; d. 1969
John S. [son of Charles E. and Geneva R.?] - b. 1907; d. 1947
DORR
Elmer E. (husb. of Laura A.) - b. 1861; d. 1949
Laura A. (wife of Elmer E.) - b. 1861; d. 1929
DOW
Dorothy P. (sister of Thelma P. ALLEY) - b. 1903; d. 1979
DOYLE
Etta A. - b. 8 October 1847; d. 13 October 1878
EDWARDS
George C. - b. 1876; d. 1919
EMERY
Abdon C. [husb. of Clara K[NOX?].] - b. 1875; d. 1931
Addie J. (wife of Julien [sic]) - b. 1867; d. 1953
Alma B. - b. 1899; d. 1967
Clara K[NOX?]. [wife of Abdon C.] - b. 1879; d. 1958
Earle L. - b. 1894; d. 1920
Eliza A. - b. 1828; d. 1915
Gladys F. (wife of Maurice C.) - b. 1906; d. 1970
Isadore O. - b. 1840; d. 1924
Julien [sic] (husb. of Addie J.) - b. 1859; d. 1943
Lucy A. (wife of William C.) - b. 1 April 1833; d. 5 June 1908
Malcolm C. [son of Julien [sic] and Addie J.] - b. 1890; d. 1890
Marion M. [wife of Roger K.] - b. 18 August 1921
Mary H. - b. 1819; d. 1846
Maurice C. (husb. of Gladys F.) - b. 1903; d. 1965
Mildred E. [dau. of Julien [sic] and Addie J.] - b. 1892; d. 1914
Roger K. [husb. of Marion M.] - b. 17 November 1919; d. 27 April 1992
Samuel N. - b. 1816; d. 1897
William C. (husb. of Lucy A.) - d. 3 December 1880 Æ 52 y., 4 m., 5 d.
FARNSWORTH
Leslie E. - b. 1922; d. 1986
Pauline M. - b. 10 June 1930; d. 6 October 1991
FLY
[Charlotte - see PRAY]
FOGG
infant (son of J. Lee and Gracie [no stones]) - d. 12 February 1899 Æ [not given]
FOSS
Fred W. [husb. of Shirley Y.] - b. 22 June 1912; d. 9 November 1979
Shirley Y. [wife of Fred W.] - b. 8 July 1923; d. 17 February 1996
FRANCIS
George M. Sr. [husb. of Rachel G.] - b. 1916; d. 1984
Phoebe F. - b. 1889; d. 1964
Rachel G. [wife of George M. Sr.] - b. 1914; d. 1994
GARLAND
Amy M. - b. 1899; d. 1996
George O. - b. December 1879; d. November 1902
James K. [husb. of Maria C.] - b. 28 October 1847; d. 16 August 1907
Lewis A. - b. 1884; d. 1963
Maria C. [wife of James K.] - b. 23 May 1851; d. 14 June 1943

Percy E. - b. 1882; d. 1934
GILBERT
Chandler E. - b. 1917; d. 1998
Ernest D. - b. 1889; d. 1946
H. Burnell - b. 1868; d. 1949
Harvey L. - b. 1878; d. 1949
Lura N. - b. 1951; d. 1959
Susie T. - b. 1877; d. 1969
GILES
Leon Philip [husb. of Rose Anna] - b. 1908; d. 1988
Rose Anna [wife of Leon Philip] - b. 1912
GONYA
Charlotte L. - b. 1901; d. 1959
Fred A. - b. 1871; d. 1957
Frederick - b. 1902; d. 1986
MaeBelle R. - b. 1873; d. 1974
GORDIUS
G. Mitchell - b. 1908; d. 1979
Hattie C. [wife of Nelson P.] - b. 1891; d. 1991
Nelson P. [husb. of Hattie C.] - b. 1880; d. 1948
Willie E. - b. 1915; d. 1989
GOTT
Clayton R. - b. 30 April 1929; d. 25 July 1970
GRANT
Adelaide E. (wife of Butler V.) - d. 5 September 1942 Æ 80 y., 5 m.
Butler V. (husb. of Adelaide E.) - d. 28 May 1927 Æ 67 y., 8 m.
Rebecca C. (wife of William H.) - d. 9 November 1899 Æ 64 y., 3 m.
William H. (husb. of Rebecca C.) - d. 7 March 1912 Æ 83 y., 1 m.
GRATEN
David Rodney (son of Walter F. and Theresa (MURPHY) [no stone]) - b. 1939; d. 1941
Henry W. [husb. of Judith K.] - b. 1877; d. 1961
Judith K. [wife of Henry W.] - b. 1887; d. 1937
Walter F. (husb. of Theresa (MURPHY) [no stone]) - b. 1921; d. 1983
GRAY
Betsey E. (wife of Joab E.) - b. 19 June 1839; d. 25 March 1917
Joab E. (husb. of Betsey E.) - b. 27 May 1835; d. 21 October 1917
GREENING
[Nellie Agnes - see THOMAS]
GRINDLE
George D. - b. 17 March 1851; d. 1 June 1909
HADLEY
[Barbara - see RICHARDSON]
Clara S. (wife of Eben M.) - b. 10 September 1816; d. 23 June 1884
Currington M. (Capt.; husb. of Eleanor H. (THOMAS)) - b. 19 December 1835; d. 25 March 1920
Dorothy M. [wife of Frederick G.] - b. 1903
Eben M. (husb. of Clara S.) - b. 23 January 1809; d. 16 March 1892
Eleanor H. (THOMAS; wife of Capt. Currington M.) - d. 14 September 1887 Æ 44 y., 11 m., 2 d.
Enos (husb. of Mary E.) - b. 1837; d. 1912
Eugene E. (son of Enos and Mary E.) - d. 7 October 1869 Æ 1 y., 18 d.

Fred L. [husb. of Minnie E.] - b. 1866; d. 1952
Frederick G. [husb. of Dorothy M.] - b. 1903
Joel M. (husb. of Lelia A.) - b. 26 July 1851; d. 1 April 1890
Josiah B. (Deacon; husb. of Zena S.) - d. 2 August 1885 Æ 86 y., 8 m.
Lelia A. (wife of Joel M.) - b. 16 February 1866; d. 12 July 1940
Mary E. (wife of Enos) - b. 1846; d. 1911
Melford [sic] O. [HADLEY?] - "lost at sea" 8 February 1841 Æ [not given]
Minnie E. [wife of Fred L.] - b. 1866; d. 1935
Olive Ann (wife of Thomas W.) - d. 10 June 1895 Æ 60 y., 8 m., 2 d.
[Rebecca - see MAYO]
Rose Blanch [sic] (dau. of Thomas W. and Olive Ann) - d. 30 April 1878 Æ 23 y., 8 m.
Thomas W. (husb. of Olive Ann) - d. 10 May 1886 Æ 59 y., 7 m.
Washington C. [HADLEY?] - b. 23 January 1849; "sailed from La Have N. S." 8 December 1876
Winslow N. (son of Amos T. and Esther [no stones]; husb. of Zeruah H.) - b. 28 April 1840; d. 15 April 1889
Zena S. (wife of Deacon Josiah B.) - d. 10 December 1871 Æ 70 y., 8 m., 10 d.
Zeruah H. (wife of Winslow N.) - d. 18 July 1879 Æ 34 y.

HALL
Arthur E. [husb. of Mary Ellen] - b. 1899; d. 1961
Ellis A. - b. 1902; d. 1945
Mary Ellen [wife of Arthur E.] - b. 1905

HAMBLEN
F. Adelle [wife of John E.] - b. 1897; d. 1982
Jack E. [husb. of Jeanne C.] - b. 1932; d. 1983
Jeanne C. [wife of Jack E.] - b. 1930
John E. [husb. of F. Adelle] - b. 1906; d. 1981
Leslie - b. 1927; d. 1941

HAMILTON
Henrietta K. [wife of Nelson E.] - b. 1914
Nelson E. [husb. of Henrietta K.] - b. 1909
Nelson E. Jr. [son of Nelson E. and Henrietta K.?] - b. 1938; d. 1993

HAMLIN
Clarice H. [wife of Philip C.] - b. 1904
Elizabeth [dau. of Philip C. and Clarice H.?] - [b. and d.?] 1926
John H. [son of Philip C. and Clarice H.?] - b. 1943; d. 1990
Philip C. [husb. of Clarice H.] - b. 1903

HAMOR
Angelia (dau. of William and Experiance [sic]) - d. 11 December 183[4 or 7?][1] Æ 16 y., 6 m., 5 d.
Aphia L. (SALSBURY [sic]; wife of Eben M.) - b. 24 February 1829; m. 1 January 1848; d. 2 October 1899
Charlie P. (son of Eben M. and Aphia L. (SALSBURY [sic])) - b. 26 November 1858; d. 4 April 1859
Christina E. [wife of Everett F.] - b. 1919
Eben M. (husb. of Aphia L. (SALSBURY [sic])) - b. 26 March 1822; m. 1 January 1848; d. 6 November 1910
Elwell S. [husb. of Helen M.] - b. 1855; d. 1918
Everett F. [husb. of Christina E.] - b. 1921; d. 1984
Experiance [sic] (wife of William) - d. 13 February 1886 Æ 87 y., 11 m., 11 d.
Helen M. [wife of Elwell S.] - b. 1862; d. 1932

[Ida M. - see RICH]
Lillian M. [HAMOR?] - b. 1865; d. 1918
Persis M. - b. 1891; d. 1945
Richard N. Sr. - b. 1920; d. 1984
William (husb. of Experiance [sic]) - d. 23 July 1866 Æ 75 y., 2 m., 22 d.
William M. Sr. - b. 1870; d. 1947
Winthrop E. (son of James E. and Roxana [sic] O. [no stones]) - b. 7 September 1852; d. 10 January 1877 Æ 24 y., 4 m., 3 d.

HARDING
[Ida A. - see BROWN]
Martha F. (wife of Seth) - b. 1830; d. 1916
Seth (husb. of Martha F.) - b. 1825; d. 1912

HAYNES
Abbie W. [wife of Richard W.] - b. 14 March 1849; d. 22 January 1895
Eugene Bolton [son of Richard W. and Abbie W.?] - b. 3 August 1888; d. 24 February 1972
Richard W. [husb. of Abbie W.] - b. 7 April 1844; d. 15 May 1919

HIGGINS
Abbie A. (wife of Leeroy [sic] E.) - b. 1862; d. 1910
Addie L. (wife of Fenelon B.) - b. 25 December 1862; d. 21 October 1953
Aldana W. - d. 23 March 1884 Æ 30 y., 6 m., 16 d.
Alexander (Capt.; husb. of Ellen A.) - b. 14 May 1828; d. 21 April 1901
Allie W. - b. 3 December 1880; d. 27 January 1908
Alma P. (wife of Capt. Nathan W.) - b. 1833; d. 1911
Alonzo (husb. of Ernesta B.) - b. 1836; d. 1906
Amanda (wife of Emery S.) - d. 2 January 1900 Æ 69 y.
Anath ([dau.?] of Isaac and Mary H.) - [no dates]
Anna P. (dau. of Joseph and Betsey) - d. 1 October 1863 Æ 27 y., 4 m., 2 d.
Archie A. [husb. of Pauline M.] - b. 1885; d. 1950
Arwilla [sic] C. (dau. of Capt. Joseph M. and Eunice H.) - d. 20 August 1870 Æ 7 y., 2 m., 9 d.
Atwater [husb. of Elmenia T.?] - b. 10 August 1822; d. 2 April 1905
Beatrice L. [wife of Carl E.?] - b. 1906; d. 1992
Betsey (wife of Joseph) - d. 11 December 1877 Æ 85 y., 2 d.
Calvin (son of Eleazer) - [no dates]
Carl E. [husb. of Beatrice L.?] - b. 1901; d. 1995
Carrie B. (wife of Eugene P.) - b. 1870; d. 1961
Charles N. - b. 21 August 1867; d. 24 April 1892
Colburn S. Jr. [husb. of Gladys L.] - b. 23 May 1904; d. 14 September 1986
Colburn S. Sr. [husb. of Eldora S.] - b. 1872; d. 1919
Cora E. (dau. of L. J. and E. L. [no stones]) - d. 22 April 1872 Æ 8 m.
David (husb. of Mary S.) - b. 31 May 1788; d. 24 March 1859
David C. [son of Carl E. and Beatrice L.?] - b. 1948; d. 1961
Edward B. (husb. of Eleanor G.) - b. 25 December 1825; d. 26 February 1912
Eldora S. [wife of Colburn S. Sr.] - b. 1872; d. 1955
Eleanor G. (wife of Edward B.) - b. 1 March 1830; d. 18 July 1899
Eleazer - [no dates]
Ellen A. (wife of Capt. Alexander) - b. 4 March 1831; d. 27 December 1908
Elmenia T. [wife of Atwater?] - b. 5 October 1818; d. 19 February 1903
Elsie Belle [dau. of Robert Bruce and Ina] - d. 29 January 1896 Æ 1 m., 4 d.
Emery S. (husb. of Amanda) - d. 1 August 1857 Æ 39 y., 9 m.
Ernesta B. (wife of Alonzo) - b. 1849; d. 1939

Eugene P. (husb. of Carrie B.) - b. 1860; d. 1942
Eugene U.[8] (son of Capt. Nathan W. and Alma P.) - b. 26 September 1859; d. 19 October 1863 Æ 4 y., 23 d.
Eunice H. (wife of Capt. Joseph M.) - d. 11 September 1892 Æ 72 y., 11 m.
Fenelon B. (husb. of Addie L.) - b. 28 April 1859; d. 22 June 1927
Gladys L. [wife of Colburn S. Jr.] - b. 1902; d. 1987
Hannah M. - b. 5 February 1828; d. 7 July 1903
Harris O. (son of Capt. Alexander and Ellen A.) - d. 12 March 1859 Æ 7 y., 3 m., 20 d.
infants (children of Fenelon B. and Addie L.) - [no dates]
Ida J. (KNOX; wife of Joseph) - d. 8 May 1893 Æ 28 y., 10 m., 5 d.
Ina [wife of Robert Bruce] - b. 1870; d. 1936
Ira L. (son of L. J. and E. L. [no stones]) - d. 16 May 1867 Æ 5 y., 3 m., 2 d.; ("drowned")
Irving F. (son of L. J. and E. L. [no stones]) - d. 19 February 1862 Æ 5 d.
Isaac (husb. of Mary H.) - b. 8 April 1800; d. 19 October 1869
Isaac (son of Isaac and Mary H.) - [no dates]
Jesse H. [husb. of Mabel H.] - b. 1877; d. 1954
Jessie G. [dau. of Robert Bruce and Ina] - d. 21 April 1889 Æ 7 w.
John S. - b. 1839; d. 1901
John T. - b. 15 May 1862; d. 20 May 1894
Joseph (husb. of Betsey) - d. 14 December 186[...][3] Æ 78 y., 1 m., 18 d.
Joseph (husb. of Ida J. (KNOX) and Phebe M.) - b. 1852; d. 1933
Joseph M. (Capt.; husb. of Eunice H.) - d. 5 February 1889 Æ 74 y., 5 m., 9 d.
Joseph W. - d. 19 November 1892 Æ 28 y., 4 m., 4 d.
Julia A. [wife of William C.] - b. 1839; d. 1933
Leeroy [sic] E. (husb. of Abbie A.) - [no dates]
Lelia A. (dau. of Capt. Alexander and Ellen A.) - d. 1 March 1859 Æ 1 y., 1 m.
Lemuel (son of Eleazer) - [no dates]
Linda M. (dau. of Joseph and Betsey) - d. 4 October 1834 Æ 18 y., 10 m., 2 d.
Lizzie A. (dau. of E[dward?]. B. and E[leanor?]. G.) - d. 13 October 1863 Æ 3 y., 11 m., 24 d.
Lovina (wife of Samuel) - d. 8 May 1872 Æ 77 y., 1 m.
Mabel H. [wife of Jesse H.] - b. 1883; d. 1957
Maretta (dau. of David H. and Eliza A. [no stones]) - d. 4 February 1867 Æ 17 y., 2 m., 15 d.
Mary H. (wife of Isaac) - b. 8 May 1804; d. 28 May 1892
Mary S. (wife of David) - b. 16 February 1808; d. 28 June 1892
Mehitable [sic] (wife of Sylvanus[2]) - b. 1821; d. 1899
Nathan W. (Capt.; husb. of Alma P.) - b. 1832; d. 1912
Nellie F. (dau. of L. J. and E. L. [no stones]) - d. 14 April 1872 Æ 3 y.
Obediah [sic] - d. 21 August 1871 Æ 56 y.
Pauline M. [wife of Archie A.] - b. 1894; d. 1959
Phebe M. (wife of Joseph) - b. 1863; d. 1937
Phineas P. (son of Isaac and Mary H.) - [no dates]
Richard Donald Sr. - b. 1923; d. 1999
Robert B. (son of Capt. Joseph M. and Eunice H.) - d. 1 June [year not given], near Salam [sic] Church, VA, Æ 19 y., 9 m., 5 d.; ("killed"; member of Co. D, 31st Maine Regiment [Civil War])
Robert Bruce [husb. of Ina] - b. 1865; d. 1950
Rubert [sic] O. (son of E[dward?]. B. and E[leanor?]. G.) - d. 19 October 1863 Æ 5 y., 6 m., 1 d.

Ruel L. (son of Fenelon B. and Addie L.) - b. 25 May 1904; d. 28 December 1925
Samuel (husb. of Lovina) - d. 1 November 1881 Æ 88 y., 7 m.
Sarah Ann (dau. of Ephraim and Lois [no stones]) - d. 21 November 1846 Æ 16 y., 11 m., 2 d.
Senora (dau. of Isaac and Mary H.) - [no dates]
Sylvanus[2] (husb. of Mehitable [sic]) - b. 1803; d. 1883
Vasconie Lamont - b. 1864; d. 1942
William C. [husb. of Julia A.] - b. 1833; d. 1912
William W. [son of Joseph and Betsey?] - "lost at sea" 18 January 1857 Æ 28 y., 9 m., 15 d.
Zalmunna (dau. of Isaac and Mary H.) - [no dates]
[...][3] (child of Capt. Joseph M. and Eunice H.) - d. 29 April 18[...][3] Æ 16 y., [...][3]

HODGDON
[Bertha - see TIBBETTS]

HODGKINS
Cecil G. - b. 1899; d. 1904
Clarissa - [no dates]
[Effie H[ODGKINS?]. - see BUTTERFIELD]
Elizabeth A. [wife of John D. Jr.] - b. 1920; d. 1994
Harley O. - b. 1901; d. 1924
J. Dallas [husb. of Marcia G.] - b. 1892; d. 1958
John D. Jr. [husb. of Elizabeth A.] - b. 1918
John L. - b. 1857; d. 1941
Lena M. - b. 1863; d. 1930
Marcia G. [wife of J. Dallas] - b. 1898; d. 1976

HOLBROOK
Jasper H. (husb. of Mary E.) - b. 1886; d. 1964
Mary E. (wife of Jasper H.) - b. 1883; d. 1952

HOOPER
Ansel L. [husb. of Marie F.] - b. 1906; d. 1972
Marie F. [wife of Ansel L.] - b. 1913; d. 1963

HUNTLEY
George H. (husb. of Sadie E.) - b. 1879; d. 1942
Sadie E. (wife of George H.) - b. 1887; d. 1969

INGALLS
Carl D. (husb. of Ellen A.) - b. 1883; d. 1943
Ellen A. (wife of Carl D.) - b. 1884; d. 1943

INGRAHAM
Angeline - b. 8 November 1830; d. 9 September 1908

IVENEY
[...] [headstone only]

IVERSON
Arthur O. [husb. of Helena H.] - b. 1912
Helena H. [wife of Arthur O.] - b. 1917; d. 1988

JELLISON
Etta G. (dau. of Henry E. and Harriet F.) - d. 3 September 1877 Æ 16 y., 6 d.
Harriet F. (wife of Henry E.) - b. 1829; d. 1898
Henry E. (husb. of Harriet F.) - b. 1827; d. 1912
Horace W. [husb. of Virginia L.?] - [d.?] 22 June 1932
Virginia L. [wife of Horace W.?] - b. 1867; d. 1934

JORDAN
Arletta E. (wife of Lowell H.) - d. 8 February 1913 Æ 20 y., 11 m., 8 d.

Florence M. - b. 1914; d. 1989
Leonia P. (wife of Lowell H.) - b. 22 September 1890; d. 15 July 1964
Lowell H. (husb. of Arletta E. and Leonia P.) - b. 18 March 1889; d. 3 March 1972

JOY
Freddie [JOY?] - [no dates]
Maria W. (wife of Melvin G.) - b. 4 July 1829; d. 19 February 1912
Melvin G. (husb. of Maria W.) - b. 27 November 1825; d. 8 September 1915; (member of Co. D, 22nd Maine Regiment [Civil War])

JOYCE
James Henry "Hank" (husb. of Phyllis G.) - b. 16 January 1913; d. 9 June 1998 Æ 85 y.
Phyllis G. (wife of James Henry "Hank") - b. 15 January 1915

KIEF
Percy H. (husb. of Tullia A.) - b. 1885; d. 1962
Tullia A. (wife of Percy H.) - b. 1886; d. 1980

KING
Charles F. [husb. of Florence E.] - b. 1870; d. 1939
Florence E. [wife of Charles F.] - b. 187[2 or 3][5]; d. 1950
Gladys [dau. of Charles F. and Florence E.] - d. [no date] Æ 3 m.
infant (dau. of [not given]) - [b. and d.?] 4 May 1974
Reginald L. [son of Charles F. and Florence E.] - b. 1906; d. 1969
Sarah H. [wife of Walter F.] - b. 1896; d. 1994
Walter F. [husb. of Sarah H.] - b. 1898; d. 1971

KITTRIDGE
B. W. (husb. of Lydia) - d. 18 May 1892 Æ 92 y., 10 m.
Charles D. - b. 1881; d. 1948
Charles W. (husb. of Judith (THOMAS)) - b. 1835; d. 1912
George - d. 18 June 1864, Petersburg, Virginia, Æ 23 y., 4 m.; ("killed"; member of Co. C, 1st Maine Heavy Artillery [Civil War])
Judith (THOMAS; wife of Charles W.) - b. 1853; d. 1924
Lydia (wife of B. W.) - d. 13 November 1890 Æ 83 y., 10 m.

KNOWLES
Andrew U. (husb. of Lavinia) - b. 17 January 1842; d. 17 November 1869
Charlie D. (son of Osborn B. and Janet B. "Jennie" (SALTER)) - d. 25 August 1874 Æ 3 m., 13 d.
[Emily - see BRANSCOM]
Freddie O. (son of Osborn B. and Janet B. "Jennie" (SALTER)) - d. 13 March 1874 Æ 1 y., 11 m.
Henry - d. 21 May 1907 Æ 75 y., 8 m., 23 d.
Janet B. "Jennie" (SALTER; wife of Osborn B.) - d. 30 May 1894 Æ 51 y., 3 m., 20 d.
John T. - d. 10 June 1860 Æ 30 y., 6 m., 4 d.
Judith B. (wife of Thomas) - d. 29 May 1876 Æ 73 y., 10 m., 18 d.
[June F. - see TUMLINSON]
Lavinia (wife of Andrew U.) - b. 5 March 1841; d. 28 May 1907
Lester U. [KNOWLES?] - b. 21 September 1867; d. 21 June 1912
Letitia G. [wife of T. Benton] - b. 11 November 1852; d. 16 June 1929
[Mary E. - see STEWART]
Osborn B. (husb. of Janet B. "Jennie" (SALTER)) - d. 6 March 1917 Æ 72 y., 4 m., 9 d.
Osborn S. (son of Osborn B. and Janet B. "Jennie" (SALTER)) - d. 14 February 1901 Æ 20 y., 5 m., 11 d.

T. Benton [husb. of Letitia G.] - b. 14 April 1839; d. 18 April 1923
Thomas - b. 26 July 1875; d. 11 July 1951
Thomas (husb. of Judith B.) - d. 29 May 1893 Æ 89 y., 7 m., 9 d.
Ulmer [KNOWLES?] - b. 26 August 1894; d. 26 February 1900

KNOX
[Clara K[NOX?]. - see EMERY]
Clarinda (wife of James) - b. 24 January 1839; d. 3 August 1922
[Ella F. - see BURNS]
Henry J. (son of James and Clarinda) - d. 10 February 1893 Æ 26 y., 3 m., 12 d.
[Ida J. - see HIGGINS]
James (husb. of Clarinda) - b. 20 May 1834; d. 13 December 1911

LEE
Estella F. [wife of George A.] - b. 1892; d. 1967
George A. [husb. of Estella F.] - b. 1903

LEIGHTON
Alfred B. Jr. - b. 26 June 1928; d. 27 February 1993
Alice M. (wife of Samuel E.) - b. 1874; d. 1964
Arlene M. - b. 1947; d. 1948
Bruce W. Jr. - b. 1971; d. 1987
Gloria J. - b. 1949; d. 1970
Samuel E. (husb. of Alice M.) - b. 1872; d. 1943

LELAND
Della C. - b. 20 September 1851; d. 13 December 1872
Martha J. [wife of Samuel H.] - b. 1853; d. 1918
Samuel H. [husb. of Martha J.] - b. 1844; d. 1915

LEONARD
Carolyn L. [wife of Lawrence D.] - b. 4 May 1908; d. 21 May 1987
Lawrence D. [husb. of Carolyn L.] - b. 1 May 1912; d. 23 February 1984

LEWIS
Orra [sic] M. - b. 8 January 1844; d. 9 March 1916

LISCOMB
E. Draper [husb. of Verna I.] - b. 1915; d. 1983
Frank E. (husb. of Cora (BURNS)) - b. 1892; d. [no date]
Cora (BURNS; wife of Frank E.) - b. 1886; d. 1940
Verna I. [wife of E. Draper] - b. 1913; d. 1995

LORD
Alice Mabel (dau. of Reuben J. and Julia M. [no stones]) - d. 21 October 1890 Æ 6 y., 1 m., 24 d.

LUNT
B. Guy [husb. of N. Evelyn] - b. 1878; d. 1942
Emma A. (wife of Capt. Watson W.) - b. 1874; d. 1954
Harold Jake - b. 1906; d. 1979
Lena R. "Judy" - b. 11 November 1920; d. 17 December 1989
N. Evelyn [wife of B. Guy] - b. 1891; d. 1963
Norris M. [son of B. Guy and N. Evelyn?] - b. 1910; d. 1924
Watson W. (Capt.; husb. of Emma A.) - b. 1873; d. 1944
William Elmer - b. 3 December 1880; d. 19 June 1921

LURVEY
Glendon G. (husb. of Louise (ASHLEY)) - b. 26 March 1915; d. 31 October 1976
Lloyd W. [husb. of Myra A.] - b. 1908; d. 1978
Louise (ASHLEY; wife of Glendon G.) - b. 2 October 1922; d. 23 October 1985
Lula G. [wife of Murray W.] - b. 1880; d. 1972

Murray W. [husb. of Lula G.] - b. 10 August 186[6 or 7][5]; d. 11 February 1957
Myra A. [wife of Lloyd W.] - b. 1908; d. 1980

MAYO

Abbie B. [wife of Jesse H.] - d. 15 April 1917 Æ 89 y., 6 m., 7 d.
Ada M. [dau. of Alfred and Sarah R.?] - b. 1857; d. 1930
Adaline R. (dau. of Capt. Thomas and Keziah) - d. 11 January 1847 Æ 19 y.
Alma L. [wife of Liston W.] - b. 1892; d. 1982
Amelia - d. 12 November 1870 Æ [not given]
[Annie N. - see ASH]
Agnes M. [wife of Lorenzo] - b. 1881; d. 1947
Alfred [husb. of Sarah R.] - b. 1819; d. 1872
[Arletta A. - see BUNKER]
Arletta Ann (dau. of Zechariah and Rebecca (HADLEY)) - d. 4 October 1843 Æ 1 y., 1 m., 2 d.
Betsey (wife of Joel) - d. 25 January 1889 Æ 85 y., 9 m., 22 d.
Beulah L. (dau. of George W. and Ida L.) - d. 11 February 1890 Æ 7 y., 4 m., 19 d.
Byron L. (son of Zechariah and Rebecca (HADLEY)) - b. 1850; d. 1863
Catharine (wife of Isaac) - [no dates]
Charlie A. (son of Rev. Gideon and Lizzie S.) - b. 1879; d. 1881
Emily (dau. of Capt. Thomas and Keziah) - d. 16 November 1834 Æ 22 y.
Fred W. (son of Rev. Gideon and Lizzie S.) - b. 1885; d. 1900
George W. (husb. of Ida L.) - d. 22 June 1926 Æ 68 y., 1 m.
Gideon (Deacon) - d. 20 March 1859 Æ 90 y., 6 m., 2 d.
Gideon (Rev.; husb. of Lizzie S.) - b. 1846; d. 1936
Gideon Jr. - d. 27 November 1846 Æ 29 y.
[Gladys M[AYO]. - see WHITTIER]
Grace E. (dau. of Rev. Gideon and Lizzie S.) - b. 1881; d. 1882
Hannah W. (dau. of James and Sarah) - d. 29 January 1826 Æ 9 y., 6 m., 12 d.
Ida L. (wife of George W.) - d. 9 January 1917 Æ 57 y., 4 m., 6 d.
Irving L. (son of Rev. Gideon and Lizzie S.) - b. 1877; d. 1879
Isaac (husb. of Catharine) - [no dates]
Isaac (husb. of Mary H. (CALLANAN)) - [no dates]; (member of Co. M, 1st Connecticut Heavy Artillery [Civil War])
James (husb. of Sarah) - d. 7 October 1863 Æ 76 y., 9 m.
Jesse H. [husb. of Abbie B.] - d. 15 March 1894 Æ 77 y., 7 m., 10 d.
Jesse U. - b. 1890; d. 1922
Joel (husb. of Betsey) - d. 7 February 1881 Æ 74 y., 12 d.
Josiah (Capt.; husb. of Lynda M. [no stone]) - d. December 1856 Æ 33 y.
Julia Maria (wife of Capt. Thomas Jr.) - d. 22 December 1855 Æ 39 y., 9 m., 25 d.
Keziah (wife of Capt. Thomas) - d. 1877 Æ [not given]
Liston W. [husb. of Alma L.] - b. 1888; d. 1949
Lizzie S. (wife of Rev. Gideon) - b. 1850; d. 1932
Lorenzo [husb. of Agnes M.] - b. 1872; d. 1964
Lorenzo (husb. of Martha H.) - b. 1820; d. 1877
Martha E. (dau. of Capt. Thomas and Lydia [no stones]) - [b. and?] d. 27 July 1864
Martha H. (wife of Lorenzo) - b. 1835; d. 1894
Mary H. (CALLANAN; wife of Isaac) - b. 1846; d. 1916[9]
Melbourn A. (son of Capt. Josiah and Lynda M. [no stone]) - d. 9 November 1860 Æ 11 y.
Rebecca (HADLEY; wife of Zechariah) - b. 1822; d. 1894
Sarah (wife of James) - d. 12 August 1831 Æ 43 y., 8 m.
Sarah Ann (dau. of James and Sarah) - d. 27 November 1846 Æ 16 y., 11 m., 2 d.

Sarah R. [wife of Alfred] - b. 1831; d. 1914
Stillie H. (son of Capt. Thomas and Lydia [no stones]) - d. 18 August 1875 Æ [...][6]
Thomas (Capt.; husb. of Keziah) - d. 10 January 1861 Æ 76 y.
Thomas Jr. (Capt.; husb. of Julia Maria) - d. 2 May 1883 Æ 74 y., 8 m.
Walter [son of Lorenzo and Martha H.?] - b. 1866; d. 1877
Willis E. - d. 7 October 1889 Æ 28 y., 4 m., 6 d.
Zechariah (husb. of Rebecca (HADLEY)) - b. 1813; d. 1869

McKAY
Annie M. [wife of Daniel W.] - b. 1843; d. 1919
Daniel W. [husb. of Annie M.] - b. 1836; d. 1915

MERCHANT
Clara R. "Dolly" [wife of George M.] - b. 11 March 1941; d. 22 February 1996
George M. [husb. of Clara R. "Dolly"] - b. 7 April 1939

MITCHELL
Audrey C. (wife of Robert Allen) - b. 1892; d. 1972
Clarence A. [husb. of Teresa R.] - b. 1905; d. 1982
Robert Allen (husb. of Audrey C.) - b. 1917; d. 1964
Teresa R. [wife of Clarence A.] - b. 1908; d. 1981

MOORE
Evadna [sic] H. [wife of Joseph N.] - b. 1922
Joseph N. [husb. of Evadna [sic] H.] - b. 1916; d. 1988

MURCH
Gladys (dau. of George W. and Gertrude E. [no stones]) - d. 22 May 1897 Æ 1 y., 2 m.

MURPHY
[Theresa - see GRATEN]

NORTON
David E. (son of Hiram T. and Lorena C.) - b. 1957; d. 1977
Hiram T. (husb. of Lorena C.) - b. 1908; d. 1978
Irad [sic] [husb. of Irene F.] - b. 1904
Irene F. [wife of Irad [sic]] - b. 1896; d. 1974
Lorena C. (wife of Hiram T.) - b. 1917

NORWOOD
[Carrie Ann - see STAPLES]
Emily B. [wife of Harvey L.] - b. 1870; d. 1907
Gerald W. - b. 1 December 1895; d. 10 May 1971
Harvey L. - b. 1934; d. 1984
Harvey L. [husb. of Emily B.] - b. 1863; d. 1944
Janett [sic] F. - b. 1908; d. 1985
Lloyd E. - b. 1899; d. 1973

PAINE
David H. (husb. of Margaret) - b. 30 April 1826; d. 15 May 1908
Donald - b. 1909; d. 1968
Etta M. (wife of Wesley T.) - d. 23 June 1901 Æ 32 y.
Margaret (wife of David H.) - b. 23 August 1829; d. 2 April 1907
Norman D. - b. 1872; d. 1957
Wesley T. (husb. of Etta M.) - b. 1865; d. 1933

PAQUET
Robert P. (son of P. F. and M. A. [no stones]) - b. 18 January 1929; d. 2 February 1933

PEACH
Arden L. [husb. of Emily B.] - d. 26 February 1900 Æ 28 y., 9 m., 28 d.

Emily B. [wife of Arden L.] - b. 1873; d. 1915
PELLETIER
Elmer S. [husb. of Maude E. (RICHARDSON)] - b. 1923; d. 1995
Maude E. (RICHARDSON; [wife of Elmer S.]) - b. 1931
PERKINS
Cora A. (wife of Frank S. [no stone]) - b. 1864; d. 1897
PHIPPEN
Adelia - b. 16 December 1883; d. 7 August 1929
Chester M. - b. 1875; d. 1942
Jean H. - d. 18 November 1896 Æ 18 y., 10 m.
Leonia A. - d. 31 August 1899 Æ 27 y., 1 m., 21 d.
Priscilla (wife of Charles [no stone]) - d. 8 December 1892 Æ 53 y., 7 m.
PORTER
Clyde T. [husb. of Gladys M.] - b. 1899; d. 1987
Gladys M. [wife of Clyde T.] - b. 1907; d. 1987
Lawrence R. - b. 3 June 1929
Raymond Earl [son of Clyde T. and Gladys M.?] - b. 1935; d. 1989
POWER
Blanche E. [wife of Frank A.] - b. 1874; d. 1944
Frank A. [husb. of Blanche E.] - b. 1860; d. 1912
Marguerite M. - b. 23 November 1914; d. 3 October 1992
PRAY
Charlotte (FLY; wife of Capt. Eben) - d. 20 July 1880 Æ 78 y., 5 m.
Eben (Capt.; husb. of Charlotte (FLY)) - d. 6 March 1882 Æ 79 y., 1 m.
Lucretia H. [dau. of Capt. Eben and Charlotte (FLY)?] - b. 1835; d. 1915
William F. (son of Capt. Eben and Charlotte (FLY)) - d. 12 August 1842 Æ 6 m.
PUFFER
Earl D. [husb. of Lenore T.] - b. 1894; d. 1972
Lenore T. [wife of Earl D.] - b. 1900; d. 1984
QUINN
Melinda W. - b. 1843; d. 1943
REED
Catharine (wife of William Jr.) - d. 27 June 1878 Æ 52 y., 4 m., 19 d.
Ellen E. [wife of Herschel E.] - b. 1867; d. 1947
Herbert D. [husb. of Lura M.] - b. 1900; d. 1981
Herschel E. [husb. of Ellen E.] - b. 1864; d. 1952
John W. (husb. of Lizzie E.) - b. 1860; d. 1918
Lizzie E. (wife of John W.) - d. 19 March 1892 Æ 31 y., 6 m., 29 d.
Lura M. [wife of Herbert D.] - b. 1905; d. 1994
Rodman V. (son of William Jr. and Catharine) - d. 27 May 1869 Æ 17 y., 10 m., 17 d.
Susan S.[7] (wife of William) - d. 21 February 1868 Æ 66 y., 4 m.
William (husb. of Susan S.) - d. 4 September 1882 Æ 93 y., 11 m., 26 d.
William Jr. (husb. of Catharine) - d. 9 March 1905 Æ 82 y., 1 m., 23 d.
RICH
Edith A. (wife of Gilman N.) - b. 12 October 1867; d. [no date]
Emma Florence [wife of Osborn Perry] - b. 1849; d. 1923
Gilman N. (husb. of Edith A.) - b. 28 October 1850; d. 2 February 1939
Ida M. (HAMOR) - b. 8 April 1854; d. 21 September 1921
Osborn Perry [husb. of Emma Florence] - b. 1848; d. 1916
RICHARDS
Addie L. (wife of George L.) - b. 1870; d. 1933

Betty - b. 1943; d. 1994
Charles D. [husb. of Dolla N.] - b. 1837; d. 1875
Charles L. [husb. of Emma L.] - b. 26 September 1927; d. 24 August 1990
David Paul - b. 30 March 1956; d. 1 April 1956
Delma T. [wife of Hoyt E.] - b. 1907; d. 1994
Dolla N. [wife of Charles D.] - b. 1839; d. 1878
[Edythe R[ICHARDS?]. - see CHURCHILL]
Emma L. [wife of Charles L.] - b. 7 April 1932
Eva H. (dau. of Capt. William B. [no stone][4] and Huldah S.) - d. 25 February 1874 Æ 15 y., 11 m., 3 d.
George L. (husb. of Addie L.) - b. 1865; d. 1952
George W. (son of Capt. William B. [no stone][4] and Huldah S.) - d. 22 July 1858 Æ 14 y., 10 m., 12 d.
Harold D. [husb. of Ida L.] - b. 22 March 1925; d. 29 April 1966
Hoyt E. [husb. of Delma T.] - b. 1902; d. 1981
Huldah S. (wife of Capt. William B. [no stone][4]) - d. 13 October 1895 Æ 79 y., 4 d.
Ida L. [wife of Harold D.] - b. 1926
Leroy - b. 1930
Marquis F. (son of Capt. William B. [no stone][4] and Huldah S.) - d. 16 October 1855 Æ 20 y., 11 m., 10 d.

RICHARDSON

Abigail (wife of Elisha) - d. 5 January 1892 Æ 97 y., 4 m., 8 d.
Albertina T. [wife of Elon F.?] - b. 8 June 1842; d. 25 March 1932
Albion (son of Capt. Eben and Jane) - d. 11 August 1848 Æ 11 y., 7 m.
Almyra J. [wife of Eben M.] - b. 13 February 1840; d. 2 September 1904
Barbara (HADLEY; [wife of Ralph M. Jr.]) - b. 12 August 1932
Bertella G. (wife of Burnham G. Sr.) - b. 1905; d. 1967
Burnham G. Jr. - b. 3 April 1924; d. 14 November 1982
Burnham G. Sr. (husb. of Bertella G.) - b. 1903; d. 1969
Eben (Capt.; husb. of Jane) - d. 4 April 1848 Æ 44 y.
Eben M. [husb. of Almyra J.] - b. 12 September 1835; d. [no date]
Elisha (husb. of Abigail) - d. 27 June 1887 Æ 87 y., 6 m., 20 d.
Elon F. [husb. of Albertina T.?] - b. 1 August 1839; d. 6 January 1929
Evelyn H. [wife of Lynwood L.] - b. 1908; d. 1981
James C. (son of Capt. Eben and Jane) - d. 20 September 1868, Wilmington, North Carolina, Æ 37 y., 7 m.
Jane (wife of Capt. Eben) - d. 8 July 1891 Æ 85 y.
Lynwood L. [husb. of Evelyn H.] - b. 1905; d. 1982
Maud E. [wife of Olin W.] - b. 22 March 1883; d. 17 August 1964
[Maude E. - see PELLETIER]
Mercie H. (dau. of Capt. Eben and Jane) - d. 15 March 1870 Æ 27 y., 10 m.
Mildred E. [wife of Rudolph E.] - b. 21 July 1913
Nelson G. - b. 14 April 1951; d. 4 February 1971
Olin W. [husb. of Maud E.] - b. 7 September 1878; d. 13 February 1969
Ralph M. Jr. [husb. of Barbara (HADLEY)] - b. 19 January 1931; d. 13 May 1997
Rudolph E. [husb. of Mildred E.] - b. 14 April 1911; d. 22 August 1995
Sylvester B. (son of Capt. Eben and Jane) - d. 17 September 1862, Antietam, Æ 19 y., 5 m.; ("killed at Antietam" [Civil War])
[...] [headstone only]

ROBBINS

Addie A. - b. 1860; d. 1936

RZASA
Susan Joyce - b. 2 January 1943; d. 30 November 1996
SALISBURY [includes SALSBURY]
Annie L. (wife of Bayard T. [no stone]) - b. 11 July 1856; d. 2 June 1915
[Aphia L. - see HAMOR]
Elliot J. (son of Reuben S. and Lydia H.) - d. 31 May 1864, Armory Sq. Hospital, Washington, D. C., Æ 21 y.; (Orderly Sergeant of Co. C, 1st Maine Heavy Artillery [Civil War])
Lydia H. (wife of Reuben S.) - d. 14 December 1872 Æ 68 y., 7 m., 11 d.
Newell - d. 14 August 1869 Æ 33 y.
Reuben S. (husb. of Lydia H.) - d. 18 August 1889 Æ 87 y., 4 m.
Thankful C. (wife of Reuben [no stone]) - d. 19 March 1889 Æ 70 y., 1 m., 19 d.
Wilson (son of Reuben S. and Lydia H.) - d. 17 April 1845 Æ 10 y., 10 m.
Westbrook (son of Reuben S. and Lydia H.) - d. 6 May 1852 Æ 11 y., 6 m.; ("was drowned")
SALTER
[Janet B. "Jennie" - see KNOWLES]
SCOTT
Judith A. - b. 4 November 1863; d. 13 August 1902
SEAVEY
Kenneth - b. 1937; d. 1976
SMITH
Lois (wife of Reuben) - d. 29 August 1879 Æ 77 y., 8 m., 3 d.
Mary Anna (dau. of Reuben and Lois) - d. 4 October 1889 Æ 42 y., 10 m.
Reuben (husb. of Lois) - d. 26 May 1875 Æ 70 y., 3 m., 18 d.
Reuben Jr. (son of Reuben and Lois) - d. 27 July 1864 Æ 24 y., 10 m., 12 d.; (member of Co. G, 8th Maine Regiment [Civil War])
Stillman H. [son of Reuben and Lois] - d. 22 June 1864, Petersburg, Virginia, Æ 20 y., 2 m., 16 d.; (member of Co. C, 1st Maine Heavy Artillery [Civil War])
[...][3] (dau. of Reuben and Lois) - d. 25 June 18[4?]6[3] Æ [...][3] y., 5 m.
[...][3] [SMITH?] - [...][3]
STAPLES
Patricia Elaine (mother of Carrie Anne NORWOOD and Christine Elaine CROWLEY [no stones]) - b. 8 July 1955; d. 9 January 1989
STEWART
infant [STEWART?] - [no dates]
Lionel S. (husb. of Mary E. (KNOWLES)) - b. 2 April 1868; d. [no date]
Mary E. (KNOWLES; wife of Lionel S.) - b. 2 January 1879; d. 4 February 1901
STOVER
Anna [wife of Rodman V.?] - b. 4 June 1875; d. 20 May 1945
Annie L. (wife of Charles H.) - b. 1853; d. 1942
Charles H. (husb. of Annie L.) - b. 1845; d. 1928
Elmer E. (son of Charles H. and Annie L.) - d. 21 May 18[...][3] Æ 5 m.
Rodman V. [husb. of Anna?] - b. 25 April 1878; d. 4 October 1931
SUMINSBEY
Abbie F. (wife of Lewis I.) - b. 1871; d. 1930
Helen L. (dau. of Lewis I. and Abbie F.) - b. 1906; d. 1993
Lewis I. (husb. of Abbie F.) - b. 1871; d. 1929
SWANSON
August S. [husb. of Dorothy M.] - b. 1897; d. 1980
Dorothy M. [wife of August S.] - b. 1910; d. 1997

SWAZEY
Dana R. Jr. - b. 1924; d. 1979
William D. - b. 4 January 1871; d. 21 November 1900
THOMAS
Alberta T. [dau. of Benjamin C. and Hel[l]en[5] Augusta?] - b. 31 August 1865; d. 16 July 1952
Augusta M. (wife of John H.) - b. 1847; d. 1917
Benjamin C. (husb. of Hel[l]en[5] Augusta) - b. 11 May 1823; d. 8 February 1899
Charles S. [THOMAS?] - b. 1870; d. 1950
Clarinda (wife of William T.) - d. 17 January 1892 Æ 71 y., 2 m., 12 d.
Edward P. [husb. of Orra [sic] F.] - b. 1874; d. [no date]
Edward P. Jr. - b. 1915; d. 1954
[Eleanor H. - see HADLEY]
Hel[l]en[5] Augusta (wife of Benjamin C.) - b. 23 May 1834; d. 16 February 1913
John (husb. of Judith (THOMPSON)) - d. 29 January 1829 Æ 51 y., 2 m., 23 d.
John H. (husb. of Augusta M.) - b. 1841; d. 1919
John William [THOMAS?] [son of William T. and Clarinda?] - d. 4 November 1845 Æ 6 m., 15 d.
Josephine P. [dau. of Benjamin C. and Hel[l]en[5] Augusta?] - b. 1860; d. 1922
[Judith - see KITTRIDGE]
Judith (THOMPSON; wife of John) - d. 14 July 1871 Æ 91 y., 10 m., 12 d.
Julia A. (dau. of Benjamin C. and Hel[l]en[5] Augusta) - b. 3 December 1856; d. 8 March 1857 Æ 3 m., 5 d.
Marilla A. (dau. of Benjamin C. and Hel[l]en[5] Augusta) - b. 22 March 1853; d. 2 October 1899
Mary Eliza (dau. of Benjamin C. and Hel[l]en[5] Augusta) - b. 21 February 1855; d. 2 January 1871 Æ 15 y., 10 m., 11 d.
Nellie Agnes (GREENING; adopted dau. of William T. and Clarinda) - d. 21 August 1879 Æ 15 y., 8 m., 12 d.
Orra [sic] F. [wife of Edward P.] - b. 1872; d. 1942
William T. (husb. of Clarinda) - d. 2 February 1890 Æ 73 y., 8 m.
THOMPSON
[Judith - see THOMAS]
TIBBETTS
Bertha (HODGDON; [wife of Henry M. Sr.]) - b. 1928
Henry M. Sr. [husb. of Bertha (HODGDON)] - b. 1920; d. 1992
TRACY
C. Irving (son of Charles and Carrie M. [no stones]) - d. 18 February 1901 Æ 3 m., 12 d.
Lena May (dau. of Charles and Carrie M. [no stones]) - d. 25 September 1895 Æ 5 m., 25 d.
Mark E. (son of Charles and Carrie M. [no stones]) - [b. and?] d. 24 December 1916
TRIPP
Charles A. - b. 1869; d. 1902
Coburn W. [TRIPP?] [husb. of Doris P.] - b. 1901; d. 1974
Doris P. [wife of Coburn W. [TRIPP?]] - b. 1905; d. 1971
L. Muriel - b. 1897; d. 1974
Lelia K. - b. 1876; d. 1954

TUMLINSON
June F. (KNOWLES; dau. of Thomas KNOWLES) - b. 2 September 1923; d. 25 December 1999
URQUHART
Alice A. - b. 1888; d. 1936
WALLS
Abbie T. [wife of William] - b. 1859; d. 1908
Ephraim [Capt.; husb. of Mary B.] - b. 1808; d. 1868
Ethel L. - b. 1878; d. 1905
Etta [WALLS?] - b. 1851; d. 1882
Florinolon T. [child of William and Abbie T.?] - d. 13 April 1892 Æ 2 y.
Harriet M. (wife of L. R. [no stone]) - b. 1842; d. 1903
infant [son of Capt. Ephraim and Mary B.] - d. 30 March 1845 Æ 8 d.
Julia M. [dau. of Capt. Ephraim and Mary B.] - d. 11 August 1847 Æ 11 m., 11 d.
May (dau. of L. R. [no stone] and Harriet M.) - b. 1866; d. 1903
Mary B. [wife of Capt. Ephraim] - b. 1810; d. 1893
William [husb. of Abbie T.] - b. 1850; d. 1919
WHITTEN
Harvey L. (husb. of Marian K.) - b. 1881; d. 1982
Marian K. (wife of Harvey L.) - b. 1887; d. 1966
WHITTIER
Gladys M[AYO]. - b. 1895; d. 1972
WILSON
Mabel A. (wife of William A.) - b. 1889; d. 1980
William A. (husb. of Mabel A.) - b. 1882; d. 1945
WOOD
Penninah R. - b. 1 November 1847; d. 24 June 1902
YOUNG
Evelyn F. [YOUNG?] - b. 1869; d. 1959
John W. - b. 1848; d. 1936
Sadie R. [YOUNG?] - b. 1888; d. 1889

Notes:
[1]Stone pitted.
[2]Sylvanus' name is in upper case letters. The *N* is backwards.
[3]Stone worn, cracked, and/or broken.
[4]A crumbling remnant of a stone adjacent to Huldah S.'s stone may belong to Capt. William B.
[5]Different on different stones.
[6]Remainder of stone below ground.
[7]There are two stones for Susan S. (wife of William REED).
[8]There are two stones for Eugene U. HIGGINS.
[9]The 9 in 1916 is upside down.

Higgins Cemetery
(Bar Harbor - 9)

Location/directions. Southeast of intersection of Indian Point Road and Oak Hill Road, Indian Point. From the traffic light at the north end of Mount Desert Island, go straight ahead (south) onto Routes 102/198. In approximately 1.9 miles, turn right onto Indian Point Road. This road intersects with Oak Hill Road on the left in about 1.7 miles. Turn left onto Oak Hill Road, and the cemetery is immediately on the left.

History. This town-owned cemetery has been called the Higgins Burial Ground (1174:677) and contains "one-tenth of an acre, more or less" (1174:678).

Notes. This cemetery is enclosed by an elaborate, gated, white, wood fence that is in need of repair and paint.There is a hole, presumably from a bullet, in the tallest monument, which is metal. Little lawn care is needed as most of the ground is covered by moss.

Names and dates on gravestones and other markers. [23 April 1999]

BRALEY
- Cassie H. - b. 1889; d. 1919

COUSINS
- Joseph (Capt.; husb. of Mary) - d. 25 February 1860 Æ 80 y., 3 m.
- Mary (wife of Capt. Joseph) - d. 1 January 1840 Æ 49 y., 4 m.

HIGGINS
- Almira (wife of Benjamin H.) - b. 6 October 1820; d. 21 June 1910
- Amasa - d. 2 February 1852 Æ 45 y., 6 m.
- Ann M. [wife of DeLorraine A.] - b. 1847; d. 1922
- Benjamin H. (husb. of Almira) - d. 24 July 1888 Æ 77 y., 6 m., 2 d.
- Benjamin H. Jr. (husb. of Louise J.) - b. 16 June 1848; d. 29 September 1928
- Betsey (wife of Jesse) - d. 22 September 1865 Æ 71 y., 6 d.
- Bloomfield (husb. of Fannie S.) - b. 25 March 1850; d. 9 September 1923
- DeLorraine A. [husb. of Ann M.] - d. 23 June 1907 Æ 65 y., 11 m., 25 d.; ("soldier rest in quiet sleep" [Civil War?])
- Ellenett (dau. of Benjamin H. and Almira) - d. 5 August 1845 Æ 3 y., 11 m.
- Fairfield (son of Benjamin H. and Almira) - d. 5 September 1852 Æ 2 y., 6 m.
- Fannie S. (wife of Bloomfield) - b. 19 July 1858; d. 27 February 1940
- H. N. - [no dates]; (member of Co. E, 25th Maine Regiment [Civil War])
- Jacob - d. 18[45?][1]
- Jared R. (son of Benjamin H. and Almira) - d. 1 June 1848 Æ 2 y., 16 d.
- Jesse (husb. of Betsey) - d. 21 June 1868 Æ 89 y., 8 m., 22 d.
- Jesse Jr. - d. 23 March 1846 Æ 31 y., 4 m., 5 d.
- Louise J. (wife of Benjamin H. Jr.) - b. 4 December 1849; d. 15 September 1910
- Myra - b. 31 December 1865; d. 18 December 1875
- Myron H. (son of Benjamin H. and Almira) - d. 2 October 1879 Æ 21 y., 10 m., 22 d.
- [S?]ophia[1] [H.?][1] (dau. of Oliver and Elizabeth [no stones]) - d. 17 February 1879 Æ 16 y., 10 m., 16 d.
- Winfield M. - b. 21 January 1880; d. 1 August 1943
- Winfield S. (son of Benjamin H. and Almira) - d. 9 April 1848 Æ 9 y., 10 m., 6 d.

JELLISON
- Myra A. - b. 19 July 1882; d. 20 April 1962

MAYO
Anna (wife of James [no stone]) - d. 18 March 1877 Æ 81 y., 3 m.
Hannah S. R. (wife of Henry [no stone]) - d. 5 August 1846 Æ 27 y., 4 m., 23 d.
NORWOOD
Clifford C. - d. 24 December 1900 Æ 16 y., 10 m., 19 d.
Violet - b. 27 April 1867; d. 19 June 1928
William H. - b. 1874; d. 1959
REED
Samuel Jr. - d. 25 October 1853 Æ 70 y., 7 m., 22 d.
RICHARDSON
Daniel (husb. of Susan D.) - b. 22 February 1787; d. 15 July 1857
Jared (son of Daniel and Susan D.) - d. 27 August 1833 Æ 18 y., 5 m., 9 d.
Lewis (son of Daniel and Susan D.) - d. 20 October 1826 Æ 6 y., 9 d.
Rhoda F. (dau. of Daniel and Susan D.) - d. 17 August 1824 Æ 8 y., 3 m., 3 d.
Susan D. (wife of Daniel) - d. 7 January 1861 Æ 69 y., 17 d.
[...]
[...][2]

Notes:
[1]Stone worn, crumbling, and/or broken.
[2]Stone worn and crumbling. This stone is adjacent to the stone of [S?]ophia [H.?] HIGGINS.

Higgins-Marcyes Burial Ground
(Bar Harbor - 10)

Location/directions. Indian Point. From the traffic light at the north end of Mount Desert Island, go straight ahead (south) onto Routes 102/198. In approximately 1.9 miles, turn right onto Indian Point Road. Follow this road for about 1.8–1.9 miles to a private driveway on the left. The cemetery is at the end of this driveway.

History. The name applied to this cemetery is only for convenience of reference in this book.

Notes. No fence encloses this cemetery. The grass is mowed and trimmed.

Names and dates on gravestones and other markers. [23 October 1999]

ATKINSON
- Sarah H. (wife of Daniel [no stone]) - d. 5 August 1851 Æ 23 y.

HIGGINS
- Ichabod (husb. of Sarah) - d. 15 April 1810 Æ 36 y.[1]
- Royal (husb. of Sarah G.) - d. 25 November 1878 Æ 72 y., 5 m., 9 d.
- Sally (dau. of Ichabod and Sarah) - d. November 1823 Æ 13 y., 6 m.
- Sarah (wife of Ichabod) - d. 14 October 1848 Æ 63 y.
- Sarah G. (wife of Royal) - d. 25 November 1880 Æ 70 y., 7 d.

MARCYES
- Asaph Alsen (son of William and Lydia) - d. 24 December 1851 Æ 17 y., 3 m.
- Lydia (wife of William) - d. 24 June 1873 Æ 77 y., 11 m.
- Nathaniel Jr. - d. 24 February 1827 Æ 30 y., 11 d.
- William (husb. of Lydia) - d. 20 January 1867 Æ 60 y., 9 m., [...][2]

WALLS
- Eddie L. (son of S. N. and Amanda L. [no stones]) - d. 25 December 1866 Æ 2 y., 11 m., 16 d.

Notes:

[1]This stone is broken and has been moved to the garage of the resident owner of the property where the cemetery is located.

[2]Inscription partly below ground.

Mount Desert Street Cemetery
(Bar Harbor - 11)

Location/directions. North side of Mount Desert Street (Route 3), in-town Bar Harbor. From the traffic light at the north end of Mount Desert Island, bear left on Route 3. Travel approximately 10.1 miles to a stop sign where Route 3 makes a right-angled turn to the left. Make this turn—this portion of Route 3 is called Mount Desert Street—and the cemetery is on the left between two churches in about 0.3–0.4 miles.

History. —

Notes. Letters and numbers on marble stones of this cemetery are much more worn than those in other cemeteries. Many unengraved pieces of stones once laying together at one side of the cemetery have been removed. During November of 1998, many stones that were laying on the ground were stood upright. Broken stones were repaired using epoxy but not modified to match the color of the stone. In a few cases, some letters and/or numbers on a stone have been obscured by the repair work.

Names and dates on gravestones and other markers.

ALLEY
- Aquaie J. [child of Capt. Frederick J. and Irene O.?] - b. 2 June 1866; d. 19 May 1886
- Frederick J. (Capt.; husb. of Irene O.) - b. 1828; d. 1911
- Irene O. (wife of Capt. Frederick J.) - b. 17 May 1838; d. 28 March 1897
- Ophelia W. [dau. of Capt. Frederick J. and Irene O.?] - b. 17 April 1859; d. 29 May 1886

ASH
- Amanda M. [mother of Israel H. and Walter R.] - d. 1 November 1903 Æ 65 y., 4 m., 16 d.
- Benjamin [husb. of Maria H.] - d. 16 January 1882 Æ 67 y.
- infant - b. 23 December 1891; d. 23 December 1891
- Israel H. (brother of Walter R.; son of Amanda M.) - b. 19 November 1863; d. 11 August 1892
- [Mariam [sic] H. - see ROBERTS]
- Maria H. [wife of Benjamin] - d. 10 August 1891 Æ 82 y., 2 m., 23 d.
- Walter R. (brother of Israel H.) - d. 28 April 1907 Æ 23 y., 9 m., 23 d.

BEVERLY
- Stephen H. - d. 16 December 1845 Æ 23 y., 13 d.
- William D. - d. 4 January 1862 Æ 26 y., 3 m., 8 d.

BREWER
- Betsey (wife of Edward Jr. [no stone]) - d. 14 September 1864 Æ 28 y., 6 m.
- Edward L. (husb. of Zena (HIGGINS)) - b. 1833; d. 1915
- Zena (HIGGINS; wife of Edward L.) - b. 1823; d. 1896

BUNKER
- Mary E. (wife of Eri [sic] L. [no stone]) - d. 23 December 1880 Æ 23 y., 5 m., 25 d.

COLE
- Abbie E. (wife of [...][1]) - d. 22 January 1884 Æ [20?][1] y., 6 m., [20?][1] d.

CONNERS
- John (husb. of Julia J.) - d. 4 October 1888 Æ 75 y., 8 m., 15 d.
- Julia J. (wife of John) - d. 9 March 1894 Æ 82 y.

COOK
- Zella B. (wife of Samuel A. [no stone]) - d. 22 January 1885 Æ 20 y., 8 m., 10 d.

CUNNINGHAM
infant (dau. of H. E. and L. M. [no stones]) - d. 25 December 1882 Æ 6 m., 6 d.
Laura A. (dau. of H. E. and L. M. [no stones]) - d. 18 May 1886 Æ 11 m., 10 d.
DAY
John W. (son of Moses and Mary B. [no stones]) - d. 1 August 1848 Æ 24 y.
DORR
Ethel Z. (dau. of Thomas T. [no stone] and Olive E.) - d. 24 January 1885 Æ 6 y., 3 m., 1 d.
Lura A. (dau. of Thomas T. [no stone] and Olive E.) - d. 17 January 1885 Æ 16 y., 2 m., 24 d.
Olive E. (wife of Thomas T. [no stone]) - d. 14 March 1885 Æ 48 y., 2 m., 14 d.
DOUGLASS
E. Woodman (son of John H. [no stone] and Margaret[t][2] H.) - d. 23 August 1881 Æ 9 m., 26 d.
H. Emery (son of John H. [no stone] and Margaret[t][2] H.) - d. 12 July 1880 Æ 1 y., 2 m., 12 d.[3]
Lucreatia [sic] K. (dau. of Rev. William S. and Priscilla [no stones]) - d. 3 August 1853 Æ 12 y.; ("was killed by falling from Cliffs on Newport Mt. Eden Me.")
Margaret[t][2] H. (wife of John H. [no stone]) - d. 2 March 1887 Æ [1?]8 y.[3]
Mary Alice (dau. of John H. [no stone] and Margaret[t][2] H.) - d. 4 January 1885 Æ 7 y., 5 m., 27 d.
EVELETH
Frances C. - d. 19 April 1883 Æ 52 y.
FROST
Gracie (dau. of George E. and L. J. [no stones]) - d. 5 January 1885 Æ 5 y., 2 m., 11 d.
infant (dau. of George E. and L. J. [no stones]) - [no dates]
GRACE
Abby A. (dau. of Moses and Hannah L.) - d. 20 [November?][1] 18[...][1]
Hannah L. (wife of Moses) - d. 14 January 1863 Æ [4?]8[1] y., 8 m., 9 d.
Moses (husb. of Hannah L.) - d. 15 October 1888 Æ 82 y., 7 m., 3 d.
GRINDLE
Georgia E. (wife of George D. [no stone]) - d. 7 November 1891 Æ 36 y., 9 m.
HAMOR
Clara B. (wife of Capt. James) - d. 12 June 1888 Æ 84 y., 6 m., 7 d.
James (Capt.; husb. of Clara B.) - d. 17 December 1873 Æ 79 y.
HAVENS
Christopher (husb. of Mary) - d. 7 April 1881 Æ 83 y.
Israel (son of Christopher and Mary) - d. 29 January 1849 Æ 22 y.
Julia E. (dau. of Christopher and Mary) - d. 1 June 1863 Æ [...][1] y.
Mary (wife of Christopher) - d. 23 October 1877 Æ 85 y.
Mercy (dau. of Christopher and Mary) - d. 8 June 1875 Æ [51?][1] y.
Sally S. (dau. of Christopher and Mary) - d. 17 February 1840 Æ [10?][1] y.
HIGGINS
Addie (dau. of Charles and Almira) - d. 24 October 1865 Æ 1 y., 5 m., 23 d.
Addie Florence (dau. of Leander A. and Mary [I. or J.][2]) - d. 24 March 1871 Æ 6 m., 14 d.
Albert F. - d. 15 March 1898 Æ 75 y., 5 m., 15 d.
Albertena (dau. of George P. and Eudora [no stone]) - d. 12 January 1849 Æ 11 m.
Almira H. (wife of Charles) - d. 21 April 1880 Æ 37 y., 4 m., 3 d.
Amos (son of Henry and Huldah) - d. August 1825 Æ 11 m.
Amos H. - d. 16 September 1859 Æ 25 y., 7 m.

Amos H. (son of Alcenus and Betsey [no stones]) - d. 15 September 1873 Æ 14 y., 10 m.
Andy - [no dates]
Angelia S. (wife of Gilbert F. [no stone]) - d. 7 January 1849 Æ 19 y., 8 m.
Ann M. (wife of Stephen) - d. 7 August 1883 Æ 69 y., 7 m.
Asa (husb. of Mercy S.) - d. 9 September 1877 Æ 73 y., 8 m.
Charles (husb. of Almira H.) - d. 29 April 1886 Æ 44 y., 2 m., 13 d.
Daniel (husb. of Hannah) - d. 11 November 1889 Æ 73 y.
Deborah (dau. of Henry and Huldah) - d. 17 July 1831 Æ 19 y.
Deborah (dau. of Henry and Huldah) - d. 15 September 1862 Æ 30 y.
Deborah (wife of Stephen) - d. 26 November 1845 Æ 74 y.
Eddie M. (son of Leander A. and Mary [I. or J.][2]) - d. 27 August 1873 Æ 4 y., 10 m., 22 d.
Ella Frances (dau. of Royal G. and Mary F.) - b. 1866; d. 1902
Ella L. (wife of Albert L. [no stone]) - b. 1 May 1853; d. 23 December 1878 Æ 25 y., 7 m., 23 d.
Emily L. (dau. of Cyrenius and Emily [no stones]) - d. 6 September 1862 Æ 21 y.
Etta J. (dau. of William H. and Mary [no stones]) - d. 19 February 18[64?][1] Æ 5y., 9 m., 22 d.
Ezra L. - d. 16 March 1855 Æ 40 y., 1 m., 26 d.
Florence A. (wife of Edwin H. [no stone]) - d. 29 August 1873 Æ 31 y.
George P. [husb. of Eudora [no stone]] - d. 7 April 1849 Æ 22 y., 8 m.
H. S. - [no dates]; (member of Co. H, 4th Maine Regiment)
Hannah (wife of Daniel) - d. 27 January 1901 Æ 83 y., 9 m.
Henry (husb. of Huldah) - d. 3 July 1843 Æ 53 y.
Hester A. (dau. of Henry and Huldah) - d. 20 December 1852 Æ 18 y., 2 m.
Huldah (wife of Henry) - d. 9 January 1882 Æ 89 y., 15 d.
Israel - d. 16 September 1852 Æ 35 y., 7 m.
Isreal [sic] (Capt.; husb. of Polly) - "lost at sea" 23 March 1823 Æ 45 y.
Laura - d. 14 December 1859 Æ 14 y.
Leander A. (husb. of Mary [I. or J.][2]) - d. 2 September 1873 Æ 34 y., 3 m.
Mamie - [no dates]
Mary C. "Lina" (dau. of Leander A. and Mary [I. or J.][2]) - d. 15 March 1885 Æ 18 y., 11 m., 21 d.
Mary F. (wife of Royal G.) - b. 1839; d. 1915
Mary H. (Miss; dau. of Capt. Stephen and Margaret [no stone]) - d. 3 June 1847 Æ 21 y., 26 d.
Mary [I. or J.][2] (wife of Leander A.) - b. 1844; d. 1926
Mercy C. (wife of Oliver 3rd) - d. 5 February 1887 Æ 83 y., 8 m.
Mercy S. (wife of Asa) - d. 9 December 1862 Æ 65 y.[4]
Oliver (husb. of Rhoda) - d. 30 January 1862 Æ [...][5]
Oliver 3rd (husb. of Mercy C.) - d. 18 February 1880 Æ [5?][...][5] y., 8 m., 2 d.
Oliver J. (son of Oliver and Rhoda) - d. 11 November 1853 Æ 28 y.
Polly (wife of Capt. Isreal [sic]) - d. 26 February 1818 Æ 36 y.
Rhoda (wife of Oliver) - d. 29 September 1871 Æ 8[3 or 9?][1] y., 2 m.
Rhoda 2nd - d. 13 August 1871 Æ [...][1]
Royal G. (husb. of Mary F.) - b. 1809; d. 1873
Sally - d. 28 August 1876 Æ 71 y.
Sarah (wife of [Capt.] Zacheus[9] [sic]) - b. 1786; d. 1869
Seth (Capt.) - d. 10 April 1860 Æ 23 y., [1?][1] m., [...][5] d.
Seth H. (son of Alcenus and Betsey [no stones]) - d. 11 November 1871 Æ [1 or 4?][1] y., 8 m.

Simon - [no dates]; (member of Co. H, 4th Maine Regiment)
Stephen (Capt.; husb. of Margaret [no stone]) - b. 31 December 1804; d. 4 September 1862 Æ 58 y.
Stephen (husb. of Deborah) - d. 19 December 1852 Æ 81 y.
Stephen (husb. of Ann M.) - d. 18 December 1891 Æ 78 y., 10 m., 10 d.
Stephen W. (son of Royal G. and Mary F.) - b. 1869; d. 1887
Zacheus [sic] - d. 3 November 1856 Æ [4 or 1?]9[1] y., 7 m., 2 d.
Zackeus[9] [sic] (Capt.; [husb. of Sarah]) - d. 1[...][5] May[6] 18[6?]7[5] Æ 85 y., 2 m.
[Zena - see BREWER]
[...am...][1,5] - d. 17 May 186[0?][1] Æ 38 y., [6?][1] m.

HOPKINS
[Bethiah - see RICHARDSON]

HOTCHKISS
Adaline (wife of John A. [no stone]) - d. 4 February 1845 Æ 34 y., 5 m.

JACKSON
Ruby (PINEO) - b. 1858; d. 1944

KANE
Sean Philip - [b. and d.?] 27 October 1979

LELAND
Adaline [sic] H. (wife of Capt. O. H. [no stone]) - d. 17 February 1858 Æ 26 y., 5 m., 16 d.
Ansel B. (son of Enoch H. and Irene) - d. 22 May 1852 Æ 5 y., 10 m.
Ellen S. (dau. of Enoch H. and Irene) - d. 25 August 1882 Æ [33?][5] y., 3 m., [...][5] d.
Enoch H. (husb. of Irene) - d. 25 February 1877 Æ 56 y., 7 m., 27 d.
Irene (wife of Enoch H.) - d. 20 March 1902 Æ 80 y., 2 m., 22 d.

LYNCH
Daniel - d. 25 January 1874 Æ 74 y.

MANCHESTER
Sarah B. - b. 1833; d. 1914

NICKERSON
Albertina - d. 15 June 1880 Æ 26 y.
Ann M. - d. 6 December 1881 Æ 31 y.
Betsey (wife of Capt. Sparrow) - d. 24 May 1869 Æ 57 y., 3 m.
Henry W. - d. 27 November 1877 Æ 26 y., 3 m.
Louisa - d. 16 July 1862 Æ 16 y., 8 m.
Sparrow (Capt.; husb. of Betsey) - d. 21 September 1859 Æ 44 y., 7 m., 19 d.

PARSONS
Harland C. (son of L. E. and Clara H. [no stones]) - d. 12 October 1884 Æ 3 y., 5 m., 13 d.

PINEO
Charles Byron - [no dates]
Flora (RODICK) - [no dates]
[Ruby - see JACKSON]

PRAY
Ella A. (dau. of E. H. and Nellie F. [no stones]) - d. 18 October 1882 Æ 1 y., 5 m., 14 d.

RICHARDS
Cassie May (dau. of [...][1] and [J.?][1] [no stones]) - d. 18 February 18[8?]1[1] Æ [...][1] m., 16 d.
E. B. - b. 1849; d. 1896
[Harbey?][1] W. (son of [...][1]) - d. [2?][1] August 1874 Æ [4?][1] m.
Henrietta C. (wife of James H. [no stone]) - d. 11 June 1880 Æ 37 y., 1 m., 27 d.

Josiah B. - d. [...][5] Æ 62 y., 10 m., 6 d.
William - d. 16 June 1893 Æ 61 y., 11 m., 16 d.

RICHARDSON

Amos (husb. of Bethiah (HOPKINS)) - d. 20 January 1877 Æ 72 y., 10 m., 11 d.
Bethiah (HOPKINS; wife of Amos) - d. 8 June 1888 Æ 81 y., 29 d.
James Small (son of Amos and Bethiah (HOPKINS)) - d. 26 January 1843 Æ 7 m., 4 d.
Sarah Rebecca - d. 5 December 1908 Æ 72 y., 6 m.

ROBERTS

Aquea S. (dau. of Tobias and Mary [no stone?]) - d. 15 November 1861 Æ 19 y., 5 m., 15 d.
Cora F. - b. 1896; d. [...][7]
George (husb. of Hannah) - d. 10 October 1862 Æ 62 y., 9 m.
Hannah (wife of George) - d. 13 April 1861 Æ 37 y., 6 m., 13 d.
John L. (son of Tobias and Mary [no stone?]) - d. 10 October 1861 Æ 16 y., 4 m., 21 d.
John Whittington (son of William Martin and Mariam [sic] H. (ASH)) - b. 22 August 1870; d. 26 November 1904
Mariam [sic] H. (ASH; wife of William Martin) - b. 1849; d. 1934
Tobias (husb. of Mary [no stone?]) - b. 19 April 1806; d. 22 October 1879
Tobias Lord - b. 1835; d. 1908
Tobias Lord - b. 8 January 1888; d. 19 November 1956
William Martin (husb. of Mariam [sic] H. (ASH)) - b. 1848; d. 1929

RODICK [includes RODRICK]

Benjamin - [no dates]; (member of Co. C, 1st Maine Heavy Artillery)
Daniel - d. 20 June 1880 Æ 79 y., 8 m., 10 d.
David (Capt.; husb. of Sally) - d. 20 January 1856 Æ 80 y., 6 m.
David Jr. (Capt.; husb. of Marian L.) - b. 1815; d. 1881
David O. [husb. of Florence E.] - b. 7 November 1893; d. 15 October 1946
Deborah (wife of Daniel [no stone?]) - d. 4 June 1861 Æ 59 y., 11 m., 14 d.
Emily (dau. of David and Betsey [no stones]) - d. 24 September 1863 Æ [...][8] y., 7 m., 6 d.
[Flora - see PINEO]
Florence E. [wife of David O.] - b. 22 May 1893; d. 18 May 1976
Fountain - b. 2 July 1844; d. 25 February 1919
Fountain (son of Thomas and Ann [no stones]) - d. 23 October 1858 Æ 3 y., 23 d.
John - d. 11 June 1854 Æ 68 y., 1 m.
Kate T. (wife of Walter E. [no stone]) - d. 20 July 1883 Æ 31 y., 3 m., 22 d.
Marian L. (wife of Capt. David Jr.) - d. 11 February 1853 Æ 35 y., 2 m., 11 d.
Milton - b. 22 February 1857; d. 16 February 1913
Milton (son of David Jr. and Marian L.) - d. 15 November 1852 Æ 6 m.
Sally (wife of Capt. David) - d. 19 February 1853 Æ 77 y., 6 m.
Thomas S. - d. 22 July 1876 Æ 51 y., 2 m., 15 d.
[...][5] (dau. of [...][1] H.) - d. 27 November 1861 Æ 10 y., 4 m., 8 d.

SALISBURY (includes SALSBURY)

Almira M. (wife of Reuben [no stone]) - d. 13 February 1866 Æ 59 y., 1 m., 2[1 or 4?][5] d.
Bethuel (Capt.; husb. of Elizabeth [no stone]) - d. 4 July 1872 Æ 65 y., 6 m., 4 d.
Ellen R. (wife of Warren H. [no stone]) - d. 26 January 1856 Æ 20 y., 5 m., 22 d.
Olevia [sic] A. (dau. of Capt. Bethuel and Elizabeth [no stone]) - d. 1 December 1865 Æ 19 y., 6 m., 4 d.

Thomas R. (son of Reuben [no stone] and Almira M.) - d. 5 January 1836 Æ [3?][1] y., [3?][1] m., [13?][1] d.

SHAW

Erma V. [wife of Norman] - b. 1905; d. 1982
Norman [husb. of Erma V.] - b. 1892; d. 1973

SMITH

Edwin F. (son of Edwin F. [no stone] and Florinda) - d. 13 December 1874 Æ 7 y., 5 m., 9 d.
Florinda (wife of Edwin F. [no stone]) - d. 20 December 1874 Æ 30 y., 4 m., 7 d.

SOPER

Laura E. (dau. of George E. and Nellie D. [no stones]) - d. 7 March 18[...]5[1] Æ 6[6] y., 6 m., 1[4?][6] d.
Ralph E. (son of George E. and Nellie D. [no stones]) - d. 30 December 1891 Æ 8 y., 6 d.

STANWOOD

Hannah (wife of Humphrey) - d. 23 April 1851 Æ 73 y.
Humphrey (husb. of Hannah) - d. 22 October 1847 Æ 80 y.

STAPLES

Isaac C. (husb. of Martha A.) - [no dates]
Martha A. (wife of Isaac C.) - d. 9 August 1862 Æ 24 y.

SUMINSBY

Deborah (wife of [...][5]) - d. 17 March 18[1?]7[5] Æ 18 y., 5 m.
Experience L. (wife of Jacob S.) - d. 19 January 1892 Æ 73 y.
Jacob S. (husb. of Sarah and Experience L.) - d. 4 July 1892 Æ 75 y., 8 m.
Sarah (wife of Jacob S.) - d. 10 March 1852 Æ 21 y., 6 m.

TABBUT

Cora A. (wife of Milton [no stone]) - d. 25 June 1886 Æ 25 y., 2 m., 2[4?][1] d.

WALLS

Ephraim H. (husb. of Clara A. [no stone]) - d. 3 January 1861 Æ 30 y., 3 m., 9 d.
Vesta E. (dau. of Ephraim H. and Clara A. [no stone]) - d. 17 February 1863 Æ 3 y., 5 m., 15 d.

WASGATT [includes WASGALT, WESCOTT]

Abby (wife of Jason) - d. 14 April 1882 Æ 82 y.
B[enjamin?]. R. (Corporal) - [no dates]; (member of Co. E, 26th Maine Regiment)
Elmer E. (son of Benjamin R. [no stone?] and Eunice S. [no stone]) - d. 30 September 1877 Æ 15 y., 7 m., 3 d.
infant (dau. of Mr. and Mrs. W. H. [no stones]) - b. 28 December 188[9?][5]; d. 29 December [...][5]
Jason (husb. of Abby) - d. 2 January 1866 Æ 66 y., 5 m.

WOODBERRY [sic]

John - d. 1 October 1875 Æ 81 y., 2 m.

YOUNG

Charlotte S. (wife of Willard W. [no stone]) - d. 23 January 1863 Æ 23 y., 2 m., 4 d.
Etta Maria (dau. of Elisha [no stone] and Priscilla [W. or J.][2]) - d. 1 February 1865 Æ 2 y., 1 m., 10 d.
Ezra H. (son of Joseph and Hannah [no stone]) - d. 13 January 1863, Washington, D. C., Æ 21 y., 4 m.; (member of 26th Maine Regiment)
George Dallas (son of Joseph and Hannah [no stone]) - d. 14 November 1872 Æ 27 y., 6 m., 17 d.
infant [YOUNG?] - [no dates]
Joseph [husb. of Hannah? [no stone]] - d. 17 June 1882 Æ 79 y., 8 m., 17 d.

Oliver H. [son of Joseph and Hannah? [no stone]] - d. 13 September 1867 Æ 17 y., 22 d.
Priscilla [W. or J.][2] (wife of Elisha [no stone]) - d. 23 December 1886 Æ 46 y.
Royal [husb. of Sarah B. (MANCHESTER)?] - b. 1843; d. 1913
Winnie J. (dau. of Elisha [no stone] and Priscilla [W. or J.][2]) - d. [...][1] August 18[7?]3[1] Æ 6 y., 10 m.

[...]

Alfred S. [brother of Katie and Lewis A.] - d. 28 April 1863 Æ 9 y., 19 d.
Andy [brother of Mamie] - [no dates]
Jonny F. (son of [...][1]) - d. [9?][1] February 1864 Æ [3?][1] m., [5?][1] d.
Katie [sister of Alfred S. and Lewis A.] - d. 18[5?]0[1] Æ [...][1] m., 18 d.
Lewis A. [brother of Alfred S. and Katie] - d. [2?]5 [August?] 186[7?] Æ [...][6]
Mamie [sister of Andy] - [no dates]
Th[...][5] - d. [...][5] Ap[ril] [...][5] Æ 69 y., [...][1] m., 7 d.
[...][1] - d. 16 March 185[...][1] Æ 39 y., 5 m., 5 d.
[...] [3; bases only]

Notes:

[1]Stone worn.
[2]Different on different stones.
[3]Dates on both stones are worn but appear to be legible. Also, the relationship of H. Emery as son of a John and Margaret is legible. Other sources will be necessary to clarify this anomaly.
[4]Remainder of stone below ground.
[5]Stone cracked and/or broken.
[6]This is now obscured by material used during the 1998 repair of stones in this cemetery.
[7]Metal marker bearing death date has been removed from the plaque.
[8]Number of years appears to be "1", but the number is followed by "yrs".
[9]Although spelling of Zacheus and Zackeus suggests otherwise, the 1850 census of Eden indicated that Sarah's husband was approximately 3 years older than her, thereby making him Zackeus HIGGINS.

Holy Redeemer Cemetery

(Bar Harbor - 12)

Location/directions. Along west side of Kebo Street between Cromwell Harbor Road and Acadia National Park's loop road. From the traffic light at the north end of Mount Desert Island, bear left on Route 3. Travel approximately 10.1 miles to a stop sign. Go straight ahead onto Kebo Street for about 0.5–0.6 miles to a stop sign. Continue through this intersection, and the cemetery is on the right in approximately 0.2–0.3 miles.

History. A monument in this cemetery reads "Holy Redeemer Cemetery/gift of/Mr. John B. How".

Notes. This cemetery is well maintained, and water is available. It is gated, but not entirely enclosed by a fence. The roads are paved or covered with finely crushed rock.

Names and dates on gravestones and other markers. [1 August 1999]

ABRAM
- Ida H. [wife of John H.] - b. 1876; d. 1949
- John H. [husb. of Ida H.] - b. 1879; d. 1961

ARATA
- Margit W. [wife of William E.] - b. 1902; d. 1998
- William E. [husb. of Margit W.] - b. 1895; d. 1985

ARGAINART
- Elise [wife of Martin] - b. 1889; d. 1976
- Martin [husb. of Elise] - b. 1905; d. 1960

BANNON
- Charles B. - b. 1905; d. 1979

BARSTON
- Frederick J. - b. 4 October 1893; d. 15 October 1918

BENNETT
- Donna M. [wife of George E.] - b. 1934
- George E. [husb. of Donna M.] - b. 1932; d. 1988

BERNARDINI
- Emanuel - b. 1846; d. 1911

BLANCHARD
- [Alice - see GRACE]
- James V. - b. 1884; d. 1933

BLANCHFIELD
- E. Maude (dau. of Patrick W. and Margaret (DWYER)) - b. 1888; d. 1966
- Elinore P. (dau. of Patrick W. and Margaret (DWYER)) - b. 1901; d. 1998
- Margaret (DWYER; wife of Patrick W.) - b. 1863; d. 1955
- Patrick W. (husb. of Margaret (DWYER)) - b. 1859; d. 1933

BLEVINS
- Charlotte E. - b. 28 February 1917; d. 3 March 2000

BOISVERT
- Blanche R. [wife of Paul A.] - b. 1907; d. 1996
- Paul A. [husb. of Blanche R.] - b. 1904; d. 1976

BOYLE
- Marion R. - b. 1893; d. 1950
- William E. - b. 1889; d. 1961

BREWER
- Dale P. [husb. of Florence G.] - b. 1911; d. 1997

Florence G. [wife of Dale P.] - b. 1910; d. 1997
BRIGNULL
Aaron F. [son of Roger L. and Elizabeth A.] - b. 6 October 1976
Elizabeth A. [wife of Roger L.] - b. 30 May 1944; d. 20 April 1991
Ember K. [dau. of Roger L. and Elizabeth A.] - b. 3 January 1979
Heather R. [dau. of Roger L. and Elizabeth A.] - b. 27 March 1974
Roger L. [husb. of Elizabeth A.] - b. 24 October 1946
BROWN
Beatrice H[AYES?]. - b. 1938; d. 1982
[Margaret - see HARRIS]
BURCH
Bridie [sic] E. (wife of Sanford A.) - b. 27 May 1913; d. 14 December 1991
Sanford A. (husb. of Bridie [sic] E.) - b. 1913; d. 1975
BURNS
Annie M. (wife of Gaylen F.) - b. 1874; d. 1952
Elizabeth M. - b. 1930
Ella F. - b. 1895; d. 1926
Gaylen F. (husb. of Annie M.) - b. 1873; d. 1955
Joseph P. - b. 29 August 1903; d. 11 November 1967
Louis G. - b. 1902; d. 1932
Marguerite - b. 15 September 1899; d. 25 March 1975
Marjorie D. - b. 1910
Martin A. - b. 1911; d. 1986
William H. - b. 1906; d. 1986
BYRNE
Mary Anne - b. 16 December 1871; d. 26 January 1942
BYRON
Alice L. [wife of Percy B.] - b. 1884; d. 1959
Percy B. [husb. of Alice L.] - b. 1883; d. 1950
CALDERWOOD
M. Clara - b. 1 June 1895; d. 19 March 1983
Mary [ELLWARD] - [no dates]
CANNING
Agatha A. - d. 26 March 1963 Æ [not given]
Blanche P. (wife of Lewis L.) - b. 1879; d. 1961
Ethelburger F. - d. 10 September 1914 Æ [not given]
"father" - d. 13 December 1916 Æ [not given]
Geraldine - b. 1920; d. 1985
Leo J. - d. 10 March 1926 Æ [not given]
Lewis L. (husb. of Blanche P.) - b. 1882; d. 1950
Margaret B. - d. 7 February 1909 Æ [not given]
"mother" - d. 17 May 1931 Æ [not given]
Philip J. - d. 5 November 1944 Æ [not given]
CANTWELL
Bridget M. - b. 1891; d. 1954
Edward T. - b. 1926; d. 1927
James L. - b. 1928; d. 1991
John F. - b. 1890; d. 1966
John F. Jr. - b. 1 July 1921; d. 20 June 1967
[Marcia C[ANTWELL?]. - see SAWYER]
Violet M. [wife of William J.] - b. 1897; d. 1989
William J. [husb. of Violet M.] - b. 1892; d. 1982

CAREY
Francis V. - b. 25 December 1917; d. 12 March 1987
CARTER
Elsie F. - b. 1893; d. 1955
Muriel E. - b. 1924; d. 1963
CASEY
John Francis - b. 3 March 1892; d. 17 March 1954
John W. (husb. of Karin L.) - b. 21 March 1915; d. 7 March 1988
Karin L. (wife of John W.) - b. 15 April 1925; d. 22 August 1981
Melena M. - b. 12 January 1896; d. 4 July 1977
Walter P. - b. 1916; "lost at sea" 1943
CLARK
Doris M. [wife of Owen J.] - b. 1905; d. 1979
"father" - b. 1860; d. 1940
"mother" - b. 1875; d. 1962
Owen J. [husb. of Doris M.] - b. 1905; d. 1984
Theodora F. - b. 1908; d. 1936
COADY
Lillian M. (wife of William F.) - b. 1889; d. 1959
[Margaret - see PAYNTER]
Uriah (brother of Margaret (COADY) PAYNTER) - b. 17 September 1922
William F. (husb. of Lillian M.) - b. 1879; d. 1946
CONNERS
Annie J. [wife of William D.] - b. 1868; d. 1942
William D. [husb. of Annie J.] - b. 1864; d. 1934
CONNOLLY
C. Edward [husb. of Helen M.] - b. 11 January 1918
Helen M. [wife of C. Edward] - b. 13 February 1920; d. 16 September 1991
CORBETT
Andrew J. [husb. of Bessie J.] - b. 1889; d. 1961
Bessie J. [wife of Andrew J.] - b. 1888; d. 1960
CORMIER
Edward A. - b. 1904; d. 1952
Helen L. - b. 1931; d. 1947
CORSON
Laura (wife of Robert) - b. 12 May 1924
Robert (husb. of Laura) - b. 1 April 1911; d. 12 July 1986
COUGH
Bernard E. (grandson of Daniel and Elvira [no stones]; son of Ezra R. and Gertrude A. (LYNCH); husb. of Helen (NORTON); father of Bernard K., Barbara, Janis, and James [no stones]) - b. 1904; d. 1978
Cora L. - b. 1907; d. 1974
Edward G. - b. 1930; d. 1984
Ezra R. (husb. of Gertrude A. (LYNCH)) - b. 1876; d. 1944
Gertrude A. (LYNCH; wife of Ezra R.) - b. 1883; d. 1968
Helen (NORTON; wife of Bernard E.; mother of Bernard K., Barbara, Janis, and James [no stones]) - b. 1907, Farmington, Maine; d. 1987
L. Vincent (husb. of Marjorie W.) - b. 7 June 1912; d. 29 September 1996
Marjorie W. (wife of L. Vincent) - b. 24 September 1919
Mary R. - b. 1915; d. 1915
Reginald - b. 1906; d. 1987

COUSINS
Rebecca Mary - b. 1869; d. 1930
CRANAFORD
Ellie - b. 1898; d. 1967
James H. (husb. of Nora) - b. 1865; d. 1954
James H. Jr. (son of James H. and Nora) - d. 27 June 1917
John B. - b. 1896; d. 1960
Nora (wife of James H.) - b. 1860; d. 1936
CURTIS
Michael Warren - b. 1933; d. 1989
DAGG
June Mary - b. 1 May 1900; d. 24 September 1990
DAIGLE
Benjamin - b. 1882; d. 1932
Catherine M. [wife of Reuben J.] - b. 13 December 1902; d. 13 July 1983
Daniel D. - b. 1870; d. 1940
Joseph E. - b. 1910; d. 1984
Judith M. [wife of Martin D.] - b. 1876; d. 1966
Julian H. - b. 1885; d. 1944
Martin D. [husb. of Judith M.] - b. 1871; d. 1966
Reuben J. [husb. of Catherine M.] - b. 26 January 1905; d. 14 December 1962
DAUGHERTY
Jack A. (husb. of Ruth A. (SIGLIN); father of Sean M., Bryan W., and Kelly R. [no stones]) - b. 25 February 1944
Ruth A. (SIGLIN; wife of Jack A.; mother of Sean M., Bryan W., and Kelly R. [no stones]) - b. 7 November 1949; d. 25 September 1997
DAVIS
Hollis M. (husb. of Virginia M.) - b. 1910; d. 1980
Virginia M. (wife of Hollis M.) - b. 1911
DAY
Mary J. - b. 8 April 1919; d. 25 July 1997
DENNERY
[Elizabeth - see McCARTHY]
DODGE
[Shirley L. - see SILK]
DOREY
Jeanne M. (wife of Parker L.) - b. 1880; d. 1952
Parker L. (husb. of Jeanne M.) - b. 1888; d. 1971
DOYLE
Edward L. Jr. (husb. of Madeleine [sic] (SILK)) - b. 1918; d. 1989
Madeleine [sic] (SILK; wife of Edward L. Jr.) - b. 1916; d. 1986
DUFFY
Catherine G. [wife of Paul H.] - b. 5 December 1920
Paul H. [husb. of Catherine G.] - b. 15 November 1918
DWYER
[Margaret - see BLANCHFIELD]
DYER
Mary E. [wife of Roger J.] - b. 1920; d. 1996
Roger J. [husb. of Mary E.] - b. 1915; d. 1983
EKOLA
Philip M. - b. 3 November 1957; d. 3 May 1974

ELLWARD [includes ELWARD]
Elizabeth M. (wife of Frank S.) - b. 1885; d. 1959
Frank S. (husb. of Elizabeth M.) - b. 1875; d. 1945
[Mary - see CALDERWOOD]
Richard G. (son of J. J. and H. A. [no stones]) - b. 1932; d. 1933
ELLS
Marie - b. 1887; d. 1982
FARRAR
Alfred Gleason [son of Guy O. and Alma L.?] - b. 13 January 1914; d. 1944
Alma L. [wife of Guy O.?] - b. 1886; d. 1967
Guy O. [husb. of Alma L.?] - b. 1883; d. 1967
Margaret E. [dau. of Guy O. and Alma L.?] - b. 1909
FARRON
Margaret - b. 14 July 1896; d. 1 November 1991
FILLIETTAZ
Anthony J. - b. 1906
Catherine C. - b. 1868; d. 1923
Catherine F. "Kay" - b. 1897; d. 1977
Dorothy A. - b. 1931
Dorothy S. - b. 1910; d. 1980
Edith L. [wife of John D.] - b. 1895; d. 1980
Henry L. - b. 1858; d. 1954
John D. [husb. of Edith L.] - b. 1901; d. 1981
Marie L. - b. 1894; d. 1987
FITZPATRICK
Edward F. (Rev.) - b. 7 March 1879, Armagh, Ireland; d. 3 December 1958
FLETCHER
Richard L. [husb. of Sharon L.] - b. 1946; d. 1978
Sharon L. [wife of Richard L.] - b. 1949
FOLEY
James - b. 1869; d. 1932
[Josephine F[OLEY?]. - see RICHARDSON]
Mary (OSLER) - b. 1883; d. 1949
Michael F. - b. 1874; d. 1967
Patricia (KELLY) - b. 1916
FOUHY
Mary - b. 1892; d. 1930
FRASER
Catherine A. - b. 1877; d. 1960
Edward L. - b. 29 June 1917; d. 20 January 1945
Marie J. [wife of William E.] - b. 1893; d. 1985
William E. [husb. of Marie J.] - b. 1885; d. 1968
FRITH
Louisa Selden - b. 29 August 1885; d. 3 November 1947
FROST
Carroll E. Jr. "Bud" [son of Carroll E. Sr. and Sadie Mary] - b. 1924; d. 1947
Carroll E. Sr. [husb. of Sadie Mary] - b. 1900; d. 1993
Sadie Mary [wife of Carroll E. Sr.] - b. 1906; d. 1992
GARLAND
Kenneth A. - b. 26 November 1919; d. 1 November 1948
GATZ
Andrew "Dutchie" - b. 1923; d. 1994

Bertha Marie - b. 1916; d. 1980
GION
Lucille A. - b. 1898; d. 1970
GOULD
Fred[e]rick[1] L. (husb. of Rachel) - b. 1885; d. 1953
Rachel (wife of Fred[e]rick[1] L.) - b. 1883; d. 1961
GOWER
Earl P. [husb. of Mary A.] - b. 1894; d. 1972
James - [b. and d.?] April 1952
James M. (Rev.) - b. 1922
Joseph - [b. and d.?] April 1952
[Kathleen A. - see PEVERINI]
Mary A. [wife of Earl P.] - b. 1891; d. 1968
GRACE
Alice (BLANCHARD; wife of Ira [no stone]) - b. 1893; d. 1918
GRAVES
Hunter Breanna - b. 14 January 1995; d. 4 May 1996
GRAY
Angus S. [husb. of Clara M.] - b. 1873; d. 1958
Clara M. [wife of Angus S.] - b. 1879; d. 1967
Reginald Francis (husb. of Rita Elizabeth) - b. 13 November 1914; d. 19 June 1992
Rita Elizabeth (wife of Reginald Francis) - b. 31 October 1921; d. 25 November 1992
HALEY
Patrick [husb. of Thresa [sic]] - b. 2 April 1845; d. 7 July 1912
Thresa [sic] [wife of Patrick] - b. 1860; d. 1918
HALL
Benedict Mark - b. 1917; d. 1990
Helen (SMALL; wife of Oliver Gray) - b. 1898; d. 1975
Hilary Martin - [b. and d.?] 26 July 1961
infant (son of Oliver Gray and Helen (SMALL)) - b. 1926; d. 1926
Oliver Gray (husb. of Helen (SMALL)) - b. 1898; d. 1971
HARRIS
Edward - b. 1867; d. 1943
"father" - b. 1865; d. 1960
Florence M. - b. 1904; d. 1986
John H. Jr. - b. 1898; d. 1929
Margaret (BROWN) - b. 1825; d. 1922
"mother" - b. 1869; d. 1926
HARTERY
Norman C. Sr. - b. 11 March 1915; d. 8 December 1994
HAYES
[Beatrice H[AYES?]. - see BROWN]
Elizabeth F. - b. 1936; d. 1949
Harold F. - b. 1910; d. 1981
Iris W. - b. 1916
HEATH
Ellen M. - b. 27 June 1874; d. 17 October 1953
Jean Louise - b. 10 May 1929; d. 4 May 1998
John C. - b. 28 April 1913; d. 7 May 1969
HERLIHY
Ada B. [wife of Daniel H.] - b. 1870; d. 1935
Daniel H. [husb. of Ada B.] - b. 1868; d. 1932

HIGGINS
Anna S. ["Ann"?] [wife of Eugene H.] - b. 1875; d. 1958
Charles E. [husb. of Edith L[URVEY?].] - b. 1906
Edith L[URVEY?]. [wife of Charles E.] - b. 1913; d. 1988
Eugene H. [husb. of Anna S. ["Ann"?]] - b. 1868; d. 1932
Francis [HIGGINS?] - [no dates]
Joanne D. [wife of Robert L. Jr.] - b. 1938
Johanna Josephine (wife of Robert Law) - b. 1911; d. 1983
Robert L. Jr. [husb. of Joanne D.] - b. 1932; d. 1986
Robert Law (husb. of Johanna Josephine) - b. 1906; d. 1996
Terrence J. (son of Robert Law and Johanna Josephine) - b. 6 September 1934; d. 27 November 1934
HUBBARD
Frederick G. [husb. of Helen M.] - b. 18 June 1895; d. 7 July 1966
Helen M. [wife of Frederick G.] - b. 1913; d. 1950
IVERSON
Lila A. - b. 1909; d. 1991
JAFFE
Barbara - [b. and d.?] 1943
JALBERT
Constance M. - b. 1922; d. 1999
JONES
Catherine E. [wife of John F. Sr.] - b. 1918; d. 1998
James J. - b. 26 June 1918; d. 3 August 1922
John [husb. of Rose A.] - b. 1886; d. 1962
John F. Sr. [husb. of Catherine E.] - b. 1916; d. 1976
Rose A. [wife of John] - b. 1888; d. 1977
KANE
Elizabeth D. [wife of Lyman J.] - b. 1919
Lyman J. [husb. of Elizabeth D.] - b. 1916; d. 1981
Lyman L. (husb. of Marjorie A.) - b. 1886; d. 1942
Marjorie A. (wife of Lyman L.) - b. 1885; d. 1947
KEISER
Alice S. (MCISAAC; dau. of Hugh D. MCISAAC and Elizabeth M.) - b. 1920; d. 1961
KELLY [includes KELLEY]
Annie M. [wife of Percy] - b. 1871; d. 1953
Constance B. - b. 1905; d. 1999
Edward T. [son of James F. and Ella R.?] - b. 1906; d. 1956
Ella R. (wife of James F.) - b. 1867; d. 1935
Ellen M. - b. 1891; d. 1963
Frank P. - b. 1901; d. 1978
Hugh N. - b. 1902; d. 1972
James F. (husb. of Ella R.) - b. 1872; d. 1940
Louis P. - b. 1910; d. 1967
[Margaret P. - see KIMBALL]
Marie W. - b. 1901; d. 1992
Martin Leo - b. 5 December 1912; d. 8 December 1966
Michael L. - b. 10 December 1953; d. 28 June 1975
[Patricia - see FOLEY]
Percy [husb. of Annie M.] - b. 1874; d. 1941
Terence J. - b. 1877; d. 1945

KENNY
[Irene - see MEAD]
John J. (Rev.) - b. 30 July 1906; d. 25 April 1985
KIMBALL
Allan R. [husb. of Margaret P. (KELLEY)] - b. 1921
Margaret P. (KELLEY; [wife of Allan R.]) - b. 1915; d. 1989
Mary Ellen - b. 30 June 1947
KIRK
Annie F. (wife of Edward) - b. 1866; d. 1936
Dorothy E. (dau. of Edward and Annie F.) - b. 1895; d. 1921
Ebba (NILSSON; [wife of Joseph Lawrence]) - b. 1892; d. 1974
Edward (husb. of Annie F.) - b. 1858; d. 1928
George E. (son of Edward and Annie F.) - b. 1894; d. 1918, France
Joseph Lawrence [husb. of Ebba (NILSSON)] - b. 1891; d. 1966
Pauline F. (dau. of Edward and Annie F.) - b. 1904; d. 1975
KLOTZ
Avon R. (husb. of Josephine M.) - b. 1914; d. 1985
Josephine M. (wife of Avon R.) - b. 1920; d. 1985
KYLE
Mary E. [wife of Thomas J.] - b. 1926
Thomas J. [husb. of Mary E.] - b. 1938; d. 1989
LANDERS
Julia L. [wife of Thomas H.] - b. 1882; d. 1918
Patricia [dau. of Thomas H. and Julia L.?] - b. 1910; d. 1911
Thomas H. [husb. of Julia L.] - b. 1875; d. 1918
LAROSA
Grace - [b. and d.?] 23 April 1943
Mary - [b. and d.?] 23 April 1943
LAWLER
James H. - b. 1912; d. 1980
Louise A. - b. 1882; d. 1961
LEATHERS
Ira B. [husb. of Katherine] - b. 14 October 1914; d. 7 July 1980
Katherine [wife of Ira B.] - b. 18 April 1915; d. 15 May 1974
LELAND
Ella M. (SILK; wife of Shirley E. [no stone]) - b. 1892; d. 1945
infant (dau. of Shirley E. [no stone] and Ella M. (SILK)) - [no dates]
LEMAY
Barbara V. - b. 1925
John W. - b. 1892; d. 1959
Richard W. - b. 1925
Susan L. - b. 1903; d. 1994
LEWEY
Frank P. - b. 1856; d. 1932
John F. - b. 1909; d. 1967
LISCOMB
Annie T. [wife of Horace H.] - b. 1888; d. 1982
Elizabeth E. [dau. of Horace H. and Annie T.?] - b. 1919
Horace F. [son of Horace H. and Annie T.?] - b. 1920
Horace H. [husb. of Annie T.] - b. 1895; d. 1939
LONG
George A. (husb. of Marjorie A.) - b. 11 October 1922; d. 13 June 1975

Marjorie A. (wife of George A.) - b. 1918
Marjorie E. (dau. of George A. and Marjorie A.) - [b. and d.?] 1 October 1949

LURVEY
Cecilia H. [wife of Wilbert F.] - b. 1874; d. 1952
[Edith L[URVEY?]. - see HIGGINS]
Wilbert F. [husb. of Cecilia H.] - b. 1879; d. 1958

LYNCH
Bernard (husb. of Mary L. (SULLIVAN)) - b. 1851; d. 1929
[Gertrude A. - see COUGH]
James B. - b. 5 June 1895; d. 18 September 1970
Lawrence V. (husb. of Mary) - b. 1898; d. 1974
Mary (wife of Lawrence V.) - b. 1901; d. 1976
Mary Frances (dau. of Lawrence V. and Mary) - b. 14 May 1943; d. 15 December 1947
Mary L. (SULLIVAN; wife of Bernard) - b. 1861; d. 1938

MACDONALD
John (husb. of Mary A.) - b. 1870; d. 1945
Mary A. (wife of John) - b. 1868; d. 1945

MACUL
Fabronia A. [wife of Henry L.] - b. 21 January 1915
Henry L. [husb. of Fabronia A.] - b. 26 January 1919; d. 23 December 1996

MAHON
Clare [sic] R. [wife of Francis J.] - b. 1910; d. 1997
Francis J. [husb. of Clare [sic] R.] - b. 1911; d. 1992

MAHONEY
Cornelius P. Jr. (son of Cornelius P. and E. A. [no stones]) - b. 1933; d. 1934

MCAVOY
Beatrice E. - b. 1897; d. 1970

MCBURNEY
Isabelle O. (wife of John J.) - b. 10 August 1910; d. 11 May 1990
John J. (husb. of Isabelle O.) - b. 11 January 1924; d. 14 October 1980

MCCARTHY
Elizabeth (DENNERY; wife of John) - b. 1858; d. 1923
Francis R. - b. 26 March 1886; d. 17 December 1946
John (husb. of Elizabeth (DENNERY)) - b. 1852; d. 1932
Mary Kathleen - b. 30 April 1896; d. 24 January 1977

MCCAULEY
Thomas - b. 1875; d. 1939

MCDERMOTT
Ellen F. - b. 11 July 1985; d. 22 August 1979

MCDOUGALL
Henrietta [wife of Mathew] - b. 1865; d. 1934
Mathew [husb. of Henrietta] - b. 1863; d. 1935

MCGRATH
Annie D. [wife of Martin J.] - b. 1880; d. 1945
M. Joseph [son of Martin J. and Annie D.?] - b. 1913; d. 1923
Martin J. [husb. of Annie D.] - b. 1882; d. 1965

MCINTOSH
Andrew J. - b. 1897; d. 1948
Bridget - b. 1859; d. 1943
Daniel - b. 1869; d. 1944

McISAAC
[Alice S. - see KEISER]
Elizabeth M. (wife of Hugh D.) - b. 1888; d. 1932
Ellen A. (wife of Maurice J. Sr.) - b. 12 December 1920
Hugh D. (husb. of Elizabeth M.) - b. 1881; d. 1944
Hugh F. - b. 1924; d. 1963
Joseph (son of Hugh D. and Elizabeth M.) - b. 1927; d. 1927
Josephine (dau. of Hugh D. and Elizabeth M.) - b. 1927; d. 1927
Maurice J. Sr. (husb. of Ellen A.) - b. 10 May 1916; d. 31 December 1981

McKAY
Ambrose J. [husb. of Mary S.] - b. 1900; d. 1977
Mary S. [wife of Ambrose J.] - b. 1897; d. 1961
Robert Edward [son of Ambrose J. and Mary S.?] - b. 13 October 1931; "lost at sea" 8 August 1949

McNAUGHTON
Mary A. - b. 1868, Armagh, Ireland; d. 1960

MEAD
Irene (KENNY) - b. 15 November 1898; d. 5 November 1989

MEDINI
Mary [wife of Nicholas] - b. 1872; d. 1940
Nicholas [husb. of Mary] - b. 1873; d. 1952

MORAN
Alta M. - b. 1893; d. 1987
John P. - b. 1885; d. 1947
John P. II - b. 1923; d. 1987

MORANG
Charlotte - b. 1921; d. 1995
G. Edgar - b. 1911; d. 1997

MORRISON
H. Dorothy (wife of Linus F.) - b. 1902; d. 1970
Linus F. (husb. of H. Dorothy) - b. 1908; d. 1979
Richard Linus - b. 5 November 1937; d. 20 October 1999

MULLHOLLAND
Leo - [no dates]
Lida - [no dates]

MURRAY
Isabelle W. (mother of Charles, James, Joseph, Theresa, and Rosalie [no stones]) - b. 1905; d. 1991

MYERS
Emma B. [wife of Howard F.] - b. 1913
Howard F. [husb. of Emma B.] - b. 1908; d. 1989

NEWDICK
Clara S. (wife of Erlon L.) - b. 1896; d. 1980
Erlon L. (husb. of Clara S.) - b. 8 March 1888; d. 16 September 1975
Richard L. - b. 1931
Robert L. - b. 1921
William A. - b. 1924

NILSSON
[Ebba - see KIRK]

NINFI
Attilio F. (husb. of Clelia A.) - b. 1869; d. 1940
Clelia A. (wife of Attilio) - b. 1892; d. 1990

NIRICH
John E. [husb. of Mary N.?] - b. 1888; d. 1969
Mary N. [wife of John E.?] - b. 1892; d. 1971
[Mary N[IRICH?]. - see ROBINSON]
NORTON
[Helen - see COUGH]
Joseph G. - b. 1905; d. 1989
O'BRIEN
James D. (Rev.) - b. 10 May 1863, Clashganiff, County Cork, Ireland; d. 6 October 1925, Bar Harbor; ("founder of the parish of our Holy Redeemer"; "Of ancient lineage, a descendant of the O'Briens of Thomond[.] He was a pious, zealous, learned priest and a princely benefactor of the Catholic Church in Maine[.] May he rest in peace!")
OSLER
[Mary - see FOLEY]
PARKER
Marguerite S. - b. 1891; d. 1974
PAYNTER
Kim E. - b. 18 October 1961; d. 19 September 1999
Margaret (COADY; sister of Uriah W. COADY) - b. 9 May 1921; d. 3 February 1993
PEVERINI
Kathleen A. (GOWER; wife of Mario [no stone]) - b. 1924; d. 1961
PHELPS
Murron Ilysh - [b. and d.?] 14 May 1998
PIERCE
Bernice A. [wife of Leon C.] - b. 1903; d. 1979
Leon C. [husb. of Bernice A.] - b. 1889; d. 1966
POLCHIES
John J. Jr. - b. 1961; d. 1990
PUGH
Constance D. (RIDER; wife of Harold D. [no stone]) - b. 1926; d. 1976
PURCELL
Patrick J. - b. 18 December 1955; d. 30 June 1991
QUAINTON
Anita Margaret - b. 9 June 1908; d. 12 February 1952
QUILTY
John [husb. of Nora] - b. 1891; d. 1944
Nora [wife of John] - d. 26 April 1972 Æ [not given]
QUIMBY
Robert E. - b. 1924; d. 1971
REDDY
Bessie E. [wife of Edward J.] - b. 1876; d. 1965
Edward J. [husb. of Bessie E.] - b. 1872; d. 1946
Henry E. - b. 16 March 1915; d. 21 June 1980
REYES
Blas - b. 1883; d. 1947
RICHARDSON
Josephine F[OLEY?]. - b. 1915
RIDER
[Constance D. - see PUGH]
George R. Jr. - b. 1905; d. 1948

RIESER
- Alice Mary - b. 1927
- Johanna [wife of John] - b. 1898; d. 1991
- John [husb. of Johanna] - b. 1897; d. 1990

ROBBINS
- Nora - b. 1901; d. 1960

ROBICHAUD
- Adeline M. [wife of Anthony G.] - b. 1880; d. 1956
- Anthony G. [husb. of Adeline M.] - b. 1876; d. 1951
- Anthony J. [son of Anthony G. and Adeline M.?] - b. 1916; d. 1972
- Oliver J. [husb. of Zelia D.] - b. 1892; d. 1965
- Zelia D. [wife of Oliver J.] - b. 1905; d. 1970

ROBINSON
- Mary N[IRICH?]. - b. 1924

RODICK
- Serenus B. - b. 1897; d. 1948

RYAN
- James E. - b. 6 July 1922; d. 12 January 1999
- James Patrick (husb. of Mary A.) - b. 20 May 1888; d. 6 January 1969
- John P. - b. 4 May 1894; d. 23 March 1963
- Mary A. (wife of James Patrick) - b. 1884; d. 1934

SABLICH
- Paul [husb. of Pauline N.] - b. 1871; d. 1957
- Pauline N. [wife of Paul] - b. 1882; d. 1980

SANER
- [Elizabeth M. - see SMITH]

SANKER
- Geraldine L. [wife of Victor L.] - b. 1913; d. 1991
- Victor L. [husb. of Geraldine L.] - b. 1912

SAWYER
- Marcia C[ANTWELL?]. - b. 1948; d. 1976

SCAMMON
- Edgar E. [son of Mary B.?] - b. 1910; d. 1978
- John R. - b. 26 February 1924; d. 18 January 1943
- Mary B. - b. 29 February 1884; d. 6 September 1943

SEAVEY
- Agatha C. [wife of Arthur L.] - b. 1905; d. 1976
- Arthur L. [husb. of Agatha C.] - b. 1907; d. 1982
- Kathleen L. (TREVITT) - b. 26 April 1945; d. 27 May 1996

SENAY
- Isabelle L. - b. 1892; d. 1957

SHEEHAN
- Albert Thomas [husb. of Mary R.] - b. 1889; d. 1954
- Mary R. [wife of Albert Thomas] - b. 1891; d. 1973

SIGLIN
- [Ruth A. - see DAUGHERTY]

SILK
- Bridget E. (WHALEN; wife of John W.) - b. 1859; d. 1932
- Catherine K. - b. 1878; d. 1957
- Clarence M. (son of John W. and Bridget E. (WHALEN); husb. of Shirley L. (DODGE)) - b. 1898; d. 1922
- Clarence W. - b. 1928; d. 1993

[Ella M. - see LELAND]
Hiram N. - b. 1894; d. 1973
J. Walter (son of John W. and Bridget E. (WHALEN)) - b. 1888; d. 1922
John W. (husb. of Bridget E. (WHALEN)) - b. 1859; d. 1940
John W. Jr. - b. 1884; d. 1960
[Madeleine [sic] - see DOYLE]
Mae W. - b. 1896; d. 1993
[Margaret - see SMITH]
Shirley L. (DODGE; wife of Clarence M.) - b. 1899; d. 1922

SMALL
Agnes A. (wife of Frederick L.) - b. 1901; d. 1976
Agnes M. (dau. of Frederick L. and Agnes A.) - [b. and d.?] 1932
Frederick C. (husb. of Mary Agnes) - b. 1869; d. 1941
Frederick L. (husb. of Agnes A.) - b. 1901; d. 1967
[Helen - see HALL]
Mary Agnes (wife of Frederick C.) - b. 1863; d. 1940

SMITH
Catherine [wife of Harry] - b. 1 December 1925
Edward M. - b. 1912; d. 1987
Elizabeth M. (SANER; wife of John J.) - b. 1906; d. 1940
Ethel M. (wife of John J.) - b. 1894; d. 1979
"father" - b. 1866; d. 1947
Florence M. [wife of Robert T.] - b. 1925
Harry [husb. of Catherine] - b. 5 August 1920; d. 27 June 1979
James Francis - b. 1 May 1901; d. 1 November 1967
John J. (husb. of Elizabeth M. (SANER) and Ethel M.) - b. 1902; d. 1980
Margaret (SILK; wife of W. Henry Sr.) - b. 1919
Mark T. - b. 1954; d. 1993
Matthew T. - b. 1965; d. 1994
"mother" - b. 1871; d. 1960
Paul V. - b. 1908; d. 1953
Robert T. [husb. of Florence M.] - b. 1925; d. 1983
W. Henry Sr. (husb. of Margaret (SILK)) - b. 1917

SPRAGUE
Adelbert (Dr.; husb. of Marguerite S.) - b. 1907; d. 1961
Marguerite S. (wife of Dr. Adelbert) - b. 1900; d. 1978

SPURLING
Donald J. - b. 1915; d. 1962
Mary T. - b. 187[0 or 3?][2]; d. 1955

STRONG
Katharine (sister of Mary) - d. 10 August 1947 Æ [not given]
Mary (sister of Katharine) - d. 15 August 1948 Æ [not given]

STROUT
Barbara J. [wife of Christopher J.] - b. 1963; d. 1994
Christopher J. [husb. of Barbara J.] - b. 1967
Lewis J. - [b. and d.?] 24 January 1953

SULLIVAN
James P. - b. 1872; d. 1934
John - b. 1865; d. 1930
[Mary L. - see LYNCH]

SWAZEY
Agnes J. - b. 1927

TOBIN
  Marguerite (dau. of Patrick F. and Veronica G. [no stones]) - b. 1915; d. 1917
TREVETT [includes TREVITT]
  Alice M. [wife of Henry A.] - b. 1910; d. 1968
  Henry A. [husb. of Alice M.] - b. 1907; d. 1959
  [Kathleen L. - see SEAVEY]
TRIPP
  Constance M. [wife of Ronald Douglas] - b. 5 August 1937
  Ronald Douglas [husb. of Constance M.] - b. 21 July 1932; d. 12 July 1965
TROPPMANN
  Margaret - [d.?] 7 October 1918
TURNBULL
  Mary C. (wife of Charles A. [no stone]) - b. 1890; d. 1924
  Sheila (dau. of Charles A. [no stone] and Mary C.) - d. 21 February 1932 Æ [not given]
VERMOT
  Louis - [d.?] 31 July 1919
WALTER
  Clementine - b. 1881; d. 1967
WEBBER
  Martin V. (husb. of Rose E.) - b. 1877; d. 1952
  Rose E. (wife of Martin V.) - b. 1887; d. 1939
WHALEN
  [Bridget E. - see SILK]
WICHELHAUSEN
  Otto Wolfgang [husb. of Ruth Hechler] - b. 1904; d. 1939
  Ruth Hechler [wife of Otto Wolfgang] - b. 1908; d. 1996
WILLEY
  Harry H. [husb. of Theresa K.] - b. 1880; d. 1959
  Theresa K. [wife of Harry H.] - b. 1880; d. 1965
WRIGHT
  James [husb. of Lucy M.] - b. 1886; d. 1973
  Lucy M. [wife of James] - b. 1895; d. 1962
YOUNG
  Merrill J. - b. 1878; d. 1952
ZULA
  Julia C. - d. 15 September 1965 Æ [not given]
  Marion I. - d. 18 April 1992 Æ [not given]
  Samuel S. - d. 10 July 1952 Æ [not given]
[...]
  [...]head[3]

Notes:
  [1]Variable spelling found on stones.
  [2]Different on different stones.
  [3]Information on metal marker faded.

Peach Cemetery
(Bar Harbor - 13)

Location/directions. Set back from west side of Norway Drive. From the traffic light at the north end of Mount Desert Island, bear left on Route 3. In approximately 4.6–4.7 miles, turn right onto Norway Drive. Travel 1.2–1.3 miles to a stop sign at the intersection of Norway Drive and Crooked Road. Continue straight on Norway Drive for another 1.2–1.3 miles to the intersection with Old Norway Drive (on the left). Across the road from this intersection is a one-story house with detached garage. The cemetery, somewhat obscured from sight, is to the right of the garage.

History. —

Notes. This cemetery is enclosed by a gated chain-link fence and is well maintained by a neighboring land owner.

Names and dates on gravestones and other markers. [19 October 1999]

BREWER
- Daniel P. [husb. of Eleanor M.] - b. 1879; d. 1960
- Eleanor M. [wife of Daniel P.] - b. 1899; d. 1988

GRAY
- Hattie E. (dau. of Adelbert and Lolia E. [no stones]) - b. 31 December 1875; d. 30 August 1893

LISCOMB
- [Mary - see PEACH]

MITCHELL
- Alphonso (husb. of May N.) - b. 1854; d. 1933
- Hattie (dau. of Alphonso and May N.) - b. 1905; d. 1905
- Lena B. [wife of Theodore R.] - b. 1906; d. 1997
- Lottie A. (dau. of George B. and Peninah A. [no stones]) - d. 26 July 1889 Æ 13 y., 5 m.
- May N. (wife of Alphonso) - b. 1872; d. 1918
- Nelson S. - b. 21 August 1889; d. 20 March 1965
- Theodore R. [husb. of Lena B.] - b. 1902; d. 1984

PEACH
- Albert C. (son of John and Mary (LISCOMB)) - d. 2 September 1862, Oil City, "P. A", Æ 20 y.; [Civil War?]
- Christopher B. (son of John and Mary (LISCOMB)) - d. 23 December 1845 Æ 9 y.
- George W. (son of John and Mary (LISCOMB)) - d. 21 March 1867, St. John's, N. B., Æ 2[6?][1] y.
- John (husb. of Mary (LISCOMB)) - d. 23 June 1900 Æ 87 y., 10 m., 11 d.
- John H. (son of John and Mary (LISCOMB)) - d. 26 November 1862, "Fort [B?]aines[1] D. C.", Æ 22 y.; [Civil War?]
- Mary (LISCOMB; wife of John) - d. 10 December 1896 Æ 86 y., 9 m., 4 d.
- Mary E. (dau. of John and Mary (LISCOMB)) - d. 14 November 1849 Æ 2 y.

SCHMITT
- Chelsea Louise - d. 30 December 1987

[...]
- infant - [b. and?] d. 1929
- [...][2]

Notes:
[1]Difficult to read. [2]Base of stone only.

Deacon Oliver's Cemetery
(Bar Harbor - 14)

Location/directions. Blagden Preserve, Indian Point. From the traffic light at the north end of Mount Desert Island, go straight ahead (south) onto Routes 102/198. In approximately 1.9 miles, turn right onto Indian Point Road. Travel on this road another 1.9 miles to a road on the right. Look for signs (2000) on a large tree indicating "Indian Point" and "The Nature Conservancy". Turn right onto this road, and park in the lot on the left. The sign "private road/residents only" applies to vehicles. A narrow trail leading to the cemetery is less than 0.4 miles up this road on the right.

History. —

Notes. The cemetery is enclosed by rope suspended between wood posts, with rope absent between one pair of adjacent posts to provide an entrance/exit. It is maintained by descendants of Deacon Oliver Higgins.

Names and dates on gravestones and other markers. [23 April 1999]

BURBANK
Emeline (HIGGINS; dau. of S[y or i]lvanus[1] [no stone] HIGGINS and Abigail K.) - d. 5 October 1863 Æ 26 y., 7 m.

HERLIHY
Belle - b. 1864; d. 1953
D. Walker - d. 26 August 1929 Æ 38 y., 2 m., 27 d.

HIGGINS
Abby B. (wife of Willard C.) - d. 27 January 1924 Æ 96 y., 11 m., 27 d.
Abigail K. (wife of S[y or i]lvanus[1] [no stone]) - d. 28 August 1856 Æ 50 y., 8 m.
Alexander H. (son of Willard C. and Abby B.) - d. 5 March 1863 Æ 2 y.
Alfonso (son of Oliver and Elizabeth [no stone]) - d. 6 October 1856 Æ 10 y., 9 m., 2 d.
Andrew J. (son of Deacon Oliver 2nd and Ruth) - d. 17 September 1838 Æ 21 y., 6 m.
Ellen (dau. of S[y or i]lvanus[1] [no stone] and Abigail K.) - d. 10 May 1848 Æ 2 y.
[Emeline - see BURBANK]
Harvey L. (son of Oliver and Elizabeth [no stone]) - d. 18 February 1881 Æ 16 y., 9 m., 28 d.; bur. Salem, N. H.
Howard P. (son of Oliver and Elizabeth [no stone]) - d. 20 November 1869 Æ 21 y., 6 m., 21 d.
infant (son of S[y or i]lvanus[1] [no stone] and Abigail K.) - [b. and?] d. 15 June 1842
infants (children of Oliver and Elizabeth [no stone]) - [no dates]
Julia J. (dau. of Willard C. and Abby B.) - d. 23 February 1863 Æ 4 y.
Julia S. (dau. of S[y or i]lvanus[1] [no stone] and Abigail K.) - d. 15 March 1863 Æ 30 y., 16 d.
Oliver (husb. of Elizabeth [no stone]) - d. 26 April 1898 Æ 77 y., 2 m., 17 d.
Oliver 2nd (Deacon; husb. of Ruth) - d. 6 February 1870 Æ 90 y.
Ruth (wife of Deacon Oliver 2nd) - d. 10 October 1849 Æ 67 y., 6 m.
Willard C. (husb. of Abby B.) - d. 20 March 1892 Æ 68 y., 1 m., 22 d.

Note:
[1]Different on different stones.

Hadley Cemetery
(Bar Harbor - 15)

Location/directions. South of Gilbert Farm Road, east of Red Rock Corner. From the traffic light at the north end of Mount Desert Island, go straight ahead (south) onto Routes 102/198. In approximately 1.6 miles on the left is the entrance to Spruce Valley Campground, on whose property the cemetery is located. Inquire at the office for permission to enter the campground and for directions to the cemetery.

History. —

Notes. This cemetery is in very poor condition. It is completely ignored and overgrown, with no discernable boundary markers. There are likely more stones here, either below ground or obscured by vegetation.

Names and dates on gravestones and other markers. [1 May 1999]
HADLEY
Amos T. (husb. of Esther) - d. 8 November 1889 Æ 86 y., 10 m., 3 d.
Edwin Eugene - b. 24 September 1877; d. 5 August 1923
[Esth]er (wife of [A]mo[s T.]) - [...][1]
John E. (husb. of Laura M.) - b. 27 August 1849; d. 26 January 1922
Laura M. (wife of John E.) - b. 9 April 1858; d. 16 January 1917
Marcia A. (dau. of Amos T. and Esther) - d. 24 May 1873 Æ 38 y., 11 m.
Mercy (wife of Simeon [no stone]) - d. 30 March 1841 Æ 64 y.
Solomon S. (son of Amos T. and Esther) - d. 1 January 1851 Æ 18 y.
Solomon [S.?][1] (son of Simeon [no stone] and Mercy) - [...][1]
[...][1]
HODGKINS
Israel L. (husb. of Huldah) - d. 24 November 1884 Æ 70 y.
Huldah (wife of Israel L.) - d. 10 February 1867 Æ 46 y.

Note:
[1]Stone worn, broken, and/or crumbling.

Thomas Cemetery
(Bar Harbor - 16)

Location/directions. Along northeast side of Bay View Drive, Eden. From the traffic light at the north end of Mount Desert Island, bear left on Route 3. In approximately 2.3–2.4 miles, turn left onto Bay View Drive. The cemetery is on the right in less than 0.1 miles.

History. The name applied to this cemetery is only for convenience of reference in this book.

Notes. The apparent boundary of the property that contains this cemetery is well marked with iron stakes. Within this boundary a new (2000) natural-wood fence has been erected. A space in the fence allows for entrance/exit. Most low, woody vegetation has been removed. A few stones are standing, but most are propped up or laying on the ground.

Names and dates on gravestones and other markers. [30 April 1999]
P.
B. [footstone only]
THOMAS
Abraham (Capt.; husb. of Jane) - d. 15 November 1838 Æ 53 y., 1 d.
Bancroft W. - d. 29 April 1878 Æ 57 y., 7 m.
George [H.?][1] (son of Nicholas J. and Nancy T. [no stones]) - d. 11 September 1846 Æ 8 m., 3 d.
Hannah (wife of Nicholas) - d. 20 May 1870 Æ 85 y.
Lafayette (son of Nicholas J. and Nancy T. [no stones]) - d. 4 April 1846 Æ [...][2]
Jane (wife of Capt. Abraham) - d. 15 January 1870 Æ 76 y.
Morton (son of Nicholas J. and Nancy T. [no stones]) - d. 27 January 1842 Æ 1 y., [3?][1] m., 6 d.
Nicholas (husb. of Hannah) - d. 18 October 1865 Æ 85 y., 5 m.
WASGATT
George B. (son of William N. and Mary [...][3] [no stones]) - d. 30 November 18[...][1] Æ 22 d.
John T. (husb. of Huldah [no stone]) - d. 22 May 1853 Æ 66 y.
Julia A. - d. 10 April 1836 Æ 13 y.; ("was interred at Deer Isle, New Brunswick")
Margaret J. D. (dau. of John T. and Huldah [no stone]) - d. 18 April 1849 Æ 19 y.

Notes:
[1]Difficult to read.
[2]Stone broken.
[3]Initial illegible.

Burn[e]s-Richardson Burial Ground

(Bar Harbor - 17)

Location/directions. Near Northwest Cove. From the traffic light at the north end of Mount Desert Island, go straight ahead (south) onto Routes 102/198. In approximately 1.9 miles, turn right onto Indian Point Road. About 1.2–1.3 miles from this turn is Fire Road #817 on the right. Approximately 0.1 miles in on this fire road, and just after the third telephone pole (the second pole on the right), turn left into the woods. The burial ground is about 100 feet from the fire road.

History. The name applied to this cemetery is only for convenience of reference in this book.

Notes. This cemetery is in very poor condition. It is completely overgrown and difficult to locate. In addition to the engraved stones are several natural stones, presumably also marking graves. A newly (1999) blazed/flagged boundary runs along the edge of the cemetery nearest Indian Point Road.

Names and dates on gravestones and other markers. [2 May 1999]

BURNES

George W. - d. 29 August 1887 Æ 22 y., 8 m., 29 d.

BURNS

Emma F. (dau. of William [no stone] and Martha) - d. 22 October 18[...][1] Æ 9 m.

Fostina F. (dau. of William [no stone] and Martha) - d. 28 February 1864 Æ 12 y., 1 m.

Martha (wife of William [no stone]) - d. 13 August 1880 Æ 64 y., 3 m., 14 d.

Walter N. (son of William [no stone] and Martha) - d. 15 January 1858 Æ 13 y., 5 m.

O.[2]

Sophronia W. (wife of [...][3]) - d. [4 or [...]4?][3] August 1859 Æ [2?][3]2 y.

RICHARDSON

Hannah R. (wife of Francis S. [no stone]) - d. 3 June 1848 Æ 30 y., 10 m.

Susan E. (dau. of Francis S. [no stone] and Hannah R.) - d. 15 November 1847 Æ 2 y., 5 m.

Notes:

[1]Stone blank.

[2]Footstone of Sophronia W. reads "S. W. O.".

[3]Stone broken.

Paine Cemetery
(Bar Harbor - 18)

Location/directions. At edge of field near woods, east of Norway Drive. From the traffic light at the north end of Mount Desert Island, bear left on Route 3. In approximately 4.6–4.7 miles, turn right onto Norway Drive. Travel 1.2–1.3 miles to a stop sign at the intersection of Norway Drive and Crooked Road. Continue straight on Norway Drive for about 0.2 miles to a private driveway on the left that leads (2000) to a gray house and small, detached barn (Blueberry Hill Farm). Inquire with the landowners for permission to visit the cemetery and for directions to it.

History. —

Notes. This cemetery is not enclosed and is not mowed.

Names and dates on gravestones and other markers. [2 August 1999]
MACKENZIE
Clara E. [wife of Daniel J.] - b. 1869; d. 1960
Daniel J. [husb. of Clara E.] - b. 1874; d. 1953
PAINE
Elizabeth C. "Lizzie" (wife of Theodore) - b. 1833; d. 1917
Jennie (dau. of Theodore and Elizabeth C. "Lizzie") - b. 30 January 1863; d. 29 August 1893
Olive (wife of Thomas) - d. 7 June 1885 Æ 84 y., 9 m.
Theodore (husb. of Elizabeth C. "Lizzie") - b. 1834; d. 1911
Thomas (husb. of Olive) - d. 25 March 1878 Æ 84 y., 6 m.
SCHMIDT-NIELSEN
Bodil Mimi - b. 1947; d. 1984

Schooner Head Cemetery (Bar Harbor - 19).

Schooner Head Cemetery
(Bar Harbor - 19)

Location/directions. Schooner Head. From the traffic light at the north end of Mount Desert Island, bear left on Route 3. Travel approximately 10.1 miles to a stop sign. Turn left onto Mount Desert Street (Route 3) and continue 0.4–0.5 miles to another stop sign. Turn right at this stop sign, following Route 3. In about 1.1–1.2 miles, bear left onto Schooner Head Road. Travel on Schooner Head Road 2.4–2.5 miles to a stop sign, and turn left. This leads to Schooner Head overlook. The cemetery can be seen with binoculars from this overlook. Facing the water, look to your left. The cemetery is toward the right portion of the cove formed by Schooner Head.

History. The name applied to this cemetery is only for convenience of reference in this book. A deed (1433:400ff.) from John S. Baer and Helen Sue Baer to D. M. Burt and M. T. Webster reserve for the Baers "and their descendants, a right of way for passage by foot only from the Schooner Head Road to the cemetery". The deed also states that Burt and Webster and "their heirs and assigns ... will not allow the cemetery to be used for any purpose other than as a burial ground" for the Baers and their descendants.

Notes. This cemetery is enclosed by a chain suspended between iron posts. Remains of an earlier iron fence are laying on the ground at the edge of the cemetery.

Names and dates on gravestones and other markers. [21 October 1999]

ALBY
  John - [no dates]; (member of Co. E, 28th Maine Regiment [Civil War])

BAER
  Juanita B. [wife of Roy S.] - b. 1886; d. 1977
  Roy S. [husb. of Juanita B.] - b. 1882; d. 1973

CLARK
  Mosses [sic] S. - d. 2 September 1850 Æ 40 y., 29 d.

LYNAM
  Hannah (wife of William) - d. 20 February 1851 Æ [...][1]
  William (husb. of Hannah) - b. 9 July 1795, Eden; d. 14 April 1857 Æ 61 y., 9 m., 5 d.

VAUGHAN
  Harry [husb. of Helen J.] - b. 1899; d. 1978
  Helen J. [wife of Harry] - b. 1903; d. 1983

[...]
  [...][2]
  [...][3]

Notes:
[1]Remainder of stone is in concrete, thereby obscuring any further information it may contain.
[2]Stone broken just above ground surface.
[3]Stone blank.

Ledgelawn Cemetery
(Bar Harbor - 20)

Location/directions. Along south side of Cromwell Harbor Road. From the traffic light at the north end of Mount Desert Island, bear left on Route 3. Travel approximately 10.1 miles to a stop sign. Go straight ahead onto Kebo Street for about 0.5–0.6 miles to a stop sign. Turn left onto Cromwell Harbor Road (no sign), and the cemetery is on the right in approximately 0.2–0.3 miles.

History. —

Notes. This cemetery is well maintained, and there is water available. A stone found behind a large rock at the back of a "turn around" near the maintenance building bears the name of Percy (son of [H?][1]. [C?][1]. and [...][1] J. Paine) - d. 10 [...][1] 18[0 or 9?]8[1] Æ 2 m.

Names and dates on gravestones and other markers. [29 May 1999]

A.
M. M. - [no dates]

ADAIR
James D. - d. 26 February 1919 Æ 66 y.

ADAMS
Edith M. - b. 1889; d. 1968

ADLER
David Lee - b. 1974; d. 1979
Harry - b. 1893; d. 1969
J. Paul - b. 1939; d. 1964

AGNESE
Ann Marie [wife of J. L. "Henri"] - b. 1908; d. 1998
J. L. "Henri" [husb. of Ann Marie] - b. 1904; d. 1990
Patricia Lynn - b. 1965; d. 1965

AHLBLAD
[...] [headstone only]

ALBEE
Arthur E. [husb. of Mattie?] - b. 1857; d. 1914
Mattie [wife of Arthur E.?] - b. 1857; d. 1925
Roy E. [son of Arthur E. and Mattie?] - b. 1888; d. 1937

ALLEN
Anna E. (wife of J. Milton [no stone]) - b. 1861; d. 1918
Berkeley LeV. (husb. of Edith (SALISBURY)) - b. 1859; d. 1934
Charles F. - b. 1858; d. 1931
Clara[15] - [no dates]
Edith (SALISBURY; wife of Berkeley LeV.) - b. 1883; d. 1963
George S. [husb. of Kathleen F. CROWLEY [name of 1st husb.]] - b. 1929
Gerald P. [husb. of Suzanne C.] - b. 1935
[Gladys A[LLEN?]. - see JORDAN]
Kathleen F. [CROWLEY [name of 1st husb.]; [wife of George S.]] - b. 1911; d. 1994
Lena R. - b. 1861; d. 1942
Lera E. - b. 7 May 1888; d. 29 February 1904
Suzanne C. [wife of Gerald P.] - b. 1938; d. 1985
William - [no dates]

ALLEY
Albion P. [husb. of Linnie G.] - b. 1861; d. 1918

Annette H. [wife of Frank O.] - b. 1894; d. 1967
Dalton E. - b. 17 July 1923; d. 1 September 1992
Everard D. - b. 1879; d. 1941
Frank O. - b. 1856; d. 1929
Frank O. [husb. of Annette H.] - b. 1895; d. 1969
Gerard F. (husb. of Vivien [sic] H.) - b. 12 July 1894; d. 4 September 1959
J. Winfield - b. 1883; d. 1923
Leona I. - b. 1913; d. 1941
Linnie G. [wife of Albion P.] - b. 1856; d. 1937
[Lucy - see YOUNG]
Maud - b. 1883; d. 1942
Sarah Adell - b. 1850; d. 1926
Sophia H. - b. 22 October 1832; d. 1 June 1910
Vivien [sic] H. (wife of Gerard F.) - b. 1894; d. 1958

AMES
Peter Grant - b. 4 May 1946; d. 26 September 1995
[...] [headstone only]

ANDRADE
Ruth K. [HIGGINS?; dau. of Harry E. HIGGINS and Etta T.?] - b. 1917; d. 1985

ANDREWS
Mina A. [wife of N. Bert] - b. 1865; d. 19[...][4]
N. Bert [husb. of Mina A.] - b. 1863; d. 1935

ANTHONY
Effie A. [wife of J. Franklin] - b. 1876; d. 1967
Ethel L. [wife of Franklin Jr.] - b. 1908; d. 1982
Franklin Jr. [husb. of Ethel L.] - b. 1906; d. 1984
J. Franklin [husb. of Effie A.] - b. 1876; d. 1944
John M. - b. 1932; d. 1983

ASH
Almira S. - b. 1841; d. 1925
Ethel M. [dau. of Orlando and Rachel Maria?] - b. 6 July 1886; d. 25 November 1890
G. [ASH?] - [no dates]
John E. [husb. of Shirley J.] - b. 22 August 1890; d. 4 September 1953
[Mamie - see EMERY]
Nathan (husb. of Sarah) - b. 1852; d. 1920
Orlando (husb. of Rachel Maria) - b. 1843; d. 1931
Rachel Maria (wife of Orlando) - b. 1854; d. 1924
Sarah (wife of Nathan) - b. 1852; d. 1933
Shirley J. [wife of John E.] - b. 9 July 1896; d. 25 March 1978

ASHTON
Charlotte (GOOCH) - b. 1919; d. 1991

ATCHERSON
Georgia A. (wife of John N.) - b. 1851; d. 1937
John N. (husb. of Georgia A.) - b. 1851; d. 1936

AUSTIN
Gerard L. [husb. of Vera G.?] - b. 1904; d. 1963
Hattie B. (wife of Leonard A.) - b. 1867; d. 1955
Leonard A. (husb. of Hattie B.) - b. 1867; d. 1930
Sylvia B. - b. 1889; d. 1967
Vera G. [wife of Gerard L.?] - b. 1912; d. 1997
Virginia D. (wife of William B.) - b. 1855; d. 1910

William B. (husb. of Virginia D.) - b. 1843; d. 1914
AVERY
Ann B. [wife of Robert H.] - b. 16 July 1928
Robert H. [husb. of Ann B.] - b. 13 February 1928; d. 20 August 1996
AYER
Robert McCormick - b. 23 September 1910; d. 23 January 1992
BABB
Alice Elena - b. 1881; d. 1917
BAKER
Blanche S. - b. 1886; d. 1949
Dorothea H. [wife of James J.] - b. 1909; d. 1996
[Emily A. [BAKER?] - see STANLEY]
James - b. 1873; d. 1925
James J. [husb. of Dorothea H.] - b. 1911; d. 1974
[Nettie - see SMITH]
BALDWIN
Sarah Sherburne - b. 5 April 1920; d. 2 January 1997
BANCROFT
Laura E. - [no dates]
BARKER
G. Ollie - b. 1921; d. 1991
BARNES
Elizabeth S. - b. 15 August 1898; d. 14 February 1981
BARRETT
Angie Grace - b. 18 October 1869; d. 20 July 1915
Edna M. - b. 1890; d. 1966
Maryhelen [sic] - b. 25 March 1940; d. 23 May 1982
BARROWS
Frank E. - b. 1874; d. 1937
BARSTOW
Alice E. (dau. of Oscar and Edna [no stones]) - d. 12 June 1911 Æ 1 y., 3 m., 18 d.
BATCHELDER
Eleanor R. (wife of Harold E.) - b. 1924; m. 19 August 1967
Harold E. (husb. of Eleanor R.) - b. 1929; m. 19 August 1967; d. 1998
BEALE
Harriet (BLAINE) - b. 29 October 1871, Augusta, Maine; d. 28 January 1958, New York
BEAN
Shirley M. - b. 9 March 1905; d. 7 January 1986
BEATON
Finley C. (husb. of Ruxpy E. (CANNING)) - b. 1849; d. [no date]
[Myrtle Ona - see HARDEN]
Norman F. - b. 1882; d. 1936
Ruxpy E. (CANNING; wife of Finley C.) - b. 1851; d. 1919
[Sarah - see SMITH]
BECK
Charles A. [husb. of Mary R.] - b. 1903; d. 1968
Mary R. [wife of Charles A.] - b. 1907; d. 1976
BENNETT [headstone: "BENNETT/MOKLER"]
Deborah - [no dates]
Florence - [no dates]
Jesalyn - [no dates]

Richard - [no dates]
BENSON
Jordan B. (Capt.) - b. 1888; d. 1945
BERNARDINI
Alma M. - b. 1886; d. 1954
James E. "Jimmie" - b. 1906; d. 1944
James J. - b. 1879; d. 1950
Minnie - b. 1876; d. 1905
BERRY
Arthur Newman [husb. of Marion (DRASHER)] - b. 1923
George F. - b. 1878; d. 1962
Henry C. - b. 1883; d. 1961
Louise N[EWMAN?]. - b. 1890; d. 1969
Marion (DRASHER; [wife of Arthur Newman]) - b. 1924
BESSEY
[Ruth A. - see CONTI]
BILLINGS
Elsie M. (wife of Earl [no stone]) - b. 1902; d. 1975
BIRCH
Lucy M[URPHY?]. [wife of Pearley [sic] D.] - b. 1891; d. 1973
Pearley [sic] D. [husb. of Lucy M[URPHY?].] - b. 1889; d. 1948
BISHOP
Harry [husb. of Isabel C.] - b. 1902; d. 1945
Isabel C. [wife of Harry] - b. 1911
BLACK
Lawrence W. [husb. of Myra J.] - b. 29 March 1914; d. 7 November 1994
Myra J. [wife of Lawrence W.] - b. 1927; d. 1975
BLAINE
[Harriet - see BEALE]
[Margaret - see DAMROSCH]
BLAISDELL
Anita R. [wife of Donald] - b. 9 October 1921
Donald [husb. of Anita R.] - b. 3 June 1919; d. 3 February 1988
BLAKE
Roy G. - b. 1899; d. 1987
Gene N. - b. 1909; d. 1979
BLOMQUIST
Jacqulyn [sic] (TRIPP) - b. 1930; d. 1977
Susan E. (dau. of Jacqulyn [sic] (TRIPP)) - b. 1959; d. 1988
BOUNAB
Joseph A. K. - b. 1875; d. 1931
BOWDEN
Jerusha A. [wife of Nathaniel F.] - b. 1837; d. 1911
Nathaniel F. [husb. of Jerusha A.] - b. 1837; d. 1911
BOYNTON
Lanie (SMALL) - b. 1 September 1953; d. 30 May 1998
[Marjorie L. - see HATT]
BRADY
[Mary - see DRAYTON]
BRAGDON
Carlyle A. - b. 1900; d. 1964
Edith Y. (wife of Henry J.) - b. 1876; d. 1936

Henry J. (husb. of Edith Y.) - b. 1854; d. 1927
Sarah E. - b. 1903; d. 1982

BRAY
Ackley N. (husb. of Cora E.) - b. 1860; d. 1926
Cora E. (wife of Ackley N.) - b. 1871; d. 1960
James L. - b. 19 January 1859; d. 5 October 1939
Lizzie N. - b. 12 June 1850; d. 8 February 1919
Marcia E. (dau. of Ackley N. and Cora E.) - d. 31 March 1904 Æ 5 y., 2 m.
Rebecca H. - b. 14 April 1832; d. 24 May 1907

BREEZE
Benjamin L. [husb. of Ethelyn M.] - b. 1905; d. 1984
Ethelyn M. [wife of Benjamin L.] - b. 1911

BRENTON
Elinor C[LEAVES?]. - b. 1915; d. 1975

BREWER
Agnes B. [wife of Irving L.] - b. 1881; d. 1959
Bernice - b. 1876; d. 1928
Harold G. - b. 1881; d. 1952
Irving L. [husb. of Agnes B.] - b. 1882; d. 1966
Lizzie L. (wife of [Loren or Loring][3] F.) - b. 1 October 1853; d. 18 November 1912
[Loren or Loring][3] F. (husb. of Lizzie L.) - b. 7 April 1853; d. [no date]
Vivian H. (dau. of [Loren or Loring][3] F. and Lizzie L.) - d. 13 May 1905 Æ 27 y., 9 m., 13 d.

BRIDGHAM
Carl E. [husb. of Florence M.] - b. 1900; d. 1970
Florence M. [wife of Carl E.] - b. 1900; d. 1975

BRIMMEKAMP
[Inge Charlotte - see WEBER]

BRODMANN
Marie ("of Konstanz Germany") - d. 6 September 1907 Æ 37 y.

BROKAW
[Elvira - see NcNAIR]

BROWN
Abbie N. [wife of Sewall W.] - b. 1903; d. 1994
Edward Daly - b. 1899; d. 1962
Sewall W. [husb. of Abbie N.] - b. 1903; d. 1992

BRUCE
D. Ann - [no dates]
Dorothy H. - b. 1908
G. Gordon - b. 1911

BRYANT
Danny Everett - b. 26 October 1942

BUCKLEY
Rea - b. 1894; d. 1955

BUDLONG
Smythe U. - b. 13 July 1925; d. 14 March 1987

BUFF
F. Stanley - b. 1909; d. 1972

BULGER
Henry F. - d. 16 November 1908 Æ 23 y., 6 m., 2 d.

BUNKER
[Alice - see DOWD]

Carolyn (DODGE; wife of John E.) - b. 1 April 1872; d. 24 November 1911
Cecil G. - b. 1910; d. 1976
[Corinne B[UNKER?]. - see SARGENT]
Euna Rich (SANFORD; dau. of George A. SANFORD and Mary Emma (MOOERS) [no stones]; wife of Maj. Stephen Sans) - b. 28 December 1877; d. 18 December 1963
Helen P. [wife of Lester E.] - b. 25 May 1924; d. 27 July 1997
[Jane - see PEACH]
Jeannette (HIGGINS; dau. of Stephen HIGGINS and Ann M. [no stones]; wife of David Albion [no stone]) - b. 24 April 1846; d. 15 January 1936
John E. (husb. of Carolyn (DODGE)) - b. 24 April 1866; d. 16 August 1918
Lena M. [wife of Ralph M.] - b. 23 April 1889; d. 13 February 1979
Lester E. [husb. of Helen P.] - b. 22 August 1914
[Marie Agnes - see HALL]
Mary (LAWRENCE; dau. of John H. LAWRENCE and Catherine (McHUGH) [no stones]; wife of Paul Sanford) - b. 13 December 1908; d. 27 June 1983
Maurice A. - b. 1899; d. 1961
Paul Sanford (son of Maj. Stephen Sans and Euna Rich (SANFORD); husb. of Mary (LAWRENCE)) - b. 26 August 1906; d. 7 July 1965
Ralph M. [husb. of Lena M.] - b. 9 July 1885; d. 8 May 1961
[Ruth - see ROHRBAUGH]
Ruth S[TAFFORD?]. - b. 1897; d. 1990
Shirley H. - b. 1885; d. 1958
Stephen Sans (Maj.; son of David Albion [no stone] and Jeannette (HIGGINS); husb. of Euna Rich (SANFORD)) - b. 1876; d. 1928

BUNTING
Kate Nowell - b. 1954; d. 1996

BURBANK
Bernice H[ARDEN?]. - b. 1875; d. 1941

BURNELL
Adam Edward - stillborn 26 June 1991

BURNS
Hilma H[AYWARD?]. - b. 21 December 1906; d. 21 March 1988
Mildred L. - b. 1950; d. 1998

BURR
Jane G. - b. 1880; d. 1956
Karl H. [husb. of Lydia A.] - b. 1866; d. 1944
Lydia A. [wife of Karl H.] - b. 1871; d. 1952

BURT
Robert H. - b. 1893; d. 1938

BURTON
Carrie G. [wife of William T.] - b. 1867; d. 1943
Doris V. - b. 1900; d. 1914
Florence I. - b. 1901; d. 1968
[Helen B[URTON?]. - see REHLANDER]
Louis R. (husb. of Marthe [sic] V.) - b. 1894; d. 1930
Marthe [sic] V. (wife of Louis R.) - b. 1894; d. 1971
William T. [husb. of Carrie G.] - b. 1869; d. 1954

BUTLER
Effie (Mrs.) - b. 1887; d. 1960
Everett H. [husb. of Margaret R.] - b. 1925
Margaret R. [wife of Everett H.] - b. 1912; d. 1986

BUTTERFIELD
[Geraldine B[UTTERFIELD?]. - see CLEAVES]
John H. (husb. of Sara [sic] A.) - b. 1873; d. 1954
[Nancy B[UTTERFIELD?]. - see THATCHER]
Sara [sic] A. (wife of John H.) - b. 1871; d. 1924
BYARD
Christine R. - b. 1890; d. 1972
Roy T. - b. 1892; d. 1958
William Ross - b. 1884; d. 1965
C.
G. E. - [no dates]
CAHILL
Joseph Henry - b. 27 December 1912; d. 29 May 1988
CAME
Carrie S. - b. 1891; d. 1956
Clifford F. - b. 1878; d. 1966
CAMP
[Ona - see EMERY]
CAMPBELL
Charlotte M. - b. 6 April 1926; d. 28 December 1926
Gretna - b. 1922; d. 1987
Phebe M. - b. 12 March 1892; d. 29 July 1986
William B. - b. 10 August 1892; d. 4 June 1950
CANNING
[Ruxpy E. - see BEATON]
CARD
Beatrice M. (wife of Harry M.) - b. 16 April 1923; d. 20 April 1996
Harry M. (husb. of Beatrice M.) - b. 1 March 1907; d. 1 January 1974
Katherine M. - b. 19 June 1902; d. 9 February 1966
CARLSON
Sigrid - b. 1888; d. 1967
CARPENTER
Phoebe S. - b. 1888; d. 1939
CARR
[Beverly - see SINCLAIR]
Ida M. - b. 23 February 1895; d. 6 December 1989
James (husb. of Sarah Cail) - b. 1865; d. 1921
Sarah Cail (wife of James) - b. 1859; d. 1909
sisters [CARR?] - [no dates]
CARROLL
Eva F. - b. 1857; d. 1933
Frank S. [CARROLL?] - b. 28 December 1899; d. 2 October 1934
Isabelle - b. 1863; d. 1913
Ralph A. - b. 16 March 1893; d. 21 March 1907
Temple C. [CARROLL?] - b. 14 September 1861; d. 12 February 1934
CARSWELL
William A. [husb. of Williamena K.] - b. 7 June 1878; d. 26 February 1965
Williamena K. [wife of William A.] - b. 6 May 1882; d. 14 September 1958
CARTER
Alden A. (husb. of Alice J.) - b. 1878; d. 1935
Aletta Y. - b. 1880; d. 1957
Alice J. (wife of Alden A.) - b. 1883; d. 1953

Alton E. - b. 1879; d. 1950
Alton R. - b. 1906; d. 1956
Avis M. (wife of Clyde Allen) - b. 1912; d. 1991
Clyde Allen (husb. of Avis M.) - b. 1907; d. 1988
Eben B. [husb. of Gertrude E.] - b. 1882; d. 1918
Edith - b. 1882; d. 1971
Elizabeth F. - b. 1877; d. 1933
[Florence - see JOHNSTON]
Florence H. - b. 1879; d. 1956
Fred L. (husb. of Helen L. (JOHNSON)) - b. 1874; d. 1945
Gerald - b. 1908; d. 1946
Gertrude E. [wife of Eben B.] - b. 1881; d. 1916
Harlan E. [husb. of Shirley J.] - b. 1922
Harold F. - b. 1877; d. 1956
[Helen - see GUPTILL]
Helen L. (JOHNSON; wife of Fred L.) - b. 1888; d. 1990
infant (son of Fred L. and Helen L. (JOHNSON)) - [b. and d.?] 18 September 1923
Jane L. (HARRIS) - b. 29 April 1938
Madalene C. - b. 1899; d. 1977
Maurice E. - b. 1911; d. 1982
[Onnolee C[ARTER?]. - see DOW]
Shirley J. [wife of Harlan E.] - b. 1922; d. 1988
Virginia A. - b. 1917; d. 1988

CASEY
Andrew C. - b. 1872; d. 1937

CHAPMAN
John S. [husb. of Marion S.] - b. 1915
Joseph K. - b. 1916; d. 1936
Marion S. [wife of John S.] - b. 1912; d. 1990
Robert - b. 1930; d. 1993

CHASE
[Lillian - see PROCTOR]
[Mary L. - see HADLEY]

CHILMAN
Arthur E. (husb. of Margaret C.) - b. 1872; d. 1954
Arthur Lester [husb. of Phyllis (TYLER)] - b. 7 August 1909
C. William - b. 1914; d. 1977
Margaret C. (wife of Arthur E.) - b. 1882; d. 1931
Oliver E. - b. 1905; d. 1980
Phyllis (TYLER; [wife of Arthur Lester]) - b. 21 July 1908

CHUDOBA
[Sally Ann - see FOX]

CHURCHILL
[Nellie - see HIGGINS]

CIRARD
Peter C. - b. 1 May 1921; d. 5 October 1963

CLARK
Bertrand E. - b. 1865; d. 1927
Bessie J. - b. 1878; d. [no date]
[Edith (FABBRI) - see MILLIKEN]
Edith R. (wife of Randolph V.) - b. 10 October 1913; d. 12 January 1982
Julia D. [wife of William E.] - b. 1854; d. 1919

Randolph V. (husb. of Edith R.) - b. 29 June 1915; d. 28 September 1980
Rowena O. - b. 16 November 1929; d. 19 November 1929
William E. [husb. of Julia D.] - b. 1848; d. 1933

CLATWORTHY
Arthur T. - b. 1911; d. 1985
Flora S. - b. 1889; d. 1979
Florence (SEAVEY; [wife of Jack?]) - b. 1921; d. 1986
Jack [husb. of Florence (SEAVEY)?] - b. 1915; d. 1989
William Sr. - b. 1884; d. 1970

CLEAVES
Adelaide E. - b. 1913; d. 1996
Alice Edna - b. 1860; d. 1931
Alonzo W. (husb. of Nancy E. (FOSTER)) - b. 1871; d. 1948
Carl Schurz [husb. of Catharene [sic] (MACLEOD)] - b. 1887; d. 1942
Catharene [sic] (MACLEOD; [wife of Carl Schurz]) - b. 1891; d. 1967
Edwin L. [husb. of Rose H.] - b. 1907; d. 1955
[Elinor C[LEAVES?]. - see BRENTON]
Elmer M. [husb. of Hazel R.] - b. 1884; d. 1957
Elnora (dau. of Alonzo W. and Nancy E. (FOSTER)) - d. 1906 Æ 2 m.
Florence (GARDNER; [wife of William L.]) - b. 1892; d. 1916
G. Prescott - b. 1867; d. 1948
George M. - b. 1877; d. 1953
George M. Jr. - b. 1911
Geraldine B[UTTERFIELD?]. (wife of Haskell H.) - b. 1902; d. 1961
Haskell H. (husb. of Geraldine B[UTTERFIELD?].) - b. 1902; d. 1980
Hazel R. [wife of Elmer M.] - b. 1892; d. 1983
Henry F. - b. 1909; d. 1954
Isabel R. - b. 1874; d. 1976
Jeanne Schell - b. 1905; d. 1954
Lora (HADLEY) - b. 1875; d. 1943
Nancy E. (FOSTER; wife of Alonzo W.) - b. 1874; d. 1939
Olive Julia - b. 1894; d. 1951
Rose H. [wife of Edwin L.] - b. 1908; d. 1991
Ruth H. - b. 1916; d. 1986
Sarah C. - b. 1951
William L. [husb. of Florence (GARDNER)] - b. 1891; d. 1966

CLEMMANS
[Edith H. F. - see FRITZ]

CLEMONS
Charlotte N. - b. 1925; d. 1976
[Deborah A. - see CLEMONS-MILLER]
Leroy Jr. - b. 1948; d. 1968

CLEMONS-MILLER
Deborah A. - b. 1951; d. 1988

COFFRON
Forest [sic] H. [husb. of Mabel A.] - b. 1889; d. 1971
Mabel A. [wife of Forest [sic] H.] - b. 1898; d. 1962
Royce - b. 1876; d. 1944

COLBY
Annie M. [wife of Stanley P.] - b. 1931
Stanley P. [husb. of Annie M.] - b. 1925; d. 1998

COLE
Allen E. - b. 1915; d. 1996
[Florence M. - see THOMPSON]
COLLIER
Esther H. [wife of Harold L.] - b. 22 April 1924
Harold L. [husb. of Esther H.] - b. 12 January 1924; d. 27 January 1979
Sargent Francis - b. 1900; d. 1968
COLLINS
Abbie L. (JORDAN; wife of William H.) - b. 1873; d. 1909
Elizabeth M. (NORTON; wife of William H.) - b. 1873; d. 1937
[Emma - see WOOD]
Harry C. - b. 1893; d. 1944
William H. (husb. of Abbie L. (JORDAN) and Elizabeth M. (NORTON)) - b. 1874; d. [no date]
COLLINS-GAY
Pauline E. - b. 2 April 1901; d. 1 September 1995
COLSON
Brenda I. [dau. of Ralph E. and Lucy O.?] - b. 7 April 1946; d. 27 October 1957
Harris H. Jr. - b. 1930; d. 1934
Lucy O. [wife of Ralph E.] - b. 22 March 1913; d. 23 January 1998
Ralph E. [husb. of Lucy O.] - b. 14 September 1901; d. 10 December 1987
CONARY
[Gladys G. - see MURCH]
CONNERS
Alfred E. (husb. of Josephine M. (HUTCHINGS)) - b. 1841; d. 1917
Alice E. - b. 1876; d. 1959
Charles E. - b. 1864; d. 1947
Dora A. (wife of Horatio B.) - b. 1847; d. 1919
Earl F. (husb. of Evelyn G.) - b. 1895; d. 1962
Eleanor B. (wife of John W.) - b. 1848; d. 1929
Evelyn G. (wife of Earl F.) - b. 1903; d. 1927
Evelyn M. - b. 1901; d. 1986
F. M. (Capt.; husb. of Marion Louise) - b. 1838; d. 1911
[Francis [sic] Marion - see RICH]
Frank H. - b. 1874; d. 1944
Hervey A. - b. 1868; d. 1938
Horatio B. (husb. of Dora A.) - b. 1843; d. 1902
John W. (husb. of Eleanor B.) - b. 1849; d. 1916
Josephine M. (HUTCHINGS; wife of Alfred E.) - b. 1841; d. 1917
Leonora (HODGKINS) - b. 27 December 1872; d. 23 April 1905
Louise S. - b. 1899; d. 1937
Marion Louise (wife of Capt. F. M.) - b. 1844; d. 1901
Mary C. - b. 1874; d. 1949
[Minnie C[ONNERS?]. - see HODGKINS]
[mother [CONNERS?] - see KEISOR]
Richmond K. - b. 1878; d. 1902
Robert H. - b. 25 April 1900; d. 25 December 1917
CONTI
Armando John [husb. of Ruth A. (BESSEY)] - b. 1897; d. 1982
Janet G. [wife of John W.] - b. 1929
John W. [husb. of Janet G.] - b. 1931
Ruth A. (BESSEY; [wife of Armando John]) - b. 1899; d. 1989

CONWAY
Addie E. (wife of W. H. [no stone]) - b. 1851; d. 1926
COONEY
Frank C. B. - b. 9 May 1893; d. 10 December 1961
Merle T. - b. 1894; d. 1950
COOPER
Llewellyn W. (Dr.; [husb. of Pauline M[ACMACKIN?].]) - b. 1926
Lorin Elizabeth - b. 30 July 1980; d. 22 June 1999
Pauline M[ACMACKIN?]. ([dau. of Oletha M. (MACMACKIN)]; wife of Dr. Llewellyn W.) - b. 1925
COPP
Frederic C. [husb. of Georgia B.] - b. 1884; d. 1960
Georgia B. [wife of Frederic C.] - b. 1884; d. 1973
CORNISH
John - b. 29 December 1894; d. 15 August 1931
COUSINS
Bessie (PAINE) - b. 8 April 1883; d. 1 March 1965
Evie [wife of Fred A.] - b. 1890; d. 1967
Fred A. [husb. of Evie] - b. 1881; d. 1933
COWAN
Clarissa H. [wife of Robert W.] - b. 1907
Robert W. [husb. of Clarissa H.] - b. 1902; d. 1990
COWING
George C. - b. 1949; d. 1988
William Richard - b. 8 November 1920; d. 28 July 1990
COX
[...] [headstone only]
CRANE
[Helen F. - see NASON]
CROSMAN
Cora A. (wife of Richard P.) - b. 1879; d. 1917
Ivis C. [child of Richard P. and Cora A.?] - d. 1914 Æ 4 d.
Richard P. (husb. of Cora A.) - b. 1867; d. 19[...][4]
Roger L. [son of Richard P. and Cora A.?] - d. 1916 Æ 3 d.
CROWLEY
James (son of Kathleen F.) - b. 1948; d. 1989
[Kathleen F. - see ALLEN]
Paul (son of Kathleen F.) - b. 1946
CRUSE
Andrew William (Capt.; [husb. of Donna Virginia (DINES)]) - b. 1898; d. 1977
Donna Virginia (DINES; [wife of Capt. Andrew William]) - b. 1909; d. 1976
CUMMINGS
Lois B. (wife of Jerremiah [sic] J. [no stone]) - d. 24 May 1910 Æ 43 y.
CUNNINGHAM
Alice M. - [no dates]
Blanche V. - [no dates]
Celia [wife of Charles] - b. 1881; d. 1971
Charles [husb. of Celia] - b. 1879; d. 1951
[Clara E. - see JOHNSTON]
Frank (husb. of Lucy Ella) - b. 1852; d. 1937
Galen A. - [no dates]
[Hazel - see NOWACK]

Helen E. [dau. of Martha E. (WEBBER)?] - b. 1904; d. 1989
Ida (HOPKINS; wife of Willard E.) - b. 1851; d. 1919
James H. - b. 9 February 1915; d. 6 October 1966
Lucy Ella (wife of Frank) - b. 1868; d. 1927
Martha E. (WEBBER) - b. 1879; d. 1907
Ralph - b. 1916; d. 1996
Willard E. (husb. of Ida (HOPKINS)) - b. 1844; d. 1922
Willard M. - d. [no date] Æ 7 m.

CURTIS
Agnes M. (wife of Warren P.) - b. 1909; d. 1954
Marcia C. - b. 1906; d. 1988
Warren P. (husb. of Agnes M.) - b. 1908; d. 1957

CUSHMAN
Myrtle F. - b. 1876; d. 1919

CUSSONS
Benjamin M. (husb. of Lydia M.) - b. 1829; d. 1916; ("G. A. R." [Civil War])
Lydia M. (wife of Benjamin M.) - b. 1849; d. 1925

D.
F. C. - [no dates]

DAIGLE
Julia I. (wife of Daniel D. [no stone]) - b. 1852; d. 1931

DAMMEYER
Eva (YOUNG; [wife of Frederick A.]) - b. 1920
Frederick A. [husb. of Eva (YOUNG)] - b. 1916; d. 1987

DAMROSCH
[Alice - see KIAER]
[Gretchen - see FINLETTER]
Margaret (BLAINE; dau. of James Gillespie BLAINE and Harriet (STANWOOD) [no stones]; wife of Walter) - b. 28 April 1865, Augusta, Maine; d. 28 July 1949, Bar Harbor, Maine
Walter (husb. of Margaret (BLAINE)) - b. 30 January 1862, Breslau, Germany; d. 22 December 1950, New York

DANEY
Doris A. - b. 1908; d. 1995
Joseph V. - b. 1854; d. 1946
Lenner E. - b. 1874; d. 1964
Marilyn L. - b. 5 July 1928; d. 6 October 1929
Vincent A. - b. 1898; d. 1972

DASO
Edith M[EGQUIER?]. - b. 4 June 1881; d. 2 March 1976

DAVIS
Charles A. - b. 1858; d. 1935
Emma L. - b. 1881; d. 1968
[Florence - see YOUNG]
Gloria A. - b. 23 November 1932; d. 23 January 1996
Henry E. (husb. of Verlie B.) - b. 28 July 1904; d. 18 May 1954
James W. - b. 14 March 1866; d. 13 July 1942
Julia A. (REYNOLDS; dau. of Katherine M. REYNOLDS) - b. 1889; d. 1953
Lincoln B. - b. 1868; d. 1943
Nancy C. (wife of William Howard) - b. 1849; d. 1935
Norman E. - b. 1910; d. 1984
Richard Slaton - b. 24 November 1940; d. 14 September 1982

Robert T. - b. 30 October 1928
Robert T. Jr. - b. 9 January 1965
Verlie B. (wife of Henry E.) - b. 20 March 1906; d. 6 February 1989
William Howard (husb. of Nancy C.) - b. 1847; d. 1917

DAY
[Mildred - see McCORMICK]

DEANE
Alberta H[AYWARD?]. - b. 1888; d. 1953

DEASY
[Blanche - see HODGKINS]
Emma M. [wife of Luere B.?] - b. 1855; d. 1938
Luere B. [husb. of Emma M.?] - b. 1859; d. 1940

DEFRANK
Mary - d. 9 October 1910 Æ 7 y., 4 m.

DEHON
Julia M. (HOFFMAN; wife of Thomas M. [no stone]) - b. 16 January 1834; d. 9 September 1916
Julia Theodora - b. 3 September 1874; d. 19 October 1949

DEVOUE
Eugene M. - b. 15 August 1901; d. 10 July 1984

DIETER
Ida J. - b. 1855; d. 1929

DINES
[Donna Virginia - see CRUSE]

DODGE
Anita T. [wife of Harold C.] - b. 1912; d. 1995
[Carolyn - see BUNKER]
Ellen S. - b. 1878; d. 1963
Harold C. [husb. of Anita T.] - b. 1904; d. 1990

DOLBEARE
Frederic R. - b. 1885; d. 1962

DOLLIVER
Dolores (wife of Robert [no stone]) - b. 10 October 1931; d. 10 November 1973
George Warren (husb. of Winnie L.) - b. 1851; d. 1903
George William (husb. of Rita J.) - b. 1889; d. 1964
George William Jr. "Buddy" [son of George William and Rita J.] - b. 1924; d. 1947
[Margaret - see WHITE]
Rita J. (wife of George William) - b. 1891; d. 1980
Winnie L. (wife of George Warren) - b. 1864; d. 1953

DOREY
Helen J[OHNSTON?]. [wife of John L.] - b. 1923; d. 1993
John L. [husb. of Helen J[OHNSTON?].] - b. 1918; d. 1996

DORITY
[Eliza Watson - see NEWMAN]

DORR
Albert B. [husb. of Eleanor M.] - b. 5 February 1896; d. 8 April 1963
B. Lillian [wife of Harvey R.] - b. 1892; d. 1982
Eleanor M. [wife of Albert B.] - b. 1899; d. 1943
Harvey R. [husb. of B. Lillian] - b. 1870; d. 1939

DOUCETTE
George L. - b. 1935; d. 1936

DOUGLAS
Alton W. [husb. of Jean S.] - b. 1902; d. 1979
Elizabeth D. - [b.?] 1 June 1923
Hedwig - b. 1894, Danzig; d. [no date]
Jean S. [wife of Alton W.] - b. 1913; d. 1996
DOUGLASS
Fannie M. - [no dates]
William H. - [no dates]
DOW
Albert W. [husb. of Onnolee C[ARTER?].] - b. 1904; d. 1965
Clara A. [wife of S. Norton] - b. 3 August 1853; d. 9 November 1930
Clarence E. [husb. of Mable [sic] M.] - b. 1875; d. 1959
Clyde V. (son of Eugene F. and Maude A.) - b. 1891; d. 1928
David H. "Skipper" - b. 28 September 1940; d. 2 March 1993
Eugene F. (husb. of Maude A.) - b. 1861; d. 1939
Harrold [sic] (son of Eugene F. and Maude A.) - b. 1900; d. 1918
Mable [sic] M. [wife of Clarence E.] - b. 1879; d. 1971
Maude A. (wife of Eugene F.) - b. 1874; d. 1939
Onnolee C[ARTER?]. [wife of Albert W.] - b. 1904; d. 1986
Phyllis M. [wife of William H.] - b. 1917; d. 1988
Ronald N. - b. 2 November 1903; d. 4 March 1911
S. Norton [husb. of Clara A.] - b. 15 August 1849; d. 27 December 1925
William H. [husb. of Phyllis M.] - b. 1913; d. 1975
DOWD
Alice (BUNKER; wife of C. Michael) - b. 15 March 1903; d. 29 July 1982
C. Michael (husb. of Alice (BUNKER)) - b. 5 April 1903; d. 19 April 1986
DOYLE
Frank James - b. 20 December 1927; d. 14 August 1972
DRASHER
[Marion - see BERRY]
DRAYTON
Mary (BRADY; "widow" of Henry Edward [no stone]) - b. 18 June 1835; d. 17 September 1910
DuBOIS
Marie [wife of Norman] - b. 1895; d. 1970
Norman [husb. of Marie] - b. 1900; d. 1986
DUNHAM
[Ella A. - see LAWFORD]
DWYER
Clement S. [husb. of Marguerite L.] - b. 18 October 1915; d. 5 June 1973
Jean L. - b. 30 April 1945; d. 24 May 1945
Marguerite L. [wife of Clement S.] - b. 18 June 1916
DYER
Donald E. [husb. of Margaret H.] - b. 1898; d. 1957
[Freda Diane - see WHITE]
[Margaret - see WHITE]
Margaret H. [wife of Donald E.] - b. 7 November 1903; d. 20 September 1994
DYMENT
[Elizabeth - see SIMPKINS]
EGAN
Carol Ann - b. 1961; d. 1973
Jacqueline M. - b. 1925; d. 1984

ELEFTHERIOU
Eleftherios Basil (Very Rev.) - b. 1906; d. 1966
Euphemia - b. 1908; d. 1983
Victoria B. - b. 1876; d. 1970
ELDER
Elizabeth - b. 1891; d. 1988
ELLIOTT
Clarice G[ETCHELL?]. [wife of Herbert E.] - b. 1909; d. 1988
Herbert E. [husb. of Clarice G[ETCHELL?].] - b. 1907; d. 1982
ELLS
Florence (SOMES; [wife of John B.]) - b. 1890; d. 1981
John B. [husb. of Florence (SOMES)] - b. 1890; d. 1971
EMERY
Ann (wife of John T.) - b. 1839; d. 1922
[Ardelle - see HADLEY]
Ceylon (husb. of Mamie (ASH)) - b. 1867; d. 1928
Edna L. [wife of Ralph S.] - b. 1872; d. 1948
Ermina T. - b. 1864; d. 1937
George [husb. of Hilda] - b. 1901; d. 1981
[Gertrude E[MERY?]. - see RODICK]
H. R. - [no dates]
Hilda [wife of George] - b. 1902; d. 1954
Howard C. - [no dates]
Howard S. (husb. of Ona (CAMP)) - b. 18 July 1894; d. 19 April 1974
Ida M. - b. 1902; d. 1981
John T. (husb. of Ann) - b. 1825; d. 1899
Lillian - b. 1859; d. 1943
Mamie (ASH; wife of Ceylon) - b. 1871; d. 1921
Newell W. - b. 1895; d. 1988
Nina M. - [no dates]
Ona (CAMP; wife of Howard S.) - b. 4 March 1897; d. 8 June 1984
Osmond - b. 1856; d. 1932
Ralph S. [husb. of Edna L.] - b. 1869; d. 1935
Stewart D. - b. 1896; d. 1973
Valerie Ruth [wife of Wellington] - b. 9 May 1918; d. 5 December 1998
Wellington [husb. of Valerie Ruth] - b. 17 January 1915; d. 22 November 1984
ENO
Amos - b. 2 August 1909; d. 29 May 1985
ETTER
John C. - b. 1891; d. 1981
Ray M. - b. 1886; d. 1969
EVANS
Elizabeth D. - b. 2 December 1923; d. 21 September 1993
John H. (husb. of Marjorie A.) - b. 1886; d. 1961
Marjorie A. (wife of John H.) - b. 1888; d. 1981
EVELETH
Eben C. - b. 1856; d. 1929
Elizabeth A. - b. 1866; d. 1942
Francis C. - b. 1899; d. 1951
Lois M. - b. 1892; d. 1971
Priscilla R. - b. 1906; d. 1979

FABBRI
[Edith - see MILLIKEN]
[Teresa - see MCMURTRY]
FADDEN
Michael Erwin - b. 13 September 1970; d. 6 January 1991
FALKENSTROM
Alice V. [wife of Arthur P.] - b. 1904; d. 1960
Arthur P. [husb. of Alice V.] - b. 1893; d. 1945
Charles F. [husb. of Evelyn A.] - b. 1903; d. 1986
Edward A. - b. 7 August 1895; d. 5 May 1961
Evelyn A. [wife of Charles F.] - b. 1898; d. 1984
Fanny M. [wife of John A.] - b. 1870; d. 1954
John A. [husb. of Fanny M.] - b. 1873; d. 1943
FARLEY
Charlotte R. [wife of Cornelius] - b. 1874; d. 1954
Cornelius [husb. of Charlotte R.] - b. 1873; d. 1969
James - b. 1872; d. 1934
Vola [sic] M. - b. 14 October 1916; d. 13 November 1968
FIELD
Mildred B. - b. 1901; d. 1974
Ralph H. - b. 1888; d. 1945
FIFIELD
Clara (HATCH; wife of George H.) - b. 1853; d. 1920
George H. (husb. of Clara (HATCH)) - b. 1852; d. 1922
[Marion - see JOY]
FINLETTER
Gretchen (DAMROSCH; [wife of Thomas K.]) - b. 3 October 1895; d. 15 December 1969, New York, New York
[Lili - see O'NEILL]
Thomas K. [husb. of Gretchen (DAMROSCH)] - b. 11 November 1893; d. 24 April 1980
FISHER
Deidre - b. 4 January 1944; d. 3 October 1997
George C. [husb. of Madeline N.] - b. 1895; d. 1977
Harry P. - b. 31 May 1886; d. 21 July 1950
Madeline N. [wife of George C.] - b. 1903; d. 1993
FLANAGAN
Olevia M. (wife of Patrick H.) - b. 1856; d. 1939
Patrick H. (husb. of Olevia M.) - b. 1861; d. 1930
FLETCHER
Henry D. [husb. of Mildred M.] - b. 1905; d. 1983
Mildred M. [wife of Henry D.] - b. 1904
FOGG
Andrew P. - b. 1905
FOLEY
Dale J. [husb. of Madeline L.] - b. 1908
Madeline L. [wife of Dale J.] - b. 1908; d. 1973
FORD
Neal E. - [b.?] 11 February 1935
FOSS [see also GARBER]
[Blanche - see PAINE]

FOSTER
Abbie M. [wife of Francis L.] - b. 1854; d. 1933
Claribel - b. 1878; d. 1918
Ella M. - b. 1852; d. 1945
Francis L. [husb. of Abbie M.] - b. 1854; d. 1938
George Fuller - b. 11 October 1889; d. 23 June 1965
Gilbert L. (husb. of Vesta S.) - b. 1872; d. 1948
James E. - b. 1846; d. 1927
[Jennie T. [FOSTER?] - see MARSHALL]
[Maxine B. - see GRAY]
[Nancy E. - see CLEAVES]
Statie M. (wife of Maj. Richard M. [no stone]) - b. 28 November 1927; d. 9 March 1999; ("buried in Arlington National Cemetery"[7])
Vesta S. (wife of Gilbert L.) - b. 1884; d. 1963
FOWLER
Douglas M. - b. 1914; d. 1976
FOX
Alice Maude (dau. of DeGrasse and Harriet [no stone]) - b. 19 February 1883; d. 26 July 1894
DeGrasse (husb. of Harriet [no stone]) - b. 23 August 1838; d. 2 October 1904
[Genevieve - see FULLER]
Sally Ann (CHUDOBA) - b. 4 March 1934; d. 24 October 1980
FRANKLIN
Sylvia - b. 3 August 1914; d. 26 October 1987
FRAYLER
Arthur L. [husb. of Margaret T.] - b. 1927; d. 1988
Margaret T. [wife of Arthur L.] - b. 1927
FRAZIER
Alan Wayne (son of R. H. and M. E. [no stones]) - b. December 1954; d. January 1955
Bradley A. - b. 1860; d. 1940
FREEMAN
Alice (WHITEHOUSE) - b. 1917; d. 1972
[...][5] - [no dates]
FRITZ
Edith H. F. (CLEMMANS; "of Folkestone, England"; wife of John) - b. 1870; d. 1951
[Elizabeth - see THORNDIKE]
John ("of Galena, Illinois"; husb. of Edith H. F. (CLEMMANS)) - b. 1855; d. 1932
FROST
Inez M. (wife of Irving G.) - b. 1880; d. 1963
Irving G. (husb. of Inez M.) - b. 1875; d. 1968
Merrill G. (son of Irving G. and Inez M.) - b. 1909; d. 1966
FULLER
Genevieve (FOX) - b. 1888; d. 1959
John Langworthy - b. 1910; d. 1992
Raymond Garfield - b. 1886; d. 1960
Ruth Parsons[13] - b. 1905; d. 1989
G.
R. W. - b. 1818; d. 1909
GABRIELSON
Annie E. - b. 1881; d. 1943

C. Louise - b. 1910
Conrad N. - b. 1872; d. 1946
Frederick C. - b. 1907; d. 1988
GAGNON
George A. - b. 1917; d. 1972
GARBER [headstone: "GARBER/FOSS"]
Barbara[14] - [no dates]
Charlie[14] - [no dates]
Evelyn[14] - [no dates]
Ralph[14] - [no dates]
GARDNER
[Florence - see CLEAVES]
Maxine E. - b. 1924; d. 1993
Onalee M. - b. 1905; d. 1931
Ruth (SHERMAN) - b. 1902; d. 1969
William S. - b. 1905; d. 1989
GARLAND
Edith - [no dates]
Ralph - [no dates]
Royce - [no dates]
GATCHELL
Walter F. (son of Earnest [sic] E. and Minnie A. [no stones]) - b. 15 July 1892; d. 12 February 1914
GEORGE
Alice E. (wife of James) - b. 1872; d. 1946
James (husb. of Alice E.) - b. 1842; d. 1921; ("G. A. R." [Civil War])
John A. [husb. of Lena P[ETERSON?].] - b. 1853; d. 1930
Lena P[ETERSON?]. [wife of John A.] - b. 1857; d. 1933
GETCHELL
Archibald L. Jr. - d. [no date] Æ 4 m., 9 d.
Archie L. - b. 1880; d. 1958
[Clarice G[ETCHELL?]. - see ELLIOTT]
Jessica H. [wife of Lawrence B.] - b. 1906
Lawrence B. [husb. of Jessica H.] - b. 1906; d. 1978
Olie M. A. - b. 1880; d. 1970
GIELING
Gladys S. [wife of John K.] - b. 1895; d. 1991
John K. [husb. of Gladys S.] - b. 1892; d. 1975
John Sherman - b. 1925; d. 1982
GIFFORD
George Merritt - b. 1874; d. 1957
GILBERT
Brenda [GILBERT?] - [no dates]
Edna May (wife of Gordon S.) - b. 1921; d. 1996
Eva Thomas - b. 1875; d. 1934
Gordon S. (husb. of Edna May) - b. 1925
GILES
Calvin L. (husb. of Grace G.) - b. 1866; d. 1955
Earl W. [husb. of Marguerite H[IGGINS?].] - b. 21 March 1889; d. 3 October 1959
Grace G. (wife of Calvin L.) - b. 1869; d. 1960
Marguerite H[IGGINS?]. [wife of Earl W.] - b. 2 September 1887; d. 27 September 1971

GILFILLAN
Edith N. [wife of James W.] - b. 1891; d. 1980
James W. [husb. of Edith N.] - b. 1893; d. 1942
GILLAM
Gertrude M. [wife of Ralph B.] - b. 15 January 1897; d. 3 October 1973
Ralph B. [husb. of Gertrude M.] - b. 5 December 1894; d. 20 November 1963
GILLEY
Charles E. - b. 1876; d. 1944
Gertrude "Sally" [wife of Morris M.] - b. 1911; d. 2000
Lena C. - b. 1884; d. 1965
Lydia A. - b. 1839; d. 1918
Morris M. [husb. of Gertrude "Sally"] - b. 1907; d. 1989
GODDARD
Agnes - b. 1879; d. 1956
GOFF
Helena E. - b. 17 August 1927; d. 28 May 1985
Jerome C. - b. 11 June 1923; d. 15 October 1989
GOLDTHWAIT
Ruth (SANDERS; [wife of Sheldon Forrest]) - b. 1908; d. 1996
Sheldon Forrest [husb. of Ruth (SANDERS)] - b. 1905; d. 1965
GONYA
David W. [husb. of Marguerite (LITTLEFIELD)] - b. 1926; d. 1987
Marguerite (LITTLEFIELD; [wife of David W.]) - b. 1932
GOOCH
Blanche G. [wife of Victor F.] - b. 1883; d. 1967
Carrol W. - b. 1916; d. 1969
[Charlotte - see ASHTON]
infant [GOOCH?] - [no dates]
Mary M. [wife of Milton A.] - b. 1877; d. 1938
Milton A. [husb. of Mary M.] - b. 1874; d. 1931
Victor F. [husb. of Blanche G.] - b. 1879; d. 1966
GOOD
Leonora (HALL) - b. 21 June 1905; d. 27 May 1980
GOODALL
Daniel M. [husb. of Emma D.] - b. 1870; d. 1935
Emma D. [wife of Daniel M.] - b. 1873; d. 1974
Mildred L. - b. 1898; d. 1931
GOODRICH
Arthur George [husb. of Winifred (JUDD)?] - b. 1898; d. 1983
[Frances - see WILLIAMS]
Winifred (JUDD; [wife of Arthur George?]) - b. 1897; d. [no date]
GOOGINS
[Ardelle M. - see HODGKINS]
Charlotte G. (wife of Grafton A.) - b. 18 October 1924; d. 4 March 1983
Grafton A. (husb. of Charlotte G.) - b. 6 December 1909; d. 14 November 1978
GORDON
Beatrice (WIGHT; [wife of Harry Leon]) - b. 1883; d. 1946
Harry Leon [husb. of Beatrice (WIGHT)] - b. 1883; d. 1949
Harry Wight - b. 1911; d. 1978
GOSS
Elmer W. (husb. of Sheila E. (RICHARDS)) - b. 1895; d. 1958
Frederick V. [husb. of Madeline L.] - b. 1 April 1892; d. 22 February 1965

M. I. [spouse of W.] - b. 1858; d. 1942
Madeline L. [wife of Frederick V.] - b. 19 June 1901; d. 24 December 1984
Sheila E. (RICHARDS; wife of Elmer W.) - b. 1901; d. 1956
W. [spouse of M. I.] - b. 1857; d. 1928

GOTT

Albert M. (husb. of Evelyn W.) - b. 1914; d. 1976
Andrew J. (Capt.; husb. of Caroline L.) - b. 18 January 1838; d. 20 December 1914
Caroline L. (wife of Capt. Andrew J.) - b. 24 June 1848; d. 17 April 1930
Evelyn W. (wife of Albert M.) - b. 1915; d. 1992
Myrtle A. [dau. of Capt. Andrew J. and Caroline L.?] - b. 14 November 1873; d. 11 August 1930

GOWER

Arlene B. - b. 1910; d. 1985
Charles M. [husb. of Clara M.] - b. 1868; d. 1931
Clara M. [wife of Charles M.] - b. 1874; d. 1953
Clarence E. - b. 1898; d. 1951
Clyde R. - b. 4 September 1897; d. 18 September 1970
Shirley A. [male] - b. 1900; d. 1939
[Thelma - see KUNKEL]

GRACE

Henrietta - b. 6 August 1845; d. 17 September 1914
Icephine - b. 13 January 1843; d. 17 February 1911

GRAFFAM

Charles E. (husb. of Eva E.) - b. 1869; d. 1938
Eva E. (wife of Charles E.) - b. 1867; d. 1929

GRAHAM

Alta V. (wife of Herbert L.) - b. 1881; d. 1957
Bethena (wife of Ernest A.) - b. 1877; d. 1942
Ernest A. (husb. of Bethena) - b. 1873; d. 1922
George Bearse - d. 23 August 1903 Æ 8 m., 17 d.
Herbert L. (husb. of Alta V.) - b. 1877; d. 1939
Mary G. - b. 1915; d. 1976
Nina J. (wife of William F[rost?].) - b. 12 August 1891; d. 10 May 1985
William F[rost?]. (husb. of Nina J.) - b. 8 May 1888; d. 17 April 1962
William Frost Jr. - b. 22 August 1922; d. 4 June 1992

GRANT

Alexander J. (husb. of Laura W.) - b. 1854, Edinburg, Scotland; d. 1927, Bar Harbor
George Allan (husb. of Margaret G.) - b. 6 June 1893; d. 26 February 1969
James C. - b. 1852; d. 1922
Laura W. (wife of Alexander J.) - b. 1874; d. 1961
Lawrence C. - b. 1909; d. 1985
Margaret G. (wife of George Allan) - b. 1894; d. 1942
[Margaret T. [GRANT?] - see WEST]
Mark B. - b. 1865; d. 1939

GRAY

Elmer (son of Arthur C. and Bertha A. [no stones]) - d. 25 August 1906 Æ 13 m.
Fannie E. [wife of Reuben N.] - b. 1873; d. 1963
Leslie B. (husb. of Susan E.) - b. 1906; d. 1973
Leslie B. Jr. [son of Leslie B. and Susan E.] - b. 8 April 1935; d. 6 October 1997
Maxine B. (FOSTER; wife of Thurle K.) - b. 1911; d. 1987
Merle H. [husb. of Pauline E.] - b. 1938
Pauline E. [wife of Merle H.] - b. 1940; d. 1984

Reuben N. [husb. of Fannie E.] - b. 1871; d. 1946
Susan E. (wife of Leslie B.) - b. 1905; d. 1972
Thurle K. (husb. of Maxine B. (FOSTER)) - b. 1912; d. 1975

GREEN
Charles V. - b. 1902; d. 1936

GRIFFIN
Esther Vanamee [wife of Hancock Jr.] - b. 1913; d. 1994
Hancock (husb. of Katharine L. M.) - b. 1882; d. 1951
Hancock Jr. [husb. of Esther Vanamee] - b. 1912; d. 1980
Katharine L. M. (wife of Hancock) - b. 1889; d. 1965

GRINDLE
Ada M. - b. 1920; d. 1995
Freeman L. - b. 1915; d. 1980
Freeman L. Sr. [husb. of Jennie M.] - b. 1885; d. 1955
Jennie M. [wife of Freeman L. Sr.] - b. 1887; d. 1981
Natalie D. - b. 1937

GROBEN
Margaret - b. 1906; d. 1975

GULLIFER
Leslie M. (husb. of Mary Ann) - b. 1871; d. 1935
Mary Ann (wife of Leslie M.) - b. 1874; d. 1916

GUPTILL
Helen (CARTER; [wife of Nathanael [sic]]) - b. 1918
Nathanael [sic] [husb. of Helen (CARTER)] - b. 1917
Zena G. - b. 26 July 1850; d. 10 July 1916

GUTHRIE
Linda (PRAY; [wife of Walter E.]) - b. 1887; d. 1976
Walter E. [husb. of Linda (PRAY)] - b. 1886; d. 1952

HADLEY
Ardelle (EMERY; wife of Benjamin L.) - b. 1853; d. 1944
Benjamin L. (husb. of Ardelle (EMERY)) - b. 1854; d. 1918
Benjamin L. ([son of Benjamin L. and Ardelle (EMERY)?]; husb. of Mary L. (CHASE)) - b. 1894; d. 1955
[Lora - see CLEAVES]
Mary L. (CHASE; wife of Benjamin L.) - b. 1892; d. 1990

HAGERTHY
Johnson Maynard [husb. of Margaret H.] - b. 1921; d. 1991
Margaret H. [wife of Johnson Maynard] - b. 1925

HALBAUER
Marguerite M. - b. 1893; d. 1978

HALEY
Dennis J. [husb. of Minnie N.?] - b. 1847; d. [no date]
Minnie N. [wife of Dennis J.?] - b. 1862; d. [no date]

HALL
[Leonora - see GOOD]
Marie Agnes (BUNKER; dau. of David Albion BUNKER [no stone] and Jeannette (HIGGINS); wife of Oliver Leigh) - b. 24 January 1874; d. 7 July 1957
Miriam A. [dau. of Oliver Leigh and Marie Agnes (BUNKER)?] - b. 17 June 1903; d. 1 January 1976
Oliver Leigh (son of Oliver Gray and S. Frances (WHITE) [no stones]; husb. of Marie Agnes (BUNKER)) - b. 6 May 1870; d. 17 November 1946

HAMERSLEY
L. Gordon Jr. [husb. of Madeline (HELLUM)] - b. 1928
Madeline (HELLUM; [wife of L. Gordon Jr.]) - b. 1930
HAMILTON
Sarah - d. 17 November 1917 Æ 68 y., 9 m., 22 d.
HAMMOND
Laura D. [wife of Oscar M.] - b. 1870; d. 1944
Oscar M. [husb. of Laura D.] - b. 1864; d. 1953
HAMOR
[Annie M. - see RODICK]
Bernie A. [son of Capt. Warren B. and Clara B.?] - b. 3 April 1864; d. 5 December 1934
Charles L. - b. 1955; d. 1985
Clara B. (wife of Capt. Warren B.) - b. 1 May 1837; d. 1 February 1906
Ella - b. 1867; d. 1950
Francis (son of Ansel A. [no stone] and Julia E.) - b. 19 November 1907; d. 13 June 1915
Julia Ann - b. 1951; d. 1993
Julia E. (wife of Ansel A. [no stone]) - b. 1866; d. 1934
Mary E. - b. 28 March 1912; d. 18 March 1989
Warren B. (Capt.; husb. of Clara B.) - b. 13 September 1837; d. 14 March 1910
HANDY
Frank W. [son of Harold W. and Nancy V.?] - b. 1927; d. 1979
Harold W. [husb. of Nancy V.] - b. 1898; d. 1983
Nancy V. [wife of Harold W.] - b. 1896; d. 1968
HANF
Andrew [husb. of Frances C.] - b. 1898; d. 1957
Frances C. [wife of Andrew] - b. 1903; d. 1996
HANSCOM
Pamelia E. [wife of Walter V.] - b. 1940
Walter V. [husb. of Pamelia E.] - b. 1937
HANSON
Adelie C. [wife of Herbert F.] - b. 1906
Grace T. (wife of Lester W.) - b. 1890; d. 1983
Harold M. [husb. of Hazel E.] - b. 1891; d. 1962
Hazel E. [wife of Harold M.] - b. 1907; d. 1983
Herbert F. [husb. of Adelie C.] - b. 1888; d. 1960
Lester W. (husb. of Grace T.) - b. 1876; d. 1955
Reginald C. - b. 1921; d. 1976
HARDEN
Almon [husb. of Delia H.] - b. 26 April 1851; d. 13 January 1938
[Bernice H[ARDEN?]. - see BURBANK]
Delia H. [wife of Almon] - b. 31 October 1851; d. 19 October 1912
[Lorinda - see WOOD]
Myrtle Ona (BEATON; wife of Maurice G. [no stone]) - b. 1896; d. 1928
HARE
Ariel (STEVENS; [wife of Charles A.]) - b. 31 October 1889; d. 25 March 1954
Charles A. [husb. of Ariel (STEVENS)] - b. 20 September 1887; d. 27 May 1951
HARKINS
Chester A. - b. 1933; d. 1934
HARPER
Albert E. - b. 1866; d. 1930

Dora M. - b. 1871; d. 1940
Eugene A. - b. 18 October 1905; d. 26 May 1969
Lawrence W. - b. 17 July 1894; d. 8 December 1963
[Shirley J. - see JOHNSTON]

HARRIMAN
Kathleen R. ("eldest daughter" of Leroy and R. Bessie) - b. 1902; d. 1989
Leroy (husb. of R. Bessie) - b. 1880; d. 1941
R. Bessie (wife of Leroy) - b. 1884; d. 1959

HARRIS
Anna P. - b. 1860; d. 1934
Cecile S. - b. 1896; d. 1990
Charles W. - b. 1901; d. 1974
Cora S. (wife of Donald) - b. 1913; d. 1993
Donald (husb. of Cora S.) - b. 1909; d. 1964
Eunice R. (wife of Rev. Wallace H.) - b. 1914; d. 1997
Eva I. - b. 1918; d. 1968
George E. - b. 1905; d. 1906
Harold L. (husb. of Hazel Page) - b. 1890; d. 1969
Hazel Page (wife of Harold L.) - b. 1905; d. 1977
James [husb. of Minnie A.] - b. 1863; d. 1947
James L. - b. 1903; d. 1984
[Jane L. - see CARTER]
Maude E. - b. 1892; d. 1975
Minnie A. [wife of James] - b. 1869; d. 1955
Rachel - b. 1879; d. 1912
Richard P. (son of Harold L. and Hazel Page) - b. 1933; d. 1980
Stanley W. - b. 1938; d. 1991
Stephanie Nicole - b. 26 September 1990; d. 28 September 1990
Wallace H. (Rev.; husb. of Eunice R.) - b. 1907

HARRISON
Andrew Townsend Thorndike - b. 1963; d. 1993

HARVEY
Fred A. (husb. of Nellie M.) - b. 1867; d. 1951
L. Marie (dau. of Fred A. and Nellie M.) - b. 1897; d. 1988
Nellie M. (wife of Fred A.) - b. 1866; d. 1915

HASKELL
Ira D. - b. 1871; d. 1942

HASS
Charles E. [husb. of Elizabeth A.] - b. 1879; d. 1952
Elizabeth A. [wife of Charles E.] - b. 1886; d. 1936
Shirley L. - b. 1902; d. 1931

HASTEY
Vera L[EIGHTON?]. - b. 26 May 1904; d. 30 January 1983

HATCH
Alvin U. Sr. (husb. of Myrtle) - b. 1900; d. 1996
[Clara - see FIFIELD]
Edward R. [husb. of Florence I.] - b. 1906; d. 1967
Florence I. [wife of Edward R.] - b. 1909; d. 1978
Myrtle (wife of Alvin U. Sr.) - b. 1905; d. 1975

HATT
Marjorie L. (BOYNTON; wife of William Orval) - b. 1929

William Orval (husb. of Marjorie L. (BOYNTON)) - b. 28 March 1925; d. 15 October 1962
HAUER
Dean - b. 1915
William "Bill" - b. 19 July 1899; d. 12 December [1989 or 1990][3]
HAVEY
Elma (STANLEY) - b. 1902; d. 1940
HAWKES
George A. - b. 17 November 1907; d. 27 June 1981
Gladys E. (wife of B. A. [no stone]) - b. 1914; d. 1983
Mary Alice (dau. of B. A. [no stone] and Gladys E.) - b. 1940; d. 1954
HAYDEN
Ethel Lee (wife of Ralph Henry) - [no dates]
Ralph Henry (husb. of Ethel Lee) - b. 1888; d. 1961
HAYDOCK
M. A. - b. 1818; d. 1903
HAYWARD
[Alberta H[AYWARD?]. - see DEANE]
Annie B. (wife of George W.) - b. 1861; d. 1932
Augusta H. (wife of Charles D.) - b. 1864; d. 1926
Charles A. [husb. of Eva H.] - b. 1880; d. 1953
Charles D. (husb. of Augusta H.) - b. 1860; d. 1947
Elizabeth (wife of Willard J.) - b. 1867; d. 1932
[Ethel H[AYWARD?]. - see SMITH]
Eva H. [wife of Charles A.] - b. 1877; d. 1958
George W. (husb. of Annie B.) - b. 1854; d. 1946
Helen - b. 1875; d. 1961
Henry - b. 1871; d. 1968
[Hilma H[AYWARD?]. - see BURNS]
Willard J. (husb. of Elizabeth) - b. 1867; d. 1945
HEAL
[S. Floy - see PATTEN]
HEATH
Dana H. Jr. [husb. of Joanne HIGDON] - b. 2 April 1948; d. 4 March 1994
[Joanne - see HIGDON]
HECHT
Samuel D. - b. 1866; d. 1947
HELLUM
Anna C. (wife of Hans A.) - b. 1870; d. 1944
Arthur C. - b. 1894; d. 1943
Blanche Q. - b. 1904; d. 1980
Dorothy L. - b. 1899; d. 1994
Grace A. - b. 1928; d. 1983
Hans A. (husb. of Anna C.) - b. 1868; d. 1934
[Madeline - see HAMERSLEY]
Ralph - b. 1902; d. 1988
HIGDON
Joanne HEATH [wife of Dana H. Jr. (1st husband)] - b. 10 May 1948; d. 15 February 2000
HIGGINS
[Abbie L. - see PEACH]
Adeline (wife of Edwin H.) - b. 1846; d. 1934

Albert L. - b. 1855; d. 1936
Alcenus - [no dates]
Allen - [no dates]
Alma G. (wife of Royal G. Jr.) - b. 1896; d. 1978
Almenia T. - b. 1886; d. 1957
Ambrose H. (husb. of Elizabeth A.) - b. 1842; d. 1910
Ambrose S. - b. 1908; d. 1971
Armida R. [wife of Thomas C.] - b. 1890; d. 1971
Arthur M. - b. 1858; d. 1920
Belle P. (wife of Lionel S.) - b. 15 July 1896; d. 11 December 1979
[Bessie H[IGGINS?]. - see MARSHALL]
Betsy - [no dates]
Blithen S. - b. 1851; d. 1915
Carolyn E. - b. 1909; d. 1982
Cecil F. (husb. of Vara [sic] G.) - b. 3 August 1906; d. 17 April 1977
Charles L. (son of Charles and Elmira [no stones]) - b. 1873; d. 1892
Charles Stephen - b. 1893; d. 1939
Charles T. [husb. of Nettie L.] - b. 1881; d. 1963
Charlotte (wife of Albert F. [no stone]) - d. 10 December 1899 Æ 74 y., 11 m., 5 d.
Clayton C. [son of Charles T. and Nettie L.?] - b. 1906; d. 1913
Clinton B. [husb. of Georgia P.] - b. 1872; d. 1918
Dorothy E. (wife of Harvard DeL.) - b. 1907; d. 1999
Edward Leander (husb. of Hortense S.) - b. 1879; d. 1936
Edward Leander Jr. (son of Edward Leander and Hortense S.) - b. 1913; d. 1917
Edwin H. (husb. of Adeline) - b. 1840; d. 1924
Elizabeth A. (wife of Ambrose H.) - b. 1844; d. 1913
Ellen E. (wife of Elvin E.) - b. 1865; d. 1942
Elvin E. (husb. of Ellen E.) - b. 1853; d. 1929
Elwood E. - b. 1926; d. 1937
Emma G. - b. 1855; d. 1919
Etta T. [wife of Harry E.] - b. 1891; d. 1942
F. Eldora [wife of Samuel N.?] - b. 1850; d. 1924
Fred A. - b. 14 July 1861; d. 20 December 1928
Freeman (son of George P. and Julia R.; husb. of Nellie (CHURCHILL)) - b. 1868; d. 1916
George H. - b. 1878; d. 1940
George P. (husb. of Julia R. and Lilla V.) - b. 1849; d. 1919
Georgia [HIGGINS?] - b. 1876; d. 1963
Georgia P. [wife of Clinton B.] - b. 1875; d. 1947
Gerald H. (son of Elvin E. and Ellen E.) - b. 1898; d. 1965
Harold F. [husb. of Myrtle B.] - b. 1882; d. 1959
Harriet H. - b. 1857; d. 1950
Harry E. [husb. of Etta T.] - b. 1887; d. 1957
Harvard DeL. (husb. of Dorothy E.) - b. 1907; d. 1995
Helena E. (wife of John R.) - b. 1920
Herbert P. (husb. of M. Blanche) - b. 1871; d. 1954
Hollis M. - b. 1883; d. 1908
Hortense S. (wife of Edward Leander) - b. 1881; d. 1941
Ida C. (wife of J. Murray) - b. 1867; d. 1956
Irene E. [wife of Randell [sic] C. Sr.] - b. 1924
J. Murray (husb. of Ida C.) - b. 1859; d. 1932
[Jeannette - see BUNKER]

John R. (husb. of Helena E.) - b. 1907; d. 1973
John T. - b. 1844; d. 1918; (member of Co. C, 1st Maine Heavy Artillery [Civil War])
Joyce Helen (dau. of Harvard DeL. and Dorothy E.) - b. 1940; d. 1991
Julia R. (wife of George P.) - b. 1846; d. 1890
Katherine G. (wife of Dr. Royal G.) - b. 1867; d. 1925
Kenneth R. - b. 1947; d. 1966
Lilla V. (wife of George P.) - b. 1859; d. 1939
Lionel S. (husb. of Belle P.) - b. 27 June 1888; d. 11 May 1974
M. Blanche (wife of Herbert P.) - b. 1870; d. 1952
[Mabel H[IGGINS?]. - see TEMPLETON]
[Marguerite H[IGGINS?]. - see GILES]
Mariam R. (dau. of Stephen and Ann M. [no stones]) - b. 31 January 1854; d. 23 December 1938
[Mary H[IGGINS?]. - see WEBBER]
Myrtle B. [wife of Harold F.] - b. 1886; d. 1982
Nellie (CHURCHILL; wife of Freeman) - b. 1864; d. 1940
Nettie L. [wife of Charles T.] - b. 1885; d. 1964
Nettie M. [wife of Thomas C.] - b. 1867; d. 1943
Norris I. - b. 1869; d. 1929
[Patricia H[IGGINS?]. - see SCHMAEDIG]
Phebe E. (wife of Albert F. [no stone]) - b. 1850; d. 1934
Ralph [HIGGINS?] - b. 1874; d. 1923
Ralph W. - b. 1910; d. 1922
Randell [sic] C. Sr. [husb. of Irene E.] - b. 1924; d. 1994
Royal G. (Dr.; husb. of Katherine G.) - b. 1867; d. 1945
Royal G. Jr. (son of Dr. Royal G. and Katherine G.; husb. of Alma G.) - b. 11 February 1895; d. 2 December 1982
[Ruth K. [HIGGINS?] - see ANDRADE]
Samuel N. [husb. of F. Eldora?] - b. 1839; d. 1918
Sherman B. - b. 1884; d. 1930
Thomas C. [husb. of Nettie M.] - b. 1848; d. 1932
Thomas C. [husb. of Armida R.] - b. 1890; d. 1953
Vara [sic] G. (wife of Cecil F.) - b. 1905; d. 1969
Victor G. - b. 1873; d. 1906
Virginia (SHIELDS) - b. 1893; d. 1977
Virginia E. - b. 21 February 1920; d. 18 April 1990
Willard H. - b. 1855; d. 1925

HILAND

Thomas (Dr.) - b. 1838; d. 1906

HILL

Alice M. [wife of Ansel B. [HILL?]] - b. 1861; d. 1927
Angelia H. [HILL?] - b. 1849; d. 1939
Ansel B. [HILL?] [husb. of Alice M.] - b. 1861; d. 1939
David W. [son of Walters G. and Sylvia L[ELAND?].?] - b. 1920; d. 1975
Sylvia L[ELAND?]. [wife of Walters G.] - b. 1888; d. 1968
Walters G. [husb. of Sylvia L[ELAND?].] - b. 31 August 1888; d. 25 January 1968

HINCH

Alice M. - b. 1866; d. 1935
Alice R. (wife of John T.) - b. 1857; d. 1928
Catherine (wife of James [no stone]) - b. 1835; d. 1910
Hattie R. - b. 1869; d. 1929

John T. (husb. of Alice R.) - b. 1862; d. 1934

HINCKLEY

George D. (husb. of Marguerite I.) - b. 18 December 1924; d. 9 December 1979
Marguerite I. (wife of George D.) - b. 9 June 1927; d. 7 August 1989

HITCH

Frank Bobo [husb. of Laura (YOUNG)] - b. 1906; d. 1952
Laura (YOUNG; [wife of Frank Bobo]) - b. 1908

HODGKINS

Amy (dau. of Chester A. and Lucy F.) - b. 1887; d. 1907
Ardelle M. (GOOGINS; wife of Edward L.) - b. 1841; d. 1928
Asa H. (husb. of Blanche (DEASY)) - b. 1893; d. 1967
Blanche (DEASY; wife of Asa H.) - b. 1887; d. 1955
Charlotte E. - b. 5 April 1903; d. 25 August 1973
Chester A. (husb. of Lucy F.) - b. 1857; d. 1917
[Dorothy H[ODGKINS?]. - see STANLEY]
Edward L. (husb. of Ardelle M. (GOOGINS)) - b. 1839; d. 1912
Eleanor W. [wife of Milton A.] - b. 28 May 1916
Esther M. [dau. of Nelson S. and Nellie F.?] - b. 1918; d. 1985
Fredonna Gladys - b. 27 September 1918; d. 9 September 1999
Grace (ROWE) - b. 1874; d. 1956
Harrison M. [husb. of Minnie C[ONNERS?].] - b. 1878; d. 1954
Irving A. - b. 1868; d. 1956
J. Robie (husb. of Mary L.) - b. 1884; d. 1943
[Lalah [sic] - see WOOD]
[Leonora - see CONNERS]
Lucy F. (wife of Chester A.) - b. 1869; d. 1925
Margaret (YOUNG; [wife of Roger Wallace]) - b. 31 August 1912; d. 10 February 1994
Maria P. - b. 1874; d. 1933
Martin H. - b. 1912; d. 1976
Mary L. (wife of J. Robie) - b. 1892; d. 1986
Milton A. [husb. of Eleanor W.] - b. 21 July 1906; d. 13 June 1994
Milton L. - b. 1910; d. 1934
Minnie C[ONNERS?]. [wife of Harrison M.] - b. 1875; d. 1944
Nellie F. (wife of Nelson S.) - b. 1892; d. 1949
Nelson S. (husb. of Nellie F.) - b. 1896; d. 1971
Roberta Vance (dau. of J. Robie and Mary L.) - b. 2 June 1919; d. 29 February 1920
Roger Wallace [husb. of Margaret (YOUNG)] - b. 16 November 1911; d. 2 April 1998
Roy (son of Chester A. and Lucy F.) - b. 1886; d. 1906
Ruth I. [dau. of Nelson S. and Nellie F.?] - b. 1916
Winfield B. - b. 31 May 1896; d. 15 February 1965

HODSON

Helen (RENWICK) - b. 10 March 1908; d. 8 April 1954
James [HODSON?] - b. 1906; d. 1972

HOFFMAN

[Julia M. - see DEHON]

HOLBROOK

Marjorie (LISCOMB; wife of Stanley) - b. 1897; d. 1982
Stanley (husb. of Marjorie (LISCOMB)) - b. 1893; d. 1973

HOLMES

Agnes V. [wife of Charles A.] - b. 1891; d. 1978

Charles A. [husb. of Agnes V.] - b. 1887; d. 1964
Joseph P. - b. 6 May 1921; d. 28 December 1972

HOOVEN
Herbert N. - b. 1898; d. 1979

HOPKINS
Amanda M. (LELAND; wife of John H.) - b. 1833; d. 1907
[Ida - see CUNNINGHAM]
John H. (husb. of Amanda M. (LELAND)) - b. 1832; d. 1907
Nelson E. - b. 1872; d. 1911
Rebecca H. (wife of Smith) - d. 25 February 1822 Æ 50 y.
Smith (husb. of Rebecca H.) - d. 15 January 1861 Æ 91 y.
Walter C. - b. 1869; d. 1912

HORNER
Mark Woolman - b. 24 August 1973; d. 14 December 1998
Robert C. - b. 7 February 1949; d. 3 October 1992
W. Rea - b. 1913; d. 1991

HOWARD
Shirlee Smith - b. 1920; d. 1978

HUCKINS
Charles Adelbert [husb. of Hilda (LELAND)] - b. 27 September 1919
Edward E. (husb. of Myrtle E.) - b. 1885; d. 1942
Hilda (LELAND; [wife of Charles Adelbert]) - b. 24 April 1918; d. 12 November 1996
Myrtle E. (wife of Edward E.) - b. 1886; d. 1971

HUNTLEY
Charles H. (husb. of Jane) - b. 1856; d. 1924
Jane (wife of Charles H.) - b. 1850; d. 19[...][4]

HUNTON
Arthur L. - b. 1878; d. 1949

HUTCHINGS
[Josephine M. - see CONNERS]

IANTOSCA
[Gilda S. - see ZERRIEN]

INGALLS
Alice J. (wife of Reginald I.) - b. 1884; d. 1979
Gerard W. [son of Reginald I. and Alice J.?] - b. 1908; d. 1967
Reginald I. (husb. of Alice J.) - b. 1884; d. 1940

JACKSON
Olive M. [wife of William E.] - b. 1922
William E. [husb. of Olive M.] - b. 1922; d. 1976

JEFFERY
Harry P. - b. 1871; d. 1946

JELLISON
Clara J. (wife of Fred A.) - b. 1857; d. 1935
Eda D. (wife of Fred C.) - d. [no date]
Fred A. (husb. of Clara J.) - b. 1855; d. 1940
Fred C. (husb. of Eda D.) - b. 1881; d. 1962
Jane (dau. of Fred C. and Eda D.) - [b. and?] d. 1910

JENKINS
Edward Kenneth [husb. of Mary L. (MARSH)] - b. 17 August 1908; d. 6 December 1972
Mary L. (MARSH; [wife of Edward Kenneth]) - b. 9 October 1914; d. 5 March 1987

JEWETT
Alton G. [husb. of Ruth E.] - b. 1907; d. 1976
Ruth E. [wife of Alton G.] - b. 1910; d. 1994
JOHNSON
[Beatrice - see LITTLE]
Carlton P. (husb. of Helen B.) - b. 1896; d. 1984
Doris [JOHNSON?] - [no dates]
Helen B. (wife of Carlton P.) - b. 1901; d. 1984
[Helen L. - see CARTER]
Jean [JOHNSON?] - [no dates]
Rose B. - b. 1904; d. 1989
JOHNSTON
Alma S. (wife of William J.) - b. 1864; d. 1920
Archie - b. 1901; d. 1965
Carol T. [wife of Mike E.] - b. 1929
Clara E. (CUNNINGHAM; wife of Lawrence E.) - b. 10 December 1898; d. 6 June 1996
Donald L. (husb. of Florence (CARTER)) - b. 28 April 1913; d. 26 March 1972
Elwin T. [husb. of Emily R.?] - b. 1867; d. 1955
Emily R. [wife of Elwin T.?] - b. 1879; d. 1969
Florence (CARTER; wife of Donald L.) - b. 4 August 1919; d. 21 March 1991
G. D. - [no dates]
Harry C. [husb. of Lucie [sic] M.] - b. 1886; d. 1957
Harry W. - b. 25 January 1918; d. 24 December 1994
[Helen J[OHNSTON?]. - see DOREY]
Lawrence E. (husb. of Clara E. (CUNNINGHAM)) - b. 19 July 1890; d. 23 March 1985
Lucie [sic] M. [wife of Harry C.] - b. 1887; d. 1984
Michael E. (husb. of Shirley J. (HARPER)) - b. 21 September 1951; d. 17 December 1988
Mike E. [husb. of Carol T.] - b. 1930
Shirley J. (HARPER; wife of Michael E.) - b. 15 August 1940
William J. (husb. of Alma S.) - b. 1864; d. 1954
JONES
Edgcomb [sic] Lee - b. 16 November 1874; d. 11 August 1937
Helen Snow - b. 1872; d. 1948
JORDAN
[Abbie L. - see COLLINS]
Albion Francis (husb. of Ellen (MOORE)) - b. 1847; d. 1906
Albion Percy (son of Albion Francis and Ellen (MOORE)) - b. 1874; d. 20 April 1876 Æ 1 y., 5 m., 16 d.
Alton T. [husb. of Mary T.] - b. 1913; d. 1996
Anna S. [wife of William R.] - b. 1865; d. 1947
Annie M. - b. 1852; d. 1929
Arno M. [husb. of Clara T.] - b. 1881; d. 1943
Catherine E. [wife of Herbert M.] - b. 1883; d. 1969
Charles A. Jr. - b. 1930; d. 1948
Charles W. - b. 1850; d. 1923
Clara T. [wife of Arno M.] - b. 1882; d. 1975
Ellen (MOORE; wife of Albion Francis) - b. 1843; d. 1898
Evelyn (KITTREDGE; [wife of Ray M.]) - b. 11 March 1911; d. 7 August 1983
Gladys A[LLEN?]. - b. 1895; d. 1979

Hannah B. - d. 8 May 1913 Æ [not given]
Herbert M. [husb. of Catherine E.] - b. 1889; d. 1937
Marion E. - b. 28 December 1905; d. 25 September 1908
Mary T. [wife of Alton T.] - b. 1915; d. 1989
Ray M. [husb. of Evelyn (KITTREDGE)] - b. 11 February 1912; d. 22 October 1986
William R. [husb. of Anna S.] - b. 1862; d. 1944

JOY
Barbara Ellen [dau. of G. Raymond and Marion (FIFIELD)] - b. 1898; d. 1984; ("native")
Eva C. (wife of Preston H. [no stone]) - b. 1866; d. 1932
G. Raymond [husb. of Marion (FIFIELD)] - b. 1877; d. 1920
Marion (FIFIELD; [wife of G. Raymond]) - b. 1877; d. 1968

JOYCE
Clar[e or a]nce[3] (husb. of Myra D.) - d. 14 January 1912 Æ 56 y., 1 m., 14 d.
Inez Frances (dau. of Clar[e or a]nce[3] A. and Myra D.) - d. 4 September 1909 Æ 15 y., 6 m., 24 d.
Myra D. (wife of Clar[e or a]nce[3] A.) - b. 2 March 1860; d. 18 March 1933

JUDD
[Alice - see STEINER]
Edith B. - b. 1874; d. 1956
[Winifred - see GOODRICH]

K.
M. T. - b. 1849; d. 1905
S. E. - b. 1850; d. 1942

KALDRO
George "Juri" - b. 17 November 1943; d. 27 April 1996

KEENE
[Addie - see PAINE]
H. Otis - b. 1894; d. 1962
Henry O. - b. 15 February 1921; d. 8 July 1994
Oliver M. - b. 1922; d. 1984
Robert G. (father of Liza [no stone]) - b. 1917; d. 1998

KEEZER
Florence Mae - b. 1890; d. 1950
Josephine S. - b. 1885; d. 1957
Vinton - b. 1914; d. 1963

KEISOR
Charles E. - b. 1875; d. 1920
father [KEISOR?] - [no dates]
Frank [KEISOR?] - [no dates]
mother [KEISOR?] [CONNERS?] - [no dates]

KELLEY
Lori Jo [dau. of Walter E. and Lucille E.] - b. 22 August 1957; d. 3 May 1999
Lucille E. [wife of Walter E.] - b. 10 December 1929
Walter E. [husb. of Lucille E.] - b. 18 December 1928

KELLIHER
Alice R. - b. 1860; d. 1905
Beatrice E. - b. 23 November 1882; d. 23 June 1948

KENT
Rosemond L. - b. 1868; d. 1930

KEUCHER
Charles A. [husb. of Ethel B.] - b. 1873; d. 1950

Ethel B. [wife of Charles A.] - b. 1879; d. 1966
KEYES
Francis Hayden - [no dates]
Ruth M. (RODICK) - b. 1929[10]
KIAER
Alice (DAMROSCH) - b. 18 May 1892; d. 23 April 1967, New York, New York
KIDD
Jane - b. 1868; d. 1965
KIEF
Jean H. [wife of Larry] - b. 1932
Larry [husb. of Jean H.] - b. 1928
KIENBUSCH
William Austin - b. 13 April 1914; d. 23 March 1980
KILBOURNE
Evelyn (STALFORD) - b. 1908; d. 1976
KING
Gurli S. - b. 1911; d. 1993
KIRK
Elizabeth [wife of Joseph?] - b. 1870; d. 1957
G. Harold - b. 1900; d. 1972
Helen Yeaton - b. 1893; d. 1989
Joseph [husb. of Elizabeth?] - b. 1867; d. 1953
KITTREDGE
[Evelyn - see JORDAN]
KNICKERBOCKER
Charlotte Erma - b. 5 May 1920; d. 4 February 1985
KNOBEL
Edith M. - b. 1895; d. 1979
KOZUBAL
Ruby (PAINE) - b. 1902; d. 1962
KUNKEL
Lawrence P. (husb. of Thelma (GOWER)) - b. 12 October 1907; d. 1 July 1976
Thelma (GOWER; wife of Lawrence P.) - b. 4 April 1913; d. 20 June 1995
LADD
Julia E. (wife of William) - b. 1850; d. 1917
William (husb. of Julia E.) - b. 1851; d. 1934
LADNER
Corrienne J. [wife of Ralph M.] - b. 1896; d. 1961
Ralph M. [husb. of Corrienne J.] - b. 1891; d. 1963
LAMBERT
David C. - b. 1901; d. 1945
G. Robert - b. 5 August 1899; d. 2 September 1981
Susan F. - b. 17 June 1901; d. 14 April 1978
LANGDON
Woodbury - b. December 1949; d. January 1950
LANGLOIS
Raoul A. - b. 1898; d. 1973
LAWFORD
Ella A. (DUNHAM; wife of Henry A.) - b. 1855; d. 1931
Henry A. (husb. of Ella A. (DUNHAM)) - b. 1858; d. 1940
Maud Hazel (wife of Arthur H. [no stone]) - b. 1893; d. 1918
[Sara [sic] - see WEBBER]

LAWN
[Neva M. - see PARKER]
LAWRENCE
Abbott E. [husb. of Gertrude S.] - b. 1857; d. 1929
Gertrude S. [wife of Abbott E.] - b. 1867; d. 1938
[Mary - see BUNKER]
LEAVITT
George A. [husb. of Lillian T.] - b. 1878; d. 1966
Lillian T. [wife of George A.] - b. 1881; d. 1958
LEE
Catherine M. "Penny" [wife of Robert J.] - b. 1917; d. 1994
Robert J. [husb. of Catherine M. "Penny"] - b. 1911; d. 1999
LEIGHTON
Ethel H. - b. 2 September 1885; d. 3 September 1977
Henry - b. 19 September 1875; d. 9 October 1954
Lawrence E. [husb. of Lida P.] - b. 1907; d. 1983
Lee S. - b. 1906; d. 1938
Louisa M. - b. 7 April 1851; d. 4 March 1928
Lida P. [wife of Lawrence E.] - b. 1908; d. 1973
[Vera L[EIGHTON?]. - see HASTEY]
LELAND
Abraham T. (husb. of Lavina H.) - b. 1842; d. 1897
[Amanda M. - see HOPKINS]
Ethel M. (wife of Harry A.) - b. 1890; d. 1953
Eugene R. [husb. of Josie K.] - b. 1871; d. 1948
Josie K. [wife of Eugene R.] - b. 1876; d. 1962
Harry A. (husb. of Ethel M.) - b. 1880; d. 1961
[Hilda - see HUCKINS]
Lavina H. (wife of Abraham T.) - b. 1843; d. 1907
Roswell (husb. of Susie (MASON)) - b. 15 April 1872; d. 16 October 1935
Susie (MASON; wife of Roswell) - b. 23 October 1876; d. 17 September 1917
[Sylvia L[ELAND?]. - see HILL]
LEONARD
Clarence L. - b. 14 April 1890; d. 15 October 1970
Mary C. - b. 1898; d. 1975
Nellie A. - b. 1884; d. 1957
Sylvia A. - b. 1911; d. 1969
LEVESQUE
William Vital (son of Peter and Arlene [no stones]) - b. 1 March 1964; d. 18 September 1964
LEWIS
Raymond S. [LEWIS?] - b. 1901; d. 1947
LIBBY
Richard E. - b. 6 October 1947; d. 20 June 1988
Seth Emerson Jr. - b. 19 August 1924; d. 26 November 1957
LINDALL
Charles E. (husb. of Maude) - b. 1860; d. 1935
Dorothy - b. 1897; d. 1915
Marjourie [sic] - [no dates]
Maude (wife of Charles E.) - b. 1874; d. 1943
LINDGREN
Emiel - b. 1864; d. 1936

Juliette - b. 1874; d. 1966
LINSCOTT
Charles C. [husb. of Eva E.] - b. 1859; d. 1941
Eva E. [wife of Charles C.] - b. 1862; d. 1926
Hazael [sic] F. [wife of Walter L.] - b. 1887; d. 1967
Walter L. [husb. of Hazael [sic] F.] - b. 1882; d. 1937
LISCOMB
Alice - b. 1913; d. 1986
Amanda L. - b. 1862; d. 1955
Andrew E. - b. 1862; d. 1931
Annie May (dau. of Horace H. and Charlotte A. "Lottie") - d. 4 April 1907 Æ 1 y., 6 m.
Berla B. [wife of Waldron D.] - b. 1912; d. 1988
Charlotte A. "Lottie" (wife of Horace H.) - b. 1880; d. 1960
Everett G. [husb. of M. Elizabeth] - b. 1889; d. 1982
Everett W. - b. 1911; d. 1979
Fred M. (son of Horace H. and Charlotte A. "Lottie") - d. 27 April 1912 Æ 5 m.
Georgia H. (wife of Shirley M.) - b. 1889; d. 1986
Horace H. (husb. of Charlotte A. "Lottie") - b. 1858; d. 1927
Irma - b. 4 June 1914; d. 9 September 1993
Lydia A. [wife of Montville S.] - b. 1 October 1888; d. 6 July 1976
M. Elizabeth [wife of Everett G.] - b. 1886; d. 1980
[Marjorie - see HOLBROOK]
Montville S. [husb. of Lydia A.] - b. 1894; d. 1976
Pauline M. [dau. of Horace H. and Charlotte A. "Lottie"] - b. 1902; d. 1928
Shirley M. (husb. of Georgia H.) - b. 1887; d. 1955
Waldron D. [husb. of Berla B.] - b. 1913; d. 1969
LITTLE
Beatrice (JOHNSON; [wife of Clarence Cook]) - b. 1899; d. 1973
Clarence Cook [husb. of Beatrice (JOHNSON)] - b. 1888; d. 1971
Edward Revere - b. 1912; d. 1970
[Laura - see MOEN]
LITTLEFIELD
[Marguerite - see GONYA]
LIVELY
Bernard - b. 1906; d. 1986
LOFGREN
James T. [husb. of Phyllis M.] - b. 16 March 1918; d. 9 August 1991
Phyllis M. [wife of James T.] - b. 1916; d. 1979
LONGTON
William H. - b. 1917; d. 1990
LORING
Charles D. (son of George J. and Laura C.) - b. 1893; d. 1945
George J. (husb. of Laura C.) - b. 1858; d. 1906
Harold A. (son of George J. and Laura C.) - b. 1904; d. 1955
Laura C. (wife of George J.) - b. 1858; d. 1950
LOVELAND
Jesse W. - b. 28 May 1931; d. 17 August 1966
LYMAN
Dorothy A. - b. 1866; d. 1904
LYMBURNER
Catherine G. [wife of Everett L.] - b. 1886; d. 1942

Everett L. [husb. of Catherine G.] - b. 1880; d. 1969
Hazel Y. [wife of Maurice F.] - b. 1891; d. 1989
Marjorie R. - b. 1908; d. 1949
Maurice F. [husb. of Hazel Y.] - b. 1884; d. 1968

LYNAM
Frederick C. [husb. of Harriet A.] - b. 1861; d. 1942
Frederick C. Jr. [son of Frederick C. and Harriet A.] - b. 1889; d. 1935
Harriet A. [wife of Frederick C.] - b. 1864; d. 1947
John S. (husb. of Nancy A.) - b. 12 January 1831; d. 11 July 1915
Nancy A. (wife of John S.) - b. 18 May 1833; d. 4 September 1905

LYNK
[...] [headstone "LYNK/LISCOMB"]

M.
N. L. - [no dates]

MACDONALD
Angus M. (husb. of Anne M.) - b. 1867; d. 1926
Anne M. (wife of Angus M.) - b. 1867; d. 1955
Lowell - b. 1899; d. 1986
Norman W. - b. 1896; d. 1973

MACGINNIS
Joseph E. (Rev.) - b. 1912; d. 1994

MACGREGOR
Gardner D. [husb. of Nina H.] - b. 1904; d. 1982
Nina H. [wife of Gardner D.] - b. 1904; d. 1988

MACKAY
Margaret (wife of Joseph J. P. [no stone]) - b. 15 May 1869; d. 21 April 1913

MACLEAN
Katherine F. [wife of Kenneth] - b. 1869; d. 1951
Kenneth [husb. of Katherine F.] - b. 1875; d. 1961

MACLEOD
Beulah P. [wife of Donald W.] - b. 1890; d. 1961
[Catharene [sic] - see CLEAVES]
Charlotte W. [wife of Donald W. Jr.] - b. 25 August 1925; d. 23 October 1992
Donald W. [husb. of Beulah P.] - b. 1883; d. 1975
Donald W. Jr. [husb. of Charlotte W.] - b. 1926; d. 1994
Ellis R. [husb. of Marion M.] - b. 1891; d. 1957
Marion M. [wife of Ellis R.] - b. 1895; d. 1984

MACMACKIN
Oletha M. - b. 1902; d. 1991
[Pauline M[ACMACKIN?]. - see COOPER]

MACQUINN
H. Robert - b. 15 August 1929
[Marilyn - see ROBINETTE]

MADDOX
[Clara - see ALLEN[15]]
Marie - [no dates]

MALCOLM
F. Marie [wife of John] - b. 1891; d. 1947
John [husb. of F. Marie] - b. 1892; d. [no date]

MANNING
Albert F. [husb. of Sadie A.] - b. 1857; d. 1940
Sadie A. [wife of Albert F.] - b. 1863; d. 1949

MANTER
John D. - b. 1959; d. 1977
MARCYES
Christine A. [wife of James E.] - b. 1894; d. 1980
James E. [husb. of Christine A.] - b. 1887; d. 1967
MARSH
[Mary L. - see JENKINS]
MARSHALL
Bessie H[IGGINS?]. - b. 1878; d. 1960
Elizabeth J. [wife of Stanley N.] - b. 1903; d. 1987
Emma J. [wife of William B.] - b. 1882; d. 1958
Eugene (son of Villa [no stone]) - b. 6 January 1900; d. 2 September 1910
George M. - b. 1866; d. 1923
Jennie T. [FOSTER?] - b. 1876; d. 1952
Stanley N. [husb. of Elizabeth J.] - b. 1905; d. 1957
William B. [husb. of Emma J.] - b. 1877; d. 1950
MARSTON
Gardner E. - d. 12 March 1912 Æ 66 y.
[Tina - see McLAUGHLIN]
MARTENS
G. [husb. of Ruth M.?] - b. 1889; d. 1955
Ruth M. [wife of G.?] - b. 1898; d. 1981
MASON
[Susie - see LELAND]
MASTERMAN
Lila [dau. of Ralph C. and Ruth G.?] - b. 1922; d. 1922
Lois Irene (dau. of Ralph C. and Ruth G.) - b. 1938; d. 1954
Ralph C. (husb. of Ruth G.) - b. 1891; d. 1977
Ruth G. (wife of Ralph C.) - b. 1902; d. 1970
MAYO
Emma I. [wife of John C.] - b. 1877; d. 1971
John C. [husb. of Emma I.] - b. 1875; d. 1951
McCORMICK
Mildred (DAY) - b. 1888; d. 1981
McCORMICK-GOODHART
Frederick Hamilton - b. 13 November 1887; d. 12 December 1938
McDANIEL
John A. - b. 1906; d. 1970
McDOWELL
Anne Roper (wife of Malcolm C.; mother of Bruce, William [no stone], and Diana [no stone]) - b. 16 April 1917, Aclare Co., Sligo, Ireland; d. 10 February 1996, Lamoine, Maine
Bruce Roper [son of Malcolm C. and Anne Roper] - b. 17 November 1943; d. 12 July 1984
Malcolm C. (husb. of Anne Roper; father of Bruce, William [no stone], and Diana [no stone]) - b. 26 January 1915; d. 19 November 1997
McFARLAND
Arthur W. - b. 2 March 1890; d. 23 October 1953
Charlotte A. [wife of William] - b. 1867; d. 1960
Chauncey A. (husb. of Mae D.) - b. 1896; d. 1977
Chauncey A. [husb. of Nancy M.] - b. 1921
Eliza (WOOD; wife of Harry S.) - [no dates]

Ella G. [wife of Sanford M.] - b. 1891; d. 1974
F. Esperance - b. 1913; d. 1990
Harry S. (husb. of Eliza (WOOD)) - [no dates]
Mae D. (wife of Chauncey A.) - b. 1895; d. 1968
Nancy M. [wife of Chauncey A.] - b. 1918; d. 1979
Pauline - b. 1916; d. 1957
Sanford M. [husb. of Ella G.] - b. 1891; d. 1964
Vernon S. Sr. - b. 1916
William [husb. of Charlotte A.] - b. 1858; d. 1926

McHUGH
[Catherine - see Mary (LAWRENCE) BUNKER]

McINTOSH
Hellen [sic] (wife of Elias [no stone]) - d. 1 July 1907 Æ 28 y.

McINTYRE
Carmen A. - b. 1894; d. 1963
Joseph N. - b. 1876; d. 1953

McKAY
Annie D. (THOMAS; wife of Daniel A.) - b. 9 July 1865; d. 9 October 19[2 or 3]1[6]
Barbara H. [wife of George C. Jr.] - b. 16 October 1920; d. 15 December 1990
[Christie - see NEVERS]
Daniel A. (husb. of Annie D. (THOMAS)) - b. 17 December 1874; d. 2 October 1910; ("drowned")
Ethel L. [wife of George C.] - b. 20 October 1885; d. 20 March 1970
Eunice M. (wife of George) - b. 1851; d. 1930
George (husb. of Eunice M.) - b. 1846; d. 1915
George C. [husb. of Ethel L.] - b. 5 December 1884; d. 10 October 1968
George C. Jr. [husb. of Barbara H.] - b. 19 July 1921
J. Whitman [husb. of Veronica M.] - b. 1901; d. 1983
Veronica M. [wife of J. Whitman] - b. 1913; d. 1969

McLAUGHLIN
Tina (MARSTON) - b. 1876; d. 1951

McLEAN
Annie - b. 1861; d. 1942
Fannie J. [wife of Harris L.] - b. 1898; d. 1984
George E. - b. 1847; d. 1926
Harris L. [husb. of Fannie J.] - b. 1895; d. 1968

McMURTRY
George Gibson (Major) - b. 6 November 1876; d. 22 November 1958
Impy[12] - b. 1958; d. 1969
Teresa (FABBRI) - b. 1898; d. 1974

McNAIR
Elvira (BROKAW; [wife of William]) - b. 1958
William [husb. of Elvira (BROKAW)] - b. 1947

McNEAL
Pauline F. [wife of Vinal R.] - b. 1920; d. 1979
Vinal R. [husb. of Pauline F.] - b. 1914; d. 1993

McNICKLE - see NICHOL

McVICAR
Duncan H. (husb. of Katherine E.) - b. 1853; d. 1923
Katherine E. (wife of Duncan H.) - b. 1860; d. 1915

MEARS
Mary E. - d. 18 August 1943 Æ [not given]

MEDEM
Olga [MEDEM?] - b. 1842; d. 1928
MEGQUIER
Arlene G. (wife of Lester C.) - b. 1910; d. 1931
[Edith M[EGQUIER?]. - see DASO]
Edna M. [wife of Olney L.] - b. 1913; d. 1999
Estelle M. (wife of Norman L.) - b. 1942
Hazel N. (wife of Lester C.) - b. 1904; d. 1988
Lester C. (husb. of Arlene G. and Hazel N.) - b. 1905; d. 1982
Norman L. (husb. of Estelle M.) - b. 1928; d. 1996
Olney L. [husb. of Edna M.] - b. 1903; d. 1994
MIDTTVEIT
Evelyn A. [wife of Nils M.] - b. 29 November 1915; d. 13 July 1991
Nils M. [husb. of Evelyn A.] - b. 12 July 1915
MILLER
Emma G. [wife of Harold E.] - b. 1926; d. 1980
Fannie M. - b. 18 June 1843; d. 1 November 1914
Harold E. [husb. of Emma G.] - b. 1921; d. 1981
Iris Margaret [dau. of William and Sarah Ann (VASS)?] - b. 1903; d. 1916
Jane B. [dau. of William and Sarah Ann (VASS)?] - b. 1896; d. 1964
Lowell [husb. of Maude E.] - b. 1906; d. 1970
Maude E. [wife of Lowell] - b. 1905; d. 1986
Sarah Ann (VASS; [wife of William]) - b. 1864; d. 1935
William [husb. of Sarah Ann (VASS)] - b. 1863; d. 1939
MILLIKEN
Edith (FABBRI) (CLARK) - b. 20 July 1920; d. 9 September 1991
J. Melvin [husb. of Minnie L.] - b. 1859; d. 1945
Minnie L. [wife of J. Melvin] - b. 1865; d. 1948
MITCHELL
Agnes H. (NASON) - b. 1881; d. 1973
Albert G. (husb. of Lura F.) - b. 1877; d. 1965
Albert L. - b. 8 February 1927; d. 15 October 1952
Allen A. - b. 1891; d. 1954
Almado (husb. of Harriet S.) - b. 1849; d. 1934
Alonzo - b. 1905; d. 1969
Annie V. (wife of Samuel D. Sr.) - b. 1887; d. 1930
Carroll A. - b. 28 April 1931; d. 17 September 1980
Charles E. - b. 1882; d. 1950
Charles E. - b. 1913; d. 1972
Clara B. - b. 1893; d. 1977
Delores [sic] M. "Dee Dee" [MITCHELL?] - b. [and d.?] 6 January 1945
Dennis Winslow - b. 15 April 1916; d. 8 January 1978
Edgar J. (Capt.) - b. 1878; d. 1959
Edwin C. (husb. of Maude E.) - b. 1878; d. 1937
Flora E. - b. 1861; d. 1946
Fred M. [son of John E. and Louise M.?] - b. 14 May 1882; d. 3 December 1955
Harriet S. (wife of Almado) - b. 1860; d. 1940
James W. - b. 1884; d. 1950
John E. [husb. of Louise M.] - b. 4 December 1847; d. 27 November 1919
Joseph F. - b. 1854; d. 1917
Joseph F. - b. 18 January 1884; d. 4 January 1927
Lillian (RICE; wife of Melvin A.) - b. 1896; d. [no date]

Louise M. [wife of John E.] - b. 14 May 1849; d. 13 May 1913
Lura F. (wife of Albert G.) - b. 1879; d. 1948
Maude E. (wife of Edwin C.) - b. 1887; d. 1955
Melvin A. (husb. of Lillian (RICE)) - b. 1896; d. 1971
Melvin G. - b. 1914; d. 1949
Samuel D. Sr. (husb. of Annie V.) - b. 1887; d. 1964
Stephen Ross - b. 11 June 1949; d. 13 January 1988
Susan May - b. 23 May 1924; d. 12 April 1995

MOEN
Laura (LITTLE) - b. 14 December 1933; d. 15 July 1993
Sandra Lie - b. 21 May 1957; d. 23 March 1998

MOKLER [headstone: BENNETT/MOKLER; see BENNETT]

MOOERS
[Mary Emma - see Euna Rich BUNKER]

MOON
Nettie M. [wife of Wilbur R.] - b. 1918; d. 1980
Wilbur R. [husb. of Nettie M.] - b. 1916; d. 1986

MOONEY
James T. [husb. of Mary A.?] - [no dates]
Mary A. [wife of James T.?] - [no dates]

MOORE
[Ellen - see JORDAN]
Franklin P. [husb. of Mary F.] - b. 1852; d. 1947
Gertrude R. - b. 1881; d. 1967
Lester L. [husb. of Ruth B.] - b. 1873; d. 1934
Mary Ann [wife of Parnel B.] - b. 22 October 1840; d. 4 November 1920
Mary F. [wife of Franklin P.] - b. 1856; d. 1932
Parnel B. [husb. of Mary Ann] - b. 7 May 1836; d. 4 August 1914
Ruth B. [wife of Lester L.] - b. 1878; d. 1955

MORHART
Carol B. [wife of Ronald F.] - b. 4 October 1935; d. 1 August 1996
Ronald F. [husb. of Carol B.] - b. 30 March 1932

MORRIS
[Kathleen - see STEVENS]

MORRISON
[Barbara - see SHEPARD]
C[harles?]. C. (Dr.; husb. of Ida M. and Harriet R.) - b. 1856; d. 1935; ("founder of this cem.")
Charles C. Jr. (Dr.; husb. of Hazel A.) - b. 1893; d. 1953
Charles C. 3rd [son of Dr. Charles C. Jr. and Hazel A.] - b. 1921; d. 1923
Elmer J. (husb. of Maud L.) - b. 1863; d. 1948
Harriet R. (wife of Dr. C[harles?]. C.) - b. 1866; d. 1933
Hazel A. (wife of Dr. Charles C. Jr.) - b. 1893; d. 1982
Ida M. (wife of Dr. C[harles?]. C.) - b. 1866; d. 1917
J. Moulton (son of Dr. C. C. and Harriet R.) - b. 1898; d. 1901
Maud L. (wife of Elmer J.) - b. 1878; d. 1940
[Mildred - see WHISTLER]
Walter A. - b. 7 July 1915; d. 13 December 1962

MORSE
[Anna - see THURBER]
Celestia G. (wife of Edward S. J.) - b. 20 October 1857; d. 4 December 1948
Edward S. J. (husb. of Celestia G.) - b. 7 May 1852; d. 12 May 1910

Harry Havelock (husb. of Sophie Bjerke) - b. 1883, Paradise, Nova Scotia; d. 1918; ("(husband and wife)/found drowned at sea/Bar Harbor Me./July 27, 1918 circa 10 A. M.")
J. Alden (husb. of Minnie A.) - b. 1869; d. 1940
Minnie A. (wife of J. Alden) - b. 1869; d. 1926
Ruth - b. 1893; d. 1981
Sophie Bjerke (wife of Harry Havelock) - b. 1887, Norway; d. 1918; [see notes on Harry Havelock]

MORTON
Avilda V. - b. 1870; d. 1963

MOSLEY
Charles E. [husb. of Mary J.] - b. 1890; d. 1972
Charles F. [husb. of Millicent A.] - b. 1858; d. 1929
Clyde W. - b. 1883; d. 1920
Gerald F. [husb. of Glennis L.] - b. 10 September 1910; d. 29 September 1994
Glennis L. [wife of Gerald F.] - b. 28 March 1911
Harriet M. - b. 1887; d. 1962
Mary J. [wife of Charles E.] - b. 1889; d. 1971
Millicent A. [wife of Charles F.] - b. 1861; d. 1949
Roy K. - b. 1875; d. 1962

MURCH
Donald E. [husb. of Hilda A.] - b. 1906; d. 1989
Frank G. - b. 1882; d. 1943
George B. (husb. of Gladys G. (CONARY)) - b. 1875; d. 1923
Gladys G. (CONARY; wife of George B.) - b. 1879; d. 1915
Hilda A. [wife of Donald E.] - b. 1906; d. 1986

MURDAUGH
Herschel Victor (husb. of Sarah Huckle) - b. 4 March 1928
Sarah Huckle (wife of Herschel Victor) - b. 17 May 1926; d. 14 March 1981

MURPHY
Benjamin [husb. of Harriet R.] - b. 1864; d. 1919
Harriet R. [wife of Benjamin] - b. 1869; d. 1953
Kasper [child of Benjamin and Harriet R.?] - b. 1897; d. 1984
[Lucy M[URPHY?]. - see BIRCH]

MURRAY
Charles W. (husb. of Elizabeth (SHEA)) - b. 4 April 1861; d. 8 December 1913
Elizabeth (SHEA; wife of Charles W.) - b. 17 May 1869; d. 23 November 1960
Frances K. (wife of Joseph M.) - b. 20 June 1898; d. 23 November 1990
Francina [wife of William S.] - b. 1905
Gerald J. - b. 29 December 1892; d. 29 September 1906
Joseph M. (husb. of Frances K.) - b. 12 March 1901; d. 10 May 1982
William S. [husb. of Francina] - b. 1899; d. 1971

NADING
Janette [sic] Lynn (dau. of A. D. and R. L. [no stones]) - b. 1981; d. 1981

NASH
Suzanne W. - b. 16 January 1947; d. 5 July 1999

NASON
[Agnes H. - see MITCHELL]
Carolyn E. (wife of Howard S.) - b. 1854; d. 1918
Charles H. (son of Howard S. and Carolyn E.; husb. of Helen F. (CRANE)) - b. 1875; d. 1930
Frank E. (son of Howard S. and Carolyn E.) - b. 1877; d. 1929

Helen F. (CRANE; wife of Charles H.) - b. 1876; d. 1927
Howard S. (husb. of Carolyn E.) - b. 1851; d. 1929
Robert H. - b. 1883; d. 1953
NEVERS
Christie (McKAY) - b. 1853; d. 1922
NEWMAN
Arthur S. (husb. of Eliza Watson (DORITY)) - b. 2 November 1852; d. 8 August 1906
Eliza Watson (DORITY; wife of Arthur S.) - b. 18 January 1860; d. 23 March 1925
[Louise N[EWMAN?]. - see BERRY]
NICHOL
Susan (dau. of Hugh McNICKLE and Mary S. K. [no stones]) - b. 19 August 1872; d. 26 July 1937
NICKELS
Ferne E. [wife of John J.] - b. 1910; d. 1986
John J. [husb. of Ferne E.] - b. 1901; d. 1972
NICKERSON
Abbie - b. 1880; d. 1970
[Harriet - see SPRATT]
Lola Bethany - b. 17 September 1930; d. 26 September 1930
Walter E. - b. 1876; d. 1961
NOLAN
Clara A. - b. 1881; d. 1930
Ethel W. - b. 1886; d. 1967
James E. - b. 1876; d. 1955
T. Pauline - b. 1908; d. 1968
NORRIS
Calvin H. (husb. of Clara E.) - b. 1856; d. 1925
Clara E. (wife of Calvin H.) - b. 1857; d. 1942
D. Sherley [sic] - b. 1880; d. 1926
NORTON
Calvin L. [husb. of Mary M.?] - b. 1875; d. 1945
Eben E. - b. 1906; d. 1978
[Elizabeth M. - see COLLINS]
James E. (husb. of Jerusha J.) - b. 1858; d. 1936
Jerusha J. (wife of James E.) - b. 1852; d. 1933
Lyda (RODICK) - b. 1880; d. 1972
Mary M. [wife of Calvin L.?] - b. 1878; d. 1950
NORWOOD
Agnes M. [wife of Forest D.] - b. 1901; d. 1976
Danielle Kara - b. 19 January 1976; d. 11 March 1976
Forest D. [husb. of Agnes M.] - b. 1895; d. 1977
Grace L. - b. 1909; d. 1984
James M. - b. 29 April 1861; d. 16 September 1914
Jennie M. [wife of Percy R.] - b. 1881; d. 1976
Lorenzo (husb. of Rose A.) - b. 1854; d. 1927
Percy R. [husb. of Jennie M.] - b. 1889; d. 1966
Rose A. (wife of Lorenzo) - b. 1868; d. 1947
NOWACK
Carl Gustave (husb. of Hazel (CUNNINGHAM)) - b. 17 April 1901; d. 13 December 1969

Hazel (CUNNINGHAM; wife of Carl Gustave) - b. 4 March 1902; d. 25 October 1994
OBER
Florence H. [wife of Harvey L.] - b. 1921; d. 1991
Harvey L. [husb. of Florence H.] - b. 1918
OGDEN
David B. (husb. of Mary Elizabeth (SHERMAN)) - b. 3 November 1849, New York, New York; d. 15 October 1923, Bar Harbour [sic]
Harriet V. C. - b. 10 January 1888, New York, New York; d. 2 November 1978, Bar Harbour [sic]
Mary Elizabeth (SHERMAN; wife of David B.) - b. 19 November 1845, New York, New York; d. 31 December 1936, Washington, D. C.
OLSTON
Mary E. - b. 1868; d. 1950
O'NEIL
George T. [husb. of Gladys F.] - b. 1914; d. 1967
Gladys F. [wife of George T.] - b. 1918; d. 1995
O'NEILL
Lili (FINLETTER) - b. 11 January 1928; d. 13 January 1997
OPDYCKE
Frances (PRESCOTT; [wife of Leonard]) - b. 1895; d. 1969
Leonard [husb. of Frances (PRESCOTT)] - b. 1895; d. 1977
OWENS
Elizabeth Espy - b. 1910; d. 1985
PAINE
Addie (KEENE) - b. 1897; d. 1987
[Bessie - see COUSINS]
Beulah E. ([1st] wife of Maynard W. Jr.) - b. 1894; d. 1926
Blanche (FOSS; "2nd wife" of Maynard W. Jr.) - b. 13 October 1907; d. 10 July 1990
Chandler B. [husb. of Etta Carlow] - b. 1918; d. 1988
Charles F. (husb. of Sarah C.) - b. 4 August 1858; d. 4 January 1942
Etta Carlow [wife of Chandler B.] - b. 1920
Harold M. (husb. of Helen E.) - b. 1898; d. 1982
Hattie L. (wife of Maynard W.) - b. 1867; d. 1942
Helen E. (wife of Harold M.) - b. 1899; d. 1950
infants (2) [children of Maynard W. and Hattie L. or Maynard W. Jr. and Beulah E.] - [no dates]
Marjorie W. - b. 1904; d. 1985
Martha J. - b. 1866; d. 1940
Maynard W. (husb. of Hattie L.) - b. 1863; d. 1927
Maynard W. Jr. (son of Maynard W. and Hattie L.; husb. of Beulah E. and Blanche (FOSS)) - b. 1891; d. 1961
Percy - b. 1896; d. 1898
Richmond G. - b. 1900; d. 1988
[Ruby - see KOZUBAL]
Sarah C. (wife of Charles F.) - b. 15 June 1860; d. 23 February 1948
Vida - b. 1903; d. 1905
Willis C. - b. 1861; d. 1931
PALMER
Harry L. - b. 1882; d. 1917
Helena C. [wife of J. A. C.] - b. 1878; d. 1954
J. A. C. [husb. of Helena C.] - b. 1884; d. 1927

PAQUET
George L. [husb. of Mary H.] - b. 1918; d. 1985
Mary H. [wife of George L.] - b. 1921
PARKER
Guy H. (husb. of Neva M. (LAWN)) - [no dates]
Isaac E. [husb. of Minnie] - b. 1864; d. 1924
Jane W. - b. 1898; d. 1970
John E. [son of Isaac E. and Minnie?] - b. 1901; d. 1955
Minnie [wife of Isaac E.] - b. 1862; d. 1922
Neva M. (LAWN; wife of Guy H.) - b. 4 January 1883; d. 22 January 1967
Priscilla L. - [no dates]
PARSONS
Annie[2] [H. or B.][3] (wife of John E.) - b. 1 January 1883; d. 26 February 1959
Aqua S. - b. 1863; d. 1951
Beryl W[ASGATT?]. - b. 1915; d. 1997
Bessie M. [dau. of John E. and Annie[2] [H. or B.][3]] - b. 1910; d. 1926
Dorothy M. (wife of Leon W.) - b. 1913; d. 1961
Georgia M. (dau. of John E. and Annie[2] [H. or B.][3]) - b. 1906; d. 1918
Gladys L. - b. 18 March 1912; d. 1 August 1986
James E. Jr. - b. 17 November 1940; d. 16 June 1989
John E. (husb. of Annie[2] [H. or B.][3]) - b. 19 October 1882; d. 17 April 1962
Leon W. (husb. of Dorothy M.) - b. 1907; d. 1979
Mark A. - b. 9 June 1975; d. 24 November 1994
[Ruth - see FULLER]
PARTRIDGE
Alma P. (wife of Arthur E.) - b. 1855; d. 1922
Arthur E. (husb. of Alma P.) - b. 1849; d. 1914
PATTEN
Charles K. "Charlie" (husb. of S. Floy (HEAL)) - b. 1871; d. 1936
S. Floy (HEAL; wife of Charles K. "Charlie") - b. 1884; d. 1923
PEACH
Abbie L. (HIGGINS) [wife of William E.?] - b. 1848; d. 1926
Betsey E. [wife of Malcolm B.] - b. 1900; d. 1993
Daisy F. - b. 1875; d. 1949
Jane (BUNKER; [wife of William E.?]) - b. 1851; d. 1934
Joseph Pearl[16] - b. 1898; d. 1953
Malcolm B. [husb. of Betsey E.] - b. 1896; d. 1977
William E. [husb. of Jane (BUNKER) and Abbie L. (HIGGINS)?] - b. 1856; d. 1927
PEARL
[Joseph[16] - see PEACH]
PENDLETON
W. R. - b. 1867; d. 1909
PENNELL
Beatrice M. [wife of Everett H.] - b. 1903; d. 1980
Everett H. [husb. of Beatrice M.] - b. 1890; d. 1967
PERKINS
Douglas Devereaux - b. 15 November 1966; d. 4 April 1999
PETERSON
Carl H. - b. 1895, Kristinehamn, Sweden; d. 1924
David A. [husb. of Marjorie B.] - b. 1895; d. 1976
[Lena P[ETERSON?]. - see GEORGE]
Marjorie B. [wife of David A.] - b. 1904; d. 1983

PETTEE
Mary F. (WOOD; wife of Leaman [no stone]) - b. 1883; d. 1915
PETTEGROW
Andy S. [husb. of Bernice A.] - b. 1884; d. 1961
Bernice A. [wife of Andy S.] - b. 1887; d. 1940
POE
[Mary Lee - see SKINNER]
POTTER
Delmont C. [husb. of Helen E.] - b. 1886; d. 1961
Helen E. [wife of Delmont C.] - b. 1891; d. 1987
R. C. P[OTTER?]. - [no dates]
V. L. P[OTTER?]. - [no dates]
POWER
Marian M. [wife of Morton A.] - b. 1909
Morton A. [husb. of Marian M.] - b. 1909; d. 1971
PRAY
[Linda - see GUTHRIE]
PREBLE
Henrietta G. - b. 1894; d. 1970
John K. [husb. of Myra E.] - b. 1874; d. 1950
[Margaret P[REBLE?]. - see ROBINSON]
Myra E. [wife of John K.] - b. 1876; d. 1965
Pauline B. [dau. of John K. and Myra E.?] - b. 1895; d. 1974
Reginald R. [son of John K. and Myra E.?] - b. 1896; d. 1970
PRESCOTT
[Frances - see OPDYCKE]
PRICE
Louis H. - b. 1910; d. 1984
PROCTER
Emily B. [wife of William] - b. 1868; d. 1949
William [husb. of Emily B.] - b. 1872; d. 1951
PROCTOR
E. Tyler [husb. of Lillian (CHASE)] - b. 13 October 1892; d. 29 June 1962
Lillian (CHASE; [wife of E. Tyler]) - b. 1890; d. 1984
PUFFER
Inez M. - b. 1874; d. 1965
RALPH
Arthur - b. 1888; d. 1972
Marie A. - b. 1896; d. 1980
RAUM
Ann C. - b. 1920; d. 1997
C. Earle [husb. of Dora B.] - b. 1899; d. 1988
Dora B. [wife of C. Earle] - b. 1899; d. 1984
RAYNES
Robert Dyer - b. 6 August 1917; d. 13 September 1993
REED
Evelyn R. - b. 20 April 1902; d. 8 January 1970
Granville E. - b. 10 May 1924; d. 30 July 1950
REGESTER
Earle T. [husb. of Jeanie P.] - b. 1898; d. 1967
Jeanie P. [wife of Earle T.] - b. 1901; d. 1987

REHLANDER
Helen B[URTON?]. - b. 1898; d. 1971
REID
[Louise - see SMITH]
RENWICK
[Helen - see HODSON]
John (husb. of Margaret) - b. 1871; d. 1950
Margaret (wife of John) - b. 1876; d. 1936
REYNOLDS
Abigial [sic] D. - b. 1824; d. 1910
Benjamin (son of George F. and Katie M. [no stones]) - d. 27 July 1910 Æ 4 y., 8 m., 28 d.
Fred E. - b. 1914; d. 1976
[Julia A. - see DAVIS]
Katherine M. - b. 1862; d. 1935
RHODES
Georgia Q. [wife of Lloyd B.] - b. 1912; d. 1995
Lloyd B. [husb. of Georgia Q.] - b. 1908; d. 1992
RICE
[Lillian - see MITCHELL]
RICH
Francis [sic] Marion (CONNERS; wife of John H.) - b. 27 May 1863; d. 9 June 1916
John H. (husb. of Francis [sic] Marion (CONNERS)) - b. 4 August 1856; d. 9 February 1928
Nettie [wife of Orient C.] - b. 17 April 1849; d. 21 September 1913
Orient C. [husb. of Nettie] - b. 1 June 1846; d. 16 April 1924
RICHARDS
Alvah [son of Heman L. and Sarah A.?] - b. 7 November 1890; d. 3 October 1891
Amelia C. (wife of George W.) - b. 1840; d. 1918
Carl L. (husb. of Katherine C.) - b. 15 September 1896; d. 16 April 1964
Fred S. [husb. of Marie Rose] - b. 1870; d. 1923
George W. (husb. of Amelia C.) - b. 1837; d. 1908
Heman L. (husb. of Sarah A.) - b. 22 January 1858; d. 3 April 1914
Loretta J. [wife of William J.] - b. 16 August 1871; d. 7 May 1947
Katherine C. (wife of Carl L.) - b. 1914
Marie E. (dau. of George W. and Amelia C.) - b. 1864; d. 1946
Marie Rose [wife of Fred S.] - b. 1872; d. 1957
Paul S. [son of Fred S. and Marie Rose?] - b. 1894; d. 1958
Sarah A. (wife of Heman L.) - b. 6 October 1863; d. 20 June 1935
[Sheila E. - see GOSS]
William B. - b. 30 May 1873; d. 17 April 1922
William J. [husb. of Loretta J.] - b. 1871; d. 1946
RICHARDSON
Adelma M. [wife of James E.] - b. 28 July 1922
Harriet J. - b. 1848; d. 1940
James E. [husb. of Adelma M.] - b. 19 May 1927
Melvin W. - b. 1878; d. 1956
Samuel O. - b. 1842; d. 1910; ("G. A. R." [Civil War])
ROBERTOFF
Alexander - b. 1851; d. 1907
ROBERTS
Bertha E. - b. 1887; d. 1984

Clara C. [dau. of Edgar L. and Susan M.?] - b. 1873; d. 1895
Cora A. (wife of Fred L.) - b. 1900; d. 1929
Edgar L. (husb. of Susan M.) - b. 1842; d. 1904
Ernest J. - b. 1876; d. 1923
Frank E. - b. 1866; d. 1921
Fred L. (husb. of Cora A.) - b. 1880; d. 1938
[Mary - see SPRAGUE]
Susan M. (wife of Edgar L.) - b. 1844; d. 1919

ROBERTSON
Glenn F.[11] - b. 1918; d. 1997
Glenyce M.[11] - b. 1931
Walter C. - b. 1922; d. 1978

ROBINETTE
James F. - b. 18 October 1933; d. 9 September 1993
Marilyn (MACQUINN) - b. 28 July 1927

ROBINS [sic]
Stanley R. - b. 5 May 1942; d. 6 September 1994

ROBINSON
Chester A. [husb. of Hazel M.] - b. 1913; d. 1983
Hazel M. [wife of Chester A.] - b. 1922; d. 1961
Margaret P[REBLE?]. [dau. of John K. PREBLE and Myra E.?] - b. 1917; d. 1975
Ronald E. - b. 1938; d. 1970

RODICK
A. Stroud [husb. of Madolin T.?] - b. 1880; d. 1969
Albert R. [husb. of Erma R.] - b. 1910; d. 1987
Alfred E. (husb. of Viola B.) - b. 1899; d. 1953
Annie M. (HAMOR; [wife of Walter E.]) - b. 1864; d. 1937
Benjamin - b. 1872; d. 1919
Clarence L. Sr. [husb. of Maxine E.] - b. 1906; d. 1973
Edward B. [husb. of Elizabeth M.] - b. 2 February 1859; d. 2 February 1901
[Effie R[ODICK?]. - see SHAND]
Elizabeth M. [wife of Edward B.] - b. 14 February 1868; d. 4 October 1928
Erma R. [wife of Albert R.] - b. 1912; d. 1994
Gertrude E[MERY?]. [wife of Harold O.] - b. 1909; d. 1990
Harold O. [husb. of Gertrude E[MERY?].] - b. 1904; d. 1989
Harry D. (husb. of Ruth M.) - b. 1879; d. 1962
John A. - b. 1914; d. 1972
John Andrew [husb. of Mary C.?] - b. 1830; d. 1914
Kenneth H. - b. 5 July 1903; d. 10 April 1950
Leon H. - b. 1896; d. 1918
[Lyda - see NORTON]
Madolin T. [wife of A. Stroud?] - b. 1882; d. 1966
Mary C. [wife of John Andrew?] - b. 1830; d. 1917
Maxine E. [wife of Clarence L. Sr.] - b. 1909
Phebe S. (wife of Serenus Higgins) - b. 1861; d. 1943
[Ruth M. - see KEYES]
Ruth M. (wife of Harry D.) - b. 1881; d. 1958
Serenus Higgins (husb. of Phebe S.) - b. 1846; d. 1904
Viola B. (wife of Alfred E.) - b. 1903; d. 1985
Walter E. Jr. [son of Walter E. and Annie M. (HAMOR)] - b. 1890; d. 1911
Walter E. [husb. of Annie M. (HAMOR)] - b. 1854; d. 1932

RODWELL
Maude M. - b. 1903; d. 1991
Rose M. - b. 1870; d. 1959
Ruby A. - b. 1908; d. 1991
Thomas S. - b. 1865; d. 1923
ROHRBAUGH
Lewis Henry (Dr.; husb. of Ruth (BUNKER)) - b. 2 July 1908; d. 10 September 1989
Ruth (BUNKER; wife of Dr. Lewis Henry) - b. 27 August 1908; d. 20 January 1992
ROLFE
Elmer M. (husb. of Geneva M.) - b. 1887; d. 1946
Geneva M. (wife of Elmer M.) - b. 1894; d. 1973
ROSS
Jean Goodwin [wife of Sherman] - b. 27 August 1920
Sherman [husb. of Jean Goodwin] - b. 1 January 1919
ROUNSEVILLE
Howard W. Jr. - b. 1951; d. 1979
ROWE
[Ella - see SAVAGE]
[Grace - see HODGKINS]
Harvard (son of Hollis E. and Lydia I.) - b. 1915; d. 1918
Hollis E. (husb. of Lydia I.) - b. 1879; d. 1959
Lydia I. (wife of Hollis E.) - b. 1890; d. 1983
RYDER
Evelyn M. [wife of George W.] - b. 12 September 1884; d. 22 November 1910
George W. [husb. of Evelyn M.] - b. 10 March 1875; d. 8 July 1962
SACHSMAN
Morton - b. 2 August 1931; d. 28 July 1975
SADLER
Charles S. [husb. of Lauretta L.] - b. 1911; d. 1958
Lauretta L. [wife of Charles S.] - b. 1906; d. 1959
Mary S. [wife of Capt. Rodney C.] - b. 1874; d. 1956
Rodney C. [Capt.; husb. of Mary S.] - b. 1871; d. 1937
SALISBURY
Amos D. - b. 8 April 1900; d. 18 June 1961
Eben A. (husb. of Mary A.) - b. 1831; d. 1909
[Edith - see ALLEN]
Elizabeth E. [wife of Marcellus E.] - b. 1864; d. 1938
Elizabeth S. (SMITH; [wife of Stephen M.]) - b. 1891; d. 1973
[Evadne S[ALISBURY?]. - see THOMPSON]
Everett J. [husb. of Everlaide M.] - b. 1871; d. 1928
Everlaide M. [wife of Everett J.] - b. 1874; d. 1899
Gladys J. [wife of Raymond E.] - b. 1910; d. 1999
Lester W. - b. 1907; d. 1930
Marcellus E. [husb. of Elizabeth E.] - b. 1862; d. 1922
Mary A. (wife of Eben A.) - b. 1829; d. 1892
Melba L. (wife of Ralph T.) - b. 1897; d. 1974
Nathan J. [husb. of Sophia S.] - b. 1841; d. 1904
Ralph T. (husb. of Melba L.) - b. 1895; d. 1987
Raymond E. [husb. of Gladys J.] - b. 1903; d. 1995
Roy S. - b. October 1882; d. September 1976
Ruth Ann - b. 1893; d. 1992

Sophia S. [wife of Nathan J.] - b. 1848; d. 1924
Stephen M. [husb. of Elizabeth S. (SMITH)] - b. 1887; d. 1920

SANBORN
Hazel M. (wife of James L.) - b. 1936
James [husb. of Mazie F.] - b. 1899; d. 1970
James L. (husb. of Hazel M.) - b. 1932; d. 1981
Mazie F. [wife of James] - b. 1907; d. 1979
Nathan Roy - b. 6 September 1930; d. 11 March 1987

SANDERS
[Ruth - see GOLDTHWAIT]

SANFORD
[Euna Rich - see BUNKER]

SARGENT
Corinne B[UNKER?]. - b. 21 March 1908; d. 13 January 1991
Fannie K. - b. 1851; d. 1919
Helen F. - b. 1905; d. 1961

SAULSBURY [sic]
Eva E. (wife of Henry N.) - b. 1876; d. 1949
Henry N. (husb. of Eva E.) - b. 1867; d. 1940

SAVAGE
Alice Ray [wife of Frederick Lincoln] - b. 5 February 1879; d. 5 February 1961
Ella (ROWE; [wife of N. Allen]) - b. 1914; d. 1995
Frederick Lincoln [husb. of Alice Ray] - b. 14 November 1861; d. 26 February 1924
N. Allen [husb. of Ella (ROWE)] - b. 1916

SAWYER
Alice L. - b. 1887; d. 1982
Elvira - b. 1869; d. 1908
Judson H. - b. 1870; d. 1939
L. Isabel - b. 1871; d. 1919
R. Carlton - b. 1908; d. 1926
Raymond L. - b. 1886; d. 1954
William R. Sr. - b. 1888; d. 1964

SCHEITLIN
Erwin H. [husb. of Maryhelen [sic]] - b. 1922; d. 1995
Joey [son of Erwin H. and Maryhelen [sic]?] - [no dates]
Maryhelen [sic] [wife of Erwin H.] - b. 1917

SCHMAEDIG
Patricia H[IGGINS?]. - b. 1949; d. 1999

SEAVEY
[Florence - see CLATWORTHY]

SEELEY
Frances Spear - b. 7 December 1908; d. 19 January 1981

SEELY
Ray Leslie - b. 1894; d. 1974

SEGAL
Ella Ruth - b. 1888; d. 1984

SHAND
Charles L. (husb. of Effie R[ODICK?].) - b. 17 July 1871; d. 6 February 1952
Effie R[ODICK?]. (wife of Charles L.) - b. 15 June 1877; d. 21 August 1930

SHEA
[Elizabeth - see MURRAY]

SHELTON
Addie E. (wife of William R.) - b. 1882; d. 1955
Charles G. - b. 1906; d. 1993
David L. (husb. of Paula Riek) - b. 18 August 1912; d. 13 March 1983
Eva L. [wife of Robert E.; mother of Sharon A., Janice M., and Paula D. [no stones]] - b. 10 January 1927
Florence B. - b. 1905; d. 1991
Paula Riek (wife of David L.) - b. 27 October 1911; d. 5 June 1980
Robert E. [husb. of Eva L.; father of Sharon A., Janice M., and Paula D. [no stones]] - b. 14 August 1922
William Leslie - b. 31 March 1910; d. 9 October 1973
William R. (husb. of Addie E.) - b. 10 March 1875; d. 19 March 1953
SHEPARD
Barbara (MORRISON; [dau. of Dr. Charles C. Jr. and Hazel A.]) - b. 1925; d. 1964
SHERMAN
Albion F. - b. 1893; d. 1941
Annie E. - b. 1863; d. 1943
Dorothy - b. 1892; d. 1964
Franklin E. - b. 1862; d. 1942
Gardiner - b. 29 December 1841; d. 10 January 1907
H. Elizabeth - b. 5 January 1949; d. 14 June 1963
Helen C. - b. 1870; d. 1956
Helen M. - b. 1894; d. 1967
Hilda H. - b. 1898; d. 1976
Mary (WHITEHEAD) - b. 1901; d. 1992
[Mary Elizabeth - see OGDEN]
Roger W. - b. 1900; d. 1961
[Ruth - see GARDNER]
Ruth N. - b. 9 November 1914; d. 2 February 1984
William E. - b. 19 January 1903; d. 14 June 1963
William H. - b. 1865; d. 1928
William H. - b. 1926; d. 1974
SHIELDS
[Virginia - see HIGGINS]
[...] [headstone only]
SIMMONS
Elsie F. - b. 31 August 1894; d. 26 February 1983
SIMPKINS
Elizabeth (DYMENT) - b. 1926; d. 1972
SINCLAIR
Beverly (CARR; wife of Horace G. [no stone]) - b. 1918; d. 1937
SKINNER
Dessa M. Jr. [husb. of Mary Lee (POE)] - b. 13 July 1905; d. 3 June 1979
Mary Lee (POE; [wife of Dessa M. Jr.]) - b. 26 October 1904; d. 18 April 1986
SLEEPER
Doris J. [wife of Reginald B.] - b. 1898; d. 1972
Reginald B. [husb. of Doris J.] - b. 8 January 1899; d. 15 August 1965
SMALL
Avery F. - b. 1882; d. 1922
Beulah W[HITMORE?]. (wife of Frank G.) - b. 1884; d. 1958
Charles H. - b. 26 January 1930; d. 12 February 1994
Elizabeth D.[17] - b. 1883; d. 1970

Frank G. (husb. of Beulah W[HITMORE?].) - b. 1885; d. 1965
John S. (son of Frank G. and Beulah W[HITMORE?].) - b. 1918; d. 1963
[Lanie - see BOYNTON]
Madeleine [sic] Rhoda - b. 1903; d. 1962

SMITH

Charles G. [husb. of Mabel S.] - b. 1880; d. 1958
Chester A. (husb. of Hattie E.) - b. 1887; d. 1951
Claudette Marie [wife of Glenn Peter] - b. 30 May 1957
Cora A. - b. 1860; d. 1929
Daniel - b. 1894; d. 1962
Earl Franklin [husb. of Lillian Rackliff] - b. 1896; d. 1992
Edna M. - b. 25 June 1882; d. 8 May 1906
Edward Freeman (husb. of Mary Josephine) - b. 1867; d. 1949
Edwin R. [husb. of Louise (REID)] - b. 1909
Elizabeth E. - b. 15 June 1892; d. 31 May 1979
[Elizabeth S. - see SALISBURY]
Elmar [sic] J. (son of Chester A. and Hattie E.) - b. 1909; d. 1910
Elmar [sic] J. (son of Chester A. and Hattie E.) - b. 1913; d. 1918
Ethel H[AYWARD?]. - b. 1890; d. 1934
F. Freemont (Dr.) - b. 1856; d. 1922
Flora (wife of James W. [no stone]) - b. 1825; d. 1906
Gertrude E. (wife of Leman [sic] L. Sr.) - b. 4 May 1908; d. 10 September 1983
Glenn Peter [husb. of Claudette Marie] - b. 18 October 1958
Harriet A. [wife of Herman D.] - b. 1855; d. 1929
Hattie E. (wife of Chester A.) - b. 1888; d. 1929
Henry M. (husb. of Nettie (BAKER)) - b. 1871; d. 1925
Herman D. [husb. of Harriet A.] - b. 1857; d. 1922
Ira - d. 1910 Æ [not given]
Kenneth E. [husb. of Theresa E.] - b. 1930
Lawrence J. (husb. of Sarah (BEATON)) - b. 1850; d. 1931
Leman [sic] L. Sr. (husb. of Gertrude E.) - b. 4 August 1900; d. 17 May 1974
Lillian Rackliff [wife of Earl Franklin] - b. 1905; d. 1986
Lincoln - d. 1921 Æ [not given]
Louise (REID; [wife of Edwin R.]) - b. 1912; d. 1993
Mabel S. [wife of Charles G.] - b. 1874; d. 1962
Mamie - b. 1895; d. 1986
[Marion - see WALLS]
Mary Josephine (wife of Edward Freeman) - b. 1869, Nova Scotia; d. 1938
Morey D. - b. 1887; d. 1945
Nettie (BAKER; wife of Henry M.) - b. 1872; d. 1920
Rhoda - d. 1910 Æ [not given]
Sarah (BEATON; wife of Lawrence J.) - b. 1852; d. 1936
Theresa “Tes” [dau. of Glenn Peter and Claudette Marie?] - b. 6 January 1988; d. 22 February 1990
Theresa E. [wife of Kenneth E.] - b. 1933; d. 1977
W. [SMITH?] - [no dates]
William Harris - b. 1931; d. 1976

SNOW

Ann C. (wife of Benjamin) - b. 1836; d. 1907
Benjamin (husb. of Ann C.) - b. 1830; d. 1914

SOMES

[Florence - see ELLS]

SOPER
Bernice O. [wife of Charles L.] - b. 1890; d. 1974
Charles L. [husb. of Bernice O.] - b. 1889; d. 1946
Everett L. - b. 1897; d. 1986
Frank - b. 1877; d. 1945
G[eorge?]. Henry (husb. of Mildred G.) - b. 1892; d. 1948
George E. (husb. of Nellie D.) - b. 1858; d. 1918
George Henry Jr. - b. 17 August 1915; d. 13 March 1949
Laura [SOPER?] - [no dates]
[Marguerite - see TONAS]
Marie [SOPER?] - [no dates]
Mildred G. (wife of G[eorge?]. Henry) - b. 1888; d. 1931
Nellie D. (wife of George E.) - b. 1859; d. 1947
SPENCER
[...] [headstone only]
SPRAGUE
Chester W. - b. 25 May 1885; d. 3 October 1949
Crystal (THOMPSON) - b. 1928
Jonathan Henry Jr. - b. 1921; d. 1991
Mary (ROBERTS) - b. 1891; d. 1965
Raymond D. Sr. - b. 1900; d. 1993
SPRATT
Alice Y. [dau. of Frank and Harriet (NICKERSON)?] - b. 1886; d. 1963
Allison H. - b. 1916; d. 1973
Anne E. - b. 1917; d. 1986
Donald H. - b. 18 October 1944; d. 15 October 1993
Frank (husb. of Harriet (NICKERSON)) - b. 1851; d. 1920
Harriet (NICKERSON; wife of Frank) - b. 1855; d. 1927
SPROUL
George A. - b. 1843; d. 1920
Jessie P. - b. 1860; d. 1950
STAFFORD
Ada A. - b. 1873; d. 1933
Carabel C. - b. 1872; d. 1961
George J. - b. 1866; d. 1921
Pamelia F. - b. 1894; d. 1980
[Ruth S[TAFFORD?]. - see BUNKER]
STALFORD
[Evelyn - see KILBOURNE]
STANLEY
Alice Williams - b. 15 July 1898; d. 2 March 1993
Blanche C. (wife of C. Bertrand) - b. 1911
C. Bertrand (husb. of Blanche C.) - b. 1898; d. 1966
Dora J. - b. 1905; d. 1974
Dorothy H[ODGKINS?]. - b. 1902; d. 1992
[Elma - see HAVEY]
Emily A. ([BAKER?]; wife of Robert E. [no stone]) - b. 1870; d. 1927
F. E. S[TANLEY?]. - b. 1859; d. 1942
George G. [husb. of Zelda M.] - b. 1890; d. 1981
George M. - b. 1905; d. 1998
H. I. S[TANLEY?]. - b. 1859; d. 1929
Robert P. - b. 1907; d. 1992

Winifred H. - b. 1908
Zelda M. [wife of George G.] - b. 1901; d. 1998

STAPLES
Doris S. [wife of Maurice N.] - b. 19 January 1909
Maurice N. [husb. of Doris S.] - b. 29 November 1908; d. 11 November 1992

STEEVES
Ada E. - b. 1899; d. 1950

STEINER
Alice (JUDD) - b. 1917

STEVENS
A. Frances (dau. of Amos F. and Mary F.) - b. 1891; d. 1952
Amos F. (husb. of Mary F.) - b. 1847; d. 1939
[Ariel - see HARE]
Emma M. [wife of Joseph A.] - b. 1864; d. 1929
Joseph A. [husb. of Emma M.] - b. 1859; d. 1932
Joseph A. Jr. [husb. of Kathleen (MORRIS)] - b. 4 June 1893; d. 30 October 1953
Kathleen (MORRIS; [wife of Joseph A. Jr.]) - b. 26 October 1893; d. 17 August 1986
Lela [dau. of Amos F. and Mary F.?] - b. 1884; d. 1967
Mary Eleanor - b. 9 September 1920; d. 18 October 1966
Mary F. (wife of Amos F.) - b. 1858; d. 1950

STEWART
Beatrice L. - b. 1900; d. 1995
Charles F. - b. 1925; d. 1980
Donald Edwin - b. 1922; d. 1931
Edwin Spencer - b. 1899; d. 1940
Hugh - d. 28 October 1904 Æ 41 y.
Neil - b. 1847; d. 1922

STOVER
J. Dorothy [wife of Walter A.] - b. 1906; d. 1987
Walter A. [husb. of J. Dorothy] - b. 1908; d. 1966

STROUT
Austin L. - b. 5 August 1921; d. 6 August 1988
Carrie L. [wife of Ora G.] - b. 1881; d. 1961
Eugene A. - b. 1886; d. 1929
Eugene W. (son of Eugene A.) - b. 1919; d. 1927
Kenneth Lee - b. 7 April 1927; d. 4 September 1998
Maurice M. (son of Marshall and Kathleen [no stones]) - b. 21 February 1936; d. 16 June 1998
Ora G. [husb. of Carrie L.] - b. 1875; d. 1943

STUART
Fred L. - d. 11 November 1904 Æ 29 y., 10 m.
Fred Leslie - b. 22 November 1904; d. 18 March 1970

STURK
Blanche (TRIPP; [wife of William H.]) - b. 1883; d. 1958
William H. [husb. of Blanche (TRIPP)] - b. 1893; d. 1946

SULLIVAN
Blanche R. (wife of George W.) - b. 1891; d. 1974
Catherine E. (wife of William B.) - b. 1856; d. 1924
Clarence ([son of George W. and Blanche R.?]; husb. of Evelyn P.) - b. 1923; d. 1989
Colby L. - b. 1930; d. 1974

Evelyn P. (wife of Clarence) - b. 1917
George W. (husb. of Blanche R.) - b. 22 February 1891; d. 15 January 1953
Joan (dau. of George W. and Blanche R.) - b. 1928; d. 1932
Walter D. - b. 1857; d. 1949
William B. (husb. of Catherine E.) - b. 1850; d. 1909

SUMINSBY
Carroll B. - b. 1892; d. 1945
Harley H. - b. 1888; d. 1912
Harriett [sic] S. - b. 1862; d. 1949
Howell K. - b. 1890; d. 1967
Inez M. - b. 1885; d. 1959
John - b. 1852; d. 1926
Virginia Eddy - b. 1892; d. 1971

SUNDERLAND
Barbara G. [wife of Riley] - b. 1920
Riley [husb. of Barbara G.] - b. 1917; d. 1993

SWAN
Thomas - b. 1905; d. 1938

SYLVIA
Elizabeth S. [wife of Ralph D.] - b. 1908; d. 1997
Floyd C. [husb. of Phyllis S.] - b. 3 October 1897; d. 25 August 1975
Gordon E. - b. 1905; d. 1968
Helen F. - b. 1912; d. 1980
Lavena D. - b. 1875; d. 1976
Phyllis S. [wife of Floyd C.] - b. 20 March 1908; d. 3 October 1987
Ralph D. [husb. of Elizabeth S.] - b. 1907; d. 1963
Thelma R. - b. 1895; d. 1949
William J. - b. 1869; d. 1934

TABBUT
A. Ralph [husb. of Nellie C.] - b. 6 May 1894; d. 16 February 1981
Donald L. - b. 5 April 1920; d. 5 March 1997
Fannie W. [wife of Leon W.] - b. 1868; d. 1960
Leon W. [husb. of Fannie W.] - b. 1867; d. 1920
Nellie C. [wife of A. Ralph] - b. 13 July 1896; d. 7 March 1995

TAIT
Milan F. - b. 9 October 1927; d. 28 March 1982
Milan F. Jr. - b. 7 March 1952; d. 10 March 1952
Robert J. - b. 23 June 1931; d. 15 February 1951

TEMME
Joel David - b. 13 February 1951; d. 24 December 1985

TEMPLETON
Mabel H[IGGINS?]. - b. 1887; d. 1976

TENAN
Emma J. - b. 1843; d. 1925

THATCHER
Arthur E. (husb. of Nancy B[UTTERFIELD?].) - b. 1882; d. 1978
Nancy B[UTTERFIELD?]. (wife of Arthur E.) - b. 1885; d. 1976

THATCHER-SHELTON
E. Allison - b. 15 April 1937; d. 27 December 1993

THOMAS
[Annie D. - see McKAY]
Ernest L. - b. 1905; d. 1969

THOMPSON
[Crystal - see SPRAGUE]
[Elizabeth D. - see SMALL]
Evadne S[ALISBURY?]. - b. 1889; d. 1981
Florence M. (COLE; wife of Orient Y.) - b. 1883; d. 1937
Harriet W. - b. 1856; d. 1933
John L. - b. 1842; d. 1929
Mary M. [wife of Verrill J.] - b. 1900; d. 1985
Orient Y. (husb. of Florence M. (COLE)) - b. 1885; d. 1951
Stephen J. - b. 1962; d. 1988
Verrill J. [husb. of Mary M.] - b. 1889; d. 1957
THORNDIKE
Augusta Baker[13] [wife of Augustus Jr.] - b. 8 March 1924
Augustus Jr. [husb. of Augusta Baker[13]] - b. 13 April 1919; d. 8 May 1993
Elizabeth (FRITZ; [wife of Robert Amory]) - b. 1908; d. 1992
Robert Amory [husb. of Elizabeth (FRITZ)] - b. 1900; d. 1972
Theodore Baker [son of Augustus Jr. and Augusta Baker[13]?] - b. 8 September 1952; d. 2 January 1987
THORNE
Bertha P. - b. 1911; d. 1974
THULIN
Helene Joerg - b. 1894, Frankfurt, Germany; d. 1986
THURBER
Anna (MORSE; [wife of Earle V.]) - b. 9 October 1886; d. 30 April 1979
Earle V. [husb. of Anna (MORSE)] - b. 21 January 1884; d. 1 December 1953
Lois E. [dau. of Earle V. and Anna (MORSE)?] - b. 1 June 1911; d. 24 July 1981
TOBIN
Charles F. - b. 1914; d. 1970
TONAS
Louis (husb. of Marguerite (SOPER)) - b. 1896; d. 1958
Marguerite (SOPER; wife of Louis) - b. 1917; d. 1988
TORREY
Dorothy - b. 1893; d. 1935
Gordon E. - b. 1913; d. 1992
Guy E. - b. 1887; d. 1937
Guy E. Jr. - b. 1919; d. 1942
Hubert Stuart - b. 1950; d. 1998
Norman S. - b. 1917; d. 1940
Payson - b. 1919
TOWN
Mina R. [wife of Willis C.] - b. 1867; d. 1948
Willis C. [husb. of Mina R.] - b. 1877; d. 1936
TRACY
Effie W. - b. 1884; d. 1943
Walter S. - b. 1872; d. 1956
TREDRIC
Edward - b. 1875; d. 1939
Matilda Casey - b. 1881; d. 1960
TRIPP
[Blanche - see STURK]
Blithen A. - b. 1879; d. 1919
Blithen A. [husb. of Kathleen G.] - b. 1908; d. 1977

Eva L. (wife of J. Eldridge) - b. 1912; d. 1976
Henry E. - b. 1876; d. 1884
J. Eldridge (husb. of Eva L.) - b. 1906; d. 1965
[Jacqulyn [sic] - see BLOMQUIST]
Joseph E. - b. 1843; d. 1919
Kathleen G. [wife of Blithen A.] - b. 1910; d. 1978
Kenneth E. [husb. of Neta R.] - b. 1909; d. 1977
Mary J. - b. 1849; d. 1926
Mary Jane - b. 1911; d. 1915
Neta R. [wife of Kenneth E.] - b. 1909; d. 1996

TRUSSELL
E. Marshall - b. 22 January 1914; d. 8 November 1985
Ethel M. - b. 1877; d. 1926
Henry H. - b. 1915; d. 1920

TUCK
Clifford L. - b. 1901; d. 1976

TURNBULL
Deborah C. - b. 25 December 1957; d. 16 September 1992

TURNER
Cassie Mae - [b. and d.?] 23 January 1986

TYLER
[Phyllis - see CHILMAN]

VAN GEMERT
Gerrit - b. 21 June 1881; d. 28 October 1965

VANIVER
Mae - b. 1887; d. 1978

VASS
[Sarah Ann - see MILLER]

WADE
Benjamin A. - b. 31 March 1938; d. 29 January 1987

WALLS
Annie May [wife of Frank L.] - b. 1883; d. 1941
Frank L. [husb. of Annie May] - b. 1876; d. 1962
Harvey G. Jr. - b. 27 November 1922; d. 9 October 1992
John T. - b. 1905; d. 1987
Joseph (husb. of Winniefred [sic] M.) - b. 1881; d. 1952
Marion (SMITH) - b. 1885; d. 1962
Ralph A. - b. 1887; d. 1971
Terrence L. - b. 15 February 1946; d. 23 April 1972
Winniefred [sic] M. (wife of Joseph) - b. 1888; d. 1972

WALPORT
James - b. 1860; d. 1927

WALTO
Patricia L. [wife of Peter A.] - b. 18 May 1951
Peter A. [husb. of Patricia L.] - b. 10 May 1945

WARD
Helen W. [wife of Otis A.] - b. 1891; d. 1989
Otis A. [husb. of Helen W.] - b. 1891; d. 1950

WARK
Avis E. (wife of Harold R.) - b. 1913
Harold R. (husb. of Avis E.) - b. 1912; d. 1965

WARREN
Dorothy A. - b. 1915; d. 1988
Ethel L. - b. 1895; d. 1969
Frances E. - b. 1921
Howard C. - b. 1916
WASGATT
Asa - b. 1906; d. 1950
[Beryl W[ASGATT?]. - see PARSONS]
Boyd "Bud" - b. 1940; d. 1991
Carolyn R. - b. 1867; d. 1938
Natalie S. - b. 1906; d. 1984
Richard D. - b. 1908; d. 1968
Vernon G. - b. 1869; d. 1932
WAY
Channing Jr. [husb. of Hermione Barret] - b. 1912; d. 1992
Hermione Barret [wife of Channing Jr.] - b. 1915; d. 1997
WAYBRET
Fred A. - b. 24 May 1880; d. 25 June 1965
WEATHERBEE
William D. - b. October 1858; d. November 1939
WEBB
Ella F. (wife of Everett C.) - b. 1873; d. 1944
Everett C. (husb. of Vyra L. and Ella F.) - b. 1863; d. 1946
Vyra L. (wife of Everett C.) - b. 1852; d. 1926
WEBBER
Burton H. Jr. - b. 3 April 1901; d. 21 September 1960
Burton H. Sr. (son of Sara [sic] (LAWFORD)[18]) - b. 29 March 1875; d. 20 August 1951
Edmund H. (husb. of Virginia E.) - b. 1895; d. 1962
Erwin C. - b. 18 August 1913; d. 30 September 1960
Glenn H. - b. 17 February 1929; d. 14 October 1980
[Martha E. - see CUNNINGHAM]
Mary H[IGGINS?]. - b. 1912; d. 1963
Parker M. (son of Burton H. Jr. and [...][5]) - b. 20 October 1930; d. 16 February 1931
Sara [sic] (LAWFORD)[18] - b. 1823; d. 1918
Virginia E. (wife of Edmund H.) - b. 1894; d. 1973
WEBER
Inge Charlotte (BRIMMEKAMP) - b. 1932; d. 1997
WELLMAN
Margie Alice [wife of Richard J.?] - b. 4 March 1882; d. 25 September 1956
Richard J. [husb. of Margie Alice?] - b. 23 June 1890; d. 1 October 1963
WESCOTT
Cecelia G. - b. 1872; d. 1959
Chester A. [husb. of Eva C.] - b. 1890; d. 1962
Eva C. [wife of Chester A.] - b. 1891; d. 1973
Frederick A. (husb. of Pearl Otto) - b. 15 March 1890; d. 21 July 1968
Gertrude Louise - b. 1906; d. 1919
Helen E. (wife of Orlando P[aine?]. Jr.) - b. 1894; d. 1986
John L. - b. 4 February 1894; d. 28 June 1953
Orlando P[aine?]. Jr. (husb. of Helen E.) - b. 2 December 1892; d. 14 February 1946
Orlando Paine - b. 1858; d. 1929
Pearl Otto (wife of Frederick A.) - b. 1893; d. 1986

WEST
Alice J. - b. 1871; d. 1948
Clara E. - b. 1891; d. 1972
Daniel M. - b. 1857; d. 1943
E. Esther - b. 1893; d. 1972
Margaret T. [GRANT?] - b. 1935
WESTRUP
Elizabeth R. [wife of Hugh G.] - b. 18 November 1886; d. 17 May 1973
Hugh G. [husb. of Elizabeth R.] - b. 21 October 1886; d. 1 January 1949
WEYMOUTH
Raymond E. Sr. - b. 1903; d. 1965
WHISTLER
Mildred (MORRISON) - b. 1895; d. 1961
WHITAM [sic]
John W. Jr. - b. 14 August 1922; d. 28 August 1922
WHITCOMB
John (husb. of Ruth W.) - b. 1905; d. 1966
Ruth W. (wife of John) - b. 1904; d. 1979
WHITE
Charles H. - b. 9 October 1909; d. 30 November 1968
Fred Kenneth (husb. of Freda Diane (DYER)) - b. 27 June 1927; d. 22 July 1995
Freda Diane (DYER; wife of Fred Kenneth) - b. 13 September 1930; d. 4 April 1997
George B. - b. 13 April 1901; d. 7 October 1947
Margaret (DOLLIVER; wife of Frank L. [no stone]) - b. 1921; d. 1989
Margaret (DYER) - b. 1879; d. 1965
William H. - b. 1913; d. 1954
WHITEHEAD
[Mary - see SHERMAN]
WHITEHOUSE
[Alice - see FREEMAN]
WHITMORE
Affie [sic] M. - b. 1865; d. 1949
Almenia B. (wife of Clarence E.) - b. 1872; d. 1942
[Beulah W[HITMORE?]. - see SMALL]
Clarence E. (husb. of Almenia B.) - b. 1868; d. 1970
Florence E. (dau. of John 2nd and Rebecca N.) - d. 7 April 1879 Æ 1 y., 10 d.
Frank E. - b. 1867; d. 1939
Gertrude Y[EATON?]. - b. 1908; d. 1974
Harold P. - b. 1888; d. 1964
John 2nd (husb. of Rebecca N.) - d. 23 September 1891 Æ 47 y., 5 m., 13 d.
Rebecca N. (wife of John 2nd) - d. 12 December 1926 Æ 79 y., 3 m., 8 d.
WHITTAKER
Carl G. [husb. of Mary M.?] - b. 1894; d. 1972
Eben K. [WHITTAKER?] - [no dates]
Ella M. [WHITTAKER?] - b. 1864; d. 1926
Mary M. [wife of Carl G.?] - b. 1893; d. 1982
WIGHT
[Beatrice - see GORDON]
WILBUR
Bertha M. (wife of Herbert T.) - b. 1879; d. 1933
Herbert T. (husb. of Bertha M.) - b. 1878; d. 1947

Herbert Tilden [Dr.; husb. of Rebecca Ormand] - b. 15 August 1911; d. 5 March 1993
Rebecca Ormand [wife of Dr. Herbert Tilden] - b. 26 July 1911; d. 7 September 1996

WILLEY
Barbara K. [wife of Roger L.] - b. 1919; d. 1990
Bertha E. (wife of Clifford M.) - b. 1877; d. 1935
Clifford M. (husb. of Bertha E.) - b. 1876; d. 1957
Clifford M. Jr. "Cliff" - b. 1911; d. 1960
Eugene W. [husb. of Harriet E.] - b. 1865; d. 1936
Fredonna [dau. of Clifford M. and Bertha E.?] - b. 1917; d. 1918
Harriet E. [wife of Eugene W.] - b. 1868; d. 1914
Lilian [sic] D. - b. 1915; d. 1998
Orrin F. - [son of Eugene W. and Harriet E.?] - b. 1898; d. 1960
Reginald [son of Clifford M. and Bertha E.?] - b. 1900; d. 1911
Roger L. [husb. of Barbara K.] - b. 1915; d. 1988

WILLIAMS
Frances (GOODRICH; [wife of Harold Thomas]) - b. 1913
Harold Thomas [husb. of Frances (GOODRICH)] - b. 1904; d. 1984

WILLIS
Clayton O. (husb. of Geraldine E.) - b. 24 January 1925; d. 19 November 1981
Geraldine E. (wife of Clayton O.) - b. 1 January 1925
Malcolm Ora [husb. of Thelma M.] - b. 1904; d. 1970
Thelma M. [wife of Malcolm Ora] - b. 1904; d. 1988

WILMARTH
Christine S. [wife of Harold E.] - b. 1895; d. 1988
Harold E. [husb. of Christine S.] - b. 4 June 1896; d. 29 December 1969

WILSON
Jennie L. - b. 1854; d. 1927

WOOD
B. H. - b. 1858; d. 1929
Dean W. - b. 1897; d. 1918; ("died in World War 1918")
[Eliza - see McFARLAND]
Eliza J. - b. 1847; d. 1909
Emma (COLLINS; wife of J. Andrew) - b. 1855; d. 1920
F. A. - b. 1851; d. 1930
F. J. - [no dates]
Harold V. Sr. [husb. of Winifred L.] - b. 18 October 1910; d. 21 September 1986
J. Andrew (husb. of Emma (COLLINS)) - b. 1856; d. 1919
Joseph Whiting [husb. of Lorinda (HARDEN)] - b. 1825; d. 1905
Lalah [sic] (HODGKINS) - b. 1900; d. 1968
Lorinda (HARDEN; [wife of Joseph Whiting]) - b. 1830; d. 1915
[Mary F. - see PETTEE]
Winifred L. [wife of Harold V. Sr.] - b. 1914; d. 1979

WOODWORTH
Elmer B. (son of Jesse and [...][5]) - d. 20 May 1911 Æ 2 y., 4 m., 20 d.
Henry Alton - b. 1908; d. 1977
Jesse - b. 1873; d. 1918
Paul D. - b. 1970; d. 1986
Queenie V. - b. 1910; d. 1988
Stephen - b. 1949; d. 1959

WYMAN
Clara E. - b. 20 September 1848; d. 8 December 1927

YEATON
- Carolyn W. - b. 1871; d. 1962
- [Gertrude Y[EATON?]. - see WHITMORE]
- Horace T. - b. 1860; d. 1940

YOUNG
- Bert Harvey (husb. of Florence (DAVIS)) - b. 1884; d. 1931
- Catherine Doran [wife of Frank Tarbox] - b. 1863; d. 1952
- Charles H. - b. 1883; d. 1959
- Dana H. [husb. of Lillian J.] - b. 1906; d. 1987
- Dennis M. - b. 5 February 1947; d. 6 March 1997
- Doris L. [wife of Morris A.] - b. 1906; d. 1995
- Elizabeth Wade - b. 1882; d. 1927
- Elvin (husb. of Mary) - d. 18 October 1895 Æ 88 y., 5 m.
- [Eva - see DAMMEYER]
- Florence (DAVIS; wife of Bert Harvey) - b. 1882; d. 1931
- Frank Tarbox [husb. of Catherine Doran] - b. 1862; d. 1941
- Hobart H. (son of Elvin and Mary) - d. 10 August 1838 Æ 3 y.
- Hobart H. [husb. of Vesta A.] - b. 1848; d. 1925
- James F. [husb. of Mary I.] - b. 1855; d. 1931
- James F. - b. 1913; d. 1945
- Judith D. [dau. of Dana H. and Lillian J.?] - b. 1938; d. 1995
- [Laura - see HITCH]
- Leonard E. (husb. of Marie F.) - b. 14 February 1880; d. 25 September 1964
- Leonard E. Jr. (son of Leonard E. and Marie F.; husb. of Marguerite S.) - b. 24 April 1916; d. 16 March 1979
- Lillian J. [wife of Dana H.] - b. 1904; d. 1997
- Lucy (ALLEY; wife of Robert D. [no stone]) - b. 18 November 1925; d. 3 December 1989
- [Margaret - see HODGKINS]
- Marguerite S. (wife of Leonard E. Jr.) - b. 23 July 1918; d. 21 February 1989
- Marie F. (wife of Leonard E.) - b. 8 April 1876; d. 21 September 1960
- Mary (wife of Elvin) - d. 1 July 1884 Æ 82 y., 4 m.
- Mary I. [wife of James F.] - b. 1855; d. 1939
- Mary J. - b. 1880; d. 1976
- Morris A. [husb. of Doris L.] - b. 1910; d. 1993
- Octavius W. [husb. of Tullia Augusta] - b. 11 November 1838; d. 20 January 1914
- Onslow (son of Elvin and Mary) - d. 18 August 1851 Æ 18 y.
- Tullia Augusta [wife of Octavius W.] - b. 29 July 1846; d. 29 June 1919
- Vesta A. [wife of Hobart H.] - b. 1854; d. 1940
- Willard - b. 1868; d. 1958

ZERRIEN
- Clara [wife of Edmund C.?] - b. 1895; d. 1984
- Edmund C. (husb. of Gilda S. (IANTOSCA)) - b. 18 July 1915; d. 31 May 1989
- Edmund C. [husb. of Clara?] - b. 16 December 1890; d. 3 February 1963
- Gilda S. (IANTOSCA; wife of Edmund C.) - b. 16 February 1916; d. 27 December 1995

[...]
- Árpád - b. 1902; d. 1904
- Boyd W. - b. 1898; d. 1938
- Forrest - [no dates]
- infant - [no dates]
- Matthew - [b. and d.?] 19 February 1998

Nick - [no dates]
Shannon E. - b. 1909; d. 1957
Vernon W. - b. 1899; d. 1962
[...][8]
[...][9]

Notes:
[1]Stone worn, cracked, and/or broken.
[2] Engraver appears to have engraved "ANNE" in error and then engraved a second *E* overlapping the right side of the original *E* to make the name appear to be "ANNIE".
[3]Different on different stones.
[4]Stone blank.
[5]Name not given.
[6]Both 2 and 3 engraved in ten's place.
[7]It is unclear whether Statie M. or Maj. Richard M. FOSTER is buried in Arlington.
[8]Stone face down, heavy.
[9]Large cross made of pressure-treated lumber.
[10]Death date on stone of Ruth M. (RODICK) KEYES is 2029.
[11]The stone containing the names of Glenn F. ROBERTSON and Glenyce M. is no longer in this cemetery.
[12]It is possible that this stone is for a family pet. George Gibson MCMURTRY's obituary in The Bar Harbor Times mentions only a wife and daughter as surviving him.
[13]To determine if this is a maiden name will require further research.
[14]It is unclear from the gravestones whether the surname is GARBER or FOSS.
[15]It is unclear from the gravestone whether the surname is ALLEN or MADDOX.
[16]It is unclear from the gravestone whether the surname is PEACH or PEARL.
[17]Her stone reads Elizabeth D. SMALL and is on a lot with a THOMPSON headstone.
[18]His Bar Harbor Times obituary reports the parents of Burton H. Webber Sr. as John and Sarah Weed Webber. The stone of Sara (LAWFORD), however, states that she is the mother of Burton H. Webber Sr. If the latter is correct, she would have been well over 50 years old when he was born.

Emery Family Burial Ground
(Bar Harbor - 21)

Location/directions. Grounds of MDI Biological Labs. From the traffic light at the north end of Mount Desert Island, bear left on Route 3. In approximately 4.2–4.3 miles, turn left onto Old Bar Harbor Road. The entrance to MDI Biological Labs is less than 0.1 miles on the left. Inquire at the office for permission to enter the grounds and for directions to the cemetery.

History. The name applied to this cemetery is only for convenience of reference in this book.

Notes. There is no discernable boundary to this cemetery. It is raked free of excessive brush.

Names and dates on gravestones and other markers. [27 December 1998]

DESISLE
- J. Frances (EMERY; dau. of Benjamin EMERY and Elmira; wife of Chesnel [no stone]) - d. 16 April 1873 Æ 32 y., 10 m.

EMERY
- Benjamin (husb. of Elmira) - b. 1808; d. 1883
- Cedelia H. - b. 1868; d. 1875
- Celia K. - b. 1853; d. 1866
- Clarence S. - b. 1853; d. 1864
- Clifford S. - b. 1855; d. 1877
- Elmira (wife of Benjamin) - b. 1809; d. 1865
- Everett - b. 1874; d. 1877
- Fannie R. - b. 1872; d. 1875
- "infant dau." - d. 25 April 1858 Æ 2 m., 19 d.
- "infant son" - b. 1854; d. 1855
- Ira L. - b. 1856; d. 1878
- [J. Frances - see DESISLE]
- Josie - b. 1877; d. 1881
- [Lydia H. - see WILCOMB]

INGALLS
- Charles A. - d. 5 March 1889 Æ 30 y.

WILCOMB
- Lydia H. (EMERY; dau. of Benjamin EMERY and Elmira; wife of Frederic [sic] [no stone]) - d. 23 April 1873 Æ 30 y., 5 m., 3 d.

Newman Grave
(Bar Harbor - 22)

Location/directions. In woods north of Route 233, on east slope of McFarland Hill. From the traffic light at the north end of Mount Desert Island, bear left on Route 3. Travel approximately 10.0–10.1 miles to the intersection of Routes 3 and 233. Just before the stop sign at the intersection, turn right onto Route 233 (Eagle Lake Road). The gravestone is in the woods to the right (north) of this road in about 2.5–2.6 miles.

History. This grave is on land that is now part of Acadia National Park.

Notes. This stone, which is detached from its base, is at the edge of an old field near a low, wet area that extends nearly to the side of Route 233.

Names and dates on gravestones and other markers. [2 April 2000]
NEWMAN
George - d. 21 April 1887 Æ 92 y., 5 m.

CRANBERRY ISLES

On 16 March 1830, five islands of the town of Mount Desert—Baker, Bear, Great Cranberry, Little Cranberry, and Sutton—incorporated as the town of Cranberry Isles. Bear Island has no cemeteries. There is one each on Baker and Sutton, and seven each on Great Cranberry and Little Cranberry.

Baker Island:
- Baker Island Cemetery (Cranberry Isles - 1)

Great Cranberry Island:
- Bunker Cemetery (Cranberry Isles - 2)
- Stanley Cemetery (Cranberry Isles - 3)
- Preble Cemetery (Cranberry Isles - 4)
- Spurling Cemetery (Cranberry Isles - 11)
- Bunker and Olson Graves (Cranberry Isles - 14)
- Harding Point Cemetery (Cranberry Isles - 15)
- Spurling Point Cemetery (Cranberry Isles - 16)

Little Cranberry Island:
- Stanley-Hadlock Cemetery (Cranberry Isles - 5)
- Merrill Family Burial Ground (Cranberry Isles - 6)
- Stanley-Gilley Cemetery (Cranberry Isles - 7)
- Sand Beach Cemetery (Cranberry Isles - 8)
- Standley Grave (Cranberry Isles - 10)
- Merrill Family Burial Ground (Cranberry Isles - 12)
- Sawtelle Graves (Cranberry Isles - 13)

Sutton Island:
- Sutton Island Cemetery (Cranberry Isles - 9)

Baker Island Cemetery (Cranberry Isles - 1) with mountains of east side of Mount Desert Island in background.

Baker Island Cemetery

(Cranberry Isles - 1)

Location/directions. In a field, near the northwest shore of Baker Island. From the cobble beach on the north shore of the island, follow the trail leading toward the interior of the island. At a concrete post turn right and follow this trail to the cemetery.

History. All persons whose graves are marked by stones are descendants of William GILLEY and Hannah (LURVEY), who moved to the island in the early 1800s from what is now Southwest Harbor.

Notes. No fence encloses this cemetery, and the grass is rarely mowed. Some stones are leaning or laying on the ground. The stone of Elisha B. Gilley is broken into several pieces and lays on the middle of another grave.

Names and dates on gravestones and other markers.

DOLLIVER

[Adeline - see GILLEY]

GILLEY

Adeline (DOLLIVER; wife of Joseph) - d. 27 March 1876 Æ 54 y., 8 m.
Charles A. - b. 27 November 1847; d. 24 November 1914
Elisha B. (husb. of Hannah M.) - d. [...][1] Æ 93 y., 10 m., 1[6?][1] d.
Hannah M. (wife of Elisha B.) - d. 11 May 1880 Æ 69 y., 4 m., 15 d.
Harriet E. "Hattie" (wife of Samuel B.) - d. 11 February 1908 Æ 51 y., 3 m., 17 d.
Joseph (husb. of Adeline (DOLLIVER)) - d. 10 July 1894 Æ 81 y., 1 m., 21 d.
Joseph W. - b. 13 October 1859; d. 5 May 1918
Samuel B. (husb. of Harriet E. "Hattie") - d. [8?][2] January 1927 Æ 70 y., 25 d.
Victor (son of Samuel B. and Harriet E. "Hattie") - b. [and d.?] 25 October 1884

STANLEY

Phebe J. (wife of Robert S.) - d. 24 April 1929 Æ 87 y., 3 m.
Robert S. (husb. of Phebe J.) - d. 29 November 1890 Æ [...][3]

Notes:

[1]Stone broken.
[2]Difficult to read.
[3]Remainder of stone below ground.

Bunker Cemetery

(Cranberry Isles - 2)

Location/directions. Along main road, Great Cranberry. From the town dock, walk straight ahead on the paved road. Soon the road curves to the left and then generally runs straight. The cemetery is along the right side of the road.

History. —

Notes. Laying in the woods behind the cemetery is a stone for Willis E. BUNKER and Rena that gives full birth and death dates. These have been incorporated into the information below. Found with this stone are footstones: "S. S. B." [Samuel S. BUNKER?], "H. A. B." [Hannah A. BUNKER?], and "A. B.", in addition to 2 broken pieces of footstones and a base with a slot for a stone. The cemetery is enclosed by a gated chain-link fence, and the grass is mowed and trimmed.

Names and dates on gravestones and other markers. [4 September 1999]

ALLEY
- Lewis H. [husb. of Lulu M.] - b. 1909
- Lulu M. [wife of Lewis H.] - b. 1895; d. [no date]

BRACY
- Anda C. (son of F. J. and Bertha E. [no stones]) - d. 13 February 1896 Æ 2 y., 4 m.
- Annie S. [wife of Wesley P.] - b. 1902; d. 1992
- Barbara A. [wife of Lester C.] - b. 3 December 1943
- Charles W. [husb. of Emma P.] - b. 1865; d. 1946
- Cynthia W. - b. 1846; d. 1911
- Emma P. [wife of Charles W.] - b. 1872; d. 1960
- James F. [husb. of Martha I.] - b. 1871; d. 1958
- Lester C. [husb. of Barbara A.] - b. 7 May 1936; d. 19 June 1990
- Martha I. [wife of James F.] - b. 1888; d. 1940
- Wesley P. [husb. of Annie S.] - b. 1906

BUNKER
- Abigail (wife of Capt. Joseph) - d. 21 September 1852 Æ 54 y., 7 m., 18 d.
- Adah A. (dau. of Capt. William P. and Hannah G.) - d. 8 April 1869 Æ 1 y., 10 m., 8 d.
- Adah H. (adopted dau. of Capt. Joseph and Mary E.) - d. 7 August 1863 Æ 8 y., 11 m., 10 d.
- Alta I. (wife of Henry A.) - b. 1877; d. 1969
- Alton H. (son of Henry A. and Alta I.) - b. 1897; d. 1943
- Amanda M. (wife of John G.) - b. 1844; d. 1910
- Annie L. (wife of Elisha G.) - b. 1890; d. 1943
- Arthur C. (Capt.; son of Capt. Thomas Jr. and Lydia M. (PREBLE)) - b. 1846; d. 1972; bur. Portland, Maine
- Atlee P. (Capt.; son of Capt. Thomas Jr. and Lydia M. (PREBLE)) - b. 1844; d. 1890, Staten Island, New York
- Benaiah (husb. of Dorcas B.) - d. 3 August 1866 Æ 81 y., 2[0 or 9?][1] d.
- Benaiah B. (husb. of Josie S.) - b. 1863; d. 1951
- Charles E. (Capt.; son of Capt. Thomas Jr. and Lydia M. (PREBLE)) - b. 1841; d. 1879, "at sea"; bur. Portland, Maine
- Clara B.[3] - b. 1874; d. 1955
- [Dorcas - see SPURLING]
- Dorcas B. (wife of Benaiah) - d. 19 June 1873 Æ 73 y., 8 m., 6 d.

Edgar A. (son of Elisha G. and Annie L.) - b. 1925; d. 8 October 1951, Yonchon, Korea; ("died in action")
Edgar F. (son of Benaiah B. and Josie S.) - d. 2 October 18[...][0 or 9?][1] Æ [...][1]
Edgar R. (son of Henry A. and Alta I.) - b. 1899; d. 1907
Elisha G. (husb. of Annie L.) - b. 1870; d. 1952
[Gaile - see COLBY]
George W. (Capt.; son of Capt. Thomas Jr. and Lydia M. (PREBLE)) - b. 1839; d. [no date]
George W. - b. 20 February 1857; d. 7 October 1914
Gertrude M. (wife of Percy E.) - b. 1884; d. 1955
Hannah A. (wife of Capt. Samuel S.) - d. 1 May 1902 Æ 80 y., 7 m., 15 d.
Hannah G. (wife of Capt. William P.) - b. 1836; d. 1925
Harriet P. (dau. of Capt. Thomas Jr. and Lydia M. (PREBLE)) - b. 1836; d. 1885
Henry A. (husb. of Alta I.) - b. 1872; d. 1941
J. H. - b. 1860; d. 1934
Joanna (wife of Capt. Thomas) - d. 24 August 1871 Æ 79 y., 9 m., 4 d.
John G. (husb. of Amanda M.) - b. 1819; d. 1902
John Melvin - b. 13 September 1868; d. 24 April 1935
John W. (son of Capt. Samuel S. and Hannah A.) - d. 25 July 1876 Æ 26 y., 3 m., 19 d.
Joseph (Capt.; husb. of Abigail) - d. 25 November 1871 Æ 74 y., 2 m., 25 d.
Joseph (Capt.; husb. of Mary E.) - d. 16 December 1896 Æ 74 y., 8 m.
Josie S. (wife of Benaiah B.) - b. 1870; d. 1958
Lily (dau. of Willis E. and Rena A.) - [b. and d.?] 22 November 1884
Lydia M. (PREBLE; wife of Capt. Thomas Jr.) - b. 1807; d. 1887
M. Rosalee (wife of Winslow E.) - b. 1919; d. 1967
Martha (dau. of Capt. Thomas and Sarah E.) - d. 9 August 1835 Æ 18 y., 1 m., 13 d.
Mary E. (wife of Capt. Joseph) - b. 15 February 1824; d. 2 December 1906
Moses S. (son of Capt. Thomas and Sarah E.) - d. 7 May 1842 Æ 15 y., 10 m., 10 d.
Moses S. (Capt.; son of Capt. Thomas Jr. and Lydia M. (PREBLE)) - b. 1842; d. 1896; bur. Portland, Maine
Norma S. - b. 1917; d. 1978
Percy E. (husb. of Gertrude M.) - b. 1887; d. 1980
Rena A. (wife of Willis E.) - b. 9 April 1856; d. 8 May 1940
Samuel (son of Capt. Samuel S. and Hannah A.) - d. 24 December 1862 Æ 7 y., 4 m., 8 d.
Samuel S. (Capt.; husb. of Hannah A.) - d. 19 July 1899 Æ 75 y., 7 m., 14 d.
Sarah E. (wife of Capt. Thomas) - d. 10 August 1852 Æ 40 y., 5 m., 20 d.
Sarah M. (dau. of Capt. Thomas Jr. and Lydia M. (PREBLE)) - b. 1852; d. [no date]
Sidney C. (wife of Warren R.) - b. 1824; d. 1918
Thomas (Capt.; husb. of Joanna and Sarah E.) - d. 7 April 1867 Æ 76 y., 6 m., 22.
Thomas Jr. (Capt.; husb. of Lydia M. (PREBLE)) - b. 1813; d. 1888
Thomas J. (Capt.; son of Capt. Thomas Jr. and Lydia M. (PREBLE)) - b. 1837; d. 1868; bur. "at sea"
Warren R. (husb. of Sidney C.) - b. 1824; d. 1870
William P. (Capt.; husb. of Hannah G.) - d. 9 November 1894 Æ 65 y., 6 m.
Willis E. (husb. of Rena A.) - b. 6 April 1855; d. 13 July 1915
Winslow E. (husb. of M. Rosalee) - b. 20 June 1912; d. 18 August 1992

COLBY
Gaile (BUNKER; dau. of Ruth (SYLVESTER) (STANLEY); [wife of Royal E.]) - b. 18 April 1935
Royal E. [husb. of Gaile (BUNKER)] - b. 3 October 1932; d. 25 May 1977
ERICKSON
John F. [husb. of Lucy H.] - b. 1866; d. 1937
Lucy H. [wife of John F.] - b. 1867; d. 1938
GILBERT
Aileen M. (wife of Clarke M.) - b. 18 November 1913
Clarke M. (husb. of Aileen M.) - b. 15 April 1910; d. 12 October 1995
Sherri K. (dau. of Clarke M. and Aileen M.) - b. 10 November 1948; d. 16 August 1996
HIGGINS
Westley [sic] K. - d. 10 June 1888 Æ 23 y., 8 m.
HOWARD
Julia E. (wife of Charles E. [no stone]) - d. 26 February 1883 Æ 19 y., 10 m., 15 d.
KINGSBURY
Comfort (wife of Ellis) - d. 10 June 1829 Æ 31 y.
Ellis (husb. of Comfort) - d. 25 January 1825 Æ 35 y.
MACALLISTER
Eugene R. - b. 1913; d. 1996
Janice M. - b. 1951
Leona A. - b. 1922
NORRIS
Martha B. (dau. of Charles and Joanna [no stones]) - d. 30 July 1849 Æ 30 y., 6 m.
PREBLE
[Lydia M. - see BUNKER]
PRESSEY
Susan P. (wife of Henry P. [no stone]) - b. 1809; d. 1875
RICE
Ada B. [wife of Charles E.] - b. 1910
Charles E. [husb. of Ada B.] - b. 1904
Elton T. - b. 1907; d. 1969
Ida C. (wife of Seth Hamilton) - b. 1874; d. 1952
Seth Hamilton (husb. of Ida C.) - b. 15 January 1872; d. 18 July 1951
RYAN
Frank J. - b. 21 April 1906; d. 25 May 1987
SALISBURY
Eva N. - b. 1878; d. 1943
SPURLING
[Clara B. - see BUNKER]
Dorcas (BUNKER; dau. of Capt. Samuel S. BUNKER and Hannah A.; wife of William S.) - d. 1 January 1876 Æ 27 y., 6 m.
Eber L. (husb. of Lena E.) - b. 24 February 1872; d. 9 October 1952
Ernest W. - b. 1880; d. 1935
Forest - b. 1907; d. 1987
Francis M. - b. 1896; d. 1958
George W. - b. 1869; d. 1933
J. M. - [no dates]
Joseph W. - d. 23 January 1887 Æ 38 y., 8 m., 24 d.
Lawrence (son of "Mr. & Mrs." Ernest W. [no stone for "Mrs."]) - [b. and d.?] 18 Aug 1909

Lena E. (wife of Eber L.) - b. 25 June 1878; d. 30 March 1942
Nellie A. - b. 1885; d. 1958
Orrington H. - d. 23 December 1899 Æ 44 y., 7 m.
Rose Marie - b. 1924; d. 1943
William S. (husb. of Dorcas (BUNKER)) - b. 23 September 1846; d. 5 June 1906

STANLEY
Eva Maria (wife of Stillman G.) - d. 12 May 1896 Æ 34 y., 1 m.
Maurice Elton (son of Stillman G. and Eva Maria) - b. 18 May 1895; d. 14 March 1911
Ruth (SYLVESTER; mother of Allison BUNKER [no stone], Gaile [sic] (COLBY) BUNKER, and Arthur BUNKER [no stone]) - b. 4 November 1906
Stillman G. (husb. of Eva Maria) - d. 16 July 1929 Æ 74 y., 2 m., 22 d.

STEELE
Willie (son of "Mr. and Mrs. Fred" [no stones]) - b. 1901; d. 1908

SWENSEN
Christopher [husb. of Elzada C.] - b. 1870; d. 1957
Elzada C. [wife of Christopher] - b. 1877; d. 1951

SYLVESTER
[Ruth - see STANLEY]

WEDGE
Lillian A. - b. 23 May 1893; d. 12 February 1936

WELLMAN
Frances L. - b. 15 February 1921; d. 4 August 1987

WHITE
George Victor - b. 1904; d. 1983

WHITNEY
Dean Spurling - b. 1937; d. 1994

[...]
[...][2] - [no dates]

Notes:
[1]Stone broken.
[2]Wooden cross, no name(s).
[3]It is unclear from the gravestone whether the surname is BUNKER or SPURLING.

Stanley Cemetery

(Cranberry Isles - 3)

Location/directions. Bulger Hill, Great Cranberry. From the town dock, walk straight ahead on the paved road. Soon the road curves to the left and then generally runs straight. Beyond the Bunker Cemetery (Cranberry Isles - 2) is a long stretch of relatively straight, flat road with fields and/or lawns on one or both sides. After this open, flat area, the road rises and curves to the left. In a short distance on the right is a dirt drive whose entrance is flanked by stone monuments. Turn right onto this drive and follow it until a less-traveled grassy road on the right leads to the cemetery.

History. This cemetery is found in the 1881 Colby Atlas.

Notes. The cemetery is bounded on three sides by chain suspended between relatively new wood posts. Several older posts with decoratively turned tops are laying on a large stump outside, but near the edge of, the cemetery. Many stones are leaning or laying on the ground.

Names and dates on gravestones and other markers. [4 September 1999]

ALLEY
- Amaziah (husb. of Ruth P.) - b. 1904; d. 1989
- Morris P. - b. 5 March 1932; d. 11 May 1953
- Ruth P. (wife of N. Gus PETERSON and Amaziah) - b. 4 June 1893; d. 23 June 1983

BIRLEM
- E. Augustus (Capt.; husb. of Emma Elvira) - b. 31 January 1841; d. 29 September 1918
- Emma Elvira (wife of Capt. E. Augustus) - b. 11 November 1855; d. 25 October 1945[4]

BULGER
- Alfred G. - b. 1851; d. 1902
- Dolly N. (wife of Michael) - d. 24 August 1894 Æ 85 y., 9 m.
- Elmer E. (son of Capt. John N. and Hannah M.) - d. 14 November 1874 Æ 3 y., 2 m., 24 d.
- Emma H. (wife of Enoch J.) - b. 1853; d. 1941
- Enoch J. (husb. of Emma H.) - b. 1849; d. 1927
- Frankie W. (son of Capt. Samuel N. and Mary L.) - d. 17 April 1870 Æ 1 m., 4 d.
- Freddie T. (son of Capt. Samuel N. and Mary L.) - d. 9 September 1864 Æ 10 m., 16 d.
- George W. (husb. of Sarah M.) - b. 3 December 1854; d. 29 June 1920
- Hannah M. (wife of Capt. John N.) - d. 31 October 1888 Æ 59 y., 21 d.
- John N. (Capt.; husb. of Hannah M.) - d. 28 May 1875 Æ 33 y., 2 m., 25 d.
- Mary L. (wife of Capt. Samuel N.) - b. 1835; d. 1925
- Michael (husb. of Dolly N.) - d. 24 November 1859 Æ 60 y.
- Samuel N. (Capt.; husb. of Mary L.) - b. 1835; d. 1918
- Sarah M. (wife of George W.) - b. 1851; d. 1924

CRANE
- Eunice ("widow" of Elisha [no stone]) - d. 25 March 1861 Æ 51 y., 9 m.
- William Henry (son of Elisha [no stone] and Eunice) - d. 16 October 1858 Æ 16 y., 3 m.

CROSBY
- Charlie C. (son of James C. [no stone] and Cora A.) - d. 2 November 18[...]4[1] Æ 3 m.

Clarence H. - b. 23 May 1892; d. 28 January 1933
Cora A. (wife of James C. [no stone]) - d. 19 June 1898 Æ 32 y.

GILLEY
Alfred H. (husb. of Catherine M.) - d. 29 December 1876, Ashtabula, Ohio, Æ 44 y., 11 m., 22 d.
Catherine M. (wife of Alfred H.) - b. 12 April 1833; d. 26 November 1910
infant (son of Alfred H. and Catherine M.) - [b. and?] d. 2 September 1865
Lucinda (dau. of William and Hannah [no stone]) - d. 18 February 1843 Æ 23 y., 1 m.[3], 18 d.
William (husb. of Hannah [no stone]) - d. 17 September 1872 Æ 90 y.

HARDING
[Ida F. - see STANLEY]

HAMOR
George R. (Capt.; husb. of Mary E.) - d. 3 March 1913 Æ 80 y., 6 m., 26 d.
Harris W. (son of Capt. George R. and Mary E.) - d. 2 November 1882 Æ 21 y., 7 m., 16 d.
Mary E. (wife of Capt. George R.) - d. 9 November 1921 Æ 83 y., 5 m., 6 d.

JOHNSON
Alma (STANLEY) - b. 1918; d. 1970
Della F. - d. 10 March 1877 Æ 19 y., 3 m., 20 d.
George O. - b. 1848; d. 1916

JOY
Arthur A. - b. 1877; d. 1915
Viola F. (dau. of George J. and Ella F. [no stones]) - d. 21 February 1911 Æ 23 y., 5 m.
Walter F. (son of George J. and Ella F. [no stones]) - b. 26 October 1890; d. 3 May 1974

LADD
Clara E. (wife of Lewis E.) - d. 24 February 1894 Æ 35 y., 5 m., 21 d.
infant (son of Lewis E. and Clara E.) - [b. and?] d. 23 February 1880
[L. M. - see WORCESTER]
Lena E. (dau. of Lewis E. and Clara E.) - d. 8 August 1876 Æ 9 d.
Lewis E. (husb. of Clara E.) - d. 17 December 1942 Æ 88 y., 10 m., 16 d.

LYMAN
[Susan Storey - see Charles Storey SHAW]

MOORE
Albion T. (Capt.) - d. 8 January 1863 Æ 33 y., 1 m., 16 d.

PETERSON
N. Gus (husb. of Ruth P. [who later married Amaziah ALLEY (*q.v.*)]) - b. 14 October 1891; d. 8 January 1929
Nils F. - b. 1916; d. 1992

PRESSEY
Bertha L. "Bertie" (dau. of John Henry and Delia H.) - d. 10 January 1889 Æ 1 y., 5 m.
Charlie H. (son of John Henry and Delia H.) - d. 2 March 1876 Æ 8 y., 5 m., 21 d.
Delia H. (wife of John Henry) - b. 1843; d. 1910
John Henry (husb. of Delia H.) - b. 27 May 1844; d. 5 May 1915

RICHARDSON
Emery Willard (son of Capt. Meltiah J. and [Mary Carrie or Carrie Mary][2]) - b. 22 July 1873; d. 8 October 1883 Æ 10 y., 2 m., 16 d.
[Mary Carrie or Carrie Mary][2] (wife of Capt. Meltiah J.) - b. 4 November 1848; d. 12 October 1920

Meltiah J. (Capt.; husb. of [Mary Carrie or Carrie Mary][2]) - b. 22 June 1828; d. 23 May 1901
Nellie G. - b. 1884; d. 1957

S.
M. O. [footstone only]

SHAW
Charles Storey (son of Samuel Parkman and Susan Storey (LYMAN) [no stones]) - b. 1946; d. 1970

SPURLING
Abigail (wife of Capt. George N. [no stone]) - d. 12 April 1852 Æ 34 y., 9 m.
Bernice M. (dau. of Warren A. and Ella Florence) - b. 1904; d. 1929
Clyde E. (son of Warren A. and Ella Florence) - b. 1910; d. 1931
Ella Florence (wife of Warren A.) - b. 5 October 1867; d. 16 October 1939
Warren A. (husb. of Ella Florence) - b. 23 June 1871; d. 23 October 1965

STANLEY
Abra[ha]m[2] C. (Capt.; husb. of Dorcas E.) - b. 4 May 1824; d. 19 November 1887; ("drowned")
Ada C. (dau. of Capt. Enoch B. and Caroline H.) - b. 1857; d. 1857
Albion M. (son of Capt. Enoch B. and Caroline H.; husb. of Minnie M.) - b. 2 June 1862; d. 2 June 1924
[Alma - see JOHNSON]
Alma M. (dau. of Edward J. and Mary S.) - d. 14 July 1886 Æ 11 y., 1 m., 15 d.
Arno P. (son of Capt. Enoch B. and Caroline H.; husb. of Mabel[le][2] E.) - b. 12 September 1865; d. 18 December 1937
Caroline H. (wife of Capt. Enoch B.) - b. 24 December 1822; d. 6 May 1907
Charles E. [husb. of Eliza B.] - b. 1883; d. 1964
Charles F. E. - d. 30 March 1851 Æ 22 y., 8 m.
Charles H. (son of Capt. Enoch B. and Caroline H.) - b. 1859; d. 3 August 1871 Æ 11 y., 8 m., 20 d.
Cora E. (dau. of Thomas F. and Luella S.) - d. 4 November 1892 Æ 7 m., 15 d.
Dorcas E. (wife of Capt. Abra[ha]m[2] C.) - d. 31 May 1877 Æ 49 y., 2 m., 8 d.
Durmont N. - b. 1928; d. 1928
Edward A. - b. 1 March 1877; d. 4 November 1904; ("drowned")
Edward J. ([son of Capt. Enoch B. and Caroline H.?]; husb. of Mary S.) - b. 1851; d. 1927
Eliza B. [wife of Charles E.] - b. 1888; d. 1967
Enoch B. (Capt.; husb. of Caroline H.) - b. 7 August 1820; d. 9 January 1903
Enoch B. Jr. (son of Capt. Enoch B. and Caroline H.; husb. of Ida F.) - b. 1849; d. 1910
Georgie B. (wife of Merrill E. [no stone]) - b. 15 May 1895; d. 15 January 1923
George S. (son of Capt. Enoch B. and Caroline H.) - b. 1853; d. [no date]
Ida F. (wife of Enoch B. Jr. and Charles H. HARDING [no stone]) - b. 1867; d. 1935
infant (dau. of Capt. Enoch B. and Caroline H.) - d. 18 May 1858 Æ 1 m.
infant (dau. of Arno P. and Mabel[le][2] E.) - [no dates]
John (Capt.; husb. of Lucinda G.) - b. 20 March 1832; d. 10 December 1894
Leah J. (wife of Lewis G.) - b. 15 April 1874; d. 10 September 1944 Æ 70 y., 4 m., 24 d.
Lewis G. (husb. of Leah J.) - b. 16 May 1869; d. 29 January 1957
Lewis W. (son of Capt. Abra[ha]m[2] C. and Dorcas E.) - d. 9 December 1853 Æ 10 m., 16 d.
Lucinda G. (wife of Capt. John) - b. 12 September 1833; d. 25 October 1925
Luella S. (wife of Thomas F.) - b. 1854; d. 1932

Mabel[le][2] E. (wife of Arno P.) - b. 1868; d. 1955
Margarett [sic] (dau. of Capt. Thomas and Mary D.) - d. 8 February 1843 Æ 31 y.
Mary (wife of Capt. Thomas Jr.) - d. 14 January 1843 Æ 54 y.
Mary C. [dau. of Capt. Enoch B. and Caroline H.?] - b. 1847; d. [no date]
Mary D. (wife of Capt. Thomas) - d. 5 February 1885 Æ 76 y., 2 m., 23 d.
Mary S. (wife of Edward J.) - b. 1855; d. 1913
Minnie M. (wife of Albion M.) - b. 18 September 1864; d. 15 June 1957
Thomas (Capt.; husb. of Mary D.) - d. 27 March 1876 Æ 86 y., 11 m., 27 d.
Thomas Jr. (son of Capt. Thomas and Mary D.) - d. 4 December 1838 Æ 25 y., 2 m., 18 d.
Thomas F. (husb. of Luella S.) - b. 1850; d. 1916
William D. (son of Capt. Enoch B. and Caroline H.) - b. 1855; d. [no date]

TEEL
Velma S. [wife of Wyman S.] - b. 1891; d. 1971
Wyman S. [husb. of Velma S.] - b. 1890; d. 1967

WORCESTER
L. M. (LADD; dau. of Lewis E. LADD and Clara E.) - b. 21 December 1881; d. 22 November 1908

Notes:
[1]Stone broken.
[2]Different on different stones.
[3]Stone reads "1 months".
[4]The obituary in The Bar Harbor Times gives the year of death as 1947.

Stanley Cemetery (Cranberry Isles - 3) on Great Cranberry Island with mountains of west side of Mount Desert Island in background.

Preble Cemetery
(Cranberry Isles - 4)

Location/directions. Great Cranberry. From the town dock, walk straight ahead on the paved road. Soon the road curves to the left and then generally runs straight and is relatively level. Just as the road begins to rise, there is a tennis court on the right. Turn right onto a gravel road immediately after the tennis court. In less than 150' a path on the left leads to the cemetery.

History. —

Notes. The cemetery is enclosed by a white picket fence that was recently (1999?) painted. A few stones, some of which are broken, are laying on the ground.

Names and dates on gravestones and other markers. [4 September 1999]

ALLEY
- Andrew E. (husb. of Clara [B. or A.][1]) - b. 1894; d. 1968
- Clara [B. or A.][1] (wife of Andrew E.) - b. 1895; d. 1965
- Leroy L. (son of Andrew E. and Clara [B. or A.][1]) - b. 29 January 1930; d. 9 September 1945

BEAL
- Barbara R. [wife of Clarence E.] - b. 1913; d. 1973
- Clarence E. [husb. of Barbara R.] - b. 1916; d. 1990

CAMPBELL
- [Dorothy - see MCFARLAN [sic]]

FEEKS
- Betsey (wife of Thomas [no stone]) - d. 15 August 1859 Æ 26 y.[2]

FERNALD [includes FURNALD]
- Amy (YOUNG; wife of Henry) - d. 23 January 1908 Æ 90 y., 11 m., 23 d.
- Henry (husb. of Amy (YOUNG)) - d. 20 November 18[8 or 9?]5[3] Æ 73 y., 2 m.
- Mary A. S. (dau. of Henry and Amy (YOUNG)) - d. 2[5?][3] [...][3,4] 1854 Æ [20?][3] d.

GILLEY
- Henrietta G. (dau. of Justus W. and Thankful C. [no stone]) - d. 14 November 1857 Æ 17 y., 8 m., 5 d.
- Justus W. (husb. of Thankful C. [no stone]) - b. 26 February 1815; d. 19 January 1860

H.
- H. [footstone only]

HARDING
- Charles - d. 27 October 1883 Æ 63 y., 3 m.
- [...][3] - d. 27 July 1860, Africa, Æ 29 y.

LADD
- Rosa L. (wife of Lewis E. [no stone] and [Edward or Edwin][1] H. SPURLING) - b. 1865; d. 1920

MACFARLAN [sic]
- Dorothy (CAMPBELL) - b. 31 January 1894; d. 12 May 1985

MOORE
- Mary S. (wife of Joseph [no stone]) - b. 1808; d. 1840

PREBLE
- Abigail C. (wife of William P.) - d. 17 January 1874 Æ 65 y., 6 m., 14 d.
- Eber C. (son of William P. and Abigail C.) - d. 24 November 1853 Æ 1 y., 6 m., 22 d.

Eber M. (son of William P. and Abigail C.) - d. 8 September 1856 Æ 1 y., 4 m., 6 d.
Eva Florence (dau. of William H. and Elmenia T. [no stones]) - d. 30 July 1879 Æ 16 y., 5 d.
Perley Russell (son of William H. and Elmenia T. [no stones]) - d. 17 December 1871 Æ 2 m., 13 d.
William P. (husb. of Abigail C.) - d. 13 April 1905 Æ 94 y., 7 d.

RICE

Caroline M. (wife of William R.) - b. 1828; d. 1910
Chester M. (son of Wilbert A. and Ella C.) - b. 3 November 1886; d. 27 February 1908 Æ 21 y., 3 m., 24 d.; ("drowned")
Ella C. (wife of Wilbert A.) - b. 1850; d. 1890
Leslie M. [husb. of Nellie M.] - b. 1882; d. 1966
Nellie M. [wife of Leslie M.] - b. 1889; d. 1971
Samuel J. (son of William R. and Caroline M.) - d. 15 July 1860 Æ 4 y., 3 m., 15 d.
Wilbert A. (husb. of Ella C.) - b. 1851; d. 1930
William R. (husb. of Caroline M.) - b. 1816; d. 1889

ROSEBROOK

Cora A. (wife of Gilbert H.) - b. 1867; d. 1954
Eben C. (husb. of Sarah J.) - b. 19 December 1835; d. 2 April 1911
Gilbert H. (husb. of Cora A.) - b. 1867; d. 1937
Harley C. (son of Gilbert H. and Cora A.) - d. 22 September 1898 Æ 4 y., 8 m., 25 d.
Jennie I. (dau. of Gilbert H. and Cora A.) - d. 28 September 1898 Æ 6 y., 3 m., 23 d.
Mildred V. (dau. of Gilbert H. and Cora A.) - d. 29 September 1898 Æ 3 y., 18 d.
Sarah J. (wife of Eben C.) - b. 1 August 1841; d. 20 July 1916

SPURLING

[Edward or Edwin][1] H. (Capt.; husb. of Rosa L. [who later or earlier married Lewis E. LADD [no stone] (*q.v.*)]) - d. 6 June 1895 Æ 32 y., 7 m.
Enoch (Capt.; husb. of Mary S.) - d. 9 November 1890 Æ 78 y., 2 m.
Frances E. (STEELE; wife of Josiah Y.) - b. 1847; d. 1913
[Georgian[n]a[1] - see STOVER]
Harvey Preble (son of Benjamin H. and Frances A. [no stones]) - d. 9 August 1877 Æ 19 d.
Josiah Y. (husb. of Frances E. (STEELE)) - b. 1844; d. 1915
Lucy A. (wife of Robert) - d. 29 November 1872 Æ 45 y., 1 m., 25 d.
Mary S. (wife of Capt. Enoch) - d. 27 December 1885 Æ 73 y., 1 m., 24 d.
Nahum Y. - b. 28 May 1837; d. 26 July 1890
Robert (husb. of Lucy A.) - d. 5 October 1881 Æ 66 y., 7 m., 22 d.
[Rosa L. - see LADD]
Smith C. - d. 9 February 1879 Æ 27 y., 1 m., 15 d.
Smith C. (Capt.) - d. 15 March 1859 Æ 34 y., 4 m., 2 d.; ("drowned")

STANLEY

Abigail C. (wife of Thomas M.) - d. 28 July 1860 Æ 22 y., 10 m.
Daniel K. (husb. of Hannah S. and Philena J.) - d. 24 March 1920 Æ 84 y., 11 m.
Hannah S. (wife of Daniel K.) - b. 1840; d. 1856
Mary H. (wife of Thomas M.) - b. 1843; d. 1927
Philena J. (wife of Daniel K.) - b. 1849; d. 1934
Thomas M. (husb. of Abigail C. and Mary H.) - b. 1827; d. 1913

STEELE
Elmira G. [wife of John B.] - b. 1845; d. 1922
[Frances E. - see SPURLING]
George F. - b. 1884; d. 1905
Irving A. - b. 1861; d. 1881
John B. [husb. of Elmira G.] - b. 1837; d. 1903
John B. Jr. - b. 1880; d. 1911
STOVER
Georgian[n]a[1] (SPURLING; wife of Samuel C.) - b. 1849; d. 1917
infant (dau. of Samuel C. and Georgian[n]a[1] (SPURLING)) - d. 18 March 1870 Æ 3 d.
Samuel C. (husb. of Georgian[n]a[1] (SPURLING)) - b. 1849; d. 1912
WEDGE
Charlie S. (son of Edward and Rosinda P. "Rose") - d. 6 April 1895 Æ 6 m.
Edward (husb. of Rosinda P. "Rose") - b. 1855; d. 1930
infant (child of Edward and Rosinda P. "Rose") - [b. and?] d. 9 November 1899
Leslie (child of Edward and Rosinda P. "Rose") - d. 10 October 1901 Æ [not given]
Rosinda P. "Rose" (wife of Edward) - b. 1862; d. 1961
YOUNG
[Amy - see FERNALD]
Josiah (husb. of Roxana) - d. 16 April 1864 Æ 74 y., 11 m., 28 d.
Roxana (wife of Josiah) - d. 10 June 1865 Æ 70 y., 2 m., 3 d.

Notes:
[1]Different on different stones.
[2]Remainder stone is in concrete, thereby obscuring any further information it may contain.
[3]Stone worn, cracked, and/or broken.
[4]Three letters in month or in its abbreviation.

Stanley-Hadlock Cemetery

(Cranberry Isles - 5)

Location/directions. Northwest end of Little Cranberry, near Hadlock Point. From the boat dock, follow the paved road to the left. Turn of this road onto the second paved road on the left. At the first intersection (with a paved road to the right and a gravel road to the left), turn left. Watch on the right in approximately 75' for a mowed path that leads to the cemetery.

History. —

Notes. This cemetery, sometimes called the Hadlock Cemetery, is not enclosed by a fence. Several stones are leaning or laying on the ground. The grass is mowed and trimmed.

Names and dates on gravestones and other markers. [4 September 1999]

BLUNT
- H. H. (HAMILTON; wife of William P.) - b. 1 March 1803; Mount Desert, Maine; d. 20 October 1895, Bolton, Massachusetts
- William P. (husb. of H. H. (HAMILTON)) - b. 31 March 1798, Portsmouth, New Hampshire; d. 23 June 1830, Ilsford [sic], Maine

BRYANT
- Lena M. (wife of Alonzo J. [no stone]) - d. 28 October 1893 Æ 23 y., 2 m., 17 d.
- Ralph A. - b. 1892; d. 1982

BUNKER
- Flora E. (wife of Francis W.) - b. 1879; d. 1955
- Francis W. (husb. of Flora E.) - b. 1880; d. 1943
- infant (son of Francis W. and Flora E.) - [b. and d.?] 3 October 1904

FORHAN
- John - “lost at sea” 13 December 1852 Æ 18 y.

GOTT
- Amanda M. (dau. of Nathaniel and Huldah H. [no stones]) - d. 27 February 1849 Æ 10 y., 8 m.
- Charles T. (son of Nathaniel and Huldah H. [no stones]) - d. 26 October 1857 Æ 16 y., 4 m., 9 d.

HADLOCK
- Edna C. (wife of George R.) - b. 1885; d. 1949
- Edwin (husb. of Mary A.) - b. 17 January 1814; d. 16 September 1875
- Edwin H. - b. 1865; d. 1938
- Elijah (son of Capt. Samuel and Sarah) - d. 1 July 1828, West Indies, Æ 32 y.
- Ella G. [wife of William E.] - b. 1911; d. 1984
- Elmer C. - b. 26 April 1909; d. 22 March 1982
- Epps (son of Capt. Samuel and Sarah) - “lost at sea” January 1831 Æ 25 y.
- Frances H. (wife of Col. William E.) - b. 1835; d. 1916
- George R. (husb. of Edna C.) - b. 1880; d. 1958
- George R. Jr. (son of George R. and Edna C.) - b. 1921; d. 1943
- Georgie (wife of Capt. Gilbert T.) - d. 6 August 1880 Æ 38 y., 11 m.
- Gilbert T. (Capt.; husb. of Georgie) - b. 1837; d. 1917
- Grace M. (wife of Walter) - b. 1871; d. 1955
- infant (dau. of Walter and Grace M.) - [no dates]
- Jonathan G. (son of Capt. Samuel and Sarah) - “lost at sea” 1 January 1831 Æ 20 y.
- Mark Dale - b. 1960; d. 1983
- Mary A. (wife of Edwin) - b. 22 July 1816; d. 23 December 1888

Samuel (Capt.; husb. of Sarah) - d. 24 September 1854 Æ 84 y.
Samuel Jr. (son of Capt. Samuel and Sarah) - "lost at sea" 1829 Æ 38 y.
Sarah (wife of Capt. Samuel) - d. 1 October 1861 Æ 90 y.
Walter (husb. of Grace M.) - b. 1870; d. 1927
Wendell Stanwood - b. 1911; d. 1978; bur. Woodbine Cemetery, Ellsworth
William E. (Col.; husb. of Frances H.) - b. 1834; d. 1911 Æ 76 y.; (member 28th Maine Regiment [Civil War])
William E. [husb. of Ella G.] - b. 1913; d. 1994

HAMILTON
[H. H. - see BLUNT]

JOY
Ella M. (wife of Alden B. [no stone]) - d. 1 September 1881 Æ 21 y., 11 m., 16 d.

KNOWLES
Samuel W. (son of Samuel H. [no stone]; grandson of Rev. George Dimock [sic] [no stone]) - d. 7 August 1855, "aboard the brig Billow", Mount Desert, Æ 21 y.

MORSE
Fannie M. - b. 1868; d. 1903

SKALING
Michael (son of David and Sarah [no stones]) - d. 19 September 1844 Æ 25 y.

SPRAGUE
James C. [husb. of Nannie E.] - b. 1864; d. 1954
Nannie E. [wife of James C.] - b. 1871; d. 1948

SPURLING
Agnes E. (dau. of Clarence Hadlock and Lenora E.) - b. 1911; d. 1920
Agnes H. [wife of Everett L.] - b. 1862; d. 1945
Clarence Hadlock (husb. of Lenora E.) - b. 10 September 1886; d. 8 August 1962
Everett L. [husb. of Agnes H.] - b. 1858; d. 1930
Lenora E. (wife of Clarence Hadlock) - d. 25 December 1912 Æ 23 y.
Serena W. - b. 1882; d. 1977; bur. Mt. Height Cemetery [Southwest Harbor - 4]

STANLEY [includes STANDLEY and STANLY]
Abram R. (husb. of Hattie M.) - d. 26 August 1892 Æ 44 y., 9 m.
Amos C. (son of [Thomas Jr. or Thomas 2nd][1] and Esther R.) - d. 29 January 1849 Æ 11 y., 10 m.
Belinda M. - b. 1846; d. 1935
Elmira G. (wife of Daniel K. [no stone]) - d. 1 April 1869 Æ 25 y., 9 m.
Emily A. (dau. of [Thomas Jr. or Thomas 2nd][1] and Esther R.) - d. 9 February 1865 Æ 19 y., 5 m.
Epps H. - b. 1843; d. 1902
Esther R. (wife of [Thomas Jr. or Thomas 2nd][1]) - d. 28 December 1862 Æ 53 y., 8 m., 17 d.
Frances G. (son [sic] of [Thomas Jr. or Thomas 2nd][1] and Esther R.) - d. 16 September 1858 Æ 2 y., 9 m.
Francis G. (son of [Thomas Jr. or Thomas 2nd][1] and Esther R.) - d. 5 August 1864, Cranberry Isles, Æ 24 y., 8 m., 21 d.; (member of Co. A, 14th Maine Regiment [Civil War])
Freddie A. (son of Tyler H. and Hannah E.) - d. 27 October 1870 Æ 1 m.
Hannah E. (wife of Tyler H.) - d. 21 April 1903 Æ 60 y.
Hattie M. (wife of Abram R.) - d. 7 September 1891 Æ 40 y., 6 m., 7 d.
Henry H. - d. 4 March 1868 Æ 37 y., 2 m.
John (husb. of Phebe) - d. 10 May 1847 Æ 82 y.
Lewis A. (son of Abram R. and Hattie M.) - d. 2 November 1873 Æ 4 y., 6 m., 7 d.

Lewis P. (son of [Thomas Jr. or Thomas 2nd][1] and Esther R.) - d. 11 January 1861 Æ 3 y., 9 m., 9 d.
Loring A. (husb. of Velma R.) - b. 1864; d. 1910
Lucinda ("consort" of [Thomas Jr. or Thomas 2nd][1]) - d. 19 September 1832 Æ 20 y.
Margaret W. (wife of Nathan S.) - b. 13 March 1841; d. 5 January 1927
Maria (wife of Peter) - d. 17 May 1869 Æ 61 y., 11 m., 10 d.
Nathan S. (husb. of Margaret W.) - b. 25 April 1842; d. 14 October 1922
Peter (husb. of Maria) - d. 7 April 1855 Æ 53 y.
Phebe (wife of John) - d. 23 January 1830 Æ 66 y.
[Thomas Jr. or Thomas 2nd][1] (husb. of Lucinda and Esther R.) - d. 16 May 1889 Æ 83 y.
Tyler H. (husb. of Hannah E.) - b. 24 May 1837; d. 31 August 1914
Velma R. (wife of Loring A.) - b. 1865; d. 1910

STANWOOD
Mary (Mrs.) - d. 18 August 1842, Boston, Massachusetts, Æ 46 y.

YOUNG
Emily [...][2] (dau. of Freeman G. and Sarah K. [no stones]) - d. 4 April 1858 Æ 9 y., 9 m., 6 d.

[...]
[...][3] - d. [2?]8[3] September 1831 Æ [...][3]

Notes:
[1]Different on different stones.
[2]Middle initial worn.
[3]Inscription very faint. Stone laying on ground.

Merrill Family Burial Ground
(Cranberry Isles - 6)

Location/directions. Little Cranberry. From the boat dock, follow the paved road to the left. In a short distance after passing a white church on the left, bear left at a fork in the road. Immediately before a small, shingled chapel on the left, follow a trail to the cemetery.

History. —

Notes. This cemetery is bounded by a chain suspended between granite posts. The grass is mowed and trimmed.

Names and dates on gravestones and other markers. [4 September 1999]

HILL

[Katharine - see MERRILL]

MERRILL

Andrew Pepperell (son of John Jr. and Helen [no stones]) - b. 12 June 1957; d. 11 August 1990

John Lee (husb. of Katharine (HILL)) - b. 22 October 1895, Brookline, Massachusetts; d. 5 November 1960, Boston, Massachusetts

Katharine Hill (HILL; wife of John Lee) - b. 23 December 1904, Augusta, Maine; d. 20 April 1962, Boston, Massachusetts

Stanley-Gilley Cemetery
(Cranberry Isles - 7)

Location/directions. Little Cranberry. From the boat dock, follow the paved road to the left. In a short distance after passing a white church on the left, bear left at a fork in the road. The cemetery is along the left side of the road immediately after a small, shingled chapel.

History. —

Notes. This cemetery, sometimes referred to as the Upper Stanley Cemetery, is bounded on three sides by a fence of concrete posts with two courses of rope stretched between them. The fourth side (parallel to the road) is bounded by an old stone wall. The grass is mowed and trimmed.

Names and dates on gravestones and other markers. [4 September 1999]

ALLEY
- Julie M. - b. 24 November 1954; d. 5 January 1998

BRADFORD
- Lena (BRYANT; wife of Lloyd C.) - b. 1932; d. 1997
- Lloyd C. (husb. of Lena (BRYANT)) - b. 1912; d. 1993

BRYANT
- Alonzo J. (husb. of Ida M.) - b. 1866; d. 1941
- Annette (LEBEL) - b. 23 May 1908; d. 22 December 1992
- Ida M. (wife of Alonzo J.) - b. 1876; d. 1960
- [Lena - see BRADFORD]
- Shirley W. (son of Alonzo J. and Ida M.) - b. 12 March 1906; d. 30 October 1918

BUNKER
- Alvah W. (husb. of Dorothy B.) - b. 1902; d. 1968
- Dorothy B. (wife of Alvah W.) - b. 1904; d. 1977
- infant (dau. of Alvah W. and Dorothy B.) - [b. and d.?] 1937
- Remona [sic] G. (dau. of Alvah W. and Dorothy B.) - b. 1924; d. 1968

CAMPBELL
- Benjamin S. [husb. of Catherine B.] - b. 30 April 1839; d. 10 November 1923
- Catherine B. [wife of Benjamin S.] - b. 21 May 1854; d. 8 February 1948

CROWLEY
- Allen C. (son of Allen C. [no stone] and Ruth L.) - d. [no date] Æ 5 d.
- Ruth L. (wife of Allen C. [no stone]) - b. 1909; d. 1935

DWELLEY
- [Elizabeth - see FERNALD]

FAULKNER
- Emma J. [wife of William J.] - b. 1890; d. 1990
- William J. [husb. of Emma J.] - b. 25 October 1890; d. 23 August 1966

FERNALD
- Arthur L. [husb. of Kathrine [sic] E.] - b. 1877; d. 1960
- Edward S. (Capt.; husb. of Lucinda G.) - d. 4 January[3] 1894 Æ 53 y., 5 m., 19 d.
- Elizabeth (DWELLEY; [wife of Francis Griffin]) - b. 18 February 1912
- Ella Frances (wife of Malcolm E. [no stone]) - b. 1907; d. 1930
- Emma J. (wife of George H.) - b. 1851; d. 1912
- Everett E. (husb. of Sadie M.) - b. 1873; d. 1958
- Francis Griffen [husb. of Elizabeth (DWELLEY)] - b. 13 August 1909; d. 29 July 1999
- Frederick G. - b. 26 September 1919; d. 13 March 1959

George H. (husb. of Emma J.) - b. 14 May 1847; d. 29 October 1932
Gerard F. - b. 28 October 1937
Ilmi M. [wife of Lewis A.] - b. 1912
Kathrine [sic] E. [wife of Arthur L.] - b. 1881; d. 1923
Lewis A. [husb. of Ilmi M.] - b. 1915; d. 1988
Lucinda G. (wife of Capt. Edward S.) - b. 1842; d. 1926
Phebe (wife of Samuel S.) - b. 28 March 1837; d. 5 September 1907
Reta [sic] R. [wife of Winfred F.] - b. 4 August 1910
Rose Marie - [b. and d.?] September 1916
Sadie M. (wife of Everett E.) - b. 1880; d. 1972
Samuel C. (son of Everett E. and Sadie M.) - b. 1906; d. 1929
Samuel F. - [b. and d.?] 1940
Samuel S. (husb. of Phebe) - d. 11 February 1888 Æ 49 y., 5 m., 4 d.
Winfred F. [husb. of Reta [sic] R.] - b. 5 May 1908; d. 9 November 1977

GILLEY
Albert W. (husb. of Emily G. and Julia F.) - b. 1845; d. 1916
Emily (wife of Capt. Samuel) - d. 7 September 1893 Æ 73 y., 2 m.
Emily G. (wife of Albert W.) - d. 15 December 1879 Æ 32 y., 6 m., 5 d.
Enoch S. (Capt.; "eldest son" of Capt. Samuel and Emily) - d. 24 December 1865 Æ 22 y., 9 m., 16 d.
George E. - b. 25 March 1848; d. 25 April 1916
infant (son of Verner A. and Wattie E.) - [no dates]
Julia F. (wife of Albert W.) - b. 1867; d. 1921
[Marcia - see MANRING]
Samuel (Capt.; husb. of Emily) - d. 27 May 1906 Æ 91 y.
Sylvia F. - b. 1913; d. 1995
Verner A. (husb. of Wattie E.) - b. 1889; d. 1950
Wattie E. (wife of Verner A.) - b. 1882; d. 1983

GRAY
Charles S. [husb. of Vivian C.] - b. 28 September 1911; d. 15 September 1987
Vivian C. [wife of Charles S.] - b. 20 September 1906

HAM
Agnes M. [wife of Arthur E.] - b. 1872; d. 1957
Albert E. [son of Arthur E. and Agnes M.?] - b. 1910; d. 1998
Arthur E. [husb. of Agnes M.] - b. 1882; d. 1963

HARRISON
Stanley H. - d. 12 March 1921 Æ 17 y., 4 m., 19 d.

JARVIS
George S. (husb. of Hannah S.) - b. 1837; d. 1913
Hannah S. (wife of George S.) - b. 18 February 1845; d. 12 October 1900[2]
infant (son of K. E. and M. E. [no stones]) - [b. and d.?] 1935
Jennie M. (wife of Oscar E.) - b. 1873; d. 1959
Oscar E. (husb. of Jennie M.) - b. 1870; d. 1928

JORDAN
Alden H. [husb. of Margaret S.] - b. 1854; d. 1938
Margaret S. [wife of Alden H.] - b. 1858; d. 1938

LEBEL
[Annette - see BRYANT]

LIBBY
Charlotte A. [wife of Clifford W.] - b. 1917; d. 1994
Clifford W. [husb. of Charlotte A.] - b. 1918; d. 1978

MANRING
Jones C. [husb. of Marcia (GILLEY)] - b. 1907; d. 1989
Marcia (GILLEY; [wife of Jones C.]) - b. 1915; d. 1999
M[AY?]O[1]
infant (dau. of William and Annie E. [no stones]) - [...][1]
MOORE
Belle (wife of Benjamin E.) - b. 1862; d. 1948
Benjamin E. (husb. of Belle) - b. 1861; d. 1927
Evelyn - b. 1897; d. 1944
PALMER
Jeffery O. - [b. and d.?] 1954
John A. (son of Robert M. and Gloria B. [no stones]) - b. 25 September 1950; d. 2 September 1983
Tracy Ann (dau. of Robert M. and Gloria B. [no stones]) - [b. and d.?] 1962
PHIPPEN
Fred W. [husb. of Inez] - b. 1870; d. 1930
Inez [wife of Fred W.] - b. 1868; d. 1957
ROSEBROOK
Jack H. - b. 2 August 1925
SPURLING
A. Rudolph (son of Fred and Nellie) - b. 1905; d. 1928
Archie S. (husb. of Lillian) - b. 1862; d. 1950
Arthur M. [husb. of Cora M.] - b. 1873; d. 1975
Cora M. [wife of Arthur M.] - b. 1877; d. 1965
Earle W. (son of Archie S. and Lillian) - b. 1901; d. 1979
Eleanor G. [wife of Elmer A.] - b. 1908
Elmer A. [husb. of Eleanor G.] - b. 1901; d. 1984
Fred (husb. of Nellie) - b. 1868; d. 1958
Irving R. (son of Fred and Nellie) - b. 1893; d. 1984
Lillian (wife of Archie S.) - b. 1863; d. 1942
Marion E. (dau. of Fred and Nellie) - b. 1902
Nellie (wife of Fred) - b. 1871; d. 1960
STANLEY
Albert W. (Capt.; son of John and Margaret; [husb. of M. H.?] [no stone]) - d. 28 July 1863, "at sea", Æ 39 y., 3 m., 23 d.
Almenia G. (wife of Capt. Benjamin Franklin) - b. 1846; d. 1922
Andrew E. Jr. [husb. of Eleanor M.] - b. 1915; d. 1981
Andrew E. Sr. - b. 4 April 1891; d. 24 April 1969
Benjamin Franklin (Capt.; husb. of Almenia G.) - b. 1842; d. 1917
Eleanor M. [wife of Andrew E. Jr.] - b. 1918; d. 1998
Elsie L. - b. 1893; d. 1938
Francis A. "Frank" [husb. of Margaret F.] - b. 16 October 1922; d. 11 November 1994
Freeman E. [husb. of Minnie E.] - b. 1876; d. 1955
John (husb. of Margaret) - d. 25 March 1864 Æ 75 y.
Joyce M. [STANLEY?] - b. 1946; d. 1947
Lewis M. (son of A[lbert?]. W. and M. H. [no stone]) - d. 3 November 1865 Æ 3 y., 2 m.
Margaret (wife of John) - d. 23 March 1874 Æ 76 y., 4 m., 12 d.
Margaret F. [wife of Francis A. "Frank"] - b. 25 October 1918; d. 14 December 1997
Minnie E. [wife of Freeman E.] - b. 1881; d. 1958
Wanita [sic] L. - b. 4 May 1948; d. 25 April 1966

Winfield E. - b. 1911; d. 1941

WAYLAND

Jane (wife of Matthew [no stone]) - d. 7 September 1866 Æ 27 y., 6 m., 21 d.

YOUNG

Hannah C. (wife of William W.) - b. 1831; d. 1918

Lulu S. [wife of William A.] - b. 1874; d. 1956

William A. [husb. of Lulu S.] - b. 1869; d. 1946

William W. (husb. of Hannah C.) - b. 1836; d. 1924

Notes:

[1]Stone broken.

[2]The 9 of 1900 is backwards.

[3]The N of "JANUARY" is backwards.

Sand Beach Cemetery
(Cranberry Isles - 8)

Location/directions. Little Cranberry. From the town dock, walk through the field toward the right to a paved road. Turn right onto this road, and the cemetery is along the left (east) side of the road.

History. —

Notes. Wood posts mark the bounday of this cemetery. On three sides a chain is suspended between the posts with two breaks along the road side for entrances/exits.

Names and dates on gravestones and other markers. [4 September 1999]

BENET
- Sula - b. 24 September 1906; d. 12 November 1982

BISCOMB
- C. John [husb. of Margery S.] - b. 1910; d. 1972
- Margery S. [wife of C. John] - b. 1917; d. 1994

BLACK
- Charles P. - b. 1845; d. 1913
- Edgar C. [husb. of Ethel R.] - b. 7 November 1884; d. 28 September 1944
- Ethel R. [wife of Edgar C.] - b. 16 July 1894; d. 1 August 1989
- Mildred E. - b. 1896; d. 1957
- Phoebe Jane - b. 1855; d. 1936

BOWMAN
- George W. (husb. of Kathleen G.) - b. 1915; d. 1994
- Kathleen G. (wife of George W.) - b. 1920

BRAGDON
- Elspeth (MACDUFFY; [wife of Marshall H.]) - b. 1897; d. 1980
- Marshall H. [husb. of Elspeth (MACDUFFY)] - b. 1906; d. 1987

BRIGHT
- Nicholas - b. 29 August 1956; d. 21 December 1988
- Stanley - b. 24 March 1910; d. 25 October 1994

CONLON
- Kevin F. - b. 20 August 1962; d. 14 January 1983
- Mary E. "May" - b. 17 August 1896; d. 12 February 1998

DEFRANCIS
- Lisa Ann - b. 30 August 1952; d. 2 January 1999

FERNALD
- Hazel (wife of Malcolm E.) - b. 1905; d. 1996
- Malcolm E. (husb. of Hazel) - b. 1902; d. 1981

FISHER
- Audrey Stevens - b. 1927
- John Kingsbury - b. 1951; d. 1998
- Paul Kingsbury - b. 1928; d. 1988

HAM
- Daniel H. [husb. of Laura A.] - b. 1869; d. 1939
- Laura A. [wife of Daniel H.] - b. 1866; d. 1937

HILL
- Anneke Johanna - b. 7 October 1938; d. 25 May 1988

KENNEDY
- Thomas F. (Rev.) - b. 19 September 1922; d. 8 June 1993

MacDUFFY
[Elspeth - see BRAGDON]
MAIN
Amos [husb. of Olive J.] - b. 6 February 1850; d. 21 December 1923
Olive J. [wife of Amos] - b. 3 April 1850; d. 22 December 1922
PEAKE
Edwin D. [husb. of Janet S.?] - b. 18 August 1903; d. 25 January 1976
Janet S. [wife of Edwin D.?] - b. 30 November 1914; d. 23 February 1986
PHILLIPS
Doris M. [wife of Maurice] - d. 1917; d. 1998
Maurice [husb. of Doris M.] - b. 1910
PHIPPEN
Fannie (wife of Samuel C.) - b. 11 February 1846; d. 15 March 1924
Harry V. [husb. of [...][1] [no stone]] - b. 19 October 1871; d. 16 December 1913
Samuel C. (husb. of Fannie) - b. 20 August 1843; d. 31 January 1932
Winfield E. [son of Harry V. and [...][1]] - d. 9 October 1898 Æ [...][1,2] m., 14 d.
PICKERING
Katrina Ruth - b. 31 October 1974; d. 12 April 1994
QUITTNER
Alfred - b. 21 June 1901; d. 22 November 1974
RAMSEY
Raymond E. [husb. of Virginia A.] - b. 1920; d. 1982
Virginia A. [wife of Raymond E.] - b. 1919
SMITH
Hildegarde F. [wife of Vernon N.] - b. 1916
Vernon N. [husb. of Hildegarde F.] - b. 1918; d. 1985
SPOFFORD
B. A. (Capt.) - b. 24 October 1829; d. 13 July 1914
SPRAGUE
Roland James - b. 12 December 1929; d. 13 March 1959
SPURLING
Annie W. (wife of Edward A.) - b. 1871; d. 1960
Edward A. (husb. of Annie W.) - b. 1863; d. 1929
Georgia A. (wife of S. Everett [no stone]) - b. 1879; d. 1920
Harry E. [husb. of Ida M.] - b. 1903
Ida M. [wife of Harry E.] - b. 1898; d. 1994
Raymond - b. 1901; d. 1988
VALDINA
[...] [headstone only]
WHIPPLE
Lucius S. - b. 1843; d. 1920
WRONKOW
George - b. 1905; d. 1989

Notes:
[1]Stone worn.
[2]At least 2 months.

Sutton Island Cemetery
(Cranberry Isles - 9)

Location/directions. Sutton Island. From dock, follow a trail straight ahead and the cemetery is on the left.

History. —

Notes. There is no enclosure around this cemetery.

Names and dates on gravestones and other markers. [31 July 1999]
BOGGS
James - b. 1919; d. 1993
CHAPIN
Andrew Clarke - b. 20 December 1973; d. 8 May 1997
D.
H. C. [footstone only]
FERNALD
[E or A]mory[1] Gil[l]man[1] (son of A. C. and N. L. [no stones]) - d. 13 March 1864 Æ 1 y., 3 m., 10 d.
Ora Elbert (son of A. C. and N. L. [no stones]) - d. 18 December 1867 Æ 2 m., 25 d.
FLEXNER
[Hortense - see KING]
HOTTEL
Hoyt Clarke [husb. of Nellie Rich[2]] - b. 1903; d. 1998
Nellie Rich[2] [wife of Hoyt Clarke] - b. 1905; d. 1994
HOWE
Frederick Gilman [husb. of Helen (KING)] - b. 1907; d. 1994
Helen (KING; [wife of Frederick Gilman]) - b. 1903; d. 1992
KING
[Helen - see HOWE]
Hortense Flexner[2] - b. 1885; d. 1973
Ruth Rodney[2] - [no dates]
Wyncie - b. 1884; d. 1961
MANLEY
Kirtland - b. 1909; d. 1975
Norris - b. 1906; d. 1973
McDONALD
Linwood A. - b. 12 April 1933; d. 28 January 1996
MOORE
Eliza (wife of Capt. William) - d. 1 June 1870 Æ 62 y., 1 m., 3 d.
William (Capt.; husb. of Eliza) - d. 12 December 1874 Æ 73 y., 5 m., 7 d.
PAINE
Alfred White - b. 1903; d. 1944
Carola (WORMSER) - b. 1908; d. 1988
Clara May - b. 1872; d. 1948
George Lyman - b. 1874; d. 1967
George Lyman Jr. - b. 1901; d. 1978
RICH
[Nellie - see HOTTEL]
RICHARDSON
Isaac (husb. of Nancy [no stone]) - d. 7 March 1874 Æ 82 y., 9 m., 26 d.
Joseph M. (son of Isaac and Nancy [no stone]) - d. 31 March 1822 Æ 4 m., 23 d.

Sophia E. (dau. of Isaac and Nancy [no stone]) - d. 11 September 1825 Æ 1 y., 2 m., 15 d.
William M. (Capt.) - d. 4 July 1864 Æ 41 y., 7 m., 18 d.

RODNEY
[Ruth - see KING]

WORMSER
[Carola - see PAINE]

Notes:
[1]Different on different stones.
[2]To determine if this is a maiden name will require further research.

Standley Grave
(Cranberry Isles - 10)

Location/directions. Little Cranberry. From the town dock, walk through the field toward the right to a paved road. Turn right onto this road and follow it past Sand Beach Cemetery (Cranberry Isles - 8) to the end of the pavement. Continue straight on a gravel road, and the grave is set back approximately 60' from the left (east) side of the road on a little rise.

History. —

Notes. The lot containing the grave is bounded by four granite posts.

Names and dates on gravestones and other markers. [24 June 2000]
STANDLEY
John - d. 17 May 1783 Æ 47 y.

Spurling Cemetery
(Cranberry Isles - 11)

Location/directions. Great Cranberry. From the town dock, walk straight ahead on the main road and, in approximately 300', turn onto the first road on the right. In about 400', the cemetery is set back from the left side of the road.

History. —

Notes. The cemetery is enclosed by a gated chain-link fence. During an August visit of one year and a late June visit of another year, it appeared that the grass had not mowed for many weeks (if at all that). Six footstones are laying outside the fence: "E. R. C." [Edgar R. COULTER?], "F. L. C." [Flora L. COULTER?], "J. M. G." [Jennie M. GOOGINS?], "A. P. S." [Arthur P. STANLEY?], "father", and a blank footstone.

Names and dates on gravestones and other markers. [29 August 1999]

BROOKS
- Barbara S. - b. 1912
- Carl A. - b. 1909; d. 1989
- "Ebbie" S. - b. 1937; d. 1952

BULGER
- [Alys Madolyn - see SPURLING]
- Dena J. (wife of Capt. William H.) - b. 17 December 1864; d. 31 October 1923
- Elva A. (wife of Capt. William H.) - d. 13 June 1875 Æ 18 y., 6 m., 5 d.
- Richard Safford - d. 10 October 1915 Æ 2 m., 22 d.
- William H. (Capt.; husb. of Elva A. and Dena J.) - b. 19 June 1845; d. 27 May 1927

CHAPMAN
- [Cora L. - see RICHARDSON]

COULTER
- Edgar R. - d. 20 September 1898 Æ 3 y., 5 m., 8 d.
- Flora L. - d. 20 November 1899 Æ 28 y., 1 m., 10 d.

DUREN
- Addie E. - b. 1886; d. 1973

GOOGINS
- Jennie M. (SPURLING; dau. of Joseph S. SPURLING and Matilda T.) - b. 27 August 1852; d. 7 June 1890

HATFIELD
- [Edna Mae - see SPURLING]

NEWMAN
- Joseph - d. 28 December 1879 Æ 90 y., 9 m., 11 d.

RICHARDSON
- Cora L. (CHAPMAN; wife of Elwood F.) - b. 1863; d. 1941
- Elwood F. (husb. of Cora L. (CHAPMAN)) - b. 1856; d. 1906

SPURLING
- Ada A. (dau. of George N. and Maria A.) - d. 6 March 1860 Æ 5 y.
- Alice J. (dau. of Capt. Benjamin and Asenath M.) - d. 9 November 1860 Æ 4 y., 2 m.
- Alys Madolyn (BULGER; [wife of Nelson Eliot]) - b. 2 December 1907; d. 10 January 1997
- Asenath M. (wife of Capt. Benjamin) - d. 10 April 1899 Æ 65 y., 4 m.
- Benjamin (Capt.; husb. of Asenath M.) - d. 4 July 1887 Æ 59 y., 3 m., 17 d.
- Charles E. [husb. of Emma F.] - b. 1850; d. 1925

Charles Samuel (husb. of Edna Mae (HATFIELD)) - b. 1880; d. 1911
Edna Mae (HATFIELD; wife of Charles Samuel) - b. 1877; d. 1967
Emma F. [wife of Charles E.] - b. 1860; d. 1934
Enoch (husb. of Hannah) - d. 26 October 1838 Æ 49 y.
George N. (husb. of Maria A.) - d. 16 January 1901 Æ 83 y.
Hannah (wife of Enoch) - d. 9 May 1856 Æ 65 y.
[Jennie M. - see GOOGINS]
Joseph S. (husb. of Matilda T.) - b. 23 August 1817; d. 6 April 1890
Lillian E. (dau. of Robert and Fannie [no stones]) - d. 13 July 1861 Æ 2 y., 4 m.
Lucelia A. (dau. of George N. and Maria A.) - d. 3 December 1857 Æ 11 w.
Maria A. (wife of George N.) - d. 18 April 1881 Æ 43 y., 5 m., 7 d.
Mary E. (dau. of Joseph S. and Matilda T.) - d. 8 March 1861 Æ 2 y., 10 m., 6 d.
Matilda T. (wife of Joseph S.) - b. 1821; d. 1912
Nelson Eliot [husb. of Alys Madolyn (BULGER)] - b. 13 June 1910

STANLEY

Arthur P. (son of Asa D. and Maria E. [no stone]) - d. 19 May 1873 Æ 9 y., 9 m., 6 d.
Asa D. (husb. of Maria E. [no stone]) - d. 12 May 1900 Æ 67 y., 11 m.
Ellen M. - b. 1842; d. 1929
Hiram L. (husb. of Nettie A.) - b. 1850; d. 1931
infant (son of Hiram L. and Nettie A.) - d. 1 October 1885 Æ 1 m., 7 d.
Nettie A. (wife of Hiram L.) - b. 1862; d. 1925
Wealthy H. (wife of Capt. A. C. [no stone]) - d. 3 November 1882 Æ 39 y., 4 m., 24 d.

TRUSSELL

Frankie E. (son of Horatio N. and Wealtha [sic] H. [no stones]) - d. 25 August 1879 Æ 6 y., 10 m., 3 d.; ("was drowned")
Freddie [TRUSSELL?][1] - [no dates]

Note:
[1]Footstone: "F. T.".

Catholic Cemetery
(Cranberry Isles - 12)

Location/directions. Little Cranberry. From the boat dock, follow the paved road to the left. In a short distance after passing a white church on the left, bear left at a fork in the road. Immediately before a small, shingled chapel on the left, follow a trail to the Merrill Family Burial Ground (Cranberry Isles - 6). This cemetery is adjacent to the further side of the Merrill Family Burial Ground.

History. The name applied to this cemetery is only for convenience of reference in this book.

Notes. Northern white-cedar trees border this cemetery and separate it from the Merrill Family Burial Ground (Cranberry Isles - 6).

Names and dates on gravestones and other markers. [4 September 1999]

BARTLETT
- Frank B. [husb. of Irene (MORSE[1])] - b. 9 July 1904; d. 2 January 1968
- Irene (MORSE[1]; [wife of Frank B.]) - b. 1 March 1909; d. 27 June 1998

LOCKE
- Reginald H. - b. 7 October 1922; d. 21 November 1993

MORSE
- Emeline H. [wife of Thomas S.] - b. 11 June 1911; d. 26 November 1992
- Frederick W. [husb. of Mary (SMITH)] - b. 1871; d. 1929
- [Irene - see BARTLETT]
- Katherine M. [dau. of Frederick W. and Mary (SMITH)?] - b. 29 March 1917; d. 20 April 1998
- Mary (SMITH; [wife of Frederick W.]) - b. 1876; d. 1962
- Thomas S. [husb. of Emeline H.] - b. 1912; d. 1984

SMITH
- [Mary - see MORSE]

Note:

[1]Prior to the stone that reads "Irene M." was a metal marker from a funeral home that gave her (presumably) maiden name as MORSE.

Sawtelle Graves
(Cranberry Isles - 13)

Location/directions. Little Cranberry. As you approach the town dock from the water, you will see the Islesford Historical Museum, a brick building, to the left. The graves are directly behind the museum.

History. —

Notes. The grave site, marked by a plaque on a boulder, is not enclosed.

Names and dates on gravestones and other markers. [4 September 1999]

BURPEE
  [Louise - see SAWTELLE]

SAWTELLE
  Eleanor Otis (dau. of William Otis and Louise (BURPEE)) - b. 17 July 1913; d. 29 March 1956
  Louise (BURPEE; wife of William Otis) - b. 9 May 1877; d. 24 January 1941
  William Otis (husb. of Louise (BURPEE)) - b. 7 July 1874; d. 22 September 1939

Bunker and Olson Graves

(Cranberry Isles - 14)

Location/directions. Great Cranberry. From the town dock, walk straight ahead on the paved road. Soon the road rises and curves to the left. After the curve is a field on the right. Turn right onto the first driveway and in approximately 85' on the left is a (perhaps mowed) path leading about 25' to the graves.

History. —

Notes. The three graves are enclosed by a low (approximately 15" high) fence of concrete posts with chain suspended between them. Between one pair of adjacent posts there is no chain, thereby providing an entrance/exit.

Names and dates on gravestones and other markers. [4 September 1999]

BUNKER
Constance Wilcock[1] - b. 6 July 1919; d. 10 January 1975
George R. - b. 1923; d. 1991
[Katherine B[UNKER]. - see OLSON]

OLSON
Katherine B[UNKER]. - b. 23 October 1951; d. 9 August 1998

WILCOCK
[Constance - see BUNKER]

Note:
[1]It is unclear from the gravestone whether this is a maiden name.

Harding Point Cemetery

(Cranberry Isles - 15)

Location/directions. Harding Point, Great Cranberry. From the town dock, walk straight ahead on the main road. Soon the road rises, curves to the left, and then runs more or less straight. From this straight section, turn left onto the paved road across from the tennis court. Follow this road generally downhill through several gentle curves and then a sharp curve to the left followed by a more or less straight section, and then another sharp curve, this time to the right. After this sharp curve and immediately before the pavement ends, turn right onto a dirt road. The third (June 2000) driveway (near telephone pole 2 $^{1}/_{2}$) on the left leads to the cemetery, which is on the left of this drive in approximately 250'.

History. The name applied to this cemetery is only for convenience of reference in this book.

Notes. The cemetery is not enclosed, but there are wood posts marking its apparent boundary. Several gravestones are laying on the ground.

Names and dates on gravegravestones and other markers. [4 September 1999]

BULGER
- Millie A. - b. 1882; d. 1976
- Oscar S. - b. 28 October 1872; d. 20 June 1943

FERNALD
- Margaret S. (wife of Samuel S. [no stone]) - d. 30 August 1867 Æ 27 y., 2 m., 22 d.

HARDING
- Dellie A. (wife of Richard J.) - b. 1 June 1852; d. 9 December 1941
- Richard J. (husb. of Dellie A.) - b. 22 March 1851; d. 21 February 1910

MANCHESTER
- Hannah (wife of Capt. Thomas) - d. 13 November 1861 Æ 87 y., 5 m.
- Thomas (Capt.; husb. of Hannah) - d. 26 January 1861 Æ 92 y., 3 m.

PHIPPEN
- Leslie R. - b. 1899; d. 1986
- Paul A. - b. 1926; d. 1985

SPURLING
- Hilda A. (wife of E. A. [no stone]) - b. 1902; d. 1987
- infant (son of E. A. [no stone] and Hilda A.) - [b. and?] d. 3 January 1925

STANLEY
- Bertha E. (wife of Gilbert Moore) - d. 2 June 1899 Æ 20 y., 7 m.
- Bertie Moore - b. 23 May 1899; d. 18 December 1918
- Frank L. (husb. of Maggie M.) - b. 1865; d. 1945
- Gilbert Moore (husb. of Bertha E.) - b. 1868; d. 1933
- Gilman J. (son of Jonathan R. and Irene) - d. 18 June 1861, Straits of Belleisle Æ 16 y., 8 m., 28 d.; ("drowned")
- Irene (wife of Jonathan R.) - d. 12 August 1889 Æ 82 y., 5 m.
- Jonathan R. (husb. of Irene) - d. 27 April 1895 Æ 91 y., 6 m.
- Lester (son of Frank L. and Maggie M.) - b. 1 June 1911; d. 13 September 1911
- Lyle (son of Frank L. and Maggie M.) - b. 1902; d. 1911
- Maggie M. (wife of Frank L.) - b. 1871; d. 1954

TRUSSELL
- Sadie A. (wife of Wilfred S.) - b. 1879; d. [no date]
- Wilfred S. (husb. of Sadie A.) - b. 1869; d. 1911

Spurling Point Cemetery
(Cranberry Isles - 16)

Location/directions. Great Cranberry. Immediately after leaving the town dock, turn right onto a flat-topped cobble ridge. In approximately 300', the path along the ridge is blocked by rugosa rose. Step down onto the beach and continue in the same direction for another 50' until there is access to the field on the left. Follow the shore side of the field, and in about 100', the stones will be visible on the left. In both 1999 and 2000, an American flag has marked one of the graves.

History. —

Notes. There is a large stone face down, thereby obscuring any information it may contain. The cemetery is in an apparently unmowed, or rarely mowed, field and has no discernable boundary markers.

Names and dates on gravestones and other markers. [4 September 1999]
HERRICK
Andrew - b. 1722[1]; d. 1812
L'GROW
Joseph - d. 25 February 1833 Æ 82 y.
S.
F. [footstone only]
SPURLING
Benjamin - d. 30 December 1836 Æ 84 y.

Note:
[1]At the grave here is a wooden marker that appears to bear a birth date of 1722. A stone, however, in the Lurvey Burial Ground (Southwest Harbor - 1) gives the birth year as 1742.

MOUNT DESERT

A resolution to incorporate the then plantation of Mount Desert passed the House of Representatives on 16 February 1789 and passed the Senate on the next day. There are no town-owned cemeteries in the town of Mount Desert. They are, therefore, either owned and maintained by a non-profit organization such as a cemetery association or owned privately and maintained or not.

Non-profit organization:
- Pretty Marsh Cemetery (Mount Desert - 1)
- Brookside Cemetery (Mount Desert - 6)
- Otter Creek Cemetery (Mount Desert - 10)
- Forest Hill Cemetery (Mount Desert - 11)
- Seal Harbor Cemetery (Mount Desert - 18)

Private or unknown oversight:
- Smith Graves (Mount Desert - 2)
- Pray Cemetery (Mount Desert - 3)
- Richardson Burying Ground (Mount Desert - 7)
- Wasgatt Cemetery (Mount Desert - 8)
- Sound Cemetery (Mount Desert - 9)
- Smallidge Cemetery (Mount Desert - 12)
- Bartlett Island -3 (Mount Desert - 13)
- Bartlett Island - 2 (Mount Desert - 14)
- Bartlett Island - 1 (Mount Desert - 15)
- Brown Cemetery (Mount Desert - 16)
- Atherton and Mikhalapov Graves (Mount Desert - 17)
- Kimball Cemetery (Mount Desert - 19)
- Bartlett Island - 6 (Mount Desert - 20)
- Bartlett Island - 5 (Mount Desert - 21)
- Carter Cemetery (Mount Desert - 22)
- Sheep Island Cemetery (Mount Desert - 23)
- Savage Graves - (Mount Desert - 24)
- Blanchard Cemetery (Mount Desert - 25)
- Kittredge Tomb (Mount Desert - 26)
- Bartlett Island - 4 (Mount Desert - 27)

Pretty Marsh Cemetery
(Mount Desert - 1)

Location/directions. Along north side of Bartlett Landing Road, Pretty Marsh. From the traffic light at the north end of Mount Desert Island, go straight ahead (south) onto Routes 102/198. In approximately 5.2 miles (and at the south end of the village of Somesville), turn right onto Pretty Marsh Road. Travel 3.5 miles to the intersection with Indian Point Road on the right. Take Indian Point Road 0.2–0.3 miles to a three-way stop. Bear left onto Bartlett Landing Road, and the cemetery is on the right in approximately 0.1–0.2 miles.

History. An 1893 deed (273:308–310) gave the "inhabitants of the Village of Pretty Marsh" an addition of "thirty two square rods more or less" to an extant and fenced in Pretty Marsh Cemetery. No earlier deed to Pretty Marsh inhabitants or to a cemetery association could be found in the index books of the Hancock County Registry of Deeds. In 1939 (671:309–310), a 3400 square foot addition was deeded to "The Pretty Marsh Cemetery Association", and in 1982 (1425:544–545), another addition was made to the cemetery.

Notes. This cemetery is well maintained. It is not enclosed by a fence.

Names and dates on gravestones and other markers. [2 May 1999]

ARDUINI
- Belinda (MACRAE) - b. 15 December 1946; d. 27 February 1997

ATHERTON
- Andrew Jackson (son of Israel and Judith (SOMES) (FREEMAN)) - d. 16 March 1836 Æ 1 y., 6 m.
- Israel (husb. of Judith (SOMES) (FREEMAN)) - b. 12 August 1802; d. 3 June 1845
- Judith ((SOMES) (FREEMAN); wife of Israel) - b. 27 October 1804; d. 23 August 1865
- Thomas W. - d. 29 July 1849 Æ 22 y., 9 m.
- William W. M. (son of Israel and Judith (SOMES) (FREEMAN)) - d. 7 March 1836 Æ 3 y.

BARRON
- Mary Ann (wife of Robert) - d. 12 January 1880 Æ 45 y., 5 m.
- Robert (husb. of Mary Ann) - d. 7 January 1910 Æ 78 y.
- Thomas W. - d. 14 March 1886 Æ 30 y.

BLANCHARD
- Hazen G. [husb. of Marion E.] - b. 1909
- Marion E. [wife of Hazen G.] - b. 1916; d. 1992

BOWDEN
- Emily A. (wife of James G. [no stone]) - d. 6 May 1850 Æ 29 y., 1 m., 6 d.
- infant (son of James G. [no stone] and Emily A.) - [no dates]

BRANSCOM [includes BRANSCOMB]
- Charles (husb. of Rebecca) - d. 18 September 1825 Æ 75 y.
- Charles (C[apt.?][1]; husb. of Joanna) - d. 15 September 1852 Æ 60 y.
- Jerusha (son of C[apt.?][1] Charles and Joanna) - d. 24 November 1826 Æ 11 m.
- Joanna (wife of C[apt.?][1] Charles) - d. 30 August 1872 Æ 75 y., 8 m.
- Rebecca (dau. of C[apt.?][1] Charles and Joanna) - d. 29 June 1839 Æ 5 y.
- Rebecca (wife of Charles) - d. 15 June 1840 Æ 100 y.

BUCHANAN
- Katherine M. (FREEMAN; wife of Pearl A.) - b. 1919; d. 1954
- Pearl A. (husb. of Katherine M. (FREEMAN)) - b. 1918

CARTER
Allen W. [husb. of Hazel R.] - b. 1903; d. 1959
Andrew J. - b. 1865; d. 1947
Benjamin F. [husb. of Frona] - b. 1860; d. 1928
Frona [wife of Benjamin F.] - b. 1863; d. 1942
Hazel R. [wife of Allen W.] - b. 1903; d. 1959
Laura E. - b. 1866; d. 1920
William F. - b. 1891; d. 1902
CHENG
Mary Eleanor (HARLOW; wife of Cheng-yin [no stone]) - b. 11 November 1935; d. 31 December 1971
CONGLETON
Cornelia A. [wife of Verner L.] - b. 1907; d. 1978
Verner L. [husb. of Cornelia A.] - b. 1901; d. 1976
COULTER
Andrew A. [husb. of Ann B.] - b. 1903; d. 1982
Ann B. [wife of Andrew A.] - b. 1909; d. 1976
CROWLEY
David L. (husb. of Rhoda R.) - "lost at sea" 17 October 1869 Æ 41 y., 9 m.
Ephraim H. - d. 16 August 1884 Æ 28 y.
Rhoda R. (wife of David L.) - d. 4 April 1896 Æ 64 y., 5 m.
CUMMINGS
Charles T. - b. 14 August 1862; d. 24 November 1927
DODGE
David B. - b. 24 September 1866; d. 23 August 1917
Emeline H. (wife of Richard B.) - d. 11 February 1886 Æ 58 y.
Hilda S. [wife of Lincoln H.] - b. 1905; d. 1958
Lincoln H. [husb. of Hilda S.] - b. 1902; d. 1978
Richard B. (husb. of Emeline H.) - d. 16 August 1897 Æ 74 y., 5 m., 28 d.
Synthia [sic] R. S. (dau. of Richard and Angelina [no stones]) - d. 22 November 1956 Æ 3 y., 1 m., 12 d.
DOE
Harold O. [husb. of Josephine (GRAY)] - b. 1893; d. 1976
Josephine (GRAY; [wife of Harold O.]) - b. 1900; d. 1990
ELIOT
[Elisabeth - see McGIFFERT]
F.
A. M. [footstone only]
FLANDERS
Elizabeth A. [wife of Reginald L.] - [no dates]
Reginald L. [husb. of Elizabeth A.] - b. 1899; d. 1991
FOOTE
Edgar Clayton (husb. of Linda F. (SMITH)) - b. 1870; d. 1954
Linda F. (SMITH; wife of Edgar Clayton) - b. 1872; d. 1965
FREEMAN
Abbie H. - d. 10 June 1872 Æ 16 y., 4 m., 11 d.
Alfrida [sic] S. - b. 1883; d. 1936
Allen E. (husb. of Lizzie E. and Nancy M.) - b. 1858; d. 1945
Benjamin T. R. (Capt.) - d. 29 April 1874 Æ 68 y.
Catherine (wife of Reuben) - b. 1742; d. [no date]
Daniel (Capt.; husb. of Mercy) - d. 14 December 1874 Æ 76 y.
Ebba S. - b. 1886; d. 1924

Elizabeth C. (wife of William M.) - d. 24 September 1904 Æ 76 y., 10 m.
F. Howard - b. 1889; d. 1897
F. Palmer (husb. of Josephine) - b. 1841; d. 1917
[Florence - see GRAY]
Gardner P. (son of Capt. Daniel [and Mercy?]) - "lost at sea" 6 September 1863 Æ 18 y.
George (husb. of Tamesin) - d. 16 April 1844 Æ 72 y.
George B. (Capt.) - d. 5 October 1872, Lewes, Delaware, Æ 33 y., 5 m., 5 d.
George H. (husb. of Mildred G.) - b. 1868; d. 1942
George W. (son of Capt. Daniel and Mercy) - d. 27 February 1870, "in Rio Janeiro S. A.", Æ 32 y.
Harvey P. - b. 1877; d. 1957
infant[2] (dau. of Reuben and Sophia [no stones]) - d. 17 August 1838 Æ [not given]
John T. (Capt.) - b. 1874; d. 1917
Joseph P. - d. 1876 Æ 8 m.
Josephine - b. 18 October 1885; d. 20 [...][4] 1894
Josephine (wife of F. Palmer) - b. 1845; d. 1926
Joshua (son of Capt. Daniel and Mercy) - d. 1 June 1872, Oregon, Æ 41 y.
[Judith - see ATHERTON]
[Katherine M. - see BUCHANAN]
Lizzie E. (wife of Allen E.) - b. 1864; d. 1903
Margaret B. (3rd wife of Capt. Reuben) - d. 2 February 1852 Æ 64 y., 11 m.
Mary J. (wife of W. H.) - b. 11 October 1838; d. 13 June 1908
Mercy (wife of Capt. Daniel) - d. 3 November 1845 Æ 44 y.
Mildred G. (wife of George H.) - b. 1887; d. 1969
Nancy M. (wife of Allen E.) - b. 1875; d. 1960
[Nellie G. - see SAUNDERS]
Nellie Snow - b. 19 January 1873; d. 30 July 1883
Palmer P. - b. 1880; d. 1898
Pearl Roger - b. 1912; d. 1986
Pearl W. - "lost at sea" 9 November 1879 Æ 24 y., 11 m.
Polly L. (2nd wife of Capt. Reuben) - d. 20 November 1829 Æ 47 y.
Prince Albert (son of Capt. Benjamin S. [no stone] and Ruth C.) - d. 5 September 1862 Æ 16 y., 10 m., 25 d.
Ralph D. (son of J. T. and Nancy L. [no stones]) - d. 7 January 1871 Æ 1 y., 8 m.
Reuben (husb. of Catherine) - b. 1740; d. 1812; [Revolutionary War veteran]
Reuben (husb. of Susan S.) - d. 8 November 1859 Æ 64 y., 2 m., 13 d.
Reuben (Capt.; husb. of Rhoda R., Polly L., and Margaret B.) - d. 19 August 1850 Æ 79 y., 4 m.
Rhoda R. (1st wife of Capt. Reuben) - d. 1 March 1813 Æ 39 y.
Ruth C. (wife of Capt. Benjamin S. [no stone]) - d. 26 September 1867 Æ 64 y.
Susan S. (wife of Reuben) - d. 13 February 1877 Æ 74 y., 9 m.
Tamesin (wife of George) - d. 23 July 1836 Æ 64 y.
W. H. (husb. of Mary J.) - b. 19 May 1836; d. 2 December 1919
Wilber S. (son of Capt. Daniel) - "lost at sea" 2 June 1865 Æ 17 y.
William H. G. - d. 10 December 1876 Æ 33 y., 10 m., 10 d.
William H. Jr.[5] - b. 15 February 1871; d. 16 March 1903
William H. Sr.[5] - b. 1915; d. 1996
William M. (husb. of Elizabeth C.) - b. 24 September 1893 Æ 71 y., 10 m.

GORDIUS
Celia - b. 1892; d. 1927

GRAY
Alice S. F. [wife of William H.] - b. 1871; d. 1964
Celia J. [wife of George W.] - b. 1910; d. 1984
Edna M. [wife of William S.] - b. 1906; d. 1987
Florence (FREEMAN; wife of Fred Edward) - b. 1873; d. 1961
Fred Edward (husb. of Florence (FREEMAN)) - b. 1873; d. 1956
George W. [husb. of Celia J.] - b. 1910; d. 1963
Hattie L. (wife of Mark H.) - b. 1870; d. 1948
[Josephine - see DOE]
Mark H. (husb. of Hattie L.) - b. 1863; d. 1933
Martha Ann [dau. of George W. and Celia J.?] - [b. and d.?] 1945
William H. [husb. of Alice S. F.] - b. 1865; d. 1937
William S. [husb. of Edna M.] - b. 1906; d. 1963
GRISWOLD
[Anne Merrill - see NOBLE]
HARLOW
Elizabeth K. S. [wife of James Hayward III] - b. 21 December 1901; d. 10 March 1997
James Hayward III [husb. of Elizabeth K. S.] - b. 1 October 1901; d. 3 July 1987
[Mary Eleanor - see CHENG]
HAYNES
Frank K. - b. 1876; d. 1939
George W. - b. 1846; d. 1917
Maria L. - b. 1847; d. 1929
HEATH
Tamesin (wife of Richard [no stone]) - d. 19 October 1839 Æ 41 y.
HOOPER
Amos (husb. of Nancy H.) - d. 27 December 1876 Æ 69 y., 2 m., 27 d.
Nancy H. (wife of Amos) - d. 14 January 1873 Æ 57 y., 6 m., 4 d.
Reuben H. (son of Amos and Nancy H.) - d. 22 August 1839 Æ 17 m., 14 d.
HYSOM
Edna Lora (RUMILL; [wife of Roscoe Hartwell]) - b. 1898; d. 1998
Roscoe Hartwell [husb. of Edna Lora (RUMILL)] - b. 1897; d. 1965
LEONARD
Ethel [wife of William P.] - b. 1895; d. 1966
George W. - b. 2 January 1896; d. 29 October 1951
Millie A. - b. 6 April 1938; d. 21 June 1999 Æ 61 y.
William P. [husb. of Ethel] - b. 1899; d. 1971
LEWIS
Lizzie M. - d. 22 July 1896 Æ 16 y., 3 m., 22 d.
[Mary L. - see SNOW]
R. S. - d. 15 March 1895 Æ 42 y., 5 m.
MACRAE
[Belinda - see ARDUINI]
John Fraser - b. 21 August 1918; d. 12 August 1993
MAYNARD
Sigrid D. - b. 1893; d. 1975
MAYO
Nancy F. - b. 5 November 1830; d. 9 June 1889
MCGIFFERT
Arthur Cushman Jr. [husb. of Elisabeth (ELIOT)] - b. 1892; d. 1993
Elisabeth (ELIOT; [wife of Arthur Cushman Jr.]) - b. 1897; d. 1991

MILLIKEN
Mel[e]tiah[3] J. - d. 24 November 1827 Æ 20 y., 5 m., 19 d.
Rachel W. (wife of Simeon) - d. 21 November 1864 Æ 88 y., 9 d.
Rufus (son of Simeon and Rachel W.) - d. 2[2 or 6][3] October 1820 Æ 5 y., 3 m., 11 d.
Sally (wife of Samuel Jr.) - d. 6 December 1833 Æ 47 y.
Samuel F. - d. 19 May 1841 Æ 21 y., 9 m., 17 d., Carlisle, Pennsylvania
Samuel Jr. (husb. of Sally) - d. 1 September 183[1 or 4?][1] Æ 55 y.
Simeon (husb. of Rachel W.) - d. 2 December 1864 Æ 85 y., 5 m., 6 d.
Simeon J. (Esq.) - d. 8 April 1835 Æ 29 y., 4 m., 18 d.
William W. - d. 5 March 1833 Æ 21 y., 3 m., 19 d.
MOFFETT
Anna (VIGUS) - b. 1838; d. 1912
NEWELL
Sadie S. [wife of Winslow L.] - b. 1871; d. 1955
Winslow L. [husb. of Sadie S.] - b. 1868; d. 1925
NOBLE
Anne Merrill (GRISWOLD) - b. 6 June 1926; d. 14 March 1998
Duncan - b. 3 September 1925; d. 11 December 1995
Duncan Griswold - b. 20 October 1955; d. 28 April 1988
PELLEGREN
Armour - b. 30 October 1893; d. 28 May 1972
PRESTON
Velma L. - b. 1893; d. 1972
READE
Florence E. - b. 1886; d. 1967
Lewis F. - b. 1882; d. 1959
Lewis F. Jr. - b. 1906; d. 1978
RUMILL
[Edna Lora - see HYSOM]
Edwin B. (Capt.; [husb. of Lettie Anna]) - b. 21 February 1860; "lost at sea" 10 October 1905
Lettie Anna [wife of Capt. Edwin B.] - b. 29 May 1864; d. 10 October 1936
SAUNDERS
Nellie G. (FREEMAN) - b. 1884; d. 1966
SEAVEY
Georgie B. [wife of Merrill L.] - b. 1909
Marguerite A. [wife of Merrill L. Jr.] - b. 1934; d. 1986
Merrill L. [husb. of Georgie B.] - b. 1905; d. 1985
Merrill L. Jr. [husb. of Marguerite A.] - b. 1932
Roger Dean - b. 1938; d. 1988
SHORT
John Gerdes - b. 1948; d. 1983
SMALLIDGE
Cora A. [wife of Nathan T.] - b. 1880; d. 1944
John N. - b. 21 February 1929; d. 31 July 1985
Lewis F. [husb. of Mazie E.] - b. 1903; d. 1981
Mazie E. [wife of Lewis F.] - b. 1906; d. 1994
Nathan T. [husb. of Cora A.] - b. 1878; d. 1963
SMITH
Allen O. [husb. of Augusta E.] - b. 1875; d. 1962
Anthelia M. [wife of John W.?] - b. 1845; d. 1880

Augusta E. [wife of Allen O.] - b. 1871; d. 1939
Bertha O. - b. 30 September 1863; d. 18 December 1917
Dexter [husb. of Emeline A.] - b. 18 September 1833; d. 21 July 1912
Emeline A. [wife of Dexter] - b. 5 February 1838; d. 8 March 1896
George W. - b. 1875; d. 1885
Harriet C. - b. 1828; d. 18 December 1848 Æ 20 y.
John [husb. of Lydia C.?] - b. 1802; d. 29 May 1841 Æ 39 y.
John A. - b. 1863; d. 1881
John W. [husb. of Anthelia M.?] - b. 1842; d. 1910
[Linda F. - see FOOTE]
Lydia C. [wife of John?] - b. 1806; d. 23 April 1871 Æ 65 y., 4 m.
Nettie E. (wife of Richmond L.) - d. 26 February 1907 Æ 62 y., 5 m., 11 d.
Reuben - b. 1835; d. 1838
Richmond L. (husb. of Nettie E.) - d. 12 December 1919 Æ 84 y., 11 m., 10 d.
Weston - b. 1830; d. 19 October 1860 Æ 30 y.

SNOW
Mary L. (LEWIS; wife of M. H. [no stone]) - d. 10 December 1918 Æ 60 y., 4 m.

SOMES
[Judith - see ATHERTON]

STALNACKE
Lillie A. - b. 1888; d. 1948

STORK
Harry [husb. of Hilda A.?] - b. 1886; d. 1959
Hilda A. [wife of Harry?] - b. 1897; d. 1990

STRØMHOLT
Edmund Ivan - b. 1944; d. 1987
Lajla Kristina - b. 18 January 1958; d. 1 December 1994

THIBODEAU
Gladis [sic] R. [wife of Von H.] - b. 1909; d. 1993
Von H. [husb. of Gladis [sic] R.] - b. 1904; d. 1991

VIGUS
[Anna - see MOFFETT]
Susan - b. 1844; d. 1929

WALLS
Edgar N. (husb. of Ida J.) - b. 1 May 1869; d. 29 October 1944
Ida J. (wife of Edgar N.) - b. 21 April 1868; d. 25 December 1927

[...]
[...][1]

Notes:
[1]Stone worn, cracked, and/or broken.
[2]Footstone: "F.".
[3]Different on different stones.
[4]Very slightly raised letters and numbers obscured by lichens.
[5]The birth and death dates for William H. FREEMAN Jr. and Sr. are correct, indicating that William Sr. is not the father of William Jr.

Smith Graves
(Mount Desert - 2)

Location/directions. Pretty Marsh. From the traffic light at the north end of Mount Desert Island, go straight ahead (south) onto Routes 102/198. In approximately 5.2 miles (and at the south end of the village of Somesville), turn right onto Pretty Marsh Road. Travel 3.5 miles to the intersection with Indian Point Road on the right. Take Indian Point Road 0.2–0.3 miles to a three-way stop. Bear left onto Bartlett Landing Road, and the single gravestone is on the right in less than 0.1 miles.

History. —

Notes. The stone is on a maintained lawn of a residence and is not enclosed.

Names and dates on gravestones and other markers. [13 August 1999]
SMITH
Daniel E.[1] (husb. of Lovina) - d. 7 April 1871 Æ 77 y.
Lovina (wife of Daniel E.) - d. 27 November 1869 Æ 76 y.

Note:
[1]Near the headstone shared by Daniel E. and Lovina is a "GAR/1861/1865" marker [Civil War].

Pray Cemetery
(Mount Desert - 3)

Location/directions. Pretty Marsh. From the traffic light at the north end of Mount Desert Island, go straight ahead (south) onto Routes 102/198. In approximately 5.2 miles (and at the south end of the village of Somesville), turn right onto Pretty Marsh Road. Travel 3.5 miles to the intersection with Indian Point Road on the right. Take Indian Point Road 0.2–0.3 miles to a three-way stop. Bear left onto Bartlett Landing Road, and the cemetery is on the left in a field in less than 0.1 miles.

History. The cemetery is on land that was part of a 102 acre parcel owned by an E. Pray in 1808 according to the Salem Towne Jr. map.

Notes. This cemetery consists of three stones—a tall monument and two smaller stones. One of the two smaller stones is laying on the ground, worn, and beginning to be obscured by grass growing over it. Several pieces of unengraved stone are laying at the base of the monument. The cemetery is not enclosed.

Names and dates on gravestones and other markers. [2 May 1999]

HODGDON

Rebecca A. (wife of Capt. Benjamin E. [no stone]) - d. 28 April 1871 Æ 21 y., 10 m.

PRAY

Ephraim (husb. of Rebecca P.) - b. 1806; d. 1889
Ephraim (husb. of Susan) - d. 25 May 1821 Æ 61 y.
Lemuel N. - b. 1838; "Lost at sea off the coast of Alaska" 1872
Rebecca P. (wife of Ephraim) - b. 1817; d. 1896
Susan (wife of Ephraim) - d. 26 January 1858 Æ 88 y.

Kenison Cemetery
(Mount Desert - 4)

Location/directions. Set back from south side of Pretty Marsh Road (Route 102). From the traffic light at the north end of Mount Desert Island, go straight ahead (south) onto Routes 102/198. In approximately 5.2 miles (and at the south end of the village of Somesville), turn right onto Pretty Marsh Road. The cemetery is on the left in about 1.6–1.7 miles.

History. This cemetery is on land that was part of lot #110, a 138 acre parcel, on the 1808 Salem Towne Jr. map. The cemetery is nearly rectangular and contains approximately 4200 square feet. Hancock County Registry of Deeds planbook 16, page 77 contains a map.

Notes. In addition to several traditional gravestones, there are seven wooden crosses, each bearing a plaque with an individual's name and birth and death dates. Also, there is a large stone with "Kenison" on one side and the names of 16 people with their age at death on the other side. The cemetery is enclosed by a northern white-cedar post and rail fence. The entrance consists of a swinging gate bearing the letter K formed by natural pieces of white-cedar cut to size and an arch containing the name Kenison spelled out in a similar manner.

Names and dates on gravestones and other markers. [2 May 1999]
DUNHAM
  Eliza Jane - d. *ca.* 1881 Æ 1 m.
  Eliza Jane (KENISON; dau. of Henry A. KENISON and Sarah S.) - b. *ca.* 1853; d. *ca.* 1881
KELLEY
  [Ella M. - see VARNUM]
KENISON
  Eliza J. (dau. of Samuel and Susan [no stone]) - d. 30 June 1854 Æ 16 y.
  [Eliza Jane - see DUNHAM]
  Ethel Noyes - b. 15 March 1895; d. 2 May 1896
  Harry B. - b. 21 May 1899; d. 13 August 1935
  Henry A. (husb. of Sarah S.) - b. 28 August 1833; d. 21 November 1911
  John (son of Henry A. and Sarah S.) - d. *ca.* 1874 Æ 8 d.
  Myra M. - b. 6 August 1871; d. 17 May 1948
  Samuel - d. 2 February 1873 Æ 75 y., 4 m., 17 d.
  Sarah S. (wife of Henry A.) - b. 17 September 1832; d. 2 September 1921
O'NEILL
  Cecil Vane (son of John and Edith E. [no stones]) - d. 5 October 1901 Æ 1 y., 7 m., 26 d.
  David H. - [d.?] 3 September 1939
  Edith K. - b. 29 April 1867; d. 29 March 1944
  Lester S. - b. 28 February 1891; d. 12 March 1950
VARNUM
  Arthur H. - [d.?] 5 June 1927
  Austin D. (husb. of Ella M. (KELLEY)) - b. 1876; d. 1934
  Ella M. (KELLEY; wife of Austin D.) - b. 1870; d. 1941
  Nayham [sic] B. (son of Austin D. and Ella M. (KELLEY)) - b. 1897; d. 1906

Oak Hill Road Cemetery
(Mount Desert - 5)

Location/directions. Along west side of Oak Hill Road, just north of intersection of Oak Hill Road and Whitney Farm Road. From the traffic light at the north end of Mount Desert Island, go straight ahead (south) onto Routes 102/198. In approximately 4.7–4.8 miles (0.5 miles of which are south of the traffic light at the intersection of Routes 198 and 102/198), turn right onto Oak Hill Road. The cemetery is on the left in about 1.5–1.6 miles.

History. This cemetery is found in the 1881 Colby Atlas. It is bordered on the east by Oak Hill Road and on the other three sides by land described in a 1987 deed (1673:305), which referred to it as "a private cemetery". It is nearly rectangular and contains approximately 5300 square feet. The name applied to this cemetery is only for convenience of reference in this book.

Notes. This cemetery's boundary is marked on three sides with an unpainted, badly deteriorating, wood post and rail fence. It appears, however, that this was, at one time, a substantial fence—each post is set onto an iron rod that is driven into a rock. Much of the groundcover is moss and needs little attention, but evidence of leaf removal indicates that this cemetery receives some care.

Names and dates on gravestones and other markers. [23 April 1999]

HAYNES
- Benjamin F. - d. 23 July 1883 Æ 61 y., 4 m.

HEATH
- George F. - d. 10 October 1862, Beaufort, South Carolina, Æ 38 y., 3 m.; (member of Co. G, 8th Maine Regiment [Civil War])
- Lewis F. - d. 10 June 1864, Cole Harbor, "V. A.", Æ 32 y., 3 m., 25 d.; (member of Co. G, 8th Maine Regiment [Civil War])

KELLIHER
- Elizabeth C. (wife of Joseph [no stone]) - d. 1 May 1848 Æ 33 y., 1 m., 24 d.

L.
- C[...][1] (wife of John [no stone]) - d. 26 May 1847 Æ 66 y., 2 m., 22 d.
- S. H. (dau. of [...][1]) - d. [7?][1] August 1830 Æ [...][1]

LEAR
- Joan S. (wife of Samuel R.) - d. 12 June 1883 Æ 69 y., 5 m., 21 d.
- Samuel R. (husb. of Joan S.) - d. 11 March 1861 Æ 54 y., 11 m., 24 d.

RICHARDSON
- George W. (son of William S. [no stone] and Lydia M.) - d. 28 February 1882 Æ 3 y.
- Hugh - d. 27 August 1879 Æ 62 y.
- Hugh (husb. of Mary) - d. 19 January 1875 Æ 83 y., 10 m.
- Lydia M. (wife of William S. [no stone]) - d. 6 April 1879 Æ 49 y., 4 m., 17 d.
- Margaret Ann P. (dau. of Hugh and Mary) - d. 24 December 1848 Æ 18 y., 3 m.
- Mary (wife of Hugh) - d. 4 July 1874 Æ 82 y., 2 m.
- Samuel H. - d. 16 September 1870 Æ 45 y.
- Wilber (son of Elisha and Abagail [sic] [no stones]) - d. 20 September 1848 Æ 20 y., 10 m.
- Windfield [sic] S. (son of George W. and Julia A. [no stones]) - d. 16 May 1865 Æ 6 y.

THOM

Anson B. - d. 22 July 1884 Æ 25 y., 2 m., 18 d.

Benjamin - d. 26 March 1881 Æ 61 y., 11 m., 17 d.

[...]

[...][2]

[...][3]

Notes:

[1]Stone worn and/or broken.

[2]This is a white, wooden cross that bears no inscription. Immediately in front of the cross is a recently replaced piece of sod of a size suggesting a cremation.

[3]This is a large stone with its top missing and the rest very worn.

Brookside Cemetery
(Mount Desert - 6)

Location/directions. Somesville. From the traffic light at the north end of Mount Desert Island, go straight ahead (south) onto Routes 102/198. In approximately 4.8–4.9 miles (0.5–0.6 miles of which are south of the traffic light at the intersection of Routes 102/198 and 102), turn right onto Brookside Road. This road leads to the cemetery.

History. The cemetery is on land that was part of a 100 acre parcel owned by Abraham Somes in 1808 according to the Salem Towne Jr. map.

Notes. This cemetery is well maintained, and there is water available. The roads were repaved in 1999.

Names and dates on gravestones and other markers. [31 May 1999]

ALLEN
- Andrew W. - d. 6 February 1875 Æ 4 y., 8 m.
- Bertha E. - b. 1897; d. 1997
- Emma A. (wife of Melville L.) - b. 20 August 1859; d. 19 July 1929
- Inez R. - d. 3 February 1875 Æ 20 y., 4 m.
- [J. Lorena[8] - see GRINDLE]
- James B. - b. 6 January 1889; d. 20 January 1971
- Melville L. (husb. of Emma A.) - b. 27 January 1862; d. 19 November 1939
- Obadiah (husb. of Sophia A.) - b. 12 April 1829; d. 9 June 1915
- Richard B. - b. 1941
- Richard O. - b. 1895; d. 1977
- Sophia A. (wife of Obadiah) - b. 8 July 1831; d. 25 April 1898
- Walter M. - b. 4 September 1890; d. 4 March 1917

ATHERTON
- Benjamin T. (Capt.; husb. of Emily E.) - d. 4 May 1894 Æ 63 y., 9 m., 3 d.; (member of Co. C, 1st Maine Heavy Artillery [Civil War])
- Emily E. (wife of Capt. Benjamin T.) - d. 22 October 1913 Æ 77 y., 10 m., 23 d.
- infant (son of [Capt. Benjamin T. and Emily E.]) - [b. and?] d. 8 May 1861
- Sumner S. [son of Capt. Benjamin T. and Emily E.] - d. 3 October 1872 Æ 5 y., 10 m.
- Vannie T. [son of Capt. Benjamin T. and Emily E.] - d. 12 September 1872 Æ 14 y., 2 m.

BABCOCK
- Dorothy S. (LETHIECQ; wife of Edward B.) - b. 1900; d. 1990
- Edward B. (husb. of Dorothy S. (LETHIECQ)) - b. 1899; d. 1927
- Sylvi [sic] A. - b. 1931; d. 1983

BABSON
- Angenoria (wife of John S.) - b. 24 February 1842; d. 3 September 1865
- Eben (Capt.; husb. of Judith (SOMES)) - b. 29 March 1792; m. 11 September 1815; d. 11 December 1841
- Eben E[lliott?]. (husb. of Phebe S.) - b. 12 March 1823; d. 28 July 1896
- Frank I. (son of John S. and Angenoria) - b. 30 January 1860; d. 26 July 1870
- Freeman - [no dates]
- John (Capt.; husb. of Susanna) - d. 21 March 1825 Æ 80 y.
- John S. (husb. of Angenoria) - b. 12 June 1833; d. 17 September 1868
- Judith (SOMES; wife of Capt. Eben) - b. 16 September 1796; m. 11 September 1815; d. 4 November 1880

Judith Lorenia (dau. of Eben E[lliott?]. and Phebe S.) - b. 9 May 1857; d. 12 November 1922
Phebe S. (wife of Eben E[lliott?].) - b. 7 December 1836; d. 24 April 1915
Susanna (wife of Capt. John) - d. September 1828 Æ 71 y.

BARNES
Carmen Schuster - b. 1924; d. 1980
Cecil [husb. of Margaret Ayer] - b. 17 April 1880; d. 25 June 1949
Hope - b. 1958; d. 1991; bur. "at sea", Stuart Island, Washington
James Paul Robert - b. 25 September 1990; d. 19 December 1991
Margaret Ayer [wife of Cecil] - b. 8 April 1886; d. 25 October 1967

BARTLETT
Grace M. [wife of Orville C.] - b. 1882; d. 1973
Orville C. [husb. of Grace M.] - b. 1878; d. 1961

BEACH
Pat Lorraine (CROSSLEY) - b. 1923; d. 1988

BEAL
David Alston (Esq.) - b. 1959; d. 1992

BECKER
Robert L. - b. 1915; d. 1991

BEEMAN
Charles R. - b. 1881; d. 1960
Elizabeth A. - b. 1917; d. 1979
Olive P. - b. 1889; d. 1971

BENSON
John Melvell [sic] - b. 13 March 1881; d. 8 January 1949
Mary M. - b. 12 June 1884; d. 4 July 1966

BICKFORD
Charles S. [husb. of Sarah F.] - b. 1846; d. 1916
Ellen K. - b. 1848; d. 1934
Frank C. - b. 1852; d. 1927
Jennie E. [dau. of Charles S. and Sarah F.] - b. 1884; d. 1891
Sarah F. [wife of Charles S.] - b. 1845; d. 1924

BLANCHARD
Abby R. - b. 1908; d. 1946
[Agnes B[LANCHARD?]. - see HANNA]
Bertha M. (wife of Everett W.) - b. 5 October 1882; d. 24 June 1977
Everett W. (husb. of Bertha M.) - b. 19 March 1881; d. 1 December 1940
"father" - b. 1858; d. 1928
Frances S. - b. 1926
Fred H. (husb. of Nettie E. (HOOPER)) - b. 1893; d. 1977
Holsey - b. 1882; d. 1946
Logan A. - b. 1898; d. 1973
"mother" - b. 1863; d. 1931
Nettie E. (HOOPER; wife of Fred H.) - b. 1897; d. 1991
Walter H. - b. 24 February 1928; d. 26 February 1995

BRANSCOM
Mildred E. [wife of Roger G.] - b. 1908
Roger G. [husb. of Mildred E.] - b. 1901; d. 1968

BROOKINGS
Frederic J. - b. 1884; d. 1933
Lillian E. - b. 1899; d. 1974

BROWN
Alton C. (Capt.; husb. of Emma M.) - b. 1879; d. 1960
Carrol E. - [b. and d.?] 1945
Charles F. (husb. of Fannie M.) - b. 1857; d. 1933
Daniel K. (husb. of Sarah N.) - b. 25 June 1837; d. 5 July 1911; (member of Co. G, 8th Maine Regiment [Civil War])
Emma M. (wife of Capt. Alton C.) - b. 1881; d. 1925
Emmons P. - b. 1919; d. 1997
Fannie M. (wife of Charles F.) - b. 1857; d. 1957
Forrest L. - b. 26 October 1907; d. 15 March 1991
George A. (son of Daniel K. and Sarah N.) - d. 8 August 1869 Æ 2 y., 10 m.
Hattie L. - b. 1873; d. 1962
Julian R. - b. 1913; d. 1982
Sarah N. (wife of Daniel K.) - b. 7 May 1839; d. 13 May 1918
W. S. (Capt.) - b. 1852; d. 1930
Walter H. - b. 4 February 1876; d. 11 August 1902

BRUSH
Howard Grafton [husb. of Sybil Reppert] - b. 6 July 1903; d. 19 August 1971
Sybil Reppert [wife of Howard Grafton] - b. 27 June 1903; d. 18 January 1978

BUCHANAN
David [husb. of Ruth] - [no dates]
Ruth [wife of David] - [no dates]

BUNKER
Arthur L. [husb. of Goldie M.] - b. 1892; d. 1965
Charles E. [son of Frances A.?] - b. 1867; d. 1937
Elton L. [son of Frances A.?] - b. 1871; d. 1954
Frances A. - b. 1845; d. 1934
Goldie M. [wife of Arthur L.] - b. 1897; d. 1993

BURNETT
[Barbara - see HENRY]

BUTLER
Bessie R. [wife of Levi W.] - b. 1881; d. 1957
Levi W. [husb. of Bessie R.] - b. 1869; d. 1947

CARPENTER
Elsie H. (wife of Ralph E.) - b. 26 February 1891; d. 25 January 1975
Ralph E. (husb. of Elsie H.) - b. 28 March 1884; d. 5 April 1939

CARTER
Dora [wife of Joseph P.] - b. 25 April 1861; d. 13 March 1927
John W. - b. 1892; d. 1973
Joseph P. [husb. of Dora] - b. 19 March 1857; d. 7 May 1918

CHARPENTIER
Arthur Aldrich - b. 1919; d. 1989

CHILLES
Ada M. [wife of George] - b. 1893; d. 1968
George [husb. of Ada M.] - b. 1887; d. 1968

CHURCHILL
Beatrice H. (HOOD; [wife of Howard Bosworth]) - b. 1905
Howard Bosworth [husb. of Beatrice (HOOD)] - b. 1901; d. 1981

CHUTE
[Mary - see HOLMES]

CIRARD
Adelard "Peter" - b. 1 September 1882; d. 25 January 1937

CLIFFORD
Virginia A. - [b. and d.?] 1960
COBB
Marian Van Vorst (COLWELL; dau. of Lino M. COLWELL and Blanche (SOMES)) - [no dates]
COLWELL
[Adelaide Somes - see HOLLAND]
Adelaide Somes (dau. of Lino M. and Blanche (SOMES)) - [no dates]
Blanche (SOMES; wife of Lino M.) - b. 1 July 1878; d. 5 November 1946
Lino M. (husb. of Blanche (SOMES)) - b. 28 January 1878; d. 20 December 1942
[Marian Van Vorst - see COBB]
CONNELL
Malcolm B. - b. 1939; d. 1978
COOMBS
John D. [husb. of Marion E.?] - b. 1891; d. 1976
Marion E. [wife of John D.?] - b. 1900; d. 1988
COUSENS
Adelaide R. [wife of Merrill E.] - b. 1909; d. 1998
Emeline R. [wife of Nathan L.] - b. 1874; d. 1961
Merrill E. [husb. of Adelaide R.] - b. 1900; d. 1974
Nathan L. [husb. of Emeline R.] - b. 1863; d. 1943
CROSBY
Vida M. - b. 1887; d. 1986
CROSSLEY
[Pat Lorraine - see BEACH]
CULVERWELL
Estella W. [wife of Tom S.?] - b. 1901; d. 1982
Tom S. [husb. of Estella W.?] - b. 1901; d. 1977
DELANEY
Margaret E. - b. 1905; d. 1996
DELUCA
Margaret A. [wife of Michael J.] - b. 1912; d. 1992
Michael J. [husb. of Margaret A.] - b. 1905; d. 1975
DEMING
Harvey F. (Dr.) - [...][1]
DICKEY
Bernice R. - b. 1924; d. 1928
Dollie - b. 1890; d. 1963
Forrest O. - b. 1886; d. 1957
George C. [husb. of Juanita B.] - b. 22 March 1919; d. 8 February 1980
Horace B. - b. 1911; d. 1928
Juanita B. [wife of George C.] - b. 17 January 1921
DILLWORTH
Eleanor Emily - b. 1934; d. 1983
DODGE
[Charlotte P. - see SOMES]
DONOHOE [sic]
Irene M. - b. October 1933; d. October 1997
DOWNEY
Ann K. - b. 1939
Franklin Robert - b. 1918; d. 1979

DREYFUS
Rosa (WYLER) - b. 7 January 1894; d. 29 August 1966
DUFF
Dennis Kevin - b. 15 March 1939; d. 12 February 1990
DUNTON
George E. [husb. of Rebecca B.] - b. 1883; d. 1969
Rebecca B. [wife of George E.] - b. 1890; d. 1986
EATON
Lucy (wife of Thomas [no stone]) - d. 6 May 1854 Æ 26 y.
EHRLICH
Gerd W. - b. 22 June 1922, Berlin, Germany; d. 7 July 1998, Towson, Maryland
EIBL
Georgia May - b. 1946; d. 1992
ELLIOTT
Hope Downing - d. 18 February 1987
EMERSON
Alma F. [wife of Sidney F.] - b. 1911; d. 1981
David B. - b. 1948; d. 1973
Sidney F. [husb. of Alma F.] - b. 1902; d. 1970
ERICKSON
Frank G. Jr. (husb. of Nancy (HUGGARD)) - b. 1929; d. 1987
Nancy (HUGGARD; wife of Frank G. Jr.) - b. 1929
Scott H. (son of Frank G. Jr. and Nancy (HUGGARD)) - b. 1954; d. 1978
ERLEWEIN
Tom - [no dates]
Virginia - [no dates]
FARLEY
Eleanor M. [wife of Everett P.] - b. 1909
Everett P. [husb. of Eleanor M.] - b. 1903; d. 1971
FENNELLY
Ann R. (wife of William) - b. 1839; d. 1912
[Flora S. - see MORRISON]
William (husb. of Ann R.) - b. 1840; d. 1912
Winsor [sic] S. "Winnie" (son of William and Ann R.) - b. 1872; d. 31 January 1875 Æ 2 y., 5 m.
FERNALD
A. C. Jr. [husb. of Helen M.] - b. 1896; d. 1988
Abraham C. (husb. of Nancy L.) - d. 14 May 1896 Æ 78 y., 6 m., 27 d.
Abraham C. Jr. [husb. of Julia S.] - b. 1860; d. 1952
Betty W. [wife of John S. Jr.?] - [no dates]
Bob - [no dates]
Burton A. [husb. of Cora B.?] - b. 1887; d. 1953
Carrie S. (wife of R. H.) - [no dates]
Cora B. [wife of Burton A.?] - b. 1890; d. 1987
Helen M. [wife of A. C. Jr.] - b. 1902; d. 1987
Herschel H. - b. 11 January 1898; d. 9 October 1898
Hollis Edmond (son of R. H. and Carrie S.) - d. 9 September 1889 Æ 5 m.
[John - see GRANT]
John S. Jr. [husb. of Betty W.?] - [no dates]
Julia S. [wife of Abraham C. Jr.] - b. 1866; d. 1947
Marjorie Somes (dau. of R. H. and Carrie S.) - d. 15 September 1894 Æ 2 y., 10 m., 12 d.

Mary A. (wife of Walter L.) - b. 1857; d. 1902
Nancy L. (wife of Abraham C.) - d. 26 October 1898 Æ 70 y., 13 d.
Norma - [no dates]
[Polly - see GRANT]
R. H. (husb. of Carrie S.) - [no dates]
Robert E. - [no dates]
Walter L. (husb. of Mary A.) - b. 1857; d. 1903
[...] [headstone only]

FOLEY
[Adelma F[OLEY?]. - see JOY]
Agnes (SOMES; wife of M. F. [no stone]) - b. 18 June 1872; d. 27 September 1900

FRANK
[Marjorie - see FULLER]

FREEMAN
[Adeline - see SOMES]
Allen E. [husb. of Doris M.] - b. 1908
Doris M. [wife of Allen E.] - b. 1910; d. 1989

FRENCH
Virginia D. [wife of William J.] - b. 1882; d. 1964
William J. [husb. of Virginia D.] - b. 1878; d. 1958

FRICK
Grace - b. 1903; d. 1979

FROST
Harriet (SILSBY) - b. 1881; d. 1953

FULLER
George Ripley II (son of Walter Atherton and Marjorie (FRANK)) - b. 1928; d. 1956
Marjorie (FRANK; wife of Walter Atherton) - b. 1892; d. 1983
Walter Atherton (husb. of Marjorie (FRANK)) - b. 1891; d. 1980

GAUDET
Joseph Resther [husb. of Marie T. Cecile] - b. 4 November 1915; d. 27 December 1994
Marie T. Cecile [wife of Joseph Resther] - b. 2 November 1918

GILLEY
[Nellie - see MACEACHERN]

GILMORE
Elizabeth Jeanne - b. 1954; d. 1998

GILPATRIC [sic]
Chadbourne - b. 1914; d. 1989
Charlotte L. - b. 1880; d. 1972
Donald S. - b. 1909; d. 1989
Margaret (KURTZ) - b. 6 August 1912; d. 10 December 1986
Roswell Leavitt - b. 1906; d. 1996
Walter H. - b. 1876; d. 1955

GILPATRICK
[Mary - see HOLMES]

GOTT
Jane R. [wife of Nathaniel] - d. [...][1] Æ 72 y., 23 d.
Nathaniel [husb. of Jane R.] - d. 29 October 1867 Æ 75 y., 11 m., 22 d.

GRANT
Agnes S. [wife of Arthur M.?] - [no dates]
Arthur M. [husb. of Agnes S.?] - [no dates]
Doris M. - b. 1899; d. 1987

George R. [husb. of Lucille C.?] - [no dates]
James (husb. of Mary W.) - b. 1860; d. 1948
James L. - b. 1895; d. 1981
John [GRANT?[7]] - [no dates]
Lucille C. [wife of George R.?] - [no dates]
Madeliene [sic] L. - b. 1906; d. 1986
Madolyn [sic] C. [wife of Walter D.] - b. 1902
Mary W. (wife of James) - b. 1869; d. 1946
Polly [GRANT?[7]] - [no dates]
Wallace M. - b. 1901; d. 1981
Walter D. [husb. of Madolyn [sic] C.] - b. 1901; d. 1984
William G. - b. 1892; d. 1967

GRAY
[Ella A. - see MASON]
Etta (wife of C. D. [no stone][5]) - b. 1876; d. 1905

GREENOUGH
[Ruth - see KELLOGG]

GRINDLE
Flora A. (wife of Dr. Robert L.) - b. 1847; d. 1933
Grace A. [wife of Dr. J. Lowell] - b. 1887; d. 1973
Harold S. [husb. of Jennie E.] - b. 1903; d. 1977
Henry A. - [b. and d.?] 1925
J. Lorena[8] - b. 1911
J. Lowell (Dr.; [husb. of Grace A.]) - b. 1877; d. 1956
Jennie E. [wife of Harold S.] - b. 1903
Marion D. (wife of Robert L.) - b. 1905; d. 1973
Robert L. (Dr.; husb. of Flora A.) - b. 1842; d. 1930
Robert L. (husb. of Marion D.) - b. 1905; d. 1966

HAMOR
Ernest L. (husb. of Nellie (PRAY)) - b. 23 January 1857; d. 5 April 1891
[Eva - see JACOBSEN]
Jonathan [husb. of Mary A.] - b. 21 May 1830; d. 2 January 1901
Mary A. [wife of Jonathan] - b. 27 October 1836; d. 1 September 1910
Nellie (PRAY; wife of Ernest L.) - b. 29 July 1860; d. 9 April 1882

HANNA
Agnes B[LANCHARD?]. - b. 14 December 1887; d. 7 June 1979
Alvin Alonzo Jr. - b. 1895; d. 1918
Thurlow H. [HANNA?] - b. 10 October 1882; d. 29 May 1959

HARGRAVES
Gordon Sweat [sic] [husb. of Nancy (SELLERS)?] - b. 1898; d. 1983
Nancy (SELLERS; [wife of Gordon Sweat [sic]?]) - b. 1898; d. 1972

HARPER
Norton S. (son of Hosea and Hannah [no stones]) - d. 11 August 1857 Æ 18 y., 4 m.

HARRIMAN
Louise E. [wife of Stearns M.] - b. 1889; d. 1964
Stearns M. [husb. of Louise E.] - b. 1892; d. 1944

HART
George O. [husb. of Katherine F.] - b. 1893; d. 1978
Katherine F. [wife of George O.] - b. 1899; d. 1997

HARTFORD
Alma A. [dau. of Lester R. and Anna M.] - b. 1940; d. 1940
Anna M. [wife of Lester R.] - b. 1920; d. 1996

Lester R. [husb. of Anna M.] - b. 1917
HASTINGS
Alfred S. (husb. of Edythe B. "Tissy") - b. 27 June 1907; d. 9 October 1993
Edythe B. "Tissy" (wife of Alfred S.) - b. 23 August 1915; d. 14 February 1997
HAYNES
Ethel V. (wife of Harry W.) - b. 1885; d. 1956
Harry W. (husb. of Ethel V.) - b. 1880; d. 1933
Joseph A. (son of Joseph and Emma G. [no stones]) - d. 4 October 1849 Æ 2 y., 4 m.
Vernon - b. 1903; d. 1909
HEATH
Herschel (Capt.; husb. of Judith S[OMES?].) - b. 14 September 1831; "sailed from La Have, N. S." 8 December 1876
Judith S[OMES?]. (wife of Capt. Herschel) - b. 23 October 1835; d. 30 September 1925
HENRY
Barbara (BURNETT; [wife of John Otto]) - b. 27 October 1924
John Otto [husb. of Barbara (BURNETT)] - b. 14 December 1925; d. 1 October 1991
Lauren [HENRY?] - [no dates]
HIBBARD
Nellie Mae - b. 16 March 1912; d. 15 April 1997
HIGGINS
A. Victor (son of Luray V. and Edith J.; husb. of Ruby L.) - b. 1907; d. 1993
Abbie E. - b. 12 April 1907; d. 7 February 1984
Addie M. [wife of Elmer M.] - b. 1 February 1905; d. 2 December 1990
Edith J. (wife of Luray V.) - b. 1882; d. 1945
Elmer M. [husb. of Addie M.] - b. 19 September 1904; d. 29 August 1975
Hannah (wife of Jesse [no stone]) - d. 11 April 1836 Æ 57 y.
Isaac C. (husb. of Mary Esther) - b. 1850; d. 1904
Isaac S. - b. 1883; d. 1942
Karl L. (son of Luray V. and Edith J.) - b. 1909; d. 1938
Luray V. (husb. of Edith J.) - b. 1882; d. 1950
Mary Esther (wife of Isaac C.) - b. 1857; d. 1897
Orin C. - b. 8 February 1897; d. 8 March 1965
Ruby L. (wife of A. Victor) - b. 1907; d. 1995
HODGDON
Fred Harold [husb. of Nancy Brown] - b. 24 September 1890; d. 21 July 1953
Nancy Brown [wife of Fred Harold] - b. 1890; d. 1985
HOLLAND
Adelaide Somes (COLWELL; [wife of Franklin Ernest]) - b. 8 June 1907; d. 8 March 1963
Franklin Ernest [husb. of Adelaide Somes (COLWELL)] - b. 23 August 1890; d. 7 September 1969
HOLMES
Charles N. - b. 17 March 1841; d. 21 July 1864
Emily A. - b. 13 May 1838; d. 31 May 1859
Eolia Bray - b. 1875; d. 1959
infant (son [of Leonard and Mary A.?]) - b. 2 August 1839; d. 16 August 1839
L. Elrie - b. 14 February 1857; d. 14 May 1937
L. Lawrie [husb. of Mary (GILPATRICK)] - b. 1886; d. 1968
Leonard (husb. of Mary A.) - b. 22 June 1814; d. 6 December 1894
Mary (CHUTE; [wife of Richard]) - b. 1917; d. 1992

Mary (GILPATRICK; [wife of L. Lawrie]) - b. 1886; d. 1978
Mary A. (wife of Leonard) - b. 22 November 1814; d. 11 October 1898
Mary E. - b. 22 October 1863; d. 28 November 1935
Myra S. (wife of Richard C.) - b. 22 April 1853; d. 9 August 1930
Richard [husb. of Mary (CHUTE)] - b. 1916
Richard C. (husb. of Myra S.) - b. 2 June 1849; d. 18 April 1899
William S. - b. 1884; d. 1964

HOOD
[Beatrice H. - see CHURCHILL]
James Walter - b. 1895; d. 1936

HOOPER
[Nettie E. - see BLANCHARD]

HOPEL
Clayton J. - b. 1922; d. 1987

HOUSE
Anita Farley [wife of Randolph D.] - b. 10 February 1929; m. 20 June 1954; d. 9 May 1994
Randolph D. [husb. of Anita Farley] - b. 6 June 1927; m. 20 June 1954

HUGGARD
[Nancy - see ERICKSON]

HUTCHINSON
Ermina (dau. of Isaac and Mary E.) - d. 6 February 1867 Æ 15 y.
Isaac (husb. of Mary E.) - d. 17 February 1892 Æ 78 y.
Lincoln - d. 9 March 1892 Æ 34 y.
Martha E. (dau. of Isaac and Mary E.) - d. 28 November 1866 Æ 18 y.
Mary E. (wife of Isaac) - d. 11 January 1901 Æ 83 y.
Mary E. (dau. of Isaac and Mary E.) - d. 28 November 1866 Æ 21 y.

HYSOM
Edith E. - b. 1869; d. 1936
Hollis R. - b. 1869; d. 1941

INGRAM
Elizabeth A. [wife of William P.] - b. 24 November 1944; d. 27 May 1978
William P. [husb. of Elizabeth A.] - b. 11 April 1943

INMAN
Henry Arthur [husb. of Roberta Crew] - b. 1869; d. 1951
Roberta Crew [wife of Henry Arthur] - b. 1874; d. 1933

INNES
Carrie E. (wife of George D.) - b. 1876; d. 1931
Edith B. [dau. of George D. and Carrie E.?] - b. 1903; d. 1967
George D. (husb. of Carrie E.) - b. 1871; d. 1944

JACOBSEN
Albert Oliver (husb. of Eva (HAMOR)) - b. 1872; d. 1947
Eva (HAMOR; wife of Albert Oliver) - b. 1877; d. 1945

JONES
Eleanor B. [wife of Thomas P. Jr.] - b. 1900; d. 1986
Thomas P. Jr. [husb. of Eleanor B.] - b. 1909; d. 1984

JORDAN
Frances C. [wife of Valdemar M.] - b. 1911; d. 1986
Valdemar M. [husb. of Frances C.] - b. 1910; d. 1995

JOY
Adelma F[OLEY?]. - b. 22 November 1837; d. 8 November 1930

KARBAN
Kathleen [wife of O. Franz] - b. 22 September 1900; d. 10 October 1982
O. Franz [husb. of Kathleen] - b. 18 September 1909
KARST
Della P. - b. 1887; d. 1959
Doris E. - b. 1907
Francis S. - b. 1913; d. 1987
KELLEY
Edward Dow - b. 27 March 1931; d. 14 August 1995
Georgia H. - b. 1907; d. 1997
Grafton L. - b. 9 August 1907; d. 24 July 1955
Heslyn L. - b. 18 August 1905; d. 13 February 1977
Ronda Gail - b. [and d.?] 19 November 1974
Shirley L. - [no dates]
KELLOGG
Ruth (GREENOUGH; wife of Capt. Branton [no stone]) - b. 26 March 1879; d. 19 February 1937
KENISTON
Emma H. - b. 1846; d. 1931
infant [KENISTON?] - [no dates]
Julia (dau. of Emma H.) - b. 1886; d. 1909
KITTREDGE
Calvin - b. 1801; d. 1855
Elizabeth - b. 1854; d. 1917
Ernest - b. 1856; d. 1943
James K. - b. 1859; d. 1863
Jane Y. - b. 1818; d. 1896
Kendal [sic] (Dr.) - b. 1773; d. 1857
Sarah W. - b. 1776; d. 1871
William - b. 1815; d. 1901
KNOX
Annie (wife of George) - b. 1858; d. 1938
Archie (son of George and Annie) - b. 1893; d. 1908
George (husb. of Annie) - b. 1862; d. 1929
Mildred S. (dau. of George and Annie) - b. 1886; d. 1914
KURTZ
Geraldine Fitzgerald [wife of Robert Fulton] - b. 16 July 1922; d. 16 February 1969
[Margaret - see GILPATRIC [sic]]
Robert Fulton [husb. of Geraldine Fitzgerald] - b. 11 March 1922
KURZENKNABE
Dorothy D. - b. 1898; d. 1974
LAFMAN
William - b. 1 March 1862; d. 28 January 1895
LANMAN
Charles R. - b. 1850; d. 1941
Edith H. - b. 1892; d. 1992
Jonathan T. - b. 1894; d. 1927
Mary H. - b. 1858; d. 1936
LAWSON
Robert C. - b. 1919; d. 1987
LEAVITT
Horace H. [husb. of Louise W.] - b. 1882; d. 1966

Louise W. [wife of Horace H.] - b. 1882; d. 1973

LELAND

Ada S. (wife of Roy J.) - b. 1893; d. 1980

Arthur L. [husb. of Mabel M. "Lena"?] - b. 17 February 1903; d. 14 February 1961

Benjamin F. (husb. of Mary A.) - b. 19 January 1828; d. 11 October 1904

Charles S. [LELAND?] (husb. of Ida M.) - b. 2 August 1864; d. 2 July 1916

Franklin W. - b. 26 September 1857; d. 24 October 1923

Ida M. (wife of Charles S. [LELAND?]) - b. 9 December 1873; d. 24 May 1939

Lena M. (dau. of Benjamin F. and Mary A.) - d. 1 June 1894 Æ 40 y., 8 m., 14 d.

Lyman L. (son of Benjamin F. and Mary A.) - d. 20 June 1860 Æ 8 y., 6 m.

Mabel M. "Lena" [wife of Arthur L.?] - b. 27 December 1906; d. 2 October 1997

Mary A. (wife of Benjamin F.) - b. 1829; d. 1922

Mildred Dazell - b. 1904; d. 1978

Nelson C. (son of Roy J. and Ada S.) - b. 1914

Roy J. (husb. of Ada S.) - b. 1890; d. 1929

LENZ

Douglas Colcock - b. 27 January 1953; d. 6 April 1996

LETHIECQ

Arline M. - b. 1897; d. 1921

Avis Somes - b. 1898; d. 1981

[Dorothy S. - see BABCOCK]

J. Albert (Dr.; [husb. of Madelle S[OMES?].]) - b. 1865; d. 1956

Madelle S[OMES?]. [wife of Dr. J. Albert] - b. 1873; d. 1942

LEVERTON

Charles H. (Rev. Dr.; husb. of Frances E.) - b. 1841; d. 1908

Frances E. (wife of Rev. Dr. Charles H.) - b. 1847; d. 1932

LISCOMB

Clara B.[3] (RICH; wife of Frank E.) - b. 27 May 1894; d. 21 February 1975

Frank E. (husb. of Clara B.[3] (RICH)) - b. 5 May 1892; d. 6 August 1983

LORD

Julia A. - d. 16 April 1914 Æ 68 y.

LORING

[Ethel - see SOMES]

LUCAS

Nita D. - b. 25 January 1881; d. 6 May 1973

LUNT

Arnold W. [husb. of Emily W.] - b. 1904; d. 1954

Emily W. [wife of Arnold W.] - b. 1904; d. 1982

MACEACHERN

Daniel Joseph (husb. of Nellie (GILLEY)) - b. 1866; d. 1935

[Margaret - see NEAD]

Nellie (GILLEY; wife of Daniel Joseph) - b. 1875; d. 1959

MACKANE

Keith A. - b. 30 December 1895; d. 12 June 1952

MALLORY

Carol F. [wife of G. Kenneth] - b. 1902; d. 1990

G. Kenneth [husb. of Carol F.] - b. 1900; d. 1986

MANHEIM

Miriam - b. 4 April 1919; d. 2 December 1996

MANNING

Frances van Antwerp - b. 15 February 1896; d. 26 December 1975

MASON
Alice E. [dau. of Timothy M. and Ella A. (GRAY)?] - b. 1879; d. 1964
Ella A. (GRAY; wife of Timothy M.) - b. 1857; d. 1936
Ella E. (wife of Harlan P.) - b. 1852; d. [no date]
Emeline (dau. of Timothy and Mary) - d. 15 May 1841 Æ 13 y.
Emily E. (RICHARDSON; wife of Timothy M.) - b. 1842; d. 1874
Freddie W. (son of Timothy M. and [Emily E. (RICHARDSON)?]) - b. 1866; d. 1873
Harlan P. (husb. of Ella E.) - b. 1845; d. 1901
Isaac [N. or T.][2] (husb. of Mary Ann) - d. 16 February 1873 Æ 39 y.; (member of Co. D, 31st Maine Regiment [Civil War])
Jeremiah (son of Timothy and Mary) - d. 3 March 1827 Æ 1 y.
Mary (wife of Timothy) - d. 15 October 1828 Æ 35 y.
Mary Ann (wife of Isaac [N. or T.][2]) - d. 27 December 1868 Æ 27 y.
Mary S. (wife of Timothy) - d. 16 June 1890 Æ 84 y., 4 m., 16 d.
Mehitabel - b. 1860; d. 1916
Mercy J. (wife of William T.) - d. 27 October 1903 Æ 78 y., 1 m., 17 d.
Timothy (husb. of Mary and Mary S.) - d. 4 October 1872 Æ 78 y.
Timothy M. (husb. of Emily E. (RICHARDSON) and Ella A. (GRAY)) - b. 22 April 1844; d. 3 August 1905
William T. (husb. of Mercy J.) - d. 17 August 1863, Bangor, Æ 42 y.; (member of 26th Maine Regiment [Civil War])

MAXCY
Caro F. (wife of Herbert B. [no stone]) - b. 1895; d. 1946

MCCONNELL
Henrietta S. [wife of Leon K.] - b. 1901; d. 1956
Leon K. [husb. of Henrietta S.] - b. 1898; d. [no date]

MCFARLAND
Gladys M. [wife of Pearl M.] - b. 1899; d. 1977
Pearl M. [husb. of Gladys M.] - b. 1891; d. 1968

MERCHANT
Eugene S. - b. 21 December 1905; d. 12 April 1996
Richard E. - b. 1926; d. 1982

MERRITT
Carrie K. (wife of Frank R.) - b. 1874; d. 1960
Frank R. (husb. of Carrie K.) - b. 1864; d. 1938

MILAND
Katherine A. - b. 1877; d. 1956

MILLER
Andrew - b. 1961; d. 1997

MITCHELL
Katie (MONIGHETTI) - b. 25 February 1978; d. 30 January 1992

MONIGHETTI
[Katie - see MITCHELL]

MORRIS
Mary E. (wife of William) - b. 7 September 1876; d. 23 February 1949
William (husb. of Mary E.) - b. 14 November 1872; d. 7 October 1918

MORRISON
Flora S. (FENNELLY) - b. 1870; d. 1908
M. Estelle [wife of Mark C.] - b. 1874; d. 1967
Mark C. [husb. of M. Estelle] - b. 1864; d. 1948

MOSHER
Ethel F. - [no dates]
Harold E. - [no dates]
MURPHY
Abbie L. - b. 1891; d. 1965
Claude L. - b. 1879; d. 1947
Claude Stanley - b. 2 February 1914; d. 28 December 1973
Eugene V. [husb. of Leona B.] - b. 1908; d. 1983
Leona B. [wife of Eugene V.] - b. 1914; d. 1998
NEAD
Margaret (MACEACHERN; wife of William M.) - b. 1898; d. 1973
William M. (husb. of Margaret (MACEACHERN)) - b. 1897; d. 1971
NEW
Eric T. - b. 4 December 1903; d. 3 February 1967
NEWTON
Florence - b. 1901; d. 1985
NORWOOD
Douglas Milton - b. 24 July 1926
Howard (husb. of Johannah) - b. 1855; d. 1914
Johannah (wife of Howard) - b. 1858; d. [not given]
Meda D. [wife of Milton W.] - b. 1892; d. 1981
Milton W. [husb. of Meda D.] - b. 1899; d. 1990
Phyllis Irene - b. 14 March 1922
NOYES
Arthur (son of John M. and Emily [no stones]) - d. 24 March 1853 Æ 3 y., 3 m., 16 d.
Charles (SMITH; adopted son of John M. and Emily [no stones])[4] - d. 4 April 1847 Æ 15 y., 5 m.
Olevia [sic] Antoinette (dau. of John M. and Emily [no stones]) - d. 2[5 or 6][2] November 1843 Æ 4 y., 10 m., 2[5 or 6][2] d.
OBER
Isaiah T. [husb. of Mary A.?] - b. 1867; d. 1928
Mary A. [wife of Isaiah T.?] - b. 1879; d. 1944
O'BRIEN
Martina B. - b. 8 June 1895; d. 26 July 1985
PALMER
Arthur Edward - b. 15 August 1908; d. 19 February 1993
Charlotte Nebel - b. 1885; d. 1966
PARKER
Alonzo W. - b. 1867; d. 1952
D. Clark - b. 16 November 1847; d. 24 December 1907
Edwin C. (husb. of Nean [sic] L. and Olivia J.) - b. 1839; d. 1907
Fred Henry - b. 1884; d. 1951
George S. - b. 23 September 1849; d. [no date]
James M. - b. 4 April 1841; d. 18 June 1864; ("killed before Petersburg"[6] [Civil War])
John H. (husb. of Sarah) - b. 8 February 1806; d. 3 October 1873
Lizzie A. - b. 9 July 1852; d. 25 May 1859
Nean [sic] L. (wife of Edwin C.) - d. 13 October 1871 Æ 29 y., 3 m.
Olivia J. (wife of Edwin C.) - b. 1841; d. 1933
Robert H. - b. 20 September 1930; d. 12 February 1951
Sarah (wife of John H.) - b. 25 April 1809; d. 2 April 1887

PARTRIDGE
Charles S. (Rev.; husb. of Phyllis S.) - b. 1923; d. 1993
Jean D. (dau. of Rev. Charles S. and Phyllis S.) - b. 1952; d. 1968
Phyllis S. (wife of Rev. Charles S.) - b. 1927
PATTERSON
Barbara Nesmith [wife of Robert Whiteley] - b. 16 January 1912; d. 17 October 1991
George [husb. of Mae K.] - b. 1884; d. 1969
Mae K. [wife of George] - b. 1891; d. 1948
Robert Whiteley [husb. of Barbara Nesmith] - b. 30 January 1905; d. 21 February 1988
PEPPER
Georgia N. - b. 1 May 1923; d. 15 July 1966
Oliver H. P. Jr. - b. 21 April 1920; d. 1 April 1962
PERKINS
Marguerite N. [wife of William F.] - b. 1891; d. 1956
William F. [husb. of Marguerite N.] - b. 1877; d. 1950
PIERCE
Dicky [sic] - b. 1935; d. 1949
Leon W. - b. 1905; d. 1998
Letha - b. 1904; d. 1993
PRAY
Charles B. [husb. of Edith H.] - b. 27 November 1835; d. 11 August 1903
Daniel E. [husb. of Melissa H.] - b. 1827; d. 1905
Edith H. [wife of Charles B.] - b. 11 September 1836; d. 15 June 1917
John F. (Capt.) - "lost at sea" 23 October 1891 Æ 29 y., 10 m.
John L. [husb. of Palma W.] - b. 1890; d. 1968
Katherine L. - b. 1862; d. 1941
Lester E. - b. 1859; d. 1927
Lucie [sic] E. - b. 1885; d. 1901
Melissa H. [wife of Daniel E.] - b. 1835; d. 1902
[Nellie - see HAMOR]
Palma W. [wife of John L.] - b. 1894; d. 1981
PRYOR
Edith (TWEEDY; wife of James Williamson [no stone]) - b. 4 March 1865; d. 16 January 1935
QUIN [sic]
Barbara Story - b. 1888; d. 1945
RAND
Dorothy P. - b. 1889; d. 1973
READ
[Tryphena - see SMITH]
REDDISH
Agatha P. [wife of Clarence N.] - b. 1898; d. 1984
Clarence N. [husb. of Agatha P.] - b. 1900; d. 1971
REDFIELD
George E. - b. 1936; d. 1992
REED
Andrew H. [husb. of Lillian E.] - b. 1857; d. 1935
Clara B. - b. 1874; d. 1954
Daniel O. (son of William and Susan S. [no stones]) - d. 25 October 1835 Æ 9 y., 1 m.
Lillian E. [wife of Andrew H.] - b. 1865; d. 1942

Samuel (son of William and Susan S. [no stones]) - d. 3 March 1833 Æ 12 y., 7 m.
Vernon Douglas - b. 1932; d. 1974
[...] [headstone only]

REYNOLDS
Alfred S. Jr. [husb. of Madeline P.] - b. 1888; d. 1955
Madeline P. [wife of Alfred S. Jr.] - b. 1902; d. 1955

RICH
[Clara B. - see LISCOMB]
Clarence W. - b. 1873; d. 1940

RICHARD
Florence B. [wife of Howard B.] - b. 1906; d. 1989
Howard B. [husb. of Florence B.] - b. 1909; d. 1990
Howard B. - b. 26 June 1939; d. 8 November 1994

RICHARDS
[Anna M. - see TWEEDY]

RICHARDSON
Achsah (dau. of Hugh and Mary [no stones]) - d. 4 September 1828 Æ 2 y., 6 m.
Adoniram J. (son of Leander [no stone] and Mary A.) - d. 14 April 1843 Æ 4 m., 15 d.
Carolyn P. [wife of Loren K.] - b. 1856; d. 1954
Clifford B. - b. 1847; d. 1930
Earl E. - b. 1896; d. 1972
Elvin A. - b. 1907; d. 1920
[Emily E. - see MASON]
Ezra G. - b. 1875; d. 1956
H. Sumner (husb. of Ida (SOMES)) - b. 6 November 1883; d. 22 December 1947
Ida (SOMES; wife of H. Sumner) - b. 25 March 1885; d. 17 March 1940
Loren K. [husb. of Carolyn P.] - b. 1853; d. 1927
Lucy A. (wife of Olin D. [no stone]) - b. 1855; d. 1930
Mabel E. (wife of William S.) - b. 1870; d. 1944
Margaret A. (wife of Edward S. [no stone]) - d. 14 February 1866 Æ 43 y.
Mark T. (husb. of Mary J.) - b. 10 March 1843; d. 4 June 1892
Martha A. [wife of Thomas M.] - b. 1869; d. 1937
Mary A. (wife of Leander [no stone]) - d. 7 August 1862 Æ 42 y., 5 m., 7 d.
Mary J. (wife of Mark T.) - b. 16 April 1849; d. 18 July 1893
Myra E. - b. 1882; d. 1958
Nellie M. - b. 1847; d. 1909
Sara [sic] A. - b. 1908; d. 1957
Thomas M. [husb. of Martha A.] - b. 1867; d. 1924
William S. (husb. of Mabel E.) - b. 1865; d. 1947

ROBINSON
George A. - b. 1922; d. 1987

RUSSELL
Richard Lawson “Dick” - b. 1940; d. 1994

SALISBURY
Abby F. (dau. of Nathan and Bethany E.) - d. 28 February 1873 Æ 23 y.
Bethany E. (wife of Nathan) - d. 18 July 1886 Æ 71 y., 8 m., 13 d.
Henrietta K. - b. 1840; d. 1903
John T. - d. 22 December 1911 Æ 68 y.
Nathan (husb. of Bethany E.) - d. 4 July 1870 Æ 63 y., 16 d.
Roscoe G. - b. 1837; d. 1903

SANDERSON
Arthur G. [husb. of Harriet (SOMES)?] - b. 1868; d. 1913
Arthur G. Jr. [husb. of Virginia S[OMES].?] - b. 1905; d. 1937
Harriet (SOMES; [wife of Arthur G.?]) - b. 1870; d. 1964
Virginia S[OMES]. [wife of Arthur G. Jr.?] - b. 1903; d. 1990
SCHWERIN
Ursula C. - b. 1924; d. 1996
SCOTT
Nancy M. - b. 1920; d. 1990
SELLERS
[Nancy - see HARGRAVES]
SHAW
Patricia Ann (TALTY) - b. 1 March 1946; d. 1 July 1999
SILSBY
Ann Eliza [wife of Dr. Edward Byron] - d. 8 November 1931 Æ 76 y., 1 m., 2 d.
Edward Byron (Dr.; [husb. of Ann Eliza]) - d. 14 October 1923 Æ 70 y., 5 m., 6 d.
[Harriet - see FROST]
SIMMONS
Alida (WESTON) - b. 1922; d. 1997
Grace M. - b. 1878; d. 1953
Joseph [husb. of Rosalind T.?] - b. 1914; d. 1986
Rosalind T. [wife of Joseph?] - b. 23 September 1915; d. 3 January 1976
SMALLIDGE
Beth [wife of Steve] - [no dates]
Steve [husb. of Beth] - [no dates]
[...] [headstone only]
SMITH
Addie B. [wife of Fred P.] - b. 1 April 1889; d. 19 November 1990
Barry Congar [sic] [husb. of Tryphena (READ)?] - b. 1878; d. 1952
Bloomfield R. (husb. of Jennie A.) - b. 1862; d. 1938
[Charles - see NOYES]
Cynthia H. (wife of William P.) - d. 7 March 1900 Æ 62 y., 4 m., 6 d.
Emily A. (wife of Pearl F.) - b. 21 July 1861; d. 27 August 1923
Fred P. [husb. of Addie B.] - b. 10 July 1886; d. 24 June 1960
Hayden Hobart - b. 1871; d. 1918
Hollis M. - b. 1886; d. 1936
Hollis M. [husb. of Julia B.] - b. 1914; d. 1968
Jennie A. (wife of Bloomfield R.) - b. 1864; d. 1942
Julia B. [wife of Hollis M.] - b. 1913
Pearl F. (husb. of Emily A.) - b. 30 October 1856; d. 16 August 1923
Sarah [SMITH?] - [no dates]
Stuart Jay - b. 26 June 1916; d. 16 December 1993
Tryphena (READ; [wife of Barry Congar [sic]?]) - b. 1890; d. 1976
William P. (husb. of Cynthia H.) - d. 8 November 1905 Æ 80 y., 1 m., 13 d.
SOMES
Abraham (husb. of Hannah and Joanna) - d. 7 September 1819 Æ 87 y.
Abraham (Capt.; husb. of Rachel B.) - d. 12 July 1845 Æ [8?]2[1] y.
Abraham (husb. of Adeline (FREEMAN)) - d. 25 August 1868 Æ 66 y., 8 m., 10 d.
Ada M. (wife of John A.) - b. 4 October 1872; d. 9 November 1949
Adeline (FREEMAN; wife of Abraham) - b. 3 November 1815; d. 5 November 1892
Adelle F. (wife of Charles P.) - d. 22 May 1890 Æ 34 y., 9 m., 22 d.
[Agnes - see FOLEY]

Almira E. (wife of George B.) - d. 1 January 1879 Æ 59 y., 4 m.
Alta M. [wife of Edward P.] - b. 1848; d. 1933
Benjamin - b. 8 January 1804; d. 25 July 1850
[Blanche - see COLWELL]
Caro M. [wife of Fred H.] - b. 1869; d. 1940
Caroline T. H. (wife of Lyman H.) - b. 6 November 1838; d. 30 April 1920
Charles E. (son of George B. and Almira E.) - d. 8 May 1885 Æ 30 y.
Charles P. (husb. of Adelle F.) - d. 7 February 1922 Æ 70 y., 3 m., 18 d.
[Charlotte J. - see THOMPSON]
Charlotte P. (DODGE; wife of Capt. Isaac) - b. 3 September 1800; d. 6 September 1872
Chauncey D. [husb. of Ethel (LORING)?] - b. 1904; d. 1984
Clara E. (wife of Thaddeus S.) - b. 29 August 1842; d. 19 July 1920
Clarissa (wife of Daniel) - d. 27 August 1841 Æ 65 y.
Clarissa B. (dau. of Daniel and Clarissa) - d. 1 September 1824 Æ 14 y., 2 m.
Daniel (husb. of Clarissa) - d. 24 June 1831 Æ 61 y.
Daniel (husb. of Sally S. (TRASK)) - d. 2 November 1882 Æ 79 y.
Dencie (wife of Isaac) - b. 18 July 1858; d. 30 May 1927
Edith D. - b. 1870; d. 1925
Edward B. (son of Daniel and Clarissa) - d. 14 April 1812 Æ 5 y., 9 m., 7 d.
Edward B. (son of Daniel and Clarissa) - d. 7 October 1833 Æ 14 y., 6 m.
Edward P. [husb. of Alta M.] - b. 1841; d. 1906
Elnora [WILLIAMS?] - b. 1932; d. 1979
Emma F. (dau. of Abraham and Adeline (FREEMAN)) - d. 12 April 1865 Æ 22 y., 10 m., 15 d.
Emma J. (wife of Henry J.) - d. 4 October 1938 Æ 97 y., 3 m.
Emma K. (wife of Lewis Jr.) - d. 4 February 1892 Æ 52 y.
Ethel (LORING; [wife of Chauncey D.?]) - b. 1903; d. 1985
Ethel B. [wife of William T.] - b. 1885; d. 1970
Eva [SOMES?] - b. 1882; d. 1977
Fred H. [husb. of Caro M.] - b. 1872; d. 1948
George A. (son of Capt. Isaac and Charlotte P. (DODGE)) - d. 5 September 1836 Æ 11 m.
George A. - b. 1853; d. 1928
George B. (husb. of Mary Jane and Almira E.) - d. 6 September 1886 Æ 76 y., 2 m.
George Lyman - b. 1857; d. 1931
Goldie G. - [no dates]
Hannah (wife of Abraham) - d. 16 March 1790 Æ [not given]
[Harriet - see SANDERSON]
Harry [SOMES?] - b. 1870; d. 1950
Harvy [sic] D. (son of Daniel and Sally S. (TRASK)) - d. 29 August 1842 Æ 5 y., 6 m., 15 d.
Henry J. (husb. of Emma J.) - d. 8 March 1887 Æ 42 y., 11 m., 10 d.
[Ida - see RICHARDSON]
infant [SOMES?] - [no dates]
Isaac (husb. of Dencie) - b. 11 July 1846; d. 15 July 1922
Isaac (husb. of Sally) - d. 3 February 1846, Fairfield, Æ 65 y.
Isaac (Capt.; husb. of Charlotte P. (DODGE)) - b. 14 February 1803; d. 7 October 1875
Jacob (husb. of Rebecca T.) - d. 2 September 1876 Æ 77 y., 4 m., 2 d.
Joanna (wife of Abraham) - d. 17 December 1831 Æ [not given]
John (husb. of Judith) - d. 9 February 1849 Æ 81 y., 2 m., 26 d.

John (husb. of Julia L.) - b. 24 September 1794; d. 10 November 1886
John A. (husb. of Ada M.) - b. 21 September 1872; d. 8 September 1930
John Grant [SOMES?] - [no dates]
John J. (husb. of Leonice H.) - b. 28 October 1841; d. 14 August 1930
John R. - [no dates]
John W. (husb. of Lucie [sic] F.) - b. 16 May 1838; d. 17 May 1913
John W. [husb. of Norma L.?] - b. 1918; d. 1981
Judith (wife of John) - d. 25 March 1850 Æ 82 y., 3 m., 25 d.
[Judith - see BABSON]
[Judith S. [SOMES?] - see HEATH]
Julia - [no dates]
Julia L. (wife of John) - b. 16 October 1812; d. 28 March 1866
Julianna (dau. of John and Judith) - d. 20 May 1812 Æ 19 m., 5 d.
Leonice H. (wife of John J.) - b. 13 September 1850; d. 24 April 1912
Lewis (husb. of Mary A.) - d. 10 October 1872 Æ 72 y.
Lewis Jr. (husb. of Emma K.) - d. 19 May 1913 Æ 81 y.
Lillian P. - b. 1871; d. 1963
Lot A. (son of Abraham and Adeline (FREEMAN)) - d. 23 November 1852 Æ 8 y., 3 m., 11 d.
Lucie [sic] F. (wife of John W.) - b. 13 March 1840; d. 2 July 1889
Lyman H. (husb. of Caroline T. H.) - b. 15 October 1833; d. 11 March 1917
[Madelle S[OMES?]. - see LETHIECQ]
Mark W. - b. 11 April 1895; d. 7 March 1919
Mary A. (wife of Lewis) - d. 21 December 1883 Æ 72 y.
Mary B. - d. 22 April 1914 Æ 56 y.
Mary Jane (wife of George B.) - d. 18 June 1845 Æ 23 y.
Morris H. - [no dates]
Nettie D. - [no dates]
Norma L. [wife of John W.?] - b. 1921; d. 1993
Rachel B. (wife of Capt. Abraham) - d. 21 March 1839 Æ 62 y.
Rebecca [SOMES?] - b. 1908; d. 1931
Rebecca T. (wife of Jacob) - b. 4 July 1817; d. 25 November 1904
Richmond L. - d. 17 November 1917 Æ 75 y.
Sally (wife of Isaac) - d. 27 May 1863 Æ 83 y.
Sally S. (TRASK; wife of Daniel) - b. 29 December 1817; d. 29 May 1904
Sarah J. - b. 19 July 1848; d. 25 March 1915
Thaddeus S. (husb. of Clara E.) - b. 2 April 1839; d. 13 January 1913
[Virginia S[OMES] - see SANDERSON]
William P. (son of Abraham and Adeline (FREEMAN)) - d. 13 October 1852 Æ 6 y., 3 m.
William T. [husb. of Ethel B.] - b. 1879; d. 1945
William T. (son of Daniel and Sally S. (TRASK)) - d. 15 September 1872 Æ 18 y.

SPEAR

Nancy Lee - b. 22 September 1949; d. 4 October 1997

SPRAGUE

James M. - b. 19 August 1934; d. 26 October 1958

SPRENGNETHER

J. L. (Dr.) - b. 31 December 1915; d. 18 July 1985

STANLEY

Ernest G. (husb. of Lucretia D. and Georgia S.) - b. 1890; d. 1979
Georgia S. (wife of Ernest G.) - b. 1890; d. 1971
J. Gilman (husb. of May F.) - b. 1864; d. 1941

Lucretia D. (wife of Ernest G.) - b. 1891; d. 1935
May F. (wife of J. Gilman) - b. 1868; d. 1946
STEVENS
Margaret P. - b. 1887; d. 1976
SWARTZ
Deborah Disston - b. 21 April 1915; d. 21 June 1996
TALTY
[Patricia Ann - see SHAW]
TATE
James William [husb. of Julia Lorena] - b. 1887; d. 1973
Julia Lorena [wife of James William] - b. 1888; d. 1974
THATCHER
Robins [sic] H. (Rev.) - b. 1904; d. 1964
THOM
Anna S. (dau. of William W. [Sr.?] and Eliza [no stone]) - d. 7 April 1812 Æ 10 m., 28 d.
Catharine M. (dau. of William W. [Sr.?] and Eliza [no stone]) - d. 8 August 1833 Æ 24 y., 1 m., 5 d.
William W. Jr. (son of William W. [Sr.?] and Eliza [no stone]) - d. 19 December 1824 Æ 10 d.
William W. Sr. [husb. of Eliza?] - [no dates]
THOMAS
Clara Jane Diana - b. 1923; d. 1961
THOMPSON
Almenia K. (wife of Capt. William) - d. 24 September 1891 Æ 86 y., 9 m., 21 d.
Charlotte J. (SOMES; only dau. of Capt. Isaac SOMES and Charlotte P. (DODGE); wife of Capt. D. S. [no stone]) - d. 16 October 1856 Æ 29 y., 1 m., 14 d.
Cornelius (husb. of Judith and Margaret) - b. 1760; d. 1835
George W. - d. 30 July 1864 Æ 27 y.; ("fell at the battle of Petersburg"; 1st Lieutenant of Co. C, 31st Maine Regiment [Civil War])
Isaac S. (son of Capt. D. S. [no stone] and Charlotte J. (SOMES)) - d. 17 November 1856 Æ 3 m.
Judith (wife of Cornelius) - d. 1792 Æ [not given]
K. K. - d. 2 November 1903 Æ 75 y., 4 m., 10 d.; bur. Ellsworth, Maine
Margaret (wife of Cornelius) - d. 1817 Æ [not given]
Sarah Frances - b. 1832; d. 1912
William (Capt.; husb. of Almenia K.) - d. 29 February 1868 Æ 75 y., 10 m., 17 d.
TRACY
Betty N. [wife of George T. Sr.] - b. 1934
George T. Sr. [husb. of Betty N.] - b. 16 August 1929; d. 6 June 1979
TRASK
[Sally S. - see SOMES]
Susan (wife of Henry [no stone]) - d. 31 August 1843 Æ 63 y.
TWEEDY
Anna M. (RICHARDS; wife of Thomas E. [no stone]) - b. 20 February 1841; d. 9 November 1923
[Edith - see PRYOR]
TYSON
Charles Roebling - b. 1914; d. 1999
[Sarah "Sally" - see VALENZUELA]
VALENZUELA
Sarah "Sally" (TYSON) de - b. 1949; d. 1987

VARNUM
Addie M. (wife of John L.) - d. 11 January 1928 Æ 69 y., 11 m.
John L. (husb. of Addie M.) - d. 21 November 1900 Æ 52 y., 8 m.
W.
Eddie - [no dates]
F. B. - [no dates]
WALKER
Mary Clayton - b. 25 January 1855; d. 24 June 1912
WASGATT
Anna S. (wife of Elisha) - d. 31 January 1884 Æ 70 y., 9 m.
Elisha (husb. of Anna S.) - d. 4 April 1885 Æ 72 y.
Thomas M. (son of Elisha and Anna S.) - d. 19 May 1863 Æ 19 y., 3 m.; (member of Co. H, 4th Maine Regiment [Civil War])
WEBBER
Carro R. - b. 1906; d. 1998
WESTON
[Alida - see SIMMONS]
Harold - b. 1910; d. 1977
Henry C. - b. 13 January 1914; d. 16 May 1969
Mary - b. 12 May 1908; d. 3 October 1975
WHITING
Andrew J. (husb. of Hittie) - b. 8 May 1830; d. 2 February 1896
Hittie (wife of Andrew J.) - b. 4 December 1831; d. 18 May 1894
WHITMORE
Kate J. - b. 2 November 1844; d. 28 February 1940
WIELAND
Joseph T. [husb. of Ruth C.] - b. 1920; d. 1994
Ruth C. [wife of Joseph T.] - b. 1926
WIGGIN
Ann M. - b. 1887; d. 1949
Corinne R. - b. 1902; d. 1974
Fred E. - b. 1878; d. 1958
WILLIAMS
[Elnora [WILLIAMS?] - see SOMES]
WILSON
C. E. - [no dates]; (member of Co. H, 1st Maine Heavy Artillery [Civil War])
Jerry - b. 1949; d. 1986
WYLER
[Rosa - see DREYFUS]
YOURCENAR
Marguerite - b. 1903; d. 1987
[...]
Madeline S.[9] - b. 1905

Notes:
[1]Stone worn and/or broken.
[2]Different on different stones.
[3]A stone for only Clara B. (RICH) LISCOMB now rests behind the maintenance shed and was likely replaced by the stone for both Clara and her husband Frank E. LISCOMB. The new stone uses R. (for RICH) as Clara's middle initial, but the stone that has been removed uses B.

[4]Two stones contain information about Charles SMITH. One, that also records information about two biological children of John M. NOYES and Emily, stands in the cemetery proper. A second one, belonging solely to Charles SMITH, lays on some granite blocks along the border of the cemetery.

[5]Although there is no stone for C. D. GRAY (husb. of Etta), there is a "G. A. R" [Civil War] marker in the space next to Etta's grave. However, if this marker is for Etta's husband, he would have been much older than his wife.

[6] Much of the time spent by Union troops in the vicinity of Petersburg was outside the city, generally referred to as "in front of Petersburg" or "before Petersburg".

[7]It is unclear from the gravestones whether the surname is FERNALD or GRANT.

[8]It is unclear from the gravestones whether the surname is ALLEN or GRINDLE.

[9]A nearby headstone reads "SOMES/SANDERSON/WILLIAMS".

Gravestone of Marguerite Yourcenar (Brookside Cemetery, Mount Desert - 6).

Richardson Burying Ground
(Mount Desert - 7)

Location/directions. Along south side of Northwood Lane (private), just west of intersection of Northwood Lane and Beech Hill Road. From the traffic light at the north end of Mount Desert Island, go straight ahead (south) onto Routes 102/198. In approximately 5.2 miles (and at the south end of the village of Somesville), turn right onto Pretty Marsh Road (Route 102). In about 0.2–0.3 miles turn left onto Beech Hill Road. (Note: this turn is easy to pass as it is just over a hill and in a curve.). In approximately 1.7–1.8 miles, turn right onto Northwood Lane. The cemetery is on the left in about 0.1–0.2 miles.

History. —

Notes. Thornton (1938) noted that the "graves are now in the shadow of great evergreen trees but the ground is cleared and the place easy of access" (p. 238). There are four pieces of one or more broken stones leaning against a tree. A portion of two words is visible on one of the pieces. This Richardson Burying Ground[1] is not enclosed, and there are no discernable boundary markers.

Names and dates on gravestones and other markers. [22 May 1999]

ATHERTON
Benjamin (husb. of Nancy (WASGOTT [sic])) - d. 12 November 1848 Æ 88 y.
Lorenzo (son of William W. and Mary [no stones]) - d. 23 April 1836 Æ 2 w.
Nancy (WASGOTT [sic]; wife of Benjamin) - [no dates]

B.
[...] [footstone only]

BILLS
Cora E. (RICHARDSON; wife of Sterling A. [no stone]) - b. 1870; d. 1893

DANBY
Emily A. (wife of William [no stone]) - d. 20 October 1910 Æ 66 y.

FARWELL[4]
Elvira (wife of Samuel [no stone]) - d. 2 April 1849 Æ 33 y.

HAMBLEN
[Sarah - see RICHARDSON]

K[ETUM?][5]
Isaac J. (son of John C. and Eleanor W. [no stones]) - d. 21 September 1833 Æ 19 y., 7 m.[8]

LADD
Daniel - d. 29 September 1834 Æ 31 y.

LANPHER
Adelmon William - b. 23 October 1894; d. 9 February 1969
Charles Warren [husb. of Juanita (MEANS)] - b. 1915; d. 1990
Elaine Alice - [b. and d.?] 1944
Elinor Ann - b. 4 August 1941; d. 13 January 1943
infant (dau. of Marcellus M. and Sophia W.) - [b. and d.?] 28 February 1912
John C. (son of Marcellus M. and Sophia W.) - [b. and d.?] 1914
Juanita (MEANS; [wife of Charles Warren]) - b. 1919
Marcellus M. (husb. of Sophia W.) - b. 1872; d. 1955
Sophia W. (wife of Marcellus M.) - b. 1873; d. 1947

MASON
Emily E. D. (wife of Capt. Timothy [D. or M.][2] [no stone]) - d. 13 February 1874 Æ 31 y., 10 m., 18 d.

Freddie W. (son of Capt. Timothy [D. or M.][2] [no stone] and Emily E. D.) - d. 26 July 1873 Æ 6 y., 11 m., 23 d.; ("drowned")
infant (son of Capt. Timothy [D. or M.][2] [no stone] and Emily E. D.) - d. [no date] Æ 4 m., 3 d.[3]

MEANS
[Juanita - see LANPHER]

R.
M. [footstone only]

RICHARDSON
Anne (WHITEMAN;. wife of Charles) - b. 24 July 1910; d. 15 June 1996 Æ 85 y.
Benjamin - d. 16 February 1866 Æ 76 y., 25 d.
Charles (husb. of Anne (WHITEMAN)) - b. 8 September 1909; d. 14 December 1987
Charlotte S. (dau. of John and Rhoda W.) - d. 14 March 1871 Æ 32 y., 8 m., 12 d.
[Cora E. - see BILLS]
Eleanor W. (wife of Nathaniel G.) - d. 30 October 1872 Æ 77 y., 1 m., 23 d.
Ella (dau. of William J. and Emily A.[7] [no stone]) - d. 7 March 1891 Æ 11 y., 6 m.
Eugene (son of J. W. and E. R. [no stones]) - d. 25 April 1889 Æ 5 m.
Ezra G. (son of William S. and Lydia M. [no stones]) - d. 10 August 1874 Æ 7 y., 5 m.
Gamage N. (husb. of Ruth H.) - b. 22 May 1840; d. 16 April 1911
George S. - b. 17 February 1853; d. 20 May 1933
Henry (son of Stephen and Margaret "Peggy"; twin brother of John) - d. 28 May 1821 Æ 9 y.
Howard P. (son of John and Rhoda W.) - "lost at sea" 1 December 1847 Æ 18 y., 4 m.
John (husb. of Rhoda W.) - b. 3 February 1800; d. 20 February 1890
John (son of Stephen and Margaret "Peggy"; twin brother of Henry) - d. 4 July 1828 Æ 16 y.
John G. (husb. of Sarah) - d. 29 January 1828 Æ 67 y.
Josie R. (dau. of John and Rhoda W.) - d. 21 August 1873 Æ 23 y., 4 m., 22 d.
Lillie (dau. of J. W. and E. R. [no stones]) - d. 11 February 1886 Æ 2 y., 8 d.
Lorenzo T. (son of William J. and Emily A.[7] [no stone]) - d. 3 July 1899 Æ 15 y.
Margaret (dau. of John and Rhoda W.) - d. 9 April 1848 Æ 14 y., 6 m.
Margaret "Peggy" (wife of Stephen) - b. 1774; d. 1862
Marion P. (dau. of William J. and Emily A.[7] [no stone]) - d. 6 August 1878 Æ 3 y.
Nathaniel G. (husb. of Eleanor W.) - d. 18 November 1861 Æ 68 y., 9 m.
Rhoda W. (wife of John) - b. 7 February 1807; d. 31 December 1879
Richard (Capt.) - d. 7 February 1869 Æ 72 y., 6 m., 19 d.
Ruth H. (wife of Gamage N.) - b. 2 July 1840; d. 18 September 1889
Sarah (wife of John G.) - d. 17 April 1810 Æ 47 y.
Sarah (HAMBLEN; wife of Stephen) - b. 2 January 1797; d. 15 February 1878
Stephen (husb. of Margaret "Peggy") - b. 1768; d. 1853
Stephen (husb. of Sarah (HAMBLEN)) - b. 30 July 1791; d. 5 September 1877
Tryphosa A. (wife of William S. [no stone]) - d. 7 September 1862 Æ 37 y., 3 m., 2 d.
Thomas J. (son of John and Rhoda W.) - d. 29 March 1866 Æ 22 y.
Viola M. (dau. of Eugene D. and Nellie A. [no stones]) - d. 22 September 1890 Æ 7 m., 13 d.
Virginia Ruffin - [no dates]
William J. (husb. of Emily A.[7] [no stone]) - d. 24 November 1892 Æ 53 y.

ROBINSON
Sarah (wife of H. C. [no stone]) - d. 31 October 1848 Æ 20 y.

Susan E. (dau. of George H. and Deborah [no stones]) - d. 11 June 1849 Æ 3 m., 11 d.

TAYLOR

Eleanor J. (wife of Israel M. [no stone]) - d. 30 March 1853 Æ 20 y., 4 m., 15 d.

WASGOTT [sic]

[Nancy - see ATHERTON]

WHITEMAN

[Anne - see RICHARDSON]

[...]

[...][6]

Notes:

[1]This is the name given by Thornton (1938, p. 236).

[2]Different middle initial on different stones.

[3]Thornton (1938) gave 6 months as age at death.

[4]Thornton (1938) gave TARWELL as Elvira's last name and noted that her burial place was "marked by a slate gravestone" (p. 237). A slate stone found in 2000 unambiguously reads FARWELL.

[5] Difficult to read.

[6]Stone broken.

[7]This is perhaps Emily A. DANBY (*q.v.*)?

[8]Remainder of stone is in concrete, thereby obscuring any further information it may contain.

Wasgatt Cemetery
(Mount Desert - 8)

Location/directions. Along east side of Beech Hill Road. From the traffic light at the north end of Mount Desert Island, go straight ahead (south) onto Routes 102/198. In approximately 5.2 miles (and at the south end of the village of Somesville), turn right onto Pretty Marsh Road (Route 102). In about 0.2–0.3 miles, turn left onto Beech Hill Road. (Note: this turn is easy to pass as it is just over a hill and in a curve.) The cemetery is on the left in approximately 2.0–2.1 miles.

History. Thornton (1938) described this cemetery "on the level plain of Beech Hill" as "a little yard where sleep many of the early pioneers of Mount Desert Island" (p. 235). She called it the "Beech Hill Burying Ground", but now [2000] a wooden sign fastened to a tree bears the inscription "Wasgatt Cemetery/c. 1840".

Notes. In 1999, no stone was found for the "young Swedish man who was drowned in Echo Lake a few years ago and whose antecedents were unknown here" (Thornton (1938), p. 236).

Names and dates on gravestones and other markers. [17 May 1999]

BABBIDGE
- Irving H. [husb. of Mary R.?] - b. 1 February 1882; d. 8 December 1938
- Mary R. [wife of Irving H.?] - b. 30 January 1894; d. 2 February 1946

BAKER
- Benjamin D. - d. 14 September 1882 Æ 82 y., 7 m.

BARTON
- Annie M. (dau. of Brunswick B. and Mary T.) - b. 1909; d. 1917
- Brunswick B. (husb. of Mary T.) - b. 1878; d. 1964
- Jennie E. (dau. of Brunswick B. and Mary T.) - b. 1904; d. 1922
- Mary T. (wife of Brunswick B.) - b. 1872; d. 1951

BLACK
- Hazel C. - b. 1919; d. 1921

BROWN
- Clarence E. (husb. of Mercy T.) - b. 1874; d. 1946
- Lyndon S. - b. 1899; d. 1920
- Mercy T. (wife of Clarence E.) - b. 1875; d. 1969
- Merle C. - b. 1902; d. 1920
- Thomas B. (son of Clarence E. and Mercy T.) - b. 7 April 1907; d. 28 October 1932

CARTER
- C. Catherine [wife of Reuben W.] - b. 1843; d. 1901
- John (husb. of Mary S.) - d. 11 March 1890 Æ 89 y., 11 m., 8 d.
- Mary S. (wife of John) - d. 18 October 1889 Æ 88 y., 7 m., 6 d.
- Reuben W. [husb. of C. Catherine] - b. 1839; d. 1935

CIRARD
- Jennie - b. 30 July 1895; d. 7 July 1944

CLARK
- Deborah (wife of John) - d. 17 November 1851 Æ 55 y.
- John (husb. of Sarah H., Deborah, and Mary E.) - d. 2 May 1857 Æ 75 y.
- Margaret D. W. (dau. of John and Sarah H.) - d. 3 September 1825[1] Æ 2 y., 2 m., 15 d.
- Mary E. (wife of John) - d. 17 November 1853 Æ 61 y.
- Mercy H. (dau. of John and Sarah H.) - d. 12 September 1825[1] Æ 5 y., 5 m.
- Sarah H. (wife of John) - d. 24[2] March 1844 Æ 39 y., 1 m.

FINNEY
Anna M. (wife of John T. [no stone]) - d. 15 January 1880 Æ 38 y.
Lydia D. (wife of Thomas B.) - b. 1815; d. 1893
Thomas B. (husb. of Lydia D.) - d. 19 July 1849 Æ 34 y., 1 m., 21 d.
GILLEY
infant (son of John M. and Mary D.) - d. 26 November 1844 Æ 3 d.
John M. (husb. of Mary D.) - d. 5 May 1864 Æ 45 y.; ("fell at the battle of the wilderness"; member of Co. D, 1st Maine Cavalry [Civil War])
Mary D. (wife of John M.) - d. 27 December 1844 Æ 26 y., 10 m.
GREENLAW
Shirley - b. 1921; d. 1988
Theodora (WAKEFIELD) - b. 1929; d. 1948
HIBBARD
Fred B. - b. 1908; d. 1969
MASON
Freddie W. (son of Ezra G. [no stone] and Louisa L.) - d. 2 March 1884 Æ 9 y., 10 m., 22 d.
Louisa L. (wife of Ezra G. [no stone]) - d. 20 September 1909 Æ 64 y., 4 m., 20 d.
MERCHANT
Gifford L. - [no dates]
Lissie M. - [no dates]
OUELLETTE
Fred - b. 1912; d. 1964
REED
Almira E. (wife of Andrew H. [no stone]) - d. 1 October 1878 Æ 19 y., 10 m., 16 d.
Jared R. - b. 20 June 1907; d. 19 October 1969
RICHARDSON
Arthur S. - b. 25 March 1895; d. 30 April 1957
Edgar N. - b. 3 October 1898; d. 15 December 1968
John G. [husb. of Mary C.] - b. 1826; d. 1902
Mary C. [wife of John G.] - b. 1835; d. 1924
William H. - b. 1 April 1873; d. 11 December 1942
ROBINSON
Henry (husb. of Joanna M.) - b. 1820; d. 1888
Ira F. [husb. of June A.?] - b. 1888; d. 1966
Joanna M. (wife of Henry) - b. 1818; d. 1903
June A. [wife of Ira F.?] - b. 1899; d. 1974
Lydia J. (dau. of Henry and Joanna M.) - d. 1845 Æ 4 y.
Martha A. (dau. of Henry and Joanna M.) - d. 1845 Æ 4[8] m.
TUA[T?][3]
Mark (Rev.) - d. 15 July 1841 Æ 33 y., 6 m.
WAKEFIELD
[Theodora - see GREENLAW]
WASGATT [includes WASGATTE and WASGOTT]
Asa (Rev.; husb. of Sarah) - d. 2[3 or 2?][4] January 187[9?][4] Æ [...5?][4] y., [...][4]
David - d. 18 December 1861 Æ 71 y.
Davis (Esq.; husb. of Rachel) - d. 27 November 1843 Æ 92 y.
Emma J. (wife of Thomas A.) - b. 20 June 1837; d. [no date]
Rachel (wife of Esq. Davis) - d. 30[5] June 1841 Æ 89 y.
Sarah (wife of Rev. Asa) - d. 29 December 1855 Æ 59 y., 4 m., 6 d.
Sarah E. (dau. of Rev. Asa and Sarah) - d. 8 July 1849, Boston, Massachusetts, Æ 28 y., 4 m., 6 d.

Thomas A. (husb. of Emma J.) - b. 10 May 1823; d. 16 May 1880

[...]

[...][6]

[...][7]

Notes:

[1]Thornton (1938) noted that 1825 was a "the year when the dread disease diphtheria swept over Mount Desert taking heavy toll among little children" (p. 236).

[2]Thornton (1938) gave the date of death as 21 March.

[3]Stone broken. Thornton (1938) gave the last name as TUEL (p. 236). The first three letters on the stone, however, are clearly TUA.

[4]Stone worn and cracked.

[5]Thornton (1938) gave the day as 3 June.

[6] Metal grave marker with all letters missing.

[7]A grave with no headstone, but its perimeter outlined by rough stones set into the ground. At this grave is a "G. A. R." marker [Civil War].

[8]The diagonal and horizontal strokes of a 4 are not evident causing this number to appear to be 1. However, the digit is followed by "mo's." implying more than 1. Also, the top of the vertical stroke resembles the top of the 4 in "1845" more than it resembles the top of the 1.

Sound Cemetery
(Mount Desert - 9)

Location/directions. Along east side of Routes 3/198. From the traffic light at the north end of Mount Desert Island, go straight ahead (south) onto Routes 102/198. In approximately 4.2–4.3 miles, at the traffic light at the intersection of Routes 102/198 and 198, turn left on Route 198. The cemetery is on the left in about 1.7–1.8 miles, approximately 0.3–0.4 miles of which are beyond (south of) the intersection with Route 233 (Eagle Lake Road).

History. —

Notes. Along the front of the cemetery is a white picket fence with an arch over the entrance. The grass is mowed and trimmed.

Names and dates on gravestones and other markers. [24 April 1999]

ABEL
- Henry R. [husb. of Nadia E.] - b. 1894; d. 1980
- Nadia E. [wife of Henry R.] - b. 1892; d. 1975

ALLEN
- Marie B. (wife of Arnold [no stone]; mother of Mady [no stone]) - b. 12 October 1916; d. 25 October 1988

BENSON
- [Villa - see TRACY]

BLAKE
- Florence E. [wife of Walter D.] - b. 1861; d. 1951
- Gertrude V. - b. 27 April 1890; d. 9 December 1970
- Walter D. [husb. of Florence E.] - b. 1859; d. 1942

BRACY
- Alice M. - b. 4 May 1883; d. 4 October 1963
- Sidney P. - b. 1870; d. 1948

BORDEAUX
- Benjamin (husb. of Mary C. (RICHARDSON)) - b. May 1824; d. October 1907
- Charles G. [husb. of Flora (REED)] - b. 1861; d. 1947
- Eva (RICE; [wife of Pearl S.?]) - b. 5 June 1892; d. 25 June 1970
- Flora (REED; [wife of Charles G.]) - b. 1862; d. 1943
- Harry E. [husb. of Leita M.] - b. 1882; d. 1960
- Leita M. [wife of Harry E.] - b. 1888; d. 1957
- Mary C. (RICHARDSON; wife of Benjamin) - b. November 1832; d. January 1908
- Pearl S. [husb. of Eva (RICE)?] - b. 18 January 1892; d. 13 August 1983

BROWN
- Arthur E. (husb. of Cora L.) - b. 1867; d. 1947
- Cora L. (wife of Arthur E.) - b. 1870; d. 1899
- John [husb. of Mary] - b. 3 February 1810; d. 2 March 1897
- Mary [wife of John] - b. 20 August 1807; d.[4] 28 November 1879

CARTER
- [Ada - see GRINDLE]

DUNTON
- Rubie Florence (wife of George E. [no stone]) - b. 12 November 1884; d. 15 April 1909

GRAY
- Melissa Jill - b. 14 July 1971; d. 22 August 1971

GRINDLE
Ada (CARTER; [wife of George E.?]) - b. 1907; d. 1943
Anna C. (wife of William S.) - b. 1875; d. 1936
George E. [husb. of Ada (CARTER)?] - b. 1899; d. 1972
Harold W. [husb. of Julia J.] - b. 1900; d. 1969
Julia J. [wife of Harold W.] - b. 1903; d. 1988
Mary L. - b. 1913; d. 1992
William S. (husb. of Anna C.) - b. 1873; d. 1942
HANSON
Harriet M. [wife of Herbert F.] - b. 1882; d. 1943
Herbert F. [husb. of Harriet M.] - b. 1888; d. [no date]
HIGGINS
[Amanda L. - see NEWMAN]
Clarence E. (husb. of Sarah E.) - b. 1871; d. 1943
Edward N. (son of Pembroke and Julia A. [no stones]) - d. 8 March 1905 Æ 25 y., 11 m., 26 d.
Edwin M. (son of Clarence E. and Sarah E.) - d. 17 December 1919 Æ 6 y.
Edwin M. (husb. of Julia) - b. 1841; d. 1922.; (member of 1st Maine Cavalry [Civil War])
Julia (wife of Edwin M.) - b. 1845; d. 1918
Mary I. [wife of Rudolph F.] - b. 1912; d. 1982
Maynard (son of Pembroke and Julia A. [no stones]) - d. 26 March 1893 Æ 19 y., 10 m.
Rudolph F. [husb. of Mary I.] - b. 1904; d. 1969
Sarah E. (wife of Clarence E.) - b. 1879; d. 1926
KETCHUM
Flora E. [wife of James H.] - b. 1897; d. 1986
James A. [KETCHUM?] - b. 1923; d. 1972
James H. [husb. of Flora E.] - b. 1897; d. 1988
MANRING
Clora [sic] T. [wife of Lewis C.] - b. 1885; d. 1969
Lewis C. [husb. of Clora [sic] T.] - b. 1888; d. 1916
McKAY
Helen G. - b. 1905; d. 1994
MORRIS
Edna P. (wife of Luke) - b. 30 April 1804; d. 31 May 1899
Luke (husb. of Edna P.) - b. 2 January 1801; d. 27 November 1880
Nancy J. (dau. of Luke and Edna P.) - d. 28 July 1864 Æ 13 y.
MURPHY
Mary E. (adopted dau. of William B. and Susan [no stone]) - d. 7 August 1870 Æ 18 y., 7 m., 18 d.
William B. (husb. of Susan [no stone]) - d. 26 May 1899 Æ 72 y., 5 m., 29 d.
NEWMAN
Amanda L. (HIGGINS; wife of G. W. [no stone]) - d. 1 September 1906 Æ 64 y., 9 m., 19 d.
NICKERSON
Alvin B. (husb. of Susan A.) - b. 1 January 1842; d. 20 August 1899
Susan A. (wife of Alvin B.) - b. 6 November 1843; d. 27 August 1908
NORWOOD
Julia M. (wife of Israel M. [no stone]) - d. 30 April 1878 Æ 45 y., 5 m., 25 d.
May (dau. of Israel M. [no stone] and Julia M.) - d. 13 January 1871 Æ 13 m. [sic], 8 d.

[Rose - see TRACY]
OUELLETTE
Harriet H. [wife of Joseph C.] - b. 1932; d. 1975
Joseph C. [husb. of Harriet H.] - [no dates]
REED
[Flora - see BORDEAUX]
RICE
[Eva - see BORDEAUX]
RICHARDSON
Bashebee C. (wife of David) - b. 25 October 1797; d. 24 September 1881
Bloomfield T. (husb. of Melissa) - b. 1840; d. 1919; (member of 1st Maine Heavy Artillery [Civil War])
[Charlotte "Lottie" - see TRACY]
Charlotte C. (wife of Capt. James M.) - b. 1839; d. 1916
David (husb. of Bashebee C.) - b. 2 September 1797; d. 5 August 1878
Freddie L. (son of Capt. James M. and Charlotte C.) - d. 11 October 1874 Æ 14 y., 3 m., 6 d.
George M. ("only son" of Capt. Benjamin [no stone] and Hannah H.) - d. 28 August 1864 Æ 18 y., 3 m., 11 d.
Gerald E. (husb. of Margaret L.) - b. 1875; d. 1938
Hannah H. (wife of Capt. Benjamin [no stone]) - d. 22 March 18[...][1] Æ 53 y.
James M. (Capt.; husb. of Charlotte C.) - b. 1837; "lost at sea" 1885
Joann M. (wife of Sibley P.) - d. 9 July 1879 Æ 59 y., 1 m., 7 d.
Margaret L. (wife of Gerald E.) - b. 1862; d. 1952
[Mary C. - see BORDEAUX]
Melissa (wife of Bloomfield T.) - d. 13 December 1904 Æ 57 y., 2 m., 24 d.
Sibley P. (husb. of Joann M.) - d. 2 May 1889 Æ 76 y., 11 m., 19 d.
ROBINSON
Abraham - d. 8 October 1864 Æ 8 y., 7 m., 8 d.
SARGENT
Cora A. [wife of Roderick H.] - b. 1867; d. 1953
Diama [sic] (wife of Giles H.) - b. 1836; d. 1877
Emily C. (wife of George W.) - b. 1858[5]; d. 1917
George W. (husb. of Emily C.) - b. 1837; d. 1903
Giles H. (husb. of Diama [sic]) - b. 1829; d. 1908
John S. [husb. of Lucy A.] - b. 1827; d. 1911
Lucy A. [wife of John S.] - b. 1825; d. 1904
Mary (wife of Stephen [no stone]) - d. 27 April 1847 Æ 29 y., 6 m.
Nina K. (dau. of George W. and Emily C.) - d. 20 September 1865[5] Æ 1 y.[5]
Roderick H. [husb. of Cora A.] - b. 1869; d. 1949
Walter - b. 1867; d. 1937
SMITH
Harry D. (husb. of Olivia H.) - b. 1889; d. [no date]
Olivia H. (wife of Harry D.) - b. 1887; d. 1942
STANLEY
Beula N. [wife of Joseph C.] - b. 1897; d. 1944
Grace B. [wife of Harvey M. "Nipper"] - b. 20 August 1904; d. 10 June 1995
Harvey M. "Nipper" [husb. of Grace B.] - b. 1903; d. 1982
Joseph C. [husb. of Beula N.] - b. 1878; d. 1950
TAYLOR
Kathy I. - b. 19 March 1956; d. 21 March 1956
Kenneth M. - b. 20 November 1908; d. 19 September 1991

TRACY
Caleb T. [husb. of Grace H.] - b. 1893; d. 1931
Caleb T. - b. 1950; d. 1976
Charlotte "Lottie" (RICHARDSON; wife of Jones) - b. 1863; d. 1939
Clarence [TRACY?] - [no dates]
Florington Y. [son of Henry and Lydia F.] - b. 10 July 1863; d. [1 or 16][2] March 1885 Æ 21 y., 8 m., 6 d.
Grace H. [wife of Caleb T.] - b. 1890; d. [no date]
Henry (husb. of Lydia F.) - b. 26 August 1817; d. 31 January 1898
infant (dau. of Henry Jr. [no stone] and Villa (BENSON)) - [no dates]
Jones (husb. of Rose (NORWOOD) and Charlotte "Lottie" (RICHARDSON)) - b. 1856; d. 1939
Julia [dau. of Jones and Rose (NORWOOD)?] - b. 1891; d. 1891
Lydia F. (wife of Henry) - b. 3 October 1823; d. 7 July 1896
Melvin Frost - b. 3 August 1901; d. 29 December 1960
Pauline H. [wife of Ralph J.] - b. 1906; d. 1986
Ralph J. [husb. of Pauline H.] - b. 1903; d. 1979
Rose (NORWOOD; wife of Jones) - b. 1857; d. 1891
Shirley D. [wife of Woodbury H.] - b. 1919; d. [no date]
Villa (BENSON; wife of Henry Jr. [no stone]) - d. 17 July 1883 Æ 30 y., 6 m., 9 d.
William B. "Willie" (son of Henry Jr. [no stone] and Villa (BENSON)) - d. 17 March 1878 Æ 4 m., 13 d.
Woodbury H. [husb. of Shirley D.] - b. 1916; d. 1986

WASGATT
Daniel H. (husb. of Rebecca C.) - d. 20 September 1897 Æ 74 y., 1 m.
Rebecca C. (wife of Daniel H.) - d. 4 January 1917 Æ 89 y., 1 m., 28 d.
Warren C. - b. 1861; d. 1927

[...]
[...][3]

Notes:
[1]Stone broken.
[2]Different on different stones.
[3]A broken bottom of a stone; next to Mary (wife of Stephen SARGENT).
[4]Mary Brown's stone reads "Deid" instead of "Died".
[5]The birth date of Emily C. (wife of George W. SARGENT), the death date and age at death of Nina K., and the relationship of Nina K. to Emily C. are all clearly readable.

Otter Creek Cemetery
(Mount Desert - 10)

Location/directions. Southeast of Route 3 and just north of entrance to Blackwoods Campground (of Acadia National Park), Otter Creek. From the traffic light at the north end of Mount Desert Island, bear left on Route 3. Travel approximately 10.1 miles to a stop sign. Turn left onto Mount Desert Street (Route 3) and continue 0.4–0.5 miles to another stop sign. Turn right at this stop sign, following Route 3. Two driveways leading to the cemetery are on the left in approximately 5.4–5.5 miles.

History. This cemetery is found in the 1881 Colby Atlas.

Notes. A chain-link fence defines a portion of this cemetery's boundary. The grass is mowed and trimmed. Several footstones or pieces of footstones are leaning against the back of a small building.

Names and dates on gravestones and other markers. [1 May 1999]
ABBOTT
Alvah L. [ABBOTT?] - b. 1906; d. 1967
ARSENAULT
Larry - b. 1904; d. 1971
Viola (GILLEY) - b. 1904; d. 1982
BABCOCK
Barbara G. [wife of William F.] - b. 1916; d. 1996
William F. [husb. of Barbara G.] - b. 1918
BAKER
James W. - b. 8 November 1969; d. 13 December 1999
Lily - b. 1904; d. 1959
BLAKE
Margret [sic] H. (GRAY; dau. of Rev. Andrew GRAY and Hannah S.; wife of Wilson [no stone]) - d. 25 January 1883 Æ 39 y., 2 m., 13 d.
BRACY
Adelma (wife of William H.) - d. 9 April 1894 Æ 28 y., 3 m.
Cora E. (wife of William H.) - d. 9 December 1882 Æ 22 y., 4 m.
David (Capt. and Deacon; husb. of Hannah) - d. 29 January 1899 Æ 77 y., 10 m., 15 d.
David [husb. of Lucy J.] - b. 1846; d. 1925
Doris (dau. of Sherley [sic] A. and Marion L.) - [no dates]
Eugene S. [son of Sherley [sic] A. and Marion L.?] - b. 1916; d. 1934
Hannah (wife of Capt. and Deacon David) - d. 23 March 1896 Æ 71 y., 2 m., 13 d.
Hannah P. (dau. of Capt. and Deacon David and Hannah) - d. 12 August 1862 Æ 6 y., 12 d.
Jennie B. (wife of William H.) - d. 15 June 1881 Æ 18 y., 2 m., 24 d.
L. H. - [no dates]; (member of Co. K, 11th Maine Regiment [Civil War])
Lucy J. [wife of David] - b. 1848; d. 1925
Marion L. (wife of Sherley [sic] A.) - b. 1888; d. 1968
Merle L. - b. 1906; d. 1981
Sherley [sic] A. (husb. of Marion L.) - b. 1888; d. 1960
William H. (husb. of Jennie B., Cora E., and Adelma) - b. 1857; d. 1940
BUNKER
A. S. - [no dates]; (member of Co. C, 1st Maine Regiment [Civil War])
Eri L. - b. 1855; d. 1926

G. F. - [no dates]; (member of Co. C, 1st Maine Regiment [Civil War])
Hattie Belle (dau. of Capt. William H. and Mary A.) - d. 27 February 1880 Æ 1 y., 14 d.
infant (dau. of Capt. William H. and Mary A.) - [b. and?] d. 17 June 1882
Lewis A. (son of Capt. William H. and Mary A.) - d. 15 May 1881 Æ 10 m.
Mary A. (wife of Capt. William H.) - b. 20 March 1853; d. 9 November 1922
Myra H. - b. 1893; d. 1940
[M. S. B[UNKER?]. - see R.]
P. S. B[UNKER?]. - b. 1814; d. 1900
S. A. - [no dates]; (member of Co. C, 1st Maine Heavy Artillery [Civil War])
William G. - b. 1808; d. 1882
William H. (Capt.; husb. of Mary A.) - b. 13 March 1836; d. 16 March 1910

BUZZELL
Clara A. [wife of George J.] - b. 1888; d. 1959
George J. [husb. of Clara A.] - b. 1891; d. 1968

BYARD
V. Esther - b. 8 January 1907; d. 17 August 1962

CAREY
Esther M. (SMITH; wife of M. L. [no stone]) - b. 1909; d. 1941
Paul C. (son of M. L. [no stone] and Esther M. (SMITH)) - b. 26 March 1929; d. 11 November 1931

CARTER
Earl R. - b. 8 May 1933; d. 1 November 1956
Mercedes L. - b. 1914
Seth E. - b. 1902; d. 1969

CLARK
Gerald H. - b. 19 August 1920; d. 9 October 1948

CORBETT
Arthur V. Jr. (son of Arthur V. and Dorothy) - d. 30 April 1929 Æ 27 d.
Arthur V. (husb. of Dorothy) - b. 31 August 1897; d. 9 July 1973
Dorothy (wife of Arthur V.) - b. 1908; d. 1963

CRANEY
Carrie A. (wife of Chester A.) - b. 1884; d. 1940
Chester A. (husb. of Carrie A.) - b. 1882; d. 1949

DAVIS
Amelia E. (wife of Thomas S.) - b. 9 October 1849; d. 31 July 1929
Andrew T. [husb. of Clara A.] - b. 1837; d. 1914
Annie - b. 1873; d. 1948
Clara A. [wife of Andrew T.] - b. 1842; d. 1923
Comfort (wife of Samuel) - d. 14 January 1880 Æ 67 y., 5 m.
[Cora G. - see JORDAN]
Elmyra F. (wife of William H. [no stone]) - d. 6 January 1894 Æ 45 y., 11 m.
Ethel J. (wife of Fountain W.) - b. 1881; d. 1932
Flora Louise (dau. of James A. and Cora G.) - b. 1903; d. 1905
Florentine R. [husb. of Joyce E.] - b. 1928; d. 1988
Fountain W. (husb. of Ethel J.) - b. 1881; d. 1955
George E. [husb. of Nettie G.] - b. 1874; d. 1942
Hattie P. (dau. of Fountain W. and Ethel J.) - b. 1912; d. 1912
James A. (husb. of Cora G.) - b. 1875; d. 1920
Joyce E. [wife of Florentine R.] - b. 1929
Lester W. (son of John W. and Lizzie [no stones]) - d. 22 November 1888 Æ 4 m.
Margaret E. [wife of Sherman A.?] - b. 1906; d. 1995

[Martha A. - see THOMAS]
Martin T. [husb. of Mildred E.] - b. 1881; d. 1933
Mildred E. [wife of Martin T.] - b. 1894; d. 1939
Nettie G. [wife of George E.] - b. 1880; d. 1968
Nettie M. (dau. of Thomas S. and Amelia E.) - d. 30 April 1879 Æ 7 m.
Samuel (husb. of Comfort) - d. 18 September 1880 Æ 71 y.
Sherman A. [husb. of Margaret E.?] - b. 1904; d. 1963
Thomas S. (husb. of Amelia E.) - b. 10 January 1844; d. 30 October 1911

DAY
Alfred S. - b. 1854; d. 1863
Cedelia - b. 1863; d. 1884
Eliza J. - b. 1829; d. 1914
Frank - b. 1862; d. 1884
Katie - b. 1856; d. 1856
Lewis A. - b. 1858; d. 1867
Lewis L. - b. 1829; d. 1903

DORR
Virgil L. - b. 1916; d. 1990

DUFFEY [includes DUFFY]
Delilah (wife of William [no stone]) - d. 8 June 1873 Æ 35 y., 7 m.
Eugene - d. "in infancy", 1878
Pamelia H. (wife of William [no stone]) - d. 1 June 1855 Æ 28 y.

EATON
Geneva V. - b. 1899; d. 1958

ELSEMORE
Doris E. [wife of Elliott G.] - b. 1902; d. 1985
Elliott G. [husb. of Doris E.] - b. 1903; d. 1966

EVANS
Augusta E. - b. 1853; d. 1930
William J. - b. 1853; d. 1927

FARNSWORTH
Elizabeth S[MITH?]. - b. 1901; d. 1957

GALLUP
Frank H. (husb. of Nira N.) - b. 29 October 1882; d. 6 November 1966
Nira N. (wife of Frank H.) - b. 21 September 1888; d. 27 January 1972

GILBERT
Nancy Ann (wife of Henry H. [no stone]) - b. 8 December 1922; d. 31 August 1985

GILLIE
Earl B. - b. 1905; d. 1940
Everett A. [husb. of Octavia J.?] - b. 1880; d. 1945
Octavia J. [wife of Everett A.?] - b. 1885; d. 1948
Walter M. - b. 1911; d. 1980

GILLEY
[Viola - see ARSENAULT]

GOTT
[Berilla B. - see SMITH]
Judy B. - b. 7 February 1946; d. 15 January 1998

GRAY
Andrew (Rev.; husb. of Hannah S.) - b. 2 September 1823; d. 24 March 1901
[Elizabeth J. - see GROVER]
Hannah S. (wife of Rev. Andrew) - d. 13 June 1884 Æ 58 y., 11 m.
[Margret H. - see BLAKE]

Sarah M. (wife of Josiah M. [no stone]) - d. 10 April 1883 Æ 79 y., 3 m.
GREELEY
Frank [son of George F. and Jane E. (TURNBULL)?] - [no dates]
George F. [husb. of Jane E. (TURNBULL)?] - d. 12 June 1889 Æ 46 y., 3 m., 11 d.
Jane E. (TURNBULL; [wife of George F.?]) - b. 1852; d. 1895
GRINDLE
Kenneth F. - b. 1 March 1924; d. 2 May 1945
Luella E. (STAPLES; wife of Oscar S.) - b. 1889; d. 1949
Oscar S. (husb. of Luella E. (STAPLES)) - b. 1894; d. 1957
GROVER
Adelbert V. (husb. of Josephine W.) - b. 1888; d. 1979
Alton C. - b. 1880; d. 1928
Elcy [sic] B. (wife of George W. [no stone]) - d. 1 January 18[...][1] Æ 61 y., 10 m.
Elizabeth J. (GRAY; dau. of Rev. Andrew GRAY and Hannah S.; wife of Gideon P.) - d. 21 August 1878 Æ 20 y., 5 m., 5 d.
[Elnora - see TUFTS]
George [husb. of Lizzie] - b. 1850; d. 1936
Gideon P. (husb. of Elizabeth J. (GRAY)) - d. 23 June 1897 Æ 48 y., 11 m., 11 d.
Josephine W. (wife of Adelbert V.) - b. 1888; d. 1972
Lizzie [wife of George] - b. 1857; d. 1940
HADLEY
Granville W. - b. 1874; d. 1920
Lucinda G. (wife of Elisha Y. [no stone]) - b. 1838; d. 1913
Samuel - d. 29 January 1888 Æ 63 y., 4 m., 14 d.
Zacheus - d. 20 January 1900 Æ 72 y.
HAGERTHY
Elmer E. - b. 1882; d. 1933
J. Maynard - b. 1890; d. 1922
HAMBLIN
Elizabeth S. - b. 1864; d. 1920
HARVEY
Fannie E. (wife of George L.) - b. 1892; d. [no date]
George L. (husb. of Fannie E.) - b. 1881; d. 1916
Marie F. - b. 1916; d. 1931
HASKELL
Susanna A. - b. 14 January 1855; d. 14 December 1934
HAYES
Anna G. - b. 1873; d. 1924
HIGGINS
infant - b. 1973; d. 1973
[Jasmine [Helen?] - see MCGARR, MCFARLAND]
Lillian O. (wife of Henry H. [no stone]) - d. 1 September 1879 Æ 19 y., 4 m., 14 d.
HOLMES
Alice M. - b. 1913; d. 1981
George Ronald - b. 26 May 1938; d. 9 August 1959
HOLT
Charles Fenton [husb. of Pearl (MACFARLAND)?] - b. 10 July 1898; d. 10 December 1966
Pearl (MACFARLAND; [wife of Charles Fenton?]) - b. 1886; d. 1973
HOPKINS
Doris A. - b. 1903; d. 1988
Margaret (wife of Eldridge [no stone]) - d. 6 May 1877 Æ 74 y.

Robert Allen "Bobby Allen" - b. 1946; d. 1970
Robert W. - b. 20 May 1928; d. 2 May 1998
IGRAS
Antoni (husb. of Dorothy) - b. 30 December 1918; d. 14 August 1996
Dorothy (wife of Antoni) - b. 2 December 1924
JACKSON
Estelle J. - b. 27 September 1886; d. 29 September 1971
JEFFERS
A. Blair - b. 1915; d. 1953
JELLISON
Betty Anne (MCFARLAND; dau. of Edward F. MCFARLAND Sr. and Jasmine [Helen?] (HIGGINS) MCGARR) - b. 10 January 1940; d. 27 August 1994
JEWETT
Arthur A. [husb. of Madeline F.] - b. 1905; d. 1984
Madeline F. [wife of Arthur A.] - b. 1919; d. 1998
JORDAN
Clarence K. (husb. of Cora G.) - b. 1869; d. 1949
Cora G. (wife of James A. DAVIS and Clarence K.) - b. 1881; d. 1953
LALLY
William - d. 5 February 1913 Æ 74 y., 3 m.
LIMEBURNER
Burke R. [husb. of F. Carmelita] - b. 1908; d. 1983
F. Carmelita [wife of Burke R.] - b. 1913; d. 1992
LISCOMB
Florence L. (wife of H. [no stone]) - d. 23 April 1899 Æ 27 y., 1 m., 8 d.
MACFARLAND [see also MCFARLAND]
[Pearl - see HOLT]
Sherman J. - b. 1865; d. 1951
MAKER
Ada A. (STANLEY; dau. of Edward STANLEY and Margaret E.) - b. 1866; d. 1895
MCFARLAND [see also MACFARLAND]
Arthur I. (son of Edward F. and Jasmine [Helen?] (HIGGINS) MCGARR) - b. 9 July 1937; d. 10 July 1939
[Betty Anne - see JELLISON]
Edward F. Sr. (husb. of Jasmine [Helen?] (HIGGINS) MCGARR) - b. 10 October 1916; d. 28 December 1957
Eugene Jesse - b. 21 April 1944; d. 4 December 1976
Jasmine [Helen?] ((HIGGINS) MCGARR; dau. of Jesse HIGGINS and Mabel (LAW) [no stones]; wife of Edward F. Sr.) - b. 1917; d. 1980
MCGARR
Beatrice W. (wife of Elmer) - b. 1890; d. 1957
Ella C. - b. 1871; d. 1948
Elmer (husb. of Beatrice W.) - b. 1900; d. 1979
Elmer E. [son of Elmer and Beatrice W.] - b. 1921; d. 1922
infant [MCGARR?] - [no dates]
[Jasmine [Helen?] (HIGGINS) - see MCFARLAND]
MCKAY
Barbara - [b. and d.?] 1938
Betsy B. [wife of George W.] - b. 26 July 1932
Eva - b. 1870; d. 1930
Florence (SAUNDERS) - b. 1906; d. 1973
George W. [husb. of Betsy B.] - b. 23 August 1930; d. 19 July 1997

Hugh E. - b. 25 July 1962; d. 10 September 1999
MILES
Annie D. - b. 1873; d. 1949
MORGAN
E. Pearl - b. 6 September 1890; d. 19 August 1983
MOULTON
Florence W. - b. 1897; d. 1960
MUISE
J. Edward [husb. of Minnie L.] - b. 1909; d. 1987
Minnie L. [wife of J. Edward] - b. 1915
NEWMAN
Archie Lee (son of Herbert L. and Esther E.) - b. 1903; d. 1907
Esther E. (wife of Herbert L.) - b. 1868; d. 1936
Herbert L. (husb. of Esther E.) - b. 1862; d. 1952
NORRIS
Jane (wife of William [no stone]) - d. 17 July 1890 Æ 79 y., 11 m.
OULTON
Florence W. - b. 1897; d. 1960
PARSONS
Cecil L. [husb. of Rozella S.] - b. 1930
Rozella S. [wife of Cecil L.] - b. 1927; d. 1962
PETERS
Bernice S. (wife of Donald A.) - b. 1910
David S. (son of Donald A. and Bernice S.) - [b. and d.?] 1932
Donald A. (husb. of Bernice S.) - b. 19[09 or 10][2]; d. 1989
PIERCE
Thomas - d. 24 February 1880 Æ 76 y., 4 m.
R.
M. S. B[UNKER?]. - b. 1833; d. 1916
RICE
[Carrie E. - see YOUNG]
Eva H. - b. 1883; d. 1965
RICHARDSON
Abbie L. (wife of John M.) - b. 20 December 1859; d. [no date]
Beulah M. [wife of John H.] - b. 1921; d. 1966
Charles S. [husb. of Maude G.] - b. 1868; d. 1937
Clarence M. [husb. of Luella] - b. 19 September 1878; d. 7 April 1953
Gerald D. (husb. of Gladys S.) - b. 1907; d. 1993
Gladys S. (wife of Gerald D.) - b. 1908
infant (son of Gerald D. and Gladys S.) - d. 1 December 1928 Æ [not given]
John H. [husb. of Beulah M.] - b. 1917
John M. (husb. of Abbie L.) - b. 26 January 1850; d. 29 March 1915
Luella [wife of Clarence M.] - b. 21 September 1887; d. 7 February 1968
Maude G. [wife of Charles S.] - b. 1879; d. 1967
Phyllis G. [wife of Wallace "Snap"] - b. 1928
Roger S. - b. 13 December 1929; d. 16 January 1967
Wallace "Snap" [husb. of Phyllis G.] - b. 1929
Wallace Sr. - b. 4 September 1908; d. 16 November 1984
SALISBURY
Harold M. (husb. of Teresa S.) - b. 1912; d. 1995
Teresa S. (wife of Harold M.) - b. 1913

SAUNDERS
Arthur G. (husb. of Vesta D.) - b. 1874; d. 1930
[Florence - see McKAY]
George B. - d. 7 July 1882 Æ 38 y., 10 m., 17 d.
Vesta D. (wife of Arthur G.) - b. 1879; d. 1955
SEELEY
Berneice [sic] [wife of Leslie] - b. 1901; d. 1963
Hubert L. [husb. of Ida E.?] - b. 1910; d. 1958
Ida E. [wife of Hubert L.?] - b. 1914; d. 1984
Leslie [husb. of Berneice [sic]] - b. 1907; d. 1975
SMITH
Arlene R. (wife of Donald G.) - b. 1925; d. 1983
Bessie G. [wife of George W.] - b. 1887; d. 1971
Berilla B. (GOTT; wife of John W.) - d. 26 November 1904 Æ 66 y., 9 m., 17 d.
Buford L. (wife of Lawrence M.) - b. 1900; d. 1983
Clifford G. "Kippy" - b. 1948; d. 1970
Donald G. (husb. of Arlene R.) - b. 1918
Elbridge V. (son of John W. and Berilla B. (GOTT)) - d. 11 June 1878 Æ 5 y., 9 m., 11 d.
[Elizabeth S[MITH?]. - see FARNSWORTH]
Ella M. - b. 1879; d. 1942
[Esther M. - see CAREY]
George W. [husb. of Bessie G.] - b. 1879; d. 1951
George W. - b. 1873; d. 1874
George William (son of Julius and Martha [no stones]) - d. 9 November 1874 Æ 1 y., 9 m., 15 d.
James H. - b. 1881; d. 1923
John (husb. of Mary D.) - b. 1843; d. 1913
John E. - b. 1863; d. 1949
John E. - b. 21 June 1925; d. 1 July 1980
John W. (husb. of Berilla B. (GOTT)) - d. 11 December 1877 Æ 42 y., 9 m., 15 d.
Julian G. - b. 29 September 1913; d. 27 July 1943
Lawrence M. (husb. of Buford L.) - b. 22 February 1898; d. 9 July 1975
Mary D. (wife of John) - b. 1844; d. 1930
Maurice E. - b. 1906; d. 1945
Maurice E. Jr. - b. 1924; d. 1980
Timothy R. (son of Donald G. and Arlene R.) - b. 1953; d. 1978
SOMERS
Beecher E. [husb. of Vena E.] - b. 31 March 1909; d. 16 January 1992
Vena E. [wife of Beecher E.] - b. 16 August 1913; d. 5 March 1986
STANLEY
Ada [STANLEY?] - [no dates]
[Ada A. - see MAKER]
Albert H. (husb. of Alice J.) - b. 1861; d. 1937
Alice J. (wife of Albert H.) - b. 1872; d. 1945
Annie P. (wife of Frederick A.) - d. 22 April 1881 Æ 33 y., 6 m., 12 d.
Charity (wife of John) - d. 15 April 1887 Æ 88 y., 6 m., 21 d.
Doris A. (wife of Hoyt A.) - b. 13 May 1914; d. 27 June 1935
Edith M. - b. 21 May 1875; d. 14 February 1914
Edward (husb. of Margaret E.) - b. 1825; d. 1913
Edward - b. 1907; d. 1939

Elizabeth A. (dau. of William and Elizabeth S.) - d. 14 March 1862 Æ 4 y., 2 m., 12 d.
Elizabeth S. (wife of William) - b. 23 March 1822; d. 12 April 1900
Eunice Y. (dau. of William and Elizabeth S.) - d. 17 March 1862 Æ 15 y., 9 m., 9 d.
Frederick A. (husb. of Annie P.) - b. 1841; d. 1915
Harold E. (son of Albert H. and Alice J.) - d. 10 February 1893 Æ 3 y.
Henry L. - b. 1861; d. 1950
Hoyt A. (husb. of Doris A.) - b. 1907; d. 1992
Jared R. (son of William and Elizabeth S.) - d. 1 March 1862 Æ 5 y., 8 m., 7 d.
John Jr. (son of John and Charity) - d. 5 April 1862 Æ 23 y., 9 m., 18 d.
John (husb. of Charity) - d. 7 May 1868 Æ 74 y., 6 m., 9 d.
John E. (husb. of Lillian A.) - b. 6 November 1863; d. 24 April 1948
Lillian A. (wife of John E.) - b. 23 October 1869; d. 26 November 1940
Margaret E. (wife of Edward) - b. 1834; d. 28 March 1887 Æ 52 y., 9 m., 23 d.
Myra A. (dau. of Albert H. and Alice J.) - d. 6 November 1895 Æ 15 d.
Nancy (dau. of John and Charity) - d. 17 October 1841 Æ 9 y., 11 m.
Otis (son of William and Elizabeth S.) - d. 28 February 1862 Æ 18 y., 7 m., 29 d.
Pauline A. (dau. of Albert H. and Alice J.) - d. 8 February 1909 Æ 4 y., 3 m., 2 d.
Thomas E. (son of William and Elizabeth S.) - d. 22 March 1862 Æ 13 y., 6 m.
Walter - b. 1865; d. 1939
William (husb. of Elizabeth S.) - b. 28 February 1820; d. 25 December 1905
William Jr. (son of William and Elizabeth S.) - d. 28 March 1862 Æ 9 y., 1 m., 22 d.

STAPLES
[Luella E. - see GRINDLE]

TAYLOR
Carlton A. [husb. of Virginia G.] - b. 25 November 1907; d. 28 March 1997
Virginia G. [wife of Carlton A.] - b. 11 January 1915

THOMAS
Alice - d. 19 July 1892 Æ 36 y., 4 m., 19 d.
Alpharetta K. - [no dates]
David (Deacon; husb. of Martha A. (DAVIS)) - b. 23 October 1826; d. [no date]
Martha A. (DAVIS; wife of Deacon David) - b. 15 January 1835; d. [no date]
Rebecca (wife of [...id?][3] [no stone?]) - [...][1,4]

TRACY
Frank Y. [husb. of Ruth D.] - b. 1884; d. 1958
Hattie J. [wife of John D.?] - b. 1874; d. 1954
John D. [husb. of Hattie J.?] - b. 1872; d. 1955
Ruth D. [wife of Frank Y.] - b. 1885; d. 1956

TRENNAM
Arnona L. [wife of Leo Z.] - b. 1921
Betty J. (wife of Richard T.) - b. 1942
Dawn Lee (dau. of Richard T. and Betty J.) - b. 11 June 1964; d. 14 June 1964
Leo Z. [husb. of Arnona L.] - b. 1917; d. 1963
Richard T. (husb. of Betty J.) - b. 1940

TRIPP
Thomas E. - b. 1876; d. 1964

TUFTS
Elnora (GROVER; wife of Harry D. [no stone]) - b. 1875; d. 1915

TURNBULL
Charles A. (husb. of Julia A.) - b. 1886; d. 1963
Charles E. [husb. of Emma J.] - b. 14 January 1851; d. 18 December 1912

Deborah C. (wife of Joseph M. M.) - b. 15 October 1808; d. 15 March 1887
Emma J. [wife of Charles E.] - b. 14 April 1869; d. 4 August 1916
[Jane E. - see GREELEY]
Joseph M. M. (husb. of Deborah C.) - b. 1 October 1804; d. 26 April 1887
Julia A. (wife of Charles A.) - b. 1892; d. 1964

WALLS

Anna L. - b. 17 March 1906; d. 9 January 1990
Austin E. - b. 1911; d. 1994
Carrie (YOUNG) - b. 1877; d. 1931
Catherine A. [wife of Glenwood M.] - b. 8 June 1938
Chester E. [husb. of Myrtle M.] - b. 1885; d. 1973
Clarissa (wife of James) - d. 22 April 1885 Æ 79 y., 7 m.
Clifford G. - d. 25 November 1918 Æ 33 y., 3 m., 15 d.
Cora B. (wife of Hillard W.) - b. 1883; d. 1954
Elbridge G. - b. 1854; d. 1927
Ellen D. - d. 1866 Æ 11 m.
Emma A. - b. 15 May 1889; d. 10 February 1974
Ernest M. - b. 1886; d. 1930
Esther R. (wife of Reginald H.) - b. 1903; d. 1966
Florence L. [wife of Greeley] - b. 10 January 1871; d. 25 November 1949
Georgia Anna - b. 1921; d. 1999
Glenwood M. [husb. of Catherine A.] - b. 18 July 1937; d. 24 February 1991
Greeley [husb. of Florence L.] - b. 1865; d. 1935
Greeley Jr. - b. 1912; d. 1966
Harvey G. [husb. of Vilda L.] - b. 3 October 1895; d. 25 March 1958
Hillard W. (husb. of Cora B.) - b. 1880; d. 1965
Ida E. [wife of Willis J.] - d. 3 April 1896 Æ 30 y., 2 m., 19 d.
James (husb. of Clarissa) - d. 12 April 1883 Æ 75 y., 6 m., 20 d.
Lora[i]na[2] D. (YOUNG; wife of Samuel) - d. 3 August 1897 Æ 80 y., 8 m.
Lorinda D. - b. 1859; d. 1900
Lydia A. - b. 1871; d. 1952
Lydia A. (wife of William H.) - d. 21 September 1883 Æ 42 y., 11 m.
Matthew Michael (son of Michael E. [no stone]) - b. 20 July 1972; d. 23 July 1972
Melinda L. ([1st] wife of Samuel J.) - b. 1840; d. 23 January 1864 Æ 24 y., 8 d.
Milton T. [husb. of Zulma T.?] - b. 1911; d. 1983
Myrtle M. [wife of Chester E.] - b. 1894; d. 1983
Otilda A. ([2nd] wife of Samuel J.) - b. 1839; d. 1916
Percy Putnam - b. 30 September 1901; d. 26 June 1921
Reginald H. (husb. of Esther R.) - b. 1905; d. 1986
Samuel (husb. of Lora[i]na[2] D. (YOUNG)) - d. 6 February 1862 Æ 51 y., 11 m.
Samuel J. (husb. of Melinda L. and Otilda A.) - b. 1835; d. 1917
Samuel L. - b. 24 June 1912; d. 30 October 1985
Samuel M. - b. 7 February 1863; d. 14 April 1948
Stanley L. - b. 24 March 1935; d. 9 September 1992
Stuart M. - b. 1933; d. 1934
Susannah E. (dau. of Samuel and Lora[i]na[2] D. (YOUNG)) - d. 13 December 1864 Æ 15 y., 11 m., 10 d.
Vilda L. [wife of Harvey G.] - b. 1901; d. 1990
William H. (husb. of Lydia A.) - d. 21 October 1899 Æ 61 y.
William T. - b. 12 September 1840; d. 27 February 1911
Willis J. [husb. of Ida E.] - b. 1862; d. 1938
Zulma T. [wife of Milton T.?] - b. 1910; d. 1989

WASS
Lawrence T. [husb. of Thelma G.] - b. 1895; d. 1979
Thelma G. [wife of Lawrence T.] - b. 1910
WHITE
Lorena (wife of Fred C. [no stone]) - b. 1875; d. 1925
WILKINSON
Homer R. [husb. of Mildred E.] - b. 1911; d. 1995
Mildred E. [wife of Homer R.] - b. 1910
WRIGHT
Evelyn M. "Evie" (wife of Lincoln C.) - b. 1873; d. 1935
infant (son of Lincoln C. and Evelyn M. "Evie") - d. 15 September 1904 Æ [not given]
Lawrence H. (son of Lincoln C. and Evelyn M. "Evie") - d. 21 September 1900 Æ 2 y., 8 m.
Lincoln C. (husb. of Evelyn M. "Evie") - d. 24 March 1906 Æ 39 y., 2 m.
YOUNG
Abbie E. (wife of John F.) - d. 7 December 1895 Æ 31 y.
Ad[a or e]line[2] M. (wife of Elbridge G.) - d. 2 April 1863 Æ 27 y., 3 m., 12 d.
Alberta B. [wife of Roy B.] - b. 1888; d. 1975
Betsy (dau. of R. J. [no stone] and Susan E.) - d. March 1858 Æ 9 m.
[Carrie - see WALLS]
Carrie E. (RICE; [wife of Charles B.]) - b. 1859; d. 1940
Charles B. [husb. of Carrie E. (RICE)] - b. 1857; d. 1933
Elbridge G. (husb. of Ad[a or e]line[2] M. and Harriet) - [no dates]
Elisha (husb. of Eunice G.) - d. 11 February 1883 Æ 92 y., 2 m., 17 d.
Eunice G. (wife of Elisha) - d. 4 December 1864 Æ 72 y., 8 m., 6 d.
Frank (son of John F. and Abbie E.) - b. 1888; d. 1908
Harriet (wife of Elbridge G.) - d. 18 August 1868 Æ 32 y., 2 m.
Herbert L. - b. 1887; d. 1963
infants (2) (dau's. of Elbridge G. and Harriet) - d. 15 August 1868
J. F. - [no dates]; (member of Co. K, 11th Maine Regiment [Civil War])
John F. (husb. of Abbie E.) - b. 1863; d. 1940
Josephine (dau. of Elbridge G. and Ad[e or a]line[2] M.) - d. 20 April 1862 Æ 4 y., 4 m., 13 d.
[Lora[i]na[2] D. - see WALLS]
Roy B. [husb. of Alberta B.] - b. 1892; d. 1968
Susan E. (wife of R. J. [no stone]) - d. 8 April 1860 Æ 29 y.

Notes:
[1]Stone broken.
[2]Different on different stones.
[3]Illegible.
[4]Remainder of stone is in concrete, thereby obscuring any further information it may contain.

Forest Hill Cemetery
(Mount Desert - 11)

Location/directions. East of Routes 102/198, near intersection of Route 3 and Routes 102/198. From the traffic light at the north end of Mount Desert Island, go straight ahead (south) onto Routes 102/198. In approximately 4.2–4.3 miles, at the traffic light at the intersection of Routes 102/198 and Route 198, turn left on Route 198. Travel about 5.2–5.3 miles on Route 198 to the intersection (on the left) with the Gatehouse Road, immediately after (south of) the Brown Mountain gate lodge. Turn left onto this road. Continue straight ahead to the cemetery; do not follow the Gatehouse Road where it turns to the right in less than 0.1 miles.

History. —

Notes. This grass is mowed and trimmed, and there is water available. The roads are paved. No fence encloses this cemetery.

Names and dates on gravestones and other markers. [20 June 1999]
ADAMS
Glenice Merrill - b. 1913; d. 1995
[Sandra - see WALLACE]
ALLEY
Donald Ashley - b. 10 January 1979; d. 11 January 1979
ANDREWS
Marie D. [wife of Schofield] - b. 1890; d. 1971
Schofield [husb. of Marie D.] - b. 1889; d. 1971
ASHLEY
Eugene S. [husb. of Velma C.] - b. 8 November 1917; d. 7 February 1998
infant [child of Irving W. and Nora L.] - [no dates]
Irving W. [husb. of Nora L.] - b. 1885; d. 1982
Nora L. [wife of Irving W.] - b. 1893; d. 1984
Velma C. [wife of Eugene S.] - b. 23 August 1917; d. 18 September 1994
BAGLEY
Ernestine (OBER; [wife of Wayne]) - b. 1911; d. 1980
Wayne [husb. of Ernestine (OBER)] - b. 1910; d. 1973
BAIN
James B. [husb. of Lucy F.] - b. 1882; d. 1953
Lucy F. [wife of James B.] - b. 1883; d. 1956
BALTZELL
Isabel P. [wife of Jean P. J.] - b. 1923; d. 1970
Jean P. J. [husb. of Isabel P.] - b. 1917; d. 1988
BARRON
Faith C. - b. 1865; d. 1943
BARTLETT
Ada (OBER) - b. 1855; d. 1929
Albert I. - b. 1873; d. 1876
Estella E. - b. 1877; d. 1932
Francis G. (husb. of Sarah F.) - b. 1836; d. 1918
Fred W. [husb. of Mabelle R.?] - b. 1875; d. 1939
Mabelle R. [wife of Fred W.?] - b. 1887; d. 1954
Nellie A. - b. 1883; d. 1929
Sarah F. (wife of Francis G.) - b. 1847; d. 1912

BARTON
[Priscilla - see MORISON]
BEALE
Lester - b. 1904; d. 1960
BEYELER
[Elizabeth B[EYELER?]. - see DOLLIVER]
Hans E. - b. 1942; d. 1989
BISHOP
[Mabel Smith - see CROMWELL]
BLACK
Lizzie (wife of Manford C.) - b. 1890; d. 1915
Manford C. (husb. of Lizzie) - b. 1870; d. 19[...][5]
Mary J. (wife of William H.) - b. 1890; d. 1954
Richard Huddy [BLACK?] - [b. and d.?] 1956
William H. (husb. of Mary J.) - b. 1883; d. 1957
BLODGETT
Gertrude H. - b. 1896; d. 1961
BOYINGTON
Blake J. [husb. of Margaret (FENNELLY)] - b. 29 March 1918; d. 30 October 1954
Margaret (FENNELLY; [wife of Blake J.]) - b. 13 January 1918; d. 18 July 1995
BRANSCOM [includes BRANSCOMB]
[Dorothy B[RANSCOM?]. - see SPURLING]
Geraldine (WAGNOR [sic]; wife of Lawrence) - b. 1905; d. 1981
J. Henry (husb. of Mary Ella) - b. 1862; d. 1927
Lawrence (husb. of Geraldine (WAGNOR) [sic]) - b. 1900; d. 1964
Mary Ella (wife of J. Henry) - b. 1868; d. 1958
Pearl E. - b. 1889; d. 1891
BROWN
Alice Jane (dau. of Sylvester [no stone] and Deborah) - d. 7 March 1862 Æ 16 y., 2 m., 3 d.
[Alice Warren - see FALLASS]
Charles W. [husb. of Mattie B.] - b. 1873; d. 1963
Deborah (wife of Sylvester [no stone]) - b. 5 May 1824, Mount Desert; d. 22 April 1865, Boston
Edward Woodman [husb. of Gwendolyn Cochran[10]] - b. 1901; d. 1993
Esther S. [wife of Florington T.] - b. 1903; d. 1972
Florington T. [husb. of Esther S.] - b. 1902; d. 1947
George H. [husb. of Madelene [sic] F.] - b. 1903; d. 1974
Gwendolyn Cochran[10] [wife of Edward Woodman] - b. 1905; d. 1994
Josephine E. (dau. of Sylvester [no stone] and Deborah) - d. 24 October 1853 Æ 6 y., 3 m., 8 d.
Madelene [sic] F. [wife of George H.] - b. 1903; d. 1974
Mattie B. [wife of Charles W.] - b. 1880; d. 1952
[Sallie - see CAREY]
Walter S. (son of Sylvester [no stone] and Deborah) - d. 11 November 1871, Boston, Æ 22 y., 5 m., 15 d.
William Averell [sic] - b. 28 September 1885; d. 29 April 1953
BUCKLIN
Charles Howard [husb. of Leola (WAGNER)] - b. 1904; d. 1957
Fred W. [husb. of Katherine F.] - b. 1871; d. 1928
Freddie W. - b. 1910; d. 1915
Horace E. [husb. of Valerie S.] - b. 1907; d. 1990

Katherine F. [wife of Fred W.] - b. 1876; d. 1950
Leola (WAGNER; [wife of Charles Howard]) - b. 1903; d. 1977
[Madeline - see ROCK]
Marjorie E. [wife of Paul R.] - b. 1909
Paul R. [husb. of Marjorie E.] - b. 1908; d. 1978
Valerie S. [wife of Horace E.] - b. 1907

BUNKER
Charles H. - b. 1866; d. 1944
Evadne P. - b. 1869; d. 1956
James P. - b. 1896; d. 1955
Zola M. - b. 1902; d. 1968

BURBANK [see DODGE]

BURCH
Kim Reed[10] - b. 1953; d. 1992
Mervin W. Sr. - b. 1915; d. 1968
Patricia J. - b. 1923; d. 1994

BURR
Edith H. [wife of Lester D.] - b. 1890; d. 1952
Eleanor (TRACY; [wife of L. Douglas]) - b. 19 December 1914; d. 20 September 1997
Jane H. [wife of Maurice H.] - b. 5 April 1917; d. 3 January 1986
L. Douglas [husb. of Eleanor (TRACY)] - b. 1 June 1914
Lester D. [husb. of Edith H.] - b. 1887; d. 1951
Maurice H. [husb. of Jane H.] - b. 11 November 1903; d. 23 January 1963

BURRILL
Matthew S. - b. 1969; d. 1976

BUTLER
James A. - b. 31 August 1861; d. 18 February 1913
[Temperance - see CARVER]

BUZZELL
[Dorothy - see GRAVES]

BYRNE
James MacGregor - [no dates]

CAREY
Sallie (BROWN; mother of Annabel and Josephine [no stones]) - b. 7 August 1893; d. 11 March 1986

CARR
Fabyan W. - b. 7 September 1921; d. 28 October 1993
Sherwood S. - b. 4 October 1925; d. 14 July 1985

CARVER
Temperance (BUTLER) - b. 8 October 1870; d. 16 March 1932

CHASE
Alberta P. [CHASE?] - [no dates]
Joseph P. Jr. - b. 5 November 1923; d. 9 March 1945
Lowell R. Sr. - b. 1924; d. 1992

CHESLOCK
Frank Edward (husb. of Margaret J.) - b. 8 March 1898; d. 12 November 1963
Margaret J. (wife of Frank Edward) - b. 1894; d. 1963

CIAVARRA
Ann (ROSENGARTEN) - b. 1943; d. 1973

COCHRAN
[Gwendolyn - see BROWN]

COFFIN
Ernest L. (Dr.) - b. 25 March 1905; d. 27 November 1984
Silas A. IV - b. 11 March 1946; d. 21 October 1946
COOMBS
Alice F[ENNELLY]. [wife of Arthur W.] - b. 1883; d. 1976
Arthur F. - d. 11 June 1999
Arthur W. [husb. of Alice F[ENNELLY].] - b. 1880; d. 1950
Dorothy F. "Cookie" - b. 1920; d. 1998 Æ 78 y.[6]
[Eleanor - see RIANHARD]
Percy E. - b. 1907; d. 1994
Thelma B. - b. 1902; d. 1974
CORSON
Isaiah - [no dates]
John W. - [no dates]
Jonas - [no dates]
Joseph (husb. of Laura Louisa) - b. 6 March 1844; d. 16 November 1909
Laura Louisa (wife of Joseph) - b. 20 February 1847; d. 2 January 1905
COUSINS
Elmer H. [husb. of Geraldine B.] - b. 1910; d. 1985
Geraldine B. [wife of Elmer H.] - b. 1914; d. 1997
COXE
Edmund P. - b. 1941; d. 1960
Helen Piper - b. 1960; d. 1998
Henry B. Jr. - b. 1898; d. 1961
CRAWFORD
Robert A. - b. 9 April 1902; d. 9 April 1911
CROCKER
infant [child of Leon H. and Verlie B.?] - [b. and d.?] 18 June 1949
Leon H. [husb. of Verlie B.] - b. 1907; d. 1992
Verlie B. [wife of Leon H.] - b. 1917
CROFOOT [sic]
Michael (Dr.; husb. of Julie [no stone]) - b. 6 September 1911; d. 6 February 1982
CROMWELL
Barbara (KISSEL; dau. of Rudolph H. KISSEL and Caroline (MORGAN) [no stones]) - b. 1901; d. 1968
Jarvis (son of Lincoln and Mabel Smith (BISHOP)) - b. 1896; d. 1992
Lincoln (son of James William and Elizabeth Stuart[10] [no stones]; husb. of Mabel Smith (BISHOP)) - b. 1865; d. 1952
Mabel Smith (BISHOP; dau. of Rev. Dr. Cornelius BISHOP and Mary Wheeler (SMITH) [no stones]; wife of Lincoln) - b. 1867; d. 1963
CROOK
Patricia E. (HERRICK; wife of Vinal R. Jr. [no stone]) - b. 14 February 1951; d. 20 July 1994
DAMON
Herbert L. - b. 17 August 1955; "lost at sea" 13 March 1989
Robert F. - b. 1924; d. 1973
Sheldon Leroy "Snick" - b. 15 April 1933; d. 18 October 1995
DANFORTH
Donald W. - b. 1923
Emily L. "Emmy Lou" - b. 1923
John W. (Dr.) - b. 1952; d. 1992

DAVIS
Celia G. [wife of Elmer C.] - b. 1884; d. 1973
Charles H. [husb. of Tena L.] - b. 1880; d. 1954
Elmer C. [husb. of Celia G.] - b. 1886; d. 1956
[Ernestine - see SAVAGE]
Philena M. [wife of Walter E.] - b. 1893; d. 1980
Robert F. - b. 1915; d. 1945
Tena L. [wife of Charles H.] - b. 1886; d. 1959
Walter E. [husb. of Philena M.] - b. 1888; d. 1947
DE PEDROSO [see SAN CARLOS DE PEDROSO]
DESISLES
Clarence E. [husb. of Inga (JOHNSON)] - b. 1873; d. 1946
Inga (JOHNSON; [wife of Clarence E.]) - b. 1880; d. 1968
DINSMORE [headstone on lot containing Frances Vaughan GARDINER's stone]
DODGE
Donald S. [DODGE?[11]] - [no dates]
Helen M. [DODGE?[11]] - [no dates]
Kay D. [DODGE?[11]] - b. 1931; d. 1991
Robert L. - [no dates]
Robert R. - [no dates]
DOLLIVER
Elizabeth B[EYELER?]. - b. 16 April 1920; d. 26 April 1998 Æ 78 y.[7]
DONNAN
David Hibbs - b. 22 April 1924
Elizabeth Pauly - b. 21 September 1953
DOUGLAS
Pauline S. (wife of Prescott M.) - b. 1905; d. 1965
Prescott M. (husb. of Pauline S.) - b. 1903; d. 1976
DUCEY
John Francis Jr. (husb. of Katharine (MUNSON) - b. 2 November 1914
Katharine (MUNSON; wife of John Francis Jr.) - b. 9 November 1916; d. 8 May 1977
DYER
Bartlett W. [brother of George] - b. 1878; d. 1950
George [brother of Bartlett W.] - b. 1875; d. 1938
EATON
Benjamin H. [husb. of Lois (WALLACE)] - b. 1915; d. 1969
Lois (WALLACE; [wife of Benjamin H.]) - b. 1913; d. 1998
ELIOT
[Carola - see GORIANSKY]
ELLIOTT
Eva M. [wife of Frank E.] - b. 1883; d. 1962
Frank E. [husb. of Eva M.] - b. 1874; d. 1946
FAGAN
Margaret - b. 24 October 1895; d. 30 August 1971
FAIRMAN
Endsley Perrine - b. 1908; d. 1998
FALLASS
Alice Warren (BROWN; [wife of Charles Henry]) - b. 6 January 1900; d. 18 April 1980
Charles Henry [husb. of Alice Warren (BROWN)] - b. 8 February 1891; d. 18 May 1982

FALT
Annie S. (SAVAGE; dau. of Capt. Augustus Chase SAVAGE and Emily (MANCHESTER); wife of James H. [no stone]) - b. 20 September 1867; d. 7 June 1897
[Edith - see FAVOUR]
Gordon H. - b. 1900; d. 1981
James H. (husb. of L. Lenora) - b. 1865; d. 1922
L. Lenora (wife of James H.) - b. 1880; d. 1956
Naomi H. - b. 1907; d. 1933
FAVOUR
Edith (FALT; wife of Paul Gordon Jr.) - b. 1916; d. 1991
Paul Gordon Jr. (husb. of Edith (FALT)) - b. 1914; d. 1984
FENNELLY
[Alice F[ENNELLY]. - see COOMBS]
Andrew E. (husb. of Eva C.) - b. 1880; d. 1953
Estelle I. [wife of Nathan] - b. 1855; d. 1920
Eva C. (wife of Andrew E.) - b. 1884; d. 1942
George H. [husb. of Mildred S.] - b. 1886; d. 1968
Isabel - b. 1853; d. 1936
[Margaret - see BOYINGTON]
Mildred S. [wife of George H.] - b. 1888; d. 1979
Nathan [husb. of Estelle I.] - b. 1854; d. 1940
Thomas - b. 1843; d. 1927
William R. - b. 1914; d. 1982
FENTON
Hilda J. - b. 1911; d. 1912
FISH
Betty G. [wife of Ernest A.] - b. 8 November 1922
Ernest A. [husb. of Betty G.] - b. 12 February 1914; d. 15 January 1999
FITCH
Lawrence E. - b. 15 December 1951; d. 25 May 1995
Ralph R. - b. 18 October 1878; d. 31 January 1970
Virginia R. - b. 20 April 1902; d. 30 November 1990
FLAGG
[Betsy - see MELCHER]
FLETCHER
Frances C. [wife of Winthrop] - b. 14 March 1917; d. 19 September 1999
Lawrence E. [son of Winthrop and Frances C.] - b. 15 December 1951; d. 25 May 1995
Winthrop [husb. of Frances C.] - b. 5 September 1918; d. 18 April 1997
FLYE
Charlotte R. [wife of Lawrence E.] - b. 1917; d. 1991
Lawrence E. [husb. of Charlotte R.] - b. 1917; d. 1992
FOGARTY
Dennis M. - b. 17 December 1949; d. 6 February 1996
FOGG
Grace P. [wife of William S.] - b. 1882; d. 1962
William S. [husb. of Grace P.] - b. 1877; d. 1964
FOSTER
Beatrice R. - b. 1892; d. 1979
Elizabeth I. [wife of J. Lealond [sic]] - b. 1904; d. 1987
Frederick A. (husb. of Sarah P.) - b. 9 February 1861; d. 15 December 1915

J. Lealond [sic] [husb. of Elizabeth I.] - b. 1901; d. 1987
John A. - b. 1916; d. 1971
Lynn - b. 1942
Margaret C. - b. 1913
Ray L. - b. 1886; d. 1980
Sarah P. (wife of Frederick A.) - b. 14 April 1869; d. 26 May 1944

FRANCIS
Bertie - [no dates]
Daniel - [no dates]
Isabell [sic] S. - d. 10 May 1918 Æ 3 m., 20 d.
John Snow - [no dates]
Juanita - [no dates]

FRATES
Manuel - d. 1926 Æ [not given]

FRAZIER
Charles H. (husb. of Ruth A.) - b. 1834; d. 9 August 1909 Æ 75 y.
Dora C. [wife of Howard C.] - b. 1868; d. 1949
Howard C. [husb. of Dora C.] - b. 1867; d. 1949
Ruth A. (wife of Charles H.) - b. 1844; d. 10 November 1928 Æ 84 y.

FROST
George Linwood (son of Melvin R. and Mary Y.) - b. 15 November 1900; d. 13 December 1904
Mary Y. (wife of Melvin R.) - b. July 1868; d. May 1909
Melvin R. (husb. of Mary Y.) - b. April 1859; d. August 1937

GARDINER
Francis Vaughan ([earlier or later a] wife of C. C. KITE and E. M. FINLETTER [no stones]) - b. 16 September 1892, Pomfret, Connecticut; d. 27 March 1985, Philadelphia, Pennsylvania

GARDNER
Fred L. [husb. of Pauline D. (KING)] - b. 1873; d. 1947
Pauline D. (KING; [wife of Fred L.]) - b. 1891; d. 1968

GATCHELL
Hester E. - b. 1923; d. 1993

GETZE
E. Bioren [husb. of Josephine F.] - b. 1899; d. 1980
Josephine F. [wife of E. Bioren] - b. 1908; d. 1995

GILKES
Arthur G. - b. 6 February 1915; d. 25 July 1999

GILLETT
Charles R. [husb. of Helen S.] - b. 1893; d. 1957
Helen S. [wife of Charles R.] - b. 1900; d. 1983

GILLEY
Mildred C. "Mimi" - b. 1913; d. 1994

GILPATRICK [includes GILLPATRICK]
Abram (husb. of Alma T.) - b. 1863; d. 1943
Abram Jr. [son of Abram and Alma T.] - b. 1910; d. 1979
Alma T. (wife of Abram) - b. 1872; d. 1934
Arthur (husb. of Mina A.) - b. 1858; d. 1941
Charles E. - b. April 1867; d. August 1906
Esther (wife of Samuel) - d. 14 June 1886 Æ 94 y., 11 m., 4 d.
Hattie Wylie (dau. of Samuel N. and Julia A.) - d. 18 September 1869 Æ 4 m., 6 d.
Julia A. (wife of Samuel N.) - b. August 1838; d. February 1909

Julia T. - [no dates]
Mina A. (wife of Arthur) - b. 1868; d. 1945
Samuel (husb. of Esther) - d. 10 February 1871 Æ 79 y., 18 d.
Samuel N. (husb. of Julia A.) - b. March 1824; d. December 1897
[...][1] L. (dau. of Samuel and Esther) - d. 23 May 1835 Æ 3 y., 9 m., 14 d.

GORDIUS
[Mary - see LUNT]

GORIANSKY
Carola (ELIOT; [wife of Lev V.]) - b. 1896, Brookline, Massachusetts; d. 1989
Lev V. [husb. of Carola (ELIOT)] - b. 1894, Kharkov, Russia; d. 1967

GRAVES
Alice T. - b. 1878; d. 1946
Alice V. - b. 1903; d. 1935
Arnold K. [husb. of Mary A.] - b. 1904; d. 1971
Benjamin C. [husb. of Harriet D.] - b. 1857; d. 1938
Bessie L. (wife of Lawris [sic] N.) - b. 1903; d. 1994
Charles (husb. of Lydia V.) - b. 1854; d. 1924
Claire C. (wife of Harvard B.) - b. 1908; d. 1944
Dorothy (BUZZELL; wife of Thomas Nelson) - b. 14 September 1930
Harriet D. [wife of Benjamin C.] - b. 1862; d. 1942
Harvard B. (husb. of Claire C.) - b. 1902; d. 1967
infant - d. 3 March 1911 Æ 7 d.
infant (dau. of Charles and Lydia V.) - [b. and?] d. 12 December 1909
John H. (son of Lawris [sic] N. and Bessie L.) - b. 1929
John Robert (son of Robert M. and Sheila L.) - b. 23 October 1949; d. 1 February 1958
Lawris [sic] N. (husb. of Bessie L.) - b. 1906; d. 1956
Lillian V. [wife of Malcolm W.] - b. 1897; d. 1966
Lydia V. (wife of Charles) - b. 1866; d. 1937
Malcolm W. [husb. of Lillian V.] - b. 1900; d. 1987
Mary A. [wife of Arnold K.] - b. 1900; d. 1980
Mary Jane [wife of Richard E.] - b. 1937
Rae D. - b. 1886; d. 1966
Richard E. [husb. of Mary Jane] - b. 1934
Robert M. (husb. of Sheila L.) - b. 1924
Scott Christopher - b. 25 December 1964; d. 25 June 1994
Sheila L. (wife of Robert M.) - b. 1926
Shirley Preston [male] - b. 7 April 1882, Franklin, Maine; d. 13 December 1917, Roxbury, Massachusetts
Thomas N. - b. 1875; d. 1919
Thomas Nelson (husb. of Dorothy (BUZZELL)) - b. 13 December 1931; d. 3 February 1992
Winifred D. - b. 1896; d. 1977
[...] headstone only

GRAY
Albert T. [husb. of Jennie F.] - b. 1894; d. 1969
Everard A. "Tator" [husb. of Jean M.] - b. 1925; d. 1990
Everett C. - b. 16 April 1906; d. 9 March 1994
Jean M. [wife of Everard A. "Tator"] - b. 1928
Jennie F. [wife of Albert T.] - b. 1895; d. 1969
Stanley W. - b. 1904; d. 1954

GREEN
[Mae P. - see KENNEDY]
GRINDLE
Chester G. (husb. of Irene M.) - b. 1902; d. 1947
Gage B. [husb. of Ruth B.] - b. 1867; d. 1958
Irene M. (wife of Chester G.) - b. 1901; d. 1967
Pauline J. - b. 1932
Porter M. - b. 1901; d. 1980
Ruth B. [wife of Gage B.] - b. 1876; d. 1956
Ruth D. - b. 1913; d. 1994
HADDAD
George J. - b. 1911
Gloria R. - b. 1928
HAMOR
Barbara L. - b. 1900; d. 1955
Cora G. - b. 1876; d. 1903
Elihu T. - b. 1901; d. 1981; bur. Weymouth Heights, Massachusetts
Ralph Jr. - b. 1899; d. 1899
HAMBLEN
Wilder S. - b. 1917; d. 1957
HARDISON
Beulah F. [wife of Charles S.] - b. 1882; d. 1945
Charles S. [husb. of Beulah F.] - b. 1876; d. 1951
HASKELL
G. Merrill [husb. of Mildred E.] - b. 1903; d. 1985
Mildred E. [wife of G. Merrill] - b. 1906
HAYNES
Carlton W. - b. 1904; d. 1960
Doris G. - b. 1912; d. 1991
Emma S. - b. 1884; d. 1965
Margaret C. [wife of Richard M.] - b. 1912
Myrtle E. - b. 1878; d. 1963
Richard M. [husb. of Margaret C.] - b. 1908; d. 1997
Roger H. - b. 1900; d. 1982
Roger H. Jr. - b. 1924; d. 1977
Walter H. - b. 1878; d. 1928
HECKSCHER
August II - b. 1913; d. 1997
HEDGES
Carl H. "Duke" - b. 1943; d. 1998
Carl W. (husb. of Faith V.) - b. 1882; d. 1956
Faith V. (wife of Carl W.) - b. 1886; d. 1936
Ruth C. - b. 1891; d. 1983
HENCKLER
Charles W. Jr. - b. 28 October 1918; d. 24 September 1969
HERKNESS
Lindsay C. - b. 1 April 1915; d. 20 July 1998
HERRICK
[Almenia - see WAGNER]
Bradford T. - b. 1901; d. 1963
Ida E. [wife of Isaac W.] - b. 1857; d. 1930
Isaac W. [husb. of Ida E.] - b. 1852; d. 1929

[Patricia E. - see CROOK]
HIGGINS
Charles A. - b. 1876; d. 1917
[Olevia [sic] A. - see REED]
Paul E. - b. 1909; d. 1917
HILL
Charles D. [husb. of Laura M.] - b. 1888; d. 1974
Daniel A. [husb. of Kathryn F.] - b. 1910; d. 1988
Kathryn F. [wife of Daniel A.] - b. 1911; d. 1996
Laura M. [wife of Charles D.] - b. 1893; d. 1964
HODGDON
Alvah L. [husb. of Lettie S.] - b. 1877; d. 1946
Annie F. (wife of Edward A.) - b. 1863; d. 1937
Edward A. (husb. of Annie F.) - b. 1863; d. 1942
Francis E. (son of Capt. Mark W. and Huldah B.) - d. 8 November 1840 Æ 4 m., 8 d.[8]
Huldah B. (wife of Capt. Mark W.) - d. 28 June 1863 Æ 37 y., 11 m., 19 d.
infant (son of Capt. Mark W. and Huldah B.) - d. 15 June 1849 Æ 4 d.
Judith C. (dau. of Capt. Mark W. and Huldah B.) - d. 14 March 1856 Æ 9 y., 6 m.
Lettie S. [wife of Alvah L.] - b. 1877; d. 1940
Mark W. (Capt.; husb. of Huldah B. [and Mary Jane]) - b. 1813; d. 1902
Mary Jane [wife of Capt. Mark W.] - b. 1822; d. 1904
Smith S. (son of Capt. Mark W. and Huldah B.) - d. 15 September 1842 Æ 6 w.
HODGKINS
Addison E. [husb. of Hilda J.?] - b. 29 February 1916; d. 3 December 1972
Hilda J. [wife of Addison E.?] - b. 25 May 1904; d. 8 September 1971
Mildred L. (dau. of Lowell G. and Daisy F. [no stones]) - d. 15 February 1900 Æ 5 y., 10 m., 11 d.
HOLLAND
Myrtle W. - b. 1890; d. 1969
Ralph D. - b. 1878; d. 1968
HOLMES
Emma R. (wife of Anson I. [no stone]) - d. 2 April 1879 Æ 22 y., 6 m., 24 d.
HOPKINS
Anne Hope van Schaack - b. 1954; d. 1977
David Luke (husb. of Katherine Disston (PORTER)) - b. 29 December 1898; d. 16 May 1976
Katherine Disston (PORTER; wife of David Luke) - b. 31 January 1903, Philadelphia, Pennsylvania; d. 22 April 1995
HOYT
Anne McM. - b. 1861; d. 1949
HUGHES
Carrie R. (wife of Dr. J. B. [no stone]) - d. 18 November 1868 Æ 42 y., 5 m.
HUNTER
Charles Welsh [sic] [husb. of Georgena [sic] Morrill[10]?] - b. 1882; d. 1966
Georgena [sic] Morrill[10] [wife of Charles Welsh [sic]?] - b. 1893; d. 1985
IVENEY
Emmons B. [husb. of Inez M.] - b. 1900; d. 1964
Frederick J. [husb. of Myrtle J.] - b. 1898; d. 1993
Inez M. [wife of Emmons B.] - b. 1904
Myrtle J. [wife of Frederick J.] - b. 1908
[...] [headstone only]

JAMES
Alfred J. Jr. "Buster" - b. 1915; d. 1992
Anna R. - b. 1891; d. 1966
infant - [no dates]
[Katherine M. - see WHITTAKER-CONTRE]
JENKINS
George E. (Major) - b. 31 March 1918; d. 13 August 1956
Jennie M. [wife of Roy G.] - b. 1915
Roy G. [husb. of Jennie M.] - b. 1915; d. 1974
JOHNSON
Elma A. ([REED?]) - b. 1883; d. 1922
[Inga - see DESISLES]
JORDAN
Cecile V. (wife of Walter H.) - b. 1898; d. 1971
George W. (husb. of Susie P.) - b. 22 February 1863; d. 17 December 1914
Henry A. - b. 2 January 1920; d. 28 September 1982
Susie P. (wife of George W.) - b. 11 May 1875; d. 31 October 1955
Walter H. (husb. of Cecile V.) - b. 25 January 1896; d. 4 March 1964
JOY
Chauncey D. (husb. of Martha M.) - b. 1863; d. 1940
George J. - b. 1861; d. 1936
Lillis P. [wife of Winfred B.] - b. 1891; d. 1981
Martha M. (wife of Chauncey D.) - b. 1863; d. 1948
Winfred B. [husb. of Lillis P.] - b. 1890; d. 1966
KELLOG
John F. III - b. 1 August 1925; d. 9 August 1998
KENNEDY
Andrew H. (husb. of Mae P. (GREEN)) - b. 5 January 1898; d. 17 April 1967
Mae P. (GREEN; wife of Andrew H.) - b. 5 March 1883; d. 10 July 1970
Margaret (dau. of Moorhead C. and Anna (SCOTT) [no stone]) - b. 1938; d. 1956
Moorhead C. (husb. of Anna (SCOTT) [no stone]) - b. 1902; d. 1995
KIMBALL
Fred E. - b. 1878; d. 1968
Katheryn [sic] D. - b. 1898; d. 1974
KING
Arthur Roy - b. 20 February 1901; d. 25 September 1962
[Pauline D. - see GARDNER]
KISSEL
[Barbara - see CROMWELL]
[Caroline (MORGAN) - see Barbara (KISSEL) CROMWELL]
[Rudolph H. - see Barbara (KISSEL) CROMWELL]
KNOX
Allen C. [husb. of Ethel A.] - b. 1919; d. 1998
Ethel A. [wife of Allen C.] - b. 1921
Stella G. [wife of William J.] - b. 1876; d. 1939
William J. [husb. of Stella G.] - b. 1875; d. 1943
LAMSON
Harriet H. [wife of Horace W.] - b. 1857; d. 1934
Horace W. [husb. of Harriet H.] - b. 1857; d. 1926
LENZ
[Lora - see MCVETY]

LERETTE
Philip A. - b. 1916; d. 1979
LIBBEY [sic]
Kenneth Wilder - b. 29 December 1943; d. 11 April 1997
LINSCOTT
Anne [wife of Arthur] - b. 1894; d. 1969
Arthur [husb. of Anne] - b. 1896; d. 1971
LIPPINCOTT
Paul Howe - b. 10 November 1940; d. 25 April 1990
LISCOMB
Cora M[EADER?]. - b. 1906; d. 1965
LLOYD
Stacy B. - b. 8 July 1908; d. 6 December 1994
LUKENS
Peter G. - b. 21 March 1969; d. 21 July 1996
LUNT
Durlin E. - b. 6 March 1910; d. 27 March 1982
Ernest E. [husb. of Helen (REID)] - b. 1889; d. 1961
Helen (REID; [wife of Ernest E.]) - b. 1904; d. 1954
Martin Gilbert [husb. of Mary (GORDIUS)] - b. 1862; d. 1932
Mary (GORDIUS; [wife of Martin Gilbert]) - b. 1865; d. 1944
LURVEY
Fred - b. 1884; d. 1940
Lester J. - b. 1890; d. 2 October 1918, "Blanc Mont, France"; ("killed in action" [World War I])
Linda E. - b. 1863; d. 1939
Reuben F. - b. 1857; d. 1939
LYNCH
Elizabeth - b. 23 September 1892; d. 10 August 1962
M.
J. [footstone only "J. M./S. B. M."]
S. B. [footstone only "J. M./S. B. M."]
MACKENZIE
Donald C. (son of William M. and Susie S.) - d. 1 April 1913 Æ 3 m.
Susie S. (wife of William M.) - b. 1882; d. 1967
William M. (husb. of Susie S.) - b. 1881; d. 1943
MACLEAN
Annie - b. 1896; d. 1975
Hughie - b. 1871; d. 1955
[Lina - see WILSON]
Philip - b. 1873; d. 1966
MACOMBER
John H. - b. 30 August 1808; d. 12 September 1898
MACW.
[Sarah - see PARKER]
MADEIRA
Alice T. [wife of Edward W.] - b. 1896; d. 1998
Edward W. [husb. of Alice T.] - b. 1892; d. 1956
MALCOLM
Edith M. [wife of Judson M.] - b. 1888; d. 1957
Judson M. [husb. of Edith M.] - b. 9 May 1889; d. 24 February 1975

MANCHESTER
Amos Melville (husb. of Emily S.) - b. December 1853; d. June 1909
Amy F. [wife of Charles T.] - b. 17 February 1888; d. 28 June 1936
Annie - b. 1852; d. 1885
Ansel L. - b. 1850; d. 1929
Charles T. [husb. of Amy F.] - b. 2 September 1888; d. 5 December 1959
Charlotte R. - b. 1897; d. 1992
Danforth B. [husb. of Lucy M.] - b. 1903; d. 1989
Danforth J. [husb. of Evelyn C.] - b. 1848; d. 1936
Edith L. - b. 15 May 1877; d. 6 August 1914
Ellen B. - b. 1880; d. 1974
Elsie B. - b. 1886; d. 1978
[Emily - see SAVAGE]
Emily S. (wife of Amos Melville) - b. November 1857; d. May 1916
Evelyn C. [wife of Danforth J.] - b. 1851; d. 1925
Flora B. - b. 5 July 1864; d. 6 October 1939
Frank E. - b. 13 August 1886; d. 13 January 1919
George A. - b. 31 July 1882; d. 26 May 1937
George A. - b. 15 March 1906; d. 31 March 1928
George E. - d. 26 October 1877 Æ 31 y., 11 m., 6 d.
Gilbert - b. 1822; d. 1825
Gilbert H. - d. 19 November 1879 Æ 33 y., 4 m., 6 d.
infant [MANCHESTER?] - [b. and d.?] 19 December 1913
infant [MANCHESTER?] - [b. and d.?] 23 May 1915
infant [MANCHESTER?] - [b. and d.?] 26 September 1917
John - b. 1763; d. 1847; ("Revolutionary soldier" [Revolutionary War])
John Jr. - b. 1795; d. 1870
John C. - b. 1824; d. 1825
John H. - b. 1898; d. 1979
Juanita C. - b. 1911; d. 1995
Julia G. - b. 1898; d. 1978
Lawrence M. - b. 1884; d. 1946
Leota H. - b. 29 April 1894; d. 14 January 1919
Linda - b. 1795; d. 1841
Linda M. - b. 1825; d. 1843
Lucy M. [wife of Danforth B.] - b. 1901; d. 1986
Manson - b. 23 December 1861; d. 21 November 1932
Mary A. (wife of Thomas) - d. 5 March 1856 Æ 28 y.
Mary E. - b. 1876; d. 1920
Melville - b. 1930; d. 1941
Minnie F. - b. 1861; d. 1953
Mona G. (wife of Russell D.) - b. 1895; d. 1975
Philena W. (wife of Thomas) - d. 15 September 1879 Æ 39 y., 7 m., 17 d.
Polly - b. 1767; d. 1857
[Rachel F. - see WOODMAN]
Russell D. (husb. of Mona G.) - b. 6 September 1895; d. 17 April 1975
Salome - b. 1810; d. 1885
Thomas (husb. of Mary A. and Philena W.) - d. 2 September 1903 Æ 82 y., 8 m.
Virgil M. - b. 1912
Warren H. - b. 1837; d. 1842
Warren H. (son of Thomas and Mary A.) - d. 20 March 1853 Æ [2?][1] y., 6 m., 19 d.
William W. - b. 1875; d. 1959

McCUE
James C. Sr. [husb. of Laura (TRACY)] - b. 1896; d. 1965
Laura (TRACY; [wife of James C. Sr.]) - b. 1890; d. 1971
McGARR
Jay Crosby [son of Robert Elliot and Shirley (REYNOLDS)] - b. 18 June 1952
Robert Elliot [husb. of Shirley (REYNOLDS)] - b. 20 October 1925; d. 8 November 199[7 or 8][2]
Shirley (REYNOLDS; [wife of Robert Elliot]) - b. 7 January 1926
McILHENNY
Polly - [no dates]
Sandra (PIERCE) - b. 13 September 1950; d. 19 February 1995
McNAUGHTON
Albert - b. 1902; d. 1976
McNULTY
Arthur E. - b. 25 July 1924; d. 22 November 1995
Charles William - b. 21 September 1919; d. 9 August 1997
Marion A. - b. 1892; d. 1935
McPHETERS
Donald Reed "Don" (husb. of Grace Eleanor "Gracie" (WILLIAMS)) - b. 5 October 1903; d. 2 February 1984
Grace Eleanor "Gracie" (WILLIAMS; wife of Donald Reed "Don") - b. 22 July 1920
McVETY
Lora (LENZ) - b. 1937; d. 1970
MEADER
Ada C. [wife of Elmer T.] - b. 1881; d. 1971
[Cora M[EADER?]. - see LISCOMB]
Elmer T. [husb. of Ada C.] - b. 1887; d. 1955
Ira E. - b. 1909; d. 1974
King T. - b. 1862; d. 1940
Merle N. [son of Elmer T. and Ada C.] - b. 1920; d. 1986
Minnie R. - b. 1882; d. 1945
MELCHER
Betsy (FLAGG; [wife of John]) - b. 8 April 1900; d. 21 April 1991
John [husb. of Betsy (FLAGG)] - b. 28 March 1895; d. 27 July 1956
MELLON
Charles Henry III - b. 1938; d. 1975
Karl Negley - b. 5 August 1937; d. 31 March 1983
MILLER
Paul Lukens - b. 6 December 1919; d. 26 July 1997
Paul Lukens Jr. "PJ" - b. 11 August 1951; d. 1 April 1993
MITCHELL
June - b. 4 January 1924; d. 25 February 1924
MONTGOMERY
Florence - b. 1889; d. 1975
MOORE
Alexander F. (husb. of Bertha E.) - b. 1848; d. 1920
Bertha E. (wife of Alexander F.) - b. 1857; d. 1927
Maude A. [wife of Walter] - b. 1872; d. 1910
Ralph A. [son of Walter and Maude A.] - b. 189[6 or 5][2]; d. 1919
Walter [husb. of Maude A.] - b. 1874; d. 1905
MORFIT
Eleanor L. [wife of Thomas Garrison] - b. 1918; d. 1974

Thomas Garrison [husb. of Eleanor L.] - b. 1915; d. 1993
MORGAN
[Caroline - see Barbara (KISSEL) CROMWELL]
MORISON
Priscilla (BARTON; wife of Samuel Eliot) - b. 1906; d. 1973
Samuel Eliot (husb. of Priscilla (BARTON)) - b. 1887; d. 1976
MORRILL
[Georgena [sic] - see HUNTER]
MULLINS
John Edward [husb. of Nona Adelle] - b. 1864; d. 1939
Nona Adelle [wife of John Edward] - b. 1880; d. 1938
MUNSON
[Katharine - see DUCEY]
MURPHY
Ai S. - b. 8 September 1907; d. 12 November 1983
Arthur A. [husb. of Clara H.] - b. 1847; d. 1928
Clara H. [wife of Arthur A.] - b. 1853; d. 1937
Clara J. [REED?] - b. 1901; d. 1969
Elizabeth M. - b. 1935
Eugene S. - b. 1873; d. 1961
Hollis D. - b. 1904; d. 1982
Leland W. [husb. of Marie A.] - b. 1928; d. 1992
Margaret E. - b. 1905; d. 1984
Marie A. [wife of Leland W.] - b. 1919
Martha M. - b. 1901; d. 1990
Maurice E. - b. 1928; d. 1989
Nida E. - b. 1882; d. 1947
Richard S. - b. 1902; d. 1938
Steven A. - b. 1952; d. 1991
NEILSON
Harry Rosengarten Jr. - b. 20 July 1928; d. 24 June 1994
NICHOLSON
Alice F. [wife of Bryant J.] - b. 1913
Bryant J. [husb. of Alice F.] - b. 14 February 1906; d. 6 June 1998 Æ 92 y.
[Emily - see SAVAGE]
NORWOOD
Douglas R. - b. 1905; d. 1980
OBER
[Ada - see BARTLETT]
Barbara P. - b. 1884; d. 1967
Berniece E. - b. 1919; d. 1961
Ernest C. - b. 1883; d. 1963
[Ernestine - see BAGLEY]
Eva P. (wife of Merritt T.) - b. 1875; d. 1940
Frank R. (Dr.; [husb. of Ina S.]) - b. 1881; d. 1960
Ina S. [wife of Dr. Frank R.] - b. 1877; d. 1963
Josephine R. - b. 1857; d. 1931
Marian L. - b. 1917; d. 1948
Mary E. - b. 1895; d. 1919
Merritt T. (husb. of Eva P.) - b. 1864; d. 1935
Otis M. - b. 1862; d. 1935
Roger F. - b. 1903; d. 1933

OKHALA
Lemke - b. 1909; d. 1954
OLSSON
Kathleen Mae "Kay" [wife of Sven V.] - b. 6 August 1913; d. 15 March 1997
Sven V. [husb. of Kathleen Mae "Kay"] - b. 9 June 1910; d. 28 June 1975
OSTERHOUT
[Miriam - see ROSENGARTEN]
OTTUM
Selina (ROBERTS) "Bean" - b. 1948; d. 1990
PACKARD
Evelyn A. [wife of Walter S.] - b. 1882; d. 1971
Walter S. [husb. of Evelyn A.] - b. 1871; d. 1958
PAGE
[Lois - see SMALLIDGE]
PARADY
Bernard B. "Bernie" (husb. of Elizabeth A. "Bette") - b. 1930; m. 15 June 1953; d. 1997
Elizabeth A. "Bette" (wife of Bernard B. "Bernie") - b. 1934; m. 15 June 1953; d. 1994
PARKER
Dudley F. [husb. of Sarah (MACW.)] - b. 24 May 1897; d. 5 March 1994
Sarah (MACW.; [wife of Dudley F.]) - b. 24 June 1901; d. 5 April 1988
PATTERSON
Andrew J. [husb. of Mildred W.] - b. 1887; d. 1966
Mildred W. [wife of Andrew J.] - b. 1889; d. 1972
PEABODY
Marietta Tree - b. 1917; d. 1991
PECKHAM
Ada F. [wife of William M.] - b. 1875; d. 1965
Ada M. [dau. of William M. and Ada F.] - b. 1906; d. 1938
Evelyn L. [wife of G. Frazier] - b. 1905
G. Frazier [husb. of Evelyn L.] - b. 1899; d. 1995
Hope M. [wife of William M. Jr.] - b. 1918
William M. [husb. of Ada F.] - b. 1873; d. 1960
William M. Jr. [husb. of Hope M.] - b. 1913; d. 1985
PERKINS
Pamela L. [wife of Val D.] - b. 1947
Val D. [husb. of Pamela L.] - b. 1946
PERRY
Charles C. [husb. of Martha A.] - b. 1844; d. 1905
Martha A. [wife of Charles C.] - b. 1849; d. 1921
PERVEAR
Ada R. (wife of Arthur H.) - b. 1872; d. 1928
Arthur H. (husb. of Ada R.) - b. 1869; d. 1937
Caroline H. [wife of Fred] - b. 1915
Fred [husb. of Caroline H.] - b. 1907; d. 1991
Guy D. - [d.?] 16 June 1937
John E. [husb. of Prudence J.] - b. 1916; d. 1998
Pamela [dau. of John E. and Prudence J.?] - b. 1948
Prudence J. [wife of John E.] - b. 1920; d. 1998
PETRIE
[Mary - see REYNOLDS]

PHELPS
John A. [husb. of Virginia S.] - b. 13 September 1921; d. 23 May 1984
Virginia S. [wife of John A.] - b. 5 February 1921
PHILLIPS
Augustus D. [husb. of Mary Craig] - b. 1898; d. 1975
Carroll A. - b. 8 February 1885; d. 1 November 1929
Cora (SAVAGE; [wife of Frederick I.]) - b. 1859; d. 1924
[Emily - see REYNOLDS]
Frederick I. [husb. of Cora (SAVAGE)] - b. 1852; d. 1926
Luther S. - b. 10 May 1891; d. 24 December 1960
Mary Craig [wife of Augustus D.] - b. 1900; d. 1973
PIERCE
C. Eliot (husb. of Dora (REDWAY)) - b. 1914; d. 1999
Dora (REDWAY; wife of C. Eliot) - b. 1920
[Sandra - see McILHENNY]
PORTER
[Katherine Disston - see HOPKINS]
RALPH
Adelma S. [wife of Isaac E.] - b. 13 August 1875; d. 15 April 1960
Isaac E. [husb. of Adelma S.] - b. 23 March 1872; d. 27 May 1951
Fred S. Jr. - [b. and d.?] 1938
S. Edward - b. 8 July 1909; d. 20 February 1991
REDWAY
[Dora - see PIERCE]
REED
Alvah L. [husb. of Lettie S.] - b. 1877; d. 1946
Annabel - b. 1862; d. 1927
Beatrice - [no dates]
[Clara J. [REED?] - see MURPHY]
E. Maitland - b. 1905; d. 1909
Edward R. - b. 1851; d. 1917
[Elma A. [REED?] - see JOHNSON]
Elwood B. - b. 1902; d. 1961
Ethel M. - b. 1884; d. 1982
Ezra D. [husb. of Lillian W.] - b. 1893; d. 1956
Florence T. - b. 1882; d. 1939
Haline F. - b. 1918; d. 1995
Harold L. - b. 1893; d. 1946
infant (son of Jared R. and Olevia [sic] A. (HIGGINS)) - [b. and?] d. 12 May 1875
Jared R. (husb. of Olevia [sic] A. (HIGGINS)) - b. 1836; d. 1920
Katharine C. - b. 1880; d. 1946
[Kim - see BURCH]
Lettie S. [wife of Alvah L.] - b. 1877; d. 1940
Lillian W. [wife of Ezra D.] - b. 1903; d. 1990
Mark H. - b. 1879; d. 1953
Mary O. - b. 1902; d. 1987
Olevia [sic] A. (HIGGINS; wife of Jared R.) - b. 1843; d. 1909
Rena - b. 1897; d. 1984
REID
[Helen - see LUNT]
RENAULT
Joseph Paul - b. 25 January 1920; d. 14 November 1999

REYNOLDS
Abbie Adelma - b. 1897; d. 1960
Abbie E. - b. 1857; d. 1945
Adelma (dau. of A[lfred?]. S. Jr. and M. C. [no stones]) - b. 10 April 1915; d. 23 January 1919
Albert R. - b. 1905; d. 1978
Albert W. - b. 1 May 1854; d. 9 February 1912
Alfred S. - b. 1859; d. 1933
Arthur W. - b. 1884; d. 1907
Austin S. (husb. of Dora K.) - b. 1878; d. 1929
Cora D. [wife of William W.] - b. 1858; d. 1924
Dora K. (wife of Austin S.) - b. 1874; d. 1955
Emily (PHILLIPS) - b. 1889; d. 1984
Foster - [b. and d.?] 1 May 1923
Hazel [R. or M.][2] - b. 1893; d. 1982
Horace Roberts [husb. of Mary Petrie[10]] - b. 1886; d. 1974
Jackson L. [husb. of Louise A.] - b. 14 October 1889; d. 17 February 1959
Keith A. [husb. of Mila M.] - b. 1923
Louise A. [wife of Jackson L.] - b. 1 October 1913; d. 14 September 1993
Mary C. - b. 1903; d. 1925
Mary Petrie[10] [wife of Horace Roberts] - b. 1886; d. 1973
Mila M. [wife of Keith A.] - b. 1931; d. 1967
Myrtle E. - b. 1893; d. 1908
Ralph W. - b. 23 November 1891; d. 6 November 1918, France
Sarah H. - b. 1864; d. 1935
[Shirley - see MCGARR]
William Eugene - b. 9 April 1894; d. 14 April 1980
William W. [husb. of Cora D.] - b. 1852; d. 1922

RIANHARD
Eleanor (COOMBS) - b. 12 February 1939; d. 16 October 1997

RIVERS
Henry Channing [husb. of Lydia (SATTERLEE)] - b. 1917; d. 1996
Lydia (SATTERLEE; [wife of Henry Channing]) - b. 1926; d. 1992

ROBERTS
Catharine G. (wife of Capt. Horace D.) - b. 27 November 1835; d. 21 November 1918
Deborah (wife of William) - d. 23 February 1876 Æ 68 y., 20 d.
Deborah M. (wife of Capt. Franklin B.) - b. 11 November 1831; d. 8 February 1917
Franklin B. (Capt.; husb. of Deborah M.) - d. 29 September 1875 Æ 48 y., 1 m.
Horace D. (Capt.; husb. of Catharine G.) - d. 7 December 1886 Æ 52 y., 9 m., 11 d.
infant (child of Capt. Franklin B. and Deborah M.) - [no dates]
Ralph V. (son of Capt. Franklin B. and Deborah M.) - d. 16 June 1886, "at sea", Æ 15 y., 11 m., 24 d.
[Selina - see OTTUM]
William (husb. of Deborah) - d. 23 December 1870 Æ 71 y., 9 m.

ROBERTSON
William G. F. - b. 1 March 1935; d. 10 August 1971

ROBINSON
Bernice W. [wife of Clyde M.] - b. 1914
Clyde M. [husb. of Bernice W.] - b. 1910; d. 1966
James E. - b. 1877; d. 1942

ROCK
Madeline (BUCKLIN) - b. 1925; d. 1991
ROGERS
Esther F. [wife of Fred M.] - b. 1908
Fred M. [husb. of Esther F.] - b. 1904
ROSENGARTEN
[Ann - see CIAVARRA]
Frederic Jr. [husb. of Miriam (OSTERHOUT)] - b. 1916; d. 1998
Miriam (OSTERHOUT; [wife of Frederic Jr.]) - b. 1923
SALISBURY
Roy Stephen - b. 28 April 1910; d. 2 November 1991
SAN CARLOS DE PEDROSO
Charlotte (WORTHEN; [wife of Jose Luis]) - b. 1926
Jose Luis [husb. of Charlotte (WORTHEN)] - b. 1914; d. 1997
SATTERLEE
[Lydia - see RIVERS]
SAVAGE
[Annie S. - see FALT]
Augustus Chase (husb. of Emily (MANCHESTER)) - b. 14 March 1832; d. 30 March 1911
Charles K. [son of George A. and Mabelle S.?] - b. 1903; d. 1979
Charles R. (son of Capt. John and Climena) - d. 7 April 1859 Æ 20 y., 1 m., 8 d.
Climena (wife of Capt. John) - d. 27 August 1884 Æ 81 y., 7 m.
[Cora - see PHILLIPS]
Emily (MANCHESTER; wife of Augustus Chase) - b. 28 August 1834; d. 25 June 1914
Emily C. (dau. of Capt. John and Climena) - d. 23 July 1858 Æ 23 y., 3 m., 27 d.
Emily (NICHOLSON) - b. 1875; d. 1941
Ernestine (DAVIS; wife of Richard Manchester) - b. 1913
George A. [husb. of Mabelle S.] - b. 1873; d. 1922
George A. Jr. [son of George A. and Mabelle S.] - b. 1911; d. 1961
H. Mardell ([SAVAGE?]; husb. of Verna F.) - b. 1892; d. 1926
[Hannah - see SMALLIDGE]
Herman L. - b. 1855; d. 1913
infants (2) (children of Capt. John and Climena) - [no dates]
John (husb. of Sarah) - d. 27 February 1816 Æ 60 y.; ("a soldier of the Revolution" [Revolutionary War])
John (Capt.; husb. of Climena) - d. 26 August 1868 Æ 67 y., 4 m.
John (son of Capt. John and Climena) - d. 25 March 1857 Æ 19 y., 10 m., 14 d.
John Chase - b. 1874; d. 1938
John Milton (son of Augustus Chase and Emily (MANCHESTER)) - d. 7 February 1858 Æ 11 m., 22 d.
John Nicholson - b. 1905; d. 1928
Julia [SAVAGE?] - [no dates]
Mabelle S. [wife of George A.] - b. 1877; d. 1965
Mary Louise - b. 1910; d. 1997
Orie E. ("infant dau." of Augustus Chase and Emily (MANCHESTER)) - [...][3]
Richard Manchester (husb. of Ernestine (DAVIS)) - b. 1908; d. 1985
Samuel T. (son of Capt. John and Climena) - d. 18 February 1865 Æ 23 y., 9 m.
Samuel T. H. (son of Capt. John and Climena) - d. 4 January 1841 Æ 10 y., 8 m., 21 d.
Samuel Thomas - b. 1906; d. 1939

Sarah (wife of John) - d. 28 December 1851 Æ 87 y.
Smith P. (son of Capt. John and Climena) - d. 15 March 1843 Æ 14 y., 10 m., 15 d.; ("was drowned")
Stephen Ralph - b. 1946; d. 1979
Verna F. (wife of H. Mardell [SAVAGE?]) - b. 1898; d. 1978

SCOTT
[Anna - see KENNEDY]

SCULL
David - b. 1917; d. 1989

SEAVEY
Ai R. [SEAVEY?] - [no dates]
Annie C. (wife of Harry V.) - b. 1885; d. 1945
Arthur - b. 1904; d. 1922
Charlotte Lorraine (dau. of Harry V. and Annie C.) - b. 24 December 1918; d. 18 July 1921
Donald R. - b. 1928; d. 1988
Harry Burton - b. 8 December 1908; d. 11 April 1962
Harry V. (husb. of Annie C.) - b. 1878; d. 1956
Hollis [SEAVEY?] - [no dates]
J. H. [SEAVEY?] - [no dates]
J. H. Jr. [SEAVEY?] - [no dates]
Margaret I. (wife of Richard B.) - b. 15 May 1847; d. 24 February 1928
Olga I. - b. 1931; d. 1967
Richard B. (husb. of Margaret I.) - b. 21 May 1845; d. 10 February 1931
Rita A. - b. 1939; d. 1973
Ruth [SEAVEY?] - b. 1905; d. 1947
"twins" [SEAVEY?] - [no dates]
V. M. [SEAVEY?] - [no dates]
William H. - b. 1900; d. 1949

SETON-JANSEN
Dirk Jan (husb. of Elisabeth [sic] Thorne[10]) - b. 24 June 1895; d. 23 December 1959
Elisabeth [sic] Thorne[10] (wife of Dirk Jan) - b. 9 October 1896; d. 22 September 1980

SINCLAIR
Amos E. (husb. of Noreva J.) - b. 1868; d. 1956
Noreva J. (wife of Amos E.) - b. 1871; d. 1951

SMALL
Charles N. [husb. of Mary P.] - b. 1872; d. 1945
Mary P. [wife of Charles N.] - b. 1879; d. 1975

SMALLIDGE
Abram G. (son of Capt. Nathan and Hannah R.) - b. 1849; d. 1849
Anna E. [wife of Samuel O.] - b. 1859; d. 1940
Arthur R. (son of Capt. Nathan and Hannah R.) - b. 1852; d. 1854
Arthur R. (son of Capt. Nathan and Hannah R.) - d. 23 March 1857 Æ 2 y., 3 m.
Clifford S. - b. 1931; d. 1980
Clifford Warren - b. 15 November 1906; d. 17 June 1936
Earl N. - b. 1911; d. 1985
[Eber or Eben][2] (son of Capt. Nathan and Hannah R.) - b. 1866; d. 12 July 1866 Æ 6 m., 18 d.
Elmer E. [husb. of S. Louise] - b. 27 April 1861; d. 28 October 1915
Galen Irving - b. 15 September 1898; "lost at sea" 10 March 1941
H. Nathalie [wife of Robert L.] - b. 20 September 1896; d. 26 August 1987
Hannah (SAVAGE; wife of Timothy 2nd) - d. 1863 Æ [not given]; bur. Otter Creek[4]

Hannah R. (wife of Capt. Nathan) - b. 1822; d. 1910
Herbert L. - b. 1860; d. 1931
Hugh D. - b. 16 July 1925; d. 7 April 1947
Inez E. - b. 1884; d. 1904
James H. - b. 1879; d. 1966
John W. - b. 1869; d. 1870
Josiah (husb. of Nancy M.) - b. 1826; d. 1905
Laura E. - b. 1876; d. 1946
Lois (PAGE) - b. 1900; d. 1966
Mary E. - b. 1851; d. 1928
Mary S. - b. 1854; d. 1938
N. Carlton - b. 1846; d. 1906
N. Irving - b. 1876; d. 1933
Nancy M. (wife of Josiah) - b. 1834; d. 1904
Nathan (Capt.; husb. of Hannah R.) - b. 1817; d. 28 December 1874 Æ 57 y., 1 m., 24 d.
Nathan R. - b. 20 December 1929; d. 5 March 1999
Proctor - b. 1847; d. 1925
[Rebecca - see STANLEY]
Robert L. [husb. of H. Nathalie] - b. 13 October 1896; d. 14 January 1982
S. Louise [wife of Elmer E.] - b. 22 April 1859; d. 3 January 1940
Samuel O. [husb. of Anna E.] - b. 1858; d. 1938
Timothy 2nd (husb. of Hannah (SAVAGE)) - d. 1866 Æ [not given]
Winfield - b. 1872; d. 1893

SMITH

Augusta Anne (wife of Victor Reginald) - b. 1873; d. 1961
C. Frances - b. 1909; d. 1929
Clarence L. - b. 21 November 1912; d. 25 February 1967
infant (son of Victor Reginald and Augusta Anne) - [b. and d.?] 17 June 1906
Lucy H. (wife of Richard A.) - b. 1919
[Mary Wheeler - see Mabel Smith (BISHOP) CROMWELL]
Richard A. (husb. of Lucy H.) - b. 1916; d. 1987
Stephen Smallidge - b. 11 September 1907; d. 29 December 1908
Victor Reginald (husb. of Augusta Anne) - b. 1873; d. 1926
Victor Reginald - b. 6 April 1912; d. 1 February 1914

SPRAGUE

Joshua S. - b. 21 April 1980; d. 26 March 1999

SPURLING

Dorothy B[RANSCOM?]. [wife of Maynard E.] - b. 1892; d. 1921
Emma M. (wife of Francis G.) - b. 1856; d. 1950
Erwin L. [husb. of Louise G.] - b. 1911; d. 1988
Francis B. - b. 12 June 1887; d. 14 December 1909
Francis G. (husb. of Emma M.) - b. 1854; d. 1944
Louise G. [wife of Erwin L.] - b. 1914; d. 1992
Maynard E. [husb. of Dorothy B[RANSCOM?].] - b. 1889; d. 1925

STANLEY

Burnham M. - b. 1902; d. 1970
C. Proctor [husb. of Mary K.] - b. 1904; d. 1992
Clarence G. (husb. of Rebecca (SMALLIDGE)) - b. 1878; d. 1965
Elizabeth L. [wife of Walter B.] - b. 1856; d. 1951
Emma R. - d. 6 October 1883 Æ 49 y., 11 m.
Frank F. (husb. of Linnie P.) - b. 1878; d. 1966

Hannah M. (wife of Capt. William) - d. 26 January 1879 Æ 80 y., 3 m., 19 d.
Linnie P. (wife of Frank F.) - b. 1883; d. 1964
Lionel Smallidge - d. 1906 Æ 8 m.
Lula M. [wife of Woodbury A.] - b. 1905; d. 1987
Mary K. [wife of C. Proctor] - [no dates]
Myra E. - b. 1882; d. 1952
Rebecca (SMALLIDGE; wife of Clarence G.) - b. 1882; d. 1956
Thomas M. - d. 5 September 1884 Æ 62 y., 6 m., 20 d.
Walter B. [husb. of Elizabeth L.] - b. 1853; d. 1933
William (Capt.; husb. of Hannah M.) - d. 31 July 1860 Æ 61 y., 10 m.
William - d. 7 March 1885 Æ 65 y., 10 m., 15 d.
Woodbury A. [husb. of Lula M.] - b. 1903; d. 1982

STUART
[Elizabeth - see Lincoln CROMWELL]

SULLIVAN
Bernice G. (wife of Sumner B.) - b. 1899; d. 1972
George C. - b. 11 June 1924; d. 26 February 1997 Æ 72 y.
Sumner B. (husb. of Bernice G.) - b. 1885; d. 1942

TATINA
Maddalena Marchi - b. 30 August 1892; d. 18 November 1984

TAYLOR
Carlton A. Jr. "Jerry" - b. 5 August 1931; d. 13 September 1953

THOMPSON
Maria Ames - b. 2 October 1921; d. 29 October 1993

THORNE
[Elisabeth [sic] - see SETON-JANSEN]

TINKER
Elmaretta L. (wife of Norton H.) - b. 1863; d. 1937
Norton H. (husb. of Elmaretta L.) - b. 1858; d. 1934

TOURTELOTTE
Erbern [husb. of Olive W.?] - b. 1929
Mildred E. [wife of Roy E.] - b. 1903; d. 1984
Olive W. [wife of Erbern?] - b. 1909
Roy E. [husb. of Mildred E.] - b. 1905; d. 1980

TOWERS
Frederic [sic] C. Jr. - b. 25 March 1961; d. 13 August 1979

TRACY
[Eleanor - see BURR]
Georgia A. [wife of Selden R.] - b. 3 September 1865; d. 30 December 1960[9]
Katharine F. [wife of Samuel. Edwin?] - b. 1891; d. 1988
[Laura - see McCUE]
Samuel Edwin [husb. of Katharine F.?] - b. 1892; d. 1955
Samuel Edwin Jr. - b. 1917; d. 1985
Selden R. [husb. of Georgia A.] - b. 23 August 1865; d. 13 October 1921

TUCKER
Anne N. - [no dates]
Milton "Butch" - [no dates]
Persis P. - [no dates]
Stacy H. - [no dates]

TURNER
Caroline S. - b. 1880; d. 1971
George E. - b. 1875; d. 1962

Harold B. - b. 1885; d. 1962
VAN DER KAR
Arthur L. (Major; [husb. of Margaret "Peg"]) - b. 1915
Margaret "Peg" [wife of Major Arthur L.] - b. 1915; d. 1986
VITELLI
Girolamo - b. 24 September 1911; d. 6 August 1995
WAGNER [includes WAGNOR]
Almenia (HERRICK; [wife of Walter Parker]) - b. 1880; d. 1951
[Geraldine - see BRANSCOM]
[Leola - see BUCKLIN]
Walter Parker [husb. of Almenia (HERRICK)] - b. 1879; d. 1955
WALLACE
Burnham E. (husb. of M. E. [no stone]) - b. 1934; d. 1972
Clayton E. - b. 1899; d. 1955
Linda Sue (dau. of Burnham E. and M. E. [no stone]) - [b. and d.?] 24 May 1955
[Lois - see EATON]
Reta [sic] M. - b. 1880; d. 1961
Sandra (ADAMS) - b. 1935; d. 1985
Shirley Woodman - b. 1 February 1924; d. 21 November 1982
WASGATT
Davis - [no dates]
Eliza J. - [no dates]
Francina - [no dates]
infant [WASGATT?] - [no dates]
James - [no dates]
Sarah - [no dates]
WHITMORE
Lora M. - b. 1863; d. 1944
WHITTAKER-CONTRE
Katherine M. (JAMES) - b. 9 March 1913; d. 15 January 1991
WILCOX
Edgar M. [husb. of Ruth R.] - b. 1899; d. 1967
Ruth R. [wife of Edgar M.] - b. 1900; d. 1990
WILLIAMS
[Grace Eleanor "Gracie" - see MCPHETERS]
WILSON
Edward (son of Lewis A. and Lina (MACLEAN)) - b. 1914; d. 1914
Lewis A. (husb. of Lina (MACLEAN)) - b. 1871; d. 1958
Lina (MACLEAN; wife of Lewis A.) - b. 1877; d. 1949
Robert D. "Buckwheat" (Dr.) - b. 29 June 1926; d. 5 June 1996
WINSLOW
Cora B. - b. 1870; d. 1946
Fay R. - b. 1901; d. 1949
Walter E. - b. 22 June 1897; d. 10 March 1949
WINTERSTEEN
Mary - b. 18 June 1871; d. 4 March 1963
WOLFERT
Frances S. - b. 5 April 1904; d. 8 October 1983
WOODMAN
Rachel F. (MANCHESTER; wife of Donald W. [no stone]) - b. 1893; d. 1976
WORTHEN
[Charlotte - see SAN CARLOS DE PEDROSO]

Charlotte Irving (wife of Nathaniel Treat) - b. 1903; d. 1983
Nathaniel Treat (husb. of Charlotte Irving) - b. 1890; d. 1974

WRIGHT
Anna Lewis [wife of Miers Fisher] - b. 15 July 1892; d. 4 May 1975
Miers Fisher [husb. of Anna Lewis] - b. 6 July 1891; d. 11 July 1945

YOUNGHANS
Abbie D. J. [wife of John W.] - b. 1888; d. 1975
John W. [husb. of Abbie D. J.] - b. 1880; d. 1973

[...]
Constantenos - [b. and d.?] 25 July 1928

Notes:
[1]Stone worn.
[2]Different on different stones.
[3]Remainder of stone below ground.
[4]No stone found in Otter Creek Cemetery (Mount Desert - 10).
[5]No ten or unit's digit given on stone.
[6]A new stone, replacing the temporary marker from which this information was taken, does not have the middle initial (F.), "Cookie", or age at death.
[7]A new stone, replacing the temporary marker from which this information was taken, does not have the day and month of birth and death, or the age at death.
[8]Relationship between Francis E. and Huldah B. (son and mother), date of birth of Huldah B., and date of death and age at death of Francis E. are all clear on the gravestones.
[9]In 1960, a 6 has been engraved on an (incorrect) 8.
[10]To determine if this is a maiden name will require further research.
[11]It is not clear from the gravestones if the surname is BURBANK or DODGE.

Smallidge Cemetery
(Mount Desert - 12)

Location/directions. North of Sinclair Road, Northeast Harbor. From the traffic light at the north end of Mount Desert Island, go straight ahead (south) onto Routes 102/198. In approximately 4.2–4.3 miles, at the traffic light at the intersection of Routes 102/198 and 198, turn left on Route 198. Travel about 6.5 miles to the village of Northeast Harbor. Turn right onto Summit Road and follow it as it curves to the right. In about 0.1–0.2 miles, turn right onto Millbrook Road. Follow this road approximately 0.3–0.4 miles to the intersection (on the left) with Sinclair Road. Turn left onto Sinclair Road, and a path leading to the cemetery is on the right in about 0.1–0.2 miles.

History. —

Notes. A portion of this cemetery is enclosed by pipes set between granite posts. There are two openings in this enclosure. Many of the pipes are rusting and/or bent. In the area adjacent to one side of the enclosed portion of the cemetery are two engraved stones and several unengraved ones that apparently mark graves. In addition, there are stumps of many large trees that were cut down in the late 1990s.

Names and dates on gravestones and other markers. [14 May 1999]

FARRIS
- [Evelyn - see KNOWLES]

GOODWIN
- Mary E. (STANLEY; dau. of Peter STANLEY and Maria [no stones]) - d. 6 February 1849 Æ 17 y.

KNOWLES
- Evelyn (FARRIS; [wife of Jerome [Henry?] Jr.]) - b. 16 May 1906; d. 26 January 1993
- Jerome [Henry?] Jr. [husb. of Evelyn (FARRIS)] - b. 24 May 1906; d. 23 May 1992
- Jerome Henry [husb. of L. Belle (SMALLIDGE)] - b. 22 August 1870; d. 26 August 1933
- L. Belle (SMALLIDGE; [wife of Jerome Henry]) - b. 17 October 1871; d. 31 October 1959

MANCHESTER
- [Comfort - see STANLEY]
- Thomas - d. 20 January 1820 Æ 23 y.

SMALLIDGE
- Asa F. [husb. of Phebe R. S.] - b. 22 September 1832; d. 2 August 1904
- Comfort M[inerva?]. - b. 13 September 1863; d. 6 June 1882
- [L. Belle - see KNOWLES]
- Phebe R. S. [wife of Asa F.] - b. 7 February 1832; d. 21 September 1899

STANLEY
- Almenia T. (wife of Nathan H.) - d. 15 February 1863 Æ 32 y.
- Comfort (MANCHESTER; wife of Joseph) - b. 3 December 1803; d. 15 November 1896
- Joseph (husb. of Comfort (MANCHESTER)) - b. 17 November 1795; d. 20 November 1873
- [Mary E. - see GOODWIN]
- Nathan H. (husb. of Almenia T.) - d. 15 December 1887 Æ 64 y., 10 m., 5 d.

Gravestone of Capt. David Bartlett (Bartlett Island Cemetery 3, Mount Desert - 13).

Bartlett Island Cemetery 3
(Mount Desert - 13)

Location/directions. East of north-south road and west of Great Cove, Bartlett Island. From the boat landing on the east side of the island, follow the road approximately 0.6 miles to a T-intersection. Turn right, and the cemetery is set back from the right side of the road in about 0.3 miles. Follow an old road for approximately 100 feet to a trail on the right that leads to the cemetery.

History. —

Notes. The cemetery is enclosed by a gated wood post and rail fence. The posts have decorative tops, and there are four courses of boards for rails. The ground vegetation, mostly moss with some ferns and spruce seedlings, is cut and trimmed.

Names and dates on gravestones and other markers. [21 August 1999]

BARTLETT

Abraham (husb. of Jerusha) - d. 25 May 1851 Æ 55 y., 6 m.

Amanda (dau. of Capt. David and Ro[si or ze]lla[1] G.) - d. 1[1 or 4?][2] April 1848 Æ [...][2]

David (Capt.; husb. of Ro[si or ze]lla[1] G.) - d. 19 March 1871 Æ 75 y., 2 m., 5 d.

David W. (son of Capt. David and Ro[si or ze]lla[1] G.) - d. 24 March 1848 Æ [5?][2] y., 1 m., 14 d.

Edwin (husb. of Joanna) - b. 17 October 1826; d. 19 September 1889

Elwell W. (son of Edwin and Joanna) - b. 28 March 1851; d. 3 October 1856

Emily (dau. of Abraham and Jerusha) - d. 14 November 1835 Æ 1 y., 6 m.

George W. - b. 11 December 1858; d. 9 February 1911

Gustina (dau. of Edwin and Joanna) - b. 13 June 1852; d. 20 January 1867

Horatio S. (son of Capt. David and Ro[si or ze]lla[1] G.) - d. 26 July 1846 Æ 6 y., 4 m., 4 d.

Hosea (son of Capt. David and Ro[si or ze]lla[1] G.) - d. 1 January 1826 Æ 3 m., 15 d.

Isaac (husb. of Isabel) - d. 18 November 1842 Æ 48 y., 7 m., 6 d.

Isabel (wife of Isaac) - d. 5 October 1871 Æ 74 y., 7 m., 8 d.

Jerusha (wife of Abraham) - d. 23 June 1871 Æ 70 y., 2 m.

Joanna (wife of Edwin) - b. 23 March 1827; d. 23 January 1899

John R. (son of James and Mary [no stones]) - d. 10 May 1839 Æ 21 y.

Mercy F. - b. 15 January 1831; d. 27 May 1898

Romelia (dau. of Capt. David and Ro[si or ze]lla[1] G.) - d. 22 July 1848 Æ 14 m., 12 d.

Ro[si or ze]lla[1] G. (wife of Capt. David) - d. 13 June 1876 Æ 74 y., 3 m., 26 d. [Rozella - see HAYNES]

Sophia F. (dau. of Edwin and Joanna) - b. 1 December 1863; d. 16 February 186[4 or 5][1]

DIX

Carrie E. (dau. of John and Emily M. [no stones]) - d. 18 December 1862 Æ 2 y., 2 m., 22 d.

FREEMAN

Paris G. (son of Daniel and Murcy [sic] [no stones]) - d. 4 September 1863 Æ 18 y., 5 m.; ("was drowned")

GILLEY

Lorenda (wife of John M. [no stone]) - d. 30 May 1867 Æ 43 y., 8 m., 10 d.

HAYNES
Benjamin F. (son of Benjamin F. [no stone] and Rozella (BARTLETT)) - d. 4 September 1863 Æ 17 y., 6 m.; ("was drowned")
Rozella (BARTLETT; dau. of Capt. David BARTLETT and Ro[si or ze]lla[1] G.; wife of Benjamin F. [no stone]) - d. 19 February 1852 Æ 31 y., 6 m., 14 d.
RAYMOND
H. C. (Capt.; husb. of Sophronia) - b. 22 January 1827; d. 11 November 1891
Sophronia (wife of Capt. H. C.) - d. 29 June 1892 Æ 55 y.
TIBBETS
Ralph E. - b. 31 January 1881; d. 17 October 1895
[...]
[El?]well[2] W. - d. [...][2]
[...][2] - d. 20 [...][2] 18[...][2] Æ [11?][2] y., 7 m., 7 d.

Notes:
[1]Different on different stones.
[2]Stone worn and/or broken.

Bartlett Island Cemetery 2
(Mount Desert - 14)

Location/directions. East of north-south road and west of Great Cove, Bartlett Island. From the boat landing on the east side of the island, follow the road approximately 0.6 miles to a T-intersection. Turn right, and the cemetery is set back from the right side of the road in about 0.3 miles. Follow an old road for approximately 100 feet to a trail on the right. Turn onto that trail, and the single grave is on the left in about 25 feet.

History. —

Notes. See below.

Names and dates on gravestones and other markers. [21 August 1999]
There are no stones—only a wire enclosure around the apparent grave site and a crucifix fastened to a tree.

Bartlett Island Cemetery 1

(Mount Desert - 15)

Location/directions. North end of Bartlett Island. From the boat landing on the east side of the island, follow the road approximately 0.6 miles to a T-intersection. Turn right, and follow this road approximately 1.4 miles to the entrance of a very large pasture. The cemetery is in the northwest portion of this pasture.

History. —

Notes. The cemetery is enclosed by a gated post and rail fence. There are four courses of round rails spiked to spruce posts. The grass is cut and trimmed. Some stones are propped up or laying on the ground.

Names and dates on gravestones and other markers. [21 August 1999]

BARTLETT

Augustus - b. 20 February 1841; d. 1 November 1888
Beulah (dau. of Quincy N. and Caddie M. [no stones]) - d. 13 October 1890 Æ 2 m.
Calvin K. - "lost at sea" 24 April 1846 Æ 23 y.
Christopher (husb. of Mary) - d. 10 August 1820 Æ 56 y.
Christopher (Capt.; husb. of Ruth) - d. 1 September 1868 Æ 70 y., 10 m., 22 d.
Christopher (Capt.) - "lost at sea" 24 April 1846 Æ 25 y.
David G. (husb. of Kathryn E.) - b. 23 June 1832; d. 28 November 1904
Etherlinda (dau. of Capt. Christopher and Ruth) - d. 1 January 1867 Æ 24 y., 11 m.
James (husb. of Mary) - "lost at sea" 24 April 1846 Æ 56 y.
James C. - d. 16 May 1886 Æ 39 y., 6 m., 28 d.
John F. - d. 14 August 1870 Æ 32 y., 1 m., 14 d.
Kathryn E. (wife of David G.) - b. 1834; d. 1910
Mary (wife of Christopher) - d. 5 March 1857 Æ 87 y., 1 m., 19 d.
Mary (wife of James) - d. 3 August 1863 Æ 71 y.
Nettie Rozenia (dau. of Quincy N. and Caddie M. [no stones]) - d. 22 September 1895 Æ 16 y.
Ruth (wife of Capt. Christopher) - d. 1 May 1899 Æ 87 y., 11 m., 10 d.
Samuel - d. 16 December 1851 Æ 38 y.

FRIEND

Benjamin (husb. of Ruth) - d. 1 October 1863 Æ 77 y., 1 m., 5 d.
Ruth (wife of Benjamin) - d. 14 September 1852 Æ 62 y., 8 m.

GALLEY

Joanna (wife of John [no stone]) - d. 3 June 1858 Æ 49 y., 8 m.

OBER

Daniel (husb. of Hannah A.) - b. 14 May 1822; d. 10 April 1896
Hannah A. (wife of Daniel) - b. 9 October 1825; d. 22 February 1902
Ida (dau. of Daniel and Hannah A.) - d. 21 February 1863 Æ 3 y., 2 m.
Ida F. (dau. of Daniel and Hannah A.) - d. 21 May 1886 Æ 17 y., 4 m., 10 d.
Mary E. (dau. of Daniel and Hannah A.) - d. 21 February 1891 Æ 19 y., 1 m., 17 d.

PEPPER

Charles H. - b. 10 January 1866; d. 11 October 1889

Brown Cemetery
(Mount Desert - 16)

Location/directions. Set back from the east side of Sargent Drive. From the traffic light at the north end of Mount Desert Island, go straight ahead (south) onto Routes 102/198. In approximately 4.2–4.3 miles, at the traffic light at the intersection of Routes 102/198 and 198, turn left on Route 198. Continue about 2.6 miles to the intersection (on the right) with Sargent Drive. Turn right onto Sargent drive, and the cemetery is on the left in aproximately 0.5–0.6 miles.

History. —

Notes. No fence encloses this cemetery, but the apparent burial area is bounded by granite. Also there is a granite retaining wall and steps at the edge of the road.

Names and dates on gravestones and other markers. [14 May 1999]
BROWN
Abbie L. (wife of Albert L.) - b. 13 February 1843; d. 4 December 1915
Albert L. (husb. of Abbie L.) - b. 9 July 1841; d. 13 December 1902; (member of Co. C, 8th Maine Regiment [Civil War])
Albert Lewis "Al" (Capt.) - b. 19 June 1906; d. 2 December 1981
NILSON
Minnie A. (wife of Ferdinand [no stone]) - b. 1869; d. 1907

Atherton and Mikhalapov Graves
(Mount Desert - 17)

Location/directions. Set back from east side of Beech Hill Road. From the traffic light at the north end of Mount Desert Island, go straight ahead (south) onto Routes 102/198. In approximately 5.2 miles (and at the south end of the village of Somesville), turn right onto Pretty Marsh Road (Route 102). In about 0.2–0.3 miles turn left onto Beech Hill Road. (Note: this turn is easy to pass as it is just over a hill and in a curve.) In approximately 1.9–2.0 miles, the stones are on the left near the trunks of three tall trees (two spruce and one birch).

History. —

Notes. The ground in front of (on the road side of) the stones is free of any obscuring woody vegetation. Recently (1999?) a limb that overhung the Atherton stones was removed. There is no enclosure.

Names and dates on gravestones and other markers. [17 May 1999]
ATHERTON
Mary (wife of William W.) - d. 25 July 1883 Æ 80 y., 3 m.
William W. (husb. of Mary) - d. 4 July 1876 Æ 76 y., 8 m.
MIKHALAPOV
George S. - d. 3 November 1971 Æ 65 y., 9 m., 7 d.

Seal Harbor Cemetery
(Mount Desert - 18)

Location/directions. West of Jordan Pond Road, Seal Harbor. From the traffic light at the north end of Mount Desert Island, go straight ahead (south) onto Routes 102/198. In approximately 4.2–4.3 miles, at the traffic light at the intersection of Routes 102/198 and 198, turn left on Route 198. Follow this road for about 5.6–5.7 miles to the intersection (on the left) with Route 3. Turn left onto Route 3. In approximately 3.0 miles, there is a T-intersection with a low monument forming an island in the road. Turn left and continue about 0.4 miles where Route 3 bears to the right and Jordan Pond Road is straight ahead. Go straight onto Jordan Pond Road, and the entrance to the cemetery is on the left in about 0.6–0.7 miles.

History. —

Notes. This cemetery is well maintained. There are many shrubs, both evergreen and deciduous, and there is water available. The roads are gravel. No fence encloses the cemetery.

Names and dates on gravestones and other markers. [11 May 1999]

ADAMS
- Mark W. - b. 18 December 1839; d. 3 September 1894

ALLAN
- Mildred H. [wife of Richard A.] - b. 1906
- Richard A. [husb. of Mildred H.] - b. 1911; d. 1991
- [...] [headstone only]

ALLEY
- Aubrey L. (husb. of Ethel V.) - b. 1875; d. 1944
- Ethel V. (wife of Aubrey L.) - b. 1884; d. 1968

ANDREWS
- E. Roberta [wife of Ernest F.] - b. 1917; d. 1977
- Ernest F. (husb. of Pearle M.) - b. 1894; d. 1962
- Ernest F. [husb. of E. Roberta] - b. 27 December 1918; d. 1 October 1993
- Pearle M. (wife of Ernest F.) - b. 1896; d. 1983

ATWOOD
- Dora S. [wife of Ernest A.] - b. 1883; d. 1950
- Edwin H. [husb. of Elizabeth F.] - b. 1910; d. 1978
- Elizabeth F. [wife of Edwin H.] - b. 1907; d. 1975
- Ernest A. [husb. of Dora S.] - b. 1870; d. 1952
- Francis J. - b. 1906; d. 1958
- Phyllis (MILLER) - b. 1907; d. 1988

BAGLEY
- Elbridge[1] L. (husb. of Georgia E.) - b. 1875; d. 1947
- Georgia E. (wife of Elbridge[1] L.) - b. 1881; d. 1946

BEARD
- [Berenice [sic] - see CANDAGE]

BERRY
- Dellcie E. [wife of William M.] - b. 1905
- Harold L. [husb. of Iva M.] - b. 1885; d. 1945
- Iva M. [wife of Harold L.] - b. 1886; d. 1953
- William M. [husb. of Dellcie E.] - b. 1906

BICKFORD
- Agnes L. [wife of Everett S. Sr.?] - b. 1891; d. 1982

Everett S. Sr. [husb. of Agnes L.?] - b. 6 May 1894; d. 7 February 1973

BILLINGS

Berniece [sic] P. - b. 9 January 1892; d. 24 May 1976
Delia E. - b. 11 March 1870; d. 4 September 1951
Evelyn (RITCHIE) - b. 15 August 1900; d. 8 November 1981
Frederick A. - b. 21 October 1862; d. 26 September 1955
John T. - b. 4 October 1900; d. 19 May 1935
[Marie - see WALCH [sic]]
Percy G. - b. 15 September 1894; d. 18 June 1984

BLAISDELL

Heman L. Jr. - b. 1915; d. 1998
Heman L. Sr. [husb. of Jennie G.] - b. 1884; d. 1965
Jennie G. [wife of Heman L. Sr.] - b. 1893; d. 1982

BLAKE

George (son of Alexander C. [no stone] and Georgie A.) - d. 16 August 1875 Æ 1 y., 10 m., 9 d.
Georgie A. (wife of Alexander C. [no stone]) - d. 23 October 1874 Æ 2[3?][2] y., 3 m., 11 d.

BLANCHARD

[...] [headstone, one side]

BOWDEN

Ada S. [wife of Arnold W.] - b. 1908; d. 1996
Arnold W. [husb. of Ada S.] - b. 1906; d. 1970

BRACY

Alice J. (dau. of Capt. John and [Barbara?]) - b. 1852; d. 1870
Augustus E. (son of Capt. John and [Barbara?]) - b. 1855; d. 1863
Barbara (wife of Capt. John) - b. 1810; d. 1866
Berila P. (wife of John) - b. 17 October 1783; d. 11 December 1873
Effie G. [wife of Herman C.] - b. 1882; d. 1982
George W. - b. 31 January 1826; d. 21 October 1899
Hannah A. (wife of Capt. John) - b. 1824; d. 1917
Herman C. [husb. of Effie G.] - b. 1866; d. 1944
John (husb. of Berila P.) - b. 22 January 1761; d. 1 February 1852
John (Capt.; husb. of Barbara and Hannah A.) - b. 1810; d. 1883
Lewis H. [husb. of Lillian P.] - b. 1911; d. 1979
Lillian P. [wife of Lewis H.] - b. 1914; d. 1985
Lucia E. (wife of Herman [no stone]) - d. 17 December 1905 Æ 20 y., 3 m., 18 d.
[Onolee - see MURCH]
Orris P. - b. 14 October 1908; d. 14 March 1970
Priscilla P. - b. 1812; d. 1902
Ulysses S. G. (son of Capt. John and Hannah A.) - b. 1870; d. 1871
William H. (son of John and Berila P.) - b. 5 November 1824; d. 4 August 1857

BREWSTER

Marie C. [wife of Merton T.] - b. 1900; d. 1957
Merton T. [husb. of Marie C.] - b. 1897; d. [no date]

BRISTOL

[Caroline - see DANA]

BROWN

Elmer F. - b. 1921; d. 1960

BRYANT

Aleta B. - b. 1905; d. 1955
Marvin L. - b. 1899; d. 1978

Peter M. - b. 11 June 1952[7]; d. 29 September 1998[7]
[Sheila B[RYANT?]. - see MURRAY]
BUNKER
[Olive J. - see Jennie Ella SMALLIDGE]
BURCH
Alfred "Joey" - [no dates]
Deborah W. - [no dates]
BURKE
John B. "Jack" [husb. of Nina C[ANDAGE].] - b. 1890; d. 1955
Nina C[ANDAGE]. [wife of John B. "Jack"] - b. 1886; d. 1970
BUTLER
Annie (wife of Samuel G.) - b. 1869; d. 1949
Clara F. [wife of Leo E.] - b. 14 January 1904; d. 10 December 1995
[Jennie - see CONARY]
Kathleen (wife of Maurice) - b. 1885; d. 1954
Leo E. [husb. of Clara F.] - b. 10 April 1897; d. 29 November 1971
Maurice (husb. of Kathleen) - b. 1892; d. 1965
[Pauline B[UTLER?]. - see WESCOTT]
Samuel G. (husb. of Annie) - b. 1854; d. 1938
CALLAHAN
Albert (son of William and Deborah P.) - d. 1 January 1878 Æ 27 y.
Alonzo R. - b. 26 June 1854; d. 4 February 1904
Deborah P. (wife of William) - d. 2 September 1896 Æ 70 y.
John W. (son of William and Deborah P.) - d. 26 November 1863 Æ 17 y., 9 m.
Mary A. (dau. of William and Deborah P.) - d. 23 December 1868 Æ 21 y.
Warren E. (son of William and Deborah P.) - d. 1 July 1879 Æ 20 y.
William (husb. of Deborah P.) - b. 3 July 1818; d. 3 February 1901
Wyman J. (son of William and Deborah P.) - d. 12 April 1892 Æ 28 y.
CAMERON
Dwight (Dr.) - b. 6 November 1912; d. 3 August 1987
Dwight F. Jr. (Rev.) - b. 1875; d. 1958
Margaret L. - b. 1918; d. 1981
CAMPBELL
Edward T. [husb. of Lena W.?] - b. 1856; d. 1920
Lena W. [wife of Edward T.?] - b. 1864; d. 1953
CANDAGE
Arthur Hilton [husb. of Meda (PRAY)] - b. 1871; d. 1915
Berenice [sic] (BEARD; wife of Byron W.) - b. 1922
Byron W. (husb. of Berenice [sic] (BEARD)) - b. 1917; d. 1984
Byron Whitefield (husb. of Margaret (SIMONTON)) - b. 1847; d. 1925
Charles A. - b. 1851; d. 1912
Evelyn H. [wife of W. C. Doane] - b. 1884; d. 1956
Laura M. (wife of Samuel W.) - b. 1875; d. 1959
Margaret (SIMONTON; wife of Byron Whitefield) - b. 1845; d. 1935
Meda (PRAY; [wife of Arthur Hilton]) - b. 1874; d. 1957
[Nina C[ANDAGE]. - see BURKE]
S. Augusta "Gusta" (wife of Samuel W.) - b. 1872; d. 1904
Samuel W. (husb. of S. Augusta "Gusta" and Laura M.) - b. 1868; d. 1935
W. C. Doane [husb. of Evelyn H.] - b. 1884; d. 1957
CARPENTER
Edward P. (husb. of Virginia (MACKENZIE)) - b. 25 June 1922

Virginia (MACKENZIE; wife of Edward P.) - b. 5 September 1924; d. 10 August 1992
CARR
Beverly [sic] A. - b. 1956; d. 1984
Norris Erwin Sr. - b. 28 September 1930; d. 26 August 1996
CARTER
Annie H. (WEBBER; wife of Wilbert L.) - b. 1857; d. 1933
Blanche M[ERCHANT?]. [wife of Harry O.] - b. 1886; d. 1970
Calvin B. - b. 1882; d. 1958
Carole (FIELD; [wife of Stetson C.]) - b. 1933; d. 1993
Cecil P. (husb. of Edythe M. [and Ida Laura]) - b. 1900; d. 1981
Earl L. [husb. of Lottie M.] - b. 1905; d. 1976
Edythe M. ([wife of Cecil P.) - b. 1903; d. 1926
Esther E. [wife of Harland A.] - b. 1901; d. 1992
Harland A. [husb. of Esther E.] - b. 1904; d. 1961
Harry O. [husb. of Blanche M[ERCHANT?].] - b. 1880; d. 1923; bur. "at Beech Hill"[3]
Ida Laura [wife of Cecil P.] - b. 1907; d. 1996
John A. - b. 1864; d. 1939
John F. - b. 1895; d. 1944
Josephine A. - b. 1878; d. 1944
Karl F. [husb. of Lyda B.] - b. 1902; d. 1971
Leslie A. - b. 1886; d. 1919
Lottie M. [wife of Earl L.] - b. 1891; d. 1969
Lyda B. [wife of Karl F.] - b. 1903
Newell Edgar - b. 15 January 1895; d. [not given]
Raymond M. - b. 11 November 1896; d. 30 August 1963
Reuben H. (husb. of Susie A.) - b. 1865; d. 1958
Stetson C. [husb. of Carole (FIELD)] - b. 1931
Susie A. (wife of Reuben H.) - b. 1860; d. 1929
Wilbert L. (husb. of Annie H. (WEBBER)) - b. 1856; d. 1918
CLEMENT
Abigail "Abby" (wife of James) - d. 8 November 1891 Æ 77 y., 1 m., 8 d.
Abram S. (son of James 2nd and Eliza J. (SOUTHARD)) - b. 2 May 1860; d. 17 October 1880
Addie L. (wife of Herbert A.) - b. 1863; d. 1941
Alanson E. (husb. of Vesta (SOUTHARD) and Jennie (LIBBY)) - b. 1855; d. 1931
Arthur M. (husb. of Cynthia R[ICHARDSON?].) - b. 1876; d. 1957
Cedelia W. (wife of John) - d. 25 June 1870 Æ 22 y., 11 m., 4 d.
Charles H. (husb. of Sarah C.) - b. 1843; d. 1932
Charlotte (HERRICK; wife of James 2nd) - b. 8 January 1821; d. 11 February 1891
Charlotte Maria [wife of Dr. James Donald] - b. 1888; d. 1986
Cynthia R[ICHARDSON?]. (wife of Arthur M.) - b. 1879; d. 1939
David A. - b. 8 June 1973; d. 21 August 1973
Deborah (wife of John [no stone]) - d. 6 September 1857 Æ 90 y.
Earl T. (son of Charles H. and Sarah C.) - d. 16 July 1890 Æ [...][4] y., 5 m., [3 or 3[...]?][4] d.
Edith M. - b. 1884; d. 1959
Edward C. [husb. of Florence A.] - b. 25 November 1909; d. 26 December 1966
Edwin (son of John and Cedelia W.) - d. 16 December 1873 Æ 7 y., 5 m., 10 d.
Edwin F. (son of Capt. Jacob and Susan U. K.) - d. 18 August 1862 Æ 17 y., 6 m., 15 d.

Eleanor F. (wife of James Donald Jr.) - b. 1925
Eliza J. (SOUTHARD; wife of James 2nd) - b. 2 May 1824; d. 19 November 1863
Florence A. [wife of Edward C.] - b. 1908; d. 1994
Frank L. B. (son of Charles H. and Sarah C.) - d. 23 April 1898 Æ 16 y., 1 m., 17 d.
Fred A. (son of Charles H. and Sarah C.) - d. 25 December 1887 Æ 1 y., 13 d.
Grace E. (wife of Leslie G.) - b. 1896; d. 1922
Herbert A. (husb. of Addie L.) - b. 1857; d. 1908
infant (son of Herbert A. and Addie L.) - [b. and?] d. 2 March 1889
Irving O. [husb. of Mary C.] - b. 1880; d. 1946
Jacob (Capt.; husb. of Susan U. K.) - d. 11 December 1852 Æ 46 y.
James (husb. of Abigail “Abby”) - d. 23 May 1887 Æ 86 y., 10 m., 15 d.
James - b. 1840; d. 1922
James 2nd (husb. of Eliza J. (SOUTHARD) and Charlotte (HERRICK)) - b. 22 March 1814; d. 5 August 1894
James Donald (Dr.; [husb. of Charlotte Maria]) - b. 1888; d. 1948
James Donald Jr. ([son of Dr. James Donald and Charlotte Maria]; husb. of Eleanor F.) - b. 1918; d. 1988
Jean (MACKAY; [wife of Stephen Caldwell]) - b. 1892; d. 1981
Jennie (LIBBY; wife of Alanson E.) - b. 1885; d. 1947
John (husb. of Cedelia W. and Olive C.) - d. 13 January 1905 Æ 66 y., 11 m.
John H. - b. 1924; d. 1983
Katherine B. [wife of Samuel J.?] - b. 1866; d. 1947
Leroy S. - b. 1883; d. 1930
Leslie G. (husb. of Grace E.) - b. 1881; d. 1940
Lydia B. (LYNAM; wife of Samuel J.) - d. 26 July 1897 Æ 48 y., 2 m., 17 d.
Mary C. [wife of Irving O.] - b. 1885; d. 1956
Maurice (son of Herbert A. and Addie L.) - d. 16 October 1895 Æ 8 m., 20 d.
Olive C. (wife of John) - d. 19 November 1898 Æ 58 y., 6 m., 1 d.
Pearl A. - b. 1886; d. 1957
Samuel J. (husb. of Lydia B. (LYNAM) [and Katherine B.?]) - b. 1848; d. 1927
Sarah C. (wife of Charles H.) - b. 1847; d. 1936
Sarah M. (dau. of James and Abigail “Abby”) - d. 13 November 1850 Æ 3 y., 8 m.
Stephen Caldwell [husb. of Jean (MACKAY)] - b. 1895; d. 1936
Susan U. K. (wife of Capt. Jacob) - d. 8 October 1894 Æ 75 y., 10 m., 7 d.
Vesta (SOUTHARD; wife of Alanson E.) - b. 1857; d. 1919

CLOSSON
G. Norman [husb. of Martena O.] - b. 1894; d. 1947
Martena O. [wife of G. Norman] - b. 1899; d. 1978

COBB
Richard A. - b. 1912; d. 1992

COLBURN
Gladys S. [wife of Raymond A.] - b. 1900; d. [no date]
Raymond A. [husb. of Gladys S.] - b. 1896; d. 1961

COLEMAN
John D. - b. 1959; d. 1971

CONARY
Henry T. [husb. of Rosalie L.] - b. 1903; d. 1951
Jennie (BUTLER; [wife of Pearl A.]) - b. 1865; d. 1932
Pearl A. [husb. of Jennie (BUTLER)] - b. 1862; d. 1939
Rosalie L. [wife of Henry T.] - b. 1914

CONVERSE
Jennie M. - b. 1861; d. 1952
COSTON
Barbara I. (HAMOR; wife of Paul A.; mother of Helen, Janie, and Paul [no stones]) - b. 6 January 1922
Charlotte A. (dau. of Earl H. and Ina E.) - d. 20 June 1919 Æ 1 y., 9 m., 26 d.
E. Eddy - b. 1915; d. 1956
Earl H. (husb. of Ina E.) - b. 1886; d. 1955
Ina E. (wife of Earl H.) - b. 1894; d. 1991
Paul A. (husb. of Barbara I. (HAMOR); father of Helen, Janie, and Paul [no stones]) - b. 30 May 1920; d. 15 January 1994
COUSINS
Flora E. (wife of Wellington) - b. 31 October 1856; d. 26 July 1915
Herbert L. - b. 1884; d. 1918
Wellington (husb. of Flora E.) - b. 20 October 1849; d. 25 June 1902
CROCKER
Michael A. - b. 1953; d. 1956
Milton E. - b. 1904; d. 1965
Ricky A. - b. 1954; d. 1956
CUMMINGS
Etta R. (wife of Capt. Fred E.) - b. 1866; d. 1938
Fred E. (Capt.; husb. of Etta R.) - b. 1865; d. 1930
DAMON
Dorothy V. [wife of Llewellyn C.] - b. 1903; d. 1970
Llewellyn C. [husb. of Dorothy V.] - b. 1902; d. 1976
M. Eleanor [wife of Waldo M.] - b. 1902; d. 1976
Waldo M. [husb. of M. Eleanor] - b. 1905; d. 1979
DANA
Caroline (BRISTOL; wife of Edward S.) - b. 30 May 1857, New Haven, Connecticut; d. 7 September 1916, Bar Harbor, Maine
Edward S. (husb. of Caroline (BRISTOL)) - b. 16 November 1849; d. 16 June 1935, New Haven, Connecticut
DAVIS
Daniel - d. 26 January 1894 Æ 57 y., 5 m., 20 d.
DeREVERE
Florence (wife of Robert F.) - b. 1887; d. 1970
Freda B. (wife of Robert E.) - [no dates]
Robert E. (son of Robert F. and Florence; husb. of Freda B.) - b. 1915; d. 1993
Robert F. (husb. of Florence) - b. 1889; d. 1985
DODGE
Albert L. [husb. of Gladys S.] - b. 1892; d. 1948
Annie M. (wife of Samuel J.) - b. 1866; d. 1911
Charles G. - b. 1887; d. 1961
Charles G. Jr. - b. 16 November 1918; d. 15 November 1987
Edwin L. (Capt.) - b. 1863; d. 1934
Gideon P. (husb. of Sarah S.) - d. 20 May 1887 Æ 79 y., 7 m., 12 d.
Gladys S. [wife of Albert L.] - b. 1893; d. 1979
Ida R. (dau. of E. W. and [S.?][4] E. [no stones]) - d. 11 September 1873 Æ 3 y., 4 m., 17 d.
J. Greeley - b. 1866; d. 1901
Lena M. - b. 1869; d. 1951
Lena M. - b. 1887; d. 1982

Lewis H. - b. 1889; d. 1916
Lewis H. - b. 1917; d. 1978
Mina M. - b. 1867; d. 1946
Percy T. - b. 1894; d. 1965
Richard Eddie - b. 1916; d. 1988
Samuel J. (husb. of Annie M.) - [no dates]
Sarah S. (wife of Gideon P.) - d. 5 June 1893 Æ 68 y., 1 m., 24 d.

DONNELL
Grace M. [dau. of Orrin A. and Laura A. (GILLEY)] - b. 1898; d. [no date]
Harvard C. [son of Orrin A. and Laura A. (GILLEY)] - b. 1894; d. 1894
Laura A. (GILLEY; wife of Orrin A.) - b. 1862; d. 1944
Orrin A. (husb. of Laura A. (GILLEY)) - b. 1859; d. 1947
Orrin A. Jr. [son of Orrin A. and Laura A. (GILLEY)] - b. 1909; d. 1942
Theodore A. - b. 1903; d. 1959

DORR
Ambrose M. - b. 1890; d. 1972
Ambrose M. Jr. - b. 1927; d. 1986
Edna L. - b. 1889; d. 1968
Elston A. - b. 1885; d. 1967
Erma E. - b. 1915; d. 1989
Esther C. - b. 1892; d. 1972
Theodore Basil - b. 15 April 1914; d. 13 October 1994
Wilbert N. - b. 5 December 1918; d. 11 December 1993

DOUGLAS
Malcolm Graham - b. 12 August 1886; d. 23 August 1947
Richard Alexander - b. 15 May 1892; d. 12 November 1990

DOW
[Nettie M. - see PHIPPEN]

DRISCOLL
Fred K. M. [husb. of Mabel H.] - b. 1892; d. 1971
Frederick M. - b. 10 September 1920; d. 12 September 1974
Jeanett [sic] (McKENZIE; [wife of Justin A.]) - b. 1871; d. 1928
Justin A. [husb. of Jeanett [sic] (McKENZIE)] - b. 1870; d. 1939
Mabel H. [wife of Fred K. M.] - b. 1891; d. 1953
[Marie D[RISCOLL?]. - see WILLIAMS]

DuLONG
Charlotte [wife of William M.] - b. 1925; d. 1997
William M. [husb. of Charlotte] - b. 1920; d. 1979

DYER
Atwood L. - b. 1896; d. 1950
Lewis B. - b. 2 August 1854; d. 14 November 1912

DYMENT
Charles E. - b. 1902; d. 1937
G. Gordon [husb. of Violet V.] - b. 1877; d. 1957
George G. Jr. - b. 3 April 1923; d. 13 July 1961
Maizie M. (wife of James K. [no stone]) - b. 1908; d. 1936
Violet V. [wife of G. Gordon] - b. 1888; d. 1962

EATON
Kenneth L. Sr. - b. 4 April 1921; d. 10 October 1995

EDDY
Ada A. (wife of George F.) - b. 1863; d. 1935
Angelia - b. 1836; d. 1904

Bertha - b. 1875; d. 1912
Clara - b. 1901; d. 1912
George F. (husb. of Ada A.) - b. 1855; d. 1930
Gregory S. - b. 1868; d. 1934
infant - [no dates]
infant (child of George F. and Ada A.) - [no dates]
Joseph - b. 1826; d. 1902

EMERY
Sarah M. (wife of Ernest [no stone]) - b. 1852; d. 1912

EUSTICE
Dora M. - b. 1893; d. 1979

FARNUM
Wayne W. - b. 1904; d. 1952

FENNELLY
Andrew (husb. of Melinda) - b. 1806; d. 1860
Melinda (wife of Andrew) - b. 1812; d. 1902

FIELD
[Carole - see CARTER]

FORD
Ida M. - b. 1857; d. 1934

FROST
Audrey M. [wife of Robert J.] - b. 1935; d. 1983
Robert J. [husb. of Audrey M.] - b. 1929

FRYE
Georgia (LUNT; [wife of Capt. Ralph John]) - b. 1895; d. 1961
Ralph John (Capt.; [husb. of Georgia (LUNT)]) - b. 10 November 1882; d. 3 April 1956

GATCOMB
John S. - b. 1868; d. 1921

GEYELIN
Frances Healy [wife of Henry Rawle] - b. 17 January 1919; d. 16 August 1988
Henry Rawle [husb. of Frances Healy] - b. 18 August 1918; d. 5 July 1998

GILLEY
Hugh M. [husb. of Ruth M.] - b. 1904; d. 1980
[Laura A. - see DONNELL]
Ruth M. [wife of Hugh M.] - b. 1905; d. 1967

GOODWIN
Elliott [sic] B. - b. 1838; d. 1917
Grace G. (wife of Herbert L. [no stone]) - b. 1868; d. 1933

GOWER
Celia G. - b. 1920; d. 1935

GRANT
[Nellie - see SMALLIDGE]

GRAY
Althea M. [wife of Samuel F.] - b. 1926
Donald M. - [no dates]
George A. [husb. of Vesta L.] - b. 1914
Irving S. Jr. - b. 17 October 1923; d. 11 May 1964
Leonard S. - b. 1900; d. 1974
Louise C. - [no dates]
Nulela - b. 1877; d. 1952
Samuel F. [husb. of Althea M.] - b. 1921

Vesta L. [wife of George A.] - b. 1917

GREEN

Abigail H. (wife of Michael[8]) - b. 1802; d. 1884
Michael[8] (husb. of Abigail H.) - b. 1811; d. 1877

GREENE

Della E. [wife of Everett E.] - b. 1892; d. 1974
Elmer Everett - b. 14 December 1915; d. 28 July 1994
Everett E. [husb. of Della E.] - b. 1889; d. 1981

GRINDLE

Alta [D. or E.][5] (wife of Arthur]) - [no dates]
Arthur (husb. of Alta [D. or E.][5]) - [no dates]
Arthur W. (husb. of Mary Z.) - b. 1932; d. 1974
Avis W. [wife of Pearl M.] - b. 1918; d. 1998
Clara A. - b. 1901; d. 1982
Edward B. - b. 6 September 1944; d. 31 January 1978
Georgia H. - b. 1891; d. 1982
Gloria M. (dau. of Arthur and Alta [D. or E.][5]) - b. 1930; d. 1930
Jay Cintron - b. 1971; d. 1991
Mary Z. (wife of Arthur W.) - b. 1935
Orris P. - b. 1883; d. 1964
Pearl M. [husb. of Avis W.] - b. 1915; d. 1972

HALL

[Helen Fowler - see WILLKIE]

HAMOR

Ada A. (THOMAS; wife of Walter M. [no stone]) - d. 28 November 1902 Æ 44 y., 9 m., 13 d.
Agnes S[MALLIDGE?]. - b. 1880; d. 1952
Albert [husb. of Sadie] - b. 1875; d. 1964
Anthony L. Jr. [husb. of Cynthia B.?] - b. 1903; d. 1991
[Barbara I. - see COSTON]
Cynthia B. [wife of Anthony L. Jr.?] - b. 1915; d. 1987
Lee S. (son of Anthony L. [no stone] and Senith L.) - b. 1926; d. 1937
Sadie [wife of Albert] - b. 1882; d. 1957
Senith L. (wife of Anthony L. [no stone]) - b. 1904; d. 1935

HARRIMAN

Alyce [sic] H[IGGINS?]. (wife of John F.) - b. 1902; d. 1968
John F. (husb. of Alyce [sic] H[IGGINS?].) - b. 1908; d. 1993

HARVEL

Dennis L. - b. 1941; d. 1992

HASKELL

Harland N. [husb. of Helen B.] - b. 1911; d. 1975
Helen B. [wife of Harland N.] - b. 1908; d. 1980

HAVEY

Lloyd C. - b. 1892; d. 1931

HAYNES

Mary Elizabeth (RICHARDSON; dau. of Hugh RICHARDSON [no stone]; “widow” of Benjamin T. [no stone] and Samuel H. RICHARDSON [no stone]) - b. 6 September 1828; d. 6 October 1908
Sylvia P[INKHAM]. - b. 1900; d. 1973

HERRICK

[Charlotte - see CLEMENT]

HERTER
Albert II - b. 6 May 1900, New York; d. 2 June 1902, Seal Harbor
HIGGINS
[Alyce H[IGGINS?]. - see HARRIMAN]
Carroll S. - b. 1904; d. 1960
Dorothy W. - b. 1921; d. 1994
Elizabeth M. [wife of Sidney A.] - b. 1876; d. 1960
Elliott J. Jr. - b. 1918
Sidney A. [husb. of Elizabeth M.] - b. 1873; d. 1941
Warren W. - b. 1941; d. 1992
HODGDON
George Toby - b. 1919; d. 1939
IRVING
Olive D. [wife of Robert E.] - b. 1898; d. 1955
Robert E. [husb. of Olive D.] - b. 1883; d. 1955
ISBISTER
Alice M. (wife of Charles [no stone]) - b. 1898; d. 1918
Elmer E. [ISBISTER?] - b. 1905; d. 1906
JEWETT
infant (son of Alton and Ruth [no stones]) - [no dates]
JORDAN
[Abigail H.[8] - see GREEN]
Alden Hale (husb. of Mercy (STEPHENS)) - b. 1829; d. 1907
[Alice (Dr.) - see SHUBERT]
Anna C. [wife of Lawrence V.] - b. 1908
Carrie E. (STANLEY; wife of George N.) - b. 1860; d. 1943
[Clarinda - see SOUTHARD]
Colgate S. (husb. of Harriett [sic] F.) - b. 22 August 1911; d. 22 December 1989
Cora Abbie (dau. of Alden Hale and Mercy (STEPHENS)) - b. 1856; d. 1876
Cora Abbie - b. 1886; d. 1963
Dora - b. 1858; d. 1927
Edwin C. (husb. of Mary G.) - b. 1884; d. 1947
Esther A. [wife of Everett G.] - b. 1881; d. 1959
Everett G. [husb. of Esther A.] - b. 1883; d. 1958
Francis Leon - b. 1905; d. 1957
Freddie Austin (son of Alden Hale and Mercy (STEPHENS)) - b. 1871; d. 1881
George Millard - b. 1888; d. 1890
George N. (husb. of Lydia) - b. 1804; d. 1863
George N. (husb. of Carrie E. (STANLEY)) - b. 1854; d. 1932
George Willis - b. 1836; d. 1914
George Willis (son of Alden Hale and Mercy (STEPHENS)) - b. 1852; d. 1853
Gertrude S. - b. 1867; d. 1923
Harriett [sic] F. (wife of Colgate S.) - b. 29 December 1910
Ina - b. 1895; d. 1978
infant - b. 1892; d. 1892
infant [child of Everett G. and Esther A.?] - b. 1909; d. 1909
John E. Sr. [husb. of Marie H.?] - b. 1904; d. 1990
Lawrence V. [husb. of Anna C.] - b. 1903; d. 1976
Lydia (wife of George N.) - b. 1805; d. 1845
Marie H. [wife of John E. Sr.?] - b. 1905
Mary G. (wife of Edwin C.) - b. 1887; d. 1953
Mary L. - b. 1892; d. 1958

Melvin J. - b. 1865; d. 1954
Melvina (dau. of George N. and [not given]) - b. 1849; d. 1865
Mercy (STEPHENS; wife of Alden Hale) - b. 1826; d. 1883
[Michael[8] - see GREEN]
Stuart E. - b. 7 June 1937; d. 16 June 1966

KINGMAN
Maurice C. - b. 1897; d. 1951

KNUDSEN
Esther A. [wife of Walter H.] - b. 1906
Walter H. [husb. of Esther A.] - b. 1904; d. 1984
Walter H. III - [b. and d.?] 6 December 1968

KVAM
Anna T. [wife of I. George] - b. 1894; d. 1953
I. George [husb. of Anna T.] - b. 1883; d. 1953

LADD
Azelle (wife of Heman W.) - b. 15 August 1862; d. 20 January 1905
Daniel (husb. of Martha B.) - b. 24 November 1825; d. 9 February 1907
Emerson D. [husb. of Lena M.] - b. 1872; d. 1942
Gilbert A. - "lost at sea" 17 November 1869 Æ 15 y.
Heman W. (husb. of Azelle) - b. 22 February 1861; d. 22 May 1932
Lena M. [wife of Emerson D.] - b. 1878; d. 1967
Martha B. (wife of Daniel) - b. 1 November 1835; d. 6 January 1898

LAMBERT
Emily S. - b. 1904; d. 1992

LEACH
Alvah L. [husb. of Mary E.] - b. 1901; d. 1976
Mary E. [wife of Alvah L.] - b. 1906; d. 1994

LeCLAIR
Edward A. - b. 1895; d. 1962

LEHR
Joan D. - b. 7 April 1924; d. 18 August 1997

LELAND
Colinette T. [wife of Lewis F.] - b. 1912; d. 1961
Lewis F. [husb. of Colinette T.] - b. 1909; d. 1982

LIBBY
[Jennie - see CLEMENT]

LISCOMB
Bessie M. - d. 4 December 1902 Æ 10 y.
Inez - d. 25 October 1912 Æ 20 y., 7 m.
Lonia - b. 1863; d. 1916
Margaret J. [wife of Ralph E.] - b. 1883; d. 1942
Ralph E. [husb. of Margaret J.] - b. 1884; d. 1945
Ruby Louise - b. 1895; d. 1918

LOWENSTEIN
Sam Davis - [b. and d.?] 10 August 1994

LUNT
[Georgia - see FRYE]

LYNAM
Albert E. - b. 1862; d. 1880
Clarence L. [husb. of Harriet M.] - b. 1854; d. 1929
Delphina H. [dau. of Eri T. and Sarah T.] - d. 18 August 1862 Æ 19 y.
Eri T. (husb. of Sarah T.) - d. 5 April 1881 Æ 62 y.

George E. [son of Eri T. and Sarah T.] - d. 25 November 1871 Æ 23 y.
Harriet M. [wife of Clarence L.] - b. 1858; d. 1939
Linda M. - b. 2 August 1842; d. 24 February 1915
[Lydia B. - see CLEMENT]
Myra L. (dau. of Eri T. and Sarah T.) - d. 4 December 1882 Æ 23 y.
Sarah T. (wife of Eri T.) - d. 29 November 1900 Æ 85 y., 6 m.
Walter E. (son of Eri T. and Sarah T.) - d. 8 August 1861 Æ 11 y.

LYNCH
Almeda A. [wife of Basil A.] - b. 1908; d. 1994
Basil A. [husb. of Almeda A.] - b. 1904; d. 1986
Bernard A. [husb. of Florence J.] - b. 25 March 1894; d. 17 August 1970
Florence J. [wife of Bernard A.] - b. 1897; d. 1991

MACCRAE [see also MCCRAE]
Judith A. ("infant dau." of Guy [no stone]) - [b. and d.?] 10 June 1933
Marilyn ("infant dau." of Guy [no stone]) - [b. and d.?] 31 October 1931
Raymond L. [husb. of Sally C.] - b. 1895; d. 1989
Sally C. [wife of Raymond L.] - b. 1897; d. 1979

MACKAY
[Jean - see CLEMENT]

MACKENZIE [see also MCKENZIE]
[Virginia - see CARPENTER]

MACNAUGHTON
Elizabeth [wife of William C.] - b. 1882; d. 1935
William C. [husb. of Elizabeth] - b. 1873; d. 1928

MARSHALL
Althea L. (dau. of David and Mable [sic] [no stones]) - b. 1909; d. 1916

MARTIN
Ernest E. - b. 1862; d. 1925
Harlan L. - b. 1887; d. 1968
Herbert A. [husb. of Nellie B.?] - b. 1869; d. 1941
Mary I. - b. 1857; d. 1924
Nellie B. [wife of Herbert A.?] - b. 1879; d. 1954

MCCORMICK
Edward J. [husb. of Mabel F.] - b. 1892; d. 1953
Mabel F. [wife of Edward J.] - b. 1889; d. 1959

MCCRAE [see also MACCRAE]
Arthur W. [husb. of Clara H.] - b. 1898; d. 1982
Clara H. [wife of Arthur W.] - b. 1904
infant - [no dates]
Iva G. [wife of Leslie E.] - b. 1897; d. 1992
James C. [husb. of Lenora E.] - b. 1868; d. 1948
Lenora E. [wife of James C.] - b. 1871; d. 1952
Leslie E. [husb. of Iva G.] - b. 1897; d. 1973

MCDONALD
Sharon (SWAN) - b. 19 March 1947; d. 17 August 1989

MCELROY
James F. [husb. of LaDonna E.] - b. 1908; d. 1983
LaDonna E. [wife of James F.] - b. 1913; d. 1998

MCKENZIE [see also MACKENZIE]
David - b. 1885; d. 1912
Fred - b. 1878; d. 1961
Gerald L. - b. 1898; d. 1928

[Jeanett [sic] - see DRISCOLL]
Minnie D. - b. 1878; d. 1970

MERCHANT
[Blanche M[ERCHANT?]. - see CARTER]

MILLER
Charles D. - b. 1901; d. 1975
[Phyllis - see ATWOOD]

MOSSMAN
Alton R. [husb. of Florence T.] - b. 20 May 1888; d. 20 May 1963
Florence T. [wife of Alton R.] - b. 25 January 1888; d. 25 June 1966

MURCH
Howard L. [husb. of Onolee (BRACY)] - b. 1910; d. 1988
Onolee (BRACY; [wife of Howard L.]) - b. 1913; d. 1978

MURRAY
Sheila B[RYANT?]. - b. 1924; d. 1968

O'DAY
Eva (WOOD; [wife of Gerald]) - b. 1904; d. 1992
Gerald [husb. of Eva (WOOD)] - b. 1900; d. 1973

ORCUTT
Fred W. (husb. of Lura G.) - b. 1871; d. 1963
Lura G. (wife of Fred W.) - b. 1879; d. 1964

OTTO
Emily S. (wife of Harry) - b. 1864; d. 1932
Harry (husb. of Emily S.) - b. 1854; d. 1932
W. Francis - b. 1904; d. 1968

PARKER
Madella (STANLEY) - b. 20 September 1846; d. 14 March 1909

PATTEN
Thomas - b. 17 May 1846; d. 23 April 1924

PEDDER
John C. - b. 1870; d. 1934

PENMAN
Georgianna (dau. of John and Georgie [no stones]) - b. 23 April 1895; d. 11 September 1895

PERKINS
Hattie M. ["infant" dau. of Morton E. and Luella M.] - [no dates]
Luella M. [wife of Morton E.] - b. 1882; d. 1968
Morton E. [husb. of Luella M.] - b. 1874; d. 1957

PETTEE
Clifton E. - b. 1898; d. 1988
Eliphalet A. [husb. of Sarah E.?] - b. 1872; d. 1962
Eugene [husb. of Mary A.?] - b. 1885; d. 1962
Marjorie L. - b. 1903; d. 1962
Mary A. [wife of Eugene?] - b. 1875; d. 1960
Sarah E. [wife of Eliphalet A.?] - b. 1875; d. 1963

PHIPPEN
Florence M. - b. 1922; d. 1992
Frank Z. (husb. of Nettie M. (DOW)) - b. 1876; d. 1916
Nettie M. (DOW; wife of Frank Z.) - b. 1886; d. 1953

PIERCE
Augustus V. (son of Ezekiel and Margaret A.) - d. 21 June 1882 Æ 9 m., 20 d.
Bernice W. (wife of Yale E.) - b. 1915

Bertha N. (wife of Walden) - b. 1864; d. 1945
Ezekiel (husb. of Sarah and Margaret A.) - d. 7 December 1890 Æ 72 y., 4 m.
George E. (Capt.; husb. of Mary M.) - b. 1846; d. 1915
Hattie V. [dau. of Walden and Nellie F.?] - b. 1888; d. 1910
Margaret A. (wife of Ezekiel) - d. 26 December 1912 Æ 76 y., 8 m., 20 d.
Mary M. (wife of Capt. George E.) - b. 1850; d. 19[...][6]
Nellie F. (wife of Walden) - d. 9 January 1896 Æ 28 y., 4 m.
Olive A. (dau. of Ezekiel and Sarah) - d. 12 May 1856 Æ 9 m., 21 d.
Sarah (wife of Ezekiel) - d. 15 September 1875 Æ 53 y., 6 m.
Stillman I. (son of Ezekiel and Sarah) - d. 2 April 1888 Æ 30 y., 11 m.
Theodore B. - d. 28 April 1892 Æ 33 y., 2 m.
Thomas M. (son of Ezekiel and Sarah) - d. 10 September 1856 Æ 4 y., 2 m.
Thomas M. 2nd - b. 1878; d. 1906 Æ 28 y.
Walden (husb. of Nellie F. and Bertha N.) - b. 1850; d. 1932
Yale E. (husb. of Bernice W.) - b. 1904; d. 1968

PINKHAM
Alton E. - b. 1907; d. 1956
Alton E. - b. 17 June 1931; d. 8 June 1974
Cora E. (wife of Simon H.) - b. 1860; d. 1890
Donald O. - d. 7 June 1936 Æ 2 d.
Florence - b. 1885; d. 1920
Fostenia B. - b. 1871; d. 1944
Frank A. - b. 1872; d. 1931
Grafton - b. 1882; d. 1974
Lizzie - b. 1871; d. 1951
Mary I. (wife of Albert C. [no stone]) - b. 1863; d. 1903
Nina L. - b. 1908; d. 1986
Rachel A. [mother of Albert C. [no stone]?] - b. 1843; d. 1919
Simon H. (husb. of Cora E.) - b. 1845; d. 1912
[Sylvia P[INKHAM]. - see HAYNES]

PRAY
[Meda - see CANDAGE]

PUNG
John - b. 28 January 1859; d. 3 May 1900

PYLE
Ann Finlay [wife of James Tolman] - b. 17 January 1916
James Tolman [husb. of Ann Finlay] - b. 8 November 1913; d. 1 April 1998

RAYFUSE
Isaac J. - b. 1865; d. 1926

RAYMOND
[...] [headstone only]

REYNOLDS
Arthur B. (husb. of Dora C.) - b. 1896; d. 1939
Dora C. (wife of Arthur B.) - b. 1894; d. 1957

RHODES
Bertha H. - b. November 1871, England; d. January 1962
Denis [sic] - b. January 1915; d. August 1941

RICHARDSON
[Cynthia R[ICHARDSON?]. - see CLEMENT]
Helen L. (wife of Shepard E.) - b. 1853; d. 1926
[Mary Elizabeth - see HAYNES]
Shepard E. (husb. of Helen L.) - b. 1846; d. 1930

RITCHIE
[Evelyn - see BILLINGS]
ROBERTS
James M. - b. 22 April 1914; d. 13 November 1992
Marion R. - b. 1919
Raymond E. - b. 1925; d. 1976
ROBERTSON
A. Maynard [husb. of Barbara A.] - b. 1916; d. 1988
Barbara A. [wife of A. Maynard] - b. 1925; d. 1988
RUMILL
Gloria (SMITH) - b. 29 February 1924; d. 3 January 1995
Katherine G. (wife of Schuyler Milton) - b. 1896; d. 1972
Robie [sic] (son of Schuyler Milton and Katherine G.) - b. 24 December 1921; d. 1 August 1924
Schuyler Milton (husb. of Katherine G.) - b. 1895; d. 1978
Schuyler Milton Jr. - b. 10 May 1920; d. 27 June 1990
RUPP
Robert S. - b. 16 November 1925; d. 28 August 1974
RUSSELL
[Flora - see TARALDSEN]
SHUBERT
Alice (JORDAN) (Dr.) - b. 1916; d. 1984
Sally Meig - b. 1955; d. 1979
SIMONTON
[Margaret - see CANDAGE]
SIMPSON
Charles Paul [husb. of Peggy (TAYLOR)] - b. 1928; d. 1996
Peggy (TAYLOR; [wife of Charles Paul]) - b. 1933
SMALLIDGE
[Agnes S[MALLIDGE?]. - see HAMOR]
Alice Marion (dau. of Chester Merrill and Nellie (GRANT)) - b. 9 September 1904; d. 27 September 1910
Chester Merrill (husb. of Nellie (GRANT)) - b. 28 July 1880; d. 23 April 1957
Clara Tracy - b. 1854; d. 1933
Dorothy Grace - b. 25 March 1891; d. 19 December 1978
E. P. - [no dates]
Eudora N. [wife of Warren] - b. 1876; d. 1972
Jennie Ella (dau. of Theodore M. and Olive J. (BUNKER) [no stones]) - b. 1869; d. 1875
John (Capt.; husb. of Mary P.) - b. 1815; d. 1875
John Francis - b. 1847; d. 1902
Joseph Warren - b. 1839; d. 1856
Mary P. (wife of Capt. John) - b. 1817; d. 1887
Nellie (GRANT; wife of Chester Merrill) - b. 25 October 1881; d. 6 October 1940
[Olive - see SOUTHARD]
Ruth Clara (dau. of Chester Merrill and Nellie (GRANT)) - b. 30 June 1906; d. 22 November 1915
Warren [husb. of Eudora N.] - b. 1868; d. 1937
Winfield Scott - b. 1854; d. 1926
SMITH
Basil L. [husb. of Mattie B.] - b. 1904; d. 1981
[Gloria - see RUMILL]

Mattie B. [wife of Basil L.] - b. 1900; d. 1942
[...] [headstone only]
SNOW
Etta K. [wife of Madison H.?] - b. 1874; d. 1952
Madison H. [husb. of Etta K.?] - b. 1864; d. 1943
SOLARI
Gary M. [husb. of Judith E.] - b. 24 January 1938; d. 26 September 1997
Helen D. - b. 1905; d. 1975
Judith E. [wife of Gary M.] - b. 27 July 1940
SOUTHARD
Alice (wife of Charles E.) - d. 27 October 1880 Æ 39 y., 3 m.
Charles E. (husb. of Alice) - b. 1836; d. 1923
Clarinda (JORDAN; wife of Stephen Jr.) - b. 1821; d. 1896
Edmund G. (son of Stephen Jr. and Clarinda (JORDAN)) - b. 1846; d. 1864
[Eliza J. - see CLEMENT]
Gilbert (son of Abram and Priscilla [no stones]) - d. 30 October 1850, New York, Æ 19 y., 5 m.
Olive (SMALLIDGE; wife of Stephen Jr.) - b. 1814; d. 1841
Sally (wife of Stephen) - b. 1791; d. 1856
Stephen (husb. of Sally) - b. 1790; d. 1841
Stephen Jr. (husb. of Olive (SMALLIDGE) and Clarinda (JORDAN)) - b. 1811; d. 1890
Stephen M. (son of Abram and Priscilla [no stones]) - d. 15 June 1864, United States Barracks Hospital, New Orleans, Louisiana, Æ 25 y.; (member of 13th Maine Regiment [Civil War])
[Vesta - see CLEMENT]
SPENCER
Martha T[RACY?]. - b. 1916; d. 1984
STANLEY
[Carrie E. - see JORDAN]
[Madella - see PARKER]
Mildred M. (wife of Francis B. [no stone]) - b. 1900; d. 1944
STEPHENS
[Mercy - see JORDAN]
STEWART
Willard Robert - b. 9 August 1926; d. 4 March 1994
STINSON
Alvin - b. 1863; d. 1930
Barbara - [no dates]
Lillian - b. 1867; d. 1938
Pauline - b. 1894; d. 1904
STREET
[Pamela Ann - see WALTON]
SULLIVAN
Dennis L. - b. 1948; d. 1996
SUPIRO
Edna D. (dau. of S. and P. A. [no stones]) - b. 13 March 1935; d. 20 March 1935
SWAN
Shannon E. - b. 30 January 1921; d. 12 January 1964
[Sharon - see McDONALD]
SWARTZ
Jason L. J. - b. 4 August 1976; d. 16 September 1980

TARALDSEN
Earl Norman [husb. of Flora (RUSSELL)] - b. 1 July 1897; d. 12 February 1985
Flora (RUSSELL; [wife of Earl Norman]) - b. 19 January 1902; d. 11 March 1995
TAYLOR
Haroldine A. - b. 24 September 1912; d. 27 December 1973
Jennie M. - b. 1915; d. 1920
Marcia L. - b. 13 November 1889; d. 16 January 1965
[Peggy - see SIMPSON]
THOMAS
[Ada A. - see HAMOR]
Robert F. Jr. - b. 1964; d. 1964
THOMPSON
Ada B. - b. 1879; d. 1973
Hannah D. [wife of Capt. Solomon S.] - b. 1815; d. 1904
Rolla F. (husb. of Viola M.) - b. 1887; d. 1960
Solomon S. (Capt.; [husb. of Hannah D.]) - b. 1816; d. 1894
Viola M. (wife of Rolla F.) - b. 1894; d. 1979
TRACY
Carolyn M. - b. 1918; d. 1932
Charles A. (husb. of Ethel E.) - b. 1873; d. 1943
Dorothy S. [wife of Ralph J.] - b. 1934
Elizabeth P. - b. 1896; d. 1970
Ethel E. (wife of Charles A.) - b. 1889; d. 1962
Gladys F. - b. 1923; d. 1932
Marjorie L. - b. 1919; d. 1932
[Martha T[RACY?]. - see SPENCER]
Ralph J. [husb. of Dorothy S.] - b. 1931
VARNUM
James O. [husb. of Kit S.] - b. 1868; d. 1945
Kit S. [wife of James O.] - b. 1872; d. 1960
Lawrence C. [husb. of Ramona G.?] - [no dates]
Leora N. [wife of Sans W.] - b. 1896; d. [no date]
Maurice [son of Lawrence C. and Ramona G.?] - b. 1918; d. 1921
Ramona G. [wife of Lawrence C.?] - [no dates]
Sans W. [husb. of Leora N.] - b. 1900; d. 1954
WALCH [sic]
Harold Gray [husb. of Marie (BILLINGS)] - b. 13 September 1922
Marie (BILLINGS; [wife of Harold Gray]) - b. 8 April 1922
WALLS
Andrew B. (husb. of Maud G.) - b. 11 November 1893; d. 12 February 1976
Charles M. (husb. of Therese D.) - b. 1900; d. 1998
Doris Louise - b. 1899; d. 1949
infant [child of Andrew B. and Maud G.] - [b. and d.?] 19 November 1914
infant [child of Andrew B. and Maud G.] - [b. and d.?] 13 October 1926
James C. [husb. of Winifred] - b. 1882; d. 1965
James C. Jr. - b. 1925; d. 1952
Jerrold W. (son of Charles M. and Therese D.) - d. 12 August 1934 Æ 1 d.
Maud G. (wife of Andrew B.) - b. 1894; d. 1937
Therese D. (wife of Charles M.) - b. 1903; d. 1996
Winifred [wife of James C.] - b. 1893; d. 1985
[...] [headstone only]

WALSH
John J. [husb. of Mary N.] - b. 1906; d. 1986
Mary N. [wife of John J.] - b. 1908; d. 1993
WALTON
Emily Ann Parker "Emmy" [dau. of Kenneth R. and Pamela Ann (STREET)] - b. 25 January 1987; d. 6 July 1995
Eva Louise [wife of Harland O.?] - b. 4 October 1938; d. 27 December 1977
Hali Jo [dau. of Harland O. and Eva Louise?] - b. 23 September 1977; d. 25 September 1977
Harland O. [husb. of Eva Louise?] - b. 28 February 1932; d. 16 July 1994
Johnny - b. 1953; d. 1954
Kenneth R. [husb. of Pamela Ann (STREET)] - b. 28 February 1947
Kenneth Roscoe [husb. of Virginia A.] - b. 1916; d. 1989
Pamela Ann (STREET; [wife of Kenneth R.]) - b. 15 October 1946
Phyllis M. [wife of William E.] - b. 1904
Virgil J. - b. 1926; d. 1988
Virginia A. [wife of Kenneth Roscoe] - b. 1921; d. 1974
William E. [husb. of Phyllis M.] - b. 1902; d. 1959
William E. Jr. - b. 17 August 1925; d. 30 September 1994
William L. - b. 1954; d. 1978
[...] [headstone only]
WARD
Harold Carl - b. 3 July 1930; d. 4 November 1930
WATSON
Charles A. [husb. of Clara M.] - b. 28 March 1927; d. 26 May 1994
Clara M. [wife of Charles A.] - b. 3 September 1929
Eileen R. [wife of Winfield J. [WATSON?]] - b. 1917
Lena J. [wife of Loring W.] - b. 1893; d. 1980
Loring W. [husb. of Lena J.] - b. 1885; d. 1961
Winfield J. [WATSON?] [husb. of Eileen R.] - b. 1916; d. 1993
WEBBER
[Annie H. - see CARTER]
WESCOTT
Florence A. - b. 1899; d. 1958
Herman Lyle - b. 6 September 1891; d. 30 July 1964
Pauline B[UTLER?]. - b. 1927; d. 1979
WHITMORE
Emma A. - b. 6 November 1859; d. 14 October 1949
John M. - b. 12 December 1860; d. 11 July 1924
Joseph H. - b. 12 December 1860; d. 18 March 1917
Mary H. (wife of Sans S.) - b. 21 August 1836; d. 1 September 1914
Sans S. (husb. of Mary H.) - b. 12 January 1822; d. 11 June 1900
Warren H. - b. 5 August 1864; d. 21 August 1920
WILLIAMS
Marie D[RISCOLL?]. - b. 1914; d. 1976
WILLKIE
Helen Fowler (HALL) - b. 28 October 1915; d. 5 March 1996
WOOD
Barry P. - b. 1933; d. 1983
Clyde E. - b. 1908; d. 1959
[Eva - see O'DAY]
George B. - b. 1856; d. 1936

Gertrude G. (wife of Howard S.) - b. 1904; d. 1978
Gloria Francis [sic] [wife of Capt. James William Jr.] - b. 1926
Harry A. [husb. of Helen H.] - b. 1876; d. 1950
Helen H. [wife of Harry A.] - b. 1878; d. 1957
Howard S. (husb. of Gertrude G.) - b. 1900; d. 1970
infant (son of Howard S. and Gertrude G.) - [b. and d.?] 1927
James William Jr. (Capt.; [husb. of Gloria Francis [sic]]) - b. 1925
Maud H. - b. 1873; d. 1962
Robert - b. 1902; d. 1920
Robert A. - b. 29 February 1936; d. 16 March 1992
Sarah B. - b. 1963; d. 1982

WRIGHT
Hollis L. [husb. of Virginia D.] - b. 1891; d. 1958
Hollis L. Jr. - b. 1913; d. 1990
Leslie D. - b. 26 March 1916; d. 21 May 1943
Virginia D. [wife of Hollis L.] - b. 1896; d. 1975

YOUNG
Walter H. (son of Loring N. and Gladys M. [no stones]) - b. 23 April 1930; d. 8 August 1930

Notes:
[1]The B of ELBRIDGE was first engraved as a D. A horizontal line changed the D to a B as it now (1999) stands.
[2]Difficult to read.
[3]There is no stone for a Harry O. CARTER in any of the 5 cemeteries along or near Beech Hill Road.
[4]Stone worn and/or broken.
[5]Different on different stones.
[6]Only "19" is engraved on the stone.
[7]Full birth and death dates were taken from a temporary marker placed on the grave prior to the current (2000) stone that gives only the years.
[8]It is unclear from the gravestones whether the surname is GREEN or JORDAN.

Kimball Cemetery
(Mount Desert - 19)

Location/directions. Kimball Road, Northeast Harbor. From the traffic light at the north end of Mount Desert Island, go straight ahead (south) onto Routes 102/198. In approximately 4.2–4.3 miles, at the traffic light at the intersection of Routes 102/198 and 198, turn left on Route 198. Follow this road for about 6.6–6.7 miles to a fork in the road at the south end of the village of Northeast Harbor. Bear left onto Kimball Road, and a path leading to the cemetery is on the right in about 0.1–0.2 miles.

History. —

Notes. This cemetery is divided into two parts—one enclosed by a stone wall and one enclosed by a iron fence. The stone of Thomas B. Ralph is outside both enclosures. Most of the lawn in this cemetery is moss and appears to require little maintenance.

Names and dates on gravestones and other markers. [13 May 1999]
HO
Christopher - b. 1966; d. 1968
KIMBALL
Abbie E. - b. 4 February 1876; d. 28 November 1927
C. Elliott (husb. of Genevieve T.) - b. 28 February 1905; d. 12 November 1958
Charlotte Emma - b. 15 November 1895; d. 24 April 1906
Clarence A. - b. 31 July 1851; d. 10 January 1935
Cora A. - b. 22 June 1874; d. 29 November 1954
Daniel (husb. of Emma) - b. 1802; d. 1887
Daniel Everett - b. 14 December 1842; d. 26 November 1911
Daniel Loren - b. 25 March 1905; d. 27 December 1906
Edmund H. - b. 15 April 1841; d. 25 February 1934
Edmund H. - b. 8 November 1906; d. 28 February 1952
Emma (wife of Daniel) - b. 1820; d. 1889
Emma E. - [no dates]
Genevieve T. (wife of C. Elliott) - b. 12 May 1907; d. 24 December 1985
George M. (son of Daniel and Emma) - b. 1862; d. 8 November 1865 Æ 2 y., 11 m., 17 d.
Gertrude R. - b. 4 March 1897; d. 13 November 1973
Hannah M. - b. 18 February 1887; d. 24 June 1984
[Ida - see SMALLIDGE]
Loren E. - b. 21 March 1855; d. 9 November 1931
Loren E. Jr. - b. 25 November 1907; d. 3 May 1969
Lucia V. - b. 25 November 1847; d. 25 June 1928
Margaret M. - b. 30 April 1899; d. 12 January 1972
Marion (MacDONALD) - b. 14 July 1902; d. 21 October 1996 Æ 94 y.
Martha - b. 17 February 1848; d. 12 November 1916
Martha - b. 30 October 1919; d. 18 February 1997
MacDONALD
[Marion - see KIMBALL]
McBRIDE
Albert Kimball - b. 6 June 1876; d. 18 February 1940
Clarence Edward - b. 2 July 1874; d. 1 October 1917
Frances Pollard - b. 30 November 1890; d. 23 August 1950
Hannah A. - b. 1839; d. 1887

RALPH
Thomas B. - b. 1857; d. 1953
SMALLIDGE
Catharine - b. 14 December 1836; d. 3 July 1926
Fred Henry - b. 25 May 1877; d. 1 September 1892
Ida (KIMBALL) - b. 1870; d. 1903
Stephen - b. 30 May 1842; d. 20 December 1908

Bartlett Island Cemetery 6

(Mount Desert - 20)

Location/directions. South end of Bartlett Island. From the boat landing on the east side of the island, follow the road approximately 0.4–0.5 miles to the first road on the left. Turn left and follow this road to the end. A trail leading approximately 100 feet to the cemetery is on the right.

History. —

Notes. The cemetery is (June 2000) in uncleared woods of spruce and fir. There are plans, however, to clear the area around the cemetery and erect a fence similar to others that enclose cemeteries on the island. One stone has the letter "S" roughly carved into it. The remaining 6 apparent graves are marked only by natural field stones.

Names and dates on gravestones and other markers.

S.

[...][1]

Note:

[1]Only the single initial "S" is carved into the stone.

Bartlett Island Cemetery 5
(Mount Desert - 21)

Location/directions. Southwest portion of Bartlett Island, between Alleys Point and Seal Cove. From the boat landing on the east side of the island, follow the road approximately 0.6 miles to the T-intersection. Turn left and follow this road about 0.5 miles to a fork. Bear left and follow this road approximately 0.5 miles to the edge of a field. The tops of a few broad-leaved trees that are in the cemetery can be seen ahead and a little to the left.

History. —

Notes. The cemetery is enclosed by an ungated fence with wood posts and stakes supporting 8 courses of wire. The grass is cut and trimmed.

Names and dates on gravestones and other markers. [21 August 1999]
ALLEY
Cordelia B. [wife of James] - b. 27 November 1814; d. 6 June 1896
James [husb. of Cordelia B.] - b. 24 March 1805; d. 10 August 1878
BAIN
Alexander G. - b. 28 October 1849; d. 28 April 1907

Carter Cemetery
(Mount Desert - 22)

Location/directions. In woods east of Beech Hill Road. From the traffic light at the north end of Mount Desert Island, go straight ahead (south) onto Routes 102/198. In approximately 5.2 miles (and at the south end of the village of Somesville), turn right onto Pretty Marsh Road (Route 102). In about 0.2–0.3 miles, turn left onto Beech Hill Road. (Note: this turn is easy to pass as it is just over a hill and in a curve.) In approximately 2.6 miles (just before the northern border of Acadia National Park property and just before an intersection on the right with Sand Point Road), there is a stone wall that runs perpendicular to the left (east) side of Beech Hill Road. Follow this stone wall, which is occasionally obscure, to the cemetery. (Near the south side of the wall, there is a ring of rocks around a spring.)

History. In 1897, a deed (318:438) from Andrew J. Carter to the "legal heirs of Andrew J. Carter" conveyed a "right of way from the ... town road to the ... burying ground" as well as "twelve square rods, more or less" that was "to be used for the purpose of a family burying ground and for no other purpose".

Notes. Some trees were recently (spring 1999?) cut. Otherwise there is no apparent maintenance to this unenclosed cemetery in the woods.

Names and dates on gravestones and other markers. [26 March 2000]
CARTER
Andrew J. (Capt.; [husb. of Clara C.]) - b. 15 March 1835; d. 20 October 1909
Clara C. [wife of Capt. Andrew J.] - b. 10 August 1839; d. 13 September 1897
Eunice (wife of Frank M.) - b. 1855; d. 1907
Frank M. (husb. of Eunice) - b. 1861; d. 1907
infant [son of F[rank]. M. [and Eunice?]?] - [no dates]
Lemuel - b. 14 October 1866; d. 30 October 1899
Maud F. (dau. of F[rank]. M. [and Eunice?]) - b. 1886; d. 1893

Sheep Island Cemetery
(Mount Desert - 23)

Location/directions. Near east edge of northern portion of Sheep Island (at north end of Somes Sound).

History. The name applied to this cemetery is only for convenience of reference in this book.

Notes. There is a single headstone and accompanying footstone on a small (approximately 6 1/2' by 6 1/2') lot whose corners are marked with granite blocks.

Names and dates on gravestones and other markers.
RICHARDSON
Josie C. (child of Bainbridge W. and Fannie D. [no stones]) - d. 22 April 1874 Æ 15 d.
Walter A. (son of Bainbridge W. and Fannie D. [no stones]) - d. 15 April 1874 Æ 8 d.

Savage Graves
(Mount Desert - 24)

Location/directions. South of Route 3, approximately north of Bear Island. From the traffic light at the north end of Mount Desert Island, go straight ahead (south) onto Routes 102/198. In approximately 4.2–4.3 miles, at the traffic light at the intersection of Routes 102/198 and 198, turn left on Route 198. Follow this road for about 5.6–5.7 miles to the intersection (on the left) with Route 3. Turn left onto Route 3. In approximately 1.4 miles, the graves are on the right between the road and the water. They are not easily visible from the road.

History. —

Notes. The stones are on a maintained lawn of a private residence.

Names and dates on gravestones and other markers.
SAVAGE
- Edward (son of Thomas [no stone] and Elmena M.) - d. 6 December 1854 Æ 2 m.
- Elmena M. (wife of Thomas [no stone]) - d. 17 July 1859 Æ 28 y.
- infant (dau. of Thomas [no stone] and Elmena M.) - d. 21 November 1855 Æ 1 m., 12 d.
- infant (son of Thomas [no stone] and Elmena M.) - d. 29 September 1853 Æ 3 d.

Blanchard Family Burial Ground
(Mount Desert - 25)

Location/directions. Set back from Blanchard Road. From the traffic light at the north end of Mount Desert Island, go straight ahead (south) onto Routes 102/198. In approximately 5.2 miles (and at the south end of the village of Somesville), turn right onto Pretty Marsh Road (Route 102). In about 0.2–0.3 miles, turn left onto Beech Hill Road. (Note: this turn is easy to pass as it is just over a hill and in a curve.) Travel about 1.1–1.2 miles to the intersection (on the right) with Blanchard Road. Turn right onto Blanchard Road, and in less than 0.1 miles on the left is a field with (2000) a mowed path leading up to the cemetery. The cemetery is not visible from the road.

History. —

Notes. The burial ground is enclosed by a wood post and rail fence that has two courses of rails and two openings for entrances/exits. Within this enclosure are two stones and some plantings further enclosed by a low, wire fence. The grass is mowed and trimmed.

Names and dates on gravestones and other markers. [22 May 1999]
BAGLEY
  [Muriel - see BLANCHARD]
BLANCHARD
  Maynard D. [husb. of Muriel (BAGLEY)] - [no dates]
  Muriel (BAGLEY; [wife of Maynard D.]) - b. 1920; d. 1965

Kittredge Tomb
(Mount Desert - 26)

Location/directions. In woods west of Routes 102/198, diagonally across the road from Babson Creek Greenhouse (2000). From the traffic light at the north end of Mount Desert Island, go straight ahead (south) onto Routes 102/198. In approximately 3.8–3.9 miles, the tomb is on the right. Alternatively, the tomb on the left about 0.3–0.4 miles north of the traffic light at the intersection of Routes 3/198 and 102/198. It cannot be seen from the road.

History. —

Notes. This tomb is located in woods with no cleared area around it. The door of a short entry way is leaning forward, but the tomb proper is sealed by granite blocks. Engraved on the door is "Doct. Kendal Kittredge & sons" as well as a single death date (see below). A stone for Dr. Kendal Kittredge is in the Brookside Cemetery (Mount Desert - 6) (*q.v.*).

Names and dates on gravestones and other markers. [6 September 1999]
KITTREDGE
Dana (son of Benjamin W. and Lydia [no stones]) - d. 26 January 1844 Æ 8 y., 2 m.

Bartlett Island Cemetery 4
(Mount Desert - 27)

Location/directions. Northwest of and visible from the boat landing, Bartlett Island. From the boat landing on the east side of the island, follow the road approximately 0.2 miles, and the cemetery is on the right.

History. —

Notes. This cemetery is enclosed by a wire fence with wood posts and stakes. Some stones are propped up.

Names and dates on gravestones and other markers. [21 August 1999]
BARTLETT
Abel B. (husb. of Olive S.) - b. 27 October 1837; d. 1 December 1910
Albert A. - d. 9 April 1863 Æ 2 y., 4 m., 3 d.
David - d. 31 January 1887 Æ 61 y.
David (husb. of Sarah H.) - d. 17 July 1864 Æ 65 y.
Isaac - d. 2 December 1886 Æ 59 y., 1 m., 3 d.; ("drowned in Bluehill Bay")
Linda May (dau. of Abel B. and Olive S.) - d. 24 April 1875 Æ 2 y., 5 m., 4 d.
Maudie (dau. of Abel B. and Olive S.) - d. 12 October 1875 Æ 1 y., 5 m.
Olive S. (wife of Abel B.) - b. 10 May 1843; d. 12 July 1912
Sarah H. (wife of David) - d. 2 February 1876 Æ 69 y., 8 m., 15 d.
DAWES
Decatur [husb. of Eliza A.] - b. 22 March 1821; d. 24 June 1895
Eliza A. [wife of Decatur] - b. 14 June 1824; d. 10 November 1895
ROBBINS
Sophia F. (wife of S. D. [no stone]) - d. 28 April 1862 Æ 27 y.

SEAVILLE

In 1838, three islands—Bartlett, Hardwood, and Robinson (now Tinker)—were separated from the town of Mount Desert and incorporated as Seaville. This town was short-lived; just 21 years later, on 24 February 1859, it was dissolved. Bartlett Island returned to Mount Desert. Hardwood and Tinker became part of Tremont, itself formerly part of Mount Desert until its separation and incorporation in 1848. Cemeteries on the islands that once comprised Seaville are reported under the towns to which these islands now belong.

SOUTHWEST HARBOR

A portion of the town of Tremont was incorporated as Southwest Harbor on 21 February 1905. That Mount Height Cemetery (Southwest Harbor - 4) is the largest cemetery in this book likely accounts for Southwest Harbor having the fewest cemeteries (12) of the five towns covered in this book.

Non-profit:
- Mount Height Cemetery (Southwest Harbor - 4)

Private or unknown oversight:
- Lurvey Burial Ground (Southwest Harbor - 1) - maintained by landowner
- Evergreen Cemetry (Southwest Harbor - 2)
- Old Burying Ground (Southwest Harbor - 3)
- Union Cemetery (Southwest Harbor - 5)
- Moore Family Burial Ground (Southwest Harbor - 6)
- King Cemetery (Southwest Harbor - 7)
- Newman Cemetery (Southwest Harbor - 8) - a few graves maintained by family members
- Doliver Grave (Southwest Harbor - 9) - no apparent maintenance to grave; stone recently (1999) repaired by a private individual
- Clark Family Burying Ground (Southwest Harbor - 10)
- Gilley Burying Ground (Southwest Harbor - 11)
- Dolliver Family Burial Ground (Southwest Harbor - 12) - maintained by Acadia National Park

Lurvey Burial Ground

(Southwest Harbor - 1)

Location/directions. Smuggler's Den Campground. From the traffic light at the north end of Mount Desert Island, go straight ahead (south) onto Routes 102/198. On the right in approximately 9.1–9.2 miles (the last 4.8–4.9 miles of which are south of the traffic light at the intersection of Routes 102/198 and 198/233), is the entrance to Smuggler's Den Campground. Inquire at the office for permission to enter the campground and for directions to the cemetery.

History. This book follows Thornton (1938) in calling this cemetery the Lurvey Burial Ground. In 1928 deeds (623:48–51), however, it was referred to as the Lurvey-Herrick cemetery.

Notes. This cemetery is enclosed by a gated wood post and wire mesh fence. One stone is tipped over and another one is broken.

Names and dates on gravestones and other markers. [6 September 1999]

GILLEY

Hannah (LURVEY; dau. of Jacob LURVEY and Hannah; wife of Capt. William [no stone]) - d. 24 March 1852 Æ 70 y.

HERRICK

Andrew - b. 1742; d. 1812; bur. "in an unmarked grave on Spurling Point Cranberry Island"[1]

Asa W. - b. 30 August 1840; d. 30 December 1898

Isaac [husb. of Lavina?] - d. 15 September 1852 Æ 57 y., 7 m.

Lavina [wife of [Isaa]c[2]?] - d. 20 July 1872 Æ 75 y., 18 d.

William (Capt.) - b. 22 December 1827; d. 25 June 1909

LURVEY [includes LERVY]

[Hannah - see GILLEY]

Hannah (wife of Jacob) - d. 1 April 1839 Æ 81 y., 7 m.

Hannah H. (dau. of Enoch and Rebecca [no stones]) - d. 5 October 1848 Æ 14 y., 6 m.

infant (son of Enoch and Rebecca [no stones]) - d. 7 April 184[6 or 7][3] Æ 2 w.

Isaac F. - d. 7 September 1863, Augusta, Maine, Æ 38 y.; (member of Co. E, 28th Maine Regiment [Civil War])

Jacob (husb. of Hannah) - b. 1761; d. 11 September 1853 Æ 92 y.; ("He was a soldier of the Revolution and was twice taken prisoner during that war." [Revolutionary War])

Jacob - b. 1844; d. 1928

Lemuel - b. 1839; d. 1923; (member of Co. D, 1st Maine Cavalry [Civil War])

Nathan Curtis (son of Enoch and Rebecca [no stones]) - d. 5 April 1848 Æ 6 m.

Notes:

[1]There is (1999) a wooden marker on Spurling Point (Cranberry Isles - 16).

[2]Stone broken and partially patched.

[3]Both numbers are engraved in the same position. It appears that 7 was engraved first and then a 6 was more coarsely carved over the 7 [to correct an erroneous 7?].

Evergreen Cemetery
(Southwest Harbor - 2)

Location/directions. Along east side of Route 102. From the traffic light at the north end of Mount Desert Island, go straight ahead (south) onto Routes 102/198. In approximately 9.1–9.2 miles (the last 4.9 miles of which are south of the traffic light at the intersection of Routes 102/198 and 198/233), the cemetery is on the left.

History. This cemetery is found in the 1881 Colby Atlas. Thornton (1938) reported that the "sum of $18 was paid for the [cemetery], which was at first called Lurvey cemetery and later changed to Evergreen to distinguish it from the old family lot" (p. 222). The "old family lot" is in Southwest Harbor and is called "Lurvey Burial Ground" (Southwest Harbor - 2) in this book.

Notes. The grass is well maintained, but some stones are leaning or laying on the ground. No fence encloses this cemetery. There is, however, along the east (back) side of the cemetery a very large stone wall that was rebuilt in "1934 [by] the boys of the C C C camp, No. 158" (Thornton (1938), p. 226). They also "replaced the broken fence with one of neat cedar rails" (p. 226). Remnants of many posts and a few rails can still be found (2000) along the north and south sides of the cemetery.

Names and dates on gravestones and other markers. [22 May 1999]

BARTLETT
- Ada M. (dau. of William H. and Mary S.) - d. 12 March 1878 Æ 7 y., 8 m., 26 d.
- Charles L. [husb. of Ida S.] - b. 1865; d. 1934
- Ida S. [wife of Charles L.] - b. 1870; d. 1946
- Mary S. (wife of William H.) - d. 20 December 1870 Æ 23 y., 6 m.
- William H. (husb. of Mary S.) - d. 29 October 1879 Æ 37 y., 7 m., 21 d.

BROWN
- Horace C. - b. 9 June 1836; d. 27 May 1906

CARROLL
- John (husb. of Rachel (LURVEY)) - d. 7 May 1867 Æ 76 y., 7 m.
- Rachel (LURVEY; wife of John; dau. of Jacob LURVEY and Hannah [no stones]) - d. 11 June 1881 Æ 90 y., 11 d.

DODGE
- Benjamin H. [husb. of Lucinda T.] - b. 2 March 1827; d. 1 June 1903; (member of Co. C, 28th Maine Regiment [Civil War])
- Edward P. (husb. of Hannah B.) - d. 1 May 1883 Æ 57 y., 6 m.
- Hannah B. (wife of Edward P.) - d. 29 July 1906 Æ 74 y., 7 m.
- Isadore L. (adopted dau. of Edward P. and Hannah B.) - d. 1 August 1884 Æ 23 y., 5 m., 5 d.
- Lucinda T. [wife of Benjamin H.] - b. 2 May 1831; d. 4 March 1911

FARQUHARSON
- William ("a native of P. E. Island") - d. 21 November 1900 Æ 37 y.

GETCHELL
- Minot (Corporal) - [no dates]; (member of Co. B, 1st Massachusetts Infantry [Civil War])

GOTT
- Ella L. (wife of Orlando T. [no stone]) - d. 4 July 1886 Æ 24 y., 9 m.

HAMBLEN
- Hattie L. (wife of Clinton F. [no stone]) - b. 26 March 1868; d. 17 April 1932

HIGGINS
Eldora M. (wife of Frank L.) - b. 1858; d. 1938
Emily M. (wife of Seth H.) - d. 17 November 1892 Æ 61 y., 9 m.
Frank L. (husb. of Eldora M.) - b. 1852; d. 1928
Grace E. (dau. of Frank L. and Eldora M.) - b. 1878; d. 1896
infant [child of Frank L. and Eldora M.?] - [b. and d.?] 1880
Seth H. (husb. of Emily M.) - d. 5 February 1877 Æ 53 y., 11 m.; (member of Co. E, 28th Maine Regiment [Civil War])
William W. [son of Seth H. and Emily M.?] - d. 5 April 1893 Æ 32 y., 5 m., 24 d.; ("drowned")
JACKSON
Edward S. - b. 1860; d. 1929
LAWLER
infant (dau. of Allen J. and Caroline R. [no stones]) - d. 22 August 1895 Æ 3 m., 12 d.
LURVEY
Abigail (wife of Samuel) - d. 18 September 1866 Æ 76 y., 10 m., 9 d.
Abigail D. (wife of Isaac) - d. 20 September 1887 Æ 91 y., 10 m., 23 d.
Alice H. (dau. of John D. and Hannah C.) - d. 14 March 1879 Æ 19 y., 1 m., 12 d.
Arthur C. [husb. of Elva M.?] - d. 24 April 1892 Æ 30 y., 2 m., 13 d.
Charles A. (son of Cyrus H. and Mary A.) - d. 4 March 1871 Æ 16 y., 3 m., 9 d.
Cyrus H. (husb. of Mary A.) - [no dates]
Elva M. [wife of Arthur C.?] - d. 22 April 1905 Æ 39 y.
Enoch - d. 3 November 1879 Æ 82 y., 4 m.
Enoch (Sgt.; husb. of Rebecca W. [no stone]) - [no dates]; (member of Co. H, 4th Maine Regiment [Civil War])
George A. - b. 1867; d. 1906
Georgie (son of Sgt. Enoch and Rebecca W. [no stone]) - d. 28 January 1867 Æ 1 y., 15 d.
Gilbert L. [husb. of Mary E.] - b. 1841; d. 1906; (member of Co. G, 18th Maine Regiment [Civil War])
Hannah C. (wife of John D.) - d. 6 June 1888 Æ 62 y., 11 m., 11 d.
infant (dau. of Levi and Lydia B.) - [b. and?] d. 5 March 1869
infant (son of John D. and Hannah C.) - [b. and?] d. [23?][1] May 1867
infants (4) (children of Cyrus H. and Mary A.) - [no dates]
Isaac (husb. of Abigail D.) - d. 21 April 1876 Æ 80 y., 9 m., 5 d.
Joann H. [wife of Samuel Jr.?] - b. 8 October 1815; d. 30 March 1907 Æ 91 y., 5 m., 22 d.
John D. (husb. of Hannah C.) - d. 28 May 1893 Æ 69 y., 10 m., 9 d.
Levi (husb. of Lydia B.) - b. 15 August 1833; d. 23 October 1902
Lydia B. (wife of Levi) - b. 16 September 1832; d. 23 June 1903
Mary A. (wife of Cyrus H.) - d. 15 September 1893 Æ 63 y., 6 m., 3 d.
Mary E. [wife of Gilbert L.] - b. 1846; d. 1927
[Maud E. - see STANLEY]
[Rachel - see CARROLL]
Samuel (husb. of Abigail) - d. 2 January 1870 Æ 76 y., 8 m., 24 d.
Samuel Jr. [husb. of Joann H.?] - d. 9 June 1893 Æ 76 y., 2 m., 17 d.
William G. - d. 30 December 1879 Æ 51 y., 5 m., 19 d.
MAYO
Isaac P. (husb. of Rosanna) - d. 12 June 1866 Æ 92 y., 25 d.
Rosanna (wife of Isaac P.) - d. 15 October 1865 Æ 83 y., 10 m., 17 d.
Ruth F. (dau. of Jacob and Hannah E. [no stones]) - d. 17 July 1894 Æ 4 m., 14 d.

MILAN
Ellen Maria (wife of Thomas) - b. 18 September 1834; d. 9 May 1915
Millie M. - b. 30 September 1876; d. 16 April 1932
Thomas (husb. of Ellen Maria) - b. 5 July 1839; d. 3 February 1906; (member of Co. H, 4th Maine Regiment [Civil War])
PERKINS
Dorothy [PERKINS?] - [no dates]; ("baby")
Irving B. [husb. of Lottie B.?] - b. 1885; d. 1955
Lottie B. [wife of Irving B.?] - b. 1875; d. 1953
SEAVEY
Mary J. - b. 1837; d. 1906
STANLEY
H. Edwin Jr. [husb. of Maud E. (LURVEY)] - b. 1869; d. 1964
Maud E. (LURVEY; [wife of H. Edwin Jr.]) - b. 1869; d. 1938
TINKER
Carroll F. (son of John R. [no stone] and Mabel A.) - b. 13 December 1901; d. 1 April 1902
infant (dau. of John R. [no stone] and Mabel A.) - [no dates]
Mabel A. (wife of John R. [no stone]) - b. 1862; d. 1915
TRUNDY
Lizzie May (dau. of Henry E. and Margaret C. [no stones]) - d. 19 February 1892 Æ 8 m., 5 d.
WALLS
Daniel Wilbert - d. 27 November 1879, "Mirago anc, St. Domingo", Æ 26 y., 3 m.
Myra S. (wife of John A. [no stone]) - d. 17 December 1906 Æ 48 y., 3 m., 5 d.
YOUNG
Charles B. - d. 8 September 1910 Æ 37 y.
Orville P. (son of Arad P. and Margaret [no stones]) - d. 25 January 1887 Æ 31 y., 3 m., 8 d.

Note:
[1]Stone cracked.

Old Burying Ground
(Southwest Harbor - 3)

Location/directions. Set back from the southeast side of High Road. From the traffic light at the north end of Mount Desert Island, go straight ahead (south) onto Routes 102/198. In approximately 10.6–10.7 miles (6.3–6.4 miles of which are south of the traffic light at the intersection of Routes 102/198 and 198/233), turn left onto Clark Point Road at the blinking light in the center of the village of Southwest Harbor. In about 0.2 miles, turn left onto High Road. The cemetery is on the right in less than 0.1 miles.

History. This cemetery is on land that was part of a 270 acre parcel owned by Ebenezer Eaton in 1808 according to the Salem Towne Jr. map. Thornton (1938) reported that the cemetery was started by Ebenezer Eaton, minister of the Congregational Church, who "allowed his parishioners to lay their dead to rest on his dry, sunny hillside in what was then his field" (p. 209).

Notes. The name used for this cemetery was taken from a weathered sign (2000) that reads, "Old burying ground/first public cemetery/on Mt. Desert Island".

Names and dates on gravestones and other markers.

ADAMS
- Gracie - d. 16 December 1889 Æ 5 y., 1 m., 13 d.

ARNOLD
- Carl F. - [...][1]
- Eulalie M. - b. 1887; d. 1888
- John M. - b. 1880; d. 1889

CLARK
- [Nancy Caroline - see COUSINS]

COUSINS
- Irene B. - d. 13 December 1887 Æ 75 y., 1 m., 13 d.
- Isaac R. (son of Nehemiah H. and Nancy Caroline (CLARK; widow of Israel CLARK)) - d. 29 March 1858 Æ 2 y.
- Nancy Caroline (CLARK; widow of Israel CLARK; wife of Nehemiah H.) - d. 23 September 1886 Æ 60 y., 7 m., 11 d.
- Nehemiah H. (husb. of Nancy Caroline (CLARK; widow of Israel CLARK)) - d. 22 March 1858 Æ 42 y.

CROCKETT
- Birtie ([dau.?] of John T. and Julia S. (FREEMAN)) - [no dates]
- John T. (husb. of Julia S. (FREEMAN)) - b. 1835; d. [no date]
- Julia S. (FREEMAN; wife of John T.) - b. 1836; d. 1910
- Katie (dau. of John T. and Julia S. (FREEMAN)) - [no dates]

DOUGLASS
- Susan (wife of Robert [no stone]) - d. April 1858 Æ 74 y.

EATON
- Abigail H. ("consort" of Rev. Ebenezer [no stone]) - d. 24 April 1830 Æ 72 y.
- Joshua Herrick - b. 20 September 1795; d. 16 December 1835 Æ 40 y.

FREEMAN
- [Julia S. - see CROCKETT]

G.
- D. R. [footstone only]

GILLEY

Clarrisa [sic] (wife of William) - d. 15 July 1837 Æ 26 y.
Elizabeth (wife of Benjamin [no stone]) - b. 3 June 1832; d. 27 October 1894
Phebe H. (wife of William) - b. 5 April 1809; d. 29 December 1893
Rebecca E. (wife of Benjamin [no stone]) - d. 25 April 1871 Æ 23 y., 2 m., 9 d.
William (husb. of Clarrisa [sic] and Phebe H.) - b. 8 July 1805; d. 6 January 1894

GOTT

Josephine (dau. of Robert and Lydia) - d. 28 May 1857 Æ 8 m.[5]
Lydia M. (wife of Robert) - d. 16 March 1891 Æ 73 y., 2 m., 14 d.
Rebecca (wife of Robert) - d. 5 April 1848 Æ 35 y.
Robert (husb. of Rebecca and Lydia M.) - [...][2]

HOLMES

Elmer E. (son of William T. and Amelia M. [no stones]) - d. 27 October 1868 Æ 7 y., 2 m., 10 d.

HOPKINS

David E. F. G.[3] (son of Allen and Clarrisa [sic] [no stones]) - d. 16 September 1857 Æ 36 y., 7 m., 16 d.
[Mary E. - see YOUNG]
Mary L. (wife of Alen [sic] [no stone]) - d. 1 November 1839[5]

MAYO

Isaac P. Jr. - d. 19 December 1842 Æ 20 y., 6 m.
Joshua - d. 10 August 1843 Æ 34 y., 8 m.

ROBERTS

Robert - b. Wales; d. 1 September 1872, "on Board U. S. S. Powhatan", Æ 28 y.

ROBINSON

Daniel Jr. (son of Daniel [no stone] and Joan[na][4]) - d. 20 March 1846 Æ 14 y., 7 m.
J. W. - [no dates]
Joan[na][4] (wife of Daniel [no stone]) - d. 1 May 1860 Æ 44 y., 17 d.
Lavinia (SAVAGE; wife of Levi) - d. 7 July 1847 Æ 33 y.
Levi (husb. of Lavinia (SAVAGE)) - b. 8 February 1808; d. [...][5]
Levi Jr. (son of Levi and Lavinia (SAVAGE)) - d. 18 September 1841 Æ 15 m.
Sarah (WHITMORE; dau. of James WHITMORE and [Rebecca or Rebeckah][4]; wife of Smith [no stone]) - d. 2 November 1850 Æ 27 y.

ROSS

L. Viola (wife of James F. [no stone]) - d. 26 September 1870 Æ 17 y., 8 m.

SAVAGE

[Lavinia - see ROBINSON]

WHITMORE

Hannah (dau. of Capt. James and [Rebecca or Rebeckah][4]) - d. 12 April 1850 Æ 17 y., 6 m.
James (Capt.; husb. of [Rebecca or Rebeckah][4]) - d. 2 February 1883 Æ 86 y., 1 m., 22 d.
John G. (son of Capt. James and [Rebecca or Rebeckah][4]) - d. 30 November 1850 Æ 16 y., 3 m.
Joseph (Capt.) - d. 24 January 1847 Æ 29 y.
[Rebecca or Rebeckah][4] (wife of Capt. James) - d. 19 March 1872 Æ 82 y., 5 m.
[Sarah - see ROBINSON]

YOUNG

Adelbert O. (son of Willard W. [no stone] and Mary E. (HOPKINS)) - d. 13 July 1862 Æ 7 y., 21 d.
Mary E. (HOPKINS; dau. of Allen HOPKINS [no stone]; wife of Willard W. [no stone]) - d. 22 September 1863 Æ 26 y., 6 m.

Notes:

[1]A tree root grown (2000) over the stone obscures any date(s).

[2]Stone broken.

[3]Footstone: "D. E. F. G. H."

[4]Different on different stones.

[5]Remainder of stone is in concrete, thereby obscuring any further information it may contain.

Mount Height Cemetery

(Southwest Harbor - 4)

Location/directions. Set back from the southeast side of Route 102. From the traffic light at the north end of Mount Desert Island, go straight ahead (south) onto Routes 102/198. In approximately 11.3–11.4 miles (0.8 miles of which are south of the blinking light in the center of the village of Southwest Harbor), is an intersection of Routes 102 and 102A. Continue straight on Route 102 and in about 0.1 miles, the entrance to the cemetery is on the left.

History. —

Notes. This cemetery is not enclosed. Roads are paved or gravel. The grass is mowed and trimmed, and there is water available.

Names and dates on gravestones and other markers. [19 September 1999]

ABBOTT
- Mildred F. - b. 26 August 1898; d. 30 May 1972

ALBEE
- Agnes M. (wife of Harry G. [no stone]) - b. 1884; d. 1936
- Cynthia S. - b. 8 June 1960; d. 8 March 1988

ALLEN
- Agnes M. - b. 1924
- Olcott A. (son of Asher and Anna M. [no stones]) - d. 14 October 1890 Æ 4 m.

ALLEY
- Calvin Carroll [husb. of Edna E.] - b. 14 September 1907; d. 13 February 1992
- Carroll M. - b. 23 October 1924; d. 9 April 1988
- Edith S. - b. 13 September 1939; d. 4 April 1979
- Edna E. [wife of Calvin Carroll] - b. 19 September 1901; d. 18 July 1991
- [Nancy M. - see BROWN]

AMIRO
- Kenneth D. [husb. of Ruth B.] - b. 1906
- Ruth B. [wife of Kenneth D.] - b. 1910; d. 1998

ANDERSON
- Emily M. [wife of Herman L.] - b. 1897; d. 1982 [see also BREWSTER]
- George W. - b. 10 March 1859; d. 22 May 1916
- Harold L. Jr. - b. 1930; d. 1997
- Herman L. [husb. of Emily M.] - b. 1891; d. 1946
- Verna W. - b. 1917; d. 1966

ANTHONY
- Alfred H. [husb. of Ella (YOUNG)] - b. 1870; d. 1953
- Ella (YOUNG; [wife of Alfred H.]) - b. 1878; d. 1941
- Harrison Edward [son of Alfred H. and Ella (YOUNG)?] - b. 1 November 1906; d. 28 December 1976

ARCHILLES
- David L. - [b. and d.?] 1953
- Shirley N. - b. 1927; d. 1964
- Wayne G. - [b. and d.?] 1953

ASH
- Linda - b. 1880; d. 1953
- Martha A. (wife of Robert) - b. 1845; d. 1929
- Robert (husb. of Zidana and Martha A.) - b. 1837; d. 1914
- Thomas W. - b. 1876; d. 1930

William [son of Robert and Zidana?] - b. 1867; d. 1871
Zidana (wife of Robert) - b. 1840; d. 1871

ATHERTON
G. Delorin (husb. of Mary J.) - b. 1848; d. 1935
Mary J. (wife of G. Delorin) - b. 1856; d. 1941

BALDWIN
[C. - see Clifton M. RICH]

BANNISTER
Hope (NORWOOD; [wife of Frank Cecil?]) - b. 1904; d. 1987
Frank Cecil [husb. of Hope (NORWOOD)?] - b. 1899; d. 1959

BARROWS
Carl W. [husb. of Elizabeth (KELLEY)] - b. 22 October 1887; d. 15 May 1972
Elizabeth (KELLEY; [wife of Carl W.]) - b. 26 September 1893; d. 26 July 1976

BARTLETT
[Emily M. - see DIX]

BATES
[Ella - see SPURLING]

BATTIS
Emily W. (wife of William L.) - b. 3 December 1840; d. 24 February 1903
William L. (husb. of Emily W.) - b. 15 January 1833; d. 10 January 1909

BAUER
Janet S. - b. 1914; d. 1978

BEAL
Ada Squires - b. 1905; d. 1981
Alston A. (son of Vinal O. and Nettie E.) - b. 1908; d. 1938
Clara M. (wife of James E.) - b. 1890; d. 1959
Edward L. [husb. of Flora L.] - b. 1892; d. 1960
Elmer L. [husb. of Prudence B.] - b. 1920
Elva L. - b. 1898; d. 1980
[Etheleen - see HAMBLEN]
Flora L. [wife of Edward L.] - b. 1892; d. 1971
James E. (husb. of Clara M.) - b. 1888; d. 1973
Harvard R. - b. 1897; d. 1967
infant [child of Maurice R. and Mamie V.?] - [b. and d.?] 1929
Mamie V. [wife of Maurice R.] - b. 1885; d. 1965
Maurice R. [husb. of Mamie V.] - b. 1894; d. 196[5 or 6][7]
Nettie E. (wife of Vinal O.) - b. 1874; d. 1967
Prudence B. [wife of Elmer L.] - b. 1920
Vinal O. (husb. of Nettie E.) - b. 1868; d. 1944
Violetta M. (dau. of James E. and Clara M.) - b. 1909; d. 1969
[Virginia - see MICHAUD]

BEAUDRY
Betty Lou - b. 8 March 1932; d. 6 October 1996

BELCHER
Helen W. [wife of Norman E.] - b. 1904; d. 1997
Norman E. [husb. of Helen W.] - b. 1899; d. 1971

BENNETT
Arlene Jane [dau. of Carl E. and Marguerite D.?] - b. 31 May 1942; d. 15 February 1943
Carl E. [husb. of Marguerite D.] - b. 4 August 1914
Charles H. [husb. of Mary E.] - b. 1922; d. 1984
Daisy M. [BENNETT?] - b. 1884; d. 1910

Fannie S. [wife of Harry] - b. 1894; d. 1964
Harry [husb. of Fannie S.] - b. 1890; d. 1965
Josephine Tröndle[13] (wife of Jack London) - b. 18 February 1914; d. 21 August 1958
Jack London (husb. of Josephine Tröndle[13]) - b. 29 September 1917; d. 4 April 1978
Malcolm S. - b. 1916; d. 1976
Margaret (wife of James E. [no stone]) - b. 1856; d. 1943
Marguerite D. [wife of Carl E.] - b. 24 November 1918; d. 2 January 1991
Mary E. [wife of Charles H.] - b. 1922; d. 1995
Stanley Roy - b. 3 September 1927; d. 22 December 1976

BENSON
[Blanche Modjeska - see NELSON]
Carey Alan - b. 25 January 1952; d. 2 October 1971
Edith Luella [dau. of Lewis F. and Elizabeth W. "Lizzie" (HITCHCOCK)?] - [b. and d.?] 1885
Elizabeth W. "Lizzie" (HITCHCOCK; wife of Lewis F.) - b. 1859; d. 1942
Frances Caroline [dau. of Lewis F. and Elizabeth W. "Lizzie" (HITCHCOCK)?] - b. 1883; d. 1934
Frank Lewis [son of Lewis F. and Elizabeth W. "Lizzie" (HITCHCOCK)?] - b. 1887; d. 1961
[Harriet - see Elizabeth Wells TRACY]
Harriet Ella [dau. of Lewis F. and Elizabeth W. "Lizzie" (HITCHCOCK)?] - [b. and d.?] 1881
Harry Parker (son of Lewis F. and Elizabeth W. "Lizzie" (HITCHCOCK)) - b. 17 January 1893; d. 21 March 1895
Lewis Albert (son of Lewis F. and Elizabeth W. "Lizzie" (HITCHCOCK)) - b. 6 September 1894; d. 12 December 1899
Lewis F. (husb. of Elizabeth W. "Lizzie" (HITCHCOCK)) - b. 1853; d. 1918
Sadie May (dau. of Lewis F. and Elizabeth W. "Lizzie" (HITCHCOCK)) - b. 1 May 1891; d. 23 September 1891

BERRY
Andrew - [no dates]
Andrew Donald - b. 19 December 1918; d. 19 October 1968
Elizabeth "Lizzie" - b. 16 August 1897; d. 16 December 1998 Æ 101 y.
Forrest I. [husb. of Mamie R.] - b. 1 November 1925
Frederick K. - b. 1922; d. 1990
Mamie R. [wife of Forrest I.] - b. 8 October 1928; d. 11 July 1990

BICKFORD
Andrew E. [husb. of Marion H.] - b. 1889; d. 1956
Arlington H. [[son of Lowell A. and Hattie J.?]; husb. of Rebecca S.] - b. 30 May 1918; d. 23 July 1983
Bertha TORREY [widow of Milton F. TORREY] - b. 1896; d. 1982
H. Chase [husb. of Lois E.] - b. 1887; d. 1960
Hattie J. [wife of Lowell A.] - b. 1893; d. 1947
Henry A. (husb. of Lillian E. (ROBINSON)) - b. 1862; d. 1940
Lillian E. (ROBINSON; wife of Henry A.) - b. 1863; d. 1926
Lois E. [wife of H. Chase] - b. 1902; d. 1961
Lowell A. [husb. of Hattie J.] - b. 1 November 1891; d. 1 May 1965
Marion H. [wife of Andrew E.] - b. 1895; d. 1986
Rebecca S. [wife of Arlington H.] - b. 30 January 1926; d. 16 October 1978
Stephanie [dau. of Arlington H. and Rebecca S.?] - b. 11 July 1953; d. October 1953

BILLINGS
Abbie D[ORR?]. (wife of Kenneth E.) - [no dates]

Alton M. [husb. of Bessie C.] - b. 22 September 1876; d. 28 October 1922
Bessie C. [wife of Alton M.] - b. 13 November 1883; d. 16 January 1931
Carolyn Ames [wife of Raymond Earl] - b. 1943
Earl E. (husb. of Elva) - b. 1892; d. 1982
Edith W. - b. 1890; d. 1923
Elva (wife of Earl E.) - b. 1885; d. 1968
Emily W. (wife of John E.) - b. 27 August 1852; d. 20 September 1933
Frances M. - b. 1902; d. 1971
Harold E. - b. 30 March 1937; d. 26 July 1997 Æ 60 y.
John D. (husb. of Rose L.) - b. 1911; d. 1988
John E. (husb. of Emily W.) - b. 27 December 1843; d. 8 December 1915
Kenneth Dorr "Kenny" (son of Kenneth E. and Abbie D[ORR?].) - b. 3 October 1945; d. 9 June 1994
Kenneth E. (husb. of Abbie D[ORR?].) - [no dates]
Raymond D. - b. 1886; d. 1966
Raymond Earl [husb. of Carolyn Ames] - b. 1934
Rose L. (wife of John D.) - b. 1904; d. 1981
[Sarah B[ILLINGS?]. - see ROBINSON]

BIRLEM [see also BIRLEN]
Charles Wallace [husb. of Margaret M.?] - b. 23 February 1914; d. 20 September 1975
[Doris - see STUBBS]
Fred Alberton (Capt.; husb. of Mary (SPURLING)) - b. 18 October 1876; d. 14 April 1950
Margaret M. [wife of Charles Wallace?] - b. 29 January 1910; d. 26 August 1989
Mary (SPURLING; wife of Capt. Fred Alberton) - b. 26 September 1877; d. 10 July 1965

BIRLEN [see also BIRLEM]
Frances M. (wife of Augustus B. [no stone]) - d. 2 February 1875 Æ 32 y., 1 m., 5 d.
Lucretia E. - d.[1] 2 May 1875 Æ 5 m.

BLACK
Allan L. (husb. of Fannie E.) - b. 1868; d. 1954
Arthur T. [husb. of Fredrica [sic] N.] - b. 1895; d. 1978
Beatrice M. [wife of Edward C.] - b. 4 October 1901
Edward C. [husb. of Beatrice M.] - b. 9 June 1895; d. 5 December 1985
Fannie E. (wife of Allan L.) - b. 1874; d. 1944
Frank - b. 1867; d. 1946
Fredrica [sic] N. [wife of Arthur T.] - b. 1897; d. 1986
Merle E. - b. 1898; d. 1981
Samuel L. - b. 1900; d. 1987
Sarah E. - b. 1875; d. 1932

BLAISDELL
Lettie F. (STANLEY; wife of Harry L. [no stone]) - b. 1884; d. 1941

BOARDMAN
Edward - d. 4 July 1906 Æ 27 y.

BOISVERT
Bernard J. [husb. of Bonnie D. L[UDWIG?].] - b. 1956
Bonnie D. L[UDWIG?]. [wife of Bernard J.] - b. 1966

BOUCHARD
Alice M[ITCHELL?]. [[dau. of Austin M. MITCHELL and Lena N.?]; wife of Normand J.] - b. 1918; d. 1972

Normand J. [husb. of Alice M[ITCHELL?].] - b. 1912; d. 1973
Normand J. Jr. "Skip" [son of Normand J. and Alice M[ITCHELL?].] - b. 1949; d. 1990

BRACY
Amanda J. (wife of Amos H.) - b. 1853; d. 1940
Amos H. (husb. of Amanda J.) - b. 1848; d. 1928

BRADFORD
Charles F. [husb. of Rebecca W.] - b. 19 February 1942
Owen F. (son of Volney S. and Hope [no stone]) - b. 1949; d. 1966
Rebecca W. [wife of Charles F.] - b. 16 June 1942; d. 30 January 1988
Volney S. (husb. of Hope [no stone]) - b. 21 December 1912; d. 21 June 1990

BRAGG
Arthur S. [husb. of Katherine L.] - b. 1914; d. 1970
Katherine L. [wife of Arthur S.] - b. 1915

BRAWN
Charlotte Evelyn - b. 1928; d. 1930
Clara - b. 1906; d. 1982
Diantha A. (wife of John A.) - b. 17 August 1841; d. 19 May 1905
Homer [husb. of Kate] - b. 1867; d. 1951
John A. (husb. of Mary E. and Diantha A.) - b. 15 April 1833; d. 19 April 1909
Kate [wife of Homer] - b. 1876; d. 1958
Lynwood - b. 1909; d. 1923
Mary E. (wife of John A.) - b. 14 January 1835; d. 21 July 1895

BREWSTER
[Emily M. - m. (1) Herman L. ANDERSON (*q.v.*), [2?] --- BREWSTER?]

BRIDGHAM
George M. - b. 1915; d. 1976

BROOKS
Charles - b. 1843; d. 1932

BROWN
[Alice - see NORWOOD]
Amos S. (husb. of Leoniece [sic] L.) - b. 1833; d. 1903; (member of Co. E., 26th Maine Regiment [Civil War])
[Antoinette - see HARMON]
Beatrice (HARPER) - b. 1918
Cora (dau. of William H.) - [no dates]
[Dorothy B[ROWN?]. - see SINCLAIR]
Edward T. [husb. of Georgia M.] - b. 1886; d. 1982
Ellen R. (wife of Harry A.) - b. 1877; d. 1968
Georgia M. [wife of Edward T.] - b. 1885; d. 1977
Harry A. (husb. of Ellen R.) - b. 1877; d. 1951
Helen (JOHNSTON; [wife of Thomas IV]) - b. 1911; d. 1980
Joann (HIGGINS; wife of William N.) - b. 1801; d. 1876
John L. (son of William N. and Joann (HIGGINS); husb. of Nancy M. (ALLEY)) - b. 1829; d. 1897
Leoniece [sic] L. (wife of Amos S.) - b. 1843; d. 1922
May W. [wife of S. B. B.] - b. 13 December 1864; d. 7 December 1939
Nancy M. (ALLEY; wife of John L.) - b. 1843; d. 1902
[Pheobe or Phoebe][2] (dau. of William H.) - [no dates]
S. B. B. [husb. of May W.] - b. 16 March 1868; d. 20 September 1944
Thomas IV [husb. of Helen (JOHNSTON)] - b. 1907; d. 1982
Wanita G. - b. 1901; d. 1974

William H. - b. 1824; d. 1860
William N. (husb. of Joann (HIGGINS)) - b. 1797; d. 1859
Winnie B. [child of John L. and Nancy M. (ALLEY)?] - b. 1875; d. 1887

BUELL
John H. (Dr.; [husb. of Marjorie W.]) - b. 1911; d. 1968
Marjorie W. [wife of Dr. John H.] - b. 1919; d. 1978
May G. - b. 1888; d. 1979

BULGER
Charles R. (husb. of Georgia F.) - b. 1885; d. 1963
Georgia F. (wife of Charles R.) - b. 1887; d. 1951
Harvey E. (husb. of Sadie A.) - b. 1883; d. 1964
Richard H. [son of Charles R. and Georgia F.?] - b. 1925; d. 1985
Sadie A. (wife of Harvey E.) - b. 1879; d. 1973

BUNKER
Edwin H. (husb. of Mary A.) - b. 24 July 1844; d. 7 April 1914
Gail P. [wife of Raymond A.] - b. 1917; d. 1995
George H. - b. 20 June 1870; d. 23 August 1944
Harry W. [son of Leslie R. and Martha L.?] - b. 1906; d. 1930
Leslie R. [husb. of Martha L.] - b. 1869; d. 1930
Martha L. [wife of Leslie R.] - b. 1874; d. 1963
Mary A. (wife of Edwin H.) - b. 24 September 1849; d. 15 February 1945
Raymond A. [husb. of Gail P.] - b. 1906; d. 1994

BURBANK
Albertenia A. (SANFORD; dau. of Capt. George E. SANFORD and Matilda J. (HADLOCK)) - b. 1842; d. 1867

BURGESS
Allie May [wife of Barclay W.] - b. 1888; d. 1961
Barclay W. [husb. of Allie May] - b. 1884; d. 1964
Ronald D. [husb. of Thelma Edna (CAMPBELL)?] - b. 1922; d. 1977
Thelma Edna (CAMPBELL; [wife of Ronald D.?]) - b. 10 February 1920; d. 16 March 1998

BURNETT
[Esther - see GOTT]

BURR
Edra F. [wife of Harry H.] - b. 8 March 1916; d. 4 March 1992
Harry H. [husb. of Edra F.] - b. 1 June 1914; d. 26 September 1986

BURRELL
Mabel (MALANSON) - b. 29 July 1892; d. 14 May 1984

BURTON
Grace D. (STANLEY; wife of Nelson D. [no stone]) - b. 8 September 1912; d. 11 November 1994

BUTLER
Esther L. [wife of Leon C.] - b. 1902; d. 1994
Jeannette P. - b. 29 July 1916; d. 27 March 1987
Leon C. [husb. of Esther L.] - b. 1910; d. 1983

CAMPBELL
[Thelma Edna - see BURGESS]

CAPEN
Milton S. [husb. of Sarah D.?] - b. 1873; d. 1962
Sarah D. [wife of Milton S.?] - b. 1880; d. 1955

CARPENTER
Alice J. - b. 1892; d. 1923

Byron S. (husb. of Hattie K.) - b. 186[5 or 6][3]; d. 1956
Hattie K. (wife of Byron S.) - b. 1874; d. 1947
Jesse P. - b. 27 September 1893; d. 21 July 1966
Rachel E. - b. 1896; d. 1897

CARR
Lurline (STANLEY) - b. 1896; d. 1975

CARROLL
[Catherine - see STANLEY]
Charles B. [CARROLL?] [husb. of Mary S. "Mae"] - b. 1902; d. 1983
David A. - b. 1938; d. 1990
Fannie E. (dau. of Capt. Jacob W. and Rebecca (WHITMORE)) - d. 16 February 1890 Æ 15 y., 10 m., 23 d.
Gertrude W. (dau. of Capt. Jacob W. and Rebecca (WHITMORE)) - b. 1873; d. 1917
Jacob W. (Capt.; husb. of Rebecca (WHITMORE)) - b. 1830; d. 1899
John [husb. of Viola T.] - b. 1875; d. 1964
[Marilyn - see LAHAYE]
Mary Ann - b. 7 May 1835; d. 29 November 1926
Mary S. "Mae" [wife of Charles B. [CARROLL?]] - b. 1908; d. 1994
Melissa F. [wife of Philip T.] - b. 1904; d. 1995
[Nellie R. - see THORNTON]
Philip T. [husb. of Melissa F.] - b. 1904; d. 1966
[Rachel C[ARROLL?]. - see PHALEN]
Rebecca (WHITMORE; wife of Capt. Jacob W.) - b. 1844; d. 1916
Robert S. - b. 1932; d. 1996
Viola T. [wife of John] - b. 1881; d. 1940

CARTER
Byron P. [husb. of Hannah R.] - b. 19 February 1854; d. 4 April 1926
Doris L. (wife of Lawrence E. Sr.) - b. 1925; d. 1999
Hannah R. [wife of Byron P.] - b. 31 October 1841; d. 23 April 1913
Laura D. - b. 1892; d. 1965
Lawrence E. Sr. (husb. of Doris L.) - b. 1923; d. 1992
Mary M. - b. 1901; d. 1956
Mildred N. [wife of Robert M.] - b. 1910; d. 1988
Raymond L. Jr. - b. 1926; d. 1986
Robert M. [husb. of Mildred N.] - b. 1905; d. 1975
Rowland C. - b. 8 January 1838; d. 20 March 1883, "at sea"

CARUSO
Frances M. [wife of Soly E.] - b. 1922; d. 1982
Soly E. [husb. of Frances M.] - b. 1896; d. [no date]

CARVER
[Aljava - see NORWOOD]

CASLIN
Charles M. - b. 8 July 1886; d. 11 August 1965

CHAFFEY
[Katie M.[14] - see SMITH]
T. Louis (husb. of Vesta E.) - b. 1870; d. 1914
Vesta E. (wife of T. Louis) - b. 1876; d. 1957

CHALMERS
Francis T. [husb. of Gussie E.] - b. 3 December 1893; d. 28 December 1985
Francis T. Jr. [son of Francis T. and Gussie E.; husb. of Mildred P.] - b. 12 July 1920; d. 14 September 1993
Gussie E. [wife of Francis T.] - b. 25 June 1897; d. 30 April 1948

Mildred P. [wife of Francis T. Jr.] - b. 29 December 1920
Wendall Dana [son of Francis T. Jr. and Mildred P.?] - b. 1953; d. 1954

CHAMBERLAIN
[Margaret - see HUTCHINS]

CHILDS
Cora E. (CLARK; wife of Edward C. [no stone]) - b. 1883; d. 1928

CIESIELKA
John [husb. of Pauline F.] - b. 1916; d. 1995
Pauline F. [wife of John] - b. 1908; d. 1986

CLARK
[Ada E. - see PARKER]
Annie D. - b. 1888; d. 1976
Bessie S. - b. 1891; d. 1974
Clarence [husb. of Florence N.] - b. 1853; d. 1940
[Cora E. - see CHILDS]
Dorinda N. (wife of Israel [no stone]) - d. 16 September 1860 Æ 23 y., 6 m.
Florence N. [wife of Clarence] - b. 1861; d. 1941
[Grace - see PEASE]
James T. [husb. of Melinda R.?] - b. 1830; d. 1902
[Josephine "Josie" - see COOMBS]
Lionel A. (husb. of Nellie M.) - b. 1855; d. 1929
Marion - b. 1893; d. 1973
Melinda R. [wife of James T.?] - b. 1834; d. 1904
Nellie M. (wife of Lionel A.) - b. 1859; d. 1938

CLEMENT
Chester III (son of Chester H. and Mildred E.) - [b. and d.?] 3 September 1945
Chester E. [husb. of Grace L.] - b. 1881; d. 1937
Chester H. ([son of Chester E. and Grace L.?]; husb. of Mildred E.) - b. 1911; d. 1984
Grace L. [wife of Chester E.] - b. 1890; d. 1987
Mildred E. (wife of Chester H.) - b. 1909; d. 1962

CLERICI
Guido - b. 1901; d. 1954

CLOSSON
Lewis E. - b. 1912; d. 1991
Phillis W[HITMORE]. - b. 1914

CLOUGH
Malcolm W. (husb. of Nina J.) - b. 24 June 1934
Nina J. (wife of Malcolm W.) - b. 7 August 1934; d. 27 August 1997

COFFEY
[Ann - see LAWLER]

COLSON
Eva (REED) - b. 1871; d. 1962
Florence [wife of Frank] - b. 1899; d. 1971
Frank [husb. of Florence] - b. 1880; d. 1971

CONARY
Alice Lessie [sic] - b. 10 November 1912; d. 25 May 1932
Elmer E. [husb. of Gertrude R.] - b. 1868; d. 1946
Elmer E. Jr. [son of Elmer E. and Gertrude R.] - b. 26 August 1905; d. 30 September 1905
Gertrude R. [wife of Elmer E.] - b. 1879; d. 1956

CONNERS
Gwendolyn H[AMOR?]. [wife of Oscar S.] - b. 1897; d. 1961
Oscar S. [husb. of Gwendolyn H[AMOR?].] - b. 1900; d. 1954
CONNORS
George (husb. of Mary) - b. 13 January 1861; d. 1 September 1919
Mary (wife of George) - b. 25 February 1865; d. 15 July 1942
COOK
[Almeda N. - see NEWMAN]
Charles E. (husb. of Zelinda J. (DOW)) - b. 1840; d. 1927; (Private, Co. F, 44th Massachusetts Infantry; Sergeant, Co. F, 5th Massachusetts Infantry [Civil War])
Zelinda J. (DOW; wife of Charles E.) - b. 1856; d. 1954
COOMBS
Amelia C. [wife of Horace C.] - b. 1900; d. 1990
Barbara (DOLLIVER) - b. 1921; d. 1996
Frederick "Freddy" [husb. of Josephine "Josie" (CLARK)] - b. 14 February 1857; d. 16 January 1858
Horace C. [husb. of Amelia C.] - b. 1901; d. 1957
Josephine "Josie" (CLARK; [wife of Frederick "Freddy"]) - b. 1 January 1864; d. 5 March 1880
CORBETT
Agnes Donnom - b. 1874; d. 1966
COUSINS
Lida E. [wife of Osborn W.] - b. 1865; d. 1951
Merle F. [husb. of Victoria V.?] - b. 1905; d. 1980
Osborn W. [husb. of Lida E.] - b. 1851; d. 1939
Victoria V. [wife of Merle F.?] - b. 1919
CRAFTS
Howard Jefferson - b. 13 January 1917; d. 25 November 1995
CRAIG
Harriet (GOTT; [wife of William Henry]) - b. 1913; d. 1976
William Henry [husb. of Harriet (GOTT)] - b. 1906; d. 1966
CRAM
Frank S. - b. 1865; d. 1940
CRANE
Kathleen Ann (KING) - b. 6 September 1938
CROCKER
Gladys M[AYO?]. - b. 1884; d. 1974
Paul Edward - [d.?] 28 October 1938
CROCKETT
Clifton M. [son of Herbert W. Sr. [no stone] and Grace A. (WING)?] - b. 30 March 1924; d. 1 October 1997
Fannie (LAWTON; wife of James) - d. 7 November 1956 Æ [not given]
Grace A. (WING; wife of Herbert W. Sr. [no stone]) - b. 1904; d. 1969
Herbert W. Jr. (son of Herbert W. Sr. [no stone] and Grace A. (WING)) - b. 1927; d. 1952
James (husb. of Fannie (LAWTON)) - d. 3 January 1941 Æ [not given]
CROWLEY
Alice L. - b. 1858; d. 1941
CUMMINGS
Geraldine [wife of Shirley] - b. 1924; d. 1957
Shirley [husb. of Geraldine] - b. 1923

CUTTER
[Mary T. - see PARKER]
DAIGLE
Michael J. - b. 1970
DALZELL
David Allan [sic] (grandson of Roger D. FOSS and Florence M.) - b. 1962; d. 1962
Everett E. [husb. of Lula B.] - b. 1899; d. 1968
Granville W. [husb. of Lydia M.] - b. 1900; d. 1960
Lula B. [wife of Everett E.] - b. 1897; d. 1975
Lydia M. [wife of Granville W.] - b. 1900; d. 1982
DAM
[Annabel - see WORCESTER]
Betty J. - b. 30 May 1926; d. 16 June 1974
Eunice B. - b. 27 March 1920; d. 7 September 1987
Samuel G. - b. 1 July 1923
DAMON
Eleanor M. [wife of Waldo M. Jr.] - b. 1927
Joseph - [b. and d.?] 29 September 1982
Waldo M. Jr. [husb. of Eleanor M.] - b. 12 April 1927; d. 13 September 1993
DANIHY
Edward T. [husb. of Susan D.] - b. 1881; d. 1949
Susan D. [wife of Edward T.] - b. 1878; d. 1948
DAVIS
[Albertine - see PLUMMER]
Bennie S. [husb. of Lillian M.] - b. 1904; d. 1971
Carrie E. - b. 1875; d. 1956
Edward C. - b. 28 December 1943
Ella (TINKER) - b. 13 March 1908; d. 31 August 1993
Grandville [sic] "Sim" [husb. of Violet B.] - b. 1897; d. 1979
Lillian M. [wife of Bennie S.] - b. 1906; d. 1959
Lynn (HINCKLEY; [wife of Ralph E. Jr.]; mother of Tammy, Robin, Ralph III, and Wendy [no stones]) - b. 11 October 1946; d. 5 October 1975
Muriel M. - b. 20 May 1908
Percy [husb. of Vera] - b. 1911; d. 1990
Ralph E. Jr. [husb. of Lynn (HINCKLEY); father of Tammy, Robin, Ralph III, and Wendy [no stones]] - b. 8 June 1945; d. 20 December 1991
Vera [wife of Percy] - b. 1918; d. 1994
Violet B. [wife of Grandville [sic] "Sim"] - b. 1895; d. 1987
DECOST
Anna M. - b. 1877; d. 1965
Rodney E. - b. 22 May 1900; d. 3 January 1919
DEMMONS
Ralph F. - b. 25 November 1907; d. 16 October 1968
DESJARDIN
Alphie J. - b. 14 June 1917; d. 27 March 1969
DEVER
Lyle H. [husb. of Pauline M.] - b. 1932
Pauline M. [wife of Lyle H.] - b. 1933
DEVINEY
[Maude - see KELLEY]
DIGGERY
[Gertrude J. - see HERRICK]

DINSMORE
George F. - b. 1883; d. 1947
DIX
Emily M. (BARTLETT; wife of John) - b. 1838; d. 1898
[Evelyn R. - see HARDING]
Hiram A. Jr. [husb. of Ida M.] - b. 1861; d. 1947
Ida M. [wife of Hiram A. Jr.] - b. 1869; d. 1956
John (husb. of Emily M. (BARTLETT)) - b. 8 April 1829; d. 10 February 1910
DOBLE
Dorothy G. [wife of Louis W.] - b. 1925
Louis W. [husb. of Dorothy G.] - b. 1925; d. 1986
DOLLIVER [includes DOLIVER]
Amos (husb. of Lizzie M.) - b. 1866; d. 1936
Ann Adele (MUISE; wife of George B.) - b. 1896; d. 1986
Arline [wife of Robert] - b. 1920
Avis H. [wife of Harold W.] - b. 21 August 1917; d. 13 September 1988
[Barbara - see COOMBS]
Barbara W. [wife of Wilder H.] - b. 1901; d. 1995
Benjamin S. [husb. of Mercey [sic] S.] - b. 21 May 1821; d. 21 June 1904
Benjamin T. (husb. of Julia E.) - b. 1860; d. 1941
Blanche (dau. of Benjamin T. and Julia E.) - b. 1892; d. 1909
Brian Lee [son of Harold W. and Avis H.?] - b. 21 January 1942; d. 9 December 1942
Calvin E. (husb. of Carolyn H.) - b. 16 October 1900; d. 12 April 1962
Carl F. (husb. of Elene M. (HAMBLEN)) - b. 1903; d. 1979
Carolyn H. (wife of Calvin E.) - b. 23 January 1917
Charles G. - d. 3 March 1867 Æ 38 y., 5 m., 3 d.
Clara (wife of Willis) - b. 1854; d. 1906
Dudley B. (Capt.; husb. of Emma J.) - d. 12 June 1885 Æ 55 y., 10 m., 14 d.
Dudley B. [husb. of Lura H.] - b. 1875; d. 1966
[Edna M. - see JELLISON]
Edith (LURVEY; wife of Lewis William) - b. 1873; d. 1940
[Eldora F. - see WARD]
Elene M. (HAMBLEN; wife of Carl F.) - b. 1907; d. 1995
Elizabeth (WORCESTER; dau. of Forester WORCESTER and Minnie) - b. 1897; d. 1925
Elsie M. [wife of Milton H.] - b. 1903; d. 1984
Emeline STANLEY (former wife of Thomas S. STANLEY; wife of Stillman S.) - d. 18 September 1895 Æ 55 y., 10 m., 6 d.
Emma J. (wife of Capt. Dudley B.) - d. 7 January 1866 Æ 27 y., 5 m.
Emma K. (dau. of Capt. Dudley B. and Emma J.) - d. 15 July 1866 Æ 7 y., 6 m., 21 d.
[Fannie - see MAYO]
Ferdinand M. [husb. of Gertrude E.] - b. 1905; d. 1984
Franklin S. (husb. of Mattie I. (MOORE)) - b. 13 April 1855; d. 25 June 1927
George B. (husb. of Ann Adele (MUISE)) - b. 1889; d. 1963
Gertrude E. [wife of Ferdinand M.] - b. 1909; d. 1995
Gwendolyn - b. 1943; d. 1992
Harold W. [husb. of Avis H.] - b. 3 February 1917; d. 29 January 1998
Henry C. [husb. of Olga W. K.] - b. 1884; d. 1945
Hiram (husb. of Lucy Ann) - b. 1823; d. 1876
infant (son of Amos and Lizzie M.) - [no dates]

James K. [son of Henry C. and Olga W. K.?] - b. 1918; d. 1988
Julia E. (wife of Benjamin T.) - b. 1866; d. 1950
Kate "Katie" (dau. of Benjamin T. and Julia E.) - b. 1895; d. [9 July 1896 Æ 1 y., 20 d. or 1897][2]
Lawrence - [b. and d.?] 1925
Lewis William (husb. of Edith (LURVEY)) - b. 1870; d. 1940
Lizzie M. (wife of Amos) - b. 1863; d. 1946
Louise (dau. of Benjamin T. and Julia E.) - b. 1889; d. 1906
Lucy Ann (wife of Hiram) - b. 1831; d. 1859
Lura H. [wife of Dudley B.] - b. 1880; d. 1966
Mary A. [wife of Stillman S.] - b. 1876; d. 1956
Mattie I. (MOORE; wife of Franklin S.) - b. 1 October 1863; d. 20 February 1945
Mercey [sic] S. [wife of Benjamin S.] - b. 8 June 1823; d. 3 January 1902
Mildred (dau. of Benjamin T. and Julia E.) - b. 1900; d. 1900
Milton H. [husb. of Elsie M.] - b. 1901; d. 1996
Minnie M. [wife of Rudolph E.] - b. 1897; d. 1979
[Miriam - see WATTS]
Morris A. [son of Stillman S. and Mary A.?] - b. 1902; d. 1997
Olga W. K. [wife of Henry C.] - b. 1889; d. 1951
Raymond E. (son of Carl F. and Elene M. (HAMBLEN)) - b. 1933; d. 1950
Robert [husb. of Arline] - b. 1911; d. 1973
Rudolph E. [husb. of Minnie M.] - b. 1898; d. 1975
Russell E. - b. 1922; d. 1985
Ruth (dau. of Benjamin T. and Julia E.) - b. 1906; d. 1910
[Sarah - see MAYO]
Stillman S. [husb. of [Emeline STANLEY and?] Mary A.] - b. 1862; d. 1942
Walter Hood (son of Calvin E. and Carolyn H.) - b. 16 November 1938; d. 27 December 1957
Wilder H. [husb. of Barbara W.] - b. 1898; d. 1994
Willis (husb. of Clara) - b. 1850; d. 1941

DORR
[Abbie D[ORR?]. - see BILLINGS]
[Alfrieda - see LEONARD]
Isabelle D. (wife of Warren A.) - d. 22 June 1919 Æ 52 y., 9 m.
Nellie (ROBINSON; [wife of Sylvester W.]) - b. 1 November 1894; d. 13 January 1991
Sylvester W. [husb. of Nellie (ROBINSON)] - b. 1 September 1888; d. 2 February 1959
Warren A. (husb. of Isabelle D.) - b. 1868; d. 1942

DOW
Charlene - b. 1927; d. 1946
Charles H. - b. 1905; d. 1964
Edith C. (dau. of George B. and Mildred W.) - [b. and d.?] 4 May 1921
George B. (husb. of Mildred W. and Vera R.) - b. 1894; d. 1967
Henry A. [husb. of Maud A.] - b. 1871; d. 1957
Karen D. - [b. and d.?] 1966
Mary L. (dau. of George B. and Mildred W.) - d. 1 February 1926 Æ 4 d.
Maud A. [wife of Henry A.] - b. 1875; d. 1962
Mildred W. (wife of George B.) - b. 1899; d. 1959
Vera R. (wife of George B.) - b. 1898; d. 1964
[Zelinda J. - see COOK]

DOWNS
Paul E. - b. 14 December 1959; d. 29 September 1994
DRISCOLL
Dennis (husb. of Rose Standish (GOTT)) - b. 1843; d. 1928
John Melvin - b. 24 December 1890; d. 22 August 1918
[Lora Mae - see HORNE]
Rose Standish (GOTT; wife of Dennis) - b. 1844; d. 1924
DUMOND
Robert S. - [b. and d.?] 14 July 1939
DUNBAR
Beatrice L. - b. 1923; d. 1938
Charles R. [husb. of Mary G.] - b. 1925; d. 1991
Dorothy (ELLIS) [wife of John Edwin] - b. 4 April 1913
Elizabeth M. - b. 9 September 1931; d. 29 September 1998
Frederick J. - b. 1920; d. 1978
Henry - b. 1914; d. 1982
Irene R. (GILLEY; [dau. of Frank L. GILLEY and Maud F. (HOLMES)?]; wife of Linwood N.) - b. 1911; d. 1940
John Edwin [husb. of Dorothy (ELLIS)] - b. 18 February 1911; d. 26 January 1991
Juanita E. - b. 1906; d. 1927
Lewis G. (husb. of Louise A.) - b. 1885; d. 1951
Linwood N. (husb. of Irene R. (GILLEY)) - b. 1904; d. 1942
Louise A. (wife of Lewis G.) - b. 1886; d. 1971
Mary G. [wife of Charles R.] - b. 1927
DUNHAM
Bessie J. [wife of Grover C.] - b. 1893; d. 1989
Celia F. [wife of Wilfred M.] - b. 15 April 1918
Grover C. [husb. of Bessie J.] - b. 1885; d. 1967
Wilfred M. [husb. of Celia F.] - b. 10 November 1918
DURANT
Mary Agnes - b. 1913; d. 1992
DYER
Deana Ann (wife of Kevin John Sr.) - b. 1962
Kevin John Sr. (husb. of Deana Ann) - b. 27 April 1965; d. 22 November 1990
EATON
Donna B. [wife of George Linwood] - b. 26 April 1921; d. 12 September 1989
George Linwood [husb. of Donna B.] - b. 19 August 1923; d. 7 February 1964
Lawrence Neal - b. 21 August 1928; d. 20 June 1971
Sally Ann - b. 1960; d. 1978
EIBLER
Elizabeth [wife of Harold] - b. 1905
Harold [husb. of Elizabeth] - b. 1902; d. 1970
EICHLER
Robert Earl [husb. of Winifred (PIKE)?] - b. 1913; d. 1987
Winifred (PIKE; [wife of Robert Earl?]) - b. 1915; d. 1992
ELLIS
Carolan [sic] (HAYWARD) - b. 1912; d. 1987; bur. 27 June 1987, "at sea"
[Dorothy - see DUNBAR]
Gertrude C. (wife of Ralph) - b. 1890; d. 1925
Michelle Dawn [ELLIS?] - [b. and d.?] 10 December 1971
Ralph (husb. of Gertrude C.) - b. 1892; d. 1933
Ralph F. (son of Ralph and Gertrude C.) - b. 1910; d. 1994

Stephenie [sic] Lorraine [ELLIS?] - [b. and d.?] 10 December 1971
EMMOTT
George R. [husb. of Verna M.] - b. 1905; d. 1987
Verna M. [wife of George R.] - b. 1906; d. 1990
EVANOFF
[Dussia - see MURPHY]
FARLEY
Albert Earl[10] - b. 2 June 1941; d. 28 November 1999
Daniel M. [son of Elwell P. and Merilyn [sic] A.?] - b. 20 April 1957; d. 17 December 1995
Edwin [husb. of Thelma V.] - b. 1895; d. 1984
Elwell P. [husb. of Merilyn [sic] A.] - b. 30 September 1930
Hattie [wife of Herman] - b. 1876; d. 1961
Herman [husb. of Hattie] - b. 1868; d. 1959
Merilyn [sic] A. [wife of Elwell P.] - b. 25 March 1931
Thelma V. [wife of Edwin] - b. 1908
FARNSWORTH
Alton E. (husb. of Emily (ROBINSON) and Edith O. (MAYO)) - b. 29 June 1866; d. 28 March 1926
Edith O. (MAYO; wife of Alton E.) - b. 15 April 1874; d. 24 June 1935
[Elizabeth F. - see RICH]
Emily (ROBINSON; wife of Alton E.) - b. 8 April 1851; d. 31 March 1905
Lottie A. (wife of Hubert G. [no stone]) - b. 1888; d. 1937
FARRAR
George [husb. of Sarah] - b. 1847; d. 1930
Millard F. [husb. of Uldene V.] - b. 1881; d. 1933
Norman D. [son of Millard F. and Uldene V.?] - b. 1917; d. 1978
Sarah [wife of George] - b. 1860; d. 1932
Uldene V. [wife of Millard F.] - b. 1891; d. 1984
FAULKINGHAM
L. Olive [wife of Thomas Frank] - b. 1892; d. 1980
Thomas Frank [husb. of L. Olive] - b. 16 November 1890; d. 22 November 1973
FERGUSON
Isabelle (McKENZIE; wife of John [no stone]) - b. 1860; d. 1933
John Witherspoon - b. 1934; d. 1998
FERNALD
Annie F. (wife of Thomas) - b. 1858; d. 1949
Dana P. [husb. of Margaret M.] - b. 1894; d. 1977
Daniel (Capt.) - b. 1808; d. 1896
Fred [husb. of Neva] - b. 1872; d. 1931
James S. (husb. of Margaret A. (MARCYES)) - b. 1843; d. 1916
Leslie W. - d. 16 November 1908 Æ 31 y.
[Louise F[ERNALD?]. - see GOULDING]
Margaret A. (MARCYES; wife of James S.) - b. 1841; d. 1918
Margaret M. [wife of Dana P.] - b. 1895; d. 1958
Myrtle A. (dau. of James S. and Margaret A. (MARCYES)) - b. 1871; d. 1909
Neva [wife of Fred] - b. 1877; d. 1955
Oliver H. (Rev.; [son of Capt. Daniel?]; husb. of Ruth A. (LAWTON)) - b. 1835; d. 1903
Orrin W. (husb. of Roxy (LELAND)) - b. 1882; d. 1952
Roxy (LELAND; wife of Orrin W.) - b. 1884; d. 1931
Ruth A. (LAWTON; wife of Rev. Oliver H.) - b. 1838; d. 1926

Thomas (husb. of Annie F.) - b. 1851; d. 1931
Waldina [sic] L. [son [sic] of James S. and Margaret A. (MARCYES)] - b. 1868; d. [no date]

FICKETT
Josephine Kroph[13] - b. 1904; d. 1994

FINNEY
John T. [husb. of Mary B.] - b. 1850; d. 1909
Mary B. [wife of John T.] - b. 1850; d. 1942

FISCHER
Carl J. - b. 1889; d. 1947

FISH
Irma - b. 1921; d. 19[88?][8] Æ 6[6?][8] y.

FLEMING
Mary T. - b. 1912; d. 1979

FOSS
Alvah E. [husb. of Martha M.] - b. 1859; d. 1921
Alvah E. [son of Clifton R. and Myrtle H.] - b. 28 September 1924; d. 4 August 1996
Clifton R. (husb. of Myrtle H.) - b. 1890; d. 1937
Fannie L. [wife of Frank C.] - b. 1881; d. 1956
Florence M. (wife of Roger D.) - b. 1894; d. 1957
Frank C. [husb. of Fannie L.] - b. 1879; d. 1946
Frederick W. - b. 1923; d. 1958
Martha M. [wife of Alvah E.] - b. 1864; d. [no date]
Myrtle H. (wife of Clifton R.) - b. 1895; d. 1959
Robert P. - b. 1897; d. 1975
Roger D. (husb. of Florence M.) - b. 1893; d. 1972

FREEDMAN
Leon J. [husb. of Phyllis G.] - b. 1913
Phyllis G. [wife of Leon J.] - b. 1913; d. 1981

FREEMAN
Ada Julia (wife of John T. R.) - b. 1837; d. 1912
Arthur H. [husb. of C. Louise] - b. 1875; d. 1944
C. Louise [wife of Arthur H.] - b. 1879; d. 1948
Carmelita M. - b. 1884; d. 1962
Charles E. - b. 1867; d. 1919
Charley C. [son of John T. R. and Ada Julia] - b. 1863; d. 1866
Emily H. [wife of James Albert] - b. 1847; d. 1928
James Albert [husb. of Emily H.] - b. 1844; d. 1916
James R. (husb. of Margaret) - b. 1810; d. 1896
John T. R. (husb. of Ada Julia) - b. 1838; d. 1916
Joseph W. - b. 1844; d. 1914
Margaret (wife of James R.) - b. 1808; d. 1888
Nettie J. - b. 1882; d. 1882

FROST
Elsie R. [wife of Raymond Lyle Jr.] - b. 14 October 1926
Raymond Lyle Jr. [husb. of Elsie R.] - b. 22 April 1926; d. 1 July 1968

FURTWENGLER
Evelyn R. [wife of Willis J.] - b. 1909; d. 1981
Willis J. [husb. of Evelyn R.] - b. 1907; d. 1990

GAFFNEY
Gerald - b. 1915; d. 1988

Louise C. - b. 1906; d. 1995
GALBREATH
Lisa Beth ([MALLINSON?]; [dau. of Charlotte C. MALLINSON?]) - b. 1951; d. 1966
GALLEY
Clarence F. - b. 12 December 1925; d. 9 April 1945
Clyde B. "Buddy" - b. 27 November 1937; d. 10 July 1964
Hiram (son of Salathiel A. [and Mary M.?]) - b. 1865; d. 19[...][4]
Mary M. (wife of Capt. Salathiel A.) - b. 1845; d. 1906
Salathiel A. (Capt.; husb. of Mary M.) - b. 1844; d. 1915
Shirley H. [husb. of Vivian E.] - b. 14 September 1893; d. 10 December 1976
Vivian E. [wife of Shirley H.] - b. 29 April 1904; d. 16 June 1975
GARLAND
Elmer G. - b. 1912; d. 1971
GEEL
Shirley Ann - b. 22 November 1981
William George II - b. 16 December 1980
GILLEY
Abbie L. [wife of George H.] - b. 1858; d. 1919
Adelbert O. (husb. of Julia I. (MOORE)) - b. 1851; d. 1906
Addie B. [wife of Wendell H.] - b. 1905; d. 1983
Alice E. - b. 1856; d. 1938
Andrew L. [husb. of Rhode M.] - b. 1873; d. 1931
Augusta G. "Gussie" [dau. of George H. and Abbie L.?] - b. 1879; d. 1931
Benjamin - b. 1824; d. 1905
Benjamin David - b. 15 January 1987; d. 5 August 1987
Bethsheba [sic] (wife of Francis) - b. 9 November 1810; d. 6 November 1894
[Clara - see SPRAGUE]
Clara M. (HARMON) - b. 1875; d. 1902
Clayton E. "Clate" [son of George H. and Abbie L.] - b. 1877; d. 1934
Donald D. (son of Adelbert O. and Julia I. (MOORE)) - d. 21 July 1894 Æ 4 m., 10 d.
Doris T. [wife of Henry O.] - b. 1898; d. 1975
Edith (STANLEY; wife of Pedrick Dyer [GILLEY?]) - b. 1877; d. 1963
Eleanor M. [wife of Richard W.] - b. 6 November 1908; d. 11 December 1999
Emma M. [wife of John H.?] - b. 1851; d. 1900
Eunice (PALMER; [wife of Philip "Phil"]) - b. 1897; d. 1987
Eunice B. [wife of George C.] - b. 1916; d. 1992
Francis (husb. of Bethsheba [sic]) - d. 19 November 1877 Æ 67 y., 5 m., 13 d.
Frank L. (husb. of Maud F. (HOLMES)) - b. 1880; d. 1920
George C. [husb. of Eunice B.] - b. 1913
George H. [husb. of Abbie L.] - b. 1849; d. 1925
Hannah B. [wife of Capt. William L.] - b. 28 July 1835; d. 12 March 1921
Harvey F. [husb. of Mabel E.] - b. 23 May 1894; d. 30 November 1950
Henry O. [husb. of Doris T.] - b. 1892; d. 1951
[Irene R. - see DUNBAR]
Joan P. [wife of Philip Jr.?] - b. 1928
John A. - b. 1907; d. 1967
John H. [husb. of Emma M.?] - b. 1848; d. 1923
Julia I. (MOORE; wife of Adelbert O.) - b. 1863; d. 1922
Leona M. (wife of Norman C. [no stone]) - b. 1929; d. 1959
Lida M. (dau. of Leverett and Rhoda E. [no stones]) - d. 18 September 1901 Æ 6 m.

Mabel E. [wife of Harvey F.] - b. 9 December 1898; d. 21 June 1982
Maud F. (HOLMES; wife of Frank L.) - b. 1883; d. 1954
Montrivelle [sic] C. - b. 1930; d. 1987
Montriville [sic] C. (husb. of Nellie H.) - b. 1862; d. 1930
Nellie H. (wife of Montriville [sic] C.) - b. 1865; d. 1933
Pedrick Dyer [GILLEY?] (husb. of Edith (STANLEY)) - b. 1866; d. 1938
Philip "Phil" [husb. of Eunice (PALMER)] - b. 1887; d. 1961
Philip Jr. [husb. of Joan P.?] - b. 1925
Rhode M. [wife of Andrew L.] - b. 1879; d. 1940
Richard W. [husb. of Eleanor M.] - b. 1906; d. 1960
Ruby B. - b. 1909; d. 1979
Rudolph A. - b. 1891; d. 1914
Wallace S. "Wally" [son of Harvey F. and Mabel E.?] - b. 29 July 1935; d. 16 April 1996
Wendell H. [husb. of Addie B.] - b. 1904; d. 1983
William L. (Capt.; [husb. of Hannah B.]) - b. 18 October 1835; d. 20 January 1912

GINN
[Alice - see MACE]
Arthur E. (husb. of Inez (TORREY)) - b. 1889; d. 1964
Inez (TORREY; wife of Arthur E.) - b. 1887; d. 1953

GODWIN
Barbara E. [wife of William J.] - b. 1930
William J. [husb. of Barbara E.] - b. 2 January 1930; d. 4 March 1974

GOGGINS
[Emma [C.?][11] - see NORWOOD]

GOLDSMITH
Doris (WHITE) - b. 1889; d. 1978

GONZALES
[Adelaide - see REED]
Arthur L. - b. 1897; d. 1979

GOODWIN
infant (child of R. Paul and Maxine) - [b. and d.?] 1942
Maxine (wife of R. Paul) - b. 1926; d. 1997
R. Paul (husb. of Maxine) - b. 1920; d. 1993

GORA
Gladys P. [wife of John H.] - b. 1919; d. 1994
John H. [husb. of Gladys P.] - b. 1909; d. 1993

GORDIUS
Alice L. [wife of Harry] - b. 1891; d. 1985
Harry [husb. of Alice L.] - b. 1885; d. 1975

GORDON
Earl [husb. of Jessie] - b. 1893; d. 1964
Jessie [wife of Earl] - b. 1889; d. 1972
[...] [headstone only]

GOTT
Abbie E. [wife of Robert?] - b. 1855; d. 1946
Ava R. [wife of Ronald W.] - b. 1915; d. 1986
Beatrice Mary (dau. of Logan Garfield and Lena M.) - b. 1920; d. 1974
Charles W. (Capt.; husb. of Evie Louise) - b. 7 May 1897; d. 27 September 1987
Chester L. [husb. of Marion W.] - b. 7 September 1918; d. 17 August 1982
Clarence G. - b. 1917; d. 1981
Earll [sic] W. [husb. of Esther (BURNETT)] - b. 1889; d. 1950

[Elizabeth - see GRAY]
Ella M. (wife of Orlando T.) - b. 1862; d. 1886
[Ellen M. - see STANLEY]
Esther (BURNETT; [wife of Earll [sic]]) - b. 15 January 1897; d. 18 August 1966
Everton L. - b. 1875; d. 1954
Evie Louise (wife of Capt. Charles W.) - b. 12 February 1902; d. 1 January 1970
Frank W. [husb. of Lucy M.] - b. 1881; d. 1951
[Harriet - see CRAIG]
infant - [no dates]
Irma Josephine - b. 1916
J. Austin - b. 1916; d. 1972
Lena M. (wife of Logan Garfield) - b. 1888; d. 1955
Leslie W. [son of Capt. Charles W. and Evie Louise?] - b. 27 May 1921; d. 26 September 1953
Logan Garfield (husb. of Lena M.) - b. 1881; d. 1958
Lucy M. [wife of Frank W.] - b. 1892; d. 1965
Marion W. [wife of Chester L.] - b. 24 March 1915; d. 16 June 1989
Matthew Wass - [b. and d.?] 1965
Milton P. [son of Frank W. and Lucy M.?] - b. 1914; d. 1985
Nathalie M. [wife of Rodney W.] - b. 1909; d. 1997
Orlando T. (husb. of Ella M.) - b. 1854; d. 1944
Phoebe E. - b. 1885; d. 1973
Robert [husb. of Abbie E.?] - [no dates]
Rodney W. [husb. of Nathalie M.] - b. 1907; d. 1997
Ronald W. [husb. of Ava R.] - b. 1910; d. 1973
[Rose Standish - see DRISCOLL]

GOULDING
Louise F[ERNALD?]. [dau. of Rev. Oliver H. FERNALD and Ruth A. (LAWTON)?] - b. 1873; d. 1963

GRAY
Arthur L.[15] - b. 22 October 1902; d. 4 September 1983
[Beatrice V. - see ROBBINS]
Chester A. - b. 1889; d. 1919
Dorothy H. [wife of Norris Irving] - b. 1923; d. 1990
[Edith - see MOORE]
Elizabeth (GOTT; wife of Henry L.) - b. 15 March 1885; d. 23 February 1971
Henry L. (husb. of Elizabeth (GOTT)) - b. 5 May 1881; d. 26 November 1947
Howard R. [husb. of Sarah R.] - b. 1903; d. 1994
Howard R. Jr. - b. 29 October 1932; d. 4 January 1996
James - b. 10 April 1862; d. 24 August 1923
James Jr. - b. 3 November 1893; d. 3 May 1917; ("killed in action")
Joseph M. [husb. of Phoebe F.] - b. 1866; d. 1944
Kathelyn E. [dau. of Henry L. and Elizabeth (GOTT)?] - b. 19 September 1905; d. 5 January 1934
Norris Irving [husb. of Dorothy H.] - b. 14 April 1922; d. 10 October 1966
Phoebe F. [wife of Joseph M.] - b. 1874; d. 1926
Pollie E. - b. 11 April 1869; d. 27 April 1950
[Sadie - see YOUNG]
Sarah R. [wife of Howard R.] - b. 1904; d. 1970

GREENING
James (husb. of Jane) - d. 19 May 1863 Æ 65 y.
Jane (wife of James) - d. 4 December 1857 Æ 65 y.

Richard (son of James and Jane) - d. 22 November 1847 Æ 16 y.
GREENLAW
[Bertha A. - see ROBBINS]
Harry B. [husb. of Maude A.] - b. 1884; d. 1955
Maude A. [wife of Harry B.] - b. 1888; d. 1957
Nellie H. [wife of Seth W.] - b. 1870; d. 1960
Seth W. [husb. of Nellie H.] - b. 1871; d. 1959
GRIFFIN
[Joy May - see MAYO]
Karl R. Sr. - b. 14 October 1923; d. 3 June 1999
Michelle Lynn - b. 1973; d. 1993
Ray W. Sr. [husb. of Violet A.] - b. 14 September 1892; d. 26 December 1945
Ray W. Jr. [son of Ray W. Sr. and Violet A.] - b. 1931; d. 1990
Violet A. [wife of Ray W. Sr.] - b. 1900; d. 1986
GRINDLE
Mary A. (wife of Horace A. [no stone]) - d. 11 November 1902 Æ 32 y.
Michael R. L. - b. 31 March 1963; d. 17 September 1985
GUITÉ
Alesa Y. [wife of Roland L.] - b. 1914; d. 1993
Roland L. [husb. of Alesa Y.] - b. 1913; d. 1967
GUNN
Letitia M. [wife of Max C.] - b. 1904; d. 1966
Max C. [husb. of Letitia M.] - b. 27 February 1902; d. 10 February 1968
GURNEY
Inez N. - b. 1857; d. 1950
[Mattie E. - see McKAY]
HAAG
Ricky C. - b. 2 December 1954; d. 9 September 1981
HAAKONSEN
Alma - b. 1895; d. 1988
HADLOCK
Elmira H. (wife of Epps L.) - d. 21 July 1901 Æ 70 y., 8 m., 9 d.
Epps L. (husb. of Elmira H.) - b. 19 September 1829; d. 6 October 1907 Æ 78 y., 17 d.
Hiram S. (husb. of Laura M.) - b. 1860; d. 1950
infant (son of Hiram S. and Laura M.) - d. 20 June 1893 Æ 3 d.
Laura M. (wife of Hiram S.) - b. 1868; d. 1939
[Marion E. - see NEWMAN]
[Matilda J. - see SANFORD]
HADVIGA
Margaret E. - b. 1884; d. 1963
HAGOPIAN
Leon G. (Dr.; husb. of Vesta S.) - b. 1882; d. 1949
Vesta S. (wife of Dr. Leon G.) - b. 1887; d. 1955
HALL
Albert G. - b. 1856; d. [no date]
Gilbert F. - b. 1918
Mildred L. - b. 1890; d. 1943
Robert D. - b. 1916
HALLOCK
Compton K. - b. 1933; d. 1981

HAMBLEN
Ben M. [husb. of Janette R.] - b. 1919; d. 1990
Bernice M. [wife of Walter H.] - b. 1885; d. 1957
Charles E. - b. 1889; d. 1952
Clinton F. - b. 1878; d. 1953
[Elene M. - see DOLLIVER]
Etheleen (BEAL; [wife of Leslie Stanwood?]) - b. 1918; d. 1996
Forrest - b. 1909; d. 1987
Frank - b. 1873; d. 1946
Gertrude (dau. of Jennie M.) - b. 1894; d. 1922
Gladys C. - b. 28 October 1913
Hilton [husb. of Jessie] - b. 1910; d. 1975
Janette R. [wife of Ben M.] - b. 1923
[Jennette [sic] H[AMBLEN?]. - see VARNUM]
Jennie M. - b. 1855; d. 1934
Jessie [wife of Hilton] - b. 1913
Leslie Stanwood [husb. of Etheleen (BEAL)?] - b. 1919; d. 1991
Levi J. - b. 1886; d. 1963
Marjorie M. [wife of Stanwood Neal] - b. 1925
Stanwood Neal [husb. of Marjorie M.] - b. 1926; d. 1987
Walter H. [husb. of Bernice M.] - b. 1883; d. 1962
[...] [headstone only]
HAMILTON
Celia M. [wife of George E.] - b. 1888; d. 1961
George E. [husb. of Celia M.] - b. 1879; d. 1942
HAMOR
[Gwendolyn H[AMOR?]. - see CONNERS]
Lee S. - b. 15 October 1942; d. 11 November 1942
Roger C. Jr. [son of Roger C. Sr.] - b. 19 October 1936; d. 22 November 1990
Roger C. Sr. - b. 18 February 1912; d. 8 November 1977
HANCOCK
Flora A. (NOYES; wife of John O.) - b. 1860; d. 1918
Grover M. - b. 1889; d. 1965
John O. (husb. of Flora A. (NOYES)) - b. 1854; d. 1924
Marguerite H. [wife of Teddie D.] - b. 1906
Teddie D. [husb. of Marguerite H.] - b. 1903; d. 1988
HANDY
[Linda C. - see TRACY]
HANNA
Nellie B. (wife of William F.) - b. 7 April 1870; d. [no date]
William F. (husb. of Nellie B.) - b. 31 March 1859; d. 13 December 1936
HANSEN
Frieda M. - b. 15 June 1910; d. 24 April 1975
Rasmus - b. 1882; d. 1929
HARDING
Charles H. [husb. of Vera E.] - b. 1883; d. 1972
Clarence E. (husb. of Hazel M. and Evelyn R. (DIX)) - b. 30 March 1895; d. 24 October 1993
David R. [husb. of Eileen A.] - b. 27 August 1920; d. 8 January 1994
Eileen A. [wife of David R.] - b. 1938
Evelyn R. (DIX; wife of Clarence E.) - b. 1902; d. 1985
Hazel M. (wife of Clarence E.) - b. 1896; d. 1948

Martha (SCOTT; [wife of William R.]) - b. 1920; d. 1998
Richard Dean (son of Clarence E. and Hazel M.) - b. 1 June 1933; d. 21 June 1933
Stephen K. (son of David [no stone?] and Doris [no stone]) - b. 1949; d. 1990
Vera E. [wife of Charles H.] - b. 1887; d. 1968
William R. [husb. of Martha (SCOTT)] - b. 1920; d. 1981

HARDY
Betty M. [wife of Carl R.] - b. 1929
Carl R. [husb. of Betty M.] - b. 1921

HARKINS
Thomas II - b. 13 July 1913; d. 30 December 1978
Thomas III - b. 1936; d. 1977

HARMAN [see also HARMON]
George L. (husb. of Lucinda G.) - b. 23 May 1834; d. 10 July 1908
Lucinda G. (wife of George L.) - b. 24 May 1835; d. 18 December 1914
Lucy A. [dau. of George L. and Lucinda G.?] - b. 1866; d. 1869

HARMON [see also HARMAN]
Antoinette (BROWN; wife of Capt. John C.) - b. 1840; d. 1921
[Clara M. - see GILLEY]
Dora E. - b. 1876; d. 1972
George (husb. of Lillian C.) - b. 1875; d. 1942
Ida F. - b. 1907; d. 1984
John C. (Capt.; husb. of Antoinette (BROWN)) - b. 1827; d. 1894
John S. - [no dates]
Lillian C. (wife of George) - b. 1873; d. 1932
Ronald C. - b. 1907; d. 1976

HARPER
Annie E. (dau. of Lyman M. and Erminie H.) - d. 19 December 1921 Æ 33 y., 7 d.
Beatrice H. [wife of W. Morton] - b. 1918
[Beatrice - see BROWN]
Blanche J. (wife [sic] of Julian Y. Jr. [no stone]) - b. 1933; d. 1949
Erminie H. (wife of Lyman M.) - b. 5 July 1856; d. 2 January 1931
Isabel E. (wife of Osmond E.) - b. 24 July 1889; d. 28 February 1959
Leslie L. - b. 29 September 1880; d. 19 December 1966
Lisa Lynn - b. 1967; d. 1989
Lyman M. (husb. of Erminie H.) - b. 22 March 1845; d. 9 April 1926
Osmond E. (husb. of Isabel E.) - b. 31 March 1887; d. [no date]
Sally F. (dau. of W. M[orton?]. and J. S. [no stone]) - b. 5 September 1947; d. 11 August 1948
W. Morton [husb. of Beatrice H.] - b. 1919; d. 1964

HASTINGS
James W. [husb. of Susie E.] - b. 1880; d. 1967
Susie E. [wife of James W.] - b. 1885; d. 1973

HAWKES
Leon R. - b. 1879; d. 1959

HAYNES
Albertina E. (dau. of Andrew H. and Caroline H.) - b. 1840; d. 1874
Andrew H. (husb. of Melinda and Caroline H.) - b. 20 May 1812; d. 21 April 1896
Andrew T. (son of Andrew H. and Caroline H.) - b. 1845; d. 1868
Caroline H. (wife of Andrew H.) - d. 11 August 1889 Æ 85 y., 11 m., 11 d.
Charles E. (husb. of Cora E. (NEWMAN)) - b. 1867; d. 1958
Cora E. (NEWMAN; wife of Charles E) - b. 1869; d. 1938
Emily M. - b. 20 February 1854; d. 10 August 1913

George E. (husb. of Sarah F.) - d. 16 January 1875 Æ 31 y., 10 m., 7 d.
Melinda (wife of Andrew H.) - d. 15 January 1838 Æ 24 y.
Sarah F. (wife of George E.) - b. 16 January 1843; d. 15 August 1931

HAYWARD
[Carolan [sic] - see ELLIS]

HEBRON
Robert L. - b. 4 September 1949; d. 3 August 1963

HENDERY
Caroline Clara - b. 1889; d. 1980

HERING
Lydia S. - b. 1872; d. 1943

HERRICK
Fannie C. [wife of William E.] - b. 1871; d. 1962
Florence M. [dau. of William E. and Fannie C.?] - b. 1904; d. 1956
Gertrude J. (DIGGERY; wife of Horace P.) - b. 25 June 1910
Hannah A. (wife of Samuel W.) - b. 1826; d. 1918
Horace P. (husb. of Gertrude J. (DIGGERY)) - b. 15 October 1901; d. 19 November 1992
Kenneth L. - b. 1907; d. 1996
Luther C. - b. 1915; d. 1998
Margaret M. - b. 1929; d. 1989
Marion E. [wife of Maynard F.] - b. 1892; d. 1964
Marjorie E. [dau. of William E. and Fannie C.?] - b. 1904; d. 1943
Maynard F. [husb. of Marion E.] - b. 1886; d. 1970
Myra N. (dau. of Samuel W. and Hannah A.) - b. 1863; d. 1946
Phyllis G. - b. 1918; d. 1972
Samuel W. (husb. of Hannah A.) - b. 1828; d. 1916
Samuel W. (son of Samuel W. and Hannah A.) - b. 1853; d. 1862
William E. [husb. of Fannie C.] - b. 1870; d. 1949

HERSEY
Jennie E. (LURVEY; wife of John E.) - b. 26 February 1862; d. 18 November 1913
John E. (husb. of Jennie E. (LURVEY)) - b. 17 May 1850; d. 26 December 1921

HIGGINS
Alice E. (wife of Edwin L.) - b. 1852; d. 1941
Athol M. - b. 1897; d. 1995
E. Leon (husb. of Nellie B.) - b. 1867; d. 1939
Edwin L. (husb. of Alice E.) - b. 1849; d. 1938
Elliott J. Sr. [husb. of Frances G.] - b. 1891; d. 1985
[Eliza - see ROBINSON]
Elizabeth E. (wife of Foster W.) - b. 1889; d. 1976
Ethel L. (wife of Fred J.) - b. 1887; d. 1967
Foster W. (son of E. Leon and Nellie B.; husb. of Elizabeth E.) - b. 1894; d. 1967
Frances G. [wife of Elliott J. Sr.] - b. 1893; d. 1979
Fred J. (husb. of Ethel L.) - b. 1881; d. 1961
George L. - b. 1889; d. 1967
Granville S. [husb. of Ida S.?] - b. 1885; d. 1967
Howe D. - b. 1894; d. 1974
Ida S. [wife of Granville S.?] - b. 1885; d. 1974
[Joann - see BROWN]
Leonard W. - b. 1914; d. 1986
Lida E. [wife of Warren H.] - b. 1896; d. 1987
Nellie B. (wife of E. Leon) - b. 1869; d. 1953

Pauline E. - b. 1895; d. 1978
[Ruby - see PICKWICK]
Warren H. [husb. of Lida E.] - b. 1888; d. 1967

HILL
Carleton P. - b. 15 December 1932; d. 30 January 1992
Carleton E. [husb. of Mildred O.] - b. 1913; d. 1997
Mildred O. [wife of Carleton E.] - b. 1913

HILTON
Billy Hugh - b. 1931; d. 1973

HINCKLEY
Henry R. - b. 1907; d. 1980
[Lynn - see DAVIS]

HITCHCOCK
[Elizabeth W. - see BENSON]
Frances B. (wife of Paul E.) - b. 1905
Paul E. (husb. of Frances B.) - b. 1894; d. 1973

HODGDON
Alice M. (wife of Hosea W.) - b. 1860; d. 1932
Alonzo A. - b. 1863; d. 1926
Charles M. (husb. of Edna F.) - b. 1905; d. 1977
Edna F. (wife of Charles M.) - b. 1899; d. 1957
Hosea W. (husb. of Alice M.) - b. 1856; d. 1910
Howard A. - b. 30 August 1895; d. 3 July 1963
Margaret "Mae" (SWEENEY) - b. 1919; d. 1989

HODGKINS
Harvey W. (Capt.; husb. of Venia C.) - b. 16 February 1849; d. 27 November 1906
Malcolm A. [husb. of Renie M.] - b. 1910; d. 1988
Mary A. - b. 9 November 1832; d. 9 May 1883
Renie M. [wife of Malcolm A.] - b. 1910; d. 1997
Venia C. (wife of Capt. Harvey W.) - b. 9 October 1854; d. 12 May 1934
Winnie (son of Mary A.) - b. 23 September 1855; d. 5 March 1876, Newfoundland

HOLMES
Amelia (wife of Thomas) - b. 1832; d. 1905
Anson I. (husb. of Avelia) - b. 1855; d. 1929
Avelia (wife of Anson I.) - b. 1851; d. 1916
El[i or ea]nor[2] (dau. of Anson I. and Avelia) - b. 15 July 1893; d. 25 December 1893
Elmer E. (son of Thomas and Amelia) - b. 17 August 1861; d. 27 October 1868
Hannah A. (dau. of Anson I. and Avelia) - b. 26 November 1889; d. 7 May 1896
infant (dau. of Anson I. and Avelia) - [b. and d.?] 3 July 1885
[Josephine - see RICHARDSON]
Lizzie B. (MAYO; wife of William H.) - b. 1861; d. 1934
[Maud F. - see GILLEY]
Thomas (husb. of Amelia) - b. 1829; d. 1910
William H. (husb. of Lizzie B. (MAYO)) - b. 1860; d. 1930

HOMER
[Jessie A. - see NEWMAN]

HOOPER
Ramona B. - b. 1929; d. 1969

HOPKINS
Anna R. (wife of John A. Jr.) - b. 29 January 1901; d. 15 August 1967
Annie S. (wife of John A.) - b. 17 May 1882; d. 26 April 1956
Celestine (wife of James S.) - b. 1910; d. 1942

Clark - b. 4 February 1833; d. 19 June 1913
Cora L. (wife of James S. [no stone]) - b. 28 October 1900; d. 26 February 1990
Harriette L. (wife of James S.) - b. 1909; d. 1989
infant (dau. of James S. [no stone] and Cora L.) - [b. and d.?] 20 June 1928
James S. - b. 30 December 1872; d. 25 February 1923
James S. (husb. of Celestine and Harriette L.) - b. 1903; d. 1972
John A. (husb. of Annie S.) - b. 7 March 1868; d. 2 March 1923
John A. Jr. (husb. of Anna R.) - b. 29 March 1901; d. 6 March 1976
Lewis James Sr. [husb. of Onalee W. "Bonnie"] - b. 4 May 1927; d. 19 September 1995
[Mary S. - see WILSON]
Onalee W. "Bonnie" [wife of Lewis James Sr.] - b. 2 July 1932
Theresa F. - b. 19 February 1933

HORNE
Byron F. (husb. of Lora Mae (DRISCOLL)) - b. 3 May 1851; d. 24 January 1932
Lora Mae (DRISCOLL; wife of Byron F.) - b. 23 July 1869; d. 7 February 1953

HOUSTON
Elmenia M. (RICHARDSON; [wife of Hiram]) - b. 1859; d. 1942
Hiram [husb. of Elmenia M. (RICHARDSON)] - b. 1846; d. 1886
Mamie E. [dau. of Hiram and Elmenia M. (RICHARDSON)] - d. 7 May 1880 Æ 3 y., 5 m., 4 d.
Mary A. - b. 1821; d. 1903

HOWE
Emily W. - b. 1881; d. 1957

HOWELL
Bertha L. [wife of William L.] - b. 1896; d. 1993
William L. [husb. of Bertha L.] - b. 1896; d. 1968

HUDSON
[...] [headstone only]

HUISMAN
Dorothy J. - b. 1914; d. 1988

HUNTLEY
Annabel N. [wife of Charles D.] - b. 1886; d. 1962
Charles D. [husb. of Annabel N.] - b. 1886; d. 1955

HUTCHINS
Frank (husb. of Margaret (CHAMBERLAIN)) - b. 1861; d. 1942
Jasper C. [husb. of Katherine E.] - b. 1897; d. 1972
Katherine E. [wife of Jasper C.] - b. 1900; d. 1982
[Lucy - see PARSONS]
Margaret (CHAMBERLAIN; wife of Frank) - b. 1863; d. 1929
[Marion - see REES]
Susie [wife of Urban] - b. 1908; d. 1994
Urban [husb. of Susie] - b. 1903; d. 1957

HYNES
Cecil [husb. of Esther] - b. 1902; d. 1971
Esther [wife of Cecil] - b. 1901; d. 1983

INMAN
Evelyn (YATES) - b. 1901; d. 1985

IVERSON
Charlotte W. [wife of Raymond W. Sr.] - b. 1928
Raymond W. Jr. [son of Raymond W. Sr. and Charlotte W.] - b. 1955; d. 1996
Raymond W. Sr. [husb. of Charlotte W.] - b. 1928

JACKSON
Richard B. - b. 1893; d. 1959
JACOBS
Kathleen N. [wife of Samuel Arthur Jr.] - b. 1929
Samuel Arthur Jr. [husb. of Kathleen N.] - b. 16 August 1926; d. 14 December 1996
JAMES
Lulu (MAYO; [dau. of Benjamin R. MAYO and Laura M. (LUNT)]) - b. 1875; d. 1942
JARVIS
Charles S. [husb. of Hattie M.] - b. 1873; d. 1947
Della M. [wife of Henry W.] - b. 1872; d. 1953
Hattie M. [wife of Charles S.] - b. 1868; d. 1939
Henry W. [husb. of Della M.] - b. 1869; d. 1948
JELLISON
Alton L. [husb. of Dorothy D.] - b. 1918; d. 1982
[Arlene - see RAMELLA]
Dorothy D. [wife of Alton L.] - b. 1917
Edna M. (DOLLIVER; wife of Linwood M.) - b. 1912
Edna May (dau. of Linwood M. and Edna M. (DOLLIVER)) - b. 1936; d. 1965
George C. (husb. of Gertrude L.) - b. 8 June 1881; d. 12 April 1962
Gertrude L. (wife of George C.) - b. 1883; d. 1940
Linwood M. (husb. of Edna M. (DOLLIVER)) - b. 1903; d. 1967
Loyd [sic] (son of George C. and Gertrude L.) - b. 1911; d. 1917
JEWETT
Barbara [wife of Melvin A.] - b. 1927
Melvin A. [husb. of Barbara] - b. 1926; d. 1992
JOCELYN
Pansy S. - b. 1889; d. 1970
JOHNSON
Bernard W. (husb. of Florence M.) - b. 1908; d. 1985
Carl R. [husb. of Dorothy M.] - b. 1924
Chester L. [husb. of E. Al[b]ertine[2]] - b. 1872; d. 1951
Dorothy M. [wife of Carl R.] - b. 1928
E. Al[b]ertine[2] [wife of Chester L.] - b. 1870; d. 1953
E. Beatrice [wife of Frank A.] - b. 1887; d. 1978
Florence M. (wife of Bernard W.) - b. 1913; d. 1984
Frank A. [husb. of E. Beatrice] - b. 1877; d. 1949
Irving A. (son of Chester and Al[b]ertine[2] [no stones]) - d. 17 April 1903 Æ 9 m., 25 d.
Lucinda S[TANLEY?]. (wife of George [no stone]) - b. 1863; d. 1947
Pauline Ruth [dau. of Chester L. and E. Al[b]ertine[2]?] - b. 1906; d. 1985
JOHNSTON
[Anna - see WELLINGTON]
Avery VanNess - b. 4 January 1973; d. 10 March 1973
Dorothy - b. 1941; d. 1958
Dorothy [wife of John] - b. 1885; d. 1953
[Helen - see BROWN]
John [husb. of Dorothy] - b. 1881; d. 1950
William V. - b. 1919; d. 1965
JONES
Georgianna - b. 1867; d. 1947
Lilly May - b. 10 June 1871; d. 29 January 1957

Nellie M. [wife of Perle Otis] - b. 1911; d. 1993
Perle Otis [son of Lilly May; husb. of Nellie M.] - b. 31 May 1902; d. 21 February 1969
JORDAN
H. Oliver [husb. of Theda [D. or A.][2]] - b. 1914; d. 1970
Harry J. (husb. of Laura V.) - b. 1882; d. 1955
Laura V. (wife of Harry J.) - b. 1889; d. 1952
Theda [D. or A.][2] [wife of H. Oliver] - b. 1918; d. 1997
JOY
Eva (MAYO) - b. 20 April 1882; d. 28 December 1948
JOYCE
Carrie E. (wife of Joseph J.) - b. 1864; d. 1962
Charles Raymond - b. 22 October 1900; d. 12 July 1958
Charles Raymond Jr. - b. 3 January 1929; d. 3 October 1984
Joseph J. (husb. of Carrie E.) - b. 1855; d. 1936
KALER
Mary W. (wife of Alberta [sic] [no stone]) - b. 1851; d. 1937
KANE
[Rose E. - see WENTWORTH]
KEENE
Mabel H. [wife of William R.] - b. 1862; d. [no date]
William R. [husb. of Mabel H.] - b. 1852; d. 1933
KELLEY
Alberta M. [wife of Thomas A.?] - b. 1886; d. 1963
Beatrice C. [wife of Carl E.] - b. 1887; d. 1974
Carl E. [husb. of Beatrice C.] - b. 1889; d. 1976
Carlton C. (husb. of Helen T.) - b. 1919; m. 7 March 1942; d. 1971
[Elizabeth - see BARROWS]
George H. ([brother of Helen E.]; husb. of Maude Deviney[13]) - b. 29 June 1884; d. 9 February 1949
H. Camilla - b. 30 September 1900; d. 1 March 1988
Helen E. [sister of George H.] - b. 13 September 1890; d. 11 December 1959
Helen T. (wife of Carlton C.) - b. 1918; m. 7 March 1942; d. 1985
James H. (son of George H. and Maude Deviney[13]) - b. 13 December 1919; d. 8 November 1936
James K. [husb. of Mary L.?] - b. 1859; d. 1939
Lester A. - b. 1921; d. 1987
Mary L. [wife of James K.?] - b. 1863; d. 1954
Maude Deviney[13] (wife of George H.) - b. 17 August 1892; d. 16 May 1936
Nahum E. - b. 4 October 1918; d. 10 August 1972
Thomas A. [son of James K. and Mary L.?; husb. of Alberta M.?] - b. 1882; d. 1964
KENT
Cora S. (wife of George E.) - b. 1876; d. 1961
G. W. (husb. of Victoria A.) - b. 1848; d. 1945
George E. (husb. of Cora S.) - b. 1866; d. 1949
Lucy F. (wife of Winfield P.) - b. 1890; d. 1932
Sheldon Samuel (Capt.; son of Lucy F. and Winfield P.) - b. 1914; d. 1968; bur. "at sea"
Victoria A. (wife of G. W.) - b. 1854; d. 1917
Winfield P. (husb. of Lucy F.) - b. 1884; "lost at sea" 1947
KIMBALL
[Hannah E. - see MAYO]

Sarah - b. 1853; d. 1937

KING

Bertha A. [dau. of Henry W. and Lucy C.?] - b. 17 January 1877; d. 5 June 1912
Edna M. - b. 1906; d. 1994
Elbert R. [son of Samuel S. and Susie B.?] - b. 1897; d. 1898
Eldred G. [son of Samuel S. and Susie B.?] - b. 1897; d. 1913
Eliza - b. 1839; d. 1935
Elizabeth T. [wife of Stanwood H.] - b. 1905
[Ethel M. - see NEWMAN]
Frances E. - b. 1863; d. 1946
Henry W. [husb. of Lucy C.] - b. 28 January 1840; d. 5 October 1906
Howard M. - b. 1876; d. 1958
infant [child of Samuel S. and Susie B.?] - [b. and d.?] 1910
[Kathleen Ann - see CRANE]
[Lottie - see REED]
Louise M. [wife of Pearl S.] - b. 1897; d. 1987
Lucy C. [wife of Henry W.] - b. 18 January 1843; d. 16 December 1928
Margaret ([wife of R]ufus) - d. [...] Æ 41 y., [...][5]
Marilyn E. [dau. of Stanwood H. and Elizabeth T.?] - [b. and d.?] 19 September 1928
Mary J. [wife of William W.] - b. 1860; d. 1941
Maud L. - b. 1875; d. 1966
Merrill B. - b. 1848; d. 1930
Merrill B. - b. 7 September 1897; d. 14 September 1963
[Nancy C. - see PARKER]
Pearl S. [husb. of Louise M.] - b. 1900; d. 1972
Reginald A. (husb. of Rena N.) - b. 1894; d. 1931
Rena N. (wife of Reginald A.) - b. 1883; d. 1961
Rufus (Capt.; husb. of Margaret) - d. 27 October 1895 Æ 78 y., 6 m., 19 d.
Samuel S. [husb. of Susie B.] - b. 1868; d. 1919
Stanwood H. [husb. of Elizabeth T.] - b. 1905; d. 1996
Susie B. [wife of Samuel S.] - b. 1873; d. 1965
Vurney L. - b. 1872; d. 1954
Wallace C. (son of Capt. Rufus and Margaret) - d. 1 May 1848 Æ 6 y., 2 m., 6 d.
Wallace E. - b. 1888; "lost at sea" 1922
William W. [husb. of Mary J.] - b. 1853; d. 1942

KNOWLES

Fred (husb. of Glennie) - b. 1859; d. 1931
Glennie (wife of Fred) - b. 1871; d. 1940
William W. [son of Fred and Glennie?] - b. 1888; d. 1965

KNOWLTON

John T. (husb. of Vilda S. (ROBBINS)) - b. 1858; d. 1923
Vilda S. (ROBBINS; wife of John T.) - b. 1864; d. 1963

KNOX

David T. - b. 1866; d. 1954

KRANTZ

Arvid Emery [son of Oscar O. and Inez E.?] - b. 18 October 1920; d. 12 December 1997
Inez E. [wife of Oscar O.] - b. 1898; d. 1963
Oscar O. [husb. of Inez E.] - b. 1888; d. 1968

KREBS

Virginia R[AMSDELL?]. - b. 1905; d. 1981

KROPH
[Josephine - see FICKETT]
LACOUNT [includes LACOUNT]
Herbert [husb. of Louise] - b. 1891; d. 1958
Louise [wife of Herbert] - b. 1892; d. 1963
Sadie A. - b. 1857; d. 1937
LAFFERTY
[Mary - see WALKER]
LAHAYE
Joan [dau. of Richard T. and Mary H.?] - [no dates]
Marilyn (CARROLL; [wife of Richard Harlan]) - b. 1930; d. 1995
Mary H. [wife of Richard T.] - b. 23 May 1910
Richard Harlan [husb. of Marilyn (CARROLL)] - b. 1932
Richard T. [husb. of Mary H.] - b. 23 December 1908; d. 2 April 1993
LAKEMAN
Emma K. (wife of Ross F. [no stone]) - b. 1902; d. 1938
LAMBERTY
Adelheid Mathilde - b. 15 July 1904; d. 8 January 1998
Hubert Franz Josef - b. 12 March 1906; d. 20 September 1982
LANE
Adrian O. - b. 1908; d. 1969
LANPHER
Alfred M. [husb. of Gladys T.] - b. 1896; d. 1966
[Arthur L.[15] - see GRAY]
Eldred G. - b. 1 December 1906; d. 28 May 1998
Gladys T. [wife of Alfred M.] - b. 1900; d. 1977
John M. [son of Alfred M. and Gladys T.?] - b. 1931; d. 1980
Lewis A. - b. 15 June 1905; d. 2 November 1993
LASH
Anstress E. (wife of John B.) - d. 19 April 1893 Æ 65 y., 2 m.
John B. (husb. of Anstress E.) - d. 1 December 1897 Æ 75 y.
LAWLER
Allen J. (husb. of Caroline (ROBINSON)) - b. 2 February 1863; d. 29 July 1933
Ann (COFFEY; wife of Christopher W.) - b. 22 February 1894; d. 17 May 1964
Caroline (ROBINSON; wife of Allen J.) - b. 23 August 1865; d. 23 January 1959
Christopher W. (husb. of Ann (COFFEY)) - b. 12 October 1893; d. 11 November 1956
Edwin A. [husb. of Vienna?] - b. 1856; d. 1930
Elizabeth [wife of John D.] - b. 1903; d. 1975
Elizabeth C. (wife of William) - d. 7 November 1905 Æ 82 y., 15 d.
Freddie (son of William and Elizabeth C.) - d. 24 September 1867 Æ 3 y., 2 m.
Frederick (son of William and Elizabeth C.) - d. 5 February 1864 Æ 9 y., 10 m.
James W. (son of William and Elizabeth C.) - d. 24 March 1877 Æ 29 y., 9 m., 19 d.
John C. [son of William and Elizabeth C.] - "lost at sea" 3 December 1872 Æ 20 y., 1 m., 9 d.
John D. [[son of Edwin A. and Vienna?]; husb. of Elizabeth] - b. 1906; d. 1997
[Lucy E. - see WHITMORE]
M. J. W. - d. 3 August 1925 Æ [not given]
[Rosemary - see THERIAULT]
Vienna [wife of Edwin A.?] - b. 1871; d. 1955
William (husb. of Elizabeth C.) - d. 24 March 1892 Æ 74 y., 7 m.

LAWRENCE
Ruth Eleanor - b. 6 March 1905; d. 17 October 1992
LAWSON
Lernice J. - b. 1928; d. 1994
[Lizabeth [sic] - see RICH]
LAWTON
Abbie May (wife of William [LAWTON?]) - b. 1855; d. 1929
Annie May (wife of J. Thomas) - b. 1869; d. 1946
Arthur F. [husb. of Edna S.] - b. 1885; d. 1950
Edna S. [wife of Arthur F.] - b. 1887; d. 1975
[Emily F. - see NEWMAN]
[Fannie - see CROCKETT]
Fred (husb. of Nettie) - b. 1863; d. 1947
Fred W. (husb. of Helen C.) - b. 1893; d. 1977
Harry [LAWTON?] - b. September 1874; d. [no date]
Helen C. (wife of Fred W.) - b. 1886; d. 1952
Hettie [LAWTON?] - b. July 1876; d. August 1942
J. Thomas (husb. of Annie May) - b. 1854; d. 1954
Nettie (wife of Fred) - b. 1861; d. 1911
[Ruth A. - see FERNALD]
William - d. 7 April 1881 Æ 56 y., 6 m.
William [LAWTON?] (husb. of Abbie May) - b. 1850; d. 1940
LEIGHTON
Belle B. [wife of George N.] - b. 1876; d. 1945
Frances J. [wife of Herbert M. Sr.] - b. 1905; d. 1980
Genevieve [wife of Harry E.] - b. 1903; d. 1970
George N. [husb. of Belle B.] - b. 1869; d. 1952
Harry E. [husb. of Genevieve] - b. 1898; d. 1979
Herbert M. Sr. [[son of George N. and Belle B.?]; husb. of Frances J.] - b. 1896; d. 1973
Juanita G. [wife of N. Everett] - b. 1920
N. Everett [husb. of Juanita G.] - b. 12 August 1916; d. 10 June 1995
Randall S. - b. 16 January 1949; d. 27 March 1983
LELAND
[Roxy - see FERNALD]
LEMONT
Julia A. [wife of Dr. Robert J.] - b. 1849; d. 1917
Robert J. (Dr.; [husb. of Julia A.]) - b. 1842; d. 1926
LEONARD
Alfrieda [sic] (DORR; [wife of Howard M.]) - b. 13 December 1912; d. 28 July 1981
Edmund J. (husb. of Laura M.) - b. 1877; d. 1921
Ferne R. (wife of John J.) - b. 1917
Howard M. [husb. of Alfrieda [sic] (DORR)] - b. 28 November 1905; d. 9 August 1974
infant (dau. of John J. and Ferne R.) - [b. and d.?] 28 March 1936
John J. (husb. of Ferne R.) - b. 1913
Laura M. (wife of Edmund J.) - b. 1884; d. 1989
LEWIS
Alton W. [husb. of Virginia M.] - b. 1917; d. 1982
Blanche M. (wife of George E.) - b. 1885; d. 1939
Chester A. Sr. - b. 24 July 1912; d. 27 December 1971
Clarence R. [husb. of Velma E.] - b. 1908; d. 1975

Eudora A. [wife of Fred] - b. 1909; d. 1996
Fred [husb. of Eudora A.] - b. 1901; d. 1971
George E. (husb. of Blanche M.) - b. 1882; d. 1954
Raymond R. - b. 29 March 1909; d. 13 November 1959
Velma E. [wife of Clarence R.] - b. 1908; d. 1986
Virginia M. [wife of Alton W.] - b. 1919
Walter C. - b. 24 July 1930; d. 1 June 1997 Æ 66 y.

LINDGREN
Burt E. [husb. of Evelyn O.] - b. 1903; d. 1981
Evelyn O. [wife of Burt E.] - b. 1905; d. 1993

LOCKHART
Andrea D. - b. 1966; d. 1998
Ida W. (wife of William L.) - b. 1920
William E. "Billy" [son of William L. and Ida W.?] - b. 1957
William L. (husb. of Ida W.) - b. 17 December 1905; d. 6 December 1964

LONG
Idabelle W[ORCESTER?]. [wife of Ralph H. Sr.] - b. 1910; d. 1998
Ralph H. Sr. [husb. of Idabelle W[ORCESTER?].] - b. 1906; d. 1972

LORD
[Clara E. - see MAYO]
Edwin G. [husb. of Ella F.] - b. 1878; d. 1955
Ella F. [wife of Edwin G.] - b. 1883; d. 1939
Hoyt K. - b. 1932
Kenneth T. - b. 1908; d. 1988
Larry L. - b. 23 July 1956; d. 24 March 1996
Winfred O. - b. 1902; d. 1981

LORING
Frances E. - b. 5 January 1933; d. 19 February 1998

LOUNSBERRY
[Ida - see PALMER]

LUDWIG
[Bonnie D. L[UDWIG?]. - see BOISVERT]
Donald G. [husb. of Helen L.] - b. 1911; d. 2000
Helen L. [wife of Donald G.] - b. 1924

LUNT
Abbie M. - b. 1870; d. 1949
Abner W. - b. 1908; d. 1975
Basil R. - b. 1872; d. 1937
Clinton A. [husb. of Marion H.] - b. 26 February 1912; d. 4 December 1997
Edward A. (husb. of Sadie Edith) - b. 1866; d. 1929
Flora L. - b. 1877; d. 1946
Harriet A. - b. 1914; d. 1997
Harry W. [husb. of Sabra A.] - b. 4 October 1884; d. 30 December 1952
[Laura M. - see MAYO]
Lenora H. [wife of Wallace L.] - b. 1913
Lincoln H. - b. 1888; d. 1889
[Louisa A. - see NORWOOD]
Marion H. [wife of Clinton A.] - b. 13 March 1909
Robert L. (son of C. W. and H. G. [no stones]) - [b. and d.?] 31 May 1967
Roland H. - b. 1857; d. 1932
Ruth A. - b. 1899; d. 1991
Sabra A. [wife of Harry W.] - b. 3 March 1898; d. 22 July 1980

Sadie Edith (wife of Edward A.) - d. 22 May 1898 Æ 33 y., 6 m., 2 d.
Shirley W. - b. 1890; d. 1976
Wallace L. [husb. of Lenora H.] - b. 1906; d. 1979

LURVEY
Abbie E. (wife of Ezra D. [no stone?]) - b. 1853; d. 1907
Arthur R. [husb. of Dorothy D.] - b. 1900; d. 1969
Charlotte E. [dau. of Ezra W. and Mary E.?] - b. 1910
Dorothy D. [wife of Arthur R.] - b. 1900; d. 1990
[Edith - see DOLLIVER]
Elmenia P. [wife of Ezra D.] - b. 1840; d. 1931
Ezra D. [husb. of [Abbie E. and?] Elmenia P.] - b. 1853; d. 1930
Ezra W. [son of Ezra D. [no stone?] [and Abbie E.?[16]]; husb. of Mary E.] - b. 1876; d. 1956
Freeman J. [husb. of Laura E.] - b. 1864; d. 1942
Grace M. (wife of Henry V.) - b. 1892; d. 1980
Henry V. (husb. of Grace M.) - b. 1886; d. 1958
Herbert W. (Capt.) - b. 1888; d. 1961
[Jennie E. - see HERSEY]
Laura E. [wife of Freeman J.] - b. 1861; d. 1917
Mary E. [wife of Ezra W.] - b. 1871; d. 1939
Persis W. (wife of Seth W.) - b. 1846; d. 1923
Rose A. (wife of Marshall [no stone]) - b. 1859; d. 1923
Seth W. (husb. of Persis W.) - b. 1848; d. 1922

LYLE
Charles Albert - b. 8 April 1936; d. 17 December 1997

MACE
Alden F. (husb. of Viola M.) - b. 1877; d. 1958
Alice (GINN; [dau. of Arthur E. GINN and Inez (TORREY)?]; wife of Raymond P.) - b. 1909
Ansel L. - b. 9 June 1910; d. 9 May 1972
Ella M. (dau. of Alden F. and Viola M.) - b. 1912; d. 24 September 1912 Æ 1 m., 16 d.
Leslie G. (son of Alden F. and Viola M.) - b. 1 November 1917; d. 16 February 191[9 or 8][2]
Raymond P. (husb. of Alice (GINN)) - b. 1905; d. 1987
Viola M. (wife of Alden F.) - b. 1885; d. 1943

MADORE
Mary I. - b. 1921; d. 1982

MAGNUSSON
Alberta M. [wife of Gustave A.] - b. 1875; d. 1926
Gustave A. [husb. of Alberta M.] - b. 1870; d. 1958

MAHLER
Joyce (STANLEY) - b. 1947; d. 1984

MALANSON [includes MALONSON; see also MALLINSON]
David W. (Capt.; husb. of Rebecca E.) - b. 3 March 1841; d. 11 June 1909
David W. [husb. of E. Marie] - b. 1889; d. 1945
E. Marie [wife of David W.] - b. 1900; d. 1997
[Mabel - see BURRELL]
Rebecca E. (wife of Capt. David W.) - b. 1859; d. 1902

MALLETT
Laura B. - b. 1899; d. 1984

MALLINSON [see also MALANSON]
Charlotte C. - b. 1926; d. 1994
[Lisa Beth [MALLINSON?] - see GALBREATH]
MANCHESTER
Frank L. (husb. of Jennette [sic] M.) - b. 1873; d. 1957
Jennette [sic] M. (wife of Frank L.) - b. 1879; d. 1932
MARCUS
Dorothy Elder - b. 1 December 1889; d. 6 June 1944
[Linda Chapin - see RAMSEYER]
MARCYES
[Margaret A. - see FERNALD]
Victorine Augusta ("eldest daughter" of D. P. and Helen A. [no stones]) - d. 8 August 1872 Æ 17 y., 8 m.
MARK
Della B. (NORWOOD) - b. 1892; d. 1993
MARSHALL
Amanda H. - b. 1851; d. 1943
Bowen F. Sr. - [no dates]
Doris M. (dau. of Simeon J. and Lucy E.) - b. 1901; d. 1929
Elmer S. Jr. - b. 22 March 1918; d. 29 August 1971
Elsie P. [wife of Roscoe C.] - b. 26 September 1905; d. 8 December 1988
[Louise M[ARSHALL?]. - see SALISBURY]
Lucy E. (wife of Simeon J.) - b. 1873; d. [no date]
Lydia Conrad - b. 6 August 1920; d. 18 March 1982
Marguerite M. (wife of Maurice C.) - b. 19 April 1883; d. 27 October 1955
Maurice C. (husb. of Marguerite M.) - b. 26 October 1883; d. 26 December 1956
Roscoe C. [husb. of Elsie P.] - b. 26 March 1911; d. 31 December 1968
Simeon J. (husb. of Lucy E.) - b. 1874; d. [no date]
MARTEL
Hester M. [wife of Wilfred John Sr.] - b. 1900
Wilfred John Jr. [son of Wilfred John Sr. and Hester M.] - b. 3 July 1924; d. 10 June 1997
Wilfred John Sr. [husb. of Hester M.] - b. 3 October 1900; d. 20 January 1997
MARTIN
Jo Anne - b. 26 August 1948; d. 31 August 1976
MASON
Helen Evelyn [dau. of Joseph B. and Mary J.?] - b. 11 November 1870; d. 9 March 1875
Joseph B. [husb. of Mary J.] - b. 16 August 1842; d. 26 June 1915
Josie Frances [dau. of Joseph B. and Mary J.?] - b. 14 November 1872; d. 9 March 1875
Katharine W. (wife of William E.) - b. 1858; d. 1957
Mark H. [son of Joseph B. and Mary J.?] - b. 9 April 1869; d. 30 January 1911
Mary J. [wife of Joseph B.] - b. 9 June 1848; d. 15 April 1932
William E. (husb. of Katharine W.) - b. 1859; d. 1937
MAYO
Agnes E. (wife of Donald K.) - b. 15 October 1894; d. 12 October 1976
Alston T. [son of Capt. Howard and Tryphosa A.?] - b. 1906; d. 1966
Augustus L. (husb. of Clara E. (LORD)) - b. 29 August 1860; d. 13 March 1910
Benjamin R. (husb. of Laura M. (LUNT)) - b. 1846; d. 1919
Byron H. (husb. of Fannie (DOLIVER) [sic]) - b. 13 March 1856; d. 14 June 1918
Clara E. (LORD; wife of Augustus L.) - b. 13 January 1868; d. 21 April 1929

Donald K. (husb. of Agnes E.) - b. 16 October 1893; d. 6 July 1924
Dudley L. - b. 1855; d. 1924
[Edith O. - see FARNSWORTH]
Eleanor R. - b. 1920; d. 1981
[Eva - see JOY]
Everett S. [son of Augustus L. and Clara E. (LORD)?] - b. 21 May 1896; d. 22 May 1896
Fannie (DOLIVER [sic]; wife of Byron H.) - b. 24 December 1858; d. 5 July 1924
Fred S. - b. 1876; d. 1949
Frederick Coombs "Freddy" [son of Jacob S. and Sarah (DOLLIVER)?] - b. 14 February 1857; d. 16 January 1858
[Gladys M[AYO?]. - see CROCKER]
Hannah E. (KIMBALL; wife of Jacob) - b. 1848; d. 1914
Howard (Capt.; [husb. of Tryphosa A.?]) - b. 1863; "lost at sea" 1917
Howard E. [son of Capt. Howard and Tryphosa A.?] - b. 1901; "lost at sea" 1917
infant (son of William I. and Annie E. [no stones]) - [b. and?] d. 17 September 1882
Irene [wife of Josiah K.] - b. 7 December 1815; d. 16 January 1899
Jacob (husb. of Hannah E. (KIMBALL)) - b. 1845; d. 1921
Jacob S. (husb. of Sarah (DOLLIVER)) - b. 14 June 1819; d. 24 April 1912
John Leman [husb. of Marion "Marnie" (BURNETT)] - b. 1887; d. 1958
Josephine Clark "Josie" [dau. of Jacob S. and Sarah (DOLLIVER)?] - b. 1 January 1864; d. 5 March 1880
Josiah K. [husb. of Irene] - b. 19 July 1810; d. 14 March 1898
Joy May (GRIFFIN; wife of Leonard Neal) - b. 10 May 1929
Laura M. (LUNT; wife of Benjamin R.) - b. 1848; d. 1927
Leonard Neal (husb. of Joy May (GRIFFIN)) - b. 19 July 1927; d. 7 January 1998
Lillian E. - b. 1889; d. 1979
[Lisa - see WILKINSON]
[Livonia A. - see NEWMAN]
[Lizzie B. - see HOLMES]
[Lulu - see JAMES]
Marion "Marnie" (BURNETT; [wife of John Leman]) - b. 1893; d. 1947
Ruth - b. 1894; d. 1894
Sarah (DOLLIVER; wife of Jacob S.) - b. 11 January 1827; d. 16 June 1898
Sim H. [husb. of Vira J.?] - b. 1867; d. 1933
Stillman [son of Augustus L. and Clara E. (LORD)?] - b. 25 August 1886; d. 27 August 1886
Tryphosa A. [wife of Capt. Howard?] - b. 1864; d. 1945
Vira J. [wife of Sim H.?] - b. 1867; d. 1960

McCAFFREY
Lawrence E. - b. 19 June 1897; d. 18 June 1959

McCASLIN
Charles M. - b. 8 July 1886; d. 11 August 1965

McENROE
Robert E. - b. 1 February 1940; d. 30 September 1970

McFARLAND
Eleanor (RHOADS; [wife of Joseph Jr.]) - b. 1898; d. 1973
Joseph Jr. [husb. of Eleanor (RHOADS)] - b. 1904; d. 1937

McINVALE
Barbara Jean - b. 1948; d. 1997
Rose - b. 1926; d. 1962

McKAY
Clarence A. (husb. of Mattie E. (GURNEY)) - b. 1890; d. 1957
John W. [son of Rufus W. and Mary?] - b. 1862; d. 1917
Mary (wife of Rufus W.) - b. 1837; d. 1913
Mattie E. (GURNEY; wife of Clarence A.) - b. 1887; d. 1927
Rufus W. (husb. of Mary) - b. 1836; d. 1914
McKENZIE
[Isabelle - see FERGUSON]
McLAUGHLIN
Robert P. Sr. - b. 1927; d. 1993
McNAUGHTON
Elizabeth S. - b. 1883; d. 1936
James - b. 1864; d. [no date]
MERCHANT
Annie S. (wife of Henry M.) - b. 1912; d. 1987
David L. (son of Henry M. and Annie S.) - b. 1946; d. 1985
Henry M. (husb. of Annie S.) - b. 1911; d. 1998
Llewellyn S. - b. 1907; d. 1981
MERRIAM
Carol Goodwin [dau. of Robert C. and Grace L.?] - b. 1928; d. 1948
Donald Phelps [son of Robert C. and Grace L.?] - b. 1926; d. 1945
Grace L. [wife of Robert C.?] - b. 1902; d. 1980
Robert C. [husb. of Grace L.?] - b. 1896; d. 1986
MICHAUD
Al M. [husb. of Virginia (BEAL)] - b. 1913
Virginia (BEAL; [wife of Al M.]) - b. 1913
MILLS
Anne Starrett (dau. of Robert C. and Elizabeth A. (STONE)) - b. 1954; d. 1986
Cora E. - b. 1888; d. 1975
Elizabeth A. (STONE; [wife of Robert C.]) - b. 1928
Jesse N. - b. 1894; d. 1972
Marion B. - b. 1893; d. 1982
Nettie M. - b. 1862; d. 1939
Olaus L. - b. 1856; d. 1939
Robert C. (husb. of Elizabeth A. (STONE)) - b. 1926; d. 1994
Sheila Louise - b. 1930; d. 1995
MILLSTEIN
Hyman (Dr.) - b. 30 May 1910; d. 4 February 1960
MITCHELL
[Alice M[ITCHELL?]. - see BOUCHARD]
Alton III (son of Alton and Janet [no stones]) - [b. and d.?] 1961
Alton L. ([son of Charles M. and Ida M.?]; husb. of Vera C.) - b. 11 April 1907; d. 29 October 1963
Austin M. [husb. of Lena N.] - b. 1892; d. 1954
Beatrice [dau. of William B. and Viola E.] - b. 8 November 1899; d. 8 January 1908
Blanche L. [wife of Elmer S.] - b. 1893; d. 1983
Charles M. (husb. of Ida M.) - b. 1865; d. 1942
Elmer S. [husb. of Blanche L.] - b. 1891; d. 1988
Everett L. [husb. of Nora L.] - b. 27 June 1895; d. 26 April 1968
George A. - b. 15 November 1915; d. 11 September 1998
Ida M. (wife of Charles M.) - b. 1864; d. 1937
infant (son of Alton. L. and Vera C.) - [b. and d.?] 1938

John Kenneth [husb. of Madeline D.] - b. 22 February 1924; d. 4 June 1993
John P. - b. 1900; d. 1924
Julius E. - b. 1902; d. 1982
Lena N. [wife of Austin M.] - b. 1897; d. 1992
Madeline D. [wife of John Kenneth] - b. 18 September 1924
Mary E. [wife of Russell] - b. 1898; d. 1971
Mary L. [wife of Nathaniel M.] - b. 1884; d. 1975
Melvin F. (husb. of Minnie E.) - b. 1870; d. 1951
Minnie E. (wife of Melvin F.) - b. 1870; d. 1950
Nathaniel M. [husb. of Mary L.] - b. 1875; d. 1948
Nora L. [wife of Everett L.] - b. 1899; d. 1986
Russell [husb. of Mary E.] - b. 1903; d. 1972
Vera C. (wife of Alton L.) - b. 25 February 1916; d. 12 April 1999
Viola E. (wife of William B.) - b. 1870; d. 1957
William B. (husb. of Viola E.) - b. 1869; d. 1936

MONOHON
Charles Edward - b. 1877; d. 1934

MOORE
Albert D. - b. 1869; d. 1944
Alice (MORRIS) - b. 17 February 1853; d. 3 March 1940
Audrey H. [wife of Harvey A.] - b. 1903; d. 1989
Belinda (wife of Lewis W.) - d. 21 January 1883 Æ 60 y., 1 m., 18 d.
Benjamin (Capt.; husb. of Eliza) - d. 29 June 1842 Æ 45 y.
Carrie M. [wife of Frank M.] - b. 1864; d. 1950
Edith (GRAY; [wife of Edwin J.]) - b. 1882; d. 1942
Edwin J. [husb. of Edith (GRAY)] - b. 1883; d. 1951
Eliza (wife of Capt. Benjamin) - d. 22 January 1891 Æ 88 y., 3 m., 14 d.
Ellen M. (wife of Capt. Peter S.) - d. 11 August 1873 Æ 36 y., 3 m., 11 d.
Enoch S. (son of Capt. Benjamin and Eliza) - d. 12 May 1851 Æ 16 y., 7 m.
Frances M. (wife of Samuel) - b. 1849; d. 1935
Frank M. [husb. of Carrie M.] - b. 1867; d. 1945
Gertrude M. [wife of Russell B.?] - b. 1885; d. 1979
Harvey A. [husb. of Audrey H.] - b. 1900; d. 1971
Henry C. - b. 1837; d. 1914
Jeremiah (husb. of Margaret) - d. 4 April 1851 Æ 56 y.
Joshua S. (Capt.) - d. 3 May 1865 Æ [...][5], 12 d.
Josie - b. 1875; d. 1959
[Julia I. - see GILLEY]
Lewis W. (husb. of Belinda) - d. 21 August 1895 Æ 72 y., 10 m., 29 d.
Margaret (wife of Jeremiah) - d. 30 March 1876 Æ 81 y., 8 m., 6 d.
Mary E. (wife of Capt. Peter S.) - d. 18 February 1919 Æ 78 y., 9 m., 19 d.
[Mattie I - see DOLLIVER]
Oliver W. - d. 26 March 1851, New York, Æ 23 y., 5 m.
Peter S. (Capt.; husb. of Ellen M. and Mary E.) - d. 17 May 1903 Æ 73 y., 6 m., 29 d.
Phebe A. (dau. of Jeremiah and Margaret) - d. 25 June 1854 Æ 17 y., 28 d.
Phillip - b. 1836; d. 1907
Royden C. - b. 28 August 1887; d. 23 October 1906
Russell B. [husb. of Gertrude M.?] - b. 31 July 1889; d. 22 January 1962
Samuel (husb. of Frances M.) - b. 1842; d. 1914

MORRILL
Charlotte E. - b. 12 April 1861; d. 9 February 1935

MORRIS
[Alice - see MOORE]
Augustus W. (son of James A. and Alice J. [no stone]) - d. 3 July 1892 Æ 19 y., 9 m.; ("drowned")
Bessie [wife of William] - b. 1909
Carrie (wife of Raymond) - [no dates]
James A. (husb. of Alice J. [no stone]) - d. 18 September 1882 Æ 47 y., 28 d.
Raymond (husb. of Carrie) - [no dates]
Rita (WALSH) - b. 4 May 1914; d. 5 July 1994
William [husb. of Bessie] - b. 1907; d. 1963

MORSE
Arvilda F. [wife of Fairfield W.] - b. 1909; d. 1992
Charlotte S. [wife of Robert C.] - b. 1910; d. 1995
Fairfield W. [husb. of Arvilda F.] - b. 1906; d. 1990
Georgia C. [wife of Grover A.] - b. 1886; d. 1970
Grover A. [husb. of Georgia C.] - b. 1885; d. 1960
Robert C. [husb. of Charlotte S.] - b. 1910; d. 1959

MOULTON
Patricia J. - b. 11 February 1935; d. 12 May 1977

MUISE
[Anne Adele - see DOLLIVER]
Annie S. (wife of Joseph) - b. 1898; d. 1976
Joseph (husb. of Annie S.) - b. 1892; d. 1975
Ronald T. - b. 24 November 1919; d. 23 August 1932

MURPHY
[Bertha C. - see NEAL]
Clarence A. "Nibby" [husb. of Jane P.] - b. 1935; d. 1989
Dennis W. [son of Joseph Walter] - b. 1955; d. 1974
Dussia (EVANOFF; wife of Lawrence K.) - b. 1912; d. 1972
Everett C. (husb. of Viola A.) - b. 1879; d. 1958
Forrest E. [husb. of L. Frances] - b. 1899; d. 1926
Harlow H. [husb. of Sadie F.] - b. 1876; d. 1924
Jane P. [wife of Clarence A. "Nibby"] - b. 1936
Joseph Walter - b. 24 September 1932; d. 20 June 1997
L. Frances [wife of Forrest E.] - b. 1901; d. 1951
Lawrence K. (husb. of Dussia (EVANOFF)) - b. 1914; d. 1991
Lida M. - b. 1889; d. 1969
Marie E. - b. 26 July 1903; d. 5 June 1999 Æ 95 y.
Paul V. [husb. of Pearl Irene[10]] - b. 1 May 1935
Pearl Irene[10] [wife of Paul V.] - b. 1 June 1937; d. 3 November 1999
Sadie F. [wife of Harlow H.] - b. 1879; d. 1929
Viola A. (wife of Everett C.) - b. 1884; d. 1977
Walter H. - b. 1898; d. 1958

MUSETTI
Julie - b. 31 May 1961; d. 25 November 1961

NASH
[Linda C. - see TRACY]

NEAL
Bertha C. (MURPHY; wife of Dr. George A.) - b. 1887; d. 1968
E. Wilder [child of Dr. Elias C. and Evelyn M. (WILDER)] - b. 1879; d. 1950
Elias C. (Dr.; husb. of Evelyn M. (WILDER)) - b. 1833; d. 1897
Essie W. (child of Dr. Elias C. and Evelyn M. (WILDER)) - b. 1877; d. 1878

Evelyn M. (WILDER; wife of Dr. Elias C.) - b. 1836; d. 1927
George A. (Dr.; [son of Dr. Elias C. and Evelyn M. (WILDER)?]; husb. of Bertha C. (MURPHY)) - b. 1872; d. 1939
Saxon K. (son of Dr. Elias C. and Evelyn M. (WILDER)) - b. 1881; d. 1898

NEARY
Grace - b. 1918; d. 1997

NELSON
Blanche Modjeska (BENSON; [dau. of Lewis F. BENSON and Elizabeth W. "Lizzie" (HITCHCOCK); wife of Freeman Leslie]) - b. 1889; d. 1970
Ellen D. [wife of Lewis F.] - b. 1924
Freeman Leslie [husb. of Blanche Modjeska (BENSON)] - b. 1885; d. 1969
Lewis F. [husb. of Ellen D.] - b. 1920; d. 1985

NEWCOMB
Mary D. - b. 1870; d. 1957

NEWMAN
Addie E. [wife of G. Everett] - b. 1885; d. 1965
Alberta L. (wife of Charles H.) - b. 1877; d. 1959
[Alma A. - see SPURLING]
Almeda N. (COOK; wife of Walter H.) - b. 1869; d. 1932
Amos B. (husb. of Viola E.) - b. 30 August 1830; d. 21 January 1916
Annabel [NEWMAN?] - [no dates]
Arthur E. (husb. of Leona G.) - b. 1898; d. 1957
Augusta (wife of Lewis F.) - b. 1863; d. 1924
Bill - b. 1864; d. 1954
Catharine W. (wife of Henry E.) - b. 1825; d. 1916
Charles H. (husb. of Alberta L.) - b. 1864; d. 1952
[Cora E. - see HAYNES]
Edgar (husb. of Jessie G.) - b. 1860; d. 1936
Emily F. (LAWTON; wife of Soulis H.) - b. 1889; d. 1918
Ethel M. (KING; wife of Lyle D.) - b. 1884; d. 1971
Eva L. - b. 12 October 1959; d. 20 September 1996 Æ 36 y.
Everett H. (Capt.; son of Henry E. and Catharine W.) - d. 2 February 1880, Long Branch, New Jersey, Æ 30 y., 10 m.; ("drowned")
G. Everett [husb. of Addie E.] - b. 1887; d. 1977
Harriet S. "Hattie" (wife of William S.) - b. 15 August 1839; d. 6 May 1901
Harry E. [husb. of Mildred G.] - b. 24 July 1887; d. 17 August 1954
Henry E. (husb. of Catharine W.) - d. 9 February 1894 Æ 75 y., 11 m., 6 d.
Hilda L. [wife of Keith B.] - b. 1931
Holsey R. (Capt.; son of Henry E. and Catharine W.) - "lost" 28 August 1876, "on coast of Labrador", Æ 29 y.
Jessie A. (HOMER; wife of Walter H.) - b. 19 October 1875; d. 19 December 1911
Jessie G. (wife of Edgar) - b. 1864; d. 1953
John D. - [no dates]
John L. (husb. of Livonia A. (MAYO)) - b. 1823; d. 1906
Jonathan - [no dates]
Keith B. [husb. of Hilda L.] - b. 30 November 1936; d. 22 July 1971
Lawrence [NEWMAN?] - [no dates]
Lena - [no dates]
Leona G. (wife of Arthur E.) - b. 1894; d. 1967
Lewis F. (husb. of Augusta) - b. 1859; d. 1953
Livonia A. (MAYO; wife of John L.) - b. 1833; d. 1903
Loren H. [son of Henry E. and Catharine W.] - b. 1855; d. 1933

Lydia J. (wife of William S.) - b. 3 February 1829; d. 16 October 1883
Lyle D. ([son of S. Ward and Marion E. (HADLOCK)?]; husb. of Ethel M. (KING)) - b. 1876; d. 1974
Malina S. (wife of Thomas M.) - b. 6 March 1838; d. 15 February 1919
Marguerite E. [wife of Thomas H.] - b. 1906; d. 1990
Marion E. (HADLOCK; wife of S. Ward) - b. 1854; d. 1945
[Marion E. - see WESCOTT]
Marnal R. (son of Lewis F. and Augusta) - b. 1887; d. 1908
Melinda (STANLEY[17]; wife of Robert S.) - b. 1833; d. 1915
Mildred G. [wife of Harry E.] - b. 1 September 1890; d. 6 October 1978
Nancy M. (SPURLING; wife of Samuel S.) - b. 1 July 1798; d. 17 September 1886
Nellie M. (wife of Robert E.) - b. 1872; d. 1929
[Ora - see SEAVEY]
Robert E. (husb. of Nellie M.) - b. 1863; d. 1947
Robert S. (husb. of Melinda (STANLEY[17])) - b. 1825; d. 1922
S. Ward (husb. of Marion E. (HADLOCK)) - b. 1852; d. 1949
Samuel S. (husb. of Nancy M. (SPURLING)) - b. 23 March 1811; d. 21 February 1902
Sarah S. - [no dates]
Soulis H. (husb. of Emily F. (LAWTON)) - b. 1891; d. 1974
Thomas H. [husb. of Marguerite E.] - b. 1903; d. 1957
Thomas M. (husb. of Malina S.) - b. 28 August 1835; d. 8 September 1942
Vesper L. - b. 23 April 1902; d. 30 May 1927
Viola E. (wife of Amos B.) - b. 29 January 1840; d. 31 December 1920
Walter H. (husb. of Jessie A. (HOMER) and Almeda N. (COOK)) - [no dates]
William Harris - [no dates]
William S. (husb. of Lydia J. and Harriet S. "Hattie") - b. 10 May 1825; d. 16 October 1901

NICE

F. Millard [husb. of S. Margaret] - b. 26 April 1911; d. 22 February 1985
S. Margaret [wife of F. Millard] - b. 18 October 1917

NIELSEN

Mercy E. - b. 1925; d. 1999

NORWOOD

Ada K. - d. 7 January 1939 Æ 68 y., 21 d.
Alice (BROWN; wife of Seth) - b. 1877; d. 1960
Alice M. (wife of Richard) - b. 1900; d. 1970
Aljava (CARVER; wife of Capt. Robie M.) - b. 22 October 1844; d. 10 June 1917
Arthur J. - b. 1889; d. 1943
Christine L. - b. 1904; d. 1970
Clarence [son of Nahum M. and Elizabeth F.?] - b. 1891; d. 1955
Daniel F. [husb. of Harriette [sic] J.] - b. 1861; d. 1924
[Della B. - see MARK]
Edna H. [wife of Emery E.] - b. 1886; d. 1989
Elizabeth F. [wife of Nahum M.] - b. 13 June 1873; d. 2 January 1969
Ellsworth T. [husb. of Mary S.] - b. 1913; d. 1972
Emery E. [husb. of Edna H.] - b. 12 December 1886; d. 22 July 1953
Emma [C.?][11] (GOGGINS; wife of Robie M. Jr.) - b. 1872; d. 1951
Ernest E. Sr. - b. 1895; d. 1961
Everett E. - b. 1898; d. 1965
George - b. 1862; d. 1931
Harriette [sic] J. [wife of Daniel F.] - b. 1864; d. 1949

[Hope - see BANNISTER]
Ida E. [dau. of Thomas O. and Louisa A. (LUNT)?] - b. 16 November 1880; d. 3 November 1919
Joseph B. (Capt.; husb. of R. May) - b. 1865; d. 1943
Lewis A. [husb. of Reta M.] - b. 1893; d. 1988
Louisa A. (LUNT; wife of Thomas O.) - b. 1846; d. 1928
M. Eugene - b. 1896; d. 1918
Marguerite H. (TORREY; wife of Harry G. [no stone]) - b. 1905; d. 1965
Mary S. [wife of Ellsworth T.] - b. 1912; d. 1990
Nahum M. [husb. of Elizabeth F.] - b. 1869; d. 1931
Percy Lord (son of Robie M. Jr. and Emma [C.?][11] (GOGGINS)) - b. 19 November 1896; d. 6 October 1897
R. May (wife of Capt. Joseph B.) - b. 1870; d. 1939
Reta M. [wife of Lewis A.] - b. 1899; d. 1966
Richard (husb. of Alice M.) - b. 1902; d. 1962
Rita S. (wife of Warren M.) - b. 1886; d. 1932
Robie M. Jr. (husb. of Emma [C.?][11] (GOGGINS)) - b. 1873; d. 1955
Robie M. (Capt.; husb. of Aljava (CARVER)) - b. 1 February 1838; d. 5 February 1909
Seth (husb. of Alice (BROWN)) - b. 1878; d. 1966
Thomas O. (husb. of Louisa A. (LUNT)) - b. 1846; d. 1923
Warren M. (husb. of Rita S.) - b. 1889; d. 1927

NOYES
Bessie M. - b. 1897; d. 1981
Clarence M. [husb. of Cora L.] - b. 1902; d. 1975
Cora L. [wife of Clarence M.] - b. 1904; d. 1986
[Flora A. - see HANCOCK]
Fred A. - b. 1868; d. 1948
George A. - b. 1916; d. 1991
James L. - b. 1900; d. 1990
John A. (husb. of June D.) - b. December 1898; d. January 1967
[Julia E. - see PARKER]
June D. (wife of John A.) - b. 1900; d. 1994
Margaret E. - b. 1905; d. 1974
Marion F. [wife of Richard W.] - b. 1924
Nellie M. - b. 1878; d. 1960
Richard W. [husb. of Marion F.] - b. 1923
Richard W. Jr. - b. 1947; d. 1967

OLIVA
Daniel - b. 21 March 1968, Caracas, Venezuela; d. 1 January 1993, Jupiter, Florida

OLSEN
John - b. 1856; d. 1921
Peter - b. 1874; d. 1944

OSBORNE
Patrick - b. 1879; d. 1945

PACKARD
Beatrice A. (WILSON) - [no dates]

PALMER
Craig Randall - [b. and d.?] 27 July 1987
[Eunice - see GILLEY]
Ida (LOUNSBERRY; wife of P. Harry) - d. 19 August 1933 Æ [not given]

Mildred A. [dau. of P. Harry and Ida (LOUNSBERRY)?] - d. 24 July 1977 Æ [not given]
P. Harry (husb. of Ida (LOUNSBERRY)) - d. 7 April 1898 Æ [not given]
PARKER
Ada E. (CLARK; [wife of William G.]) - b. 1850; d. 1917
Andrew E. (husb. of Ida M.) - b. 1875; d. 1957
Dora L. - b. 1875; d. 1973
Fred C. (son of William G. and Ada E. (CLARK)) - b. 1886; d. 1903
George H. (husb. of Nancy C. (KING)) - b. 1873; d. 1927
George R. (son of Joseph G. and Mary T. (CUTTER)) - b. 1840; d. 1859
Grace M. (wife of Jess[i]e[2] L.) - b. 1881; d. 1974
Harriet (dau. of Andrew E. and Ida M.) - d. 4 February 1916 Æ 5 d.
Helen (WRIGHT; [wife of James Andrew]) - b. 1922; d. 1993
Ida M. (wife of Andrew E.) - b. 1874; d. 1952
infants (2) - [no dates]
James A. (husb. of Julia E. (NOYES)) - b. 22 August 1859; d. 8 November 1925
James Andrew [husb. of Helen (WRIGHT)] - b. 1916; d. 1993
James E[verett?]. ([son of James A. and Julia E. (NOYES)?]; husb. of Julia N.) - b. 16 September 1890; d. 21 November 1972
Jess[i]e[2] L. (husb. of Grace M.) - b. 1881; d. 1966
Joseph G. (husb. of Mary T. (CUTTER)) - b. 1805; d. 1843
Julia E. (NOYES; wife of James A.) - b. 11 August 1863; d. 10 November 1915
Julia N. (wife of James E[verett?].) - b. 31 December 1891; d. 3 September 1974
Mary C. (dau. of William G. and Ada E. (CLARK)) - b. 1869; d. 1948
Mary T. (CUTTER; wife of Joseph G.) - b. 1807; d. 1859
Nancy C. (KING; wife of George H.) - b. 1872; d. 1904
William G. (son of Joseph G. and Mary T. (CUTTER); husb. of Ada E. (CLARK)) - b. 1832; d. 1890
PARRITT
Ralph E. [husb. of Valora B.?] - b. 1891; d. 1966
Valora B. [wife of Ralph E.?] - b. 1898; d. 1987
PARSONS
[Gladys M. - see REED]
Joseph Allen - b. 1875; d. 1955
Lucy (HUTCHINS; wife of Harland A. [no stone]) - b. 1922; d. 1953
PEASE
Grace (CLARK; [wife of Jesse H.]) - b. 1848; d. 1917
Jesse H. [husb. of Grace (CLARK)] - b. 1836; d. 1901
PENLEY
Geneva H. - b. 1916; d. 1979
PERKINS
Adella A. [wife of F. Dwight] - b. 1905
Alton S. - b. 1907; d. 1984
F. Dwight [husb. of Adella A.] - b. 1902; d. 1981
Jessie L. - b. 1891; d. 1956
PERRY
Janet [wife of Wendell] - b. 1932; d. 1995
Wendell [husb. of Janet] - b. 1918
PETERSEN
Elizabeth (wife of Thorwald) - b. 1866; d. 1943
Thorwald (husb. of Elizabeth) - b. 1849; d. 1929

PETTEGROW
Alice M. - b. 1871; d. 1947
Barbara J. [wife of Wyman B.] - b. 1949
Clyde L. [husb. of Leola R.] - b. 1908; d. 1955
Earl S. - b. 1907; d. 1944
Howard E. [son of Clyde L. and Leola R.?] - b. 1935; d. 1958
Leola R. [wife of Clyde L.] - b. 1912; d. 1969
Wyman B. [husb. of Barbara J.] - b. 1949

PHALEN
Rachel C[ARROLL?]. - b. 17 October 1913; d. 30 July 1999

PHILLIPS
Carrie Frances (wife of Joseph D.) - b. 26 March 1863; d. 30 December 1892
Clara D. (wife of Joseph D.) - b. 14 September 1872; d. 11 December 1964
Joseph D. (husb. of Carrie Frances and Clara D.) - b. 17 December 1857; d. 20 July 1942
Lawrence D. [husb. of Maud G.] - b. 1903; d. 1971
Maud G. [wife of Lawrence D.] - b. 1902; d. 1987

PHIPPEN
Deborah Susan - b. 4 July 1959; d. 21 June 1991
Harold D. [son of John D. and Viola O.?] - b. 1907; d. 1932
John D. [husb. of Viola O.] - b. 1867; d. 1935
Ralph O. [husb. of Virginia M.] - b. 1900; d. 1980
Shirley M. - b. 1922; d. 1999 Æ 77 y.
Viola O. [wife of John D.] - b. 1874; d. 1967
Virginia M. [wife of Ralph O.] - b. 1917

PICKWICK
Desmond F. [husb. of Ruby (HIGGINS)] - b. 1915; d. 1992
Ruby (HIGGINS; [wife of Desmond F.]) - b. 1913

PIERCE
Leon W. Jr. [husb. of Ramona S.] - b. 1926
N. Allen - b. 1883; d. 1960
Ramona S. [wife of Leon W. Jr.] - b. 1929; d. 1980

PIKE
[Winifred - see EICHLER]

PINKHAM
Bertha C. - b. 1879; d. 1959
Dorothy E. [wife of Emery P.] - b. 1906; d. 1988
Emery P. [husb. of Dorothy E.] - b. 1900; d. 1976
Helen R. (STANLEY; dau. of E[noch?]. A. STANLEY and E[mma?]. B[eatrice?].; [wife of Roger E.]) - b. 1931; d. 1985
Ira O. - b. 11 July 1926; d. 1 May 1996
Joseph A. - b. 1929; d. 1992
Roger E. [husb. of Helen R. (STANLEY)] - b. 1928; d. 1978

PLUMMER
Albertine (DAVIS; dau. of Carrie E. DAVIS) - b. 1895; d. [no date]

POTTER
Charlotte (RUST; wife of Wilson [no stone]) - b. 1878, Cleveland, Ohio; d. 1947, Southwest Harbor, Maine
John R. - b. 1914; d. 1996
Rust (son of Wilson [no stone] and Charlotte (RUST)) - b. 1908; d. 1918

PREBLE
Phebe E. - b. 1840; d. 1918

RAMELLA
  Arlene (JELLISON; dau. of Linwood M. JELLISON and Edna M. (DOLLIVER)) - b. 1931; d. 1955
RAMIERZ [sic]
  N. Barbara - b. 1929; d. 1981
RAMSDELL
  Almon F. - b. 1873; d. 1946
  Bruce E. - b. 1904; d. 1950
  Ernest P. (husb. of Pauline V.) - b. 1910
  Faith W. (wife of Ralph L.) - b. 1919
  Mary A. - b. 1876; d. 1966
  Pauline V. (wife of Ernest P.) - b. 1914
  Ralph L. (husb. of Faith W.) - b. 1918; d. 1948
  Rebecca K. - b. 25 September 1918; d. 23 August 1978
  [Virginia R[AMSDELL?]. - see KREBS]
RAMSEYER
  Frank Wells [husb. of Linda Chapin (MARCUS)] - b. 1905; d. 1974
  Linda Chapin (MARCUS; [wife of Frank Wells]) - b. 1909; d. 1975
RANDALL
  Chaney W. - b. 1879; d. 1951
  Edwina [dau. of Samuel W. and Emma B.?] - b. 1880; d. 1882
  Elvena [dau. of Samuel W. and Emma B.?] - b. 1880; d. 1881
  Emma B. (wife of Samuel W.) - b. 1854; d. 1916
  Fred S. [son of Samuel W. and Emma B.?] - b. 1877; d. 1877
  Gertrude L. [dau. of Samuel W. and Emma B.?] - b. 1884; d. 1971
  Samuel W. (husb. of Emma B.) - b. 1849; d. 1901
RAY
  Comfort K. [wife of William H.?] - b. 12 August 1829; d. 17 March 1892
  William H. [husb. of Comfort K.?] - d. 15 March 1881 Æ 51 y., 10 m., 19 d.
REA
  William H. - b. 1857; d. 1918
REDLON
  Eugene F. [husb. of LaVerne E.] - b. 1918; d. 1984
  LaVerne E. [wife of Eugene F.] - b. 1921
REED
  Adelaide (GONZALES) - b. 17 September 1878; d. 27 September 1936
  Annie [wife of Lester] - b. 1899; d. 1953
  Arthur L. [husb. of Bertha C.] - b. 1924
  Bertha C. [wife of Arthur L.] - b. 1924
  Bloomfield (husb. of Vesta S.) - b. 7 September 1858; d. 26 April 1919
  Edna M. (wife of Ralph D.) - b. 1915; d. 1937
  Elmer L. - b. 15 December 1902; d. 17 September 1971
  Eugene H. [husb. of Susie M.] - b. 1881; d. 1957
  [Eva - see COLSON]
  Fannie E. [wife of Ferdinand E.] - b. 1872; d. 1944
  Ferdinand E. [husb. of Fannie E.] - b. 1879; d. 1939
  Flavilla M. [wife of Lyle A.] - b. 1904; d. 1992
  Flora L. [wife of Ralph E.] - b. 1908; d. 1986
  Forrest A. [husb. of Mildred E.] - b. 1891; d. 1964
  Gladys M. (PARSONS) - b. 1910; d. 1968
  H. Wesley [husb. of Minerva M.] - b. 1906; d. 1968
  infant [child of Raymond W. Jr. and Margaret T.] - [b. and d.?] 11 April 1958

infant [REED?] - [b. and d.?] 1916
Lester [husb. of Annie] - b. 1885; d. 1963
Lottie (KING) - b. 1890; d. 1957
Lyle A. [husb. of Flavilla M.] - b. 1905; d. 1991
Margaret T. [husb. of Raymond W. Jr.] - b. 1924; d. 1995
Mark David (son of David E. and Janice L. [no stones]) - b. 27 November 1959; d. 28 November 1959
Mark E. (son of David E. and Janice L. [no stones]) - b. 8 July 1964; d. 25 November 1982
Mildred E. [wife of Forrest A.] - b. 1891; d. 1988
Minerva M. [wife of H. Wesley] - b. 1906; d. 1983
Minnie F. (ROBBINS; wife of Wilbert) - b. 1867; d. 1927
Ralph D. (wife of Edna M.) - b. 1915; d. 1997
Ralph E. [husb. of Flora L.] - b. 1901; d. 1974
Raymond W. (husb. of Violet M.) - b. 1893; d. 1964
Raymond W. Jr. [husb. of Margaret T.] - b. 1922
Susie M. [wife of Eugene H.] - b. 1882; d. 1972
Vesta S. (wife of Bloomfield) - d. 21 August 1884 Æ 21 y.
Violet M. (wife of Raymond W.) - b. 1896; d. 1963
Wilbert (husb. of Minnie F. (ROBBINS)) - b. 1862; d. 1931

REES
Marion (HUTCHINS; [dau. of Frank HUTCHINS and Margaret (CHAMBERLAIN)?]) - b. 18 April 1899; d. 13 April 1982

REYNOLDS
Agnes B. (wife of John) - b. 1888; d. 1957[12]
Charles P. [husb. of Doris E.] - b. 1913; d. 1996
Doris E. [wife of Charles P.] - b. 1916; d. 1987
Isabelle - d. [no date] Æ 14 m.
John (husb. of Agnes B.) - b. 1880; d. 1961
John - b. 1886; d. 1966
Joseph D. [husb. of Margaret B.] - b. 1913; d. 1958
Louis - b. 1895; d. 1955
Margaret B. [wife of Joseph D.] - b. 1916

RHOADS
[Eleanor - see MCFARLAND]

RICE
Annie H. [wife of Harry Freeman] - b. 1888; d. 1964
Dorothea R. (SANFORD; dau. of Capt. George E. SANFORD and Matilda J. (HADLOCK)) - b. 1862; d. 1899
Effie W. [wife of Capt. Warren G.] - b. 1908; d. 1997
Harry Freeman [husb. of Annie H.] - b. 1882; d. 1963
Harry Freeman Jr. [son of Harry Freeman and Annie H.] - b. 8 April 1916; d. 30 August 1994
Warren G. (Capt.; [husb. of Effie W.]) - b. 1906; d. 1988

RICH
Charles H. [husb. of Mary L.] - b. 1892; d. 1967
Charles H. - b. 10 April 1949; d. 1 July 1992
Clifton M. (son of J. and C. (BALDWIN) [no stones]; husb. of Elizabeth F. (FARNSWORTH)) - b. 1881; d. 1970
Donald D. [husb. of Lizabeth [sic] (LAWSON)] - b. 21 October 1913; d. 12 January 1997

Elizabeth F. (FARNSWORTH; dau. of A. FARNSWORTH and C. [no stones]; wife of Clifton M.) - b. 1887; d. 1969
Gerald P. - b. 1 June 1937
Jack R. - b. 13 September 1938
Lizabeth [sic] (LAWSON; [wife of Donald D.]) - b. 1912; d. 1978
Lyford Judson [RICH?] (Capt.) - b. 25 June 1916; d. 24 December 1990
M. Cecil (son of Clifton M. and Elizabeth F. (FARNSWORTH)) - b. 1926; d. 1941
Mark J. (son of F. J. and V. L. [no stones]) - b. 1964; d. 1964
Mary L. [wife of Charles H.] - b. 1894; d. 1977
Maurice S. - b. 13 February 1913; d. 19 September 1988
Roger C. (son of Clifton M. and Elizabeth F. (FARNSWORTH)) - b. 1913; d. 1996
Roxann - b. 1948; d. 1964
Vera A. - b. 12 December 1918; d. 2 May 1996

RICHARDSON
Artemas J. [husb. of Martha M.?] - b. 1893; d. 1958
Arthur T. [husb. of Ida M.] - b. 23 April 1857; d. 5 October 1916
Clara A. [wife of Hollis H.] - b. 1906; d. 1971
Clytie N. [wife of George H.] - b. 1890; d. 1962
Eben F. - b. 1863; d. 1940
Effie M. (wife of Stephen) - b. 1871; d. 1960
[Elmenia M. - see HOUSTON]
Eugene D. [husb. of Nellie A.] - b. 1869; d. 1947
George H. [husb. of Clytie N.] - b. 1901; d. 1980
Hollis H. [husb. of Clara A.] - b. 1894; d. 1973
Ida M. [wife of Arthur T.] - b. 27 June 1862; d. 28 October 1923
Josephine (HOLMES; dau. of William H. HOLMES and Lizzie B. (MAYO)) - b. 1894; d. 1960
Martha M. [wife of Artemas J.?] - b. 1891; d. 1972
Mary R. [dau. of Artemas J. and Martha M.?] - b. 1923; d. 1985
Nellie A. [wife of Eugene D.] - b. 1874; d. 1964
Stephen (husb. of Effie M.) - b. 1866; d. 1945

RIDDLE
John C. W. - b. 24 April 1921; d. 7 April 1979
Mary F. - b. 28 February 1895; d. 2 March 1989

RINALDI
Dorothy A. (wife of Paul) - b. 1915; d. 1969
Paul (husb. of Dorothy A.) - b. 1901; d. 1989

ROBBINS
Abbie T. (wife of Wellington C.) - b. 1889; d. 1982
Agnes M. (wife of John E.) - b. 1881; d. 1966
Beatrice V. (GRAY; [wife of Watson Wayne]) - b. 17 December 1937
Bertha A. (GREENLAW; wife of Pearl S.) - b. 8 August 1845; d. 23 June 1930
Blanche I. [wife of Watson C.] - b. 1922
Calvin A. [son of Lem S. and Lizzie M.?] - b. 12 May 1928; d. 5 June 1986
Chester C. [husb. of Pheobe [sic] E.] - b. 1881; d. 1947
Clifford F. [husb. of Ethel R.] - b. 1904; d. 1978
Clifford M. [husb. of Pansy L.] - b. 1880; d. 1967
Colson H. (husb. of Lizzie A. (SPRAGUE)) - b. 1858; d. 1935
Dorothy Mae (dau. of Edgar H. and E. J. [no stone]) - b. 1904; d. 1906
Dorothy S. (wife of Lloyd P.) - b. 1920; d. 1991
Edgar H. (husb. of E. J. [no stone]) - b. 14 November 1883; d. 10 March 1920
Edwin W. [son of Wellington C. and Abbie T.?] - b. 1919; d. 1979

Eliza (wife of Howard P.) - b. 1848; d. 1928
Ethel R. [wife of Clifford F.] - b. 1905; d. 1978
Eugene S. [husb. of Eva E.] - b. 1904; d. 1994
Eva E. [wife of Eugene S.] - b. 1903; d. 1984
Evelyn P. - b. 1900; d. 1990
Fred M. [husb. of Lillie S.] - b. 1865; d. 1943
George C. (husb. of Louisa A.) - b. 1885; d. 1970
Georgia M. - b. 1903; d. 1990
H. Kenneth - b. 1906; d. 1968
Howard P. (husb. of Eliza) - b. 1837; d. 1918
infant (son of Lem S. and Lizzie M.) - [no dates]
Jay L. - b. 1897; d. 1961
John E. (husb. of Agnes M.) - b. 1866; d. 1933
Lem S. (husb. of Lizzie M.) - b. 1890; d. 1987
Lettie F. - b. 1882; d. 1958
Lillie S. [wife of Fred M.] - b. 1869; d. 1959
Lizzie A. (SPRAGUE; wife of Colson H.) - b. 1857; d. 1912
Lizzie M. (wife of Lem S.) - b. 1903; d. 1997
Lloyd P. (husb. of Dorothy S.) - b. 1908; d. 1966
Louisa A. (wife of George C.) - b. 1885; d. 1988
Louise A. (dau. of George C. and Louisa A.) - b. 1919; d. 1937
[Minnie F. - see REED]
Pansy L. [wife of Clifford M.] - b. 1881; d. 1967
Pearl S. (husb. of Bertha A. (GREENLAW)) - b. 26 September 1840; d. 22 July 1915
Pheobe [sic] E. [wife of Chester C.] - b. 1885; d. 1974
[Vilda S. - see KNOWLTON]
Vola N. - b. 1888; d. 1964
Watson C. [husb. of Blanche I.] - b. 1910; d. 1993
Watson Wayne [husb. of Beatrice V. (GRAY)] - b. 23 April 1936; d. 2 November 1998
Wellington C. (husb. of Abbie T.) - b. 1888; d. 1974

ROBERTS
Annie - b. 1855; d. 1938
Mina E. [wife of Robert H.] - b. 1887; d. 1957
Robert H. [husb. of Mina E.] - b. 1885; d. 1957
Wesley C. - b. 1917; d. 1988

ROBERTSON
Aaron (husb. of Nancy J.) - b. 1850; d. 1928
Howard S. (son of Aaron and Nancy J.) - b. 1879; d. 1907 Æ 28 y.
Nancy J. (wife of Aaron) - b. 1861; d. 1932
Walter C. - b. 1882; d. 19[...][4]

ROBINSON
Abbie H. [wife of Thomas S.?] - b. 1851; d. 1918
Abigail (WHITMORE; wife of James) - b. 1829; d. 1906
Agnes M. (wife of Lewis K.) - b. 3 November 1875; d. 13 March 1916
Alice G. - b. 1924; d. 1985
Alice W. (wife of Oliver W.) - b. 1914
Alton L. [husb. of Anna T.?] - b. 1892; d. 1967
Anna T. [wife of Alton L.?] - b. 22 December 1905; d. 19 August 1998 Æ 92 y.[9]
Arthur L. [husb. of Carrie M.] - b. 1889; d. 1959
Barbara W. (wife of Richard G.) - b. 11 January 1917; d. 12 June 1992

Benjamin M. (husb. of Eliza (HIGGINS)) - b. 8 May 1826; d. 30 August 1901
Byron L. [husb. of Mary C.] - b. 15 June 1899; d. 2 June 1971
[Caroline - see LAWLER]
Carrie M. [wife of Arthur L.] - b. 1879; d. 1929
Celestia G. (wife of Ralph J.) - b. 1875; d. 1961
Cheston (son of Smith and Lydia S.) - b. 1865; d. 1913
Colburn W. [son of James and Abigail (WHITMORE)?] - b. 1849; d. 1867; ("drowned")
Davis B. [husb. of Marjorie B.] - b. 1904; d. 1970
Eliza (HIGGINS; wife of Benjamin M.) - b. 3 May 1830; d. 27 October 1914
Ella M. (TORREY; wife of Herbert L.) - b. 1860; d. 1937
[Emily - see FARNSWORTH]
Fred P. (husb. of Nellie E.) - b. 1868; d. 1937
Harold N. (husb. of Marion A.) - b. 1909; d. 1987
Herbert L. (husb. of Ella M. (TORREY)) - b. 1859; d. 1933
Hilda V. [dau. of Byron L. and Mary C.?] - b. 1932; d. 1957
Howard E. (husb. of D. E. [no stone]) - b. 1896; d. 1972
Ida S. (wife of Lewis K.) - b. 1881; d. 1944
James (husb. of Abigail (WHITMORE)) - b. 1824; d. 1881
James E. [husb. of Lucie D.] - b. 1854; d. 1929
Lawrence S. - b. 1897; d. 1980
Lewis K. (husb. of Agnes M. and Ida S.) - b. 8 February 1874; d. 25 January 1958
[Lillian E. - see BICKFORD]
Lucie D. [wife of James E.] - b. 1859; d. 1942
Lydia S. (wife of Smith) - b. 1829; d. 1903
Marion A. (wife of Harold N.) - b. 1911; d. 1979
Marjorie B. [wife of Davis B.] - b. 1909; d. 1983
Marjorie H. - b. 1910; d. 1991
Mary C. [wife of Byron L.] - b. 1904; d. 1997
Maurice H. (son of Howard E. and D. E. [no stone]) - b. 1923; d. 1952
Minnie A. [dau. of James and Abigail (WHITMORE)?] - b. 1859; d. 1863
[Nellie - see DORR]
Nellie E. (wife of Fred P.) - b. 1875; d. 1949
Oliver W. (husb. of Alice W.) - b. 1906; d. 1962
[Rachel S. - see WHITMORE]
Ralph J. (husb. of Celestia G.) - b. 1870; d. 1923
Richard G. (husb. of Barbara W.) - b. 29 October 1914; d. 19 April 1993
Samuel N. - b. 1843; d. 1919
Sarah A. [dau. of James and Abigail (WHITMORE)?] - b. 1864; d. 1866
Sarah B[ILLINGS?]. - b. 19 December 1880; d. 10 December 1957
Sarah S. [dau. of James and Abigail (WHITMORE)?] - b. 1862; d. 1863
Smith (husb. of Lydia S.) - b. 1819; d. 1885
Thomas S. [husb. of Abbie H.?] - b. 1850; d. 1916
Walter M. - b. 1867; d. 1928

ROMER

Phillip - b. 1865; d. 1946

ROSS

Frankie E. (son of James F. and Phebe A. [no stones]) - d. 27 October 1879 Æ 5 y., 7 m., 9 d.

ROWE

Alice (dau. of John S. and Amanda C.) - d. 8 September 1888 Æ 1 y., 13 d.
Amanda C. (wife of John S.) - b. 1865; d. 1955

John A. (Capt.) - b. 1892; d. 1942
John S. (husb. of Amanda C.) - b. 1865; d. 1932
Vergie L. - d. 3 October 1908 Æ 19 y.

ROWELL
Albert - b. 1874; d. 1964
Herman - b. 1875; d. 1929

RUSSELL
Marjorie F. [wife of Maynard F.] - b. 1910; d. 1985
Maynard F. [husb. of Marjorie F.] - b. 1906; d. 1986

RUST
[Charlotte - see POTTER]

SALISBURY [see also SALSBURY]
Archie R. [husb. of Celia E.] - b. 1879; d. 1935
Celia E. [wife of Archie R.] - b. 1876; d. 1945
Louise M[ARSHALL?]. [dau. of Maurice C. MARSHALL and Marguerite M.?] - b. 12 October 1909; d. 21 March 1945

SALSBURY [see also SALISBURY]
May S. [wife of Nate] - b. 1893; d. 1985
Nate [husb. of May S.] - b. 1888; d. 1963

SANFORD
[Albertenia A. - see BURBANK]
[Dorothea R. - see RICE]
George E. (Capt.; husb. of Matilda J. (HADLOCK)) - b. 1812; d. 1873
George E. - b. 1846; d. 1871
Matilda J. (HADLOCK; wife of Capt. George E.) - b. 1826; d. 1898
Samuel C. - b. 1852; d. 1933

SANNER
June H. [wife of Walter W.] - b. 1924
Walter W. [husb. of June H.] - b. 1920; d. 1989

SARGENT
Mina M. - b. 1890; d. 1953
Perry L. - b. 1870; d. 1947
Vinnie M. - b. 1872; d. 1934

SAVAGE
Alma A. (wife of Thomas SEAVEY [no stone]; wife of Smith R.) - b. 1870; d. 1947
Carrie Ethel (dau. of Thomas R. and Nellie O.) - b. 7 May 1879; d. 18 September 1896
Ernest (son of Thomas [no stone] and Mary A.) - b. 1861; d. 1882
Eugene (son of Smith R. and Mary V.) - [no dates]
Fannie N. (wife of Capt. Thomas) - d. 21 October 1893 Æ 60 y., 1 m., 7 d.
[Hazel Winifred - see TIBBETTS]
Mary A. (wife of Thomas [no stone]) - b. 1836; d. 1876
Mary V. (wife of Smith R.) - b. 1854; d. 1881
Nellie O. (wife of Thomas R.) - b. 10 February 1854; d. 10 September 1935
Smith R. (husb. of Mary V. and Alma A.) - b. 1850; d. 1929
Thomas (Capt.; husb. of Fannie N.) - d. 21 August 1889 Æ 66 y., 6 m., 17 d.
Thomas R. (husb. of Nellie O.) - b. 1 September 1852; d. 30 October 1925

SAWYER
Allen J. [son of Charles W. and Evelyn?] - b. 1923; d. 1923
Charles W. [husb. of Evelyn] - b. 1898; d. 1970
Edward E. [son of Emmons P. and Mary L.?] - b. 1895; d. 1917
Emmons P. [husb. of Mary L.] - b. 1859; d. 1928

Evelyn [wife of Charles W.] - b. 1903; d. 1982
Hollis W. - b. 1904; d. 1956
Lila M. (wife of Ralph R.) - b. 1897; d. 1996
Marie - b. 1886; d. 1911
Marion S. [wife of Paul A.] - b. 1889; d. 1986
Mary L. [wife of Emmons P.] - b. 1881; d. 1937
Nancy - b. 1838; d. 1920
Paul A. [husb. of Marion S.] - b. 1891; d. 1971
Ralph R. (husb. of Lila M.) - b. 1900; d. 1968
Samuel N. - [no dates]
William P. - b. 1827; d. 1899

SCHENK
Oliver Wendell - b. 1903; d. 1996

SCOTT
[Martha - see HARDING]

SEAVEY
[Alma A. - see SAVAGE]
Harriet M. (wife of Thomas H.) - b. 1875; d. 1928
Laurie A. - b. 1964; d. 1985
Ora (NEWMAN; wife of Oscar R.) - b. 1900; d. 1975
Oscar R. (husb. of Ora (NEWMAN)) - b. 6 March 1895; d. 3 April 1974
Thomas H. (husb. of Harriet M.) - b. 1872; d. 1959

SHEDD
Maud M. (wife of George H. [no stone]) - b. 1889; d. 1937

SHIVELY
Beatrice B. [wife of Carl E.] - b. 1910; d. 1961
Carl E. [husb. of Beatrice B.] - b. 1908; d. 1966

SILVA
Katherine - b. 1939; d. 1940
[Nettie - see SMILY]

SIMMONS
Nettie B. (wife of C. A. [no stone]) - d. 13 August 1895 Æ 32 y., 8 m., 22 d.

SINCLAIR
Charlotte - [no dates]
Dorothy B[ROWN?]. [wife of Harvard E.] - b. 1905; d. 1993
Harvard E. [husb. of Dorothy B[ROWN?].] - b. 1905; d. 1977

SKYE
[Robin Starr - see Thomas B. SWEENEY and Patricia R. SWEENEY]

SMILY
Nettie (SILVA) - b. 1904; d. 1980

SMITH
Alice E. (wife of Clarence L.) - b. 1886; d. 1965
Alice J. [dau. of Clarence L. and Alice E.?] - b. 1914; d. 1932
Carl C. - b. 31 January 1897; d. 29 October 1897
Carroll F. (son of Albert and Helen L. [no stones]) - d. 21 February 1917 Æ 10 m., 11 d.
Clarence E. [husb. of Robena B.] - b. 1910; d. 1967
Clarence L. (husb. of Alice E.) - b. 1879; d. 1964
Daisy L. (wife of Rueben [sic] M.) - b. 1890; d. 1976
David N. (husb. of Donna M.) - b. 1931; d. 1992
David N. Jr. (son of David N. and Donna M.) - b. 1955; d. 1984
Donna M. (wife of David N.) - b. 1930

Frank L. - b. 1854; d. 1920
Franklin - [no dates]
Herman L. - b. 1886; d. 1969
infant (son of [Carl C.?]) - [b. and d.?] 30 October 1879
Josephine M. [wife of Walter K.] - b. 1912; d. 1993
Katie M.[14] (CHAFFEY) - b. 1900; d. 1925
Lora B. - b. 1897; d. 1949
Malcolm H. (son of Albert and Helen L. [no stones]) - d. 30 March 1915 Æ 1 m., 21 d.
Robena B. [wife of Clarence E.] - b. 1911; d. 1998
Rueben [sic] M. (husb. of Daisy L.) - b. 1891; d. 1946
Theolyn - [no dates]
Walter K. [husb. of Josephine M.] - b. 1909; d. 1991

SNOW
[Edna M. - see WILSON]

SOMES
Arthur L. (husb. of Lucy C.) - b. 1869; d. 1941
Hallie M. (wife of Raymond P.) - b. 1891; d. 1983
Lucy C. (wife of Arthur L.) - b. 1863; d. 1936
Mildred M. (wife of Raymond P.) - b. 1900; d. 1932
Raymond P. (husb. of Mildred M. and Hallie M.) - b. 1893; d. 1983

SOUKUP
Elizabeth (STANLEY; [wife of William T.]) - b. 12 May 1900; d. 27 September 1977
William T. [husb. of Elizabeth (STANLEY)] - b. 3 May 1898; d. 14 October 1954

SOULIS
Frank A. [son of James H. and Henrietta?] - b. 2 September 1876; d. 2 December 1898
Henrietta (wife of James H.) - b. 3 October 1838; d. 29 December 1940
James [son of James H. and Henrietta?] - b. 26 June 1874; d. 27 September 1874
James H. (husb. of Henrietta) - b. 22 March 1842; d. 5 February 1918
Walter H. [son of James H. and Henrietta?] - b. 15 July 1871; d. 5 March 1884

SPRAGUE
Bertha M. [wife of Donald E.] - b. 1911; d. 1998
Clara (GILLEY) - b. 1889; d. 1910
Donald E. [husb. of Bertha M.] - b. 1911; d. 1989
[Lizzie A. - see ROBBINS]
Harold E. [husb. of Marion G.] - b. 1906; d. 1992
Louise P. [wife of Roy Neil] - b. 1933
Marion G. [wife of Harold E.] - b. 1912; d. 1989
Ralph W. - b. 1905; d. 1973
Roy Neil [husb. of Louise P.] - b. 1929; d. 1991

SPURLING
Alma A. (NEWMAN; dau. of John L. NEWMAN and Livonia A. (MAYO); wife of Henry E.) - b. 1878; d. 1955
Annie M. [wife of Millard S.] - b. 1877; d. 1928
Annie R. [wife of George H.] - b. 1852; d. 1936
Blanche E. [wife of William F.] - b. 1886; d. 1960
Charles [son of Robert and Fannie?] - b. 14 July 1856; d. 28 November 1893
[Dorothy - see WHITNEY]
Ella (BATES; [wife of J. Elwood]) - b. 1877; d. 1979
Emerson F. [son of Millard S. and Annie M.?] - b. 1914; d. 1980

Esther M. - b. 20 August 1895; d. 13 January 1984
Fannie (wife of Robert) - b. 8 April 1837; d. 6 May 1916
Geneva M. [dau. of William F. and Blanche E.?] - b. 1910; d. 1978
George H. [husb. of Annie R.] - b. 1845; d. 1936
Henry E. (husb. of Alma A. (NEWMAN)) - b. 1872; d. 1923
J. Elwood [husb. of Ella (BATES)] - b. 1882; d. 1960
Kirsten J. - b. 1920
[Mary - see BIRLEM]
Millard S. [husb. of Annie M.] - b. 1877; d. 1967
Minnie E. - b. 1877; d. 1963
[Nancy M. - see NEWMAN]
Robert (husb. of Fannie) - b. 4 March 1830; d. 3 February 1916
Serena W. [see also Cranberry Isles - 5] - b. 27 January 1882; d. 14 September 1977
Sheldon E. - b. 1907
William F. [husb. of Blanche E.] - b. 1884; d. 1967

STANLEY

Abigail (wife of Joshua M.) - d. 12 November 1858 Æ 59 y., 2 m., 10 d.
Abigail N. "Abbie" (wife of William) - d. 3 July 1908 Æ 79 y., 8 m.
Adeline - b. 1890; d. 1979
Albra M. [wife of Leverett S.] - b. 1901; d. 1965
Allan P. [husb. of Mildred A.] - b. 1901; d. 1979
Alice M. [wife of Richard H.] - b. 1890; d. 1970
Ambrose A. (husb. of Ellen M. (GOTT)) - b. 1847; d. 1911
Ann M. [wife of Clifford R.] - b. 1907; d. 1969
Barbara L. - b. 27 February 1949; d. 25 March 1949
Bertha E. (wife of Chester W.) - b. 1901; d. 1968
Carroll [husb. of Elizabeth W.] - b. 1902; d. 1992
Catherine (CARROLL; wife of William B.) - b. 1832; d. 1911
Charles E. - b. 1833; d. 1904
Charles E. (husb. of Rebecca G.) - b. 1844; d. 1928
Charles L. [husb. of Rose] - b. 1862; d. 1924
Chester W. (husb. of Bertha E.) - b. 1900; d. 1971
Clark [STANLEY?] - [no dates]; ("baby")
Clifford R. [husb. of Ann M.] - b. 1897; d. 1988
Cynthia B. - b. 1889; d. 1952
Derby [husb. of Edith W.] - b. 1886; d. 1947
[Edith - see GILLEY]
Edith W. [wife of Derby] - b. 1886; d. 1980
[Elizabeth - see SOUKUP]
Elizabeth W. [wife of Carroll] - b. 1891; d. 1973
Elizabeth W. (wife of Everett G.) - b. 1877; d. 1949
Ellen M. (GOTT; wife of Ambrose A.) - b. 1849; d. 1935
Elmer A. - b. 1863; d. 1935
Emma Beatrice (wife of Enoch A.) - b. 1895; d. 1937
[Emeline - see DOLLIVER]
Enoch A. (husb. of Emma Beatrice) - b. 1897; d. 1977
Ernest (son of Melinda NEWMAN[17]) - b. 186[4 or 6][2]; d. 193[6 or 5][2]
Everett G. (husb. of Elizabeth W.) - b. 1874; d. 1951
F. Vondell - b. 1867; d. 1936
Freddie (son of John L. and Mary L.) - d. 18 January 1881 Æ 4 y., 3 m., 15 d.
[Grace D. - see BURTON]
Grace H. [wife of Leroy Q.] - b. 1892; d. 1954

H. Dean - b. 1887; d. 1954
Harold F. (husb. of Sylvia R.) - b. 1898; d. 1979
Harold L. [husb. of Lena M.] - b. 1892; d. 1972
Herbert A. [husb. of Ulrica B.] - b. 1872; d. 1950
Hiram F. (son of Joshua M. and Abigail) - d. 22 September 1866 Æ 26 y., 8 m., 14 d.
Hiram M. (son of Thomas S. and Emeline) - d. 11 July 1891, "at sea", Æ 20 y., 6 m.; ("drowned")
Hugh L. [husb. of Marguerite L.] - b. 1921; d. 1986
infant (son of Arthur and Charlotte [no stones]) - [no dates]
infant (son of Everett G. and Elizabeth W.) - d. 9 April 1914 Æ 2 d.
Isaac F. (husb. of Minnie C.) - b. 1 December 1870; d. 22 March 1953
John B. - b. 1920; d. 1984
John L. (husb. of Mary L.) - b. 25 April 1841; d. 5 July 1922
Joshua M. (husb. of Abigail) - d. 23 July 1852 Æ 54 y.
[Joyce - see MAHLER]
Julia A. - b. 1838; d. 1928
Lena M. [wife of Harold L.] - b. 1897; d. 1965
Leroy Q. [husb. of Grace H.] - b. 1890; d. 19[...][4]
Lester F. - b. 24 March 1926; d. 25 April 1971
[Lettie F. - see BLAISDELL]
Leverett S. [husb. of Albra M.] - b. 1894; d. 1968
[Lucinda S[TANLEY?]. - see JOHNSON]
Lucy W. - b. 1867; d. 1949
[Lurline - see CARR]
Lyman L. [husb. of Vira R.] - b. 1862; d. 1937
Malcolm W. - b. 1917; d. 1982
Marguerite L. [wife of Hugh L.] - b. 1913; d. 1992
Mary Ann - b. 1850; d. 1920
Mary L. (wife of John L.) - b. 15 October 1853; d. 21 February 1924
[Melinda - see NEWMAN]
Merrill E. Jr. [son of Merrill E. Sr. and Minnie A.] - b. 1939
Merrill E. Sr. [husb. of Minnie A.] - b. 1894; d. 1970
Mildred A. [wife of Allan P.] - b. 1900
Minnie A. [wife of Merrill E. Sr.] - b. 1905; d. 1974
Minnie A. [wife of William S.] - b. 1875; d. 1964
Minnie C. (wife of Isaac F.) - b. 7 September 1871; d. 10 November 1963
Morris E. - b. 19 July 1916; d. 28 November 1974
Nancy G. (wife of William D.) - b. 1854; d. 1932
Rebecca G. (wife of Charles E.) - b. 1851; d. 1950
Richard H. [husb. of Alice M.] - b. 1884; d. 1966
Richard W. (son of Everett G. and Elizabeth W.) - d. 19 April 1908 Æ 6 m., 12 d.
Rose [wife of Charles L.] - b. 1862; d. 1905
Ruth (dau. of Everett G. and Elizabeth W.) - d. 12 October 1910 Æ 23 d.
Sylvia R. (wife of Harold F.) - b. 1893; d. 1970
Thomas C. (son of William B. and Catherine (CARROLL)) - b. 1877; d. 1901
Thomas S. (husb. of Emeline) - d. 30 March 1885 Æ 58 y., 8 m., 25 d.
Ulrica B. [wife of Herbert A.] - b. 1873; d. 1938
Vira R. [wife of Lyman L.] - b. 1866; d. 1919
Warren D. [son of Derby and Edith W.?] - b. 1920; d. 1948
Wilder N. [son of Enoch A. and Emma Beatrice?] - b. 8 September 1936; d. 12 April 1994

William (husb. of Abigail N. "Abbie") - d. 12 February 1903 Æ 76 y., 9 m., 2 d.
William B. (husb. of Catherine (CARROLL)) - b. 1832; d. 1910
William D. (husb. of Nancy G.) - b. 1855; d. 1950
William S. [husb. of Minnie A.] - b. 1865; d. 1950
Willie T. (son of William and Abigail N. "Abbie") - d. 24 March 1862 Æ 6 m., 7 d.

STANWOOD
Raleigh E. - b. 1911; d. 1995

STAPLES
Albert (husb. of Emily) - b. 1870; d. 1958
Emily (wife of Albert) - b. 1874; d. 1951

STERLING
[Jane - see STERN]

STERN
Jane (STERLING) - b. 1915; d. 2000

STETSON
Seth Frank - b. 16 June 1887; d. 11 October 1918

STEWART
Frank W. (husb. of Lucy H.) - b. 1863; d. 1945
George H. (son of Frank W. and Lucy H.) - b. 1906; d. 1927
infant [child of Frank W. and Lucy H.] - [b. and?] d. 1911
Lucy H. (wife of Frank W.) - b. 1870; d. 1957

STONE
[Elizabeth A. - see MILLS]

STUBBS
Doris (BIRLEM; wife of Winfield Loud) - b. 8 October 1917; d. 22 August 1990
Winfield Loud (husb. of Doris (BIRLEM)) - b. 18 December 1908; d. 13 March 1988

SULLIVAN
Donald Sr. [husb. of Maude] - b. 1909; d. 1981
Donald I. Jr. (husb. of Sandra J.) - b. 1935; d. 1993
Goldie M. (wife of James W.) - b. 1887; d. 1927
infant (dau. of Donald I. Jr. and Sandra J.) - [b. and d.?] 28 October 1959
James W. (husb. of Goldie M.) - b. 1884; d. 1969
Maude [wife of Donald Sr.] - b. 1906; d. 1996
Sandra J. (wife of Donald I. Jr.) - b. 1938

SUTHERLAND
[Vernamae - see WORCESTER]

SWEENEY
[Margaret "Mae" - see HODGDON]
Patricia R. (wife of Thomas B.; mother of Robin Starr SKYE [no stone]) - b. 25 January 1928, Missouri
Thomas B. (husb. of Patricia R.; father of Robin Starr SKYE [no stone]) - b. 11 May 1927, California; d. 23 August 1993, Southwest Harbor, Maine

TAPLEY
Cheryl C. [wife of Theodore L.?] - b. 1954
LaRita [wife of Lewis M.] - b. 1 September 1916; d. 1 April 1992
Lewis M. [husb. of LaRita] - b. 15 May 1916; d. 8 November 1985
Theodore L. [husb. of Cheryl C.?] - b. 1940; d. 1986

TARVIS
Frankie (son of J. and F. [no stones]) - b. 1911; d. 1915

TAYLOR
Arthur L. (husb. of Hattie B.) - b. 1875; d. 1973
Harriet - b. 1838; d. 1930

Hattie B. (wife of Arthur L.) - b. 1888; d. 1988
TEAGUE
Dunham - [no dates]
Fidelia M. (wife of Nathaniel Jr.) - d. 31 March 1903 Æ 55 y.
George E. (Capt.; husb. of Martha Cornelia) - "lost at sea" March 1877 Æ 42 y.
Henry N. - b. 2 June 1875; d. 2 October 1951
Martha Cornelia (wife of Capt. George E.) - b. 4 October 1840; d. 24 June 1915
Mary - [no dates]
Nathaniel Jr. (husb. of Fidelia M.) - d. 22 December 1885 Æ 39 y., 9 m.; (member of Co. F, 31st Maine Regiment [Civil War])
TEEL
Raymond L. - b. 9 February 1900; d. 20 February 1976
TEMPLE
Burton A. [husb. of Dorothy L.] - b. 17 November 1907; d. 20 February 1990
Dorothy L. [wife of Burton A.] - b. 3 May 1921
TENAN
Edgar G. [husb. of Nellie M.] - b. 1894; d. 1950
Nellie M. [wife of Edgar G.] - b. 1888; d. 1962
TERRY
George W. - b. 1922; d. 1983
THERIAULT
Eugene Carroll [husb. of Rosemary (LAWLER)] - b. 1926; d. 1996
Rosemary (LAWLER; [wife of Eugene Carroll]) - b. 1921
THOMS
[Addie - see TORREY]
THORNTON
Nellie R. (CARROLL; [wife of Seth S.]) - b. 25 October 1871; d. 3 February 1958
Seth S. [husb. of Nellie R. (CARROLL)] - b. 18 December 1862; d. 17 July 1920
THURLOW
Dorothy M. - b. 1940; d. 1959
Edith M. - b. 1901; d. 1949
James Earl [husb. of Mildred Helen] - b. 1903; d. 1982
Madella M. - b. 1906; d. 1958
Mildred Helen [wife of James Earl] - b. 1916; d. 1989
THURSTON
Alice M. (wife of Eugene S.) - b. 18 December 1883; d. 22 July 1944
Daisy W. (wife of Maurice S.) - b. 1878; d. 1945
Dorothy M. [wife of Kermit W.] - b. 1913; d. 1995
Effie F. - b. 1920; d. 1988
Eugene S. (husb. of Alice M.) - b. 30 January 1881; d. 21 April 1961
Eugene S. [husb. of Helen M.] - b. 1920; d. 1992
Geraldine H. - b. 1924; d. 1960
Helen M. [wife of Eugene S.] - b. 1921; d. 1973
Kermit W. [husb. of Dorothy M.] - b. 4 May 1911; d. 19 November 1974
Leslie W. - b. 1921
Marie M. - b. 1921; d. 1971
Maurice S. (husb. of Daisy W.) - b. 1876; d. 1962
TIBBETTS
Hazel Winifred (SAVAGE; wife of Raymond W. [no stone]) - b. 27 March 1896; d. 13 May 1923
TINKER
[Ella - see DAVIS]

Everett Elmer - b. 11 December 1888; d. 1 August 1958
TORREY
Addie (THOMS; wife of Capt. Charles P.) - b. 1852; d. 1891
Archie [son of Maynard V. and Georgia A.?] - b. 1911; d. 1911
[Bertha - see BICKFORD]
Bertha M. (wife of Capt. Charles P.) - b. 1868; d. 1948
Charles P. (Capt.; husb. of Addie (THOMS) and Bertha M.) - b. 1850; d. 1924
[Ella M. - see ROBINSON]
Everett S. ([son of Fred M. and Jessie B.?]; husb. of Reta [sic] M.) - b. 21 September 1895; d. 27 February 1969
Florence F. [wife of Percy E.] - b. 1903; d. 1989
Fred M. (husb. of Jessie B.) - b. 1858; d. 1932
Georgia A. [wife of Maynard V.] - b. 1884; d. 1959
[Inez - see GINN]
infant (dau. of Capt. Charles P. and Bertha M.) - [b. and d.?] 14 October 1897
Jessie B. (wife of Fred M.) - b. 1861; d. 1941
Lewis G. - b. 1884; d. 1945
[Marguerite H. - see NORWOOD]
Maynard V. [husb. of Georgia A.] - b. 1882; d. 1942
Milton F. - b. 1893; d. 1932
Percy E. [husb. of Florence F.] - b. 1901; d. 1989
Reta [sic] M. (wife of Everett S.) - b. 1901; d. 1997
TORRN
William "Bill" - b. 1930; d. 1983
TOWER
Elmer M. Jr. - b. 1920; d. 1944
Kate E. [wife of William J.] - b. 1866; d. 1931
William J. [husb. of Kate E.] - b. 1869; d. 1950
TRACEY [see also TRACY]
Kenneth L. [son of Lawrence M. and Lucy M.?] - b. 7 August 1924; d. 21 August 1961
Lawrence M. [husb. of Lucy M.] - b. 25 May 1899; d. 14 November 1970
Lucy M. [wife of Lawrence M.] - b. 9 March 1902; d. 13 August 1967
TRACY [see also TRACEY]
Elizabeth Wells (dau. of Merle Elliott and Harriet (BENSON) [no stones]) - b. 27 May 1908; d. 23 April 1910
Henry (husb. of Linda C. (NASH) HANDY) - b. 1849; d. 1925
Linda C. (NASH; "widow" of Marcus H. HANDY [no stone]; wife of Henry) - b. 1847; d. 1915
Mary E. [wife of Merrill A.] - b. 1887; d. 1968
Merrill A. [husb. of Mary E.] - b. 1893; d. 1974
TRASK
Allie M. (wife of Robert D.) - b. 1879; d. 1967
Belle M. (wife of William S.) - b. 1882; d. 1944
Henry A. - d. 23 October 1930 Æ 36 y., 11 m., 12 d.
Joseph L. [husb. of Marjorie A.] - b. 1904; d. 1988
Margaret - b. 1896; d. 1908
Marjorie A. [wife of Joseph L.] - b. 1903; d. 1991
Robert D. (husb. of Allie M.) - b. 1885; d. 1930
William S. (husb. of Belle M.) - b. 1873; d. 1927
TRENHOLM
Chana M. [wife of Douglas?] - b. 1881; d. 196[...][6]

Douglas [husb. of Chana M.?] - b. 1878; d. 197[...][6]
Gertrude L. [wife of Richard E.] - b. 1922; d. 1974
Richard E. [husb. of Gertrude L.] - b. 1921; d. 1976

TRUNDY
A. Elwell - b. 1903; d. 1978
Alice J. (wife of Rufus N.) - b. 1864; d. 1942
H. Alton (husb. of Linnie E.) - b. 1878; d. 1967
Henry E. (husb. of Margaret C.) - b. 1851; d. 1929
Linnie E. (wife of H. Alton) - b. 1882; d. 1951
Margaret C. (wife of Henry E.) - b. 1851; d. 1931
Rufus N. (husb. of Alice J.) - b. 1860; d. 1939
Thelma S. - b. 1913

TURNER
Fillmore D. - b. 13 December 1915; d. 14 April 1976

VAN HORN
Eleanor R. [wife of William H.] - b. 1895; d. 1960
William H. [husb. of Eleanor R.] - b. 1889; d. 1963

VARNUM
Jane Lee [dau. of John R. Sr. and Jennette [sic] H[AMBLEN?].] - b. 4 September 1942; d. 28 December 1942
Jennette [sic] H[AMBLEN?]. [[dau. of Charles E. HAMBLEN?]; wife of John R. Sr.] - b. 1922
John R. Sr. [husb. of Jennette [sic] H[AMBLEN?].] - b. 1917; d. 1995

VINE
Alfred W. [husb. of Nettie B.] - b. 15 May 1913; d. 18 February 1993
Nettie B. [wife of Alfred W.] - b. 18 September 1917; d. 26 February 1987

WAKEFIELD
Annie M. - b. 1910; d. 1990

WALKER
Eleanor K. (wife of Joseph C.) - b. 1909
Joseph C. (husb. of Eleanor K.) - b. 1897; d. 1986
Mary (LAFFERTY) - b. 1905; d. [no date]; bur. "at sea"

WALLACE
Clarence E. - b. 1901; d. 1949

WALLS
Abbie S. [wife of Arthur D.] - b. 1901; d. 1972
Arthur D. [husb. of Abbie S.] - b. 1896; d. 1969
Fred A. [husb. of Katherine B.] - b. 1888; d. 1949
Jacob B. (husb. of Thursea [sic] O.) - b. 1856; d. 1919
Katherine B. [wife of Fred A.] - b. 1873; d. 1957
Maude H. (dau. of Jacob B. and Thursea [sic] O.) - b. 1891; d. 1907
Nellie I. - b. 23 March 1919
Thursea [sic] O. (wife of Jacob B.) - b. 1860; d. 1940

WALSH
[Rita - see MORRIS]
Norman J. - b. 8 May 1912; d. 3 August 1965

WARD
Charles S. [husb. of Susie F.] - b. 1875; d. 1944
Eldora F. (DOLIVER [sic]; wife of William H. Jr.) - b. 1868; d. 1938
Franklin [son of William H. Jr. and Eldora F. (DOLIVER [sic])] - b. 1900; d. 1963
George A. (husb. of Thelma D.) - b. 1885; d. 1943
George Malcolm [son of Malcolm S. and Margaret L.?] - b. 1927; d. 1933

John P. - b. 1891; d. 1963
Madeline (dau. of William H. Jr. and Eldora F. (DOLIVER [sic])) - b. 1905; d. 1908 Æ 3 y., 3 m., 26 d.
Malcolm S. [husb. of Margaret L.] - b. 1904; d. 1983
Margaret L. [wife of Malcolm S.] - b. 1906; d. 1974
Susie F. [wife of Charles S.] - b. 1881; d. 1968
Thelma D. (wife of George A.) - b. 1891; d. 1973
William H. Jr. (husb. of Eldora F. (DOLIVER [sic])) - b. 1871; d. 1921

WARDWELL
Florence - b. 7 September 1903; d. 26 July 1982

WASS
Emma W. [wife of Lester L.] - b. 7 December 1908; d. 2 February 1988
Gerald W. [son of Lester L. and Emma W.?] - b. 27 September 1932; d. 17 June 1995
Henry Bucknam (husb. of Thirza [sic] C.) - b. 21 November 1906; d. 5 June 1986
Jones E. [husb. of Winifred L.] - b. 1881; d. 1956
Lester L. [husb. of Emma W.] - b. 22 September 1905; d. 27 April 1987
Thirza [sic] C. (wife of Henry Bucknam) - b. 6 March 1917
Winifred L. [wife of Jones E.] - b. 1882; d. 1977

WATSON
Audree W[HITMORE?]. - b. 1925; d. 1951
Betty O. [wife of Willis B.] - b. 1889; d. [no date]
Willis B. [husb. of Betty O.] - b. 1884; d. 1962

WATT
Grace V. [wife of S. George] - b. 1901; d. 1956
S. George [husb. of Grace V.] - b. 1898; d. 1972

WATTS
Charles Augustus (husb. of Miriam (DOLIVER [sic])) - b. 1854; d. [no date]
Miriam (DOLIVER [sic]; wife of Charles Augustus) - b. 1859; d. 1938
Susan Henrietta (dau. of Charles Augustus and Mariam (DOLIVER [sic])) - [b. and d.?] 6 August 1893

WEAVER
Earle R. - b. 17 October 1938; d. 22 December 1974

WEDGE
Ethel M. [wife of Oscar G.] - b. 1891; d. 1995
Linwood B. - b. 1913; d. 1961
Mildred E. [wife of Norman K.] - b. 6 October 1917; d. 14 March 1994
Norman K. [husb. of Mildred E.] - b. 18 September 1919; d. 31 October 1995
Oscar G. [husb. of Ethel M.] - b. 1887; d. 1967

WELLINGTON
Anna (JOHNSTON) - b. 1918; d. 2000

WELLS
Leon J. (Dr.) - b. 3 February 1884; d. 19 June 1978

WELTON
Edith C. [wife of Theodore L.] - b. 7 November 1923; d. 27 August 1982
Theodore L. [husb. of Edith C.] - b. 15 January 1923; d. 5 March 1975

WENTWORTH
Alonzo R. [husb. of Elsie M.] - b. 1903; d. 1972
Alton R. (husb. of Rose E. (KANE)) - b. 9 June 1924; d. 30 March 1993
Ann E. - b. 1925; d. 1990
Elsie M. [wife of Alonzo R.] - b. 1909
Kathleen M. [wife of Lou E.] - b. 1916; d. 1970

Lou E. [husb. of Kathleen M.] - b. 1908; d. 1994
Rose E. (KANE; wife of Alton R.) - b. 16 October 1924; d. 9 February 1989
Timothy M. (son of Alton R. and Rose E. (KANE)) - b. 3 March 1956; d. 12 August 1987

WESCOTT
Fred W. (husb. of Marion E. (NEWMAN)) - b. 1876; d. 1933
Marion E. (NEWMAN; [dau. of S. Ward NEWMAN and Marion E. (HADLOCK)?]; wife of Fred W.) - b. 1890; d. 1976

WEST
James C. - b. 1874; d. 1944

WHITE
Aquaie (wife of Leslie F. Sr.) - b. 1886; d. 1950
[Doris - see GOLDSMITH]
Leslie F. [husb. of Myrtle L.] - b. 1921
Leslie F. Sr. (husb. of Aquaie) - b. 1891; d. 1967
Mary E. [wife of Russell B.] - b. 1917
Myrtle L. [wife of Leslie F.] - b. 1916
Russell B. [husb. of Mary E.] - b. 1915

WHITMORE
[Abigail - see ROBINSON]
[Audree W[HITMORE?]. - see WATSON]
Edna M. (wife of John L.) - b. 1890; d. 1978
Eleanor G. (wife of Jay N.) - b. 1901; d. 1992
George C. (husb. of Ruby A.) - b. 12 June 1864; d. 22 August 1940
Gladys E. [wife of James F.] - b. 1887; d. 1977
Isaac S. (husb. of Rachel S. (ROBINSON)) - b. 18 March 1820; d. 24 May 1906
James F. [husb. of Gladys E.] - b. 1875; d. 1951
Jay N. (husb. of Eleanor G.) - b. 1896; d. 1984
John L. (husb. of Edna M.) - b. 1879; d. 1933
Lucy E. (LAWLER; wife of William H.) - b. 1849; d. 1934
Mary S. (dau. of William H. and Lucy E. (LAWLER)) - b. 15 October 1888; d. 28 December 1923
Mildred S. - b. 1892; d. 1987
[Phyllis W[HITMORE]. - see CLOSSON}]
Rachel S. (ROBINSON; wife of Isaac S.) - b. 28 August 1828; d. 8 March 1903
Raymond C. - b. 1889; d. 1971
[Rebecca - see CARROLL]
Ruby A. (wife of George C.) - b. 8 August 1868; d. 30 November 1938
Thomas L. (son of John L. and Edna M.) - b. 31 July 1914; d. 8 September 1914
Tyler A. [son of John L. and Edna M.?] - b. 1911; d. 1947
Wilbur C. (son of William H. and Lucy E. (LAWLER)) - b. 11 October 1873; d. 25 November 1874
William H. (husb. of Lucy E. (LAWLER)) - b. 1847; d. 1914

WHITNEY
Andrew J. - d. 27 November 1911 Æ 74 y., 18 d.
Dorothy (SPURLING; [dau. of J. Elwood SPURLING and Ella (BATES)?]; [husb. of Philmore Allen]) - b. 1911; d. 1998
Elhanan W. (husb. of Eliza Ann) - d. 11 September 1893 Æ 82 y., 6 m.
Eliza Ann (wife of Elhanan W.) - d. 21 September 1888 Æ 72 y., 7 m., 13 d.
Philmore Allen [husb. of Dorothy (SPURLING)] - b. 1913; d. 1995

WILBUR
Donald E. [husb. of Virginia Y.] - b. 31 August 1901; d. 16 November 1985

James F. [son of Donald E. and Virginia Y.?] - b. 29 April 1943; d. 24 May 1991
Virginia Y. [wife of Donald E.] - b. 22 June 1905; d. 23 June 1986
WILDER
[Evelyn M. - see NEAL]
WILKINSON
Holley A. - b. 1886; d. 1970
Lisa (MAYO) - b. 1887; d. 1965
WILLEY
Guilford B. [husb. of M. Eula] - b. 1907; d. 1984
M. Eula [wife of Guilford B.] - b. 1904; d. 1980
WILLIAMS
Harriet H. - b. 1889; d. 1965
Margaret E. [wife of Owen H.] - b. 1916
Owen H. [husb. of Margaret E.] - b. 1919; d. 1998
WILSON
Augustus A. (husb. of Mary S. (HOPKINS) and Edna M. (SNOW)) - b. 1864; d. 1950
Beatrice A. [wife of Sherril S.] - b. 1902; d. 1983
[Beatrice A. - see PACKARD]
Charles H. (husb. of Susie I.) - b. 1886; d. 1962
Curtis J. - b. 22 July 1958; d. 21 September 1978
Edna M. (SNOW; wife of Augustus A.) - b. 1873; d. 1936
Howard Edwin - b. 6 December 1928; d. 20 August 1966
infant [WILSON?; child of Sherril S. and Beatrice A.?] - [no dates]
Mary S. (HOPKINS; wife of Augustus A.) - b. 1866; d. 1909
Sherril S. [husb. of Beatrice A.] - b. 1893; d. 1968
Susie I. (wife of Charles H.) - b. 1883; d. 1937
WINCEY
Caroline C. (dau. of David and Esther) - d. 15 April 1866 Æ 21 y., 2 m., 15 d.
David (husb. of Esther) - d. 28 July 1892 Æ 89 y., 8 m.
Esther (wife of David) - d. 24 January 1869 Æ 66 y.
WING
[Grace A. - see CROCKETT]
WOODS
Bernard Allen - b. 1934; d. 1967
Donald E. - b. 1932; d. 1989
Lowell E. - b. 27 June 1935; d. 16 August 1993
WOOSTER
Nettie E. - b. 1881; d. 1960
WORCESTER
Alfred Small [husb. of Vernamae (SUTHERLAND)] - b. 1913; d. 1978
Annabel (DAM; [wife of Ben Conley Jr.]) - b. 1921; d. 1979
Ben Conley (husb. of Sophie E.) - b. 1882; d. 1978
Ben Conley Jr. [husb. of Annabel (DAM)] - b. 1921
Donald O. [[son of Orman C. and Helen W.?]; husb. of Mary L.] - b. 1924
[Elizabeth - see DOLLIVER]
Forester (husb. of Minnie) - b. 1873; d. 1922
Frederick C. [husb. of Mabel E.] - b. 1899; d. 1970
Helen W. [wife of Orman C.] - b. 1902; d. 1996
[Idabelle W[ORCESTER?]. - see LONG]
Mabel E. [wife of Frederick C.] - b. 1900; d. 1994
Mary L. [wife of Donald O.] - b. 1922

Minnie (wife of Forester) - b. 1876; d. 1957
Orman C. [husb. of Helen W.] - b. 1901; d. 1994
Shayne Conley (son of Mark Conley and Priscilla (ST. JOHN) [no stones]; brother of Megan Leigh [no stone]) - b. 15 October 1969, Fairbanks, Alaska; d. 26 May 1999, San Francisco, California
Sophie E. (wife of Ben Conley) - b. 1887; d. 1966
Vernamae (SUTHERLAND; [wife of Alfred Small]) - b. 1917; d. 1971
[...] [headstone only]

WORKMAN
Augustus A. - b. 1873; d. 1959
Lena E. - b. 1893; d. 1969
Velma A. - b. 1925
Warren A. - b. 1926

WORSTER
Arthur R. - b. 16 September 1919; d. 15 August 1987

WRIGHT
[Helen - see PARKER]

YATES
[Evelyn - see INMAN]
G. Edith - b. 1895; d. 1982
Lloyd D. - b. 1903; d. 1996
Maya - b. 1932; d. 1974
Ronald S. - b. 1956; d. 1982

YOUNG
Alice C. - b. 1879; d. 1964
Athalanie M. (wife of Guy V. [YOUNG?]) - b. 1888; d. 1971
Edwin D. - b. 1911; d. 1973
[Ella - see ANTHONY]
Francis C. - b. 1903; d. 1984
Fred E. - b. 1872; d. 1959
Geneva B. - b. 1862; d. 1946
George H. [husb. of Sadie (GRAY)] - b. 15 January 1899; d. 8 August 1963
Guy V. [YOUNG?] (husb. of Athalanie M.) - b. 1871; d. 1936
John F. - b. 1848; d. 1929
Martha F. - b. 1906; d. 1987
Rolfe N. - b. 1917
Sadie (GRAY; [wife of George H.]) - b. 24 July 1898; d. 29 July 1986

[...]
F. E. [footstone only]
Valore (sister of Viola A. MURPHY) - b. 1884; d. 1946

Notes:
[1]The stone of Lucretia E. BIRLEN reads *Bied* rather than *Died*.
[2]Different on different stones.
[3]Different dates on 2 markers—a metal marker from a funeral home and the gravestone.
[4]No ten or unit's digit given on stone.
[5]Stone crumbling and/or broken.
[6]No unit's digit given on stone.
[7]Both a 5 and a 6 are engraved in the unit's position. According to State of Maine vital records, Maurice R. BEAL d. 7 December 1965 Æ 71 y., Ellsworth.

[8]The information for Irma FISH is from a temporary marker in which her date of death and age at death are unclearly pressed into the surface.

[9]Information from temporary marker that has been replaced by a stone that bears only the years of birth and death.

[10]Temporary marker gave middle name. Stone has only initial.

[11]Difficult to read.

[12]The 7 of 1957 is upside down on the stone of Agnes B. REYNOLDS.

[13]It is unclear from the gravestone(s) whether this is a maiden name.

[14]It is unclear from the gravestone whether Katie M. was a CHAFFEY who married a SMITH or a SMITH who married a CHAFFEY.

[15]It is unclear whether Arthur L. was a GRAY or a LANPHER.

[16]Relationships are unclear from the gravestones.

[17]It is unclear from the gravestones whether STANLEY is a former married name.

Union Cemetery
(Southwest Harbor - 5)

Location/directions. Southwest of Route 102A, behind Manset Union Church. From the traffic light at the north end of Mount Desert Island, go straight ahead (south) onto Routes 102/198. In approximately 11.3–11.4 miles (about 0.8 miles of which are south of the blinking light in the village of Southwest Harbor), turn left onto Route 102A. The church and cemetery are on the right in about 0.8–0.9 miles.

History. A deed (54:500; 10 January 1831) from Nicholas Tucker to the Committee for the [church?] Proprietors referred to the "Burying-ground". Thornton (1938) noted that during "the summer of 1934 this churchyard was cleared of bushes and underbrush by the boys of the C C C camp, Company 158."

Notes. Stones in this cemetery are generally in poorer condition—both in readability and in position— than stones in most other cemeteries in the area. This cemetery is enclosed by a post and rail fence with one space between a pair of adjacent posts for an entrance/exit. Except for two rails that are broken, the fence is in good condition.

Names and dates on gravestones and other markers. [29 May 1999]

ADAMS
- Ann Maria (dau. and "only child" of John and Mary Ann) - [b. and d.?] 17 [...][1] 185[8?][1]
- John (husb. of Mary Ann) - b. 24 December 1801; d. 7 May 1892
- Mary Ann (wife of John) - b. 21 October 1816; d. 13 April 1897

BOWDEN
- Cyntha [sic] M. (dau. of Twisden and Patience [no stones]) - d. 8 December 1852 Æ 15 y., 8 m.

BROWN
- infant (dau. of Capt. William N. and Joan[na][3] [no stones]) - [no dates]
- Jno. [Jonathan] - [no dates]; (Revolutionary War soldier)
- Mercey C. (dau. of Capt. William N. and Joan[na][3] [no stones]) - d. 16 June 1851 Æ 16 y.
- Nathan C. (son of Capt. William N. and Joan[na][3] [no stones]) - d. 17 December 1831 Æ 4 w.
- Nathaniel H. (son of Capt. William N. and Joan[na][3] [no stones]) - d. 10 May 1846 Æ 4 y.
- Robert H. (son of Capt. William N. and Joan[na][3] [no stones]) - d. 10 January 1858 Æ 30 y.

DOLLIVER [includes DOLIVER]
- Joseph T. (son of Peter [no stone] and Phebe J.) - d. 12 November 1850 Æ 19 y., 28 d.
- Lemuel (Capt.) - d. 24 May 1887 Æ 50 y., 2 m.
- Phebe J. (wife of Peter [no stone]) - d. 1[8?][1] [August?][1] 18[...][1] Æ 76 y., 2 m.

HIGGINS
- Sarah D. (wife of Nathaniel [no stone]) - d. 5 April 1855 Æ 33 y.

HODGKINS
- Bryant[2] - [no dates]
- Louisa D.[2] - d. 1902 Æ [not given]

HOPKINS
- Mary A. (wife of Clark [no stone]) - d. 13 July 1893 Æ 57 y., 9 m.

KEENE
- Lucy C. (wife of Reuben F.) - d. 25 July 1893 Æ 73 y.

Reuben F. (husb. of Lucy C.) - d. 22 May 1889 Æ 74 y.; (member of Co. A, 13th Maine Regiment [Civil War])

KING

E. N. K[ING?]. [footstone only]

Lucy - d. 19 April 1839 Æ 33 y., 8 m., 15 d.

M[argaret?]. (wife of Capt. Rufus) [footstone only]

R[ufus?]. (Capt.; husb. of Margaret) [footstone only]

Rufus W. (son of Capt. Rufus and Margaret [no stones]) - d. 8 November 1857 Æ 13 y., 6 m., 17 d.

W. C. K[ING?]. [footstone only]

William - d. 9 March 1834 Æ 4 y., 10 m.

LANGLY

Esther (wife of Phillip [sic] [no stone]) - d. 26 May 1868 Æ [...][1] y., 6 m.

M.

P. [spouse of R. F.?] [footstone only]

R. F. [spouse of P.?] [footstone only]

MAYO

Cordelia H. (dau. of Joshua and Livonia [no stones]) - d. 1 November 1850 Æ 15 y., 4 m.

McKENZIE

Angelia (dau. of William and Delia [no stones]) - d. 24 September 1849 Æ 7 y., 6 m.

MOORE [includes MORE]

Andrew W. - b. 18 October 1839; d. 8 April 1906

Benjamin Franklin ("oldest son" of Capt. Benjamin S. [no stone] and Rebecca) - d. 3 July 1843 Æ 17 y., 7 m., 12 d.

Gilbert H. (son of Capt. Benjamin S. [no stone] and Rebecca) - d. 20 December 1850 Æ 22 y., 4 m.

John (husb. of [S]usan[1]) - d. 12 March 1881 Æ 83 y., 1 m., 19 d.

Phebe Maria (dau. of Capt. Benjamin S. [no stone] and Rebecca) - d. 22 October 1834 Æ 2 y., 3 m., 4 d.

Rebecca (wife of Capt. Benjamin S. [no stone]) - d. 20 June 1898 Æ 92 y., 5 m., 21 d.

[S]usan[1] (wife of John) - d. 12 June [...][1] Æ 62 y., [10?][1] m., 11 d.

NEWMAN

Laura (wife of Capt. R. S. [no stone]) - d. 3 November 1860 Æ 26 y., 11 m.

R.

J. [footstone only]

RAFANEL [includes RAFNEL]

Augustus (husb. of Nancy) - d. 14 October 1845 Æ 82 y.

Nancy (wife of Augustus) - d. 7 May 1842 Æ 89 y., 9 m., 13 d.

Simeon (son of Augustus and Nancy) - b. Mount Desert; d. 12 December 1820 Æ 27 y.

SMITH

Carlie [sic] C. (son of Frank L. and Katie N. [no stones]) - d. 29 October 1897 Æ 9 m.

infant ("first infant son" of Frank L. and Katie N. [no stones]) - [b. and?] d. 30 October 1879

STANLEY [includes STANLY]

Calvin J. (son of Horace E. and M. A. [no stone]) - d. 30 December 1894 Æ 23 y., 4 m.

Horace E. (husb. of M. A. [no stone]) - d. 20 February 1895 Æ 55 y., 8 m.

Isaac - d. [...][1] Æ [...][1]

Mary A. (wife of William [no stone]) - d. 19 February 1851 Æ 20 y., 5 m.
Mary Etta B. (dau. of Capt. Peter S. and Sarah N.) - d. 8 November 1851 Æ 13 y., 4 m.
Peter S. (Capt.; husb. of Sarah N.) - b. 5 June 1808; d. 17 January 1892
Sarah N. (wife of Capt. Peter S.) - d. 20 February 1864 Æ 50 y., 11 m., 23 d.

TUCKER
Amanda M. (dau. of Nicholas and Bets[e]y[3] [no stone]) - d. 21 October 1833 Æ 3 y., 2 m., 19 d.
Andrew (son of Nicholas and Bets[e]y[3] [no stone]) - b. 21 November 1817; d. 22 April 1819
Horace D. (son of N. C. and S. L. [no stones]) - d. 25 June 1860 Æ 1 y., 4 m., 10 d.
Nicholas (husb. of Bets[e]y[3] [no stone]) - d. 14 July 1839, "in a foreign land", Æ [63?][1] y.

WARD
Andrew (son of Capt. William H. and Hannah E.) - d. 2 September 1869 Æ 2 m.
Benjamin Jr. (son of Capt. Benjamin and Margaret) - d. 3 October 1850 Æ 18 y.
Benjamin (Capt.; husb. of Margaret) - d. 23 April 1866 Æ 73 y., 6 m., 20 d.
Hannah E. (wife of Capt. William H.) - d. 11 May 1886 Æ 36 y.
Margaret (wife of Capt. Benjamin) - d. 23 December 1879 Æ 81 y., 2 m., 20 d.
Miriam S. (dau. of Capt. Benjamin and Margaret) - d. 8 January 1851 Æ 15 y.
Nettie (dau. of Capt. William H. and Hannah E.) - d. 10 January 1875 Æ 1 y., 10 m., 6 d.
William H. (Capt.; husb. of Hannah E.) - d. 16 August 1902 Æ 72 y., 6 m., 27 d.

Notes:
[1]Stone worn and/or broken.
[2] The names of Bryant and Louisa D. HODGKINS are on one side of a large stone that is laying on the ground, thereby obscuring any name(s) and date(s) that may be on the other side.
[3]Different on different stones.

Moore Family Burial Ground
(Southwest Harbor - 6)

Location/directions. At edge of field northeast of Route 102A. From the traffic light at the north end of Mount Desert Island, go straight ahead (south) onto Routes 102/198. In approximately 11.3–11.4 miles (about 0.8 miles of which are south of the blinking light in the village of Southwest Harbor), turn left onto Route 102A. In approximately 2.2–2.3 miles on the left (and immediately after a small trailer park) is a building from which take-out food is sometimes served. The cemetery is behind this building, but visible from Route 102A only when approaching from the south.

History. The name applied to this cemetery is only for convenience of reference in this book.

Notes. Presence of wood posts with holes to hold rails is evidence of a former fence along at least three sides of this cemetery. Four of the eight stones are laying on the ground. All woody vegetation has been cut to the ground in two strips approximately three feet wide that border opposite ends of the cemetery. Grass is mowed.

Names and dates on gravestones and other markers. [29 May 1999]
MOORE [includes MOOR]
Ferdinand P. (son of John S. and Joanna B.) - d. 3 October 1872, State Hospital, New Haven, Connecticut, Æ 15 y., 6 m.
Joann S. (wife of Esq. Joseph) - d. 19 January 1863 Æ 66 y., 7 m., 28 d.
Joanna B. (wife of John S.) - d. 17 January 1932 Æ 92 y., 10 m., 25 d.
John S. (husb. of Joanna B.) - d. 19 April 1914 Æ 86 y., 6 m., 28 d.
Joseph (Esq.; husb. of Joann S.) - d. 17 November [1873?][1] Æ 79 y., 3 m., 13 d.
Lanie F. (son of Esq. Joseph and Joann S.) - d. 19 September 1862 Æ 21 y., 11 m., 13 d.
Margaret S. (dau. of Esq. Joseph and Joann S.) - d. 17 January 1866 Æ 47 y., 5 m., 9 d.
Melville - b. 26 April 1834; d. 19 December 1912

Note:
[1]Stone broken.

King Cemetery

(Southwest Harbor - 7)

Location/directions. From the traffic light at the north end of Mount Desert Island, go straight ahead (south) onto Routes 102/198. In approximately 11.3–11.4 miles (about 0.8 miles of which are south of the blinking light in the village of Southwest Harbor), turn left onto Route 102A. In approximately 1.2 miles, turn left onto Kings Lane. In less than 0.1 miles, a wide trail on the right leads to the cemetery.

History. —

Notes. There appears to be no regular maintenance in this cemetery. Discarded food containers and tire tracks can be found along the trail leading to the cemetery. A heavy, double stone is laying face down (2000) and needs to be lifted to reveal the names and dates. The top of the stone reads "Mother" and "Father".

Names and dates on gravestones and other markers. [29 May 1999]

BILLINGS
- D. G. B[ILLINGS?]. [footstone only]
- Davis C. - d. 12 October 1872, "in the Bay of Honduras", Æ 24 y., 4 m.
- Reuben (husb. of Sarah W.) - d. 25 August 1899 Æ 87 y., 10 m., 24 d.
- Sarah W. (wife of Reuben) - d. 15 April 1872 Æ 56 y., 3 m., 7 d.

KING
- Adelaide V. (wife of Joseph L.) - d. 13 May 1928 Æ 77 y., 10 m., 24 d.
- D. [KING?] [footstone only][1]
- David (Capt.; husb. of Lucy and Emma) - d. 11 August 1880 Æ 76 y., 7 m.
- Emma (wife of Capt. David) - d. 6 April 1876 Æ 66 y., 2 m., 7 d.
- Everett D. (son of Joseph and Adelaide V.) - d. 8 December 1880 Æ 4 y., 4 m., 13 d.
- Frances M. (dau. of Capt. David and Emma) - d. 6 August 1862 Æ 18 y., 11 m., 8 d.
- Joseph L. (husb. of Adelaide V.) - d. 22 August 1901 Æ 66 y., 11 d.
- Josephine M. (wife of Leslie S.) - b. 21 August 1879; d. 12 October 1910
- Leslie S. (husb. of Josephine M.) - b. 1879; d. 1936
- Lucy (wife of Capt. David) - d. 19 April 1839 Æ 33 y., 8 m., 15 d.
- P. M. [KING?] [footstone only][1]

MOORE
- Hazel D. (dau. of Fairfield H. and Helen F. [no stones]) - d. 1 January 1896 Æ 8 m., 7 d.

PARKER
- infant (son of James A. and Julia E. [no stones]) - [b. and?] d. 13 April 1889

Note:

[1]D. K. and P. M. K. are footstones on adjacent graves. The headstones are worn, broken, and/or crumbling.

Overgrown Newman Cemetery (Southwest Harbor - 8). American flag is at the grave of Gilbert H. Moore who died in the Civil War.

Newman Cemetery
(Southwest Harbor - 8)

Location/directions. From the traffic light at the north end of Mount Desert Island, go straight ahead (south) onto Routes 102/198. In approximately 11.3–11.4 miles (about 0.8 miles of which are south of the blinking light in the village of Southwest Harbor), turn left onto Route 102A. In approximately 1.6–1.7 miles, turn left onto an unnamed dirt road (or if named, with no sign). This road runs along a large field that is enclosed by a wood fence. The cemetery is on the left in approximately 0.1 miles. It is so overgrown with vegetation that it is easy to miss.

History. Amos B. Newman sold (481:410; 29 May 1911) to the "inhabitants of the town of Southwest [Harbor]" an eight foot by fourteen foot parcel that was a "lot of land in the addition to the Newman Cemetery ... to be used by said inhabitants for a burial lot".

Notes. This cemetery is in very poor condition. There has been mowing around six stones, but otherwise, nothing is done—what remains of a fence is falling down, and vegetation is growing unchecked throughout.

Names and dates on gravestones and other markers. [9 January 2000]

BILLINGS
- Fannie (wife of Reuben [no stone]) - d. 23 April 1880 Æ 63 y., 10 m., 22 d.

CRAM
- Hannah G. (STANLEY; wife of George O. [no stone]) - d. 29 December 1869 Æ 33 y., 1 m.

DOLLIVER [includes DOLIVER]
- Alvah - d. 29 August 1896 Æ 44 y., 1 m., 10 d.
- Fanny S. (wife of John Jr. [no stone]) - d. 23 March 1866 Æ 40 y.
- Julia S. A. (dau. of John Jr. [no stone] and Fanny S.) - d. 17 October 1849 Æ 2 y., 9 m., 24 d.
- Lydia J. (wife of Benjamin S. [no stone]) - d. 10 July 1845 Æ 21 y., 10 m., 18 d.
- Thomas S. (son of John Jr. [no stone] and Fanny S.) - d. 23 September 1849 Æ 3 y., 5 m., 14 d.

FORESMAN
- Harriet de Peyster (WELLES) - b. 8 June 1939; d. 30 August 1996

GETCHELL
- [Lucy T. - see STANLEY]

HIGGINS
- Harvey L. (son of Alfred E. and Amanda [no stones]) - d. 18 June 1885 Æ 7 m., 26 d.

HODGDON
- Ann (wife of Enoch [no stone]) - d. 10 October 1846 Æ 26 y.

MOORE
- Benjamin A. (Capt.; husb. of Julia A.) - b. 29 June 1822; d. 1 February 1898
- Betsey L. (wife of Thomas) - b. 1 December 1818; d. 5 May 1904
- Ezekiel (Capt.; husb. of Mary) - b. 29 June 1809; d. 3 May 1899
- Gilbert H. - d. 16 May 1864 Æ 23 y., 11 m., 7 d.; ("who fell in defence [sic] of his country" [Civil War])
- Julia A. (wife of Capt. Benjamin A.) - b. 2 December 1823; d. 5 May 1909
- Mary (wife of Capt. Ezekiel) - b. 18 April 1817; d. 22 June 1887
- Rachel (wife of Philip [no stone]) - d. 19 November 1825 Æ *ca.* 23 y.
- Samuel [husb. of Sarah?] - d. 10 October 1839 Æ 68 y.

Sarah [wife of Samuel?] - d. 12 March 1861 Æ 88 y.
Thomas (husb. of Betsey L.) - d. 28 May 1858 Æ 47 y.
Welch - d. 7 February 1845 Æ 42 y.

MORRIS
Abraham [husb. of Susan] - d. 16 August 1885 Æ 79 y., 6 m.
Susan [wife of Abraham] - d. January 1898 Æ 76 y.

NEWMAN
Adelbert A. (son of John L. and Livonia A. [no stones]) - d. 22 January 1871 Æ 17 y.
Alma A. (dau. of John L. and Livonia A. [no stones]) - d. 14 June 1863 Æ 4 y.
Archie A. (son of John L. and Livonia A. [no stones]) - d. 11 November 1889 Æ 17 y., 10 m., 11 d.; ("drowned")
Benjamin S.[1] (husb. of Eliza) - b. 23 August 1814; d. 18 September 1887
Dolly (wife of Thomas) - d. 8 February 1878 Æ 81 y., 21 d.
E. H. (Capt.; son of [...][3]) - d. [...][3] February [...][3], Long Br[...][3] Æ [...]0[2] y.; ("drowned")
Eliza[1] (wife of Benjamin S.) - b. 31 October 1818; d. [no date]
Emily (wife of John L. [no stone]) - d. 13 November 1850 Æ 22 y.
H. R. (Capt.) - "lost at Labrador" 28 August 1876 Æ 29 y.
infant (dau. of John L. [no stone] and Emily) - [b. and?] d. 13 November 1850
John D. - d. 1 August 1840 Æ 19 y., 4 m.
Thomas (husb. of Dolly) - d. 9 January 1861 Æ 75 y., 11 m., 7 d.

SAKOIAN
Frances Cherpic Wilkin - b. 8 October 1912; d. 3 March 1989
Vartkes "Sark" - b. 28 April 1915; d. 27 August 1991

STANLEY
Fanny (wife of Capt. Sans) - d. 19 November 1849 Æ 52 y., 1 m.
[Hannah G. - see CRAM]
Holsey - d. 2 February 1880 Æ 26 y., 7 m., 2 d.
John - d. 2 June 1867 Æ 61 y., 9 m.
John 2nd - d. 28 June 1866 Æ 33 y., 8 m., 22 d.
John E. - b. 14 March 1850; d. 20 August 1908
Lucy T. (GETCHELL; wife of Sans) - b. 20 November 1836; d. 9 March 1903
Samuel S. - d. 2 April 1871 Æ 28 y., 5 m.; ("drowned on Georgies")
Sans (husb. of Lucy T. (GETCHELL)) - b. 3 June 1827; d. 16 August 1900
Sans (Capt.; husb. of Fanny) - b. 14 May 1791; d. 26 July 1858

T.
A. [footstone only]

WELLES
Catharine Bedlow Fish van Alstyne - b. 2 August 1906; d. 18 June 1983
Edward Randolph II (Bishop) - b. 20 April 1907; d. 15 April 1991
Edward R[andolph?]. III (Admiral) - b. 17 January 1941; d. 9 February 1994
[Harriet de Peyster - see FORESMAN]

YOUNG
Mary E. (wife of Guy V. [no stone]) - b. 3 October 1872; d. 10 May 1901

Notes:
[1]Benjamin S. and Eliza NEWMAN's names are on one side of a monument that is laying on the ground. A second side is blank, and the remaining two sides are in contact with the ground and cannot be seen.
[2]Difficult to read.
[3]Below ground.

Doliver Grave
(Southwest Harbor - 9)

Location/directions. In woods, east of Route 102 and west of Route 102A. Access is by foot from Hillcrest Circle. From the traffic light at the north end of Mount Desert Island, go straight ahead (south) onto Routes 102/198. In approximately 11.3–11.4 miles (about 0.8 miles of which are south of the blinking light in the village of Southwest Harbor), there is an intersection of Routes 102 and 102A. Continue straight on Route 102 about 0.4 miles, and turn left onto Hillcrest Circle. In less than 0.1 miles, bear left onto a gravel road. In approximately 0.1–0.2 miles, there is a road on the left that leads in the general direction of the grave. From this point travel should be on foot. More specific directions to this stone are not given here to protect it from further vandalism. The stone bears the marks of two bullets and is located in the general vicinity of discarded white goods, a half a dozen or so abandoned automobiles, and other debris.

History. —

Notes. This stone was repaired in 1999 by a private individual.

Names and dates on gravestones and other markers. [18 June 2000]
DOLIVER [sic]
Peter - d. 15 August 1871 Æ 73 y., 3 m., 18 d.

Gravestone of Peter Doliver (Southwest Harbor - 9). Above his name, note the two marks caused by bullets.

Clark Family Burying Ground
(Southwest Harbor - 10)

Location/directions. Along west side of Claremont Road. From the traffic light at the north end of Mount Desert Island, go straight ahead (south) onto Routes 102/198. In approximately 10.6–10.7 miles (6.3–6.4 miles of which are south of the traffic light at the intersection of Routes 102/198 and 198/233), turn left onto Clark Point Road at the blinking light in the center of the village of Southwest Harbor. In about 0.6–0.7 miles is an intersection on the left with Claremont Road. (The angle of the sign for Claremont Road makes it difficult to read from Clark Point Road, so look for a sign for the Claremont Inn). Turn left onto Claremont Road, and the cemetery is on the left in less than 0.1 miles.

History. This cemetery is on land that was part of a 270 acre parcel owned by Ebenezer Eaton in 1808 according to the Salem Towne Jr. map.

Notes. The cemetery is mowed and enclosed by a wire mesh fence with metal posts. A sign on a tree reads "CLARK FAMILY/BURYING GROUND".

Names and dates on gravestones and other markers. [29 May 1999]

CARROLL
- [Grace - see CLARK]

CLARK
- Alice L. (dau. of Seth H. and Lucy W.) - d. 16 December 1853 Æ 3 y., 5 m., 3 d.
- Amanda A. (dau. of Edwin and Phebe A. [no stone]) - b. 7 June 1865; d. 28 November 1879
- Augustus (husb. of Ida C.) - b. 1846; d. 1938
- Caroline (wife of Henry H.) - b. 20 June 1813; d. 17 December 1898
- Edwin (husb. of Phebe A. [no stone]) - b. 15 June 1838; d. 25 November 1870
- Gertrude (wife of Edwin [no stone]) - b. 15 July 1871; d. 30 September 1904
- Grace (CARROLL; wife of Roderick P.) - b. 21 November 1882; d. 6 September 1949
- [Henrietta - see ROBINSON]
- Henry - b. 17 August 1841; d. 30 April 1919
- Henry H. (husb. of Caroline) - b. 2 February 1811; d. 21 January 1897
- Hilda Louise - b. 20 June 1903; d. 16 October 1923
- Ida C. (wife of Augustus) - b. 1854; d. 1930
- Israel - b. 15 October 1836; d. 17 August 1865
- Lucy W. (wife of Seth H.) - d. 19 August 1899 Æ 82 y.
- Mercy - d. 2 December 1868 Æ 81 y., 7 m., 26 d.
- Nathan - d. 21 March 1848 Æ 67 y., 7 m., 16 d.
- Nathan [husb. of Philena C.] - b. 11 January 1843; d. 3 March 1907
- Philena C. [wife of Nathan] - b. 6 February 1846; d. 16 October 1921
- Roderick P. (husb. of Grace (CARROLL)) - b. 16 May 1880; d. 13 February 1965
- Seth H. (husb. of Lucy W.) - d. 16 March 1896 Æ 80 y.

ROBINSON
- A. J. (Capt.; husb. of Henrietta (CLARK)) - b. 8 March 1834; d. 21 March 1912
- Bertha E. (dau. of Capt. A. J. and Henrietta (CLARK)) - d. 6 March 1894 Æ 32 y.
- Henrietta (CLARK; wife of Capt. A. J.) - b. 24 December 1840; d. 20 July 1908

STANLEY
- Charles E. [husb. of Josephine S.] - b. 24 November 1848; d. 28 November 1899
- Josephine S. [wife of Charles E.] - b. 9 February 1846; d. 2 June 1926

Gilley Burying Ground

(Southwest Harbor - 11)

Location/directions. South of Fernald Point Road. From the traffic light at the north end of Mount Desert Island, go straight ahead (south) onto Routes 102/198. In approximately 9.7–9.8 miles (5.4–5.5 miles of which are south of the traffic light at the intersection of Route 102/198 and Route 198), turn left onto Fernald Point Road. In about 0.2 miles the road rises and curves to the left. On the right in this curve is a paved drive that leads to the cemetery. The cemetery is on the right in approximately 0.1 miles.

History. This cemetery is on land that was part of a 100 acre parcel owned by William Gilley in 1808 according to the Salem Towne Jr. map. "Gilley Burying Ground" is the name used by Thornton (1938, p. 214).

Notes. An elaborately constructed fence along one end of the cemetery and along part of the opposite end is falling down. Many large and nearly buried boulders along the side of the cemetery next to the road suggest some sort of stone wall at one time. Some gravestones are leaning or laying on the ground.

Names and dates on gravestones and other markers. [20 May 1999]

CRANE
- Abigail B. (wife of John T. G. [no stone]) - d. 10 February 1870 Æ 84 y., 2 m.
- Elisha B. (Capt.) - d. 22 June 1843 Æ 38 y., 3 m., 3 d.

DAY
- Benjamin G. (son of Henry E. and Abigail P. [no stones]) - d. 19 November 1863 Æ 16 y., 10 m.
- Delphenia G. (dau. of Henry E. and Abigail P. [no stones]) - d. 22 November 1863 Æ 1 y., 1 m.
- Emeline C. (dau. of Henry E. and Abigail P. [no stones]) - d. 24 October 1863 Æ 10 y., 8 d.
- Mahala - b. 1825; d. 1907

DODGE
- Gertie L. (dau. of L. M. and T. E. [no stones]) - d. 18 January 1876 Æ 3 y., 6 m., 6 d.

FISKE
- [Emeline Holmes - see HAMOR]

GILLEY
- Abigail C. (wife of Benjamin) - d. 7 August 1881 Æ 82 y., 2 m., 27 d.
- Benjamin (husb. of Abigail C.) - d. 9 September 1875 Æ 78 y., 2 m., 9 d.
- Carrie C. (wife of Charles B.) - d. 3 December 1879 Æ 28 y., 3 m.
- Charles B. (husb. of Delphina I. and Carrie C.) - b. 2 December 1841; d. 25 November 1901
- Cordelia S. (wife of Stephen M.) - b. 2 December 1833; d. 24 December 1907
- Delphina I. (wife of Charles B.) - d. 22 February 1861 Æ 19 y., 2 m.
- Jennie F. (dau. of Stephen M. and Cordelia S.) - d. 17 June 1872 Æ 12 y., 4 m., 14 d.
- Orin Leslie (son of Charles B. and Delphina I.) - d. 16 August 1861 Æ 8 m., 12 d.
- Stephen M. (husb. of Cordelia S.) - b. 29 April 1829; d. 28 January 1910; (member of Co. G, 1st Maine Heavy Artillery [Civil War])

HAMOR
- Emeline Holmes (FISKE; wife of Seth H.) - b. 1832; d. 1913

Seth H. (husb. of Emeline Holmes (FISKE)) - b. 1826; d. 21 October 1880 Æ 54 y., 7 m.

HIGGINS

Lucretia P. (dau. of Robert and Mary [no stones]; granddau. of Leonard HOLMES and Mary) - d. 10 November 1878 Æ 39 y., 12 d.

HOLMES

[Ann L. P. or Louisa A.][1] (wife of Lewis [no stone]) - d. 2 November 1898 Æ 75 y., 9 m., 15 d.

Catharine (dau. of Lewis [no stone] and [Ann L. P. or Louisa A.][2]; twin of Emeline) - d. 11 July 1846 Æ 12 d.

Emeline (dau. of Lewis [no stone] and [Ann L. P. or Louisa A.][2]; twin of Catharine) - d. 9 July 1846 Æ 10 d.

Estella J. (dau. of John M. and Mahala [no stone]) - d. 20 June 1852 Æ 15 m.

John M. (husb. of Mahala [no stone]) - d. 10 June 1864 Æ 39 y., 10 m., 20 d.

Leonard (husb. of Mary) - d. 15 January 1869 Æ 80 y., 10 m., 19 d.

Lewis E. (son of Lewis [no stone] and [Ann L. P. or Louisa A.][1]) - d. 30 October 1849 Æ 5 y., 8 m., 19 d.

Mary (wife of Leonard) - d. 6 April 1876 Æ 83 y., 8 m.

REYNOLDS

Mercy C. (wife of William D.) - d. 15 September 1896 Æ 70 y., 6 m., 10 d.

Sarah R. (wife of Bion B. [no stone]) - d. 15 January 1896 Æ 38 y., 17 d.

William D. (husb. of Mercy C.) - b. 1825; d. 1901

ROBBINS

David M. (husb. of Lydia M.) - b. 5 July 1830; d. 5 January 1907

Ellen F. (dau. of David M. and Lydia M.) - d. 6 February 1864 Æ 4 y., 4 d.

Lydia M. (wife of David M.) - d. 27 March 1875 Æ 37 y., 9 m.

ROGERS

Frederick G. (son of Rev. Charles and Jennie [no stones]) - d. 13 August 1881 Æ 3 y., 8 m.

TARR

Andrew (Capt.; husb. of Susan) - d. 4 May 1875 Æ 79 y.

Susan (wife of Capt. Andrew) - d. 20 May 1890 Æ 91 y., 10 m., 11 d.

Note:

[1]Different on different stones.

Dolliver Family Burial Ground

(Southwest Harbor - 12)

Location/directions. Seawall Campground (Acadia National Park). From the traffic light at the north end of Mount Desert Island, go straight ahead (south) onto Routes 102/198. In approximately 11.3–11.4 miles (about 0.8 miles of which are south of the blinking light in the village of Southwest Harbor), turn left onto Route 102A. The entrance to Seawall Campground is on the right in approximately 3.1–3.2 miles. Inquire at the ranger station for directions.

History. The name applied to this cemetery is only for convenience of reference in this book. In a deed (806:331; 21 November 1957) to John D. Rockefeller Jr. and Martha B. Rockefeller, Laura Haynes Dolliver reserved for herself and "her heirs and assigns, the right of access on foot in a reasonable location to the cemetery lot measuring about thirty feet by thirty five feet ... for the purpose of maintaining said cemetery lot and the graves therein". The Rockefellers, and later the United States which obtained the land from them (819:486; 3 April 1958), promised that "there shall be no further burials made in said cemetery lot" and that they "will not destroy the graves nor remove the bodies in said cemetery lot, and ... will take all reasonable steps to prevent vandalism".

Notes. The cemetery is enclosed by a wire mesh fence with wood posts with an opening between one pair of adjacent posts. The grass is mowed.

Names and dates on gravestones and other markers. [6 September 1999]

DOLLIVER [includes DOLIVER]

Aggie S. (dau. of William [H.?][2] and [M?]...s[3] [no stones]) - d. 17 June 1884 Æ 3 y., 5 m., 6 d.

Edward "Uncle Ed" - d. [no date] Æ 79 y., 8 m.; ("California Pioneer")

Fanny [wife of John S.?][1] - d. 13 September 1875 Æ 73 y., [...][1]

Hattie F. (dau. of William [H.?][2] and [M?]...s[3] [no stones]) - d. 11 March 1860 Æ 1 y., 3 m., 15 d.

John S. [husb. of Fanny?][1] - d. 22 January 1864 Æ 63 y., 9 m.

Note:

[1]Fanny's stone is broken.

[2]Difficult to read.

[3]Stone cracked and broken.

TREMONT

On 3 June 1848, a portion of the town of Mount Desert was incorporated as the town of Mansel. In a few days more than two months (8 August 1848), the name was changed to Tremont. This town has more cemeteries (at least 33) than any other town covered in this book.

Federal:
Kelley Cemetery (Tremont - 7)
Norwood Grave (Tremont - 30)

Non-profit:
Hillrest Cemetery (Tremont - 9)
McKinley Cemetery (Tremont - 11)
Benson Cemetery (Tremont - 13)

Town, private, or unknown oversight:
Hodgdon Cemetery (Tremont - 1)
Center Cemetery (Tremont - 2)
Ober Cemetery (Tremont - 3)
Hodgdon and Stewart Graves (Tremont - 4)
Seal Cove Cemetery (Tremont - 5)
Flye Cemetery (Tremont - 6)
Tinker-Pomroy Cemetery (Tremont - 8)
Rich Cemetery (Tremont - 10)
Billings Graves (Tremont - 12)
Head of the Harbor Cemetery (Tremont - 14)
Murphy Cemetery (Tremont - 15) - no apparent care
Carver Tomb (Tremont - 16)
Heath Cemetery (Tremont - 17)
Reed Point Cemetery (Tremont - 18)
James Reed Cemetery (Tremont - 19)
Langley Cemetery (Tremont - 20) - no apparent care
Tinker Island Cemetery (Tremont - 21)
Babbidge-Murphy Burial Ground (Tremont - 22)
Rumill-Dodge Cemetery (Tremont - 23)
Norwood Cemetery (Tremont - 24)
Wentworth-Walls-Norton Cemetery (Tremont - 25)
Dix Burying Ground (Tremont - 26)
Crockett Point Cemetery (Tremont - 27)
Richtown Cemetery (Tremont - 28)
Murphy Hill Cemetery (Tremont - 29) - no apparent care
Gott Island Cemetery (Tremont - 31)
Benjamin Norwood Cemetery (Tremont - 32)
Washburn Grave (Tremont - 33)

Hodgdon Cemetery
(Tremont - 1)

Location/directions. Set back from east side of Route 102. From the traffic light at the north end of Mount Desert Island, go straight ahead (south) onto Routes 102/198. In approximately 5.2 miles (and at the south end of the village of Somesville), turn right onto Pretty Marsh Road (Route 102). A driveway that passes by the cemetery is on the left in about 4.8–4.9 miles. Immediately before the driveway is a large rock with "Hodgdon Pond/Farm" engraved in it. The picket fence surrounding part of the cemetery and some of the stones can be seen from a parking place just beyond the driveway.

History. This cemetery is on land that was part of lot #4, a 108 acre parcel, on the 1808 Salem Towne Jr. map.

Notes. Except for one lot that is enclosed by a white picket fence that needs paint, the stones are standing or laying in an unmaintained area of trees and lower, but unchecked, vegetation.

Names and dates on gravestones and other markers. [23 May 1999]

BILLINGS
- Jane (wife of Deacon John) - d. 16 January 1873 Æ 97 y., 11 m., 20 d.
- John (Deacon; husb. of Jane) - d. 10 February 1860 Æ 79 y., 6 m.

CLONEY
- Isabelle E. (wife of Raymond H. [no stone]) - b. 1904; d. 1933

H.[1]
- N.[1]

HODGDON
- Ann (wife of Joseph T.) - d. 6 March 1833 Æ 78 y.
- Charles A. (husb. of Mabelle H. (NORWOOD)) - b. 1873; d. 1907
- Charlotte G. (dau. of Charles A. and Mabelle H. (NORWOOD)) - b. 1903; d. 1908
- [Elisha or Elisher][2] B. (husb. of Nancy and Mary [no stone]) - d. 22 May 1863 Æ 75 y., 6 m.
- infant (son of [Elisha or Elisher][2] B. and Nancy) - d. 15 June 1817 Æ 2 d.
- Isabelle B. (wife of William W.) - b. 2 February 1831; d. 18 January 1918
- Joseph T. (husb. of Ann) - d. 15 September 1816 Æ 68 y.
- Mabelle H. (NORWOOD; wife of Charles A.) - b. 1876; d. 1950
- Marjorie I. (dau. of Charles A. and Mabelle H. (NORWOOD)) - b. 1897; d. 1914
- Nancy (wife of [Elisha or Elisher][2] B.) - d. 15 September 1834 Æ 38 y.
- Nancy R. (dau. of [Elisha or Elisher][2] B. and Mary [no stone]) - d. 24 December 1855 Æ 19 y., 3 m.
- R. M. - [no dates]; (member of Co. F, 3rd Maine Regiment [Civil War])
- William W. (husb. of Isabelle B.) - b. 15 January 1834; d. 12 August 1904
- Winfield (son of [Elisha or Elisher][2] B. and Mary) - d. 17 May 1852 Æ 5 y.

NORWOOD
- [Mabelle H. - see HODGDON]

Notes:

[1]Headstone reads only "Aunt Meenie" and "20th century".

[2]Different on different stones.

Center Cemetery
(Tremont - 2)

Location/directions. North of north end of Cape Road. From the traffic light at the north end of Mount Desert Island, go straight ahead (south) onto Routes 102/198. In approximately 5.2 miles (and at the south end of the village of Somesville), turn right onto Pretty Marsh Road (Route 102). Travel on Route 102 about 5.1–5.2 miles to the intersection with Cape Road on the right. Turn right onto Cape Road, and in less than 0.1 miles, take the first right and then immediately the right fork. This drive leads to the cemetery.

History. —

Notes. A portion of the boundary is marked by a wire fence with wood posts. The grass is well maintained, but there are a few stones leaning, laying on the ground, and/or broken.

Names and dates on gravestones and other markers. [23 May 1999]
ALDEN
John (son of "Mr. and Mrs. Charles E." [no stones]) - b. 18 February 1906; d. 5 December 1914
BARTLETT
Everett J. - b. 1917; d. 1982
Grace L. (wife of Henry D. [no stone]) - b. 3 June 1898; d. 3 February 1924
Wallace R. - b. 1908; d. 1952
BILLINGS
Almira C. (dau. of Elisha H. and Abigail S. [no stones]) - d. 8 May 1839 Æ 3 w.
Rachel S. (Mrs.) - b. 5 November 1806; d. 9 June 1879 Æ 73 y., 6 m., 4 d.
BUTLER
Alice M. [wife of William L.?] - b. 1889; d. 1925
Andrew J. (husb. of Lena E.) - b. 18 August 1838; d. 26 March 1922; (member of Co. D, 31st Maine Regiment [Civil War])
Chester A. - b. 1881; d. 1967
Everett W. [husb. of Wilhemean [sic]?] - b. 1916; d. 1981
George - d. 1 January 1844 Æ 69 y., 8 m., 14 d.
George F. (son of George W. and Myra F.) - b. 1907; d. 1931
George W. (husb. of Myra F.) - b. 1874; d. 1942
Harold D. - b. 1919; d. 1979
Herbert G. [husb. of Katherine A. (HOOPER)?] - b. 1883; d. 1942
Hollis Burton - b. 4 April 1923; d. 16 February 1991
John I. - b. 30 March 1905; d. 24 April 1961
Katherine A. (HOOPER; [wife of Herbert G.?]) - b. 1906; d. 1936
Lena E. (wife of Andrew J.) - b. 28 April 1845; d. 7 January 1933
Myra F. (wife of George W.) - b. 1884; d. 1931
Wilhemean [sic] [wife of Everett W.?] - b. 1918; d. 1993
William L. [husb. of Alice M.?] - b. 1877; d. 1943
CAMPBELL
Byron L. (husb. of Mary E.) - b. 11 November 1891; d. 20 August 1960
C. H. [footstone only]
Ernest Alton Sr. - b. 5 September 1927; d. 12 September 1995
Mary E. (wife of Byron L.) - b. 7 November 1896; d. 21 October 1987
Vivian I. (JOHNSON) - b. 1925; d. 1959

CARTER
Audrey J. (dau. of Willis B. and Lucy L.) - b. 1901; d. 1903
Benjamin P. [husb. of Helen A.] - b. 1884; d. 1949
Helen A. [wife of Benjamin P.] - b. 1890; d. 1975
Joseph P. (husb. of Mercy J.) - b. 1829; d. 1897
Lucy L. (wife of Willis B.) - b. 1872; d. 1934
Mercy J. (wife of Joseph P.) - b. 1832; d. 1905
Willis B. (husb. of Lucy L.) - b. 1877; d. [no date]
CHAPMAN
Addie A. (wife of Melville [no stone]) - b. 4 November 1875; d. 8 May 1900
CLARK
Abigail C. (wife of David [no stone]) - d. 8 February 1859 Æ 45 y., 10 m.
Albion L. (son of David [no stone] and Abigail C.) - d. 28 March 1859 Æ 2 y., 4 m.
Mary K. - b. 1808; d. 1896
CLINKARD
Alfred H. - b. 29 August 1881; d. 19 December 1936
Alfred Harper - b. 1857; d. 1944
[Flora M. - see STEWART]
Joanna F. (wife of William H.) - d. 21 January 1900 Æ 74 y.
Lewis W. - b. 1887; d. 1941
Martin L. - d. 2 July 1886 Æ 35 y., 4 m., 28 d.
William H. (husb. of Joanna F.) - b. 23 July 1823; d. 26 July 1907
CLOUGH
Alberta R. - b. 1912; d. 1996
COOKE
Mavis E. - b. 1906; d. 1995
Roy A. N. - b. 1917; d. 1980
DOW
Cornelius M. (son of Capt. Thurlow and Harriet M.) - d. 4 June 1855 Æ 8 y., 2 m.
Elnora T. (dau. of William and Isabel M.) - d. 11 Jan 1870 Æ 22 y., 7 m., 22 d.
Ephraim (husb. of Rebecca) - b. 12 February 1781; d. 25 May 1872
Harriet M. (wife of Capt. Thurlow) - d. 9 June 1883 Æ 58 y., 10 m., 27 d.
Isaac C. (husb. of Rebecca H.) - b. 1837; d. 1919; ("G. A. R." [Civil War])
Isabel M. (wife of William) - d. 27 December 1890 Æ 74 y.
John W. (son of Isaac C. and Rebecca H.) - b. 1879; d. 1898
Mary A. - b. 1856; d. 1905
Rebecca (wife of Ephraim) - b. 3 June 1785; d. 3 February 1855
Rebecca H. (wife of Isaac C.) - b. 1845; d. 1912
Reuben B. (son of William and Isabel M.) - d. 19 March 1866 Æ 24 y., 10 m., 5 d.
Reuben E. (son of Isaac C. and Rebecca H.) - b. 1874; d. 28 April 1876 Æ 2 y., 2 m., 23 d.
Thurlow (Capt.; husb. of Harriet M.) - d. 22 January 1891 Æ 70 y., 7 m.
William (husb. of Isabel M.) - d. 19 June 1907 Æ 93 y., 10 m., 16 d.
FARRELL
Basil A. (son of Luella B. KELLEY) - b. 1918; d. 1984
GALLEY
[....] [headstone only]
GRAY
Deda B. (wife of James A.) - b. 1866; d. 1935
Frances C. - b. 28 June 1917; d. 29 December 1996 Æ 79 y.
James A. (husb. of Deda B.) - b. 1858; d. 1933

H.
Hannah (wife of W[...][1]) - d. 23 March 1841 Æ 75 y., 6 m.
W[...][1] (husb. of Hannah) - d. [...][1] Æ [...][1]
HARPER
Alfred Jr. (Capt.) - d. 7 September 1861 Æ 29 y., 4 m., 2 d.
Alfred L. (husb. of Jane) - d. 17 January 1873 Æ 69 y., 7 m.
Ansel L. (husb. of May) - b. 26 March 1876; d. 18 August 1952
Clifford E. - b. 22 December 1883; d. 8 February 1884
Edward C. (husb. of Fannie E.) - b. 1859; d. 1934
Elizabeth (wife of William Sr.) - b. 1798; d. 1896
Ermina Townley (SOMES; dau. of John C. SOMES and Joann; wife of William Jr. [no stone]) - b. 5 April 1830; d. 26 June 1856 Æ 26 y., 2 m., 20 d.
Fannie E. (wife of Edward C.) - b. 1862; d. 1948
Hannah E. (wife of William) - b. 25 December 1838; d. 22 February 1915
Hannah W. [wife of Phillip [sic] S.] - b. 3 May 1842; d. 28 June 1925
Jane (wife of Alfred L.) - d. 15 August 1880 Æ 78 y., 10 m., 15 d.
John W. (son of William and Hannah E.) - d. 13 April 1862 Æ 9 m., 13 d.
[Mary - see PASCOE]
Mary Elizabeth (dau. of William Sr. and Elizabeth) - d. 21 September 1854 Æ 16 y., 11 m.
Mary S. (wife of Reuben A.) - d. 9 June 1895 Æ 59 y., 25 d.
May (wife of Ansel L.) - b. 10 May 1878; d. 31 August 1966
Phillip [sic] S. [husb. of Hannah W.] - b. 20 April 1827; d. 20 May 1876
Reuben A. (husb. of Mary S.) - b. 8 October 1828; d. 30 July 1904
William (husb. of Hannah E.) - d. 31 January 1888 Æ 58 y., 2 m., 9 d.
William Sr. (husb. of Elizabeth) - d. 5 March 1858 Æ 64 y.
HODGDON
Alexander (husb. of Lydia and Mary [no stone]) - d. 30 January 1855 Æ 65 y.
Bernice L. (dau. of Frank L. and Idella [no stones]) - d. 18 June 1898 Æ 8 y., 2 m.
infant (son of Alexander and Mary [no stone]) - d. 18 January 1828 Æ [not given]
John F. Sr. [husb. of Verna F.] - b. 15 March 1895; d. 2 February 1974
Lydia (wife of Alexander) - d. 28 March 1835 Æ 31 y.
Verna F. [wife of John F. Sr.] - b. 1905
William - d. 15 April 1864 Æ 45 y., 6 m., 13 d.
HOOPER
[Katherine A. - see BUTLER]
HOWLAND
Ermine B. (wife of Ralph K. [no stone]) - b. 1888; d. 1952
J.
C. C. - [no dates]
C. W. - [no dates]
JOHNSON
Chester A. (husb. of Hazel R.) - b. 1897; d. 1955
Hazel R. (wife of Chester A.) - b. 1902; d. 1973
Larry E. - b. 2 June 1932; d. 2 February 1996
[Vivian I. - see CAMPBELL]
KANE
Rudolph - [b. and d.?] 1929
KELLEY
Alden A. (husb. of Luella B.) - b. 1894; d. 1951
Alfred Harry - b. 14 August 1921; d. 8 October 1958
Luella B. (wife of Alden A.) - b. 1898; d. 1979

M. E. [spouse of R. F.?] - [no dates]
Maurice E. [husb. of Patricia A.?] - b. 6 June 1925; d. 26 February 1975
Patricia A. [wife of Maurice E.?] - b. 18 August 1940; d. 6 October 1997
R. F. [spouse of M. E.?] - [no dates]
Rudolph E. - b. 22 March 1920; d. 17 February 1944
KENNY [includes KENNEY]
Mary M. (wife of Michael) - d. 24 February 1884 Æ 88 y.
Michael (husb. of Mary M.) - d. 5 October 1844 Æ 45 y.
Peter - d. 15 April 1861 Æ 23 y., 9 m., 15 d.
LALLEY
Thomas - d. 19 December 1869 Æ 63 y.
LEONARD
Clara A. - b. 1872; d. 1924
Guy W. - b. 1891; d. 1911
Samuel G. - b. 1868; d. 1946
McINTIRE
Lucy A. (wife of Miles M.) - b. 1896; d. 1979
Miles M. (husb. of Lucy A.) - b. 20 May 1898; d. 21 March 1949
Ralph T. (son of Miles M. and Lucy A.) - b. 1927; d. 1944
MORISON
Peter Greene - b. 1917; d. 1969
MURPHY
Allen Wayne [husb. of Eva Jean] - b. 2 March 1935
Arlene V. [wife of Ernest D.?] - b. 1922; d. 1978
[Brenda M[URPHY?]. - see NEVELLS]
Delmont H. (husb. of Mabel H.) - b. 1883; d. 1963
Donald M. - b. 15 August 1928; d. 27 November 1992
Ernest D. [husb. of Arlene V.?] - b. 1924; d. 1977
Ernest D. Jr. - b. 1952; d. 1955
Eva Jean [wife of Allen Wayne] - b. 4 March 1941; d. 4 October 1999
Florence [wife of Gus] - [no dates]
G. Merton - b. 27 February 1885; d. 22 March 1899
Gus [husb. of Florence] - [no dates]
James H. [husb. of Sheila H.] - b. 1907; d. 1983
Mabel H. (wife of Delmont H.) - b. 1884; d. 1939
Ralph M. Sr. - b. 1919; d. 1963
Richard A. - b. 24 September 1931; d. 26 June 1959
Russell Albert - b. 17 January 1922; d. 2 April 1996
Sheila H. [wife of James H.] - b. 1911; d. 1982
NEVELLS
Brenda M[URPHY?]. (wife of Peter [no stone]) - b. 1955; d. 1973
OBER
Amanda (dau. of Capt. Isaiah and Emma W. [no stones]) - d. 23 November 1832 Æ 1 m., 4 d.
Hannah M. (wife of James W.) - b. 4 June 1843; d. 23 May 1910
Isaac W. (husb. of Joanna) - d. 17 March 1861 Æ 85 y., 9 m., 11 d.
James W. (husb. of Hannah M.) - b. 29 October 1839; d. 29 September 1906
Joanna (wife of Isaac W.) - d. 24 April 1861 Æ 88 y., 7 m.
Mahala S. - b. 11 January 1801; d. 22 June 1879 Æ 78 y., 5 m., 11 d.
PASCOE
James [husb. of Mary (HARPER)] - b. 1877; d. 1949
Jim [son of James and Mary (HARPER)] - [no dates]; ("baby")

Mary (HARPER; [wife of James]) - b. 1869; d. 1944
REALE
Anna H. [wife of Edward T. Sr.] - b. 1933
Edward T. Sr. [husb. of Anna H.] - b. 9 February 1930; d. 17 July 1990
REED
Jet - b. 1875; d. 1919
Lorraine Lee (dau. of Wendell and Rosemary (SMALLIDGE) [no stones]) - b. 6 May 1935; d. 13 November 1935
ROBBINS
Aphia (wife of David) - d. 10 January 1868 Æ 68 y., 9 m.
David (husb. of Aphia) - d. 6 November 1834 Æ 39 y., 1 m.
Marion H. (dau. of Capt. John E. and Georgia A. [no stones]) - b. 26 September 1885; d. 3 October 1888
Sophronia F. - b. 7 July 1831; d. 1 March 1901
Temperence (dau. of David and Aphia) - d. 24 June 1826 Æ 7 y., 9 m.
ROBINSON
Clifford L. [son of James E. and Grace A.?] - b. 1904; d. 1981
Grace A. [wife of James E.] - b. 1876; d. 1906
Isabella B. - b. 1910; d. 1980
James E. [husb. of Grace A.] - b. 1877; d. 1941
James E. Jr. [son of James E. and Grace A.] - b. 1906; d. 1906
SCOTT
Marguerite C. [wife of Robert W.] - b. 1912
Robert W. [husb. of Marguerite C.] - b. 1905; d. 1990
SMALLIDGE
Robert I. - b. 21 April 1922; d. 16 April 1960
SMITH
Marye [sic] Harrold [sic] - b. 1916; d. 1995
SOMES
Abraham (son of John C. and Joann) - d. 31 December 1851 Æ 28 y., 7 m.
Angelina M. - b. 24 May 1869; d. 18 September 1933
[Ermina Townley - see HARPER]
George R. - d. 1 October 1858 Æ 24 y., 10 m., 28 d.
Joann (wife of John C.) - d. 23 July 1868 Æ 69 y., 5 m.
John C. (husb. of Joann) - d. 30 May 1862 Æ 65 y.
Matilda (dau. of John C. and Joann) - d. 15 Ma[...][2] 1825 Æ [2 digits][2] d.
Rachel H. (dau. of John C. and Joann) - d. 25 December 1830 Æ 11 y., 10 m., 19 d.
STANLEY
Juanita H. [wife of Perley Lyman] - b. 11 November 1927
Lyman Perley - b. 1945; d. 1945
Perley Lyman [husb. of Juanita H.] - b. 13 July 1922; d. 12 December 1994
Perley Lyman - b. 1946; d. 1949
STEWART
Clara E. (wife of Capt. Lorenzo W.) - b. 2 November 1856; d. 3 March 1922
Emmie B. (wife of Capt. Lorenzo W.) - d. 6 September 1880 Æ 37 y., 10 m., 22 d.
Flora M. (CLINKARD; wife of Lorenzo E.) - b. 10 May 1866; d. 5 April 1929
George F. (husb. of Henrietta M.) - b. 1872; d. 1948
Henrietta M. (wife of George F.) - b. 1879; d. 1960
Letitia Mae - b. 1901; d. 1964
Lorenzo E. (husb. of Flora M. (CLINKARD)) - b. 8 June 1865; d. 16 December 1919
Lorenzo W. (Capt.; husb. of Emmie B. and Clara E.) - b. 4 August 1842; d. 1 August 1933

Lucinda (wife of Mathew [sic]) - d. 29 July 1882 Æ 77 y., 3 m., 5 d.
Mathew [sic] (husb. of Lucinda) - d. 8 June 1875 Æ 77 y., 1 m., 6 d.

WELLINGTON

John C. (husb. of Lucille H.) - b. 8 April 1920
Lucille H. (wife of John C.) - b. 10 July 1921; d. 21 July 1969

Notes:

[1]Stone broken. Husband's initial is from footstone.
[2]Stone worn and pitted.

Ober Cemetery
(Tremont - 3)

Location/directions. Set back from northwest side of Cape Road. From the traffic light at the north end of Mount Desert Island, go straight ahead (south) onto Routes 102/198. In approximately 5.2 miles (and at the south end of the village of Somesville), turn right onto Pretty Marsh Road (Route 102). Travel on Route 102 about 5.1–5.2 miles to the intersection with Cape Road on the right. Turn right onto Cape Road, and the cemetery is on the right in about 0.3–0.4 miles.

History. —

Notes. The grass of the cemetery proper as well as that of a path leading to it is mowed by the town. No fence encloses the cemetery, but survey markers were found (2000) at three of the likely corners.

Names and dates on gravestones and other markers. [23 May 1999]

BUTLER
- Beatrice I. [wife of Clarence W.] - b. 1914; d. 1960
- Clarence W. [husb. of Beatrice I.] - b. 24 March 1908; d. 8 September 1966
- Lawrence A. - b. 21 October 1912; d. 24 March 1968

CAMPBELL
- Collin A. (husb. of Emma J.) - b. 1837; d. 1928
- Emma J. (wife of Collin A.) - b. 1854; d. 1916

DOW
- Josie - [no dates]

FARRELL
- William J. - d. 31 January 1878 Æ 50 y., 6 m., 22 d.

HARPER
- Glendon L. - b. 13 March 1893; d. 31 December 1958
- Sarah Matilda (wife of Alfred Jr. [no stone]) - d. 24 March 1854 Æ 18 y., 5 m., 10 d.

HERRICK
- Fannie (OBER) - b. 18[6?]8[3]; d. 1910

HODGDON
- Elizabeth S. (wife of Samuel) - b. 19 March 1830; d. 13 January 1921
- George Lynwood [HODGDON?] - b. 1901; d. 1905
- Joel K. (husb. of Lizzie E. J.) - b. 1851; d. 1939
- Leona S. - b. 16 October 1886; d. 15 March 1899
- Lizzie E. J. (wife of Joel K.) - d. 2 September 1889 Æ 32 y., 11 m.
- Rebecca (wife of Samuel [no stone]) - d. 13 June 1873 Æ 84 y., 10 m., 6 d.
- Samuel (husb. of Elizabeth S.) - b. 12 December 1822; d. 21 December 1902
- Seth S. (son of Samuel and Elizabeth S.) - d. 2 October 1861 Æ 1 y., 7 m., 17 d.

KENNEY
- [Ellen - see OBER]

OBER [includes OBEAR]
- Abbie T. - b. 4 February 1877; d. 7 December 1897
- Aram T. - b. 1835; d. 1919
- Caroline B. (wife of Capt. William) - d. 26 October 1856 Æ 27 y., 11 m., 23 d.
- Edna [OBER?] - b. 30 August 1902; d. 28 October 1902
- Ellen (KENNEY; wife of Capt. William) - b. 1837; d. 1909
- [Fannie - see HERRICK]
- Henrietta (wife of John W. [no stone]) - d. 19 March 1871 Æ 21 y., 19 d.

Isiphenia H. (dau. of Deacon William and Martha) - d. 16 March 1860 Æ 17 y., 10 m., 8 d.
James (son of Deacon William and Martha) - d. 19 March 1835 Æ 7 m., 26 d.
Leon C. (son of George S. and Linda C. [no stones]) - d. 14 May 1890 Æ 2 m., 20 d.
Margaret Ann (dau. of Deacon William and Martha) - d. 11 September 1853 Æ 21 y., 3 m.
Martha (wife of Deacon William) - d. 19 April 1871 Æ 73 y., 1 m., 5 d.
Nellie Mary (dau. of Capt. William and Ellen (KENNEY)) - d. 20 March 1865 Æ 8 m., 8 d.
Ralph F. (son of Capt. William and Ellen (KENNEY)) - d. 25 March 1862 Æ 1 y., 2 d.
[Serena S. - see WINSLOW]
Seth Randall (son of Capt. William and Caroline B.) - d. 22 January 1857 Æ 2 y., 8 m., 8 d.
Will A. - b. 1872; d. 1908
William (Capt.; husb. of Caroline B. and Ellen (KENNEY)) - d. 3 September 1893 Æ 70 y., 11 m., 19 d.
William (Deacon; husb. of Martha) - d. 26 February 1867 Æ 66 y., 9 m., 14 d.

ROBBINS
Abra[ha]m[1] (Capt.; husb. of Martha O.) - b. 24 September 1824; d. 5 February 1905
Addison O. (husb. of Emma J.) - b. 2 December 1833; d. 22 January 1908
Emma J. (wife of Addison O.) - b. 27 March 1838; d. 5 March 1900
Henry N. (husb. of Phebe A.) - b. 1851; d. 1930
infant (son of Capt. Abra[ha]m[1] and Martha O.) - d. 12 February 1852 Æ 12 d.
Martha O. (wife of Capt. Abra[ha]m[1]) - b. 23 January 1828; d. 23 March 1903
Phebe A. (wife of Henry N.) - b. 1858; d. 1930
Viola N. (dau. of Capt. Abra[ha]m[1] and Martha O.) - d. 23 March 1868 Æ 1 y., 6 m., 7 d.

ROBINSON
Abram R. (son of John H. and Mary H. [no stones]) - d. 25 January 1887 Æ 18 y., 10 d.
Walter (son of John and Hannah [no stones]) - d. 24 December 1870 Æ 24 y., 9 m.

STROUT
Olive A. - b. 1957; d. 1975

WHITE
Lovisa [wife of Michael] - b. 1816; d. 1895
Michael [husb. of Lovisa] - b. 1809; d. 1869

WINSLOW
Serena S. (OBER; dau. of Deacon William OBER and Martha; wife of Sumner [no stone]) - d. 10 March 1861 Æ 21 y., 1 m., 1 d.

WONG
Tony - b. 1903; d. 1972

[...]
[...][2] - d. 26 December [...][2] Æ 51 y., [...][2]

Notes:
[1]Different on different stones.
[2]Stone broken.
[3]The inscription was marked in wet concrete and is difficult to read.

Hodgdon and Stewart Graves
(Tremont - 4)

Location/directions. On private land off Carter Road. From the traffic light at the north end of Mount Desert Island, go straight ahead (south) onto Routes 102/198. In approximately 5.2 miles (and at the south end of the village of Somesville), turn right onto Pretty Marsh Road (Route 102). Travel on Route 102 about 5.1–5.2 miles to the intersection with Cape Road on the right. Turn right onto Cape Road, and in approximately 1.2–1.3 miles, the Carter Road is on the right. The Carter Road leads to a fork in the road in about 0.1–0.2 miles. The left fork leads to the property containing the gravestones, which are under a large spruce tree in a field.

History. This cemetery is on land that was part of lot #11, a 146 acre parcel, on the 1808 Salem Towne Jr. map.

Notes. There is no enclosure around the area containing the graves and no apparent maintenance other than mowing the field in which they occur.

Names and dates on gravestones and other markers. [11 March 2000]
HODGDON
Charity (wife of Capt. Hosea) - d. 12[1] December 1864 Æ 41 y., 8 m., 24[1] d.
Hosea (Capt.; husb. of Charity) - d. 15 January 1867 Æ 41 y., 20 d.
STEWART
Albion[2] K. P. - d. 11 February 1852 Æ 27 y., 3 m., 9 d.

Notes:
[1]Both the 12 and 24 were clear in August 1996, but they were no longer present in March 2000 due to a break in the stone.
[2]Difficult to read. Only the *b*, *i*, and *n* of Albion could be made out. The name is clear in a photograph taken several years ago by Ray Robbins.

Seal Cove Cemetery

(Tremont - 5)

Location/directions. Along west side of Route 102 a short distance north of outlet of Seal Cove Pond. From the traffic light at the north end of Mount Desert Island, go straight ahead (south) onto Routes 102/198. In approximately 5.2 miles (and at the south end of the village of Somesville), turn right onto Pretty Marsh Road (Route 102). The cemetery is on the right in about 6.9–7.0 miles.

History. —

Notes. A low wire mesh fence with wood posts and a wrought iron gate encloses the cemetery. The lawn is well maintained, but some stones are leaning, laying on the ground, and/or partially buried.

Names and dates on gravestones and other markers. [23 May 1999]

ASHLEY
- Bernice (dau. of Roland B. and Caroline E.) - b. 1888; d. 1976
- Caroline E. (wife of Roland B.) - b. 1859; d. 1941
- Roland B. (husb. of Caroline E.) - b. 1852; d. 1945

ATCHERSON
- James R. - b. 25 August 1918; d. 11 July 1970

ATHERTON
- Benjamin (Deacon; husb. of Rachel) - d. 19 October 1884 Æ 92 y., 25 d.
- Rachel (wife of Deacon Benjamin) - [no dates]
- [Rachel A. - see FULLER]

BILLINGS
- Abby A. - b. 25 March 1855; d. 26 February 1857
- Fernando W. - b. 28 August 1860; d. 28 February 1861
- Hannah S. (DOW; wife of Stephen) - b. 21 December 1836; d. 25 July 1914
- [Harriet - see SWAIN]
- Ina May (dau. of Stephen and Hannah S. (DOW)) - d. 26 November 1873 Æ [8 or 6?][1] y., 5 m.
- Stephen (husb. of Hannah S. (DOW)) - b. 3 June 1833; d. 19 May 1909

BROWN
- [Mary Norton - see NORWOOD]
- Phebe C. (wife of William S. [no stone]) - d. 9 July 1886 Æ 30 y., 6 m.

BUTLER
- Emerline [wife of James M.?] - b. 1818; d. 1856
- Fred E. [husb. of Virgelia M.] - b. 1896; d. 1956
- James M. (husb. of [Emerline and?] Lucy J.) - b. 1815; d. 1878
- Lucy J. (wife of James M.) - b. 1833; d. 1915
- Virgelia M. [wife of Fred E.] - b. 1898; d. 1987
- William J. (son of James M. and Lucy J.) - b. 1857; d. 9 December 1879 Æ 22 y., 4 m., 7 d.

CARTER
- Ella (WALLS; [wife of Roland L.?]) - b. 1864; d. 1955
- Roland L. [husb. of Ella (WALLS)?] - b. 1879; d. 1953

CARY
- Calvin Judson (son of Rev. Calvin L. [no stone]) - d. 8 October 1834 Æ 2 y., 1 m.

COOMBS
- Alice B. (HARPER; dau. of Capt. Nehemiah A. HARPER and Sophronia D.) - b. 1867; d. 1956

CUNNINGHAM
Josiah [husb. of Martha R.] - b. 2 August 1812; d. March 1886
Martha R. [wife of Josiah] - b. 18 June 1798; d. 6 November 1884
DOW
[Hannah S. - see BILLINGS]
Mary S. [wife of Samuel?] - b. 16 January 1793; d. 21 November 1855
Samuel [husb. of Mary S.?] - b. 31 May 1788; d. 31 October 1861
FULLER
Charles C. (Esq.; husb. of Juli[a]ette[2] [no stone] and Rachel A. (ATHERTON)) - d. 10 October 1863, Tremont, Maine, Æ 41 y., 10 m., 26 d.; (member of Co. A, 28th Maine Regiment [Civil War])
Ella L. (WILBUR; wife of George Ripley) - b. 27 November 1870; d. 22 May 1963
Emma Everett (dau. of Esq. Charles C. and Juli[a]ett[2] [no stone]) - d. 22 August 1853 Æ 1 y., 4 m., 15 d.
George Ripley (husb. of Ella L. (WILBUR)) - b. 15 September 1857; d. 28 June 1937
infant (son of Esq. Charles C. and Juli[a]ette[2] [no stone]) - [b. and?] d. 30 December 1849
infant (dau. of Esq. Charles C. and Juli[a]ette[2] [no stone]) - [b. and?] d. 8 April 1852
Nellie C. (dau. of Esq. Charles C. and Rachel A. (ATHERTON)) - d. 12 September 1876 Æ 17 y., 7 m., 5 d.
Rachel A. (ATHERTON; wife of Esq. Charles C.) - b. 25 April 1828; d. 1 January 1891
GOODWIN
Frederic B. (son of Frederic B. and Allie B. [no stones]) - d. 28 October 1893 Æ 8 m., 20 d.
GOTT
Joseph - d. 20 December 1873 Æ 67 y., 4 m., 19 d.
Martha L. - b. 1 August 1816; d. 1 November 1890
HAMBRO
Joseph - d. 27 November 1937 Æ [not given]
HARPER
[Alice B. - see COOMBS]
Carroll E. (son of Seth A. Sr. and Sylvia M.) - b. 28 January 1930; d. 1 May 1944
Clyde H. Sr. - b. 1931; d. 1990
Dean L. [HARPER?] - b. 16 July 1960; d. 2 August 1960
infant (son of Capt. Nehemiah A. and Sophronia D.) - d. 5 September 1880 Æ 1[6?][1] [d.?][1]
J. William (husb. of Minnie A.) - b. 1871; d. 1956
James W. - b. 1927; d. 1980
Julia K. [wife of Julian Y.] - b. 1907; d. 1988
Julian Y. [husb. of Julia K.] - b. 1898; d. 1970
Minnie A. (wife of J. William) - b. 1870; d. 1951
Nehemiah A. (Capt.; husb. of Sophronia D.) - b. 1834; d. 1897
Seth A. Sr. (husb. of Sylvia M.) - b. 1894; d. 1977
Sophronia D. (wife of Capt. Nehemiah A.) - b. 1839; d. 1917
Sylvia M. (wife of Seth A. Sr.) - b. 1896; d. 1986
William M. (son of Seth A. Sr. and Sylvia M.) - [b. and?] d. 9 August 1926
HEATH
Louisa (dau. of Esq. William [no stone]) - d. 28 August 1819 Æ 14 y.
Sally (wife of Thomas) - d. 24 September 1825 Æ 40 y.
Thomas (husb. of Sally) - d. 31 August 1845 Æ 60 y.

HENDERSON
Marguerite A. - b. 28 May 1922; d. 9 January 1970
HODGDON
Bernice L. (dau. of Frank L. and Idella J.) - b. 1891; d. 1899
Edgar W. (son of George S. and Lillie B.) - b. 26 March 1893; d. 3 January 1912
Frances E. (wife of Leroy R.) - b. 1860; d. 1932
Frank A. (Dr.) - b. 1892; d. 1964
Frank L. (husb. of Idella J.) - b. 1869; d. 1941
Fred E. [husb. of Gladys L.] - b. 1892; d. 1966
George S. (husb. of Lillie B.) - b. 6 April 1871; d. 10 May 1905
Gladys L. [wife of Fred E.] - b. 1891; d. 1978
Idella J. (wife of Frank L.) - b. 1873; d. 1940
John F. (Capt.; husb. of Myra F.) - b. 1 January 1843; d. 13 November 1897
Kendal [sic] Kittredge - b. 8 August 1824; d. 8 October 1902
Leroy R. (husb. of Frances E.) - b. 1849; d. 1926
Lillie B. (wife of George S.) - d. 31 July 1899 Æ 27 y., 6 m.
Mary A. (wife of Gilbert H. [no stone]) - b. 5 August 1848; d. 21 January 1895
[Maud - see LANGSTROTH]
Myra F. (wife of Capt. John F.) - b. 9 September 1847; d. 28 December 1936
Ruth W. - b. 1917; d. 1960
LANGSTROTH
Maud (HODGDON; wife of Walter) - b. 1867; d. 1943
Walter (husb. of Maud (HODGDON)) - b. 1866; d. 1945
LATTY [includes LATTEY]
Frank - b. 1878; d. 1943
John G. (husb. of Mercie B.) - d. 13 June 1901 Æ 94 y., 10 m., 21 d.
John T. - d. 26 February 1865 Æ 24 y., 8 m.
Mercie B. (wife of John G.) - d. 4 May 1881 Æ 73 y., 4 m., 26 d.
Mercy M. "Mert" (wife of Richmond L.) - d. 22 March 1903 Æ 52 y.
Riche [sic] (son of Richmond L. and Mercy M. "Mert") - d. 1 January 1899 Æ 5 y., 21 d.
Richmond L. (husb. of Mercy M. "Mert") - d. 19 August 1930 Æ 82 y., 7 m., 15 d.
MATHEW [sic]
Mary L. (wife of Charles [no stone]) - d. 4 March 1871 Æ 27 y., 13 d.
MURPHY
Josie H. (wife of David N. [no stone]) - b. 28 March 1875; d. 30 November 1895
Myrtle I. (dau. of David N. [no stone] and Josie H.) - b. 4 July 1895; d. 19 January 1897
NORWOOD
Ida M. (wife of Capt. Willard S.) - b. 1857; d. 1941
[Lizzie[4] - see SAWYER]
Mary Norton (BROWN; wife of Oliver M.) - d. 22 February 1900 Æ 86 y., 5 m.
Oliver M. (husb. of Mary Norton (BROWN)) - d. 5 February 1879 Æ 66 y.
Shubel D. (son of Oliver M. and Mary Norton (BROWN)) - "lost at sea" 11 June 1857 Æ 16 y., 11 m., 15 d.
Willard S. (Capt.; husb. of Ida M.) - b. 1844; d. 1911
Wood W. [1st husb. of Lizzie?] - d. 1 March 1896 Æ 44 y., 4 m., 19 d.
OBER
Albert L. - b. 1864; d. 1933
Eliza (Mrs.) - d. 14 March 1825 Æ 33 y., 1 m., 5 d.
Isaac M. (Capt.) - "lost at sea" December 1853 Æ 45 y.; ("lost at sea in the gale of Dec. 1853")

John E. [son of Joseph W. and Martha J.] - b. 1866; d. 1925
Joseph W. [husb. of Martha J.] - b. 1836; d. 1905
Leslie C. - b. 1845; d. 1928
Martha J. [wife of Joseph W.] - b. 1839; d. 1921
Zeruiah - b. 1816; d. 1880

PIERCE
Dellie L. (wife of Rev. E. Nelson [no stone]) - d. 12 December 1888 Æ 26 y., 10 m.
Eliza M. (wife of George M. [no stone]) - d. 28 September 1859 Æ 44 y., 3 m.

POWERS
Angeline S. (wife of Capt. James Studley) - b. 1834; d. 1931
James Studley (Capt.; husb. of Angeline S.) - b. 1835; d. 1907

REED
Elmer Jesse Sr. (husb. of Sadie A.) - b. 21 June 1907; d. 13 December 1992
Sadie A. (wife of Elmer Jesse Sr.) - b. 1920; d. 1974

ROBBINS
Lucy E. (wife of Charles Jr. [no stone]) - d. 14 December 1873 Æ 20 y., 6 m., 20 d.
Sherman W. - b. 3 June 1883; d. 21 April 1924
Sidney B. - b. 1904; d. 1957

RUMILL
Arthur H. (husb. of Lelia A.) - b. 1883; d. 1948
Basil G. (son of Capt. Joseph H. and Eliza A.) - d. 30 January 1896 Æ 1 y., 4 m., 7 d.
Eliza A. (wife of Capt. Joseph H.) - b. 1857; d. 1919
Joseph H. (Capt.; husb. of Eliza A.) - b. 1855; d. 1924
Lelia A. (wife of Arthur H.) - b. 1883; d. 1967
Madalene [sic] B. ("infant" dau. of Arthur H. and Lelia A.) - [no dates]

SAWYER
Abigail M. (wife of Joshua) - d. 2 May 1862 Æ 74 y.
Benjamin (husb. of Charlotte F. D.) - b. 1817; d. 1892
Caleb H. (husb. of Clara D.) - b. 1828; d. 1902
Charles R. - b. 1861; d. 1943
Charlotte F. D. (wife of Benjamin) - b. 1828; d. 1890
Clara D. (wife of Caleb H.) - b. 1832; d. 1919
Clara D. (dau. of Benjamin and Charlotte F. D.) - d. 11 October 1881 Æ 23 y., 8 m., 11 d.
Eben P. - b. 1865; d. 1938
Emily J. (dau. of Benjamin and Charlotte F. D.) - b. 1861; d. 1922
Eva L. - b. 1863; d. 1888
Herbert L. - b. 1870; d. 1952
Joshua (husb. of Abigail M.) - d. 7 May 1869 Æ 84 y., 5 m., 12 d.
Joshua Jr. (son of Joshua and Abigail M.) - d. 8 January 1831 Æ 20 y., 10 m.
Lizzie[4] - b. 1858; d. 1939
Richard M. - b. 1903; d. 1941
Willard (son of Joshua and Abigail M.) - d. 7 August 1842 Æ 22 y.; ("was drowned by falling from ship Chili off Valparaiso")
William E. (son of Benjamin and Charlotte F. D.) - b. 1866; d. 1906; bur. "at sea"

SPRAGUE
Josephine (wife of Eugene H. [no stone]) - b. 1880; d. 1954

STANLEY
Avild[i]a[2] B. (wife of John B.) - d. 8 January 1891 Æ 60 y., 9 m.
Bowen - b. 8 November 1862; d. 4 March 1934
Elmer B. (husb. of Josie B.) - b. 1864; d. 1944

Isaac - d. 9 November 1903 Æ 43 y., 11 m.
John B. (husb. of Avild[i]a[2] B.) - d. 31 January 1893 Æ 64 y., 11 m.
John L. - b. 27 November 1855; d. 27 November 1898
Josie B. (wife of Elmer B.) - b. 1872; d. 1936
M. Elva - b. 22 August 1855; d. 8 December 1945
Martha E. [dau. of John B. and Avild[i]a[2] B.] - d. 31 May 1853 Æ 2 y., 3 m.

STICKNEY
Rodney E. (son of Frank E. and Grace M. [no stones]) - d. 27 December 1892 Æ 17 y., 5 m., 27 d.

SWAIN
Harriet (BILLINGS) - b. 1809; d. 1879

SWAZEY [includes SWASEY]
Dana R. Sr. - b. 21 January 1895; d. 30 November 1959
Annie J. (YOUNG; wife of Edwin V. [no stone]) - b. 1874; d. 1928
Jessie Mae [SWAZEY?] - b. 1877; d. 1948
Joseph B. - b. 27 May 1925; d. 14 October 1944
Joseph E. [husb. of Sarah L.] - b. 1843; d. 1925
Lillian A. (dau. of Joseph and Almira [no stones]) - d. 25 August 1895 Æ 19 y., 6 m., 17 d.
Olive M. - b. 1903; d. 1985
Sarah L. [wife of Joseph E.] - b. 1862; d. 1935
[...] [headstone only]

TAYLOR
Gladys - b. 1899; d. 1968

TINKER
Abby S. (dau. of William L. and Amanda B. [no stones]) - d. 21 April 1856 Æ 6 d.
Amanda (dau. of William L. and Amanda B. [no stones]) - d. 10 September 1857 Æ 3 m.
Edward S. (son of William L. and Amanda B. [no stones]) - d. 15 May 1858 Æ 5 w.
infant (dau. of William L. and Amanda B. [no stones]) - d. 15 June 1858 Æ [not given]
Leonora M. (dau. of William L. and Amanda B. [no stones]) - d. 21 November 1857 Æ 10 y., 7 m., 15 d.
Willie (son of William L. and Amanda B. [no stones]) - d. 21 April 1858 Æ 6 y., 9 m.

WADE
Benjamin L. (husb. of Nellie M.) - d. 5 May 1874 Æ 26 y., 20 d.
Nellie M. (wife of Benjamin L.) - d. 4 October 1872 Æ 21 y., 8 m.

WALLS
Chester F. - b. 1881; d. 1907
[Ella - see CARTER]
Etta H. (wife of Wills D.) - b. 1863; d. 1934
infant (son of [not given]) - [b. and d.?] 1896
Jacob B. (husb. of Sophronia D.) - b. 1822; d. 1902
James M. - b. 1857; d. 1902
John (Capt.; husb. of Mary A. [no stone]) - d. 1 December 1893 Æ 68 y.
John W. (son of Capt. John and Mary A. [no stone]) - d. 11 July 1891 Æ 26 y.
Rose (wife of Watson) - b. 12 May 1854; d. 29 July 1940
Sophronia D. (wife of Jacob B.) - b. 1828; d. 1898
Watson (husb. of Rose) - b. 26 August 1851; d. 3 June 1924
Wills D. (son of Jacob B. and Sophronia D.; husb. of Etta H.) - b. 1851; d. 1919

WILBUR
    [Ella L. - see FULLER]
YOUNG
    [Annie J. - see SWAZEY]
[...]
    Ralph - b. 1913; d. 1957
    [...][1]
    [...][3]
    [...][3]

Notes:
    [1]Stone worn and/or broken.
    [2]Different on different stones.
    [3]Base of stone only.
    [4]Lizzie SAWYER's name is on the same gravestone as Wood W. NORWOOD's.

Flye Cemetery
(Tremont - 6)

Location/directions. East of Route 102 and south of outlet of Seal Cove Pond. From the traffic light at the north end of Mount Desert Island, go straight ahead (south) onto Routes 102/198. In approximately 5.2 miles (and at the south end of the village of Somesville), turn right onto Pretty Marsh Road (Route 102). Travel about 7.3–7.4 miles to the first drive on the left after the bridge. Take the left fork, and watch on the right for a mowed path that leads to the cemetery.

History. This cemetery is on land that was part of lot #18, a 95 acre parcel, on the 1808 Salem Towne Jr. map.

Notes. A white, wood fence encloses the cemetery. The grass is well maintained, but several stones are laying on the ground.

Names and dates on gravestones and other markers. [23 May 1999]

FLYE
- Athalaney (dau. of James and Hannah [no stones]) - d. 8 April 1834 Æ 18 y., 4 m.
- [Eldora R. - see OBER]
- Eliza S. (wife of Hiram) - b. 8 October 1820; d. 13 June 1900
- [Hannah G. - see HEATH]
- Hiram (husb. of Eliza S.) - b. 20 October 1811; d. 29 March 1892
- infant (dau. of Hiram and Eliza S.) - d. 19 March 1840 Æ [not given]
- James (Capt.) - d. 1 March 1825 Æ 18 y.
- Joseph M. - d. 14 June 1875 Æ 25 y.
- Lucinda F. (dau. of Hiram and Eliza S.) - d. 9 July 1854 Æ 10 y., 4 m., 24 d.
- Vondel J. - b. 6 July 1862; d. 28 February 1925

HEATH
- Adelle F. - b. 5 September 1872; d. 18 August 1909
- H. F. ("our mother") - d. 29 March 1871 Æ 86 y., 3 m.
- Hannah G. (FLYE; wife of Joinville A.) - b. 13 October 1848; d. 8 November 1918
- Joinville A. (husb. of Hannah G. (FLYE)) - d. 31 January 1872 Æ 28 y.

OBER
- Albert E. (Capt.; husb. of Eldora R. (FLYE)) - d. 17 December 1874; bur. "at sea"
- Eldora R. (FLYE; dau. of Hiram FLYE and Eliza S.; wife of Capt. Albert E.) - d. 8 October 1872 Æ 27 y., 12 d.
- infant [child of Julius H. and Maud S.] - [b. and d.?] 17 October 1891
- Julius H. (husb. of Maud S.) - b. 11 October 1869; d. 30 December 1915
- Maud S. (wife of Julius H.) - b. 15 July 1872; d. 2 May 1898

REED
- Athalany F. (dau. of Capt. Ezra D. and Lorenia F.) - d. April 1837 Æ 3 y., 9 m.
- Ezra D. (Capt.; husb. of Lorenia F.) - d. 24 May 1897 Æ 89 y., 10 m., 7 d.
- Lorenia F. (wife of Capt. Ezra D.) - d. 3 June 1883 Æ 69 y., 8 m.
- S. M. - [no dates]; (member of Co. H, 16th Maine Regiment [Civil War])

SPRAGUE
- Eugene H. [SPRAGUE?] - "lost at sea" 30 March 1903 Æ 28 y.
- Inez F. (dau. of Capt. Lemuel R. and Nancy M.) - d. 9 October 1872 Æ [single digit; stone broken] y., 5 m., 9 d.
- Lemuel R. (Capt.; husb. of Nancy M.) - d. 20 March 1915 Æ 82 y.
- Nancy M. (wife of Capt. Lemuel R.) - d. 5 January 1908 Æ 71 y., 8 m.
- Udolph [sic] M. (son of Capt. Lemuel R. and Nancy M.) - d. 18 December 1891 Æ 20 y.

Kelley Cemetery

(Tremont - 7)

Location/directions. Along north side of Seal Cove Road. From the traffic light at the north end of Mount Desert Island, go straight ahead (south) onto Routes 102/198. In approximately 5.2 miles (and at the south end of the village of Somesville), turn right onto Pretty Marsh Road (Route 102). Travel on Route 102 about 7.5–7.6 miles, and turn left onto Seal Cove Road. The cemetery is on the left in approximately 0.8 miles.

History. This cemetery is on land that is now part of Acadia National Park.

Notes. There is no fence, and no boundary markers are evident.

Names and dates on gravestones and other markers. [23 May 1999]

FARLEY
- infant (son of E. and T. [no stones]) - [b. and d.?] 1930
- Loring E. - d. 9 April 1896 Æ 38 y.
- Stanley Alden - [b. and d.?] 19 December 1937

HIGGINS
- Jennie - b. 1900; d. 1924

KELLEY [includes KELLAY]
- Anna (wife of James) - d. 8 April 1870 Æ 89 y., 9 m.
- Annie R. (wife of George M. [no stone]) - d. 8 June 1891 Æ 44 y., 5 m., 8 d.
- Dorcas F. (wife of James) - b. 1819; d. 1898
- G. - b. 26 February 1881; d. 15 June 1963
- George W. [son of James and Dorcas F.] - b. 1843; d. 1866
- Ina Rose - b. 1900; d. 1904
- James (husb. of Dorcas F.) - b. 1815; d. 1894
- James (husb. of Anna) - d. 27 August 1859 Æ [6 or 7?]3[1] y., 10 m.
- John W. (Capt.; husb. of Mary L. [no stone]) - "lost at sea" 17 December 1874 Æ 34 y., 4 m., 10 d.
- Mehitable [sic] N. (wife of George M. [no stone]) - d. 13 May 1850 Æ 30 y., 2 m., 26 d.
- Orville C. [son of James and Dorcas F.] - b. 1850; d. 1878
- Phebe M. (wife of Nahum B. [no stone]) - d. 30 January 1892 Æ 38 y., 8 m.
- Ray C. (son of Capt. John W. and Mary L. [no stone]) - d. 7 August 1876 Æ 6 y., 8 m., 27 d.
- Sarah A. (wife of George M. [no stone]) - d. 18 April 1879 Æ 43 y., 8 m., 7 d.
- Thomas A. [son of James and Dorcas F.] - b. 1853; d. 1879

Note:

[1]Both a 6 and a 7 are engraved in the ten's place.

Tinker-Pomroy Cemetery
(Tremont - 8)

Location/directions. East of Dix Point Road. From the traffic light at the north end of Mount Desert Island, go straight ahead (south) onto Routes 102/198. In approximately 5.2 miles (and at the south end of the village of Somesville), turn right onto Pretty Marsh Road (Route 102). Travel on Route 102 about 9.0–9.1 miles and in a sharp curve to the left, turn right onto Dix Point Road. In approximately 0.3–0.4 miles on the left, just over the crest of a hill, is a drive that leads by the entrance (on the left) to the cemetery.

History. This cemetery is on land that was part of lot #20, a 58 acre parcel, on the 1808 Salem Towne Jr. map.

Notes. This cemetery is not enclosed and no boundary markers are evident, although there appears to have been a recent (1999?) survey of an abutting parcel. The grass is mowed and trimmed. Most of the old stones are leaning or laying on the ground.

Names and dates on gravestones and other markers. [25 March 2000]

EATON
- infant (dau. of Francis M. and Laura M.) - [no dates]
- infant (son of Francis M. and Laura M.) - [no dates]
- Francis M. (husb. of Laura M.) - b. 10 January 1856; d. 14 March 1928
- Laura M. (wife of Francis M.) - b. 4 February 1855; d. 1 November 1907

FOX
- John Large [husb. of Mary Anna] - b. 14 February 1908; [m. 26 February 1973?]
- Mary Anna [wife of John Large] - b. 15 September 1910; [m. 26 February 1973?]

GOODWIN
- Burdell M. - b. 1897; d. 1984
- H. Donald Sr. - b. 30 July 1931; d. 15 December 1979
- Harvey - [no dates][1]
- Henry - [no dates][1]
- Henry A. - b. 1877; d. 1944
- John - [no dates][1]
- Richard C. [husb. of Ruth M.] - b. 1922; d. 1999
- Roy Irving III - b. 4 February 1980; d. 6 February 1980
- Ruth M. [wife of Richard C.] - b. 1919; d. 1988

GOTT
- Elmer E. - b. 1862; d. 1899
- Harry H. - b. 1890; d. 1909

JONES
- Barbara A. (NORCROSS; dau. of Theo M. NORCROSS) - b. 4 June 1937; d. 27 August 1984

KERN
- Charles Lewis - b. 1 October 1969; d. 14 August 1997

MARSHALL
- Edwin L. (husb. of Lettie F.) - b. 3 March 1871; d. 22 January 1969
- Lettie F. (wife of Edwin L.) - b. 9 September 1874; d. 5 December 1968

MILLER
- Hannah M. (dau. of William A. and Sarah J. [no stone]) - d. 14 January 1852 Æ 7 m.
- William A. (husb. of Sarah J. [no stone]) - d. 9 December 1854 Æ 33 y.

MITCHELL
- Charles B. (husb. of Nancy A.) - b. 1857; d. 1927

Lettie H. (dau. of Charles B. and Nancy A.) - b. 5 September 1895; d. 14 November 1910
Nancy A. (wife of Charles B.) - b. 1859; d. 1937

NORCROSS
[Barbara A. - see JONES]
Theo M. - b. 28 March 1905; d. 19 December 1982

POMROY
Abner (Capt.; husb. of Caroline) - b. 10 December 1820; d. 25 May 1906
Alton A. [husb. of Cretia S.] - b. 12 August 1868; d. 10 February 1921
Caroline (wife of Capt. Abner) - b. 9 May 1835; d. 26 July 1902
Clinton D. [POMROY?] (husb. of Ruth B.) - b. 1904; d. 1962
Cretia S. [wife of Alton A.] - b. 7 March 1873; d. 28 July 1957
David Abner - b. 14 July 1912; d. 22 December 1954
infant (child of John W. and Lissie M.) - [b. and?] d. 13 September 1908
John G. (son of John W. and Lissie M.) - d. 17 September 1900 Æ 1 y., 1 m.
John L. (son of John W. and Lissie M.) - d. 1888 Æ 3 m.
John W. (husb. of Lissie M.) - b. 1856; d. 1935
Lissie M. (wife of John W.) - b. 1864; d. 1927
Michael W. - b. 1955; d. 1955
Nettie M. (STAPLES) - b. 28 June 1885; d. 20 October 1926
Pansy P. (dau. of John W. and Lissie M.) - d. 1891 Æ 10 m.
Rodney A. (son of John W. and Lissie M.) - d. 12 September 1905 Æ 1 y., 1 m., 6 d.
Ronald O. - b. 1930; d. 1955
Ruth B. (wife of Clinton D. [POMROY?]) - b. 1910; d. 1980

STAPLES
[Nettie M. - see POMROY]

TINKER
Abbie (wife of Capt. George B.) - d. 20 January 1892 Æ 62 y., 5 m.
[Elerson or Ellison][4] D. (son of Capt. George B. and Abbie) - d. 10 February 1878 Æ 2 m.
Elizabeth D. - b. 13 November 1813; d. 6 October 1910
George B. (Capt.; husb. of Abbie) - d. 30 October 1893 Æ 66 y., 5 m., 12 d.
George G. - b. 18 December 1860; d. 5 June 1913
Hannah Margaret (Miss) - b. 7 July 1830; d. 3 April 1850
Harriet M.[2] (wife of Capt. James) - d. 7 January 1882 Æ 63 y., 4 m., 27 d.
infant (son of William and Ann [no stones]) - [b. and?] d. 6 March 1850
James (son of Capt. J. and S. A. [no stones]) - d. 15 November 1882 Æ 6 m., 23 d.
James[2] (Capt.; husb. of Harriet M.) - d. 23 April 1893 Æ 72 y.
James (Capt.; husb. of Sally) - d. 23 April 1851 Æ 70 y., 3 m., 16 d.
James Jr. (Capt.; son of Capt. James) - "lost at sea" 23 January 1882 Æ 29 y., 3 m., 2 d.
Saddie [sic] A. (dau. of Capt. George B. and Abbie) - d. 4 May 1885 Æ 29 y., 11 m., 24 d.
Sally (wife of Capt. James) - d. 21 April 1888 Æ 101 y., 2 m., 28 d.
William D. (Capt.) - "lost at sea" 4 August 1854 Æ 39 y.; ("whose vessel was run down and sunk by Steamer Governor"[3])
Willie M. - d. 9 December 1896 Æ 15 y., 2 m.

WENTWORTH
Katherine (dau. of A. R. and C. L. [no stones]) - b. 8 May 1928; d. 28 June 1963
Millicent S. (dau. of A. R. and C. L. [no stones]) - b. 23 February 1929; d. 1 January 1931

Rosemary (dau. of A. R. and C. L. [no stones]) - b. 10 November 1934; d. 27 October 1935

Notes:

[1]Henry, Harvey, and John GOODWIN share a single stone bearing their names and the words "babies" and "together again".

[2]Stones of both Capt. James TINKER and his wife, Harriet M., are broken and have been repaired. The repair of his stone was unsuccessful, and its top leans (2000) against a tree near the grave.

[3]If there is any further information on this stone, it is below ground.

[4]Different on different stones.

Hillrest Cemetery
(Tremont - 9)

Location/directions. Along south side of Route 102 and north side of Clark Point Road. From the traffic light at the north end of Mount Desert Island, go straight ahead (south) onto Routes 102/198. In approximately 5.2 miles (and at the south end of the village of Somesville), turn right onto Pretty Marsh Road (Route 102). The cemetery is on the right in about 9.5–9.6 miles, at the corner of Route 102 and Clark Point Road.

History. This cemetery is on land that was part of lot #23, a 200 acre parcel, on the 1808 Salem Towne Jr. map.

Notes. This cemetery is enclosed by a chain-link fence. The lawn is mowed and clipped, and other maintenance (*e.g.*, cutting down shrubs and filling uneven places with dirt) is evident.

Names and dates on gravestones and other markers. [6 September 1999]
AUSTIN
Clarence I. [husb. of Edith H.] - b. 16 June 1870; d. 4 August 1956
Edith H. [wife of Clarence I.] - b. 5 October 1879; d. 19 December 1952
B.
W. A. [footstone only]
BARBOUR
Sarah H. (wife of Thomas F.) - b. 4 September 1890; d. 28 October 1989
Thomas F. (husb. of Sarah H.) - b. 4 January 1874; d. 9 May 1944
BARTLETT
Leita M. (wife of Reginal [sic] L.) - b. 1912; d. 1975
Reginal [sic] L. (husb. of Leita M.) - b. 1907
BEERS
Bernice H. - b. 4 July 1905; d. 2 April 1991
Karen [BEERS?] - b. 10 February 1956; d. 21 June 1991
BERGERON
Joseph C. (husb. of Sadie M. (JOYCE)) - b. 18 October 1893; d. 8 April 1933
Joseph H. (son of Joseph C. and Sadie M. (JOYCE)) - b. 1926; d. 1948
Sadie M. (JOYCE; wife of Joseph C.) - b. 10 June 1895; d. 6 April 1976
BILLINGS
Caynell B. [wife of Elmer E.] - b. 1910; d. 1982
Elmer E. [husb. of Caynell B.] - b. 1909; d. 1992
BLACK
Bessie E. (wife of Everett J.) - b. 1899; d. 1984
David C. Jr. - b. 28 February 1971; d. 11 June 1987
Everett J. (husb. of Bessie E.) - b. 1893; d. 1936
BRAGG
Cora E. (wife of Oscar L.) - b. 1874; d. 1956
Herbert I. [husb. of Marjorie L.] - b. 1903; d. 1990
Marjorie L. [wife of Herbert I.] - b. 1903; d. 1991
Oscar L. (husb. of Cora E.) - b. 1868; d. 1949
BRANSCOM
Nan M. (wife of Capt. Charles E. [no stone]) - b. 13 February 1855; d. 4 November 1895
BREWER
Eugene B. (husb. of Julia F.) - b. 1871; d. 1939

Julia F. (wife of Eugene B.) - b. 1875; d. 1950
BRIDGES
Arabella [wife of Fred E.] - b. 1866; d. 1940
Fred E. [husb. of Arabella] - b. 1862; d. 1940
BROMLEY
Muriel (LUNT) - b. 1896; d. 1948
BROWN
Eleanor (WALLS; [wife of Eugene K.]) - b. 1930
Eugene K. [husb. of Eleanor (WALLS)] - b. 1926
BUTLER
Martha A. (wife of Charles [no stone]) - d. 15 December 1852 Æ 18 y., 2 m.
CARTER
[Susie M. - see LUNT]
CARVER
[Sylvia - see MANN]
CLANCY
Mildred E. - b. 23 July 1864; d. 23 June 1910
CLARK
George E. (son of James T. and Melinda R. [no stones]) - d. 29 January 1861 Æ 4 y., 10 m., 23 d.
Nancy C. (LOPAUS; wife of David [no stone][2]) - d. 17 October 1851 Æ 52 y.
William A. (husb. of Zulma S.) - d. 28 October 1889 Æ 56 y.
Zullie M. (dau. of William A. and Zulma S.) - d. 21 March 1864 Æ 9 m., 22 d.
Zulma S. (wife of William A.) - b. 28 October 1833; d. 20 February 1913
CLOSSON
Doris I. (wife of Everett N.) - b. 1903; d. 1980
Everett N. (husb. of Doris I.) - b. 1904; d. 1971
COLBETH
Arthur E. [husb. of Dorothy A.] - b. 1929
Dorothy A. [wife of Arthur E.] - b. 1933; d. 1985
COLE
Alberta H. [wife of Oscar E.] - b. 23 April 1927
Oscar E. [husb. of Alberta H.] - b. 19 May 1924; d. 20 February 1999
COLSON
Fred H. - b. 1905; d. 1976
George N. Jr. (son of G. N. and F. M. [no stones]) - b. 1916; d. 1927
CROCKETT
Herbert W. Sr. [husb. of Phyllis (FARLEY)] - b. 1906; d. 1980
Phyllis (FARLEY; [wife of Herbert W. Sr.]) - b. 1926
DAIGLE
Ruby H. - b. 5 March 1931; d. 24 February 1990
Steven A. Sr. - b. 24 March 1954; d. 8 September 1992
DAVIS
Edwin M. Sr. - b. 14 January 1925; d. 19 July 1998
Ethel M. (wife of Fred M.) - b. 1900; d. 1961
Fred M. (husb. of Ethel M.) - b. 1894; d. 1961
Lulu Mae (dau. of Fred M. and Ethel M.) - b. 8 January 1917; d. 24 January 1917
DAWES
[Margaret - see MURPHY]
DICKENS
Eva M. - b. 1901; d. 1938
infant (dau. of William S. and Katie L.) - b. [and d.?] 11 May 1894

Katie L. (wife of William S.) - b. 1 February 1862; d. 11 January 1902 Æ 39 y., 11 m., 10 d.
[Rhoda C. - see HARKINS]
Silas B. (son of William S. and Katie L.) - b. 15 May 1891; d. 20 May 1891 Æ 5 d.
William S. (husb. of Katie L.) - b. 7 May 1853; d. [no date]

DIX
Alice V. (wife of Capt. William) - d. 4 August 1899 Æ 55 y., 3 m., 25 d.
Apphia (wife of Capt. Jonathan T.) - d. 26 December 1850 Æ 50 y.
Christopher B. (Capt.; husb. of Eliza A.) - d. 15 August 1904 Æ 76 y., 10 m., 5 d.
Colin N. [son of Hiram A. and Emily J.?] - b. 1 November 1867; d. 24 October 1897
Eliza A. (wife of Capt. Christopher B.) - d. 23 March 1900 Æ 62 y., 4 m., 18 d.
Elmar [sic] C. (son of Capt. Christopher B. and Eliza A.) - d. 6 April 1876 Æ 15 m.
Emily J. (wife of Hiram A.) - b. 15 January 1834; d. 10 June 1905
Ernest L. - "lost at sea" 26 May 1903 Æ 33 y., 11 d.
Frederick W. (son of Capt. William and Sarah J.) - d. 2 October 1886, "at sea", Æ 25 y., 11 m., 12 d.
George[3] (Capt.; husb. of Sally and Julia M.) - d. 16 December 1894 Æ 86 y., 6 m.
George R. (son of Reuben and Judith S.) - b. 1856; d. 1877, "at sea"
Hannah A. [dau. of Reuben and Judith S.] - b. 1863; d. 1865
Hiram A. (husb. of Emily J.) - b. 30 September 1832; d. 16 August 1917
infant (son of Capt. Christopher B. and Eliza A.) - b. [and d.?] 29 May 1869
infant (son of Capt. Christopher B. and Eliza A.) - d. 6 January 1872 Æ 3 w.
Iona Jane (dau. of Reuben and Judith S.) - b. 1860; d. 20 June 1864 Æ 4 y., 20 d.
Jonathan T. (Capt.; husb. of Apphia) - d. 6 October 1885 Æ 89 y.
Judith S. (wife of Reuben) - b. 1832; d. 1905
Julia M. (wife of Capt. George) - d. 4 January 1884 Æ 52 y., 10 m., 24 d.
Maria (LUNT; wife of Capt. Robert B.) - b. 1839; d. 1924
Maria L. (dau. of Capt. William and Sarah J.) - d. 20 October 1859 Æ 2 y., 2 m., 2 d.
Mary A. [dau. of Reuben and Judith S.] - b. 1858; d. 1917
Mary J. - b. 18 August 1845; d. 4 March 1909
Myra F. (dau. of Capt. William and Sarah J.) - d. 23 January 1869 Æ 5 w., 3 d.
Orie E. (child of Capt. Christopher B. and Eliza A.) - d. 4 August 1870 Æ 1 m., 15 d.
Reuben (husb. of Judith S.) - b. 1830; d. 1915
Robert B. (Capt.; husb. of Maria (LUNT)) - d. 7 April 1901 Æ 63 y., 4 m.
Sally[3] (wife of Capt. George) - d. 9 April 1855 Æ 42 y.
[Sarah - see EYE]
Sarah J. (wife of Capt. William) - d. 5 June 1879 Æ 42 y., 9 m., 13 d.
Stilman [sic] (son of Capt. George and Sally) - d. 24 May 1838 Æ 4 m.
Valdor M. (son of Capt. Robert B. and Maria (LUNT)) - d. 17 January 1878 Æ 2 y., 1 m., 7 d.
Vandalia T. (dau. of Hiram A. and Emily J.) - d. 1 January 1866 Æ 6 y., 9 m., 27 d.
William (Capt.; husb. of Sarah J. and Alice V.) - b. 1826; d. 1910

DOW
Clara J. - b. 1937; d. 1982
Daniel M. [husb. of Martha Jane] - b. 15 August 1857; d. 19 March 1922
Martha Jane [wife of Daniel M.] - b. 29 May 1863; d. 14 March 1945
[Polly - see WENTWORTH]

EATON
Eva M. (wife of Roy F.) - b. 1890; d. [no date]
Roy F. (husb. of Eva M.) - b. 1890; d. 1947

ELDRIDGE
Frank W. (husb. of Jennie B.) - b. 1913
Jennie B. (wife of Frank W.) - b. 1913; d. 1999
Kathleen E. (dau. of Frank W. and Jennie B.) - b. 1947; d. 1949
ENNIS
Marilyn (JOYCE) - b. 23 May 1926; d. 27 November 1990
EVERBECK
Leroy P. [husb. of Virginia A.] - b. 1923
Richard C. [son of Leroy P. and Virginia A.?] - b. 1942; d. 1997
Virginia A. [wife of Leroy P.] - b. 1923
EYE
Eugene D. - b. 1875; d. 1952
[Mary - see MELCHER]
Sarah (DIX) - b. 1849; d. 1947
FARLEY
Eva M. (wife of Giles H. [no stone]) - b. 13 February 1880; d. 3 March 1903
Evelyn L. [wife of Merle A.] - b. 1892; d. 1955
Floyd C. - b. 24 May 1915; d. 6 June 1990
[Hilda - see WALKER]
Melvin L. - b. 1918; d. 1988
Merle A. [husb. of Evelyn L.] - b. 1891; d. 1964
[Phyllis - see CROCKETT]
Ronald A. - b. 1910; d. 1988
Ronald Jr. - b. 1945; d. 1950
FARRELL
Addie C. [wife of Albion H.] - b. 1873; d. 1948
Albion H. [husb. of Addie C.] - b. 1870; d. 1968
FERNALD
Flora A. (dau. of O. H. [no stone] and Hannah A.) - d. 3 April 1882 Æ 20 y., 8 m.
Hannah A. (wife of O. H. [no stone]) - d. 29 October 1864 Æ 28 y., 1 m., 16 d.
FINLAY
Henry - b. 1915
John F. - b. 23 June 1918; d. 24 March 1999 Æ 80 y.
Margaret - b. 1927
FUQUA
Madeline V. (GORDIUS; dau. of Calvin M. GORDIUS and Bessie E.) - b. 10 September 1916; d. 6 January 1998
GILLEY
Hannah W. (wife of Lewis W.) - b. 1846; d. 1923
infant (dau. of Lewis W. and Hannah W.) - b. 7 July 1866; d. [no date] Æ 7 w.
infant (dau. of Lewis W. and Hannah W.) - b. 24 May 1868; d. [no date] Æ 4 w.
Lewis W. (husb. of Hannah W.) - b. 1843; d. 1907
GORDIUS
Bessie E. (wife of Calvin M.) - b. 1894; d. 1922
Calvin M. (husb. of Bessie E.) - b. 1882; d. 1963
[Madeline V. - see FUQUA]
GOTT
Ambrose T. (husb. of Anna D. "Annie") - b. 1848; d. 1900
Anna D. "Annie" (wife of Ambrose T.) - b. 1850; d. 1921
C. Lewis (husb. of Margaret H.) - b. 1888; d. 1947
Charles A. - b. 1876; d. 1940

Lucy Leona (REED; wife of Benjamin J. [no stone]) - b. 16 July 1892; d. 10 January 1919
Margaret H. (wife of C. Lewis) - b. 1890; d. 1984
Rubie M. [son [sic] of Ambrose T. and Anna D. "Annie"] - d. 20 March 1870 Æ 18 m.

GRAHAM
Donald M. [husb. of Hazel H.] - b. 1919
Hazel H. [wife of Donald M.] - b. 1929
Kenneth B. - b. 25 January 1919; d. 8 November 1995
Ruth - b. 1916; d. 1997

GRAY
Clinton E. (husb. of Rena V.) - b. 1889; d. 1949
Rena V. (wife of Clinton E.) - b. 1884; d. 1967

HAMBLEN
Leslie E. [husb. of Wilda V.] - b. 1878; d. 1924
Wilda V. [wife of Leslie E.] - b. 1886; d. 1953

HAMOR
Rhoda A. - b. 31 July 1918; d. 24 October 1991

HANNA [includes HANNAH]
Abbie L. (wife of Capt. William) - b. 19 August 1840; d. 17 June 1904
Alvin A. [son of Capt. William and Abbie L.?] - b. 1861; d. 1946
Dora M. - b. 1865; d. 1941
William (Capt.; husb. of Abbie L.) - b. 1833; d. 1916

HARDY
Freddie H. (son of H. J. and E. [K. or R.?][9] [no stones]) - d. 27 January 1885 Æ 5 m.

HARKINS
infant [HARKINS?] - [b. and d.?] 1915
James E. Sr. - b. 1922; d. 1990
Rhoda C. (DICKENS; wife of Thomas) - b. 1888; d. 1968
Robert E. - b. 1908; d. 1971
Thomas (husb. of Rhoda C. (DICKENS)) - b. 1878, Scotland; d. 1950

HAWTHORN
Robert K. (husb. of Winifred B.) - b. 1881; d. [no date]
Winifred B. (wife of Robert K.) - b. 1899; d. 1935

HIGGINS
Benjamin E. - b. 21 March 1889; d. 7 January 1983
Helen H. (wife of Myron E.) - b. 1898; d. 1933
Myron E. (husb. of Helen H.) - b. 1899; d. 1969

HODGDON
Albert E. [husb. of Zulma N.] - b. 1900; d. 1997
Zulma N. [wife of Albert E.] - b. 1894; d. 1992

INGALLS
Austin H. (husb. of Beulah A.) - b. 1902
Beulah A. (wife of Austin H.) - b. 1904; d. 1945
[Constance - see ROBERTS]
George Frank - b. 1848; d. 1930
Nancy (LOPAUS) - b. 5 July 1853; d. 5 February 1899
Nellantonie (wife of Otis Henry) - b. 1883; d. 1959
Nettie (dau. of Otis Henry and Nellantonie) - b. 17 February 1909; d. 19 February 1909
Lettie (dau. of Otis Henry and Nellantonie) - b. 17 February 1909; d. 19 February 1909

Otis Henry (husb. of Nellantonie) - b. 27 June 1869; d. 17 February 1945

JOYCE

Carlton (son of Ernest C. and Helen B.) - b. 1925; d. 1928
Charles Henry - b. 26 November 1932; d. 24 September 1961
Delia V. [wife of Harry B.] - b. 1872; d. 1953
Ernest C. (husb. of Helen B.) - b. 1893; d. 1976
Harry B. [husb. of Delia V.] - b. 1870; d. 1949
Helen B. (wife of Ernest C.) - b. 1905; d. 1991
Lessie Emeline - b. 2 October 1902; d. 5 April 1994
[Marilyn - see ENNIS]
Myrtle I. (dau. of Ernest C. and Helen B.) - b. 1923; d. 1927
[Sadie M. - see BERGERON]

KANE

Gertrude L. (wife of Jason P.) - b. 1876; d. 1963
Jason P. (husb. of Gertrude L.) - b. 1867; d. 1934
Joseph P. [husb. of Laura J.] - b. 1902; d. 1993
Laura J. [wife of Joseph P.] - b. 1902; d. 1953[5]
Priscilla Jean - b. 1939; d. 1997

KELLEY

Eva L. (wife of James R.) - b. 1871; d. 1933
infant (child of James R. and Eva L.) - b. 1894; d. 1894
James R. (husb. of Eva L.) - b. 1867; d. 1945
Lucy J. [wife of Woodrow W.] - b. 1912; d. 1994
Vernon R. (son of James R. and Eva L.) - b. 1896; d. 1907
Winnie B. (dau. of James R. and Eva L.) - d. 1 December 1892 Æ 2 y., 9 m.
Woodrow W. [husb. of Lucy J.] - b. 1912; d. 1991

KIRKPATRICK

David E. [husb. of Martha D.] - b. 26 January 1923; d. 6 April 1995
Martha D. [wife of David E.] - b. 1919

KOFFER

Margaret - b. 1901; d. 1995

LAMBERT

[Hannah - see LOPAUS]

LARRABEE

Earl R. - [no dates]
Kattie [sic] L. - [no dates]
Ronald P. - [no dates]

LATTY [includes LATTEY]

Abra[ha]m[6] R. (husb. of Letitia B. (SPRAGUE)) - d. 18 March 1879 Æ 36 y., 6 m., 25 d.
Douglass [sic] (son of Vernon H. and Stella M.) - b. 1901; d. 1924
Flora M. (THURSTON; wife of Harry E.) - b. 1891; d. 1983
Harry E. (husb. of Flora M. (THURSTON)) - b. 1887; d. 1926
Jay (son of Vernon H. and Stella M.) - d. 17 June 1902 Æ 1 y., 17 d.
John T. (son of Abra[ha]m[6] and Letitia B. (SPRAGUE)) - d. 2 July 1870 Æ 2 y., 5 m., 24 d.
Letitia B. (SPRAGUE; wife of Abra[ha]m[6] R.) - b. 1843; d. 1943
Stella M. (wife of Vernon H.) - b. 1876; d. 1953
Vernon (son of Vernon H. and Stella M.) - b. 1906; d. 1921
Vernon (son of Douglass [sic] and Madolin [sic] [no stone]) - b. 1923; d. 1924
Vernon H. (husb. of Stella M.) - b. 1876; d. 1956
Woodbury H. - b. 1898; d. 1926

LAWSON
Carl C. Sr. [husb. of Daisy M.] - b. 1892; d. 1976
Daisy M. [wife of Carl C. Sr.] - b. 1896; d. 1986
Dora M. (wife of Harold G.) - b. 1888; d. 1948
Dorothea E. - b. 1920; d. 1994
Edwin W. [husb. of Elsie L.] - b. 1899; d. 1994
Elsie L. [wife of Edwin W.] - b. 1901; d. 1993
Gardner [son of Harold G. and Dora M.?] - b. 1909; d. 1995
George G. (husb. of Wilhemean) - b. 1859; d. 1933
Harold G. (husb. of Dora M.) - b. 1887; d. 1945
infant (son of Perry L. and Vera M.) - [b. and d.?] 1924
Leonard E. Jr. - [b. and d.?] 9 February 1973
Perry L. (husb. of Vera M.) - b. 1905; d. 1990
Perry L. Jr. [son of Perry L. and Vera M.] - b. 26 April 1926; d. 19 January 1992
Stephanie Ann - [b. and d.?] 14 October 1974
Vera M. (wife of Perry L.) - b. 1907; d. 1985
Wilhemean (wife of George G.) - b. 1863; d. 1929
LEONARD
Julia A. - b. 1843; d. 1921
LOPAUS
Abraham W. (son of Abraham W. and Dorcas J. [no stone]) - d. 4 October 1851 Æ 8 y., 11 m.
Abraham W. (son of Samuel [Watson?] and Hannah [(LAMBERT)?]; [husb. of Dorcas J. [no stone]?]) - d. 12 December 1842 Æ 24 y.
Alonzo A. - b. 2 July 1843; "lost at sea" 21 October 1887
Andrew L. (Capt.; husb. of Rachel M.) - b. 1811; d. 1889
Anna R. "Annie" (wife of Roscoe G.) - b. 24 March 1844; d. 28 June 1920
Ashbury A. (husb. of Eunice L.) - b. 1877; d. 1937
Austin L. (son of Edwin E. and Mildred M.) - b. 1902; d. 1902
Edwin E. (husb. of Mildred M.) - b. 1879; d. 1956
Eunice L. (wife of Ashbury A.) - b. 1878; d. 1936
Hannah (LAMBERT; wife of Samuel Watson) - b. 1780; d. 23 August 1849 Æ 69 y.
Mildred M. (wife of Edwin E.) - b. 1881; d. 1967
[Nancy C. - see CLARK]
[Nancy - see INGALLS]
Rachel M. (wife of Capt. Andrew L.) - d. 19 March 1876 Æ 68 y.
Roscoe Deless (son of Roscoe G. and Anna R. "Annie") - b. 13 October 1867; d. 22 January 1870 Æ 2 y., 3 m., 9 d.
Roscoe G. (husb. of Anna R. "Annie") - b. 9 October 1845; d. 20 June 1912
Sally (dau. of Samuel [Watson?] and Hannah [(LAMBERT)?]) - d. 4 December 1832 Æ 21 y.
Samuel C. - "lost at sea" November 1865 Æ 24 y.
Samuel Watson (husb. of Hannah (LAMBERT)) - b. 1776; d. 186[...][9]
William W. (son of Samuel [Watson?] and Hannah [(LAMBERT)?]) - d. 20 [March?][4] 18[4?]0[4] Æ 26 y.
LUNT
Abbie F. [wife of Capt. George W.] - b. 1858; d. 1946
Albion K. P. (Capt.; husb. of Miriam M.) - d. 9 May 1884 Æ 60 y., 4 m., 20 d.
Andrew P. (Capt.; husb. of [Laurania or Lurana][6] M.) - b. 6 June 1823; d. 23 November 1897
Anna May (wife of William H.) - b. 1866; d. 1940
Annie M. (wife of Walter S.) - b. 1872; d. 1959

Charles E. (son of Capt. Charles H. and Rhoda R.) - d. 25 June 1864 Æ 12 y., 9 m.
Charles H. (Capt.; husb. of Rhoda R.) - d. 13 January 1856, "Auxcayes, St. Domingo", Æ 29 y., 10 m., 10 d.
Charles P. (Capt.; husb. of Susie M. (CARTER)) - b. 1856; d. 1924
Edward P. (son of Capt. Andrew P. and [Laurania or Lurana][6] M.) - b. 1856; d. 29 December 1856 Æ 11 m.
Eliza A. (wife of Capt. Amos C. [no stone]) - d. 2 March 1883 Æ 74 y., 3 m., 8 d.
Frank W. (husb. of Mary P.) - b. 1852; d. 1930
Frankie (son of Frank W. and Mary P.) - d. 15 June 1893 Æ 3 m.
George W. (Capt.; [husb. of Abbie F.]) - b. 1848; d. 1938
Helen L. (wife of Capt. William P. [no stone]) - d. 18 December 1875 Æ 19 y., 3 m., 6 d.
Heslyn A. - b. 1893; d. 1903
John R. (Capt.; husb. of Katie P.) - d. 14 November 1874 Æ 42 y., 10 m., 15 d.
Katie P. (wife of Capt. John R.) - d. 15 November 1877 Æ 39 y., 4 m., 22 d.
[Laurania or Lurana][6] M. (wife of Capt. Andrew P.) - b. 1828; d. 1914
Lincoln W. (son of Capt. Andrew P. and [Laurania or Lurana][6] M.) - b. 1861; d. 1868
[Maria - see DIX]
Mary P. (wife of Frank W.) - b. 1855; d. 1954
Miriam M. (wife of Capt. Albion K. P.) - d. 14 January 1892 Æ 65 y., 2 m., 23 d.
[Muriel - see BROMLEY]
Nancy G. (wife of Roland H.) - d. 3 January 1920 Æ 74 y., 9 m.
Rena M. - b. 1878; d. 1964
Rhoda R. (wife of Capt. Charles H.) - d. 27 May 1899 Æ 70 y., 4 m., 19 d.
Robert F. - b. 28 October 1932; d. 22 May 1977
Roland H. (husb. of Nancy G.) - b. 23 March 1834; d. 6 September 1902
Rudolph Grantley (son of Walter S. and Annie M.) - b. 9 March 1902; d. 30 October 1902
Susie M. (CARTER; wife of Capt. Charles P.) - b. 1872; d. 1936
Walter S. (husb. of Annie M.) - b. 1873; d. 1928
William H. (husb. of Anna May) - b. 1856; d. 1939

LURVEY
[Caroline - see PUMROY]

LYONS
Brenda Jean [dau. of Edward William and Inez Alma] - b. 26 August 1956; d. 12 October 1956
Edward William [husb. of Inez Alma] - b. 1930; d. 1974
Inez Alma [wife of Edward William] - b. 1932

MACDIARMID
Cora - b. 1885; d. 1961

MANN
Horace Eugene - b. 1898; d. 1972
Jason Carver - b. 1968; d. 1988
Sylvia (CARVER) - b. 1896; d. 1971

MCDONALD
Kirby - b. 1910; d. 1986

MCINTIRE
Gordon T. - b. 19 March 1956; d. 21 August 1998

MELCHER
Mary (EYE) - b. 1872; d. 1957

MERCHANT
infant (son of H. Jr. and H. A. [no stones]) - b. 1946; d. 1946
MILLIKEN
Catharine (wife of Simeon [no stone]) - d. 10 September 1881 Æ 75 y., 10 m., 10 d.
MITCHELL
Mary Jane (wife of Robert [no stone]) - d. 14 March 1862 Æ 19 y., 1 m.
MOREY
Elizabeth S. (wife of Otis W.) - d. 4 February 1870 Æ 41 y., 8 m., 11 d.
Otis W. (husb. of Elizabeth S.) - d. 8 April 1887 Æ 62 y., 6 m.
MOULDEN [includes MOULDING]
Hannah (wife of James) - b. 1835; d. 1912
James (husb. of Hannah) - b. 1830; d. 1899
Mary A. (dau. of James and Hannah) - d. 5 July 1870 Æ 6 y., 3 m., 16 d.
[Phebe M. - see THURSTON]
MURPHY
Addie B. (wife of Pearl E.) - b. 1889; d. 1945
Albion (husb. of Hannah E.) - b. 12 November 1850; d. 7 May 1910
Alton R. [son of William A. and Emma F.?] - b. 1870; d. 1950; ("caretaker of the cemetery")
Augustus W. [son of William A. and Emma F.?] - b. 1872; d. 1942
Eldora M. [wife of John T. Jr.] - b. 1923
Emma F. (wife of William A.) - b. 1847; d. 1880
Ernest A. - b. 1884; d. 1934
Flora B. [wife of Isaac T.] - b. 1867; d. 1946
George W. (Capt.; husb. of Lillian F.) - b. 1863; d. 1915
Georgia I. (dau. of Capt. George W. and Lillian F.) - d. 2 April 1896 Æ 6 m., 12 d.
Hannah E. (wife of Albion) - d. 24 January 1902 Æ 38 y., 1 m., 13 d.
Isaac T. [husb. of Flora B.] - b. 1860; d. 1938
John T. [husb. of Viola A.] - b. 1870; d. 1957
John T. Jr. [husb. of Eldora M.] - b. 12 July 1911; d. 26 August 1971
Joseph Delbert [son of Joshua and Margaret Dawes[11]?] - b. 1871; d. 1944
Joshua (husb. of Margaret Dawes[11]) - b. 1830; d. 1895
[Katherine M. - see WALLS]
Leonard L. - b. 1906; "lost at sea" 1929
Lillian F. (wife of Capt. George W.) - b. 1864; d. 1911
Margaret Dawes[11] (wife of Joshua) - b. 1833; d. 1917
Maynard H. [son of William A. and Emma F.?] - b. 1874; d. 1894
Pearl E. (husb. of Addie B.) - b. 1881; d. 1962
[Rhoda - see PIERCE]
Rodney P. - b. 1909; d. 1979
Viola A. [wife of John T.] - b. 1877; d. 1965
William A. (husb. of Emma F.) - b. 1846; d. 1927
[...]arston[10] - b. 8 January 1876; d. 18 February 1949
NORTON
Lemuel (Rev.) - d. 18 September 1866 Æ 81 y., 3 m.
NORWOOD
Dennis E. (husb. of Ella M.) - b. 1870; d. 1956
Ella M. (wife of Dennis E.) - b. 1871; d. 1915
Emily R. (wife of James T.) - b. 1857; d. 1903
Esther H. - b. 1894; d. 1973
George W. (husb. of Nida M.) - b. 1882; d. 1946
James F. - b. 1914; d. 1986

James T. (husb. of Emily R.) - b. 1855; d. 1905
Maynard H. - b. 1893; d. 1948
Melissa E. (wife of Capt. William G.) - d. 23 February 1890 Æ 50 y., 6 m., 13 d.
Nida M. (wife of George W.) - b. 1875; d. 1954
Thelma E. - b. 1932; d. 1932
W. J. Jr. - b. 1933; d. 1934
William G. (Capt.; husb. of Melissa E.) - d. 7 May 1899 Æ 66 y., 27 d.
Willie E. (son of Thomas O. and Louisa A. [no stones]) - d. 12 May 1874 Æ 1 y., 3 m.

P.
C. [footstone only]

PERVEAR
Beatrice M. [PERVEAR?] - b. 22 July 1902; d. 25 April 1984
John G. (husb. of Lucinda F.) - b. 1881; d. 1961
Lucinda F. (wife of John G.) - b. 1882; d. 1928

PIERCE
Rhoda (MURPHY; dau. of Joshua MURPHY and Margaret Dawes[11]) - b. 1860; d. 1924

POMROY [see also PUMROY]
Cretia V. [POMROY?] - b. 1929; d. 1949
Irene C. [POMROY?] - b. 1931; d. 1949
John M. - b. 3 November 1934; d. 20 August 1998
Milton Lee [husb. of Velma A.?] - b. 7 November 1898; d. 17 March 1968
Velma A. [wife of Milton Lee?] - b. 14 June 1901; d. 22 June 1984

PUMROY [see also POMROY]
Caroline (LURVEY; wife of Capt. John) - d. 25 October 1889 Æ 68 y., 4 m., 27 d.
John (Capt.; husb. of Caroline (LURVEY)) - d. 23 September 1873 Æ 62 y., 17 d.

REED
Adelbert H. [husb. of Lula H.] - b. 1879; d. 1961
Alfred William - b. 1902; d. 1978
Basil E. - b. 1893; d. 1905
Benjamin B. - b. 1867; d. 1938
Benjamin B. (husb. of Sarah A.) - b. 1832; d. 1893
Charles Elmer [son of Alfred William?] - b. 1929; d. 1929
Doris A. [wife of W. Stanley] - b. 1915
[Dorothy - see WELLS]
Edmund B. (Capt.) - d. 31 December 1880 Æ 21 y., 9 m.
Edmund B. [husb. of Kathlyn [sic] M.] - b. 1880; d. 1970
Emma A. (wife of Capt. Nathan A.) - b. 1858; d. 1932
Eunice (wife of Capt. George) - d. 16 July 1884 Æ 49 y., 1 m., 6 d.
Gardner A. (son of Hollis G. and Lillian M.) - b. 14 May 1912; d. 9 September 1976
George (Capt.; husb. of Eunice) - b. November 1834; d. 19 July 1893
Georgie - b. 1899; d. 1931
Hannah E. (dau. of William and Sarah) - d. 5 February 1864 Æ 15 y., 11 m.
Herbert S. - b. 1892; d. 1918
Hollis G. (husb. of Lillian M.) - b. 1888; d. 1967
Hollis G. "Junior" (son of Hollis G. and Lillian M.) - b. 1920; d. 1926
Jacob B. (son of William and Sarah) - d. 14 May 1861 Æ 36 y., 2 m.
John W. (husb. of Rose E. (WHITE)) - b. 1855; d. 1929
Julia L. (dau. of Benjamin B. and Sarah A.) - d. 24 December 1856 Æ 6 m., 20 d.
Kathlyn [sic] M. (dau. of Hollis G. and Lillian M.) - b. 1916; d. 1928
Kathlyn [sic] M. [wife of Edmund B.] - b. 1882; d. 1965

Leon G. (son of Capt. Nathan A. and Emma A.) - d. 25 February 1883 Æ 5 y., 5 m., 6 d.
Lillian M. (wife of Hollis G.) - b. 1889; d. 1973
[Lucy Leona - see GOTT]
Lula H. [wife of Adelbert H.] - b. 1884; d. 1968
Nathan A. (Capt.; husb. of Emma A.) - b. 1857; d. 1912
Robert Bradley [REED?] - [b. and d.?] 27 June 1992
Rose E. (WHITE; wife of John W.) - b. 1847; d. 1918
Sarah (wife of William) - d. 12 January 1871 Æ 65 y.
Sarah A. (wife of Benjamin B.) - b. 1835; d. 1917
Sylvia L. - b. 1872; d. 1970
Toby Michial [sic] [REED?] - [b. and d.?] 27 June 1992
W. Stanley [husb. of Doris A.] - b. 1918
William (husb. of Sarah) - d. 8 June 1869 Æ 75 y.
Zulma C. (dau. of Benjamin B. and Sarah A.) - d. 1 October 1874 Æ 13 y., 6 m.

RICH
Ambrose T. [husb. of Margaret M.] - b. 16 January 1830; d. 9 July 1904
Ann M. [wife of James H.] - b. 1 August 1932; d. 24 September 1984
Charles E. (son of Gilbert L. and Eudora D. [no stones]) - d. 17 August 1875 Æ 8 y., 5 m., 5 d.
Cora E. (wife of James H.) - b. 1885; d. [no date]
Elzada V. (wife of Thomas S.) - d. 27 April 1912 Æ 51 y.
Ernest E. - b. 18 August 1906; d. 23 September 1946
Ethel V. [wife of Jasper E.] - b. 1900; d. 1990
James H. (husb. of Cora E.) - b. 1877; d. 1946
James H. [husb. of Ann M.] - b. 25 June 1932
Jasper E. [husb. of Ethel V.] - b. 1905; d. 1996
Margaret M. [wife of Ambrose T.] - b. 7 July 1837; d. 25 September 1912
Margaret P. (wife of Elias [no stone]) - d. 16 June 1878 Æ 40 y., 5 m., 18 d.
Mildred W. [wife of Robert F.] - b. 1917
Nellie B. (wife of Capt. Willard F.) - b. 1880; d. 1957
Robert F. [husb. of Mildred W.] - b. 1915; d. 1981[1]
Thomas S. (husb. of Elzada V.) - d. 7 August 1907 Æ 66 y.
Willard F. (Capt.; husb. of Nellie B.) - b. 1858; d. 1938
Willard M. (son of Capt. Willard F. and Nellie B.) - b. 1898; d. 1906

ROBBINS
Freddie - [no dates]
Gracie [wife of Lawrence] - b. 1952; d. 1986
Ida E. (wife of Wilder L.) - b. 1907; d. 1953
Lawrence [husb. of Gracie] - b. 1954
Lena A. (wife of Wilder B.) - b. 4 January 1866; d. 6 April 1926
Myrtle M. [wife of Raymond E.] - b. 2 September 1904; d. 13 September 1997
Raymond E. [husb. of Myrtle M.] - b. 6 November 1895; d. 5 January 1977
Wilder B. (husb. of Lena A.) - b. 9 April 1852; d. 26 September 1926
Wilder L. (husb. of Ida E.) - b. 1897; d. [no date]

ROBERTS
Constance (INGALLS) - b. 1926; d. 1978

ROBINSON
Elizabeth B. [wife of Linwood J.] - b. 1906; d. 1968
Harold G. - b. 12 June 1912; d. 22 July 1970
Linwood J. [husb. of Elizabeth B.] - b. 1905; d. 1959
Vesta M. - b. 1889; d. 1949

William G. - b. 1880; d. 1945
ROMER
Willis E. (son of Joseph and Julia [no stones]) - d. 2 April 1875 Æ 4 y., 2 m., 1 d.
RUMILL [includes RUMELL]
Archie Roy (son of Loren W. and Myra E.) - d. 27 October 1891 Æ 3 m., 28 d.
Barnard (husb. of E. N.[8]) - d. 30 January 1871 Æ 71 y., 5 d.
Eliza C. (wife of Capt. Joseph B.) - b. 1836; d. 1931
E. N.[8] (wife of Barnard) - d. 5 June 1879 Æ 80 y., 3 m., 6 d.
George W. (Capt.) - d. 14 November 1884, "at sea", Æ 26 y., 7 m., 15 d.
Joseph B. (Capt.; husb. of Eliza C.) - d. 16 June 1893 Æ 65 y., 8 m., 11 d.
Loren W. (husb. of Myra E.) - b. 1863; d. 1951
Myra E. (wife of Loren W.) - b. 1867; d. 1960
Nettie J. (wife of Robie M.) - b. 1869; d. 1939
[Reta [sic] G. - see SPRAGUE]
Robie M. (husb. of Nettie J.) - b. 1867; d. 1915
SAWYER
Burton C. [husb. of Mildred A.] - b. 1917; d. 1999
Mildred A. [wife of Burton C.] - b. 1917; d. 1990
SEAVEY
Alice A. (wife of Edwin W.) - b. 1875; d. 1956
Barbara L. [dau. of Frank G. and Letha M.] - b. 1918; d. 1921
Edwin W. (husb. of Alice A.) - b. 1872; d. 1950
Edwin W. [husb. of Flora A.] - b. 11 May 1894; d. 31 January 1975
Flora A. [wife of Edwin W.] - b. 1911; d. 1976
Frank G. (husb. of Letha M.) - b. 1895; d. 1966
Frank G. Jr. (son of Frank G. and Letha M.) - b. 18 October 1917; d. 20 January 1967
Helen E. [wife of William W.] - b. 1933; d. 1990
Irving E. [husb. of Voilet [sic] S.] - b. 1910; d. 1974
Lawrence R. - b. 8 April 1938; d. 30 April 1963
Letha M. (wife of Frank G.) - b. 1896; d. 1967
Maury L. - b. 24 February 1969; d. 15 March 1995
Rosetta M. [wife of Wilbur E.] - b. 1930
Voilet [sic] S. [wife of Irving E.] - b. 1915; d. 1973
Wilbur E. [husb. of Rosetta M.] - b. 1922; d. 1981
William W. [husb. of Helen E.] - b. 1931
SMITH
Emery Weston - b. 23 August 1921; d. 24 March 1997
SPRAGUE
Jennie M. (wife of Capt. Winfield S.) - d. 3 November 1886 Æ 34 y., 10 m.
Leroy Southard - b. 12 September 1925; d. 14 August 1998
[Letitia B. - see LATTY]
Reta [sic] G. (RUMILL; dau. of Robie M. RUMILL and Nettie J.) - b. 1897; d. 1936
Winfield S. (Capt.; husb. of Jennie M.) - d. 22 August 1909 Æ 59 y., 10 m.
SPRIGGS
Madeline A. (wife of Melvin T.) - b. 1915; d. 1988
Melvin T. (husb. of Madeline A.) - b. 1915
SPURLING
Benjamin F. (Capt.; husb. of Hannah M.) - "lost at sea" October 1853 Æ 33 y.
Hannah M. (wife of Capt. Benjamin F.) - d. 26 April 1856 Æ 31 y., 9 m., 20 d.
STANLEY
Clarence E. - b. 1911; d. 1964

Eugene M. [husb. of Florence E.] - b. 1866; d. 1943
Florence E. [wife of Eugene M.] - b. 1878; d. 1956
Harvard A. - b. 30 June 1918; d. 27 March 1972

THURSTON

Ambrose (Capt.; husb. of Elmira B.) - d. 12 August 1885 Æ 69 y., 10 m.
Bradley W. [THURSTON?] - b. 1925; d. 1938
Carrie F. ([2nd?] wife of Henry W.) - b. 1872; d. 1959
Edith M. [dau. of Wills D. and Harriet M. "Hattie"] - b. 1903; d. 1985
Elmira B. (wife of Capt. Ambrose) - d. 17 February 1898 Æ 79 y.
Elwyn L. [son of Wills D. and Harriet M. "Hattie"?] - d. 22 February 1918 Æ [not given]
[Flora M. - see LATTY]
Fred W. [husb. of Rena E.] - b. 1878; d. 1959
George H. (husb. of Maud M.) - b. 1861; d. 1934
Gertrude K. [wife of Herbert W.] - b. 1888; d. 1972
Gracie E. (dau. of Wills D. and Harriet M. "Hattie") - d. 1 April 1901 Æ 4 m., 12 d.
Harriet M. "Hattie" (wife of Wills D.) - b. 1874; d. 1940
Henry W. (husb. of Carrie F. and Maria S.) - b. 1858; d. 1945
Herbert W. [husb. of Gertrude K.] - b. 1887; d. 1966
Lula R. [wife of William H.] - b. 1884; d. 1966
Maria S. ([1st?] wife of Henry W.) - d. 18 May 1883 Æ 23 y., 5 m., 15 d.
Mary A. (wife of Capt. James [no stone]) - d. 17 January 1879 Æ 43 y., 1 m., 10 d.
Mary G. (wife of Solomon G.) - b. 7 June 1835; d. 3 November 1910
Maud M. (wife of George H.) - b. 1868; d. 1920
[My?]ra[4] Ja[ne?][4] (dau. of Nelson [no stone] and Sylvia A.) - [...][4]
Percy W. [son of Wills D. and Harriet M. "Hattie"?] - b. 1902; d. 1918
Phebe M. (MOULDEN; wife of Watson J.) - b. 1865; d. 1937
Rena E. [wife of Fred W.] - b. 1886; d. 1973
Rena M. - b. 1865; d. 1905
Solomon G. (husb. of Mary G.) - b. 13 March 1830; d. 14 February 1913
Sylvia A. (wife of Nelson [no stone]) - d. 14 June 1870 Æ 22 y., 6 m.
Watson J. (husb. of Phebe M. (MOULDEN)) - b. 1863; d. 1924
William H. (Capt.) - d. 4 August 1900 Æ 34 y., 8 m., 7 d.
William H. [husb. of Lula R.] - b. 1886; d. 1957
Wills D. (husb. of Harriet M. "Hattie") - b. 1867; d. 1935
Winfield W. (son of Solomon G. and Mary G.) - d. 11 June 1870 Æ 1 y., 2 d.

TITUS

Nellie A. (dau. of Joseph H. and Lucy A. [no stones]) - d. 5 December 1873 Æ 4 y., 6 m., 20 d.
Nellie A. (dau. of Joseph H. and Lucy A. [no stones]) - d. 19 April 1879 Æ 3 y., 3 m., 21 d.

TOLMAN

Eva F. [wife of Oscar A.?] - b. 1892; d. 1975
Harriet Gertrude - b. 1880; d. 1958
Oscar A. [husb. of Eva F.?] - b. 1875; d. 1967

TRASK

[Marjorie - see WALLS]

W.

H. G. [footstone only]

WALKER

Hilda (FARLEY; [dau. of Merle A. FARLEY and Evelyn L.?]) - b. 1928; d. 1947

WALLS
Alvin A. (husb. of Bessie R.) - b. 1892; d. 1988
Andrew Jr. (husb. of Hannah G.) - d. 16 December 1879 Æ 51 y., 3 m., 14 d.
Bessie R. (wife of Alvin A.) - b. 1898; d. 1980
[Eleanor - see BROWN]
G. Eugene Jr. [husb. of Marjorie (TRASK)] - b. 1925
Granville E. (husb. of Lurlene B.) - b. 1901; d. 1932
Hannah G. (wife of Andrew Jr.) - d. 1 April 1883 Æ 48 y., 9 m.
infant (dau. of Alvin A. and Bessie R.) - [b. and d.?] 30 August 1923
Katherine M. (MURPHY; wife of Otis M.) - b. 1872; d. 1952
Lurlene B. (wife of Granville E.) - b. 1904; d. 1992
Marjorie (TRASK; [wife of G. Eugene Jr.]) - b. 1932
Otis M. (husb. of Katherine M. (MURPHY)) - b. 1867; d. 1928
WEBSTER
Daniel W. (son of Capt. Sullivan and Eliza W.) - d. 14 January 1856 Æ 1 y., 5 m., 10 d.
Della S. [wife of Sullivan C.] - b. 1883; d. 1940
Eliza W. (wife of Capt. Sullivan) - d. 15 July 1887 Æ 66 y.
Fred M. - b. 18 March 1910; d. 24 May 1969
Hannah E. (dau. of Capt. Sullivan and Eliza W.) - d. 26 January 1851 Æ 9 m., 4 d.
Henry T. (husb. of Julia L.) - b. 1843; d. 1914
Ida (dau. of Capt. Sullivan. and Eliza W.) - d. 2 December 1856 Æ 4 w.
infant (dau. of Capt. S. W. and A. T. [no stones]) - [b. and?] d. 3 September 1879
Julia Floella (dau. of Henry T. and Julia L.) - d. 25 June 1870 Æ 4 y., 2 m., 8 d.
Julia L. (wife of Henry T.) - b. 1841; d. 1919
Maud N. (wife of William H.) - b. 1881; d. 1962
Melissa M. (dau. of Henry T. and Julia L.) - d. 27 June 1870 Æ 1 y., 11 m., 4 d.
Samuel S. (Capt.; son of Capt. Sullivan and Eliza W.) - d. 30 September 1860 Æ 19 y., 3 m.
Sullivan (Capt.; husb. of Eliza W.) - d. 26 April 1863 Æ 52 y., 3 m.
Sullivan C. [husb. of Della S.] - b. 1878; d. 1967
William H. (husb. of Maud N.) - b. 1873; d. 1943
WELLS
Dorothy Reed[11] - b. 1913; d. 1983
WENTWORTH
Alonzo A. [husb. of Polly (DOW)] - b. 1871; d. 1959
Ann M. [wife of Robert L.] - b. 1944
George W. - b. 1898; d. 1984
Polly (DOW; [wife of Alonzo A.]) - b. 1876; d. 1952
Robert L. [husb. of Ann M.] - b. 1946; d. 1998
Wills Dow - b. 1915; d. 1995
WHITE
[Rose E. - see REED]
WHITTLESEY
Ina F. [wife of John J.] - b. 1886; d. 1977
John J. [husb. of Ina F.] - b. 1878; d. 1949
Marjorie T. - b. 1912; d. 1991
Stephen M. - b. 1917; d. 1996
WOOSTER
Fred L. - b. 1897; d. 1979
Joseph E. (husb. of Myra J.) - b. 1872; d. 1955
Myra J. (wife of Joseph E.) - b. 1875; d. 1945

[...]
[...][7]

Notes:
[1] Engraved on a natural stone setting at this grave is "Round Is. 6/12/81".
[2]There is a worn and broken stone next to hers that may belong to David.
[3]See stone for Sally Dix in Dix Burying Ground (Tremont - 26).
[4]Stone worn and/or broken.
[5]The unit's digit was originally engraved as 8, but then part of the 8 was filled to create a 3.
[6]Different on different stones.
[7]Grave outlined with stones.
[8]Headstone broken. Footstone: "E. N. R."
[9]There is no digit in the unit's place.
[9]Difficult to read.
[10]This name was written on paper inside a "temporary" marker, and a portion of the paper was obscured by a plastic protective covering when this record was made. In March of 2000, after the snow had melted, the piece of plastic was found a few feet from the marker, but the paper is gone.
[11]It is unclear from the gravestone whether this is a maiden name.

Rich Cemetery
(Tremont - 10)

Location/directions. Along west side of Route 102, near mouth of Cousins Creek emptying into Bass Harbor. From the traffic light at the north end of Mount Desert Island, go straight ahead (south) onto Routes 102/198. In approximately 5.2 miles (and at the south end of the village of Somesville), turn right onto Pretty Marsh Road (Route 102). The cemetery is on the left in about 11.5–11.6 miles. There is good parking in a pull out across Route 102.

History. The cemetery is on land that was part of a 160 acre parcel owned by Stephen Richardson in 1808 according to the Salem Towne Jr. map.

Notes. No fence currently encloses this cemetery, but there is evidence of a previous one—about a half dozen rocks along the side of the cemetery nearest the road have iron rods, now broken and rusting, driven into them. The grass is mowed and trimmed. A once very tall monument for several members of the RICH family is now broken into several pieces.

Names and dates on gravestones and other markers. [30 May 1999]

ALBEE
- Clista L. (wife of Forest [sic] L.) - b. 1897; d. [no date]
- Erma B. [wife of Myron E.] - b. 1908; d. 1980
- Forest [sic] L. (husb. of Clista L.) - b. 1893; d. 1942
- Georgia A. [wife of James H.] - b. 1881; d. 1949
- James H. [husb. of Georgia A.] - b. 1879; d. 1959
- Judith Lynne - b. 15 February 1960; d. 10 March 1979
- Linda M. (wife of Millard F.) - b. 1 May 1860; d. 29 December 1929
- Millard F. (husb. of Linda M.) - b. 27 March 1848; d. 19 February 1906
- Myron E. [husb. of Erma B.] - b. 1901; d. 1973

BEALE
- Douglas D. [husb. of Irma E.] - b. 1905
- Irma E. [wife of Douglas D.] - b. 1909; d. 1974

BUNKER
- Myra G. (wife of Lowell A. [no stone][5]) - b. 11 February 1886; d. 14 October 1918

CLOSSON
- Frances M. (wife of John F.) - b. 1885; d. 1950
- John F. (husb. of Frances M.) - b. 1878; d. 1952

COOPER
- Carrie S. (GALLEY; dau. of Capt. George B. GALLEY [no stone] and Jessie B.) - d. 4 March 1897 Æ 17 y., 3 m., 24 d.

DODGE
- Edward C. (husb. of Sarah A.) - b. 1 July 1825; d. 3 March 1894
- Sarah A. (wife of Edward C.) - b. 24 November 1827; d. 18 February 1907
- William E. - b. 4 April 1849; d. 3 January 1888

DORR
- Mabel B. - b. 1881; d. 1937

DOW
- Bert B. [husb. of Viola H.] - b. 27 July 1895; d. 16 December 1961
- Louise M. [wife of Pearl H.] - b. 1912; d. 1997
- Pearl H. [husb. of Louise M.] - b. 1900; d. 1981
- Viola H. [wife of Bert B.] - b. 1891; d. 1975

FALVEY
[Ethel - see RICH]
FINCKE
[Margaret - see MACDUFFIE]
GALLEY
[Carrie S. - see COOPER]
Jessie B. (wife of Capt. George B. [no stone]) - d. 11 August 1881 Æ 28 y., 6 m.
Lucretia S. - b. 1879; d. 1937
Olive S. (wife of William F.) - b. 1844; d. 1916
Shirley F. - b. 1908; d. 1923
William F. (husb. of Olive S.) - b. 1839; d. 1918
GOTT
Collista F. (MULLIN; wife of Solomon T.) - b. 1853; d. 1940
Solomon T. (husb. of Collista F. (MULLIN)) - b. 1848; d. 1924
HALLETT
Lula Agnes (dau. of Benjamin and Gertrude M. [no stones]) - d. 19 November 1907 Æ 4 y., 10 m.
HAMBLEN
Margaret A. (dau. of Levi and Lucretia [no stones]) - d. 20 December 1851 Æ 4 y.
Millicent F. (TRASK; dau. of George TRASK and Emily) - b. 1903; d. 1981
KELLEY
Edward [husb. of Fay] - b. 1896; d. 1980
Fay [wife of Edward] - b. 1894; d. 1957
LATTY
Margaret C. [wife of Richard F.] - b. 1912; d. 1964
Margaret G. - b. 1932; d. 1993
Richard F. [husb. of Margaret C.] - b. 1910; d. 1985
MACDUFFIE
Malcolm A. [husb. of Margaret (FINCKE)] - b. 1902; d. 1976
Margaret (FINCKE; [wife of Malcolm A.]) - b. 1904; d. 1985
MORONG
Eliza J. (SMITH; wife of William E.) - b. 15 October 1848; d. 21 December 1928
Herbert N. (son of William E. and Eliza J. (SMITH)) - b. 11 June 1872; d. 9 November 1900
William E. (husb. of Eliza J. (SMITH)) - [no dates]
MULLIN
[Collista F. - see GOTT]
MURPHY
George F. (husb. of Wavie [A. or L.][1]) - b. 1885; d. 1965
Harold E. - b. 1917; d. 1935
Harriet F. (dau. of George F. and Wavie [A. or L.][1]) - b. 1912; d. 1916
Richard L. (son of George F. and Wavie [A. or L.][1]) - b. 1911; d. 1931
Wavie [A. or L.][1] (wife of George F.) - b. 1883; d. 1961
PARKER
Max C. [husb. of Sylvia A.] - b. 1916; d. 1991
Sylvia A. [wife of Max C.] - b. 1920; d. 1971
RICH
Angus M. (son of John T. and Margaret) - b. 1840; d. 17 January 1854 Æ 13 y., 3 m.
Charlotte B. "Lottie" (wife of John M.) - b. 185[4 or 6][1]; d. 1925
Clarrisia [sic] (wife of Samuel G.) - b. [...][2] 181[4?][2]; d. 13 November 1890
Elias (husb. of Sally) - d. 14 December 1867 Æ 88 y., 1 m., 22 d.

Ethel (FALVEY; wife of Frank Pettigrove) - b. 12 December 1888; d. 15 May 1972
Eugene (son of John T. and Margaret) - b. 1867; d. 1868
Frank Pettigrove (husb. of Ethel (FALVEY)) - b. 18 July 1887; d. 19 November 1923
John M. (husb. of Charlotte B. "Lottie") - b. 1853; d. 1919
John T. (husb. of Margaret) - d. 4 July 1880 Æ 66 y., 11 m., 8 d.
Loren D. [husb. of Sidney S.] - b. 2 February 1845; d. 9 January 1923
Lucy A. (dau. of John T. and Margaret) - b. 1860; d. 1860
Margaret (wife of John T.) - d. 16 February 1895 Æ 72 y.
Melinda H. - b. 1841; d. 1896
Orville C. (son of John M. and Charlotte B. "Lottie") - d. 26 June 1880 Æ 1 y., 8 m., 14 d.
Sally (wife of Elias) - d. 6 December 1882 Æ 90 y., 5 m., 8 d.
Samuel G. (husb. of Clarrisia [sic]) - d. 23 April 1871 Æ 62 y., 4 m., 8 d.
Sarah (dau. of Elias and Sally) - d. 28 January 1854 Æ 15 y., 8 m.
Sidney S. [wife of Loren D.] - b. 24 July 1849; d. 26 February 1914
Thomas G. (son of John T. and Margaret) - b. 1847; d. 1857
Tyler F.[6] (son of John T. and Margaret) - d. 23 May 1864 Æ 22 y., 4 m.; ("killed at the battle of the wilderness"; Sergeant of Co. H, 16th Maine Regiment [Civil War])

ROMER [includes ROAMER]
Angus Eugene [son of James C. [no stone] and Ann B.] - d. 11 December 1873 Æ 17 y., 5 m.
Angus M. (son of James C. [no stone] and Ann B.) - d. 17 November 1854 Æ 9 m.
Ann B. (wife of James C. [no stone]) - d. 7 May 1858 Æ 30 y., 8 m.

SMITH
[Eliza J. - see MORONG]

TRASK
C. Orville [husb. of Esther M.] - b. 1908; d. 1961
Emily (wife of George) - b. 1884; d. 1981
Esther M. [wife of C. Orville] - b. 1909
George (husb. of Emily) - b. 1877; d. 1958
[Millicent F. - see HAMBLEN]

WALLACE
Adelbert J. (husb. of Elzora E.) - b. 1854; d. 1915
Eliza S. (wife of James B.) - b. 1833; d. 1907
Elzora E. (wife of Adelbert J.) - b. 1855; d. 1929
James B. (husb. of Eliza S.) - b. 1830; d. 1871
James Burdene (son of James B. and Eliza S.) - d. 20 February 1879 Æ 7 y., 3 m.
Jay W. [husb. of Leila C.] - b. 1888; d. 1957
Leila C. [wife of Jay W.] - b. 1894; d. 1974
Marcia (dau. of Adelbert J. and Elzora E.) - d. 3 January 18[8?]7[2] Æ 5 y., 1[2?][2] d.
Sidney E. - b. 1879; d. 1935

YOUNG
Francis K. (husb. of [...][2]) - d. 19 January 1890 Æ 76 y.
[...][2] (wife of Francis K.) - d. 19 August 1874 Æ [...][2,3] y., [...][2,4] m.

Notes:
[1]Different on different stones.
[2]Stone broken.
[3]Two digits. First digit is not curved; *i.e.*, 1 or 4 or 7. Second digit has a rounded lower portion, perhaps a 9.

[4]Single digit with a rounded lower portion.
[5]A very large stone with Myra G. BUNKER's name on one side is tipped over obscuring any information that may be on the other side.
[6]Thornton (1938) gave the middle initial as E.

McKinley Cemetery

(Tremont - 11)

Location/directions. Along east side of Route 102A, Bass Harbor. From the traffic light at the north end of Mount Desert Island, go straight ahead (south) onto Routes 102/198. In approximately 5.2 miles (and at the south end of the village of Somesville), turn right onto Pretty Marsh Road (Route 102). In about 12.2–12.3 miles, go straight ahead, leaving Route 102; do not follow Route 102 as it curves to the left. Travel approximately 0.3 miles to a stop sign, and then turn right onto Route 102A. The cemetery is on the left in about 0.3 miles. Alternatively, from the traffic light at the north end of Mount Desert Island, go straight ahead (south) onto Routes 102/198, but do not turn right onto Pretty Marsh Road. Approximately 13.0 miles from the traffic light at the beginning, go straight ahead following the sign to Bass Harbor instead of staying to the right on Route 102. The cemetery is on the left in about another 0.5–0.6 miles.

History. This cemetery is on land that was part of a 100 acre parcel owned by Joshue Norwood in 1808 according to the Salem Towne Jr. map. The cemetery is found in the 1881 Colby Atlas. Recently, the associations of the McKinley and Hillrest cemeteries merged.

Notes. This cemetery is enclosed by a chain-link fence and is well maintained. Some stones lean or lay on ground. All stones appear (2000) to have been cleaned recently as they bear few or no lichens.

Names and dates on gravestones and other markers. [4 September 1999]

ALLBY

Lydia W. (wife of Capt. William [no stone]) - d. 24 June 1873 Æ 45 y., 4 m., 29 d.

BARRON

Annie M. (wife of Thomas W. [no stone]) - b. 1859; d. 1905

[Maud L. - see TORREY]

BICKFORD

Daniel K. (son of John R. and Abigail K. [no stones]) - d. 25 July 1863, California, Æ 34 y.

Isaac V. (son of John R. and Abigail K. [no stones]) - d. 13 January 1870 Æ 16 y., 3 m., 11 d.

Jacob S. (son of John R. and Abigail K. [no stones]) - d. 23 August 1864 Æ 26 y., 8 m., 23 d.

Joseph W. (Capt.; son of John R. and Abigail K. [no stones]) - d. 24 August 1864, Havana, Cuba, Æ 31 y., 1 m., 10 d.

BLACK

Helen B. (dau. of Allan L. and Fannie R. [no stones]) - d. 26 April 1895 Æ [10?][1] m., 21 d.

BRAGG

[Violet M. - see MILLER]

BUNKER

Estella B. - b. 1877; d. 1937

May R. (GOTT; dau. of Capt. Israel L. GOTT and Eliza S.) - d. 3 March 1906 Æ 35 y., 8 m., 3 d.

BURNHAM

Daniel (Capt.) - d. 3 August 1815 Æ 30 y.

CARTER

Bertha L. ("infant dau." of Mary [no stone]) - [b. and?] d. 1933

Roy Wilber [sic] - b. 1895; d. 1918
CLEVELAND
[Amanda H. - see HIGGINS]
CLOSSON
Fred H. (husb. of Mavilla M.) - b. 1863; d. 1938
infant (son of Fred H. and Mavilla M.) - d. 8 September 1903 Æ 29 d.
Mavilla M. (wife of Fred H.) - b. 1862; d. 1960
COUSENS
Clara G. (wife of Merrill E.) - b. 1906; d. 1933
Merrill E. (husb. of Clara G.) - b. 1900
COVILL
Clarence F. - b. 1866; d. 1903; ("Father of nine[.] Drowned fishing off the coast of Nova Scotia[.] Found May 18, 1904 by Sylvester Gott and buried with gratitude from all our family[.]")
DAVIS
[Irene - see DAWES]
DAWES [see also DAWS]
Irene Davis[8] - d. 20 February 1913 Æ 56 y., 10 m., 20 d.
Vera F. (dau. of Nelson and Eva B. [no stones]) - d. 5 August 1889 Æ [not given]
DAWS [see also DAWES]
Lizzie A. (dau. of David G. and Sarah J. [no stones]) - d. 29 September 1875 Æ 15 y., 11 m., 8 d.
DIX
Almira T. [wife of Charles B.] - b. 1838; d. 1919
Charles B. [husb. of Almira T.] - b. 1836; d. 1906
George H. (son of John P. and Harriet E. [no stones]) - d. 19 November 1863 Æ 1[3] y., 5 m., 6 d.
DIXON
Robert A. - d. 5 December 1846 Æ 26 y.
DODGE
Ezra H. (husb. of Mercy) - d. 25 November 1848 Æ 83 y.
Lucy M. [wife of William H. C.] - b. 1862; d. 1946
Mercy (wife of Ezra H.) - d. 27 April 1860 Æ 78 y., 5 m.
William H. C. [husb. of Lucy M.] - b. 1866; d. 1947
DOLLIVER
Clifford Harding (husb. of Florence (SANBORN)) - b. 16 December 1876; d. 8 March 1957
Florence (SANBORN; wife of Clifford Harding) - b. 28 December 1895; d. 8 January 1982
DONALDSON
Rupert R. (son of William R. and Linda E. [no stones]) - d. 28 December 1900 Æ 3 m., 27 d.
EATON
Amos (Capt.; husb. of Betsey and Joan N.) - d. 30 October 1855 Æ 78 y.
Betsey (wife of Capt. Amos) - d. 20 January 1862 Æ 76 y., 8 m.
Daniel B. (husb. of Isabelle C.) - d. 23 April 1894 Æ 6[7 or 5?][1] y., 1 m., 6 d.
Eddie [EATON?] - [no dates]
Isabelle C. (wife of Daniel B.) - d. 6 February 1916 Æ 86 y., 6 m., 20 d.
James H. - d. 23 January 1905 Æ 57 y.
Joan N. (wife of Capt. Amos) - "lost at sea" 5 July 1873 Æ 62 y., 9 m.
Joshua (Capt.; husb. of Lydia D.) - d. 24 September 1882 Æ 66 y., 3 m., 3 d.
Joshua D. (son of Capt. Joshua and Lydia D.) - d. 19 July 1846 Æ 1 y., 6 m., 22 d.

Lydia D. (wife of Capt. Joshua) - d. 12 March 1883 Æ 67 y., 8 m., 23 d.

GOTT

[Abbie B. - see TURNER]

Alonzo (son of James S. and Martha [no stones]) - d. 16 August 1862 Æ 11 y., 10 m., 28 d.

Annie M. - b. 1871; d. 1944

Augustus - b. 1885; d. 1955

Charles M. - b. 25 April 1892; d. 3 February 1943; ("Lost in North Atlantic when ship was torpedoed on way to Greenland.")

Clyde Foster (son of Sylvester and Esther [F. or O.][2]) - d. 11 January 1903 Æ 1 y., 8 m., 12 d.

Cora K. (dau. of William E. and Gertrude M.) - b. 1900; d. 1918

Decator S. (husb. of Sarah M.) - b. 19 May 1847; d. 6 February 1918

Eliza S. (wife of Capt. Israel L.) - b. 1848; d. 1924

Esther [F. or O.][2] [wife of Sylvester L.] - b. 1877; d. 1957

Gertrude M. (wife of William E.) - b. 1882; d. 1949

Gladys E. (dau. of William E. and Gertrude M.) - b. 1897; d. 1926

[Grace E. - see MCKAY]

Heman L. - b. 1879; d. 1963

Isaac (Deacon; husb. of Polly) - d. 27 March 1866 Æ 81 y., 11 m., 17 d.

Israel L. (Capt.; husb. of Eliza S.) - b. 1839; d. 1920

John M. (husb. of Lizzie E.) - b. 25 December 1859; d. 27 April 1938

John V. (WEBSTER; adopted son of Deacon Isaac and Polly) - d. 7 January 1854 Æ 16 y., 25 d.

Joseph (husb. of Lucy) - d. 30 April 1839 Æ 70 y.

Lizzie E. (wife of John M.) - b. 16 July 1871; d. 12 March 1907

Lucy (wife of Joseph) - d. 26 July 1848 Æ 80 y., 4 m.

[May R. - see BUNKER]

Peter (Capt.; husb. of Puah) - "lost at sea" 15 December 1838 Æ 52 y.

Polly (wife of Deacon Isaac) - d. 3 March 1856 Æ 70 y., 2 m., 2 d.

Puah (wife of Capt. Peter) - d. 31 March 1882 Æ 95 y., 3 m.

Sarah M. (wife of Decator S.) - b. 29 February 1852; d. 26 September 1921

Solomon (son of Capt. Israel L. and Eliza S.) - d. 9 July 1895 Æ 32 y., 2 m., 15 d.

Sylvester L. [husb. of Esther [F. or O.][2]] - b. 1865; d. 1957

William E. (husb. of Gertrude M.) - b. 1867; d. 1954

HIGGINS

Alfred E. (husb. of Amanda H. (CLEVELAND)) - b. 1852; d. 1914

Amanda H. (CLEVELAND; wife of Alfred E.) - b. 1864; d. 1924

Norman V. (son of Alfred E. and Amanda H. (CLEVELAND)) - b. 1888; d. 1911

HOLDEN

Grace M. (dau. of Simeon Amasa and Hannah Augusta) - b. 8 September 1871; d. 8 July 1872

Hannah Augusta (wife of Simeon Amasa) - b. 6 March 1850; d. 25 February 1920

Pauline Vernette (dau. of Simeon Amasa and Hannah Augusta) - b. 20 May 1887; d. 31 August 1902

Simeon Amasa (husb. of Hannah Augusta) - b. 14 July 1844; d. 9 May 1901

HOLMES

Edna Ella (dau. of Lewis H. and Mary A. (SPEAR)) - d. 11 July 1877 Æ 2 y., 4 m., 1 d.

Guy L. - b. 1896; d. 1941

infant (dau. of Lewis H. and Mary A. (SPEAR)) - d. 4 June 1879 Æ 4 d.

Katie May (dau. of Lewis H. and Mary A. (SPEAR)) - d. 8 August 1898 Æ 16 y., 1 m., 20 d.
Lewis H. (husb. of Mary A. (SPEAR)) - b. 1848; d. 1925
Mary A. (SPEAR; wife of Lewis H.) - b. 1852; d. 1926

JOHNSON
Mary W. (wife of Myrtle) - d. 5 March 1886 Æ 89 y., 5 m.
Myrtle (husb. of Mary W.) - d. 5 February 1872 Æ 76 y., 25 d.

JORDAN
Sarah B. (dau. of Melatiah and Susan [no stones]) - d. 6 September 1844 Æ 19 y., 5 m., 11 d.

KENT
Elizabeth - d. 15 March 1886 Æ 72 y., 1 m., 2 d.

LADD
William H. N. (son of Daniel and Priscilla [no stones]) - d. 19 July 1846 Æ 11 y., 5 m., 12 d.

MANCHESTER
Elizabeth W. (wife of Moses) - b. 13 April 1833; d. 15 February 1915
Eunice - d. 17 June 1841 Æ 28 y., 6 m.
Moses (husb. of Elizabeth W.) - d. 12 January 1894 Æ 79 y.
Stephen - d. 16 June 1835 Æ 28 y., 9 m.
Thomas - d. 25 February 1848 Æ 39 y.
William S. - b. 1859; d. 1933

MARTIN
infants (twin dau's. of A. L. and L. M. [no stones]) - d. 28 February 1844 Æ 1 d.

MCKAY
Charles L. (husb. of Grace E. (GOTT)) - b. 1885; d. [no date]
Grace E. (GOTT; wife of Charles L.) - b. 1896; d. 1920

MCMULLIN [see also MULLIN][5]
Austin B. (son of Francis and Mary E.) - d. 4 March 1871 Æ 9 y., 2 m., 12 d.
Francis (husb. of Mary E.) - b. 1822; d. 1906
Frank (son of Francis and Mary E.) - b. 1856; d. 1917
Fred P. (son of Francis and Mary E.) - d. 23 January 1870 Æ 8 m., 15 d.
Lucy (wife of William) - d. 24 September 1883 Æ 83 y., 11 m., 14 d.
Mary E. (wife of Francis) - b. 1825; d. 1905
Nancy J. - d. 25 August 1899 Æ 74 y., 7 m.
William (husb. of Lucy) - d. 11 March 1863 Æ 76 y., 15 d.

MILLER
Violet M. (BRAGG; wife of George J. [no stone]) - b. 1902; d. 1931

MORGAN
Charlie A. - b. 1908; d. 1909
infant[7] [MORGAN?] - [no dates]
Ruby A. - b. 1872; d. 1912

MULLIN [see also MCMULLIN][5]
Delia P. - d. 22 August 1889 Æ 27 y., 7 m., 22 d.
Hannah (wife of William) - d. 29 November 1894 Æ 7[3?][1] y., 8 m., 20 d.
Hannah Abby (dau. of William and Hannah) - d. 26 November 1860 Æ 10 y., 6 m., 1 d.
William (husb. of Hannah) - d. 3 January 1899 Æ 78 y., 1 m., 4 d.

MURCH
Donald M. (son of Harland F. and Carrie S. [no stones]) - [no dates]

MURPHY
George (husb. of May E.) - b. 1855; d. 1942

May E. (wife of George) - b. 1855; d. 1924

NORWOOD

Amanda E. - b. 10 June 1872; d. 18 October 1918

Joshua (husb. of Ruth) - d. 27 January 1815 Æ 72 y.

Ruth (wife of Joshua) - d. October 1837 Æ "about 95" y.

PERRY

Deborah R. (wife of Henry M. [no stone]) - d. 14 January 1860 Æ 21 y., 8 m., 5 d.

RICH

[Ardell - see WILSON]

Benjamin H. (son of Zebadiah [sic] T. and Eunice N. [no stone]) - d. 13 January 1845 Æ 3 m., 19 d.

Eunice (dau. of Zebadiah [sic] T. and Eunice N. [no stone]) - d. 18 December 1855 Æ 5 y., 5 m., 10 d.

Hattie M. (dau. of Zebadiah [sic] T. and Eunice N. [no stone]) - d. 27 January 1864 Æ 18 y., 11 m., 27 d.

infant (dau. of Ambrose T. [no stone] and Lucy D.) - d. 21 January 1854 Æ [not given]

Lucy D. (wife of Ambrose T. [no stone]) - d. 10 January 1854 Æ 17 y., 8 m.

Lydia Wilson[8] - b. 30 June 1839; d. 20 September 1912

Zebadiah [sic] T. (husb. of Eunice N. [no stone]) - d. 8 March 1870 Æ 57 y., 6 m., 26 d.

RICHARDSON

A. - d. 22 September 1820 Æ 49 y.

Abraham (Capt.; husb. of Deborah N.) - b. 5 February 1809; d. 31 August 1878 Æ 69 y., 6 m., 26 d.

Abraham L. (son of Capt. Abraham and Deborah N.) - d. 8 July 1860 Æ 20 y., 2 m., 25 d.

Amy (wife of Thomas) - d. 11 February 1826 Æ 61 y.

Daniel E. (son of Capt. Abraham and Deborah N.) - d. 21 July 1873 Æ 23 y., 5 m., 12 d.

Deborah N. (wife of Capt. Abraham) - d. 31 March 1859 Æ 49 y., 11 m., 2 d.

E. Maude (wife of Wilmer E.) - b. 1852; d. 1896

Eliza Ann (dau. of Capt. Abraham and Deborah N.) - d. 25 February 1855 Æ 17 y., 6 m., 22 d.

Ella May (wife of Herbert P.) - b. 31 March 1866; d. 24 January 1916

Eugene A. (son of Capt. Abraham and Deborah N.) - d. 4 August 1874 Æ 26 y., 4 m., 17 d.

Frances A. (wife of P. W.) - b. 1843; d. 1929

Hannah (wife of Capt. Moses) - d. 23 October 1835 Æ 32 y., 9 m.

Herbert P. (husb. of Ella May) - b. 1863; d. 1938

infant (dau. of Capt. Abraham and Deborah N.) - d. 10 September 1853 Æ 6 d.

John C. (son of Capt. Abraham and Deborah N.) - d. 5 January 1862, Washington, D. C., Æ 30 y., 2 m., 19 d.

Lucy M. (wife of Oscar A.) - b. 29 April 1850; d. 8 March 1918

Mercy E. D. (dau. of Capt. Abraham and Deborah N.) - d. 31 October 1843 Æ 9 m., 20 d.

Moses (Capt.; husb. of Hannah and Priscilla D.) - b. 10 August 1802; d. 31 October 1887

Oscar A. (husb. of Lucy M.) - b. 6 August 1846; d. 19 August 1878

P. W. (husb. of Frances A.) - b. 1839; d. 1918

Priscilla D. (wife of Capt. Moses) - b. 20 November 1807; d. 22 December 1895

Simeon J. M. (son of Capt. Moses and Priscilla D.) - d. 11 June 1853 Æ 15 y., 11 m.
Sophina H. (dau. of Capt. Moses and Priscilla D.) - d. 25 January 1853 Æ 13 y., 7 m.
Spencer H. (son of Capt. Moses and Priscilla D.) - d. 13 March 1846 Æ 20 m.
Thomas (husb. of Amy) - d. 4 October 1855 Æ 92 y.
Warrington P. - b. 2 September 1904; d. 3 November 1923
Wilmer E. (husb. of E. Maude) - b. 1851; d. 1889

ROBBINS
Charles D. (husb. of Sarah M.) - b. 1831; d. 1914
Sarah M. (wife of Charles D.) - b. 1834; d. 1918
[...] [headstone only]

SANBORN
[Florence - see DOLLIVER]

SMITH
Alwilda (WILEY; wife of Emery [no stone]) - b. 1858; d. 1908

SPEAR
Abbe S. (dau. of Dr. William A. and Hannah B.) - d. 2 August 1847 Æ 3 y., 8 m., 17 d.
Hannah B. (wife of Dr. William A.) - d. 27 October 1892 Æ 70 y., 7 m., 14 d.
[Mary A. - see HOLMES]
William A. (Dr.; husb. of Hannah B.) - d. 3 March 1899 Æ 85 y.

STANLEY [includes STANDLEY]
Adaline [sic] A. (wife of James) - d. 27 May 1883 Æ 60 y., 2 m., 27 d.
Benjamin W. (husb. of Ellen M.) - b. May 1830; d. September 1910
Dellie (son of Benjamin W. and Ellen M.) - d. 23 September 1875 Æ 3 y., 3 m.
Ellen M. (wife of Benjamin W.) - d. 24 September 1889 Æ 49 y., 8 d.
Everett A. [husb. of Laura M.] - b. 1862; d. 1924
infant (son of Eugene M. and Florence E. [no stones]) - [b. and?] d. 31 May 1905
James (husb. of Adaline [sic] A.) - b. 1824; d. 1900
Laura M. [wife of Everett A.] - b. 1870; d. 1961
Nelson (son of Thomas and Persilla [no stones]) - d. 1 March 1846 Æ 3 y., 3 m.
Smith H. (son of Thomas and Persilla [no stones]) - d. 15 July 1835 Æ 21 m.
Thomas Jr. (son of Thomas and Celia [no stones]) - d. 7 May 1861 Æ [...][1]
Warren (son of Eugene M. and Florence E. [no stones]) - d. 4 May 1908 Æ 4 d.
William (son of Thomas and Persilla [no stones]) - d. 10 April 1839 Æ 16 m.

STEWART [includes STEUART]
Alonzo A. - "lost at sea" 1 March 1874, "in Lat. 33° 13" [sic] North, Long. 73° 3" [sic] West", Æ 24 y., 10 m., 15 d.
Edward B. - d. [...][1] Æ [...][1]

STUART
Sarah A. (wife of A. K. P. [no stone]) - d. 5 December 1853 Æ 26 y., 5 m., 18 d.

THURSTON
Charles William - d. 24 December 1909 Æ 57 y., 16 d.
Frank (son of John and Delia [no stones]) - d. 20 March 1874 Æ 2 y., 1 m., 20 d.
John (Capt.; husb. of Nancy) - d. 20 November 1865 Æ 65 y., 4 m., 3 d.
Nancy (wife of Capt. John) - d. 23 April 1862 Æ 58 y., 8 m., 5 d.

TORREY
Mary A. (wife of Samuel) - b. 1853; d. 1935
Maud L. (BARRON; wife of Lewis G. [no stone]) - d. 9 September 1909 Æ 26 y., 7 m., 13 d.
Samuel (husb. of Mary A.) - b. 1849; d. 1896

TURNER
Abbie B. (GOTT; wife of Clarence A.) - [no dates]
Clarence A. (husb. of Abbie B. (GOTT)) - [no dates]
Marion Eunice (dau. of Clarence A. and Abbie B. (GOTT)) - b. 1896; d. 1910
Millie Vernett (dau. of Clarence A. and Abbie B. (GOTT)) - d. 21 October 189[3 or 4][4] Æ 23 d.
VERRILL [includes VERREL]
Elizabeth A. (wife of Capt. Isaac G. [no stone]) - d. 1 March 1879 Æ 42 y., 7 m., 9 d.
Henry J. (son of John Jr. and Mary Jane [no stone]) - d. 10 November 1865 Æ 17 y., 6 m.
infants (sons of Capt. John and Mary G.) - [no dates]
Isaac W. (son of John Jr. and Mary Jane [no stone]) - d. 13 January 1870 Æ 15 y., 8 m., 22 d.; ("drowned")
John (Capt.; husb. of Mary G.) - b. 1808; d. 1883
John Jr. (husb. of Mary Jane [no stone]) - d. 19 October 1872 Æ 45 y.
Mary (dau. of Capt. John and Mary G.) - d. 7 March 1846 Æ 14 y., 6 m., 7 d.
Mary G. (wife of Capt. John) - b. 1811; d. 1894
Serena T. (dau. of [Capt.?][6] John [and Mary G.?][6]) - d. 9 December 1853 Æ 21 y., 3 m.
Sylvester N. - d. 28 May 1901 Æ 31 y., 7 m., 10 d.
WEBSTER
[John V. - see GOTT]
WELCH
Susan A. (wife of John [no stone]) - d. 27 August 1855 Æ 21 y., 10 m.
WILEY
[Alwilda - see SMITH]
WILSON
Ardell (RICH; wife of Leslie M. [no stone]) - d. 10 March 1890 Æ 17 y., 6 m.
Anna A. (wife of John S. [no stone]) - d. 29 September 1879 Æ 71 y., 11 d.
Clara C. (dau. of John G. and [Sally or Sallie][4] A.) - d. 26 August 1870 Æ [1?]7[1] y., 7 m., [...][1] d.
James L. (husb. of Lydia A. [no stone]) - d. 20 August 1880 Æ 49 y., 2 m., 7 d.
John G. (husb. of [Sally or Sallie][4] A.) - d. 18 November 1915 Æ 86 y., 3 m., 18 d.
John W. (son of James L. and Lydia A. [no stone]) - d. 20 November 1872 Æ 7 m., 8 d.
[Lydia - see RICH]
Myra A. - d. 22 January 1910 Æ 46 y., 5 m., 8 d.
Nancy C. [WILSON?] - d. [2?]1[1] July 18[61?][1] Æ 16 y., [8?][1] m., 2[0?][1] d.
Ralph P. - d. 11 July 1900 Æ 23 y., 6 m.
[Sally or Sallie][4] A. (wife of John G.) - d. 23 October 1907 Æ 74 y., 3 m., 16 d.
Sara [sic] L. (dau. of C. H. and S. L. [no stones]) - [no dates]
Sarah A. (dau. of James L. and Lydia A. [no stone]) - d. 12 April 1858 Æ 11 m., 16 d.
YOUNG
Abbie W. (wife of John F. [no stone]) - d. 15 November 1880 Æ 28 y., 2 m., 24 d.
[...]
Nathan (son of Luther E. and Alvena [no stones]) - d. 27 December 1907 Æ 7 y., 3 m.

Notes:
[1]Stone worn and/or broken.

[2]Although both F. and O. are given as middle initials for Esther GOTT, F. is probably the correct one as the O. likely stands for OSIER, her maiden name.
[3]Number of years is clearly 1, but it is followed by "yrs".
[4]Different on different stones.
[5]Name on Austin B. and Fred P's stones is MULLIN. Name on their parents' stone is MCMULLIN.
[6]Stone broken and repaired with concrete.
[7]Second N in "INFANT" is backwards.
[8]It is unclear if this is a maiden name.

Billings Graves
(Tremont - 12)

Location/directions. On private land off Carter Road. From the traffic light at the north end of Mount Desert Island, go straight ahead (south) onto Routes 102/198. In approximately 5.2 miles (and at the south end of the village of Somesville), turn right onto Pretty Marsh Road (Route 102). Travel on Route 102 about 5.1–5.2 miles to the intersection with Cape Road on the right. Turn right onto Cape Road, and in approximately 1.2–1.3 miles, the Carter Road is on the right. Follow the Carter Road to a fork in about 0.1–0.2 miles. The right fork leads to the property containing the cemetery.

History. This cemetery is on land that was part of lot #11, a 146 acre parcel, on the 1808 Salem Towne Jr. map.

Notes. These stones are completely overgrown by shrubs and small trees. Recording the inscription required crawling on hands and knees.

Names and dates on gravestones and other markers.
BILLINGS
Pearl J. (son of J. M. and [V. or M.?][1] A. [no stones]) - d. 1 February 1878 Æ 1[5?][1] y., 10 m.
[...]
[...][2]

Notes:
[1]Difficult to read.
[2]Only the base of a stone was found. It is not the base of the Pearl J. BILLINGS stone because the holes in this base and the holes in the BILLINGS stone do not align. A photograph in the collection of Ray Robbins indicates that this may belong to Mary [wife of John BILLINGS] - d. 20 J[...][1] 187[1?][1].

Benson Cemetery
(Tremont - 13)

Location/directions. Lopaus Point. From the traffic light at the north end of Mount Desert Island, go straight ahead (south) onto Routes 102/198. In approximately 5.2 miles (and at the south end of the village of Somesville), turn right onto Pretty Marsh Road (Route 102). Travel on Route 102 about 11.3–11.4 miles, and turn right onto the road leading to Bernard. In approximately 0.4–0.5 miles (and shortly after the Bass Harbor Memorial Library, a brick building on the right), turn right onto Lopaus Point Road. The cemetery is on the left in about 0.4–0.5 miles.

History. —

Notes. This cemetery is enclosed by a gated chain-link fence. The lawn is well maintained.

Names and dates on gravestones and other markers. [30 May 1999]

B.
- C. B. [footstone only]

BALDWIN
- Bessie May (dau. of William and Josie [no stone]) - d. 28 June 1894 Æ 4 m., 10 d.
- Betsey (wife of James) - d. 6 July 1891 Æ 65 y.
- James (husb. of Betsey) - b. 1828; d. 1911
- William (husb. of Josie [no stone]) - d. 4 March 1903 Æ 46 y.

BEADLESTON
- [Emma - see PRAY]

BENSON
- Almira (HEATH; dau. of William HEATH [no stone]; wife of Capt. Benjamin [Jr.][4]) - b. 6 September 1801; d. 12 March 1850
- Anna K. "Ann" (wife of Capt. Benjamin) - d. 12 October 1880 Æ 83 y., 8 m.
- Bartlett (son of Capt. Benjamin and Anna K. "Ann") - d. 1 January 1833 Æ 12 m.
- Benjamin (Capt.; husb. of Hannah and Anna K. "Ann") - d. 12 August 1859 Æ 87 y.
- Benjamin [Jr.][4] (Capt.; husb. of Almira (HEATH) and Jessie (GRAHAM)) - b. 10 July 1801; d. 23 September 1875 Æ 74 y., 2 m., 13 d.
- Benjamin [2nd][3] (husb. of Harriet M.) - b. 1816; d. 1897
- Caroline E. [wife of Daniel G.] - b. 1855; d. 1915
- Clara (dau. of Benjamin [2nd][3] and Harriet M.) - d. 16 December 1860 Æ 5 d.
- Daniel G. [husb. of Caroline E.] - b. 1858; d. 1931
- Eliza A. (dau. of Capt. Benjamin [Jr.][4] and Jessie (GRAHAM)) - b. 28 January 1862; d. 1 May 1865
- Eva M. (LAWSON; wife of James B.) - b. 1857; d. 1950
- Eva W. [wife of Ralph G.] - b. 1899; d. 1988
- Flora (dau. of Benjamin [2nd][3] and Harriet M.) - d. 15 August 1859 Æ 5 m.
- Franklin (son of Benjamin [2nd][3] and Harriet M.) - d. 23 November 1857 Æ 9 y., 3 m.
- Hannah (wife of Capt. Benjamin) - d. 7 September 1828 Æ 56 y.
- [Hannah - see GOTT]
- Hannah H. (dau. of Capt. Benjamin [Jr.][4] and Almira (HEATH)) - b. 15 May 1836; d. 30 July 1912
- Harriet M. (wife of Benjamin [2nd][3]) - b. 1823; d. 1905
- Henry C. (son of Capt. Benjamin [Jr.][4] and Almira (HEATH)) - d. 30 August 1879 Æ 47 y., 10 m., 27 d.
- infants (4) (children of William H. and Lucy A. (NOONAN)) - [no dates]

James B. (husb. of Eva M. (LAWSON)) - b. 1856; d. 1926
Jessie (GRAHAM; dau. of Moses GRAHAM and Jane [no stones]; wife of Capt. Benjamin [Jr.]^{4}) - d. 18 September 1870 Æ 48 y., 2 m., 25 d.
John (son of Capt. Benjamin and Hannah) - d. 28 June 1825 Æ 21 y.
Julia A. - d. 14 June 1910 Æ 72 y., 7 m.
Lilly (dau. of Benjamin [2nd]^{3} and Harriet M.) - d. 4 June 1858 Æ 4 d.
Lucy A. (NOONAN; wife of William H.) - d. 10 May 1905 Æ 74 y., 6 m., 10 d.
Mary E. - b. 10 August 1845; d. 2 November 1915
Matthew - b. 2 August 1830; d. 26 October 1890
Ralph G. [husb. of Eva W.] - b. 1893; d. 1975
Rosa E. (dau. of James B. and Eva M. (LAWSON)) - b. 16 May 1882; d. 7 May 1902
[Rosamond - see PINCHETTI]
Samuel P. (son of Capt. Benjamin [Jr.]^{4} and Almira (HEATH)) - d. 8 September 1875 Æ 30 y.
William H. (husb. of Lucy A. (NOONAN)) - d. 14 October 1877 Æ 49 y., 9 m., 27 d.
William M. (son of Benjamin [2nd]^{3} and Harriet M.) - d. 21 August 1864 Æ 14 y., 6 m., 12 d.

BOOTH
Rhoda Ermina (dau. of Capt. George and Dorcas J. [no stones]) - d. 7 October 1851 Æ 2 y., 2 m.

COLLINS
[Sarah - see LAWSON]

CONDON
Hiram H. [husb. of Mabel L.] - b. 1871; d. 1957
Mabel L. [wife of Hiram H.] - b. 1882; d. 1965

DALBY
John K. - b. 1849; d. 1905

GOTT
Almena (dau. of Capt. Daniel [no stone] and Hannah (BENSON)) - d. 19 November 1867 Æ 30 y., 6 m.
Caroline (dau. of Capt. Daniel [no stone] and Hannah (BENSON)) - d. 2 January 1862 Æ 20 y., 9 m., 15 d.
Hannah (BENSON; dau. of Capt. Benjamin BENSON and Hannah; wife of Capt. Daniel [no stone]) - d. 9 December 1871 Æ 65 y., 1 m.
Lucy (wife of [Capt.?] Daniel [no stone]) - d. 14 February 1832 Æ 23 y., 1 m., 17 d.
Lydia (dau. of [Capt.?] Daniel [no stone] and Lucy) - d. 19 February 1847 Æ 19 y.

GRAHAM
[Jessie - see BENSON]

HANSCOM
Mabelle - b. 1880; d. 1931

HARDING
James - d. 5 April 1853 Æ 67 y.

HEATH
[Almira - see BENSON]

HESSAY
Ann E. (wife of William) - d. 11 June 1874 Æ 68 y.
William (husb. of Ann E.) - d. 26 July 1867 Æ 71 y.

HINTON
Harriet C. - b. 1904; d. 1984

JACKSON
  Ella May - b. 1856; d. 1923
  Fred B. - b. 1884; d. 1913
  Helen E. - b. 1890; d. 1919
  Mary Almira - b. 1851; d. 1884
  Thomas W. - b. 1848; d. 1919
LAWSON
  [Eva M. - see BENSON]
  Capt. George (husb. of Hannah B.) - d. 2 April 1870 Æ 44 y., 8 m., 18 d.
  Hannah B. (wife of Capt. George) - d. 9 December 1865 Æ 31 y., 5 m.
  infant [son of Capt. George and Hannah B.?][1] - [no dates]
  John (husb. of Sarah (COLLINS)) - b. 2 December 1796, Driffield, Yorkshire, England; d. 22 December 1856
  Leon M. (son of Capt. George and Hannah B.) - d. 12 September 1860 Æ 4 y., 8 m.
  Robert - b. 1839; d. 1913
  Sarah (COLLINS; wife of John) - b. 4 October 1803, Youlthrope, Yorkshire, England; d. 9 April 1884
LYFORD
  Joseph - b. 1918; d. 1992
  Philip [husb. of Ruth (PRAY)] - b. 1887; d. 1950
  Ruth (PRAY; [wife of Philip]) - b. 1894; d. 1977
MCRAE
  Lucy B. (wife of Capt. Colin [no stone]) - d. 4 September 1860 Æ 36 y., 5 m.
MITCHELL
  Benjamin - d. 30 June 1817 Æ 1[8?][2] y., 10 m., 1[...][2] d.
  Charles (husb. of Rhoda) - d. 25 September 1844 Æ 57 y.
  Charles (husb. of Marietta B.) - d. 18 March 1861 Æ 40 y., 10 m.
  Emma D. (wife of John B. [no stone]) - d. 13 August 1859 Æ 23 y., 7 m.
  Lucy (wife of William G.) - d. 17 November 1860 Æ 22 y., 4 m.
  Marietta B. (wife of Charles) - d. 21 February 1872 Æ 38 y.
  Rhoda (wife of Charles) - d. 25 April 1888 Æ 92 y., 6 m.
  Rhoda M. (dau. of Charles and Rhoda) - d. 20 January 1862 Æ 23 y., 7 m.
  William G. (husb. of Lucy) - d. 26 May 1861 Æ 31 y., 9 m.
NEWBURY
  Hannah (dau. of Benjamin [no stone] and Mary Ann) - d. 23 July 1853 Æ 17 m. [sic]
  Mary Ann (wife of Benjamin [no stone]) - b. 14 April 1833; d. 7 November 1859
NOONAN
  [Lucy A. - see BENSON]
PINCHETTI
  Irvin [husb. of Rosamond (BENSON)] - b. 1919
  Rosamond (BENSON; [wife of Irvin]) - b. 1929
PRAY
  Annie M. [wife of Franklin P.] - b. 1854; d. 1940
  Arthur - b. 1877; d. 1951
  Emma (BEADLESTON) - b. 1875; d. 1947
  Franklin P. [husb. of Annie M.] - b. 1853; d. 1918
  [Ruth - see LYFORD]
SAWYER
  Ahira - d. 16 May 1895 Æ 27 y.
THURSTON
  Eliza A. (wife of James) - b. 15 September 1824; d. 10 October 1857
  James (husb. of Eliza A.) - b. 10 November 1822; d. 12 July 1901

James G. - d. 31 March 1879 Æ 33 y., 3 m., 24 d.
VAN HORN
Marion - b. 18 February 1896; d. 29 January 1903
WATSON
Barron Crowell III - b. 22 July 1923; d. 6 July 1997
WEBSTER
Hannah G. (wife of Capt. Sullivan [no stone]) - d. 29 October 1838 Æ 25 y., 9 m.
[...]
infant - [b. and d.?] 1 January 1895

Notes:
[1]This stone reads "brother" and is next to the stone of Leon M. (son of Capt. George and Hannah B.).
[2]Stone worn.
[3]Some stones omit "2nd".
[4]Some stones omit "Jr.".

Head of the Harbor Cemetery
(Tremont - 14)

Location/directions. West of Marsh Road. From the traffic light at the north end of Mount Desert Island, go straight ahead (south) onto Routes 102/198. In approximately 5.2 miles (and at the south end of the village of Somesville), turn right onto Pretty Marsh Road (Route 102). Travel on Route 102 about 12.0–12.1 miles, and turn left onto Marsh Road (just before the Tremont School and Town Office/Hall). A drive leading to the cemetery is on the left in approximately 0.2–0.3 miles.

History. —

Notes. The grass is mowed and trimmed. A single lane, dead end, grass road runs the length of the cemetery. A chain-link fence runs along most of one side of the cemetery, and iron posts are set along the back and most of the other side. A single, old, wood post was found standing in line with the iron posts.

Names and dates on gravestones and other markers. [30 May 1999]
ABBOTT
Eunice H. (wife of William N.) - d. 11 January 1898 Æ 82 y., 11 d.
William N. (husb. of Eunice H.) - d. 31 August 1902 Æ 82 y., 10 m.
ALBEE
Daniel (husb. of Mary J.) - b. 1832; d. 1902
Jonathan (husb. of Rhoda) - d. [no date] Æ 63 y.
Judson D. (husb. of Margaret R.) - b. 16 July 1842; d. 25 November 1916
Margaret R. (wife of Judson D.) - b. 10 November 1846; d. 24 July 1870
Mary J. (wife of Daniel) - b. 1838; d. 1880
Mary M. (wife of William E.) - b. 1869; d. 1955
[Olivette S. - see FARLEY]
Rhoda (wife of Jonathan) - d. [no date] Æ 87 y.
William E. (husb. of Mary M.) - b. 1867; d. 1944
BARR
[Mary G. - see BENSON]
BENSON
Benjamin B. (husb. of Mary G. (BARR)) - b. 1827; d. 1907
David Wentworth (husb. of Lydia S.) - b. 19 February 1836; d. 4 October 1900
Edward W. (son of Benjamin B. and Mary G. (BARR)) - b. 1867; d. 1870
Lydia S. (wife of David Wentworth) - d. 17 September 1886 Æ 46 y., 4 m., 17 d.
Mary G. (BARR; wife of Benjamin B.) - b. 1836; d. 1877
BILLINGS
Emeline L. (wife of John M. [no stone]) - d. 24 January 1890 Æ 39 y., 3 m., 27 d.
BLACK
Gilbert F. [husb. of Helena G.] - b. 1912
Helena G. [wife of Gilbert F.] - b. 1909; d. 1997
BOOTH
Dorcas J. (MITCHELL; wife of Capt. George) - d. 19 September 1883 Æ 62 y., 1 m.
George (Capt.; husb. of Dorcas J. (MITCHELL)) - d. 26 November 1871 Æ 48 y., 8 m.
George W. (son of Capt. George and Dorcas J. (MITCHELL)) - d. 29 March 1884 Æ 24 y.
[Lucy B[OOTH?]. - see NORWOOD]

BREWER
Mattie E. (wife of Merrill F. [no stone]) - b. 1885; d. 1905
BROWN
Elizabeth J. (dau. of James T. and Sarah [no stones]) - d. 9 November 1853 Æ 12 y., 6 m.
CARROLL
[Sarah - see KITTREDGE]
CLARK
Antoinette (dau. of Eaton and Julia A.) - d. 7 June 1858 Æ 16 y., 5 m., 20 d.
Eaton (husb. of Julia A.) - d. 22 February 1874 Æ 61 y.
Elizabeth N. (wife of Wilford E.) - b. 11 January 1848; d. 4 October 1928
Isabel C. - b. 26 January 1854; d. 8 April 1922
Julia A. (wife of Eaton) - d. 29 July 1895 Æ 78 y., 7 m., 25 d.
[Julia A. - see HOLDEN]
Wilford E. (husb. of Elizabeth N.) - d. 14 June 1879 Æ 31 y., 4 m., 3 d.
CLOSSON
Carrie B. (wife of Charles L.) - b. 1884; d. 1924
Charles L. (husb. of Carrie B.) - b. 1874; d. 1942
Irene L. - b. 1905; d. 1995
Maynard S. (Capt.) - b. 1901; d. 1971
Norman H. III "Buddy" - b. 30 July 1971; "missing at sea" 25 February 1991
COUGH
Caroline C. [dau. of Daniel [no stone] and Elvira?] - d. 27 May 1880 Æ 1 y., 1 m., 2 d.
Elvira (wife of Daniel [no stone]) - d. 10 December 1897 Æ 52 y., 5 m., 21 d.
George D. [son of Daniel [no stone] and Elvira?] - d. 30 May 1897 Æ 15 y., 8 m., 6 d.
infant [dau. of Daniel [no stone] and Elvira?] - d. 25 June 1884 Æ "no days"
infant [son of Daniel [no stone] and Elvira?] - d. 15 November 1887 Æ 9 m., 5 d.
Mary H. [dau. of Daniel [no stone] and Elvira?] - d. 27 September 1890 Æ 19 y., 9 m., 10 d.
Rena R. [dau. of Daniel [no stone] and Elvira?] - d. 21 October 1879 Æ 3 y., 28 d.
DANBY
David W. (son of William and Susan Maria) - d. 14 May 1870 Æ 14 y., 3 m., 19 d.
Susan Maria (wife of William) - d. 8 April 1896 Æ 65 y., 18 d.
W. Franklin (son of William and Susan Maria) - d. 13 November 1865 Æ 7 y., 11 m.
William (husb. of Susan Maria) - b. 1835; d. 1925
DAWS
Joseph (husb. of Mary) - d. 5 August 1885 Æ 89 y., 5 m.
Mary (wife of Joseph) - d. 22 March 1885 Æ 84 y., 5 m.
DAY
[Linda M. - see DODGE]
DODGE
Charles H. (Capt.; husb. of Rose E.) - b. 1856; d. 1908
Elizabeth (MARVIN; wife of Capt. John S.) - b. 1811; d. 1904
John S. (Capt.; husb. of Elizabeth (MARVIN)) - d. 5 August 1854 Æ 53 y.
Linda M. (DAY; wife of Thomas E. O.) - b. 1842; d. 1911
Marvin (son of Capt. John S. and Elizabeth (MARVIN)) - d. 31 August 1847 Æ 2 y., 6 m.
Mervin (son of Capt. John S. and Elizabeth (MARVIN)) - d. 1 December 18[...]0[1] Æ 5 y., 6 m., 20 d.

Rose E. (husb. of Capt. Charles H.) - b. 1862; d. 1932
Thomas E. O. (husb. of Linda M. (DAY)) - b. 1841; d. 1934; (member of Co. G, 1st Maine Heavy Artillery [Civil War])

DORNFELD
Frederick W. [husb. of Thelma G.] - b. 1903; d. 1973
Paul C. - b. 21 April 1925; d. 25 December 1973
Thelma G. [wife of Frederick W.] - b. 1905; d. 1995

DORR
Dexter (son of Lester L. and Maud M. [no stone]) - b. 1907; d. 1928
Eliza L. (wife of John W.) - b. 15 October 1855; d. 6 November 1915
John W. (husb. of Eliza L.) - b. 1861; d. 19[...][5]
Lester L. (husb. of Maud M. [no stone]) - b. 5 October 1884; d. 10 March 1928

DOW
Mary H. [wife of Philip E.] - b. 1937
Philip E. [husb. of Mary H.] - b. 1939

FALVEY
Everett N. - b. 1900; d. 1950
[Linda - see GOSSELIN]

FARLEY
Albert - b. 1842; d. 1925
Alice M. (dau. of William and Olivette S. (ALBEE)) - b. 1894; d. 1895
Beulah [wife of Raymond?] - b. 1897; d. 1971
Dorothy V. [wife of Robert] - b. 1908; d. 1986
Earle W. (husb. of Lyllis F.) - b. 1893; d. 1970
Eli Otis (son of William and Olivette S. (ALBEE)) - b. 1881; d. 1883
Leon E. (son of Thomas and Rebecca H. (KELLEY)) - b. 1888; d. 18 June 1890 Æ 2 y., 3 m.
Lyllis F. (wife of Earle W.) - b. 1906; d. 1965
Olivette S. (ALBEE; wife of William) - b. 1857; d. 1902
Raymond [husb. of Beulah?] - b. 1893; d. 1984
Rebecca H. (KELLEY; wife of Thomas) - b. 1854; d. 1930
Robert [husb. of Dorothy V.] - b. 1907; d. 1981
Thomas (husb. of Rebecca H. (KELLEY)) - b. 1851; d. 1925
William (husb. of Olivette S. (ALBEE)) - b. 1845; d. 1933

GALLANT
Andrew J. Jr. - b. 24 June 1927; d. 10 April 1963
Rose Edna - b. 20 June 1931; d. 3 July 1993

GALLEY
Arabelle (wife of Fred D.) - b. 1860; d. [no date]
Etta L. (dau. of Leonard R. and Bessie E. [no stone]) - [b. and d.?] 12 March 1912
Fred D. (husb. of Arabelle) - b. 1865; d. 1934
Leonard R. (husb. of Bessie E. [no stone]) - b. 1891; d. 1924

GAUDET
[Mildred C. - see PETTIGROVE]

GODFREY
Lewis (son of G. L. and C. H. [no stones]) - d. 27 May 1862 Æ 11 m., 20 d.

GOODWIN
Rachel E. - b. 1935; d. 1990

GOSSELIN
Linda (FALVEY) - b. 1863; d. 1927

GOTT
Lewis Freeman (husb. of Vesta S. (MURPHY)) - b. 1857; d. 1926

[Lydia J. - see MITCHELL]
Vesta S. (MURPHY; wife of Lewis Freeman) - b. 1861; d. 1943

HAMBLEN
Edwin F. - b. 6 June 1916; d. 18 November 1988
Evelyn P. (RICH) - b. 1885; d. 1973
Joan E. - b. 20 February 1936; d. 4 November 1997

HIGGINS
Fred W. - b. 1886; d. 1930
Warren H. - b. 1914; d. 1963

HOLDEN
Cummings M. (husb. of Julia A. (CLARK)) - b. 12 June 1837; d. 5 December 1895
Emma E. (wife of Capt. William [no stone]) - b. 18 October 1832; d. 17 August 1909
infant (son of Frank P. and Gertrude [no stones]) - [b. and d.?] 1 November 1898
Isiphenia A. (dau. of Capt. William E. and Isiphenia M.) - d. 3 February 1853 Æ 3 y., 6 m., 13 d.
Isiphenia M. (wife of Capt. William E.) - d. 25 January 1861 Æ 44 y., 1 m.
Julia A. (CLARK; wife of Cummings M.) - b. 16 November 1843; d. 12 February 1916
William E. (Capt.; husb. of Isiphenia M.) - d. 13 September 1878 Æ 66 y., 6 m.

JACKSON
Violet E. - b. 1889; d. 1949

JOHNSON
Mary A. (wife of Frank H. [no stone]) - b. 14 November 1851; d. 15 October 1915

KELLEY
Aldred M. [wife of Vernon M.] - b. 1923; d. 1993
Alice N. [wife of Vernon M. Sr.] - b. 1909; d. 1978
Cora B. [wife of Shirley R.] - b. 1889; d. 1962
Earlene N. [wife of Raymond W.] - b. 21 November 1934
Edward (son of Jacob M. and Lizzie M.) - d. 31 August 1895 Æ 1 y., 4 m., 11 d.
Jacob M. (husb. of Lizzie M.) - b. 1865; d. 1951
Joseph W. [husb. of Rose B.] - b. 1898; d. 1992
Lizzie M. (wife of Jacob M.) - b. 1867; d. 1957
[Rebecca H. - see FARLEY]
Raymond W. [husb. of Earlene N.] - b. 1 March 1931
Rose B. [wife of Joseph W.] - b. 1900; d. 1961
Shirley R. [husb. of Cora B.] - b. 1889; d. 1964
Vernon M. [husb. of Aldred M.] - b. 1930; d. 1984
Vernon M. Sr. [husb. of Alice N.] - b. 1908; d. 1974

KITTREDGE
Ella M. (wife of Osborne M.) - d. 26 September 1896 Æ 50 y., 11 m., 10 d.
Hawley C. (son of Osborne M. and Ella M.) - d. 10 March 1878 Æ 1 y., 10 m., 10 d.
Osborne M. (husb. of Ella M.) - d. 31 March 1928 Æ 83 y., 7 m., 11 d.
Sarah (CARROLL; wife of Wilford H.) - b. 1880; d. 1960
Wilford H. (husb. of Sarah (CARROLL)) - b. 1881; d. 1950

LAMSON
Grace L. [wife of Guy V.?] - b. 1881; d. 1934
Guy V. [husb. of Grace L.?] - b. 1877; d. 1936

LATTY
Beatrice P. [wife of Rodney G.] - b. 1914
John [husb. of Sylvia M.] - b. 1880; d. 1961

Rodney G. [husb. of Beatrice P.] - b. 1908; d. 1993
Roger Leslie - b. 6 August 1913; d. 14 January 1971
Sylvia M. [wife of John] - b. 1886; d. 1962

LUNT
Chestena (REED; wife of Elwell P.) - b. 1883; d. 1931
Elwell P. (husb. of Chestena (REED)) - b. 1870; d. 1960
infant[2] - [no dates]
L. N. M.[2] [LUNT?] - d. 5 December 1930 Æ [not given]
Lester E. - b. 22 November 1903; d. 15 May 1984
Salem[2] - b. 1854[3]; d. 1929

MALLINSON
Lissie M. [wife of Robert R.] - b. 1918; d. 1975
Robert R. [husb. of Lissie M.] - b. 30 January 1919; d. 15 August 1995

MARSHALL
Joshua L. - b. 1842; d. 1905

MARVIN
[Elizabeth - see DODGE]

McDONALD
Angus [husb. of Anna L.] - d. 1 December 1876 Æ 53 y.
Anna L. [wife of Angus] - b. 1833; d. 1914

McRAE
Angus - b. 1863; d. 1934
Colin (husb. of Vesta Spear[6]) - b. 1822; d. 1900
Vesta Spear[6] (wife of Colin) - b. 1842; d. 1916

MITCHELL
[Dorcas J. - see BOOTH]
Frank S. (husb. of Lydia J. (GOTT)) - b. 1855; d. 1947
John B. - b. 5 July 1825; d. 10 May 1913
Linda G. - b. 7 April 1843; d. 16 February 1909
Lydia J. (GOTT; wife of Frank S.) - b. 1855; d. 1929

MOORE
Ernest F. (husb. of Mary A.) - b. 1861; d. 1933
Mary A. (wife of Ernest F.) - b. 1859; d. 1928

MURPHY
Annabelle [L. or E.][4] (wife of Winfield P.) - b. 1912; d. 1998
Arthur A. (son of Winfield P. and Annabelle [L. or E.][4]) - b. 1930; d. 1942
Ernest A. "Billy" - b. 1935; d. 1976
Mertie L. - b. 1912; d. 1996
[Vesta S. - see GOTT]
Winfield P. (husb. of Annabelle [L. or E.][4]) - b. 1882; d. 1960

NELSON
Geraldine H. [wife of John F.] - b. 5 June 1906; d. 27 August 1983
John F. [husb. of Geraldine H.] - b. 25 November 1907; d. 12 February 1988

NEWBURY
Ada [dau. of James and Frances] - [no dates]
Frances [wife of James] - b. 1830; d. 1912
James [husb. of Frances] - b. 1829; d. 1899
Jane [dau. of James and Frances] - [no dates]

NEWMAN
Julia M. - b. 27 November 1854; d. 26 September 1940

NICE
David C. (husb. of Nancy C.) - b. 1842; d. 1911

John H. [husb. of Letha M.] - b. 1876; d. 1943
Letha M. [wife of John H.] - b. 1890; d. 1988
Nancy C. (wife of David C.) - b. 1851; d. 1921

NORTON
Addie D. - b. 25 September 1866; d. 5 August 1959

NORWOOD
Abraham (son of Capt. John F. and Lydia J.) - d. 27 February 1854 Æ 5 m., 22 d.
Charles H. (husb. of Sylvia M.) - b. 1 March 1855; d. 9 February 1926
Charlotte K. [dau. of Capt. Ezra and Lucy B[OOTH?].?] - b. 1888; d. 1970
Ezra (Capt.; husb. of Lucy B[OOTH?].) - b. 1851; d. 1900
Jasper E. [husb. of Phyllis A.] - b. 1881; d. 1961
John F. (Capt.; husb. of Lydia J.) - d. 7 July 1903 Æ 88 y., 6 m.
Llewellyn J. [son of Capt. Ezra and Lucy B[OOTH?].?] - b. 1874; d. 1946
Lucy B[OOTH?]. (wife of Capt. Ezra) - b. 1851; d. 1887
Lydia J. (wife of Capt. John F.) - d. 16 February 1896 Æ 85 y.
Phyllis A. [wife of Jasper E.] - b. 1906; d. 1997
Sylvia M. (wife of Charles H.) - b. 29 June 1856; d. 10 September 1912

PECKHAM
Gussie (son of James A. and Luc[y or ie][4] B.) - d. 7 December 1871 Æ 3 m.
James A. (husb. of Luc[y or ie][4] B.) - b. 1838; d. 1905
Luc[y or ie][4] B. (wife of James A.) - b. 1837; d. 1905

PETTIGROVE
Alice M. (dau. of Frank E. [no stone] and Elizabeth S.) - d. 1 October 1870 Æ 3 m.
Carl W. (husb. of Mildred C. (GAUDET)) - b. 2 February 1878; d. 2 May 1923
Clarence H. (husb. of Etta A. and Cora L.) - b. 1875 d. 1937
Cora L. (wife of Clarence H.) - b. 1889; d. 1971
Elizabeth S. (wife of Frank E. [no stone]) - b. 1851; d. 1924
Etta A. (wife of Clarence H.) - b. 4 November 1881; d. 26 April 1911
Mildred C. (GAUDET; wife of Carl W.) - b. 1884; d. 1945

REED
[Chestena - see LUNT]
Giles Almond (son of Eugene H. and Susie M. [no stones]) - b. 25 December 1903; d. 20 February 1904

RICH
Almira F. (wife of M[aurice?]. R. [no stone?]) - d. 25 December 1887 Æ 51 y., 9 m., 23 d.
Alvah D. - b. 3 April 1872; d. 3 September 1908
Amelia A. (wife of Levi C.) - b. 31 August 1832; d. 29 January 1920
C. Winifred (wife of Leslie J.) - b. 1877; d. 1960
[Evelyn P. - see HAMBLEN]
Everett N. (son of Levi C. and Amelia A.) - d. 21 July 1889 Æ 8 y., 1 m.
Everett R. - b. 18 November 1902; d. 23 September 1920
Fred J. (husb. of Mary M.) - b. 1858; d. 1913
infant (dau. of Fred J. [no stone] and Vienna S. (RICH)) - [no dates]
John (husb. of Rhoda R.) - d. 1 October 1875 Æ 75 y., 7 m., 23 d.
Jonathan (husb. of Rosannah B.) - d. 28 September 1907 Æ 71 y., 3 m., 9 d.
Leslie J. (husb. of C. Winifred) - b. 1874; d. 1948
Levi C. (husb. of Amelia A.) - b. 4 September 1846; d. 23 January 1926
Lisa Jean - [b. and d.?] July 1963
Mandy A. (wife of Maurice R.) - b. 21 February 1836; d. 14 April 1915
Mary M. (wife of Fred J.) - b. 1872; d. 1956
Maurice R. (husb. of Mandy A.) - b. 22 December 1833; d. 11 August 1911

Reuben D. (husb. of Sarah J. [no stone]) - b. 1827; d. 1863
Reuben ("only son" of Reuben D. and Sarah J. [no stone]) - d. 10 August 1864 Æ 5 y., 5 m., 3 d.
Rhoda R. (wife of John) - d. 25 May 1876 Æ 84 y., 8 m., 21 d.
Rosannah B. (wife of Jonathan) - d. 12 January 1916 Æ 74 y., 8 m., 13 d.
Samuel H. (husb. of Sarah S.) - b. 14 November 1807; d. 18 June 1892
Sarah S. (wife of Samuel H.) - b. 21 September 1815; d. 30 April 1893
Vienna S. (RICH; "only dau." of Jonathan RICH and Rosannah B.; wife of Fred J. [no stone]) - d. 8 April 1889 Æ 25 y., 8 m., 16 d.

RICHARDSON
Helen D. - b. 30 October 1884; d. 26 May 1962
Julia A. (wife of W. Z. [no stone]) - d. 14 December 1870 Æ 24 y.

ROBBINS
Charles (Capt.; husb. of Mary A.) - b. 1853; d. 1940
Jessie F. - [no dates]
Katie A. - [no dates]
Mary A. (wife of Capt. Charles) - b. 1856; d. 1910
Maude E. - [no dates]

ROCHE
John Joseph - b. 3 July 1886; d. 12 April 1976

ROSSI
Nolan Natale Sr. - b. 25 December 1925; d. 27 January 1995

RUMILL
Euphemia D. (wife of George C. Sr.) - b. 1914; d. 1973
George C. Jr. - b. 1934; d. 1978
George C. Sr. (husb. of Euphemia D.) - b. 1909; d. 1977

S.
O. E. [footstone only]

SAWYER
Alberta (wife of Joshua A.) - b. 1868; d. 1948
Alice Maude (dau. of Salem T. and Clara A. [no stone]) - d. 15 April 1871 Æ 8 m., 5 d.
Caroline E. (wife of Capt. Jacob) - d. 19 July 1894 Æ 72 y., 5 m.
Chester J. (husb. of Leona G.) - b. 1892; d. 1934
E. Kingsbury (son of Capt. Jacob and Caroline E.) - d. 22 May 1858 Æ 13 y., 5 m., 16 d.
Freelove M. [wife of Henry W.] - b. 1896; d. 1971
George R. - b. 1896; d. 1918
Harriett [sic] (dau. of Chester J. and Leona G.) - d. 14 February 1918 Æ 2 y., 9 m.
Henry W. [husb. of Freelove M.] - b. 1890; d. 1971
Herbert G. (husb. of Iona H.) - b. 1871; d. 1927
infant (son of Capt. Jacob and Caroline E.) - d. 30 October 1857 Æ 8 d.
infant (son of Lewis F. and Vienna B.) - [b. and?] d. October 1876
Iona H. (wife of Herbert G.) - b. 1873; d. 1950
Jacob (Capt.; husb. of Caroline E.) - b. 26 July 1813; d. 28 April 1897
Joshua A. (husb. of Alberta) - b. 1859; d. 1932
Kenneth E. [husb. of Margaret Mary] - b. 1914; d. 1993
Leona G. (wife of Chester J.) - b. 1890; d. 1987
Lewis F. (husb. of Vienna B.) - b. 10 December 1842; d. 16 September 1919
Margaret Mary [wife of Kenneth E.] - b. 1918; d. 1998
Salem T. (husb. of Clara A. [no stone]) - d. 15 July 1870 Æ 29 y., 5 m.
Vienna B. (wife of Lewis F.) - b. 6 March 1848; d. 1 January 1903

SMITH
Rufus Weston - b. 18 August 1893; d. 19 November 1966
SPEAR
[Vesta - see MCRAE]
STANLEY
Charles E. (husb. of Hettie [sic] N.) - b. 1851; d. 1925
Hettie [sic] N. (wife of Charles E.) - b. 1850; d. 1935
Randall O. (son of Charles E. and Hettie [sic] N.) - b. 1883; d. 1940
Roger Merrill [husb. of Ruth M.] - b. 14 May 1916; d. 16 September 1975
Ruth M. [wife of Roger Merrill] - b. 1916
STEVENS
Eliza Jane (wife of Robert) - d. 2 May 1899 Æ 81 y.
Robert (husb. of Eliza Jane) - d. 4 August 1866, on board "Barque Maria Scammell on voyage from Valparaiso to Boston", Æ 45 y.
THURSTON
Elfreida (wife of Fred V.) - b. 1898; d. 1936
Fred V. (husb. of Elfreida) - b. 1894; d. 1960
Julia A. (wife of Charles W. [no stone]) - b. 1856; d. 1934
WATSON
Viola Helen [wife of Willis] - b. 1860; d. 1940
Willis [husb. of Viola Helen] - b. 1859; d. 1928
WHEATON
Edward B. [husb. of Georgia A.] - b. 1873; d. 1952
Georgia A. [wife of Edward B.] - b. 1898; d. 19[...][5]
WHITE
Charles A. [husb. of Phoebe M.?] - [d.?] 1933
Phoebe M. [wife of Charles A.?] - b. 1862; d. 1912
WILSON
Ethel M. (wife of Leslie M.) - b. 20 October 1879; d. 28 September 1925
Leslie M. (husb. of Ethel M.) - b. 25 September 1869; d. 10 July 1958
YOUNG
John M. - b. 27 October 1941; d. 24 December 1996
Manuel L. [husb. of Mildred E.] - b. 1913; d. 1982
Mildred E. [wife of Manuel L.] - b. 1915
Philip L. - b. 1913; d. 1980

Notes:
[1]Stone broken.
[2]Information marked in concrete before it set.
[3]The 4 is backwards.
[4]Different on different stones.
[5]Stone blank.
[6]To determine if this is a maiden name will require further research.

Murphy Cemetery
(Tremont - 15)

Location/directions. East of Kelleytown Road. From the traffic light at the north end of Mount Desert Island, go straight ahead (south) onto Routes 102/198. In approximately 5.2 miles (and at the south end of the village of Somesville), turn right onto Pretty Marsh Road (Route 102). Travel on Route 102 about 7.7–7.8 miles, and turn left onto Kelleytown Road. In about 0.5–0.6 miles on the left is an old drive now (2000) blocked by two large rocks and bordered on its left by four old apple trees. Downhill from this drive are the gravestones, one of which is visible in the winter from the drive.

History. —

Notes. This cemetery has no clear boundary and is not maintained.

Names and dates on gravestones and other markers. [23 October 1999]
MURPHY
Emma F. (wife of William A. [no stone]) - d. 24 November 1880 Æ 32 y., 11 m., 29 d.
[...]ard[1] H. (son of William A. [no stone] and Emma F.) - d. 18 October 1894 Æ 20 y., 5 d.
[...]
[...][2]

Notes:
[1]Stone worn.
[2]This is only a base of a stone [possibly belonging to William A.?], which, together with Emma F.'s, flank the stone of [...]ard H.

Carver Tomb
(Tremont - 16)

Location/directions. In woods, west of Route 102. From the traffic light at the north end of Mount Desert Island, go straight ahead (south) onto Routes 102/198. In approximately 5.2 miles (and at the south end of the village of Somesville), turn right onto Pretty Marsh Road (Route 102). Travel on Route 102 about 7.7–7.8 miles, and turn right onto Rumill Road. The tomb is in the woods beyond the detached garage of the large white house on the right.

History. —

Notes. This tomb is located in woods with no cleared area around it. Following some vandalism, it was sealed to prevent further entry.

Names and dates on gravestones and other markers. [19 March 2000]
There are no names engraved on any visible (1997) portion of this tomb.[1]

Note:
[1]According to the great great granddaughter of Wills CARVER and the owner of property adjacent to that containing the tomb, it contains the remains of Wills CARVER, Nancy (his first wife), and Albert CARVER.

Heath Cemetery

(Tremont - 17)

Location/directions. In woods, west of Route 102 and north of south end of Cape Road. From the traffic light at the north end of Mount Desert Island, go straight ahead (south) onto Routes 102/198. In approximately 5.2 miles (and at the south end of the village of Somesville), turn right onto Pretty Marsh Road (Route 102). Travel on Route 102 about 7.1–7.2 miles to an old woods road on the right. Follow this woods road (on foot) to several large stones on the right. Turn right after these stones and follow a wide trail. Watch on the left, about 55' after passing through a break in a stone wall, for a trail that cuts slightly back. Follow this trail to the cemetery.

History. This cemetery is on land that was part of a 100 acre parcel owned by William Heath in 1808 according to the Salem Towne Jr. map.

Notes. Until this year (2000), this cemetery was completely overgrown. Both the cemetery proper and an old woods road and path leading to it (and beyond) have recently been cleared of large, woody vegetation. The cemetery is not enclosed, but a stone wall runs along two sides.

Names and dates on gravestones and other markers. [30 May 1999]

ALLEN
- [Elizabeth - see Hannah HEATH]
- [Hannah - see HEATH]
- [Nehemiah - see Hannah HEATH]

ATHERTON
- Alonzo P. - d. 2 November 1872 Æ 37 y., 5 m., 14 d.
- Bertha [ATHERTON?][1] - d. 11 September 1866 Æ 2 y., 8 m., 13 d.

HEATH
- Alvena D. M. [wife of William W. A.] - b. 1843; d. 1925
- Fred W. - b. 1869; d. 1953
- Hannah (ALLEN; dau. of Nehemiah ALLEN and Elizabeth [no stones]; wife of Esq. William) - b. 1768, Beverly, Mass.; m. 1786; settled on Mount Desert 1789; d. 29 July 1854 Æ 86 y.
- J. Julian - b. 1874; d. 1931
- John William (Capt.; son of William Jr. and Catharine [sic] [no stones]) - d. 30 August 1849 Æ 23 y., 27 d.
- Louisa M. - b. 1872; d. 1958
- Victor A. - b. 1878; d. 1962
- William (Esq.; husb. of Hannah (ALLEN)) - m. 1786; d. 6 September 1840 Æ 76 y.; ("a worthy soldier of the American Revolution" [Revolutionary War])
- William W. A. [husb. of Alvena D. M.] - b. 1834; d. 1912

KITTREDGE
- Edwin [husb. of Louisa H.] - d. 31 January 1891 Æ 79 y.
- Louisa H. [wife of Edwin] - [...][2]

Notes:

[1]Her footstone reads "B. A.", and her grave is adjacent to the grave of Alonzo P. Atherton.

[2]Stone of Edwin KITTREDGE and Louisa is tipped forward so far that only the information near the top is visible.

Reed Point Cemetery
(Tremont - 18)

Location/directions. Near north shore of Seal Cove. From the traffic light at the north end of Mount Desert Island, go straight ahead (south) onto Routes 102/198. In approximately 5.2 miles (and at the south end of the village of Somesville), turn right onto Pretty Marsh Road (Route 102). Travel on Route 102 about 7.2–7.3 miles, and turn right onto the south end of Cape Road. Follow Cape Road approximately 1.1–1.2 miles to a dirt road on the left (the second road/drive on the left after the water). Turn left onto this road, and watch on the left for a field containing a mowed path leading to this cemetery as well as to Tremont - 19 and Tremont - 32. In about 50 feet, the path divides. Follow the left branch down the hill, and watch on the left of the granite posts near a stone wall.

History. The name applied to this cemetery is only for convenience of reference in this book.

Notes. Seven granite posts mark the boundary of the burial area. The grass is mowed.

Names and dates on gravestones and other markers. [30 May 1999]
There are no stones giving the name(s) of the deceased, only two markers with United States flags—one with "Post 105 G. A. R." and the other "Veteran 61–65" with "O F L" clockwise around the margin [Civil War].

James Reed Cemetery
(Tremont - 19)

Location/directions. West of Cape Road and south of private road leading to Reed Point. From the traffic light at the north end of Mount Desert Island, go straight ahead (south) onto Routes 102/198. In approximately 5.2 miles (and at the south end of the village of Somesville), turn right onto Pretty Marsh Road (Route 102). Travel on Route 102 about 7.2–7.3 miles, and turn right onto the south end of Cape Road. Follow Cape Road approximately 1.1–1.2 miles to a dirt road on the left (the second road/drive on the left after the water). Turn left onto this road, and watch on the left for a field that contains a mowed path leading to this cemetery as well as to Tremont - 18 and Tremont - 32. In about 50 feet, the path divides. Follow the right branch to the cemetery.

History. The name applied to this cemetery is only for convenience of reference in this book.

Notes. Flanking the path leading to the cemetery are two granite posts. A third post, matching the others stands in the cemetery. The stones are in a mowed area around four large spruce trees.

Names and dates on gravestones and other markers. [30 May 1999]

GORDIUS
- Augustus [husb. of Vilda M.] - b. 1844; d. 1918
- Vilda M. [wife of Augustus] - b. 1846; d. 1918

LALLY
- Nancy (wife of William [no stone]) - d. 13 March 1873 Æ 32 y., 7 m., 26 d.

LUNT
- George B. (son of Abner and A. F. [no stones]) - d. 27 October 1894 Æ 29 y., 2 m., 20 d.

N.
- C. S. [footstone only]

NUTTER
- David (Capt.; son of Lewis and Mehetable [sic] [no stones]) - d. 21 April 1854 Æ 18 y., 9 m.

REED [includes READ]
- Calvin M. (husb. of Mary A.) - b. 1853; d. [no date]
- Ira W. (husb. of Sarah M.) - d. 6 September 1894 Æ 74 y.
- James[1] (husb. of Martha) - d. 24 September 1838 Æ 67 y.
- Martha (wife of James) - d. 14 June 1877 Æ 102 y., 6 m., 1 d.
- Mary A. (wife of Calvin M.) - b. 1855; d. 1905
- Mary M. (dau. of James and Tryphena [no stones]) - d. 25 March 1853 Æ 22 y., 1 m.
- Myra C. (dau. of Calvin M. and Mary A.) - d. 1 October 1895 Æ 15 y., 1 m.
- Sarah M. (wife of Ira W.) - d. 1 December 1898 Æ 72 y., 10 m., 25 d.

SAUNDERS
- Matilda (wife of Paul F. [no stone]) - d. 11 June 1873 Æ 32 y., 6 m.

STANLEY
- James C. (son of George and Susan M. [no stones]) - d. 4 August 1853 Æ 10 m.

Note:

[1]James is represented by two stones. One is worn and broken, but in March 2000, the number 24 can be discerned at the bottom edge of one of the pieces. This is likely a portion of the death date that is clear on the stone shared with his wife.

Langley Cemetery
(Tremont - 20)

Location/directions. East of Cape Road. From the traffic light at the north end of Mount Desert Island, go straight ahead (south) onto Routes 102/198. In approximately 5.2 miles (and at the south end of the village of Somesville), turn right onto Pretty Marsh Road (Route 102). Travel on Route 102 about 5.1–5.2 miles to the intersection with Cape Road on the right. Turn right onto Cape Road. In approximately 1.1–1.2 miles on the left is a private drive leading to the property containing the cemetery. Facing away from the house and toward the field that slopes away from the house, follow the edge of the field on your left. After crossing a new (1999?) gravel road that ends/begins just a few feet into the woods, you will see a portion of the woods that juts into the field. The four headstones are in that portion of the woods.

History. —

Notes. The four stones found are in the woods where vegetation is growing unchecked. The stones are leaning or laying on the ground. There are no apparent boundaries.

Names and dates on gravestones and other markers. [11 March 2000]
HARPER
Ida F. (dau. of Capt. N. A. and Sophronia D. [no stones]) - d. 24 January 1861 Æ 1 y., 1 m., 10 d.
LANGLEY
Jacob C. (son of John and Catherine [no stones]) - d. 10 December 1852 Æ 3 m., 6 d.
John H. (son of John and Catherine [no stones]) - d. 12 October 1853 Æ 12 y., 8 m.
Samuel D. (Capt.) d. 17 January 1862 Æ 25 y., 21 d.

Gravestone of Capt. Jonathan Tinker (Tinker Island Cemetery, Tremont - 21).

Tinker Island Cemetery
(Tremont - 21)

Location/directions. Tinker Island. This cemetery is visible from the rocky beach at the southeastern edge of the island.

History. —

Notes. The unenclosed cemetery is in an unmowed, grassy area.

Names and dates on gravestones and other markers. [10 June 2000]
LELAND
A[bb?]y[1] A. T. (dau. of [...][1] and [...][1,2] [M or W?][1,2] - d. [9?][1] May 1837 Æ 6 m., 13 d.
TINKER
Ada B. A. (dau. of Capt. John F. and Phebe [sic] [no stone]) - d. 15 December 1853 Æ 12 y., 4 m.
Hannah D. (wife of Capt. James T.) - d. 16 April 1849 Æ 21 y.
James T. (Capt.; husb. of Hannah D.) - d. 9 August 1839, "N. Y.", Æ 27 y.
John F. (Capt.; husb. of Phebe [sic] [no stone]) - "lost at sea" 4 February 1845 Æ 38 y., 7 m.; ("lost at sea from the brig Gulnar[e or c?][1] off Cape Hatteras")
Jonathan (Capt.) - d. 2 January 1852 Æ 73 y.

Notes:
[1]Stone worn.
[2]Initials only given on stone.

Babbidge-Murphy Burial Ground
(Tremont - 22)

Location/directions. West of Kelleytown Road. From the traffic light at the north end of Mount Desert Island, go straight ahead (south) onto Routes 102/198. In approximately 5.2 miles (and at the south end of the village of Somesville), turn right onto Pretty Marsh Road (Route 102). Travel on Route 102 about 7.7–7.8 miles, and turn left onto Kelleytown Road. In about 0.7–0.8 miles, there is a private road/driveway on the right. On the left (south) side of this driveway, before it rises toward a private residence, is a flat, cleared area. The cemetery, not visible from the drive, is just beyond this cleared area.

History. —

Notes. This cemetery is enclosed by a gated, wire-mesh fence with metal posts. The woody vegetation is cut by the owners of the property that includes the cemetery.

Names and dates on gravestones and other markers. [23 October 1999]
BABBIDGE
Isabel H. (wife of Joseph) - b. 18 June 1833; d. 11 April 1902
Joseph (husb. of Isabel H.) - b. 12 April 1834; d. 7 May 1867
GOTT
[Margaret - see MURPHY]
MURPHY
Isaac S. (husb. of Margaret (GOTT)) - b. 26 December 1839; d. 25 April 1919
Margaret (GOTT; wife of Isaac S.) - b. 1851; d. 1885
[...]
[...][1]

Note:
[1]Two rough stones mark two children's graves according to property owners.

Rumill-Dodge Cemetery
(Tremont - 23)

Location/directions. On private land on Dodge Point. From the traffic light at the north end of Mount Desert Island, go straight ahead (south) onto Routes 102/198. In approximately 5.2 miles (and at the south end of the village of Somesville), turn right onto Pretty Marsh Road (Route 102). Travel on Route 102 about 8.2–8.3 miles, and turn right onto Dodge Point Road. The cemetery is in a field on the left in approximately 0.8 miles.

History. This cemetery is on land that was part of a 145 acre parcel owned by Ezra Dodge in 1808 according to the Salem Towne Jr. map.

Notes. The cemetery is not enclosed, but three of four corners are marked, according to a 1993 deed (2104:98), by a 15" spruce tree, an 8" apple tree, and a monument, all of which were observed in 2000.

Names and dates on gravestones and other markers. [30 May 1999]

D.
M. [footstone only][1]

DODGE
Clarissa (wife of Deacon Ezra) - d. 11 May 1878 Æ 81 y., 10 m., 19 d.
Ezra (Deacon; husb. of Clarissa) - d. 8 May 1857 Æ 63 y., 3 m., 3 d.
S. Ambrose - d. 16 October 1866 Æ 29 y., 8 m., 17 d.

GRISWOLD
Penelope (PARKMAN; wife of Roger [no stone]) - b. 12 April 1896; d. 23 December 1959

PARKMAN
[Penelope - see GRISWOLD]

POMROY
Margaret (wife of Captain John [no stone]) - d. 11 October 1844 Æ 19 y.

RUMILL
Calvin L. (Captain; husb. of Louisa H.) - b. 25 April 1826; d. 12 June 1907
Louisa H. (wife of Captain Calvin L.) - d. 8 October 1884 Æ 48 y., 5 m., 5 d.
William A. - d. 3 September 1891 Æ 50 y., 4 m., 20 d.

THOMAS
Abbie S. (wife of William B. [no stone]) - d. 20 March 1897 Æ 52 y., 2 m.

Note:
[1]This footstone is at the foot of Clarissa DODGE's grave.

Norwood Cemetery
(Tremont - 24)

Location/directions. Along west side of Richtown Road. From the traffic light at the north end of Mount Desert Island, go straight ahead (south) onto Routes 102/198. In approximately 5.2 miles (and at the south end of the village of Somesville), turn right onto Pretty Marsh Road (Route 102). Travel on Route 102 about 10.3–10.4 miles, and turn right onto Richtown Road. The cemetery is on the right in approximately 0.2 miles.

History. —

Notes. This cemetery is enclosed by a gated chain-link fence. The grass is mowed and trimmed.

Names and dates on gravestones and other markers. [30 May 1999]

NORWOOD
- Alvin Jr. - b. 1908; d. 1942
- Alvin Sr. - b. 1878; d. 1956
- Arthur G. - b. 1879; d. 1959
- Avis - b. 1918
- Carrie E. - b. 1893; d. 1973
- Clyde E. - b. 16 February 1910; d. 22 February 1986
- Dalton M. - b. 13 September 1916; d. 25 August 1975
- Harold E. - b. 1924; d. 1996
- Harry - b. 1906; d. 1975
- Hollis G. - b. 2 June 1930; d. 13 November 1998
- R. S. N[ORWOOD?]. [footstone only]
- Ralph W. - b. 1912; d. 1991
- William - d. 29 March 1857 Æ 76 y.

WORCESTER
- Jennie C. - b. 1885; d. 7 April 1940 Æ 54 y., 4 m., 23 d.

Wentworth-Walls-Norton Cemetery
(Tremont - 25)

Location/directions. In woods across Clark Point Road from Hillrest Cemetery (Tremont - 9). According to Robbins (1994), this cemetery is "on the northeast side of [a] path and about one third of the way from the Ambrose Rich house to the Norton field" (p. 239).

History. —

Notes. Information below was taken from photographs by Ray Robbins.

Names and dates on gravestones and other markers.
WALLS
Melissa (dau. of Capt. [...][1] and Sarah) - d. 20 November 1851 Æ 9 y., 6 m., 15 d.
[...]
[...][1,2] - d. 8 September 1850 Æ 19 y., 8 m.; ("was drowned in the Bay of Chalurt")

Notes:
[1]Stone broken.
[2]The name Daniel is used in the verse at the bottom of the stone.

Dix Burying Ground
(Tremont - 26)

Location/directions. Along south side of private drive, east of Dix Point Road. From the traffic light at the north end of Mount Desert Island, go straight ahead (south) onto Routes 102/198. In approximately 5.2 miles (and at the south end of the village of Somesville), turn right onto Pretty Marsh Road (Route 102). Travel on Route 102 about 9.0–9.1 miles and, in a sharp curve to the left, turn right onto Dix Point Road. In nearly 0.5 miles, where the town road ends, a private drive is on the left (east). The cemetery is along the right (south) side of this driveway as one approaches the house.

History. The cemetery is on land that was part of lot #22, a 95 acre parcel, according to the 1808 Salem Towne Jr. map.

Notes. There is no enclosure around this cemetery. It is cleared but not mowed. All stones are standing, but with one (Hannah APPLETON's) propped against a rock because it has broken at the base. The boundary is marked by iron rods.

Names and dates on gravestones and other markers. [30 May 1999]

APPLETON
Hannah (wife of Frances [sic] W. [no stone]) - d. 7 August 1804 Æ 30 y.

DIX
Eunice (wife of William) - d. 2 November 1849 Æ 77 y.
Sally[1] (wife of George[1] [no stone]) - d. 9 April 1855 Æ 42 y.
William (husb. of Eunice) - d. 17 August 1814 Æ 38 y.

PUMROY
Mary B. (wife of William [no stone]) - d. 23 September 1856 Æ 70 y., 7 m.

Note:
[1]See stones for Capt. George DIX and Sally DIX in Hillrest Cemetery (Tremont - 9).

Crockett Point Cemetery

(Tremont - 27)

Location/directions. Crockett Point. From the traffic light at the north end of Mount Desert Island, go straight ahead (south) onto Routes 102/198. In approximately 5.2 miles (and at the south end of the village of Somesville), turn right onto Pretty Marsh Road (Route 102). Travel on Route 102 about 11.3–11.4 miles, and turn right onto the road leading to Bernard. In approximately 0.1-0.2 miles, turn left onto Crockett Point Road. The cemetery sets back from this road on the left in a little more than 0.1 miles.

History. —

Notes. There are two distinct parts of this cemetery—an older, unmaintained portion and a newer portion with recent gravestones.

Names and dates on gravestones and other markers. [1 April 2000]

ALBEE [see also ALBY]
Clyde W. (son of James H. and Georgie D. [no stones]) - d. 17 October 1899 Æ 6 m.

ALBY [see also ALBEE]
George W. (son of William and Abigail [no stones]) - d. 10 November 1847 Æ 16 y.
Mary (dau. of William and Abigail [no stones]) - d. 14 February 1845 Æ 18 y.

BUTLER
Amy (wife of Capt. Charles) - d. 7 April 1901 Æ 79 y.
Charles (Capt.; husb. of Amy) - d. 4 July 1896 Æ 77 y.

DOWNIE
Barbara P. [wife of David W.] - b. 1924; d. 1992
David W. [husb. of Barbara P.] - b. 1921

GALLEY
George B. (husb. of Emma [no stone]) - d. 8 September 1850 Æ 33 y., 10 m.; ("drowned")
Hannah (wife of John) - d. 10 September 1844 Æ 49 y., 4 m.
infant (son of W. F. and O. S. [no stones]) - d. 7 December 1868 Æ 18 d.
John (husb. of Hannah) - d. 28 October 1850 Æ 67 y.
Sadie (dau. of Fred D. and Belle [no stones]) - d. 15 August 1898 Æ 2 y.
Sylvester (son of George B. and Emma [no stone]) - d. 5 July 1847 Æ 8 y.

PETTIGROVE
Clarence B. - b. 20 May 1926; d. 26 August 1990
Florence B. [wife of Halsey C.] - b. 1905; d. 1988
Halsey C. [husb. of Florence B.] - b. 1901; d. 1980

STUPAK
Vera Boyd - b. 1909; d. 1999

Richtown Cemetery
(Tremont - 28)

Location/directions. Set back from northeast side of Richtown Road. From the traffic light at the north end of Mount Desert Island, go straight ahead (south) onto Routes 102/198. In approximately 5.2 miles (and at the south end of the village of Somesville), turn right onto Pretty Marsh Road (Route 102). Travel on Route 102 about 10.3–10.4 miles, and turn right onto Richtown Road. A path leading to the cemetery, which is visible from the road, is on the left in approximately 0.4–0.5 miles.

History. —

Notes. The cemetery is bordered by tall northern white-cedar trees.

Names and dates on gravestones and other markers. [30 May 1999]
PARSONS
M. Louise - b. 1913; d. 1935
Maurice R. - b. 1922; d. 1940
Nadia May (RICH) - b. 1878; d. 1935
RICH
Ardell (dau. of Maurice P. and Daty [no stone]) - d. 14 January 1870 Æ 18 y., 9 m.
Charlotte I. [wife of L. Neal] - b. 1929
Chauncey G. - b. 1875; d. 1939
[Datie R. - see THURSTON]
Delilah A. (dau. of Elias Jr. and Emil[y or ie][1] P.) - d. 7 March 1869 Æ 5 y., 2 m., 24 d.
Elias Jr. (husb. of Emil[y or ie][1] P.) - d. 1 February 1896 Æ 69 y., 3 m., 22 d.
Emil[y or ie][1] P. (wife of Elias Jr.) - d. 16 March 1902 Æ 70 y., 9 m., 4 d.
Frank B. (husb. of Goldie C.) - b. 1882; d. 1976
Goldie C. (wife of Frank B.) - b. 1889; d. 1966
L. Neal [husb. of Charlotte I.] - b. 1928; d. 1989
Leslie G. - b. 1902; d. 1957
Lois H. (THURSTON; wife of Maurice P.) - b. 1843; d. 1922
Margaret (wife of Jonathan [no stone]) - d. 19 April 1817 Æ 37 y.
Maurice P. (husb. of Daty [no stone]) - d. 18 August 1879 Æ 73 y., 7 m., 23 d.
Maurice P. (husb. of Lois H. (THURSTON)) - b. 1841; d. 1892; ("G. A. R." [Civil War])
[Nadia May - see PARSONS]
Roy U. - b. 1873; d. 1944
Sarah A. (wife of John R. [no stone]) - d. 6 April 1880 Æ 42 y., 4 m., 17 d.
Ulysses S. - b. 1878; d. 1951
THURSTON
Datie R. (RICH; wife of John S.) - b. 1851; d. 1927
Elias [THURSTON?] - [no dates]
Ethel [THURSTON?] - [no dates]
Harold Lynn (son of John S. and Datie R. (RICH)) - d. 27 June 1880 Æ 2 m., 10 d.
John S. (husb. of Datie R. (RICH)) - b. 1853; d. 1924
Lillie [THURSTON?] - [no dates]
[Lois H. - see RICH]

Note:
[1]Different on different stones.

Murphy Hill Cemetery
(Tremont - 29)

Location/directions. West of Route 102. From the traffic light at the north end of Mount Desert Island, go straight ahead (south) onto Routes 102/198. In approximately 5.2 miles (and at the south end of the village of Somesville), turn right onto Pretty Marsh Road (Route 102). Travel on Route 102 about 7.9–8.0 miles, and turn right onto a private driveway. Inquire at the house for permission to visit the cemetery and directions to it.

History. The cemetery is on land that was part of lot #19, a 108 acre parcel, according to the 1808 Salem Towne Jr. map.

Notes. This cemetery is in very poor condition. Some stones are broken or laying on the ground, covered with moss and/or almost buried in duff, and a large tree fallen into the cemetery. There are remnants of barbed and non-barbed wire along part of three sides.

Names and dates on gravestones and other markers. [23 October 1999]

GOTT
- B. F. (Rev.; husb. of Ermina E.) - b. 24 May 1861; d. [no date]
- Elizabeth Gott - b. 1897; d. 1970
- Ermina E. (wife of Rev. B. F.) - b. 25 January 1871; d. 13 January 1917
- infant ["baby brother" of Elizabeth?] - b. 1903; d. 1903
- John M. (husb. of Nancy T.) - b. 1813; d. 1907
- [Lydia - see MITCHELL]
- Nancy T. (wife of John M.) - d. 29 July 1888 Æ 68 y., 3 m.

MERCHANT
- Arthur M. (son of Llewellyn M. and Cora Arletta) - d. 7 September 18[...][1] Æ 3 m.
- Cora Arletta (wife of Llewellyn M.) - d. 4 February 1890 Æ 28 y.
- Hannah M. (wife of Llewellyn M.) - d. 16 October 1923 Æ 50 y., 5 m.
- Llewellyn M. (husb. of Cora Arletta and Hannah M.) - b. 1858; d. 1937
- Mary Elizabeth - [b. and d.?] 9 June 1942
- Sandra Rae - [b. and d.?] 2 October 1938

MITCHELL
- Lydia (GOTT; wife of Robert [no stone]) - d. 2 June 1883 Æ 86 y., 5 m.

MURPHY [includes MURPHEY]
- George (husb. of Hannah C.) - d. 27 March 1842 Æ 82 y.
- Hannah C. (wife of George) - d. 16 June 1863 Æ 96 y., 3 m.
- Harvey F. (son of Israel and Mercy [no stones]) - d. 1 September 1861 Æ 23 y.
- Jacob V. (son of Israel and Mercy [no stones]) - d. 10 September 1847, "at sea on board Brig Neptune", Æ 17 y., 9 m., 10 d.
- Thomas V. (son of Israel and Mercy [no stones]) - d. 3 July 1847, "at sea on board Nasau", Æ 20 y., 1 m., 15 d.

RICH
- Albion K. P. (Capt.; husb. of Hattie L.) - d. 8 December 1895 Æ 59 y., 8 m., 18 d.
- Hattie L. (wife of Capt. Albion K. P.) - d. 18 November 1890 Æ 42 y., 17 d.

YOUNG
- Harriet A. (wife of Francis [no stone]) - d. 20 May 1857 Æ 31 y., 6 m., 14 d.

Note:
[1]Stone broken.

Gravestone of Mary Norwood (Tremont - 30).

Norwood Grave
(Tremont - 30)

Location/directions. North of Seal Cove Road on what is now a knoll because surrounding land was removed for gravel. From the traffic light at the north end of Mount Desert Island, go straight ahead (south) onto Routes 102/198. In approximately 5.2 miles (and at the south end of the village of Somesville), turn right onto Pretty Marsh Road (Route 102). Travel on Route 102 about 7.5–7.6 miles, and turn left onto Seal Cove Road. In about 0.7–0.8 miles, there is a small pull-out on the left (north) side of the road. Walk into the woods to the edge of the former gravel pit, and follow the boundary of the pit to your right.

History. This stone stands is on land that is now part of Acadia National Park.

Notes. A grave adjacent to Mary NORWOOD's is marked by an unengraved fieldstone.

Names and dates on gravestones and other markers. [18 June 2000]
NORWOOD
Mary (wife of Jonathan [no stone]) - d. 20 November 1846 Æ 57 y.

Gravestone of Elizabeth Gott (Gott Island Cemetery, Tremont - 31).

Gott Island Cemetery
(Tremont - 31)

Location/directions. Great Gott Island. From the boat dock, follow a mowed (2000) path that passes to the right of a small, red (2000) building. This path leads by the cemetery.

History. —

Notes. The cemetery is enclosed by a white, wood fence.

Names and dates on gravestones and other markers. [18 June 2000]

ASH
- Ethel Maud (dau. of Orlando and Rachel M. [no stones]) - d. 25 November 1890 Æ 4 y., 4 m., 19 d.

BABBIDGE
- Louis W. (son of Frank A. and Lura B. [no stones]) - d. 3 April 1906 Æ 1 y., 3 d.
- Martin V. (husb. of Susan G.) - b. 10 October 1836; d. 10 November 1916
- Susan G. (wife of Martin V.) - b. 27 February 1840; d. 22 September 1918

BALDWIN
- Birgit - b. 10 August 1960; d. 17 June 1988

BARTON
- James Jr. - [no dates]; (member of Reed's Co., 7th Massachusetts Regiment [Revolutionary War])

BULGER
- Frances H. (wife of A. G. [no stone]) - d. 11 March 1887 Æ 25 y., 4 m., 20 d.

CATES
- [Judith S. - see MOORE]

DANA
- Katharine Simmons - b. 30 May 1910; d. 23 October 1989
- Marshal Murat Halstead - b. 17 February 1908; d. 3 October 1968

DEMAN
- Patricia K. [wife of Paul M.] - b. 1 February 1927, Washington, D. C.
- Paul M. [husb. of Patricia K.] - b. 6 December 1919, Antwerp, Belgium; d. 21 December 1983, New Haven, Connecticut

DRISCOLL
- William Perry (son of Dennis and Rose [no stones]) - d. 27 December 1883 Æ 7 m., 16 d.

GILLIS
- Benjamin Robert - b. 1965, Princeton, New Jersey; d. 1991, Masai Mara, Kenya

GOTT
- Avis (dau. of Collins M. and Elizabeth [no stones]) - b. 1 March 1920; d. 15 March 1920
- B[e or i]rlin[1] A. (husb. of Blanche H.) - b. 1877; d. 1955
- Bertha M. (dau. of William E. and Emma L.) - d. 14 September 1907 Æ 7 m., 18 d.
- Blanche H. (wife of B[e or i]rlin[1] A.) - b. 1890; d. 1980
- Daniel - d. 1 [...][2] 1838 Æ 21 y., 1 m.
- Daniel Jr. - b. 23 December 1739; d. 7 June 1814 (private, Continental Line [Revolutionary War])
- Elizabeth (wife of Deacon Nathaniel) - d. 15 May 1844 Æ 77 y.
- Emma L. [wife of William E.] - b. 1877; d. 1954
- Erastus L. (husb. of Rachel W.) - b. 1843; d. 1922
- Hannah (wife of Samuel M.) - d. 30 December 1899 Æ 82 y., 9 m., 22 d.

Hollis M. - b. 1916; d. 1994
James A. - b. 1865; d. 1901
Margaret (dau. of B[e or i]rlin[1] A. and Blanche H.) - b. 31 July 1908; d. 11 August 1926
Martin V. - b. 1867; d. 1898
Montelle D. - b. 1881; d. 1963
Nathaniel (Deacon; husb. of Elizabeth) - d. 27 January 1841 Æ 78 y.
Paris - b. 1873; d. 1898
Rachel W. (wife of Erastus L.) - b. 1845; d. 1901
Russell L. (son of B[e or i]rlin[1] A. and Blanche H.) - b. 1910; d. 1991
Ruth M. (dau. of Collins and Elizabeth [no stones]) - d. 17 June 1909 Æ 5 d.
Samuel M. (husb. of Hannah) - d. 19 November 1895 Æ 82 y.
[Sara J. - see NELSON]
Susannah (MILLIKEN; dau. of Samuel MILLIKEN and Susannah [no stones] "of Mount Desert" ; wife of William "of Tremont") - d. 6 June 1859 Æ 77 y., 6 m., 17 d.
William (husb. of Susannah (MILLIKEN)) - d. 18 February 1856 Æ 78 y., 4 m.
William E. [husb. of Emma L.] - b. 1874; d. 1939
William P. - d. 24 April 1883 Æ 32 y., 6 m., 11 d.; ("drowned")

GRINDLE
infant [GRINDLE?] - [no dates]
infant [GRINDLE?] - [no dates]
Jennie [GRINDLE?] - b. 1875; d. 1920
Lewis M. - [b. and?] d. 2 May 1906
Venita H. - d. 17 May 1905 Æ 5 m.

HAMBLEN
Daniel (husb. of Hannah) - [no dates]
Hannah (wife of Daniel) - [no dates]

HARDING
Jennie H. [wife of William H.] - b. 14 April 1865; d. 13 February 1942
Mary A. (wife of Charles [no stone]) - b. 7 November 1821, Brixton, England; d. 6 July 1895
William H. [husb. of Jennie H.] - b. 5 June 1857; d. 3 February 1925

HOLMES
Edward M. [husb. of Jane M.] - b. 1910
Jane M. [wife of Edward M.] - b. 1908; d. 1983

JONES
Bertha M. (wife of Harold [no stone]) - b. 1893; d. 1920

KENWAY
James Salisbury - b. 18 June 1955; d. 22 February 1990

MARTIN
Sarah M. (wife of Lewis R. [no stone]) - d. 15 October 1878 Æ 36 y., 6 m., 15 d.

MILLER
Henry F. - d. 19 September 1889 Æ 62 y., 6 m.

MILLIKEN
[Susannah - see GOTT]

MOORE [includes MOOR]
Alice (POTTER; [wife of Holsey N.]) - b. 29 June 1883; d. 26 July 1957
Asenath (wife of Capt. Phil[l]ip[1]) - d. 29 July 1852 Æ 49 y., 8 m., 19 d.
Betty "Jo" - b. 7 May 1953; d. 27 October 1999
Enoch N. (Capt.; husb. of Lucinda and Laura A.) - d. 26 May 1908 Æ 70 y., 1 m., 15 d.

Fanny S. - d. 31 August 1834 Æ 1 y., 7 m.
Flavilla R. (wife of George B.) - d. 10 March 1879 Æ 36 y., 3 m.
George B. (husb. of Flavilla R.) - d. 4 April 1876 Æ 37 y., 7 m., 13 d.
Harvey (son of Capt. Enoch N. and Laura A.) - d. 31 August 1895 Æ 15 y., 11 m., 14 d.
Helen - b. 22 October 1906; d. 1 July 1995
Holsey N. [husb. of Alice (POTTER)] - b. 19 October 1881; d. 13 June 1921
infant (son of Capt. Phil[l]ip[1] and Mary E.) - d. 25 April 1854 Æ 1 d.
Judith S. (CATES; adopted dau. of Capt. Phil[l]ip[1] and Asenath) - d. 2 October 1852 Æ 22 y., 9 m., 21 d.
Laura A. (wife of Capt. Enoch N.) - d. 7 May 1915 Æ 65 y., 2 m., 17 d.
Lovina (wife of Philip) - b. 1878; d. 1956
Lucinda (wife of Capt. Enoch N.) - d. 4 July 1859 Æ 17 y., 4 m., 16 d.
Mary E. (wife of Capt. Phil[l]ip[1]) - d. 28 November 1888 Æ 74 y., 7 m., 14 d.
Mary E. (dau. of Capt. Phil[l]ip[1] and Mary E.) - d. 4 January 1858 Æ 1 y., 11 m., 5 d.
Philip (husb. of Lovina) - b. 1871; d. 1937
Phil[l]ip[1] (Capt.; husb. of Asenath and Mary E.) - d. 10 April 1880 Æ 80 y., 7 m., 3 d.

MORGAN
Calvin - b. 1943; d. 1992

MORRILL
Caroline L. - b. 1872; d. 1894
Charline Leslie (dau. of Leslie W. and Ruth C.) - b. 30 August 1923; d. 21 September 1923
Leslie W. (husb. of Ruth C.) - b. 1894; d. 1980
Ruth C. (wife of Leslie W.) - b. 1897; d. 1988

MULLER
Franz Theo. ("a Native of Bremen[,] Germany") - b. 28 February 1829; d. 9 July 1892

MURPHY
Benjamin (husb. of Jane A.) - d. 10 March 1886 Æ 60 y.
Jane A. (wife of Benjamin) - d. 23 March 1898 Æ 75 y.

NELSON
Sara J. (GOTT; dau. of B[e or i]rlin[1] A. GOTT and Blanche H.) - b. 1912; d. 1990

POTTER
[Alice - see MOORE]

SPAHR
Ann (TYLER; wife of Christian Carson Febiger "Kit") - b. 1947
Christian Carson Febiger "Kit" (husb. of Ann (TYLER)) - b. 1937; d. 1991

STAPLES
Amos W. (husb. of Isabelle H.) - b. 1868; d. 1946
Isabelle H. (wife of Amos W.) - d. 25 January 1922 Æ 48 y., 6 m.
Susie G. [STAPLES?] - b. 1879; d. 1902

THURSTIN
Susanna - d. 16 December 1844 Æ 19 y., 9 m., 2 d.

TRASK
Charles A. - d. 23 August 1903 Æ 27 y., 9 m., 23 d.
Lorenzo S. (Capt.; husb. of Margaret C.) - d. 10 October 1909 Æ 60 y., 6 m.
Margaret C. (wife of Capt. Lorenzo S.) - b. 16 August 1847; d. 21 June 1924
Pearl E. (son of William S. and Belle M. [no stones]) - d. 14 April 1912 Æ 11 y., 4 m., 8 d.

TYLER
[Ann - see SPAHR]
WELCH
John V. - d. 10 October 1889 Æ 30 y., 11 m., 21 d.
Lawrence (husb. of Rachel) - b. 13 February 1817, Waterford, Ireland; d. 4 April 1894 Æ 77 y., 1 m., 22 d.
Rachel (wife of Lawrence) - d. 27 May 1902 Æ 75 y., 5 m., 15 d.
[...]
Herman O. - b. 1893; d. 1963
Lewis E. - b. 1890; d. 1901
Nellie H. - b. 1853; d. 1930
Oliver J. - b. 1850; d. 1908

Notes:
[1]Different on different stones.
[2]Stone broken.

Benjamin Norwood Cemetery
(Tremont - 32)

Location/directions. Reed Point, south of bar leading to/from Moose Island. From the traffic light at the north end of Mount Desert Island, go straight ahead (south) onto Routes 102/198. In approximately 5.2 miles (and at the south end of the village of Somesville), turn right onto Pretty Marsh Road (Route 102). Travel on Route 102 about 7.2–7.3 miles, and turn right onto the south end of Cape Road. Follow Cape Road approximately 1.1–1.2 miles to a dirt road on the left (the second road/drive on the left after the water). Turn left onto this road, and watch on the left for a field that contains a mowed path leading to this cemetery as well as to Tremont - 18 and Tremont - 19. In about 50 feet, the path divides. Follow the left branch down the hill, and pass on the right of the granite posts of Tremont - 18. Continue following this path to the cemetery, which borders the left edge of the path.

History. The cemetery is on land that was part of a 102 acre parcel owned by a J. Reed in 1808 according to the Salem Towne Jr. map.

Notes. The burial area is not enclosed, and there are no evident boundary markers. The graves are in an open area under tall spruce trees. Several stones are held upright by sticks. The stones, and presumably graves also, are oriented at various angles to each other.

Names and dates on gravestones and other markers. [26 March 2000]
NORWOOD
- Benjamin - d. 22 February 1857 Æ 60 y.
- Benjamin H. (son of Benjamin and Esther [H. or N. or M.?][1] [no stone]) - d. 27 July 1853 Æ 13 y.
- George M. (son of Benjamin and Esther [H. or N. or M.?][1] [no stone]) - d. 28 February 1856 Æ 29 y., 4 m.
- Lois M. (dau. of Benjamin and Esther [H. or N. of M.?][1] [no stone]) - d. 5 April 1829 Æ 5 y.

REED
- Benjamin (son of Benjamin and Lorenia F. [no stones]) - d. 30 March 1856 Æ 7 m.
- Henry A. (son of Benjamin R. and Lorena N. [no stones]) - d. 28 October 1876, Vinal Haven [sic], Æ 15 y., 11 m., 28 d.; ("drowned")
- Howard N. (son of Benjamin and Lorenia F. [no stones]) - d. 5 March 1854 Æ 9 m.

Note:
[1]Stone worn.

Washburn Grave
(Tremont - 33)

Location/directions. Great Gott Island.

History. —

Notes. Information below was taken from a rubbing by Lyford Stanley.

Names and dates on gravestones and other markers.
WASHBURN
Lorraine - b. 1917; d. 1982

TRENTON

A small portion of the north end of Mount Desert Island is part of Trenton. There are no cemeteries on this land.

“Man’s work is from sun to sun, but woman’s work is never done.”

INDEX

NOTES

NOTES

NOTES

NOTES

NOTES

NOTES

NOTES

Harvey's 1st teaching job on
Cranberry Islands
Coast Guard used to take him
in boat to bring back & forth

Barbara played saxophone with
a band at odd fellows hall on
Swans Island

Gene Taro took us to Cranberry Island
Malcolm McDuffy took us on a picnic
Took me lobstering
minister

1/2 Kelley's Drunks Ned was
Joe & Shelley hated it

Jack Rice would show up drunk at
Kenney farm. Grandma Kenney would
pour any alcohol down sink. Jack would cry

NOTES

CEMETERIES OF CRANBERRY ISLES AND THE TOWNS OF MOUNT DESERT ISLAND

ORDER FORM

(Please photocopy)

Name: ____

Address: ____

Town/city: ______________________ State: ____________

E-mail: ________________________ Zip code: __________

Please send _____ copies @ $35.00 ____________

Maine 5% sales tax ($1.75 per book)
(for addresses in Maine) ____________

Shipping
first book - $6.00
each additional book - $2.00 ____________

TOTAL ____________

Thank you for your order. Please make checks payable to:

V. F. Thomas Co.
P. O. Box 281
Bar Harbor, Maine 04609-0281

If you have any questions or wish to place an order,
please call: 207-266-5748 (= 207-BOOKS-4-U) or e-mail: info@vfthomas.com

Visit our web site: http://www.vfthomas.com